THE NIV
APPLICATION
COMMENTARY

From biblical text . . . to contemporary life

PROVERBS

THE NIV APPLICATION COMMENTARY

From biblical text . . . to contemporary life

PAUL E. KOPTAK

ZONDERVAN®

GRAND RAPIDS, MICHIGAN 49530 USA

ZONDERVAN.COM/
AUTHORTRACKER

We want to hear from you. Please send your comments about this book to us in care of zreview@zondervan.com. Thank you.

ZONDERVAN®

The NIV Application Commentary: Proverbs
Copyright © 2003 by Paul E. Koptak

Requests for information should be addressed to:

Zondervan, *Grand Rapids, Michigan 49530*

Library of Congress Cataloging-in-Publication Data

Koptak, Paul E., 1955 –
    Proverbs / Paul E. Koptak.—1ˢᵗ ed.
       p. cm.—(The NIV application commentary)
    Includes bibliographical references and indexes.
    ISBN-10: 0–310–21852–7
    ISBN-13: 978-0-310-21852-4
    1. Bible. O.T. Proverbs—Commentaries. I. Title. II. Series.
BS1465.53.K67 2003
223'.7077—dc21
                             2003008670
                             CIP

This edition printed on acid-free paper.

Printed in the United States of America

---

12 • 12 11 10 9

Contents

The NIV Application Commentary Series

When complete, the NIV Application Commentary
will include the following volumes:

To see which titles are available,
visit our web site at www.zondervan.com

NIV Application Commentary
Series Introduction

THE NIV APPLICATION COMMENTARY SERIES is unique. Most commentaries help us make the journey from our world back to the world of the Bible. They enable us to cross the barriers of time, culture, language, and geography that separate us from the biblical world. Yet they only offer a one-way ticket to the past and assume that we can somehow make the return journey on our own. Once they have explained the *original meaning* of a book or passage, these commentaries give us little or no help in exploring its *contemporary significance*. The information they offer is valuable, but the job is only half done.

Recently, a few commentaries have included some contemporary application as *one* of their goals. Yet that application is often sketchy or moralistic, and some volumes sound more like printed sermons than commentaries.

The primary goal of the NIV Application Commentary Series is to help you with the difficult but vital task of bringing an ancient message into a modern context. The series not only focuses on application as a finished product but also helps you think through the *process* of moving from the original meaning of a passage to its contemporary significance. These are commentaries, not popular expositions. They are works of reference, not devotional literature.

The format of the series is designed to achieve the goals of the series. Each passage is treated in three sections: *Original Meaning, Bridging Contexts,* and *Contemporary Significance.*

THIS SECTION HELPS you understand the meaning of the biblical text in its original context. All of the elements of traditional exegesis—in concise form—are discussed here. These include the historical, literary, and cultural context of the passage. The authors discuss matters related to grammar and syntax and the meaning of biblical words.[1] They also seek to explore the main ideas of the passage and how the biblical author develops those ideas.

---

1. Please note that in general, when the authors discuss words in the original biblical languages, the series uses a general rather than a scholarly method of transliteration.

After reading this section, you will understand the problems, questions, and concerns of the *original audience* and how the biblical author addressed those issues. This understanding is foundational to any legitimate application of the text today.

THIS SECTION BUILDS a bridge between the world of the Bible and the world of today, between the original context and the contemporary context, by focusing on both the timely and timeless aspects of the text.

God's Word is *timely*. The authors of Scripture spoke to specific situations, problems, and questions. The author of Joshua encouraged the faith of his original readers by narrating the destruction of Jericho, a seemingly impregnable city, at the hands of an angry warrior God (Josh. 6). Paul warned the Galatians about the consequences of circumcision and the dangers of trying to be justified by law (Gal. 5:2–5). The author of Hebrews tried to convince his readers that Christ is superior to Moses, the Aaronic priests, and the Old Testament sacrifices. John urged his readers to "test the spirits" of those who taught a form of incipient Gnosticism (1 John 4:1–6). In each of these cases, the timely nature of Scripture enables us to hear God's Word in situations that were *concrete* rather than abstract.

Yet the timely nature of Scripture also creates problems. Our situations, difficulties, and questions are not always directly related to those faced by the people in the Bible. Therefore, God's word to them does not always seem relevant to us. For example, when was the last time someone urged you to be circumcised, claiming that it was a necessary part of justification? How many people today care whether Christ is superior to the Aaronic priests? And how can a "test" designed to expose incipient Gnosticism be of any value in a modern culture?

Fortunately, Scripture is not only timely but *timeless*. Just as God spoke to the original audience, so he still speaks to us through the pages of Scripture. Because we share a common humanity with the people of the Bible, we discover a *universal dimension* in the problems they faced and the solutions God gave them. The timeless nature of Scripture enables it to speak with power in every time and in every culture.

Those who fail to recognize that Scripture is both timely and timeless run into a host of problems. For example, those who are intimidated by timely books such as Hebrews, Galatians, or Deuteronomy might avoid reading them because they seem meaningless today. At the other extreme, those who are convinced of the timeless nature of Scripture, but who fail to discern its timely element, may "wax eloquent" about the Melchizedekian priesthood to a sleeping congregation, or worse still, try to apply the holy wars of the Old Testament in a physical way to God's enemies today.

The purpose of this section, therefore, is to help you discern what is timeless in the timely pages of the Bible—and what is not. For example, how do the holy wars of the Old Testament relate to the spiritual warfare of the New? If Paul's primary concern is not circumcision (as he tells us in Gal. 5:6), what *is* he concerned about? If discussions about the Aaronic priesthood or Melchizedek seem irrelevant today, what is of abiding value in these passages? If people try to "test the spirits" today with a test designed for a specific first-century heresy, what other biblical test might be more appropriate?

Yet this section does not merely uncover that which is timeless in a passage but also helps you to see *how* it is uncovered. The authors of the commentaries seek to take what is implicit in the text and make it explicit, to take a process that normally is intuitive and explain it in a logical, orderly fashion. How do we know that circumcision is not Paul's primary concern? What clues in the text or its context help us realize that Paul's real concern is at a deeper level?

Of course, those passages in which the historical distance between us and the original readers is greatest require a longer treatment. Conversely, those passages in which the historical distance is smaller or seemingly nonexistent require less attention.

One final clarification. Because this section prepares the way for discussing the contemporary significance of the passage, there is not always a sharp distinction or a clear break between this section and the one that follows. Yet when both sections are read together, you should have a strong sense of moving from the world of the Bible to the world of today.

THIS SECTION ALLOWS the biblical message to speak with as much power today as it did when it was first written. How can you apply what you learned about Jerusalem, Ephesus, or Corinth to our present-day needs in Chicago, Los Angeles, or London? How can you take a message originally spoken in Greek, Hebrew, and Aramaic and communicate it clearly in our own language? How can you take the eternal truths originally spoken in a different time and culture and apply them to the similar-yet-different needs of our culture?

In order to achieve these goals, this section gives you help in several key areas.

(1) It helps you identify contemporary situations, problems, or questions that are truly comparable to those faced by the original audience. Because contemporary situations are seldom identical to those faced by the original audience, you must seek situations that are analogous if your applications are to be relevant.

(2) This section explores a variety of contexts in which the passage might be applied today. You will look at personal applications, but you will also be encouraged to think beyond private concerns to the society and culture at large.

(3) This section will alert you to any problems or difficulties you might encounter in seeking to apply the passage. And if there are several legitimate ways to apply a passage (areas in which Christians disagree), the author will bring these to your attention and help you think through the issues involved.

In seeking to achieve these goals, the contributors to this series attempt to avoid two extremes. They avoid making such specific applications that the commentary might quickly become dated. They also avoid discussing the significance of the passage in such a general way that it fails to engage contemporary life and culture.

Above all, contributors to this series have made a diligent effort not to sound moralistic or preachy. The NIV Application Commentary Series does not seek to provide ready-made sermon materials but rather tools, ideas, and insights that will help you communicate God's Word with power. If we help you to achieve that goal, then we have fulfilled the purpose for this series.

The Editors

General Editor's Preface

PAUL KOPTAK, THE AUTHOR of this fine commentary on the book of Proverbs, tells us that in its original setting Proverbs was used as a "course of study designed to foster wisdom, using literary-rhetorical resources" as teaching methods. That is, this book teaches applied knowledge—wisdom.

This makes Proverbs an extremely important book. Wisdom is in short supply these days. Look around and one finds plenty of knowledgeable people. Look in other places and one finds plenty of goodhearted people. But we look hard to find people both goodhearted and knowledgeable—or, put a better way, people who have learned how to integrate their hard-won knowledge with their grace-imparted goodness.

You see, Westerners live in a culture that suffers from having separated knowledge from ethics. Because of the importance and influence of science and technology in our world, we live with the notion that one can know things without knowing how those same things should be used. Scientists working on the atomic bomb, for example, could pretend that all they were doing was extending the frontiers of knowledge when in fact they were creating knowledge that could be used for horrific human ends. No wisdom there, for sure.

Wisdom is not an easy nut to crack, however. If it were so easy, it wouldn't be in such short supply. What makes it difficult? At least five things:

(1) Wisdom often seems *cryptic*. That is, it is often hard to understand, not because the content is so difficult but because it is usually radical and subversive. That is, it usually goes against established cultural norms, norms geared toward economic success or political power. It takes ears specially trained in the ways of the gospel to hear the wisdom of many proverbs. "Ears to hear," Jesus called them. Otherwise, how could you hear someone say, "He who is trustworthy conceals a matter," without thinking of Enron and concealment and corporate greed and think that the writer of that proverb may be more than just a little bit out of touch?

(2) Wisdom often seems *ambiguous*. Ambiguity is the very thing one would think wisdom was designed to do away with. But Proverbs teaches us that that is not true. Wisdom is sometimes found in the interaction between two proverbs rather than the statement of just one:

> Do not answer a fool according to his folly,
>   or you will be like him yourself.
> Answer a fool according to his folly,
>   or he will be wise in his own eyes. (26:4–5)

We have to read both, we have to understand both, and then we have to read both and understand them together before wisdom emerges.

(3) Wisdom, like everything else human, is *culture specific*. Wisdom in one culture is not always wisdom in another. Thus, when we read in Proverbs 7 about the virtues of a good woman, one of the questions engendered is, what are the virtues of a good man? As Paul Koptak shows us, Proverbs contains some wisdom but not all wisdom. It is the product of a culture that didn't think to warn its daughters about men to avoid, as Proverbs 7 warns young men about women to avoid. It takes some effort to convert this message for twenty-first century women.

(4) Wisdom takes *courage* to implement. It is not enough to see what action is required by the knowledge you attain. You have to do more than recognize and acknowledge the action wisdom requires, you have to do it as well. It is not enough to say that most basic and earliest Christian creed, "Jesus is Lord." We must also act in ways that acknowledge that Jesus *is* Lord—by obeying, loving, and relating to Jesus as Lord.

(5) Finally, wisdom is *broadminded*. It teaches us that not just any old actions implied by our knowledge will do. Our actions must be measured by the extent to which they contribute to God's plan: the building of the kingdom of God, human flourishing, the well-being of the whole creation. But trying to work out the ciphers of future effects from today's causes is not so easy.

Perhaps the greatest of all the lessons of Proverbs is this—that the wisdom it extols is hard to find but most worthy of seeking.

Terry C. Muck

Author's Preface

A PROVERB ATTRIBUTED to Joseph Joubert says, "The one who teaches learns twice." I know that has been true for me. As I have taught from the book of Proverbs in person and now here in print, I have come to a stronger sense of appreciation for those who have handed down this tradition of wisdom from one generation to the next. So much of who we are grows out of what we have been given. Therefore, I am grateful to the scholars, students, and pastors who have been my teachers and conversation partners as I have studied and spoken. Whatever is helpful in the book can in some way be traced to them.

I am also thankful for the generous support of the board, administration, and faculty of North Park Theological Seminary, particularly for sabbatical time dedicated to this project. I would often begin a day's work with a prayer of thanks for the opportunity to spend it in study and reflection. The friendship and encouragement of my former teachers Fredrick Carlson Holmgren and C. John Weborg have meant a great deal, especially for our conversations about biblical wisdom.

The editors of the series—Robert Hubbard, Tremper Longman III, Terry Muck, and John Walton—read the first pages and made helpful comments. Tremper also read the entire first draft and proved that "iron sharpens iron," graciously using his own expertise in Proverbs to help me clarify my position on a number of interpretive issues. Klyne Snodgrass offered valuable feedback on the introduction, and Ken Litwak did the same for selected chapters. Thanks go to the staff at the Brandel Library and student assistants Mark Carlson, Jennifer Dunahoo, Cheryl Green, Denise Johnson, and Dennis White. Brian Simpson proofread the entire manuscript and checked the Scripture references. Conversations with psychologists Sam Alibrando, Jeffrey Slutsky, and Patrick Thyne kept the discussions on marriage and family grounded in reality. A special word of thanks goes to the editors at Zondervan, especially to Verlyn Verbrugge for his help in making the writing more direct and clear.

Above all my wife, Linda, added to the joy of our life together with her constant encouragement, often asking what I had learned about

Author's Preface

Proverbs that day, sometimes saying that she could tell I was enjoying myself. Thankful for her laughter and wisdom, this husband stands up to call her blessed. On the occasion of our twentieth wedding anniversary, this book is dedicated to her.

Paul E. Koptak
North Park Theological Seminary

Abbreviations

AB	Anchor Bible
AEL	*Ancient Egyptian Literature: A Book of Readings*, 3 vols., ed. M. Lichtheim (Berkeley: Univ. of California Press, 1971, 1976, 1980)
ANET	*Ancient Near Eastern Texts Relating to the Old Testament*, ed. J. B. Pritchard, 3d ed. (Princeton: Princeton Univ. Press, 1969)
AThR	*Anglican Theological Review*
Bib	*Biblica*
BibInt	*Biblical Interpretation*
BibSac	*Bibliotheca Sacra*
BLS	Bible and Literature Series
BTB	*Biblical Theology Bulletin*
BWL	*Babylonian Wisdom Literature*, ed. W. G. Lambert (Winona Lake, Ind.: Eisenbrauns, 1996)
BETL	Bibliotheca ephemeridum theologicarum lovaniensium
BLS	Bible and Literature Series
BST	The Bible Speaks Today
BZAW	Beiheft zur Zeitschrift für die alttestamentliche Wissenschaft
CBOT	Coniectanea biblica (Old Testament)
CBQ	*Catholic Biblical Quarterly*
CBQMS	Catholic Biblical Quarterly Monograph Series
DBS	Daily Bible Studies
EBC	*Expositor's Bible Commentary*
FOTL	Forms of Old Testament Literature
GKC	*Gesenius' Hebrew Grammar*, ed. E. Kautzsch, trans. A. E. Cowley, 2d ed. (Oxford: Clarendon, 1910)
GTJ	*Grace Theological Journal*
HBIS	History of Biblical Interpretation Series
HS	*Hebrew Studies*
HTR	*Harvard Theological Review*
ICC	International Critical Commentary

Abbreviations

IDB	*Interpreter's Dictionary of the Bible*
IDBSup	*Interpreter's Dictionary of the Bible Supplementary Volume*
Int	*Interpretation*
ISBE	*The International Standard Bible Encyclopedia*, 4 vols., rev. ed. G. W. Bromiley (Grand Rapids: Eerdmans, 1979, 1982, 1986, 1988)
ITC	International Theological Commentary
JBL	*Journal of Biblical Literature*
JCR	*Journal of Communication and Religion*
JNSL	*Journal of Northwest Semitic Languages*
JQR	*Jewish Quarterly Review*
JSOT	*Journal for the Study of the Old Testament*
JSOTSup	Journal for the Study of the Old Testament Supplement Series
JTS	*Journal of Theological Studies*
LXX	Septuagint (Greek translation of the Old Testament)
MT	Masoretic Text
NAC	New American Commentary
NASB	New American Standard Bible
NCBC	New Century Bible Commentary
NIB	*The New Interpreter's Bible*
NICOT	New International Commentary on the Old Testament
NIDOTTE	*New International Dictionary of Old Testament Theology and Exegesis*, 5 vols., ed. W. A. VanGemeren (Grand Rapids: Zondervan, 1997)
NIV	New International Version
NJB	New Jerusalem Bible
NRSV	New Revised Standard Version
NSBT	New Studies in Biblical Theology
OBO	Orbis biblicus et orientalis
OTE	*Old Testament Essays*
OTG	Old Testament Guides
OTL	Old Testament Library
OTM	Old Testament Message
OTP	*The Old Testament Pseudepigrapha*, 2 vols., ed. J. H. Charlesworth (Garden City, N.Y.: Doubleday, 1983–1985)
RB	*Revue biblique*
REB	Revised English Bible
SAOC	Studies in Ancient Oriental Civilizations

SBLDS	Society of Biblical Literature Dissertation Series
SJOT	*Scandinavian Journal of the Old Testament*
TDOT	*Theological Dictionary of the Old Testament*, 12+ vols., ed. G. J. Botterweck and Helmer Ringgren (Grand Rapids: Eerdmans, 1974–)
TNIV	Today's New International Version
TNK	Tanak (Jewish Publication Society)
TOTC	Tyndale Old Testament Commentaries
TynBul	*Tyndale Bulletin*
TWOT	*Theological Wordbook of the Old Testament*, 2 vols., ed. R. L. Harris, G. L. Archer, B. K. Waltke (Chicago: Moody Press, 1980)
VT	*Vetus Testamentum*
VTSup	Vetus Testamentum Supplements
WBC	Word Biblical Commentary
WMANT	Wisenschaftliche Monographien zum Alten und Neuen Testament
ZAH	*Zeitschrift für Althebräistik*
ZAW	*Zeitschrift für die Alttestamentliche Wissenschaft*
ZBK	Zürcher Bibelkommentare

Introduction

MANY CHRISTIANS HAVE a love-hate relationship with the book of Proverbs. We love the sparkle and punch of the individual proverbs and can quote many from memory. Some, like "Pride goes before a fall," have made their way into everyday conversation, although the actual proverb is, "Pride goes before destruction, a haughty spirit before a fall" (Prov. 16:18). But many of us find it frustrating to try to read or study this book, let alone teach or preach from it. Some portions sound like tedious advice we never asked for (another word might be nagging), while other parts mystify us with riddles and cosmic symbolism. It sometimes seems easier to draw memorable quotes from the book of Proverbs and let it go at that.

This state of affairs shouldn't surprise us, for we are a society that loves sayings and aphorisms. Advertising and television comedies create the catch phrases that pepper our conversations; a day spent listening for the sayings that inundate and shape our lives would end up with quite a list![1] There is also a renewed interested in wisdom in our time, but often it takes the form of sentimental life lessons or management pep talk. Real wisdom that not only observes how life works but also asks ultimate questions about how and why life is to be lived is not as popular. Wisdom of this sort is usually relegated to the back of the shopping mall bookstore in the philosophy and religion section, while guides to health, wealth, and success in life are placed up front to greet customers as they walk in.

Biblical wisdom surprisingly offers both, but on its own terms. We will do ourselves and the book a disservice if we think of Proverbs as the kind of success handbook we find in the self-help section. This commentary is written in hope that more Christians will study the wisdom of the book of Proverbs in its entirety, as it was meant to be heard, in home Bible studies, Christian education classrooms, and pulpits. Those who undertake such a study will discover the kind of wisdom that finds its beginning in the fear of the Lord.

---

1. Alyce McKenzie imagines what such a day would be like in *Preaching Proverbs: Wisdom for the Pulpit* (Louisville: Westminster John Knox, 1996), xi–xii.

Introduction

Studying the Book of Proverbs

STUDENTS WHO HAVE tried to teach and preach from Proverbs have told me that they sometimes find it hard to move beyond the obvious meaning of so many of the teachings and sayings, and they fear they will appear to be as superficial as a sound bite when they preach. They worry that the short-hand of the proverbs can become a shortcut around reasoned argument and appeal. They have also heard scholars say that proverbs, once removed from their social context, are lifeless. In all, these students hope to recover some sense of Israel's experience of God that gave rise to the book so the proverbs can do their work and speak to new situations. They also want to learn how to do the reflection that is necessary if one is to probe deeply into the wisdom of the book.

This commentary is designed to help the reader appreciate the similarities and differences between the world of the biblical writers and our own. It seeks to integrate historical and literary methods of study to bridge the gap between the two.[2] While some distinction of aims in method should be made, the study of rhetorical and literary forms can build a bridge between ancient understanding of a text and contemporary readings. Historical research keeps interpretations grounded; literary study keeps interpretation from being stuck in the past.[3]

In all methods of study, the primary concern is for the *theology* of the texts and the place of that theology in the larger theological outlook of the Old and New Testaments. Some interpreters distinguish exegesis (what the texts themselves say) from biblical theology (the relationship between the different theologies of the many texts of Scripture) and biblical hermeneutics (explanation of the encounter between the worldview of the Bible and our own).[4] Throughout the commentary, we will strive to stay focused on the witness of Proverbs to God's work in the ancient world so that we can celebrate what God is doing now in our own days.

The book begins with the heading "The proverbs of Solomon" (1:1), yet the book is much more than a simple collection of sayings. For the purposes of this introduction, we will begin with the smallest unit (i.e., what is a

---

2. Some believe the two should be kept separate; see P. F. Craffert, "Relationships Between Social-Scientific, Literary, and Rhetorical Interpretations of Texts," *BTB* 26 (Spring 1996): 45–55.

3. O. H. Steck, *Old Testament Exegesis: A Guide to the Methodology* (Atlanta: Scholar's Press, 1995), 3–16.

4. R. P. Knierim, "On the Task of Old Testament Theology," in *A Biblical Itinerary: In Search of Method, Form and Content: Essasys in Honor of George W. Coats*, ed. E. E. Carpenter (JSOTSup 240; Sheffield: Sheffield Academic Press, 1997), 151–66.

proverb?) and work our way to the larger unit of the entire book (i.e., what is this book of Proverbs?).

What Is a Proverb?

THE STRANGE TRUTH discovered by researchers in folklore and communication studies is that almost everyone can recognize a proverb but hardly anyone can give an adequate definition. Paremiologists (students of proverbs) continue to propose and debate definitions, so A. Taylor's famous statement about the "indefinable qualities" of a proverb is encouraging: "An incommunicable quality tells us this sentence is proverbial and that one is not."[5] Wolfgang Mieder gathered fifty definitions from nonexperts and condensed them into: "A proverb is a short sentence of wisdom," highlighting the proverb's brevity and observational quality.[6] Other definitions do the same: "Proverbs are short sentences drawn from long experience" (M. Cervantes, *Don Quixote*, 1605); "much matter decocted into a few words" (T. Fuller, *The Worthies of England*, 1662); "the wit of one and the wisdom of many" (Lord J. Russell, *Quarterly Review*, 1850).[7] One famous description is memorable in itself: A proverb has three qualites: shortness, sense, and salt.

A functional view comes from Kenneth Burke, who defined a proverb as a shorthand for situations in life that recur often enough that people feel the need to have a name for them.[8] Proverbs name and size up situations, giving those who use and hear them guidance on how to respond. Proverbs, then, are speech-acts that teach, cajole, taunt, and reprove, depending on how they are used. When the king of Aram threatened to level Samaria, the king of Israel answered in defiance, "One who puts on his armor should not boast like one who takes it off" (1 Kings 20:11). When his disciples asked Jesus when and where the kingdom of God would come, he assured them that no one would miss it: "Where there is a dead body, there the vultures will gather" (Luke 17:37). Burke thought that all poetry (even the poetry of the Bible) can be understood as "complex variants" of the capacity of proverbs to name a situation and embody the attitudes that go with it. Thomas Long adds that

---

5. A. Taylor, *The Proverb* (Cambridge, Mass.: Harvard Univ. Press, 1931), 3.

6. W. Mieder, *Proverbs Are Never Out of Season: Popular Wisdom in the Modern Age* (New York: Oxford Univ. Press, 1993), 18–40.

7. L. and R. Flavell, *Dictionary of Proverbs and Their Origins* (New York: Barnes & Noble, 1993), 2.

8. K. Burke, *The Philosophy of Literary Form* (Berkeley: Univ. of California Press, 1973), 2–3. Burke first published this essay in 1941.

proverbs do not give advice as much as ask the question: Is this a situation that the name fits?[9]

Proverbs are found scattered throughout the Old and New Testaments. David used a popular proverb to declare his good intentions to Saul: "As the old saying goes, 'From evildoers come evil deeds,' so my hand will not touch you" (1 Sam. 24:13). The Hebrew word for "saying" here is *mašal*, which is also the first word of the book, "the *proverbs* of Solomon." *Mašal* was used for prophetic proverbs (Ezek. 16:44; 18:2–3) and parables (Ezek. 17:2; 24:3–5), but also for taunts (Isa. 14:4; Mic. 2:4; Hab. 2:6), oracles (Num. 23:70, as well as the longer discourse sections of Job, see Job 27:1; 29:1). Jesus also quoted common proverbs, such as "Physician, heal yourself" (Luke 4:23), and many of his parables also have a proverbial ring about them (Matt. 13:52–53; Mark 3:23; Luke 6:39; 8:10). Other teachings of Jesus appear to have been inspired by the book of Proverbs (Luke 14:7–11).

As hard as it may be to define the term, we can at least conclude that the *mašal* is a saying that stimulates thought and provides insight. It connects with the human capacity to think in terms of comparisons.[10] One model proposes that the *mašal* is an "ethnic genre" that draws from personal and collective memory and experience. The *mašal* provides a model of reality— or better, a model *for* reality—using analogy to connect the saying with the actual life situation of the audience.[11] In sum, readers of the book of Proverbs must keep in mind that its proverbs are never simple ancient deposits of wisdom; rather, they are sayings designed to provoke a response in those who hear them and relate them to life. See also the excursus "Reading the Sentence Proverbs" in the discussion of chapter 10.

What Is the Book of Proverbs?

ANYONE WHO HAS read or skimmed Proverbs in one sitting will notice that the book is written in a variety of literary forms. While we are most familiar with the short catchy sayings, the first major section of the book was written in a form that most resembles a series of lectures (chs. 1–9). The end of the book brings together a confession, a series of numerical sayings, a final lecture, and an acrostic poem of praise (chs. 30–31).[12] Therefore, the book

---

9. T. Long, *Preaching and the Literary Forms of the Bible* (Philadelphia: Fortress, 1989), 59.

10. K. Snodgrass, "Parables and the Hebrew Scriptures," in *To Hear and Obey: Essays in Honor of Fredrick Carlson Holmgren*, ed. B. Bergfalk and P. E. Koptak (Chicago: Covenant Publications, 1997), 164–77.

11. S. Niditch, *Folklore and the Hebrew Bible* (Minneapolis: Augsburg Fortress, 1993), 67–87.

12. A detailed list of wisdom forms can be found in D. Garrett, *Proverbs, Ecclesiastes, Song of Songs* (NAC 14; Nashville: Broadman, 1993), 29–38.

of Proverbs can best be described as a wisdom anthology or collection. Because there are seven subheadings in the book that name speakers or compilers (1:1; 10:1; 22:17; 24:23; 25:1; 30:1; 31:1), we can more properly speak of a collection of collections.

Why do people make collections of proverbs, and how do the compilers expect them to be used? One contemporary bibliography of proverbs has 9,051 entries, most of them proverb collections.[13] Some collections are created to preserve oral traditions and make them available to researchers, others simply to entertain. Fortunately, the book of Proverbs itself tells us that its sayings were collected with three purposes in mind: to teach wisdom, form character, and encourage an obedient relationship with the Lord (see the comments on 1:1–7).

With this information in mind, we can now ask: What is the book of Proverbs? Here is a definition that will help us understand the way the book presents itself. The book of Proverbs is:

a course of study (a collection of wisdom teachings and sayings)
designed to foster wisdom (the development of discernment and character)
using literary-rhetorical resources (juxtaposition and metaphor)

A Course of Study

THE BOOK OF Proverbs presents itself as a course of study in three major sections. Readers will readily observe that the first two-thirds of the book are divided between instruction and sentence proverbs respectively. The voice of the instructor resumes again in the last third. A three-part structure suggests itself.[14]

Part 1   1:1–9:18 — Instruction
Part 2   10:1–22:16 — Sentence Proverbs
Part 3   22:17–31:31 — Miscellany: Instruction, Sentences, and Additional Forms

---

13. O. Moll, *Sprichwörterbibliographie* (Frankfurt: Vittorio Klostermann, 1958), noted in W. Mieder, *International Proverb Scholarship: An Annotated Bibliography*, 2 vols. (New York and London: Garland, 1982, 1990). See also W. Mieder and A. Dundes, *The Wisdom of Many: Essays on the Proverb* (New York and London: Garland, 1981).

14. P. W. Skehan, "Wisdom's House," in *Studies in Israelite Poetry and Wisdom* (Washington, D. C.: Catholic Biblical Association of America, 1971), 27–45, proposes a similar three-part structure.

Following a short prologue, a series of extended wisdom teachings allow us to listen in on the education of a young man coming of age. The young man's mother and father urge him again and again: "Hear my son!" Scattered among these lessons are speeches of Wisdom, who invites young men to her feast of teaching (1:8–9:18). The middle and largest portion of the book is devoted to a collection of "Proverbs of Solomon," individual wisdom sayings that are sometimes gathered around repetitions of word or theme (10:1–22:16). These anonymous sayings also speak of a son whose wise choices makes his parents glad. A third section of the book is a miscellaneous collection of instructions and individual sayings that concludes with a mother advising her son (22:17–31:31).[15]

This three-part course of study brings together parental instruction, community sayings, and traditional words of the wise in a series of lessons one must master before moving on to the next unit. For readers, this means one completes the lessons of chapters 1–9, learning wisdom and fear of the Lord, before going on to practice deciphering and connecting the individual sayings in chapters 10–22. The third and final course leads the reader into more nuanced use of forms and symbolism (chs. 22–31), challenging the reader to develop competence in a variety of genres.

Designed to Foster Wisdom

THE OPENING VERSES (1:1–7) explain that this course of study was designed to foster wisdom, and this commentary hopes to show that this wisdom encompasses all of life; it unites belief and action. Wisdom is concerned with what one understands but also what one does with that understanding. Wisdom is about developing both discernment and character.

Every good teacher knows that education is more than passing on a body of knowledge; it nurtures a person's growth in knowledge and discernment. In the book of Proverbs, much is said about discipline and discretion (1:2–4), the ability to use knowledge and judgment to make wise decisions for the good of one's self and one's community. Wisdom is as much about seeing clearly as it is about making decisions and acting. To do what is right, one

---

15. D. A. Dorsey, *The Literary Structure of the Old Testament: A Commentary on Genesis–Malachi* (Grand Rapids: Baker, 1999), 187, proposes a five-part structure.

   a Two-part introduction (1:1–7; 1:8–9:18)
      b Solomon's proverbs—first collection (10:1–22:16)
         c Words of the wise (22:17–24:34)
      b' Solomon's proverbs—second collection (25:1–29:27)
   a' Two-part conclusion (30:1–33; 31:1–31)

must be able to discern what that good is in a variety of situations, and wisdom promises to teach how that may be done.

Discernment and character are both necessary for wise living; they are inseparably related. Years ago I listened as an InterVarsity campus staff member explained to our college fellowship that God is just as interested in the kind of people we are as in the good works that we do. Character, he said, is the foundation for godly living, and he drew a diagram of a house set on a firm foundation to illustrate the point. Biblical wisdom unites the process of becoming mature persons with the larger scheme of God's purposes for all creation. It guides the way we live in our bodies and our communities by encouraging the development of virtues.[16]

Using the Rhetorical Resources of Juxtaposition and Metaphor

FOR THIS COURSE of study to be effective in instilling wisdom, the learner must come to see, accept, and believe that wisdom really is the best path for life. In other words, education as it is found in the book of Proverbs employs elements of *rhetoric*; it must persuade the learner (ancient and contemporary) that its view of life is a good one and that its lessons are worth learning. Instructive lectures and witty proverbs have this in common: They both use every available means of persuasion to shape outlook and character. Many of the proverbs about speaking share this view (4:24; 15:23, 31). They look to the facility of speech as a means for establishing righteousness and justice in the world. Hear, for example, how Lemuel's mother urges him to speak out for justice: "Speak up for those who cannot speak for themselves, for the rights of all who are destitute. Speak up and judge fairly; defend the rights of the poor and needy" (31:8–9).

For the purposes of our definition, we begin by noting that biblical rhetoric shares the concern for the "means of persuasion" of classical Greek rhetoric, but also observe that it takes a very different path to achieve its ends. (1) Biblical rhetoric is concrete. Greek rhetoric states and illustrates whereas the Bible most often describes reality, leaving the reader to draw conclusions. (2) Biblical rhetoric uses parataxis, not syllogisms; words like "whereas," "therefore," and "consequently" are not often found. Instead, biblical rhetoric relies on juxtaposition, such as the comparison of Jairus's daughter and the

---

16. J. R. Wilson, "Biblical Wisdom, Spiritual Formation, and the Virtues," in *The Way of Wisdom: Essays in Honor of Bruce K. Waltke*, ed. J. I. Packer and S. K. Soderlund (Grand Rapids: Zondervan, 2000), 297–307.

woman with a hemorrhage.[17] The book of Proverbs juxtaposes characters, such as personified Wisdom and Folly in chapter 9, and single proverbs, such as in the famous pair of 26:4–5, illustrating both sides of dealing with the fool:

> Do not answer a fool according to his folly,
>> or you will be like him yourself.
> Answer a fool according to his folly,
>> or he will be wise in his own eyes.

Binary structures prevail, not only in the parallelism of the verses but also in paired images: light and dark, two paths, righteous and evil, and especially oppositions. One learns to read the book of Proverbs by closely watching for the binary oppositions.[18]

Related to the strategy of juxtaposition is the use of metaphor to draw a comparison between insight and image. Metaphor is so widespread throughout the Bible that we often overlook its presence or we relegate it to a position of lesser importance by speaking of ornamentation or style. We need to keep in mind that metaphor is one of the Bible's "controlling modes of thought," a "perspective" or way of seeing something in terms of something else.[19] For example, when the parental teacher wants to speak of wisdom's rewards, the point can be made explicitly (3:1–10) or indirectly by speaking of Woman Wisdom as a tree of life (3:13–18).

I often refer to a distinction between *practical teaching*, which is direct, usually spoken in the imperative, and *poetic teaching*, which uses imagery as a form of indirect communication. Practical teaching is generally found in the instructions of the parent to the son while poetic teaching is most concentrated in the sayings, but the distinction should not be held too tightly. The instructions make much use of metaphor, as in the image of the road and the division of the two ways, and most majestically in the image of Woman Wisdom. So also, the individual sayings often speak their message directly ("It is not good to be partial to the wicked or to deprive the innocent of justice,"

---

17. R. Meynet, *Rhetorical Analysis: An Introduction to Biblical Rhetoric* (JSOTSup 256; Sheffield: Sheffield Academic Press, 1998), 172–77.

18. K. Egan, *Teaching As Story Telling: An Alternative Approach to Teaching and the Curriculum* (London: Routledge, 1988). Egan shows how good teachers use binary oppositions to make content clear and compelling.

19. On "modes of thought," see N. Frye, *The Great Code: The Bible and Literature* (San Diego and New York: Harcourt, Brace, Jovanovich, 1982), 54; on "perspective," see K. Burke, "The Four Master Tropes," in *A Grammar of Motives* (Berkeley: Univ. of California Press, 1945), 503–5.

18:5). Why metaphor? It not only teaches truth in unique and interesting ways, it speaks to the heart. Education in wisdom is too important to be trusted with anything less.

 THE NIV APPLICATION Commentary Series asks each of its authors to treat three areas of interpretation: the original meaning of a text, steps taken in bridging contexts, and the contemporary significance of a text. The first task, discerning the original meaning of a biblical text, requires that the student of Proverbs examine the ancient faith and culture of Israel as well as the larger context of wisdom in the ancient Near East.

Wisdom in the Ancient Near East

ONE MAY STUDY historical context in a variety of ways, examining political history, cultural practices, and belief systems, often consulting archaeological research; but whatever the interest, the student of biblical wisdom literature is primarily occupied with texts, biblical and extrabiblical. One scholar of ancient Near Eastern studies has said that ancient texts have a horizontal axis, the historical circumstances and lived experience that produced them in a particular time and place, and a vertical access, earlier texts that inspired them and later texts that react to them.[20]

Use of extrabiblical texts is a recent development; the nineteenth century discovery of the Rosetta Stone unlocked the scores of manuscripts written in hieroglyphics and ancient scripts. As a result, scholars discovered that many texts were similar to the extended teachings and proverbial sayings collected in the book of Proverbs. The study of biblical wisdom literature has profited enormously from the study of these texts, although the extent to which they should be compared is vigorously debated. For example, W. McKane's distinction between extended instructions and short proverbial sayings is observed in this commentary, even while his theory that earlier secular wisdom texts were later given a religious overhaul is not.[21] The cultures of Egypt and Mesopotamia used both instructions and proverbs.

---

20. W. W. Hallo, ed., *The Context of Scripture* (Leiden: Brill, 1997), xxvi.

21. W. McKane, *Proverbs: A New Approach* (London: SCM, 1970), 51–208. Thirty years after its publication, this introduction to "International Wisdom" is still essential reading. For a challenge to McKane's theory, see S. Weeks, *Early Israelite Wisdom* (Oxford: Clarendon, 1994), 53–73, who argues that sufficient evidence is lacking.

Introduction

Mesopotamia and Canaan

THE EARLIEST TEXT, *The Instructions of Shuruppak*, may date as early as 2500 B.C. It records the words of a wise man urging his son to accept his teaching. Most of the teachings give a simple directive followed by a motivating reason for the command.

Do not make a guarantee for some; the person will have a hold on you.

Do not go to a place of strife; the strife will make you a witness.

You should not curse with violence; it comes back to the hand![22]

There are also a number of proverb collections. One Sumerian proverb recommends thrift: "Build like a lord, live like a slave! Build like a slave, live like a lord!"[23] Although this literature shows a distinct use of instructional and proverbial forms, few scholars claim that any of these sayings inspired the proverbs of the Bible. Some, noting their separation of wisdom and religion, believe these texts should not be called wisdom literature at all.[24]

More comparisons are made with the writing associated with a wise man from the Neo-Babylonian court of Esarhaddon (681–669 B.C.). The figure of Ahiqar was widely known in the ancient world over a long period of time, even receiving mention in the apocryphal book of Tobit (Tobit 1:21–22). In a late fifth-century B.C. Aramaic manuscript uncovered in Egypt, the sayings attributed to Ahiqar are introduced with the story of his nephew's plot to discredit him before the king. When he is vindicated, Ahiqar finds his nephew, puts him in chains, administers a beating, and then recites the teachings, presumably because the young man had not learned any wisdom the first time he heard them!

Spare not your son from the rod; otherwise, can you save him [from wickedness]?

If I beat you my son, you will not die; but if I leave you alone, [you will not live].[25]

These aphorisms, riddles, fables, instructions, and brief sayings may have originated in Syria and were added latter to the narrative from Mesopotamia.

---

22. "The Instructions of Shuruppak," *ANET*, 594–95 and *BWL*, 92–95.

23. B. Alster, *Proverbs of Ancient Sumer: The World's Earliest Proverb Collections*, 2 vols. (Bethesda, Md.: CDL Press, 1997). Proverbs appear as early as 2600 B.C. and are often found on tablets used to teach writing to scribes.

24. W. G. Lambert, *Babylonian Wisdom Literature* (Winona Lake, Ind.: Eisenbrauns, 1996), 1.

25. "Ahiqar: A New Translation and Introduction," trans. J. Lindenberger, in *Old Testament Pseudepigrapha*, 2 vols. (Garden City, N.Y.: Doubleday, 1985), 2:498; *ANET*, 428 (cf. Prov. 23:13–14).

Like the book of Proverbs, they advise readers on relating to kings and speak of wisdom as a divine gift.

Egypt

ALTHOUGH PROVERBS WERE not unknown to the Egyptians, most of the literature that is comparable to the book of Proverbs comes in the form of extended instructions given by an elder to a younger man addressed as "my son." It is not certain whether the relationship depicted was real parenthood or that of a teacher and student. The instruction offered to teach a young man what he needed to know to succeed in life. Whether the teaching came from a ruler (e.g., Ptahhotep, Kagemni, Merikare) to his son, a teacher (e.g., Amenemhet, Duauf) to court officials, or a scribe (e.g., Ani) to his son, all made the basic assumption that "there is no one born wise."[26]

Topics varied from instruction to instruction, but a general list of subjects includes choosing one's friends and associates, proper behavior before superiors, responsible use of the power of speech, integrity in business and community relationships, and acceptance of the will of God. Such concerns were not limited to instructions but permeated the Egyptians' outlook on life and death. One of the earliest tomb inscriptions presents a standard list of virtues in which the deceased claims to have "done justice," such as rescuing the weak, giving bread to the hungry and clothes to the naked, respecting father, and pleasing mother. "I spoke truly, I did right, I spoke fairly, I repeated fairly."[27]

Much scholarly attention has been given to the strong resemblance of Proverbs 22:17–24:22 and the "Instruction of Amenemope."[28] Arguments that one inspired the other, most assuming that the Egyptian text came first, are tenuous and add little to our understanding of Proverbs. It should also be remembered that themes and phrases comparable with Amenemope arc found throughout the book of Proverbs, not just in chapters 22–24.[29]

---

26. "The Instruction of Ptahhotep," *AEL*, 1:63; *ANET*, 412.

27. "Inscription of Nefer-Seshem-Re Called Shesi," *AEL*, 1:17.

28. R. Murphy provides a balanced assessment of the question in *Proverbs*, 290–94, and *The Tree of Life*, 23–25. See also J. H. Walton, "Cases of Alleged Borrowing," in *Ancient Israelite Literature in Its Cultural Context* (Grand Rapids: Zondervan, 1989), 192–97; and N. Whybray's review of research in *The Book of Proverbs: A Survey of Modern Study* (HBIS 1; Leiden: Brill, 1995), 6–14, 78–84.

29. See J. Ruffle, "The Teaching of Amenemope and Its Connection with the Book of Proverbs," *TynBul* 28 (1977): 29–68; reprinted in R. B. Zuck, *Learning from the Sages: Selected Studies on the Book of Proverbs* (Grand Rapids: Baker, 1995), 293–331.

Introduction

In the last few years the picture of Israelite adaptation of ancient Near Eastern wisdom has received some challenges, especially concerning the lack of explicit reference in the biblical texts to court schools and professional teachers of wisdom. The instruction of Proverbs 1–9 seems to be directed toward life in general, not life at the court, and only a few sections of Proverbs 10–22 and 25–29 concern kings, and even these may have their origins among everyday people. The question of foreign wisdom's influence on Israel is related to the question of the social context of education in ancient Israel. Were there schools similar to those depicted in texts from Egypt and Mesopotamia? How did education take place in Israel?

Social Situation: Schools, Courts, or Clan?

THE EARLIEST REFERENCE to schools in Israel is found in the apocryphal book of Sirach (Sir. 51:23), which names a "house of study" in the second century B.C., some eight hundred years after David and Solomon. While the evidence from the Bible and inscriptions indicates that writing was used and taught from a very early time, there is no mention of a school. Evidence for schools has been extrapolated from biblical texts, inscriptions from Palestine, and texts discovered throughout the ancient Near East, and scholars have reached opposite conclusions. Some say the silence on the existence of schools in Israel shows that none existed, while others say that the presence of schools was so widespread that no mention of them needed to be made.

The idea of Israelite schools was developed on analogy with the presence of schools in Egypt, Mesopotamia, and probably Ugarit. One hypothesis takes the presence of similar vocabulary and images in the biblical Proverbs as evidence that such ideas were passed on through schools.[30] Yet no evidence brought forth to date is sufficient to support the analogy, nor does it require the presence of schools.[31]

Literacy is not stressed in Israelite wisdom literature; rather, the emphasis is placed on hearing, whereas Egyptian texts make a number of references

---

30. N. Shupak, "The 'Sitz-im-Leben' of the Book of Proverbs in the Light of a Comparison of Biblical and Egyptian Wisdom Literature," *RB* 94:1 (1987): 98–119, and *Where Can Wisdom be Found?* (OBO 130; Göttingen: Vandenhoeck & Ruprecht, 1993), 339. Similarities include the heated and cool-tempered persons (cf. Prov. 19:19), weighing of hearts (24:12), and chambers of the belly ("inmost being," 20:30).

31. J. Crenshaw, "Education in Ancient Israel," *JBL* 104 (1985): 601–15; and "The Contemplative Life," in *Civilizations of the Ancient Near East*, ed. J. Sasson (New York: Scribners, 1995); both reprinted in *Urgent Advice and Probing Questions: Collected Writings on Old Testament Wisdom* (Macon, Ga.: Mercer Univ. Press, 1995). See also F. W. Golka, "The Israelite Wisdom School or 'The Emperor's New Clothes,'" in *The Leopard's Spots: Biblical and African Wisdom in Proverbs* (Edinburgh: T. & T. Clark, 1993), 4–15.

to writing. Instead of postulating formal schools for which there is little evidence, one could envision "family guilds specializing in crafts of various kinds."[32] One model sets Israelite wisdom instruction in the house of the courtier training a son to succeed him in service.[33] In sum, it appears that while similarities to Egyptian wisdom may be noted in the book of Proverbs (esp. in chs. 1–9 and 22–24), the biblical and archaeological evidence suggests that wisdom instruction in Israel took place in the family or clan, not in schools as we think of them.[34]

Author and Date

THE ATTRIBUTION OF the book to Solomon (Prov. 1:1) sends us to the notice in 1 Kings 4:29–34 that he received his wisdom as a gift of God. That text praises Solomon's wisdom and insight as he is credited with speaking three thousand proverbs, composing a thousand and five songs, and exploring the world of nature. Earlier in that book, we read that Solomon asked God for this wisdom (3:2), and earlier still, David charged his son Solomon to act in wisdom, repaying those who had done evil to his father (2:6, 9). Solomon's epitaph lifts up his wisdom as the most notable aspect of his reign (11:41), portraying him as a "wise son who brings joy to his father" (Prov. 10:1).

Yet there is a shadow that falls over Solomon's reign. He also loved many foreign women, who turned his heart after other gods (1 Kings 11:1–13). The kingdom was torn away from his son Rehoboam, who was left with only one of the eleven tribes. Rehoboam refused the wise counsel of his advisors, and as a result he suffered a rebellion and the loss of the northern territory of Israel (12:1–20). So Solomon was also remembered for his apostasy and a dynasty that was only kept in place by the mercy of God. In sum, while Solomon was like the wise son of Proverbs, he also resembled the young men who go astray (Prov. 7:1–27; 9:13–18; 31:1–13) and had a son who did the same.

The attribution to Solomon at the head of the book and its link with Solomon's patronage of wisdom sets the book of Proverbs in that historical context. Yet the contemporary reader may be surprised that foreign names

---

32. J. L. Crenshaw, "The Perils of Specializing in Wisdom: What I Have Learned from Thirty Years of Teaching," in *Urgent Advice*, 594, and *Education in Ancient Israel: Across the Deadening Silence* (New York: Doubleday, 1998).

33. B. K. Waltke, "The Book of Proverbs and Ancient Wisdom Literature," *BibSac* 139 (1979): 221–38; reprinted in *Learning from the Sages: Selected Studies on the Book of Proverbs*, ed. R. B. Zuck (Grand Rapids: Baker, 1995), 49–65.

34. J. D. Martin, *Proverbs* (OTG; Sheffield: Sheffield Academic Press, 1995), 18–31; D. W. Jamieson-Drake, *Scribes and Schools in Monarchic Judah* (Sheffield: JSOT Press, 1991), 138–57.

are credited with some sections of the book.[35] Of the seven superscriptions that organize the book of Proverbs, three name Solomon (1:1; 10:1; with "the men of Hezekiah," 25:1), two name "the wise" (22:17; 24:23), and the last two name Agur (30:1) and Lemuel (along with his mother, 31:1), persons about whom we know hardly anything.

Arguments about authorship often go hand in hand with attempts to date the material, but dating is difficult, especially when working with a book that is an anthology of texts. Who could date the entries in a Norton Reader without the introductions? The earlier view that single proverbs came before the extended instructions has been overturned by the discovery of late proverbs and early instructions. Both types of literature can be documented in extrabiblical texts written before Solomon ruled. A more recent view, noting verbal and thematic similarities between chapters 1–9 and 31 and correspondences with the postexilic social situation, suggests a work of editorial shaping that placed those chapters as a frame around chapters 8–30, sometime after the return from exile.[36] The differences in literary form in Proverbs make some sort of collection and shaping more than likely, but this hypothesis says little about the relative age of the components and smuggles in the older view. Even while it is logical to assume that an introduction is written last (the way we were taught in school), the claim that chapters 1–9 are introductory says more about editorial work than composition.[37]

Therefore, there is no compelling reason to doubt that Solomon is to be associated with much of the book as author and patron, even as we recognize that it is not possible to discern by any scholarly criteria what is directly attributable to Solomon and what is the work of later hands who carried on his tradition of wisdom. So it is that his name appears first, perhaps as tribute and dedication, the way Webster's name appears on today's editions of the dictionary he wrote long ago. "The people of Israel, no less than any one man, is ultimately also the author of Proverbs."[38]

---

35. B. S. Childs, *Introduction to the Old Testament As Scripture* (Philadelphia: Fortress, 1979), 553. Childs believes that the ascriptions to Agur and Lemuel indicate that the first verse credits Solomon with a general responsibility for the whole book, 548.

36. C. V. Camp, *Wisdom and the Feminine in the Book of Proverbs* (BLS 11; Sheffield: Almond Press, 1985).

37. Against the view of M. V. Fox, *Proverbs 1–9*, 6, 48–49. However, Fox's skepticism about various attempts to date Prov. 1–9 in the mid-fifth century B.C. rightly argues that correspondences between text and context do not rule out other social-historical contexts. So, for example, Fox suggests that personified Wisdom may be a response to Greek philosophy, but he adds that while this and other characteristics "allow for a Hellenistic dating, they do not prove it."

38. W. G. Plaut, *The Book of Proverbs: A Commentary* (New York: Union of American Hebrew Congregations, 1961), 10.

Perhaps more important, this book of Proverbs offers the wisdom that was given to Solomon to all who would read its pages and heed its lessons. Just as Solomon sought wisdom above the power of wealth and was given both, so readers of Proverbs in identification with Solomon are urged to make the same choice. It is often said that difficult situations require the "wisdom of Solomon." It is available because he and those who came after him have bequeathed it to us in this book.[39]

ONCE WE HAVE discerned an ancient writer's message and purpose to the best of our ability, how are we to build a bridge between that original situation and our own? This commentary recommends three related approaches to the question: a concern for rhetorical effects, a study of the canonical context, and a reflection on the theological message.

Rhetorical Effects

IF WE ASSUME that the Scriptures were written to bring about changes in the lives of those who read, hear, and reflect on them, we will take care to discover the rhetorical effects a passage was designed to achieve. Rhetorical effects are those changes in belief, attitude, or action that come about as the product of intentional communication. If, for instance, Proverbs 9:1–6 and its picture of Wisdom's feast was designed to create a desire for wisdom and a hunger for her teachings, then we will carry over that understanding of the intended outcome as we make application for today. While every commentary engages in this process to a greater or lesser extent, the renewed appreciation among biblical scholars for the intended *effects* of biblical texts will be central to our study.[40] It is also this concern that keeps biblical study grounded in the life of the church (i.e., what some call *the ethics of interpretation*[41]).

---

39. R. E. Clements has suggested that "for the most part the proverbs and admonitions of the wise men of ancient Israel have little to gain or lose by being ascribed to Solomon. They are intended to be true and memorable in themselves, rather than on account of their notable authorship" ("Solomon and the Origins of Wisdom in Israel," in *Perspectives on the Hebrew Bible: Essays in Honor of Walter J. Harrelson*, ed. James L. Crenshaw [Macon, Ga.: Mercer Univ. Press, 1988], 25).

40. D. Patrick and A. Scult, *Rhetoric and Biblical Interpretation* (Sheffield: JSOT Press, 1990), 12, define rhetoric as "the means by which a text establishes and manages its relationship to its audience in order to achieve a particular effect."

41. S. Fowl, "The Ethics of Interpretation; or, What's Left Over After the Elimination of Meaning," in *The Bible in Three Dimensions: Essays in Celebration of the Fortieth Anniversary of the Department of Biblical Studies, University of Sheffield*, ed. D. J. A. Clines, S. E. Fowl, and S. E. Porter (Sheffield: JSOT Press, 1990), 379–98.

Therefore, readers must not only attend to literary forms, techniques and structures, juxtaposition and metaphor as discussed in earlier sections, they must also look for the function such features are meant to perform. That is, they must look at their rhetorical strategy and ask how these texts are intended to inform and persuade. In studying a passage, one looks at the terms and images that are associated, those that are set in contrast, those that lead the reader along a movement and progression, and those that mark transformations. The approach can be summarized in a series of questions: What goes with what? What is versus what? What leads to something else? What is changed or becomes new?

Attention to these relationships and the structures they reveal give some clues to the writer's persuasive purpose. In addition, readers can also look for the connection with the joys and sorrows of human experience, the point at which readers identify with the speaker, characters, or action. In the hands of a skilled communicator, identification with readers becomes a powerful rhetorical strategy.[42]

A related concern has to do with the community that written texts establish with their readers (and hearers), that is, how writers establish a relationship with readers through a written text. Interestingly enough, the book of Proverbs not only speaks to the business of getting along with others in families and communities, it creates a community, as all texts do with their readers.[43] Students of the book of Proverbs are invited to live in *this* community of believers, created by teachers and speakers and sages, who use words to draw people together instead of driving them apart. This book of Scripture, then, is not only about wise speech and action, it also imparts words of wisdom as it addresses its readers and hearers. The book itself takes on the role of sage and teacher, becoming the reader's guide and friend.

Teaching takes place as readers identify themselves with the sons who are addressed at the beginning and end of the book (as well as a number of points in between, 10:1; 13:1; 15:20; 23:26). Alongside the depiction of a young man's education is a recurring symbol of home: The young man leaves his role as son in his parents' home to establish a household of his own (Gen.

---

42. For more detailed descriptions of this approach, see P. E. Koptak, "Reading Scripture with Kenneth Burke: Genesis 38," in *To Hear and Obey: Essays in Honor of Fredrick Carlson Holmgren*, ed. B. J. Bergfalk and P. E. Koptak (Chicago: Covenant Publications, 1997): 84–94, and "Rhetorical Identification in Preaching," *Preaching* 14 (November/December 1998): 11–18.

43. J. B. White, *When Words Lose Their Meaning: Constitutions of Language, Character, and Community* (Chicago: Univ. of Chicago Press, 1984), 14–20. For White, language in general and reading in particular have three functions: to establish a relationship between writer and reader, to form individual character, and to constitute and reconstitute culture.

2:24; Prov. 31:10–31). As he learns and grows, he also must know how to relate to the larger community, treating neighbors well, avoiding any association with wicked men and adulterous women, and loving wisdom. In churches and seminary classes, a number of women have spoken to me about the difficulty of identifying with such a masculine role, and admittedly, more work is required of female readers. Even so, the symbolism can be transposed into terms that apply to men and women, speaking to such topics as relation to parents, choice of spouse, and reputation in the community.

A good example of this comes from Alice Ogden Bellis, who transposed the warnings about the adulteress in Proverbs 7 into terms her daughters could readily understand. In a letter to them she spoke about the seductions that would come from young men as well as from the larger culture:

> Do not be misled by handsome faces, by beautiful bodies, by the right clothes, or the correct manners. Especially do not be deluded by flatterers who tell you that you are beautiful (of course you are!) and then ask you to give them your body or your soul.... Rather spend your time with men of substance and worth. A good man is hard to find, but he is more precious than jewels.[44]

While the symbolism requires some work of translation to be applicable to persons of all ages and both genders, it speaks to universal issues.

Canonical Context

WHEN INTERPRETERS USE a canonical approach, they recognize that the historical context in which a Scripture text was produced and shaped is not the only context to be considered. It is also necessary to study the final form of the book, its place in the larger biblical canon, and the process by which that canon was shaped.[45] In other words, scholars, preachers, and teachers study the final form of text, inquiring about its norming function and the strategic questions it was designed to answer. Similarities in vocabulary and theme as well as other connections with the rest of the Old Testament suggest that the book of Proverbs was given its final form as a response to the story of Israel as recorded in the Old Testament (commands, historical

---

44. A. Ogden Bellis, "The Gender and Motives of the Wisdom Teacher in Proverbs 7," in *Wisdom and Psalms: The Feminist Companion to the Bible, Second Series*, ed. A. Brenner and C. R. Fontaine (Sheffield: Sheffield Academic Press, 1998), 90–91.

45. E. Dyck, "Canon As Context for Interpretation," in *The Act of Bible Reading: A Multidisciplinary Approach to Biblical Interpretation*, ed. E. Dyck (Downers Grove, Ill.: InterVarsity Press, 1996), 33–64. See also D. F. Morgan, *Between Text and Community: The "Writings" in Canonical Interpretation* (Minneapolis: Fortress, 1990).

narratives, and prophecy), a response that offers another way of describing a life lived in obedience and trust.

Put another way, the book of Proverbs is engaged in a conversation with
the rest of the Old Testament, a conversation that points to the common
ground that lies between the covenant God made with Israel and God's
instruction in wisdom found in Proverbs. A good example is the common
language of fatherly discipline found in Deuteronomy 8:5 and Proverbs
3:11–12. One is set in the context of covenant, the other in the context of
wisdom, yet both state that obedient sonship is a matter of growth and
receiving correction.

The interpreter is therefore interested in the interactions that take place
among Scripture texts, one shedding light on another, particularly when a text
makes allusion to a person or event in Israel's story.[46] Clues to such intertextual relationships can be found by using a concordance to highlight common
vocabulary. So we shall see that personified Wisdom picks up biblical images
of creation to insist that she understands the way the world works and can
pass on her secrets (see the comments on chs. 3 and 8).

Moreover, the canonical approach also insists that we read Old Testament
texts in the context of the Christian Bible and look to see how Old Testament
themes are developed there.[47] The image of wisdom present at creation is central to the New Testament's understanding of the nature of our Lord Jesus
Christ (John 1; Col. 1; Heb. 1; see "Wisdom in the New Testament" later in
this introduction). We do not read these later understandings back into the
Old Testament texts, but rather look to see how the Old Testament provides the language to describe what God has done in sending Jesus into the
world he made.

In sum, we will look at texts that come before and after Proverbs in our
Bibles to set its message in the larger context of God's word to the church.
This work of canonical study is a necessary foundation for the third step in
bridging contexts, that of theological reflection.

---

46. See M. Garsiel, *The First Book of Samuel: A Literary Study of the Comparative Structures,
Analogies and Parallels* (Ramat-Gan: Revivim, 1985). On inner-biblical interpretation, see M.
Fishbane, *Biblical Interpretation in Ancient Israel* (Oxford: Clarendon, 1985).

47. C. J. Scalise, *From Scripture to Theology: A Canonical Journey into Hermeneutics* (Downers
Grove: InterVarsity Press, 1996). Scalise argues that interpreters must explain how each biblical text fuctions as authority for the Christian church. See also Scalise, *Hermeneutics As Theological Prolegomena: A Canonical Approach* (Macon: Mercer Univ. Press, 1994).

Theological Reflection

ONCE RHETORICAL STRATEGIES and canonical contexts have been examined, the last step before moving on to talk about application or contemporary significance is to reflect on a text's theology.[48] By theological reflection, I mean a discussion of a Scripture passage's teaching about the character of God and its relation to the gospel of Jesus Christ. In this way, the interpreter should show how a passage contributes to a biblical theology of the subjects discussed. A guiding rule of thumb for this step in interpretation will ask what each passage teaches about God, how that teaching is good news, and how it relates to the good news of the gospel. Certainly that good news also tells us about ourselves and life as it was meant to be lived in this world. Our goal will be to determine how the passage portrays God's character and actions in the world of the past so that we can determine what God is doing today.

Responses of praise, trust, and obedience can follow from this reflection. But theology always comes first. "One must read the Bible theologically before reading it morally."[49] So, for example, we will ask what the book of Proverbs has to say about God before going on to discuss the human response, namely, the "fear of the Lord" (see comments in "Contemporary Significance," below). While Proverbs' portrait of God is many faceted, three features stand out.

(1) Yahweh created the world by wisdom. The statement of Proverbs 3:19, "By wisdom the LORD laid the earth's foundations," is developed as personified Wisdom places herself on the scene: "I was there when he set the heavens in place ... when he marked out the foundations of the earth" (8:27–29). Yahweh creates and gives life, and Wisdom claims a role, just as she claims to lead those who follow her on the path of life (8:35; 9:11; 14:26–27). Yahweh blesses with health, wealth, and honor through the work of Wisdom who holds these gifts of God in her hand (3:5–10; 16). God's life-giving work is mediated by Wisdom, who, like God, delights in humankind (8:31); Wisdom is an expression of God's love!

(2) Yahweh in wisdom rules and judges the world. While it is not stated explicitly that Yahweh governs through the agency of wisdom, it is clear that Woman Wisdom's prescriptions for a king's righteous and just actions are modeled after divine rule (8:15–16; 15:10–12; 31:4–9). Proverbs' instructions for fair dealing frequently pull back the curtain to show Yahweh who

---

48. See R. Schultz, "Integrating Old Testament Theology and Exegesis: Literary, Thematic and Canonical Issues," in *NIDOTTE*, 185–205.

49. J. Sanders, "Hermeneutics," in *IDBSup* (Nashville: Abingdon, 1962), 402–7.

watches (15:3; 24:18) and acts (16:4–5; 21:12), repaying good and evil actions in kind. Yahweh looks out for the poor and opposes the wicked who take advantage of them. Such a view of a divine judge assumes a sovereign rule of this world that at times seems paradoxical from our limited viewpoint (16:1–7, 33).

(3) Yahweh gives wisdom to those who seek it. He not only gives and preserves life by means of wisdom, he offers that same wisdom to humans as a guide for choosing life-giving ways over ways that lead to death. In other words, wisdom is one of God's ways to protect and preserve life. To those who seek it and call out for it, wisdom comes as a gift (and with it knowledge of God); in a sense, in giving wisdom, God is giving of himself (2:1–6). This gift protects and saves; it keeps its followers from receiving or doing harm (2:7–22). There is a reciprocal relationship at work. As one lives wisely, the good that one does to others returns, partly because that is the way the world works, but ultimately because that is the way God works in the world.

In sum, the book of Proverbs works to assemble a beautiful mosaic picture of our God who acts in wisdom to give, preserve, and protect human life in all its physical and social dimensions.[50] More wonderful still is the news that God gives this wisdom to humans so they may walk through this world in ways that honor God. This work of God sustains the life of individuals, but it also maintains the life of households, communities, and entire nations, giving each the instructions on righteousness, justice, and equity they need to thrive (1:3). God demonstrated his love for Israel not only in deliverance and covenant (Deut. 7:7–11) but also in many acts of kindness "towards, and on behalf of Israel as a people," including sending the gift of wisdom.[51] Or, seen from another angle, just as God acted to save Israel from its enemies as reported in the historical books, here God acts in love to preserve Israel in times of peace by means of wisdom.

Wisdom in the Old Testament

DESCRIPTIONS OF WISDOM take different shape in different Old Testament contexts. In some, wisdom is knowledge related to a technical skill—for example, Bezalel's skill in crafting artistic designs with silver and gold, stone, and wood (Ex. 31:3). In other contexts, wisdom refers to more general knowl-

---

50. On this topic, see L. Boström, *The God of the Sages: The Portrayal of God in the Book of Proverbs* (Stockholm: Almqvist and Wiksell, 1990).

51. R. E. Clements, "Israel in Its Historical and Cultural Setting," in *The World of Ancient Israel: Sociological, Anthropological and Political Perspectives*, ed. R. E. Clements (Cambridge: Cambridge Univ. Press, 1989), 7–10. See also L. Purdue, J. Blenkinsopp, J. J. Collins, C. Meyers, *Families in Ancient Israel* (Louisville: Westminster John Knox, 1997), 225–49.

edge learned from experience, especially from observation of the creation—for example, the lowly ant models diligence and foresight (Prov. 6:6–8). In general, we can say that wisdom involves knowing what to do in a given situation; skill in crafts or skill in living well both require that a person has learned how to "do the right thing."

Yet wisdom is also a gift from God, a revelation given to those who cry out and seek it (2:1–6); although it is hidden from humans, God knows how to find it (Job 28:1–28). We therefore come to know wisdom in a series of its multifaceted aspects, in part rather than in whole (cf. 1 Cor. 13).[52] Users of this commentary will need to remember to let the word wisdom take its meaning from the way it is used in the literary context first and the lexicon second.

When Proverbs speaks of wisdom, it answers the question, What does a person need to come of age, to become mature and take on the responsibilities of adult life? Wisdom was and is often associated with age in the cultures of the world (cf. Job 12:12). In the Bible, one needs wisdom to function as an adult in relation to God and society.

Biblical wisdom shares these concerns with the commandments (or, to use the Hebrew word for the commandments and teaching, *torah*). In this way, wisdom is complementary to *torah* but comes at these matters from another direction. God teaches through observation and experience as well as divine command, although the distinction between the two is never so defined as to isolate one from the other. So, for example, whereas the commandment says, "Honor your father and mother" (Ex. 20:12; Deut. 5:16), Proverbs says, "A wise son brings joy to his father, but a foolish son grief to his mother" (Prov. 10:1). The commandment says, "You shall not steal" (Ex. 20:15; Deut. 5:19); Proverbs says, "Ill-gotten treasures are of no value, but righteousness delivers from death" (Prov. 10:2).

One might go a little farther and say that experience and observation together persuade the wise of the truth of *torah*. It is *torah* tested in the crucible of experience, and one can draw from that crucible examples of how wisdom works in real life. Examples of wisdom in Proverbs, but also in Job, Ecclesiastes, a number of the psalms, and perhaps even the Song of Songs, join together to say: See, this way of life works—sometimes in ways we did not expect (see Job and Ecclesiastes)—and one need not be afraid to bring the teaching of *torah* to experience to be tested by it. In wisdom literature the rule of God described in the *torah* takes on personal suffering (Job), the contradictions of life (Ecclesiastes), and the presence of evil in this world

---

52. E. M. Curtis, "Old Testament Wisdom: A Model for Faith-Learning Integration," *Christian Scholar's Review* 15/3 (1986): 213–27.

(Proverbs) and affirms that God's instructions can be trusted. Experience ultimately will not contradict them.[53]

Similarly, the wisdom of Proverbs has much in common with the story of Israel as recorded in the books sometimes called the Former Prophets (Joshua, Judges, 1–2 Samuel, and 1–2 Kings) and the Latter Prophets (Isaiah, Jeremiah, Ezekiel, and the twelve minor prophets).[54] For example, Wisdom tells her hearers that "the upright will live in the land, and the blameless will remain in it; but the wicked will be cut off from the land, and the unfaithful will be torn from it" (Prov. 2:21–22). Readers will recall that Israel and Judah were both removed from the land just as the Lord had warned (Deut. 28:64). Wisdom in Proverbs offers another way of understanding what went wrong in the life of the nation. The historical and prophetic books condemned Israel for its idolatry and injustice; as the saying goes, theology is always reflected in sociology, the way we treat others. So also, Proverbs urges fear of the Lord as the antidote to idolatry, and fair dealing in word and deed instead of injustice.

In sum, biblical wisdom literature was written and handed on from generation to generation to offer encouragement to those struggling with their faith. (1) It first of all gives permission to ask the questions, to bring Scripture face to face with experience and experience face to face with Scripture. It is often the young, the sons and daughters of the faithful, who ask such questions, and they are encouraged to do so by the wisdom writings.

(2) It lets people of experience speak and bear witness in answer to those questions: parents teaching sons (Proverbs), sufferers and philosophers locked in debate (Job), an old king reflecting on what is really valuable (Ecclesiastes), and a community of faith that tested these words and passed them on. These were all experienced people. They weren't there for the Exodus, the commands at Sinai, the wanderings in the desert; they weren't there for the crisis of apostasy, prophecy, and conquest. They were, however, seasoned and thoughtful about what they heard in the tradition and what they saw with their eyes. They concluded that Scripture and experience do not contradict one another; their message for us is that obedience and trust worked then and still work now.[55]

---

53. Emerging Judaism identified wisdom with *torah*, as seen in Sir. 24:23 and in 19:20, "All wisdom is fear of the Lord and in all wisdom is the fulfillment of the Law." See R. Murphy, *The Tree of Life*, 78–79.

54. In the Hebrew canon, the major division after "The Torah" is called "The Prophets." It includes the historical books Joshua through 2 Kings and the prophetic books Isaiah through Malachi (except for Ruth, Lamentations, and Daniel, which are found in the third major division, "The Writings").

55. G. Wilson describes the relationship between wisdom and traditional teachings of covenant and law as "holy tension . . . a tension *through* which they provide needed 'words of wisdom'" ("Wisdom," *NIDOTTE*, 4:1277).

What does this have to do with the book of Proverbs? The larger context of wisdom literature supports the suggestion that the book is to be read as the education of a young man receiving the instruction of those older and more experienced than he. He is called to desire and choose wisdom, to master the wisdom teaching of proverbs, maxims, and riddles—all with the goal of learning "the fear of the LORD." Readers are to walk through this education in wisdom with the young man, receiving the teaching of these elders and testing that teaching with their own experience of life (on readers who are not young men, see the earlier discussion). Moreover, the testing takes place as readers see the teachings of the rest of the Old Testament confirmed by another voice of Scripture.

The Wisdom of Proverbs and the New Testament

THE BIBLE OF the Christian church, Old and New Testaments, finds its center in the revelation of God through the person of Jesus Christ. For this reason, we turn our attention toward the New Testament's use of the book of Proverbs and the wisdom tradition of which it is a part. It has been my experience that time spent in study of the book of Proverbs and biblical wisdom tunes the ear for echoes of these writings throughout the New Testament. We know from the writings of emerging Judaism that biblical wisdom and the book of Proverbs had a significant influence on the development of Jewish life and thought. For example, the *Wisdom of Jesus Ben Sirach* not only presents a personification of Woman Wisdom similar to that of the book of Proverbs, it begins and ends with acrostic poems in homage to the book as well.

Both the *teachings* of Jesus as recorded by the Gospel writers and the portrait of the *person* they present are inspired by the book of Proverbs. (1) Jesus taught in ways that resemble the teaching of the sages; he not only used proverbs and comparisons to drive his point home, he talked at length about wisdom: "Everyone who hears these words of mine and puts them into practice is like a wise man who built his house on the rock" (Matt. 7:24); "wisdom is proved right by her actions" (Matt. 11:19; cf. Luke 16:8). In the Synoptic Gospels, Jesus used paradox ("the first will be last") and hyperbole ("better to lose an eye") to get across the unexpected reversals that will come with the kingdom of God.[56] Therefore, one of the titles we may ascribe to Jesus is that of sage or wisdom teacher (cf. Matt. 13:52), one greater in wisdom than Solomon (12:42).

---

56. W. A. Beardslee, "Uses of the Proverb in the Synoptic Gospels," *Int* 24 (1970): 61–73; reprinted in Mieder and Dundes, *The Wisdom of Many*. See also A. P. Winton, *The Proverbs of Jesus: Issues of History and Rhetoric* (Sheffield: Sheffield Academic Press, 1990).

(2) The Gospels, especially John, portray Jesus as more than a teacher of wisdom, but wisdom come in a person.[57] Christians who read personified Wisdom's declarations in Proverbs 8 cannot help but hear echoes of the hymn to the Word in John 1:1–14. How shall we give account for these echoes? We might look to a principle of analogy that is operative throughout the Old and New Testaments. As the Gospel writers struggled for words to describe the wondrous person of Jesus, they borrowed the language of Wisdom in a transferal of her attributes and blessings to him, just as they showed how Jesus was like Moses when he provided bread in the desert and like Elijah when he brought a child to life. Jesus is like Wisdom as she is described in Proverbs: "All that the early Jews or others sought in wisdom and her benefits, the Fourth Evangelist now maintains can be found in Jesus."[58]

(3) Questions often arise concerning this use of the poem in Proverbs 8: Is Christ foreshadowed in the book of Proverbs? The answer is yes and no— yes in that the description of Wisdom provides the concepts and language to describe Christ, no in that the composer and editors of the book did not view it as pointing ahead to the salvation of God come in a person. Does the transfer of this description to the Son of God (John 1:1–14; Col. 1:15–17; Heb. 1:1–2) mean that we can think of him as feminine and address Christ using the feminine *Sophia*? We must remember that while the Bible uses a number of feminine images to describe God, it never speaks to or about God as "she." Similarly, Jesus is like Woman Wisdom but is not to be identified with her.[59] Rather, Christ is proclaimed as the wisdom of God and the power of God (1 Cor. 1:24; cf. Col. 2:2–3).

Therefore, the Christian who reads Proverbs can develop a new appreciation for the significant contribution of the book to the New Testament view of Jesus and what it means to follow this man who both taught wisdom and embodied wisdom in his person. Wisdom is not to become the forgotten voice of the Old Testament, nor is it only to be treated in Old Testament studies. Bible studies and sermons from the Gospels and New Testament let-

---

57. B. Witherington III, *Jesus the Sage: The Pilgrimage of Wisdom* (Philadelphia: Fortress, 1994). See also F. W. Burnett, "Wisdom," in *Dictionary of Jesus and the Gospels*, ed. J. B. Green and S. McKnight (Downers Grove, Ill.: InterVarsity Press, 1992), 873–77.

58. Witherington, *Jesus the Sage*, 370, n. 102, reminds us that John chose the term *logos* (word) and not *sophia* (wisdom). For a discussion of Paul's use of *sophia*, see J. S. Lamp, *First Corinthians 1–4 in Light of Jewish Wisdom Traditions: Christ, Wisdom and Spirituality* (Lewiston, N.Y.: Mellen, 2000), 117–88.

59. Also, the language for describing wisdom in the apocryphal Wisdom of Jesus Ben Sirach and Wisdom of Solomon provides a variety of words and images that are transferred to Jesus. The question is explored in greater detail in the comments for chs. 1, 3, and 8, where Woman Wisdom appears.

ters can do much to restore this long neglected subject of wisdom to the life of Christian communities. To facilitate teaching and preaching, this commentary will look to New Testament texts to shed light on those parts of Proverbs that treat common themes.[60]

IN THE PREVIOUS sections we have seen that Proverbs is so much more than a book of good advice and life lessons, even though it offers both. Its vision of true wisdom calls students from every age to maturity and community—maturity, because one must learn to use wisdom in making good decisions for life, and community, because we need teachers, advisors, and coworkers to make the rule of God visible by the way we live.

For this reason, we may need to unlearn the idea that Proverbs is a book of principles that allow us to predict or even control how life will turn out, a collection of promises that we can cash in like coupons. My seminary teacher in Old Testament used to say that "barking dogs never bite—most of the time."[61] He meant to teach us that proverbs describe the way life usually works, not how it always works or must work. We fool ourselves if we think that we are in a position to become masters of our fates just because we've learned to pay attention to outcomes.

Therefore, it is a mistake to assume that "train up a child" comes as a promise from God, as many brokenhearted parents have realized. Solomon and the sages who followed him never claimed that their observations were promises that God was duty-bound to fulfill. They understood that the wicked sometimes prosper for a time and that the righteous often suffer, but they also knew that God does not stop being God when circumstances seem to point the other way. Instead, these writings show us how life in this God-created universe works so we can work with it and not against it.

It is not only important to understand the nature of proverbs and how they work, but to remember that they were written to people who lived a long time ago in an oriental, agrarian society. When we consider the vast differences

---

60. For help in preaching from the book of Proverbs, see E. Achtemeier, *Preaching from the Old Testament* (Louisville: Westminster John Knox, 1989); and D. Gowan, *Reclaiming the Old Testament for the Christian Pulpit* (Atlanta: John Knox, 1980), for chapters on wisdom literature. T. Long, *Preaching and the Literary Forms of the Bible*, and A. M. McKenzie, *Preaching Proverbs*, have chapters dedicated to the book of Proverbs.

61. F. C. Holmgren, "Barking Dogs Never Bite, Except Now and Then: Proverbs and Job," *AThR* 61 (1979): 341–53.

between the ancient cultures that first heard these proverbs and our own, we will think carefully before we act on what we think the proverbs teach and prescribe. In fact, we should be a bit surprised that so much of what is said rings true to our ears, testimony that many situations and problems in life are still with us today. Still, this sense of recognition should never lull us into a false sense of certainty that our understanding of these sayings is correct. The commentary will seek to point out such differences so readers can enter into the process of interpretation.

One way to draw a connection between the ancient world of Proverbs and our own is to remember that these teachers assume that their readers are also interested in the book's theology and spirituality. There is an experience of God behind theology, and that theology stands behind its prescriptions for wise living. Rather than treating the Bible (and the book of Proverbs) as a collection of proof texts or a list of rules for behavior, we will seek to build on what a passage says about God and God's will to develop theological guidelines for contemporary practice.

While we acknowledge that the Bible does not contain prepackaged responses to ethical questions or a finely scripted list of what believers should do in every situation, we also strongly affirm that Scripture can and does reveal knowledge of God and God's will for us.[62] In the book of Proverbs, the proper response to God is summed up as "the fear of the LORD," the beginning of wisdom that guides all a person's attitudes and actions. Wisdom in action is best described as a life of virtuous character, that is, a life of faithfulness.[63]

Fear of Yahweh

AS THE OLD saying goes, "Fools rush in where angels fear to tread." A wise person knows when to be afraid; the fool fears nothing (or the wrong thing) and pays the price. The saying is never more true than when used to speak about one's relationship with God. The book of Proverbs opens with "the fear of the LORD [as] the beginning of knowledge" (1:7, and knowledge of God, 2:5; 9:10) and closes with the praise of the woman who "fears the LORD" (31:30). Everything in between reminds the reader again and again that one does right, not only because it benefits others and ultimately benefits oneself, but because it pleases God.

We may understand this truth better as we look at the many proverbs concerning the righteous king. The king is to judge rightly (16:10–12; 20:8, 26;

---

62. D. Atkinson, *Pastoral Ethics* (Oxford: Lynx Communications, 1994), 12–13.

63. D. Gill lists faithfulness as the first of the virtues in *Being Good: Building Moral Character* (Downers Grove, Ill.: InterVarsity Press, 2000), 103–13.

24:24–25); he is not to spend his resources on women and drink but is to speak for the rights of the poor and needy (31:1–9). A righteous king's wrath is like a lion's roar, a messenger of death (16:14; 19:12; 20:2), so he should be obeyed and feared. Fear of God and king are identified in 24:21–22: "Fear the LORD and the king, my son, and do not join with the rebellious, for those two will send sudden destruction upon them, and who knows what calamities they can bring?" Just as one would not want to displease a human king, so a wise person seeks to please the God who rules heaven and earth, both for the joy of bringing him pleasure and from a fear of bringing displeasure. Fear of the Lord is "worshipful submission"[64] or "reverent obedience."[65]

For the ancients, fear of the Lord was a sign of recognition that the universe has a ruler and that the proper response before a ruler is to bow. The same response is appropriate today. I do not often quote what actors playing clergy say on TV, but one exchange has stayed in my mind. In offering advice to a parishioner, this minister said, "Early on I learned two things that have helped me make my way in life. The first is that there is a God, and the second is that I am not him." While it sounds obvious, I take this advice as a reminder that the cosmos has a kind and just ruler who rightfully calls people to account for their behavior. So Jesus told many a parable about kings and their subjects to communicate God's gracious authority.

Fear of the Lord requires that we remove ourselves as the center of authority in our self-made universes. In Bertolucci's film *The Last Emperor,* the Chinese boy-king comes to a sudden realization of the power that he holds over others. Wishing to impress his new teacher with a show of authority, he orders his cousin and classmate to drink the bottle of ink from his inkwell, and the cousin obeys. The teacher is appalled at the boy's lack of concern for anyone but himself, yet he also sees his work cut out for him: to teach this king who has not yet gained the wisdom to match his authority.

Yet false kings and petty tyrants that we are, we make the same mistakes, acting only in our own interests and often appearing like spoiled children. Thus, the teachers and sages of Proverbs lead us to wisdom and maturity by pointing to persons who both exercise and submit to authority, much as the centurion related Jesus' authority to his own (Luke 7:6–9). In Proverbs, parents teach children to submit to the community elders and king, while the king answers to God and the people (20:26–28).

While the biblical books we call wisdom books recommend fear of the Lord (see also Job 28:28; Eccl. 12:13–14), the phrase is especially prominent in Proverbs, coming as a kind of evangelistic sermon that calls readers to

64. Kidner, *Proverbs,* 59.
65. Hubbard, *Proverbs,* 48.

take on this basic orientation toward life and God. In other words, just as we seek to introduce family and friends to Jesus as Savior and Lord, our mothers and fathers of the faith in Israel called their children and neighbors to faith and obedience by talking about fear. For today's Christian, the fear of the Lord also means that one has made the foundational decision to trust Jesus as Lord of one's life. To say that we believe in Jesus but to refuse to acknowledge him as Lord of creation and Lord of our lives is to live like the fool, in dangerous denial of the facts. Proverbs, seeing that danger, offers more than tips for success or even for moral guidance; it holds out wisdom as an invitation to relationship with a loving Lord.

Character and Virtue

A SECOND BUT no less important concern of Proverbs is for character formation that leads to faithfulness. If it is a mistake to reduce Proverbs to a book of good advice, it is equally wrong to elevate its counsels to some lofty ideal of human life that has no bearing on everyday choices. Proverbs, if nothing else, zeroes in on the choices we face, and in recommending one way over another, it describes the kind of persons we can become and ought to be. So we are advised to speak truth and not falsehood (14:25; 15:4), to walk in humility and not pride (18:12; 15:25), to practice diligence instead of sloth (18:9), to show generosity instead of greed (18:11).

The proverbs do not give directions for what to do in every situation; instead, they present the qualities of character that guide us in the many decisions we will face in life. It can be encouraging to remember that there is a reciprocal relationship between decision making and character formation. While godly character influences the decision to, for instance, practice self-control over one's tongue, each time we choose to tell the truth, avoid gossip, and offer encouragement instead of unfair criticism we also strengthen the character quality of self-control. Virtues, as they are practiced, become a habit.

The virtues of Proverbs may be summarized in the word "faithfulness" (3:3). In the Scriptures, faithfulness takes on a number of expressions: obedience to commands (Ex. 20:1–12; Matt. 5:19), imitation of Christ and other biblical figures (1 Cor. 4:16; Eph. 5:1; 1 Thess. 1:6; Heb. 6:12; 13:7), and virtue, the cultivation of godly and faithful character (1 Tim. 2:2; 4:8; 6:6, 11). In Proverbs, faithful people fear the Lord and therefore consider the effects their actions have on others (Prov. 14:8, 15; 15:28). They seek to preserve good relations with them, to bring them good and not harm. In New Testament language, they seek to practice love; the famous text of 1 Corinthians 13:4–7 takes on new significance after a study of Proverbs. Just as fear of the

Lord turns our reference point away from ourselves as the final authority, so faithfulness turns our attention toward others as we seek to practice the social virtues of righteousness, justice, and fairness (Prov. 1:3).

In the world of Proverbs, faithfulness seems to move in ever-widening concentric circles from the individual to the family, to the larger household, to the community, and ultimately to the nation and its rulers. So also the church must not neglect Proverbs' emphasis on a gathered people of character, or what some are calling the "communities of character."[66] These communities join together as personalities that practice what is fair, honest, and kind.

Communities, like individuals, exhibit character.[67] We must ask ourselves whether our churches are becoming communities of character where truth is spoken, power politics rejected, generosity practiced, and peace maintained. I believe that they are, but I also know that there are many congregations where no pastor wants to go. It should not surprise us that the church becomes more conflicted as our culture becomes more contentious. True, we do not stop being people of our times when we gather as a Christian fellowship, but we must also be models of what is timeless. It is an irony that often some virtues (clean living) are held up to the exclusion of others (honesty, fairness, and tolerance).

While we ought not move directly from the ideal of a righteous Israel to that of a righteous America, we should observe that the wisdom of Proverbs has a great deal to say about how a nation should exhibit a righteous character, and we should call our government and its leaders to that standard. Many of wisdom's teachings do work even when practiced without a faith commitment. But first things first. Our call for righteousness in our nation should be made credible by the church's demonstration of the faithfulness found in Proverbs. The book should be read to learn what we may become as a church as well as individuals.

For all the above reasons, it is my hope that this commentary will help spark a renewed sense of the importance of biblical wisdom—and Proverbs in particular—in sermons and studies. We usually consult a commentary when we have to teach or preach from a passage, and that is especially appropriate here, for this book of Proverbs would have us become wise teachers. The ultimate goal of the book is to move its readers from students to teachers, those who take what is given and pass it on to the next generation (as implied in 4:1–9). The book of Proverbs is not only concerned that we

---

66. After S. Hauerwas, *A Community of Character: Toward a Constructive Christian Social Ethic* (Notre Dame, Ind.: Univ. of Notre Dame Press, 1981).
67. See W. P. Brown, *Character in Crisis: A Fresh Approach to the Wisdom Literature of the Old Testament* (Grand Rapids: Eerdmans, 1996).

become wise, but that we teach others to fear God and live in faithful relationships with others through love of wisdom. Just as the woman who "fears the LORD" is to be praised at the gate (31:30–31), let Wisdom as she is found in the book of Proverbs be praised in our Bible studies and pulpits![68]

---

68. Throughout the commentary, use of "Yahweh" signifies the tetragrammaton YHWH (NIV, "LORD").

Outline of Proverbs

Part 1

I. "The Proverbs of Solomon Son of David, King of Israel" (1:1–9:18)
   A. Prologue (1:1–7)
   B. Instructions (1:8–9:18)

Part 2

II. "The Proverbs of Solomon" (10:1–22:16)
   A. Mostly Antithetical Proverbs (10:1–15:33)
   B. Mostly Synonymous Proverbs (16:1–22:16)

Part 3

III. "The Sayings of the Wise" (22:17–24:22)
IV. "Further Sayings of the Wise" (24:23–34)
V. "More Proverbs of Solomon, Copied by the Men of Hezekiah King of Judah" (25:1–29:27)
   A. Mostly Synonymous Proverbs (25:1–27:27)
   B. Mostly Antithetical Righteous/Wicked Proverbs (28:1–29:27)
VI. "The Sayings of Agur Son of Jakeh" (30:1–33)
   A. Agur's Confession (30:1–14)
   B. Numerical Sayings (30:15–33)
VII. "The Sayings of Lemuel King of Massa, Which His Mother Taught Him" (31:1–31)
   A. Mother's Instruction (31:1–9)
   B. Acrostic Poem (31:10–31)

Select Bibliography on Proverbs

Commentaries

Aitken, K. T. *Proverbs*. DBS. Philadelphia: Westminster, 1986.

Clifford, Richard. J. *Proverbs: A Commentary*. OTL. Louisville, Ky.: Westminster John Knox, 1999.

Cox, D. *Proverbs, with an Introduction to Sapiential Books*. OTM. Wilmington, Del.: Glazier, 1982.

Delitzsch, F. *Biblical Commentary on the Proverbs of Solomon*. Commentary on the Old Testament 6. Reprinted. Grand Rapids: Eerdmans, 1982 (orig. 1873).

Farmer, K. A. *Proverbs and Ecclesiastes*. ITC. Grand Rapids: Eerdmans, 1991.

Fox, Michael V. *Proverbs 1–9: A New Translation with Introduction and Commentary*. AB 18A. New York: Doubleday, 2000.

Garrett, Duane A. *Proverbs, Ecclesiastes, Song of Songs*. NAC 14. Nashville: Broadman, 1993.

Goldingay, John. "Proverbs." Pages 584–608 in *The New Bible Commentary 21st Century Edition*. Leicester, England: Inter-Varsity Press, 1994.

Harris, S. L. *Proverbs 1–9: A Study of Inner-Biblical Interpretation*. SBLDS 150. Atlanta: Scholar's Press, 1995.

Hubbard, David A. *Proverbs*. Communicator's Commentary 15. Dallas: Word, 1989.

Kidner, Derek. *The Proverbs: An Introduction and Commentary*. TOTC 15. Downers Grove, Ill.: InterVarsity Press, 1964.

McKane, William. *Proverbs: A New Approach*. OTL. Philadelphia: Westminster, 1970.

Meinhold, Arndt. *Die Sprüche*. 2 volumes. ZBK 16. Zürich: Theologischer Verlag Zürich, 1991.

Murphy, Roland E. *Wisdom Literature: Job, Proverbs, Ruth, Canticles, Ecclesiastes and Esther*. FOTL. Grand Rapids, Mich.: Eerdmans, 1981.

————. *Proverbs*. WBC 22. Nashville: Nelson, 1998.

Murphy, Roland E., and Elizabeth Huwiler. *Proverbs, Ecclesiastes, Song of Songs*. NIBCOT, Peabody Mass.: Hendrickson, 1999.

Perdue, Leo G. *Proverbs*. Interpretation. Louisville: Westminster John Knox, 2000.

Plaut, W. G. *The Book of Proverbs: A Commentary*. New York: Union of American Hebrew Congregations, 1961.

Ross, Allen. P. "Proverbs." Pages 881–1,134 in volume 5, *EBC*. Grand Rapids, Mich.: Zondervan, 1991.

Scott, R. B. Y. *Proverbs, Ecclesiastes*. AB 18. New York: Doubleday, 1965.

Toy, C. H. *A Critical and Exegetical Commentary on the Book of Proverbs*. ICC. Edinburgh: T. & T. Clark, 1899.

Van Leeuwen, Raymond C. "The Book of Proverbs." Pages 19–264 in volume 5, *NIB*. Nashville: Abingdon, 1997.

Waltke, Bruce. *Proverbs*. NICOT. Grand Rapids: Eerdmans, forthcoming.

Whybray, R. N. *Proverbs*. NCBC. Grand Rapids/London: Eerdmans/Marshall Pickering, 1994.

Related Works

Achtemeier, E. *Preaching from the Old Testament*. Louisville: Westminster John Knox, 1989.

Alster, B. *Proverbs of Ancient Sumer: The World's Earliest Proverb Collections*. 2 volumes. Bethesda, Md.: CDL Press, 1997.

Alter, R. *The Art of Biblical Poetry*. New York: Basic Books, 1985.

Atkinson, D. *The Message of Proverbs: Wisdom for Life*. BST. Downers Grove, Ill.: InterVarsity Press, 1996.

Boström, L. *The God of the Sages: The Portrayal of God in the Book of Proverbs*. Stockholm: Almqvist and Wiksell, 1990.

Brown, W. P. *Character in Crisis: A Fresh Approach to the Wisdom Literature of the Old Testament*. Grand Rapids: Eerdmans, 1996.

Bryce, G. E. *A Legacy of Wisdom: The Egyptian Contribution to the Wisdom of Israel*. Lewisburg, Pa.: Bucknell Univ. Press; London: Associated Univ. Presses, 1979.

Camp, C. V. *Wisdom and the Feminine in the Book of Proverbs*. BLS 11. Sheffield: Almond, 1985.

Clements, R. E. *Wisdom in Theology*. Grand Rapids: Eerdmans, 1992.

Clifford, R. J. *The Wisdom Literature*. Nashville: Abingdon, 1998.

Crenshaw, J. L. "Education in Ancient Israel." *JBL* 104 (1985): 601–15.

_____. *Education in Ancient Israel: Across the Deadening Silence*. New York: Doubleday, 1998.

Estes, D. J. *Hear My Son: Teaching and Learning in Proverbs 1–9*. NSBT. Grand Rapids: Eerdmans, 1997.

Flavell, L. and R. *Dictionary of Proverbs and Their Origins*. New York: Barnes and Noble Books, 1993.

Fontaine, C. *Traditional Sayings in the Old Testament*. BLS 5. Sheffield: Almond, 1985.

Foster, R. J. *Money, Sex, and Power: The Challenge of the Disciplined Life*. San Francisco: Harper and Row, 1985.

Gammie, J., and L. Perdue, eds. *The Sage in Israel and the Ancient Near East.* Winona Lake, Ind.: Eisenbrauns, 1990.

Gill, D. *Being Good: Building Moral Character.* Downers Grove, Ill.: InterVarsity Press, 2000.

Golka, F. W. *The Leopard's Spots: Biblical and African Wisdom in Proverbs.* Edinburgh: T. & T. Clark, 1993.

Habel, N. C. "The Symbolism of Wisdom in Proverbs 1–9." *Int* 26/2 (April 1972): 131–57.

Heim, K. M. *Like Grapes of Gold Set in Silver: An Interpretation of Proverbial Clusters in Proverbs 10:1–22:6.* BZAW 273. Berlin/New York: Walter de Gruyter, 2001.

Hildebrandt, T. A. "Proverb." Pages 233–54 in *Cracking Old Testament Codes: A Guide to Interpreting the Literary Genres of the Old Testament.* Ed. D. B. Sandy and R. L. Giese Jr. Nashville: Broadman and Holman, 1995.

_____. "Proverbial Pairs: Compositional Units in Proverbs 1–29." *JBL* 107/2 (1988): 204–24.

Holmgren, F. C. "Barking Dogs Never Bite, Except Now and Then: Proverbs and Job." *AThR* 61 (1979): 341–53.

Hybels, B. *Making Life Work: Putting God's Wisdom into Action.* Downers Grove, Ill.: InterVarsity Press, 1998.

Jobes, K. H. "Sophia Christology: The Way of Wisdom?" Pages 226–50 in *The Way of Wisdom: Essays in Honor of Bruce K. Waltke.* Ed. J. I. Packer and S. K. Soderlund. Grand Rapids: Zondervan, 2000.

Kalugila, L. *The Wise King: Studies in Royal Wisdom as Divine Revelation in the Old Testament and its Environment.* CBOT 15. Lund: Liber Läromedel/Gleerup, 1980.

Lambert, W. G. *Babylonian Wisdom Literature.* Winona Lake, Ind.: Eisenbrauns, 1996.

Lichtheim, M. *Ancient Egyptian Literature.* 2 volumes. Berkeley: Univ. of California Press, 1980.

Long, T. *Preaching and the Literary Forms of the Bible.* Philadelphia: Fortress, 1989.

Longman III, T. *How to Read Proverbs.* Downers Grove, Ill.: InterVarsity Press, 2002.

Maier, C. C. "Conflicting Attractions: Parental Wisdom and the 'Strange Woman' in Proverbs 1–9." Pages 98–108 in *Wisdom and Psalms: A Feminist Companion to the Bible (Second Series).* Ed. A. Brenner and C. R. Fontaine. Sheffield: Sheffield Academic Press, 1998.

Marcus, R. "The Tree of Life in Proverbs." *JBL* 62 (1943): 117–20.

Martin, J. D. *Proverbs.* OTG. Sheffield: Sheffield Academic Press, 1995.

McCreesh, T. P. *Biblical Sound and Sense: Poetic Sound Patterns in Proverbs 10–29.* Sheffield: JSOT Press, 1991.

McKane, W. "Functions of Language and Objectives of Discourse According to Proverbs, 10–30." Pages 166–85 in *La sagesse de l'Ancien Testament*. Ed. M. Gilbert. BETL 51. Leuven: Leuven Univ. Press, 1990.

McKenzie, A. *Preaching Proverbs: Wisdom for the Pulpit*. Louisville, Ky.: Westminster John Knox, 1996.

Melchert, C. F. *Wise Teaching: Biblical Wisdom and Educational Ministry*. Harrisburg, Pa.: Trinity Press International, 1998.

Meynet, R. *Rhetorical Analysis: An Introduction to Biblical Rhetoric*. JSOTSup 256. Sheffield: Sheffield Academic Press, 1998.

Mieder, W. *International Proverb Scholarship: An Annotated Bibliography*. 2 volumes. New York and London: Garland, 1982, 1990.

_____. *Proverbs Are Never Out of Season: Popular Wisdom in the Modern Age*. New York: Oxford Univ. Press, 1993.

Mieder, W., and A. Dundes. *The Wisdom of Many: Essays on the Proverb*. New York and London: Garland, 1981.

Morgan, D. F. *The Making of Sages: Biblical Wisdom and Contemporary Culture*. Harrisburg, Pa.: Trinity Press International, 2002.

Murphy, R. E. "The Faces of Wisdom in the Book of Proverbs." Pages 337–45 in *Mélanges bibliques et orientaux en l'honneur de M. Henri Cazelles*. Ed. A. Caquot and M. Delcor. Neukirchen-Vluyn: Neukirchener Verlag, 1981.

_____. "The Kerygma of the Book of Proverbs." *Int* 20 (1966): 3–14.

_____. *The Tree of Life: An Exploration of Biblical Wisdom Literature*. 2d ed. Grand Rapids: Eerdmans, 1996.

_____. "Wisdom and Eros in Proverbs 1–9." *CBQ* 50 (1988): 600–603.

Nel, P. J. *The Structure and Ethos of the Wisdom Admonitions in Proverbs*. BZAW 158. Berlin: Walter de Gruyter, 1982.

Newsom, C. A. "Woman and the Discourse of Patriarchal Wisdom: A Study of Proverbs 1–9." Pages 142–60 in *Gender and Difference in Ancient Israel*. Ed. P. L. Day. Minneapolis: Fortress, 1989.

Niditch, S. *Oral World and Written Word: Ancient Israelite Literature*. Louisville, Ky.: Westminster John Knox, 1996.

Odell Gilchrist, M. "Proverbs 1–9: Instruction or Riddle?" *Proceedings of the Eastern Great Lakes and Midwest Biblical Societies* 4 (1984): 131–45.

Overland, P. "Did the Sage Draw from the Shema?" *CBQ* 62 (July 2000): 424–40.

Packer, J. I., and S. K. Soderlund, eds. *The Way of Wisdom: Essays in Honor of Bruce K. Waltke*. Grand Rapids: Zondervan, 2000.

Parkinson, R. B. *Voices from Ancient Egypt: An Anthology of Middle Kingdom Writings*. Norman: Univ. of Oklahoma Press, 1991.

Patrick, D., and A. Scult, *Rhetoric and Biblical Interpretation*. Sheffield: JSOT Press, 1990.

Perry, T. A. *Wisdom Literature and the Structure of Proverbs*. University Park, Pa.: Pennsylvania State Univ. Press, 1993.

Pritchard, J., ed. *Ancient Near Eastern Texts Relating to the Old Testament*. 3d ed. Princeton: Princeton Univ. Press, 1969.

von Rad, G. *Wisdom in Israel*. Nashville: Abingdon, 1972.

Roth, W. M. W. *Numerical Sayings in the Old Testament: A Form Critical Study*. VTSup 13. Leiden: Brill, 1965.

_____. "The Numerical Sequence x/x+1 in the Old Testament." *VT* 12 (1962): 300–311.

Scherer, A. *Das Weise Wort und Seine Wirkung: Eine Untersuchung zur Komposition und Redaktion von Proverbia 10, 1–22*. WMANT 16. Neukirchen-Vluyn: Neukirchener Verlag, 1999.

Schneider, T. R. *The Sharpening of Wisdom: Old Testament Proverbs in Translation*. Pretoria: Old Testament Society of South Africa, 1992.

Schroer, S. "Wise and Counseling Women in Ancient Israel: Literary and Historical Ideals of the Personified *HOKMA*." Pages 67–84 in *A Feminist Companion to Wisdom Literature*. Ed. A. Brenner. Sheffield: Sheffield Academic Press, 1995.

Schultz, R. L. "Unity or Diversity in Wisdom Theology? A Canonical and Covenantal Perspective." *TynBul* 48 (1997): 271–306.

Scoralick, R. *Einzelspruch und Sammlung*. BZAW 232. Berlin: Walter de Gruyter, 1995.

Shupak, N. *Where Can Wisdom be Found?* OBO 130. Göttingen: Vandenhoeck and Ruprecht, 1993.

Skehan, P. W. *Studies in Israelite Poetry and Wisdom*. CBQMS 1. Washington, D. C.: Catholic Biblical Association, 1971.

Snell, D. *Twice-Told Proverbs and the Composition of the Book of Proverbs*. Winona Lake, Ind.: Eisenbrauns, 1993.

Taylor, A. *The Proverb*. Cambridge, Mass.: Harvard Univ. Press, 1931.

Van Leeuwen, R. C. *Context and Meaning in Proverbs 25–27*. SBLDS 96. Atlanta: Scholars Press, 1988.

_____. "Liminality and Worldview in Proverbs 1–9." *Semeia* 50 (1990): 111–44.

Waltke, B. K. "The Book of Proverbs and Ancient Wisdom Literature." *BibSac* 136 (July-September 1979): 221–38.

_____. "Old Testament Interpretation Issues for Big Idea Preaching." Pages 41–52 in *The Big Idea of Biblical Preaching: Connecting the Bible to People*. Ed. K. Willhite and S. Gibson. Grand Rapids: Baker, 1998.

Walton, J. H. *Ancient Israelite Literature in its Cultural Context*. Grand Rapids: Zondervan, 1989.

Washington, H. C. *Wealth and Poverty in the Instruction of Amenemope and the Hebrew Proverbs*. SBLDS 142. Atlanta: Scholars Press, 1994.

Weeks, S. *Early Israelite Wisdom*. Oxford: Clarendon, 1994.

Westermann, C. *Roots of Wisdom: The Oldest Proverbs of Israel and Other Peoples*. Louisville, Ky.: Westminster John Knox, 1995.

Whybray, R. N. *The Book of Proverbs: A Survey of Modern Study*. HBIS 1. Leiden: Brill, 1995.

_____. *The Composition of the Book of Proverbs*. JSOTSup 168. Sheffield: JSOT Press, 1994.

_____. *Wealth and Poverty in the Book of Proverbs*. JSOTSup 99. Sheffield: JSOT Press, 1990.

_____. "Yahweh Sayings and Their Contexts in Proverbs 10:1–22:16." Pages 153–65 in *La sagesse de l'Ancien Testament*. Ed. M. Gilbert. Leuven: Leuven Univ. Press, 1990.

Williams, J. G. *Those Who Ponder Proverbs: Aphoristic Thinking and Biblical Literature*. Sheffield: Almond Press, 1981.

Winton, A. P. *The Proverbs of Jesus: Issues of History and Rhetoric*. Sheffield: Sheffield Academic Press, 1990.

Wilson, J. R. "Biblical Wisdom, Spiritual Formation, and the Virtues." Pages 297–307 in *The Way of Wisdom: Essays in Honor of Bruce K. Waltke*. Ed. J. I. Packer and S. K. Soderlund. Grand Rapids: Zondervan, 2000.

_____. *Gospel Virtues: Practicing Faith, Hope, and Love in Uncertain Times*. Downers Grove, Ill.: InterVarsity Press, 1998.

Witherington, B. III., *Jesus the Sage: The Pilgrimage of Wisdom*. Philadelphia: Fortress, 1994.

Zuck, R. B. *Learning from the Sages: Selected Studies on the Book of Proverbs*. Grand Rapids: Baker, 1995.

Proverbs 1:1–7

T HE PROVERBS OF Solomon son of David, king of Israel:
²for attaining wisdom and discipline;
for understanding words of insight;
³for acquiring a disciplined and prudent life,
doing what is right and just and fair;
⁴for giving prudence to the simple,
knowledge and discretion to the young—
⁵let the wise listen and add to their learning,
and let the discerning get guidance—
⁶for understanding proverbs and parables,
the sayings and riddles of the wise.

⁷The fear of the LORD is the beginning of knowledge,
but fools despise wisdom and discipline.

Original Meaning

T HESE SEVEN VERSES form a distinct unit of introduction. An introduction, contrary to much of our common experience in listening to popular speakers, is not a warm-up or a time for pleasantries. Biblical writers waste no time with anything less than matters of highest priority. They go to the heart of the matter, especially when dealing with first things: "In the beginning God created the heavens and the earth" (Gen. 1:1); "in the beginning was the Word" (John 1:1). At the beginning of Proverbs we have an introduction that declares without apology that "the fear of the LORD is the beginning of knowledge" (1:7).

We should always pay attention to beginnings and endings of literary works because writers tend to put their most important thoughts and images there. We should pay especially close attention to a literary introduction when it includes a phrase that is also found in the work's conclusion. In this case, "fear of the LORD" not only concludes this prologue and the first part of the book of Proverbs (i.e., chs. 1–9; cf. 9:10), it also appears at the end of the entire book (31:30). The writer's use of this framing device of *inclusio* tells us to watch for "the fear of the LORD" as it recurs throughout the Proverbs and guides our reading of it. For now we observe that as Yahweh is the source of every beginning, so our fear of him (worship and faithfulness) is the beginning of the study of wisdom as well as its primary goal.

The introduction, most of it one long Hebrew sentence, not only honors the book of Proverbs with the names of its most revered kings, Solomon and David, it states the book's purpose. In a series of Hebrew infinitive verbs (six in all after verse 2; infinitives begin every verse but verses 5 and 7), we readers are told not only what the book is (a collection of *mešalim*) and who receives the credit for the collection (Solomon),[1] but what the book is *for*. In a word, this book was written to pass on wisdom. Such a statement of introduction was not unusual in the ancient world. Egyptian instructions in wisdom often named the speaker and recipient as part of their statement of purpose: to pass on wisdom for successful living from one generation to the next. So Ptahhotep taught his son, "There is no one born wise."[2]

We should also notice that this introduction includes a list of literary forms ("proverbs and parables, the sayings and riddles of the wise"), reasons for studying them ("for attaining wisdom . . . for giving prudence"), and qualities of character that readers should cultivate ("a disciplined and prudent life, doing what is right and just and fair"). Finally, the prologue describes different sorts of people who will read and respond to the teaching of this book ("the simple . . . the young . . . the wise . . . [and] fools").

The different terms for wisdom, knowledge, and understanding have puzzled commentators, who have tried to determine what distinguishes one from another. Some have looked for patterns and progressions.[3] Others have been content to say that the many terms are brought together to show that no one word can describe the reality and splendor of wisdom. Kidner put it well, comparing the prologue to a prism that breaks "the plain daylight of wisdom (*hokmah*) into its rainbow of constituent colors."[4]

The first of the purpose clauses says that the proverbs are "for attaining wisdom and discipline" (1:2). "Wisdom" in its most general meaning is the acquired learning that helps one know what to do in a given situation.[5] It includes knowledge and skill, whether that skill is applied to craft work (Isa. 40:20) or to the business of right living, as it is here. In this prologue, the Hebrew root *hkm* is used twice of wisdom (Prov. 1:2, 7) and twice for the wise persons who both acquire and teach it (1:5, 6). Therefore, one learns wisdom from those who are farther along in the process (cf. 12:15; 13:20). Yet such

---

1. See the introduction on these topics.

2. *AEL*, 1:63; *ANET*, 413 (sec. 40).

3. W. P. Brown, *Character in Crisis*, 23−30, sees a chiastic or mirror pattern that distinguishes: comprehensive intellectual virtues (1:2a and 7), literary expressions of wisdom (1:2b and 6), instrumental virtues (1:3a and 4−5), and, at the center position of greatest importance, moral and communal virtues (1:3b).

4. Kidner, *Proverbs*, 36.

5. See the section "Wisdom in the Old Testament" in the introduction.

wisdom does not come apart from a right relationship to the Lord, here expressed as "fear." Therefore, before going on, this prologue wants us to know that wisdom, taught by elders and received in the fear of God, is the primary goal for human life.

"Wisdom" is in first position as an indication of its primary importance (1:2), yet wisdom does not stand alone. It is paired with "discipline," not only here but again in 1:6. "Discipline" (*musar*) basically refers to instruction, especially in the sense of correction. The word is used for God's discipline in Deuteronomy 11:2; Isaiah 26:16; and Psalm 50:17. Some of the proverbs use it for corporal punishment (Prov. 13:24; 22:15; 23:13). When paired with "wisdom" (*ḥokmah*), discipline means submitting to instruction in order to reach the goal of wisdom. "Listen to advice and accept instruction (*musar*), and in the end you will be wise" (19:20; cf. 23:23). The pairing of wisdom and discipline suggests that both are a way of life that one comes to know and learn.[6] No one is born wise or without the need for discipline.

Discipline (*musar*) is also paired with "a prudent life" (*śekel*)—a term for practical wisdom (1:3; cf. 16:22).[7] Throughout Scripture, *śekel* refers to understanding and insight that can lead to good ends (Ezra 8:18) or bad (Dan. 8:25). It speaks of the ability to size up a situation and respond accordingly. When tempered with discipline, this practical wisdom leads one along good paths.

The second half of verse 3 continues to describe the disciplined and prudent life; it is characterized by actions that are "right and just and fair." The break in the series of infinitive verbs adds extra emphasis on this trio of virtues (in Hebrew they appear in noun forms, "righteousness, justice, and equity"). We will meet them again in the next chapter, where they speak of how and why God gives wisdom (2:9). This triad is at the center of the prologue's structure, and its goal for life is at the heart of the whole book.[8] Righteousness, justice, and equity are also often used of God in the Psalms (Ps. 9:8; 33:5; 89:14; 96:10; 97:2; 103:17), and as attributes of God they set the standard for human interaction (58:1). They appear throughout Proverbs to show us how disciplined and prudent living is recognized.[9]

In Proverbs 1:4 we meet, for the first time, the person who is to receive this instruction in wisdom. That person is "simple" or "untutored" (*peti*; some

---

6. Scott, *Proverbs*, 36.

7. Fox, *Proverbs 1–9*, 36, understands *śekel* as insight, "the ability to grasp the meanings or implications of a situation or message," combining understanding and expertise.

8. Brown, *Character in Crisis*, 42. See also footnote 3. Brown sees a chiastic structure in verses 2–7 with these three terms at the center focus.

9. Whybray, *Proverbs*, 32.

translations even use "ignorant"),[10] more lacking in instruction than intelligence. Remember that the statutes of the Lord make the simple wise (Ps. 19:8). The simple can be led astray (Prov. 1:10 uses the same root for "entice"), so there is sometimes a sense of "gullible" or "naive" included as well. It is a significant term, for we will see in this same chapter that personified Wisdom rebukes the simple for remaining in ignorance (1:22). So also both Wisdom and Folly address their invitations to the simple in chapter 9.

The term "simple" is set in parallel with "the young"; thus, it seems that the first objects of wisdom teaching are those who need education in every area of life. They are to learn "prudence," "knowledge," and "discretion." "Prudence" is here used as a positive description of hidden, private thoughts. Not saying everything that comes to mind has its advantages, but if thoughts are hidden in deceit, they appear as shrewdness or even cunning or scheming (Gen. 3:1; Ex. 21:14; Josh. 9:4). Likewise, "discretion," the ability to make plans, can, when used for evil purposes, become the kind of craftiness that the Lord condemns (Prov. 12:2).[11] "Knowledge," by contrast, is a positive term that will receive a greater positive charge in 1:7 by its association with the fear of Yahweh.

Verse 5 brings another group of persons into view. Wisdom instruction is not only for the unlearned; the "wise" also listen and continue to learn while the "discerning get guidance" or strategies (see 11:14; 20:18; 24:6; 12:5 for a negative sense). The Hebrew grammar of the first phrase will allow a jussive sense of "let the wise hear." But whether the statement is directive or descriptive, it is clear that the character of learners determines their actions and the actions of learners reveal character.

Who are these wise ones? Coming after mention of the simple, the term "wise" may indicate those who are more experienced and accomplished in learning, those who would require skills of discernment that are more finely honed.[12] Contrasted with the fools who are mentioned in 1:7, the wise are any who choose to follow the path of learning instead of passing it by. By placing the wise and discerning between the simple and the fools, the writer highlights the inevitable decision that all must make. The simple must choose to become one of the wise or by default will become one of the fools.

In 1:6, the last of the purpose clauses, "for understanding" (*lᵉhabin*), takes as its object "proverbs and parables, the sayings and riddles of the wise." Two

---

10. Scott, *Proverbs*, 33.

11. McKane, *Proverbs*, 265, noting that both terms "border on the pejorative," takes this as an indication that early wisdom teaching was secular and pragmatic to a fault. But there is no reason to look to a hypothetical history of the text to explain the jarring use of terminology here.

12. Scott L. Harris, *Proverbs 1–9: A Study of Inner-Biblical Interpretation* (SBLDS 150; Atlanta: Scholar's Press, 1995), 191–93.

of the terms appear in the headings that divide the book into its parts: "proverbs" (10:1; 25:1) and "sayings" (lit., "words of" 22:17; 30:1; 31:1). Just as wisdom and discipline give "understanding" (also *lᵉhabin*) of "words of insight" in 1:2, so here the wise acquire learning that aids in understanding these ancient wisdom forms. The forms do not only teach wisdom, they offer training in interpreting its puzzles. Wisdom teaching was not typically communicated directly or in anything like our prose essay or magazine article. Proverbs and parables, sayings and riddles, all hide in order to reveal. They require some work and some exercise of wit on the part of the reader to crack the combination lock. There seems to be some higher level of learning at work than that offered to the simple and young in 1:4.

The "proverb" and "parable" both compare in order to instruct. It is less clear what the "sayings" (lit., "words") of the wise and their "riddles" refer to, especially since few of the teachings or independent proverbs in the book of Proverbs take the form of a riddle (chs. 30 and 31 may). Another biblical reference may provide a clue. Psalm 49:3–4 uses "words of wisdom" and sets "proverb" (*mašal*) in synonymous parallel with "riddle" (*ḥidah*) to introduce a wisdom teaching on the transience of wealth. The psalm ends with a comparison: "A man who has riches without understanding is like the beasts that perish" (Ps. 49:20).

Riddles seem to have been a popular form of entertainment and display of wit in the ancient world. Samson posed a riddle to his wedding guests (Judg. 14:12, apparently a widespread custom),[13] and the Queen of Sheba tested Solomon's wisdom with riddles (1 Kings 10:1). Riddles are a form of indirect communication. Therefore, Numbers notes with wonder that the Lord did not speak in riddles to Moses but rather "face to face, clearly" (Num. 12:8). The riddle hides its meaning in order to demonstrate cleverness, both of the one who contrives the puzzle as well as the one who solves it.[14]

Yet Psalm 49 and most, if not all, of the book of Proverbs do not take the form of a riddle as much as they present indirections that warrant reflection. It may be that a two-stage process of learning is envisioned in this book of Proverbs, one in which the more advanced learners go on to tackle the harder puzzles of the proverbs (or other wisdom teaching). With this in mind, we note that the instructions of chapters 1–9 are more direct (at least on the surface) than the proverbs and other kinds of independent sayings that follow in chapters 10–22. If so, then this prologue also tells the reader not to skip over the introductory chapters!

13. V. Hamp, "חִידָה," *TDOT*, 4:321.
14. McKane, *Proverbs*, 266.

In 1:7 the composer of this introduction has saved the most important teaching for last, but this end is also a beginning, since the verse ushers the reader into the book of Proverbs. The Hebrew word for "beginning" (*rēšiʾt*) has the sense of what comes first, what stands at the head of the line. Therefore, it can refer to what is first in time, a beginning (some go as far as to say a source), but also it can designate what is first in importance. "Fear of the LORD" comes closest to describing worship and the practice of religion in the book of Proverbs.[15] Fear of Yahweh is also central to the wisdom teaching of Job (Job 28:28) and Ecclesiastes (Eccl. 12:13). While injunctions to fear gods are not unique to Israel, the Hebrew Bible gives it an emphasis not found in any other ancient Near Eastern literature.[16]

"Fear of the LORD" in Proverbs is certainly the most important of the "sayings of the wise." It appears as a key theme that is sounded repeatedly throughout the book. Each time it appears, "fear of the LORD" is paired with a phrase or partner to highlight a different dimension of this essential attitude. This pairing reminds the reader that without it there can be no instruction in wisdom. "Fear of the LORD" leads to knowledge of God (2:5; 9:10); hatred of evil, pride, and arrogance (8:13); long life (10:27); avoidance of death (14:27); and wisdom, humility, honor, and wealth (15:33; 22:4).

As noted earlier, "fear of the LORD" also serves as an inclusio, a framing device that marks the beginning and the end of the book of instruction (chs. 1–9; 9:10 is similar to 1:7) and the end of the book of Proverbs (31:30). We also note that "knowledge," "wisdom," and "discipline" (Heb. *daʾat, hokmah,* and *musar*) appear here in 1:7 in the same order as when the words were first introduced in 1:2. This second framing device takes us back to the beginning of the prologue as it looks ahead to all that follows.

We learn about fear and foolhardiness in 1:7 by reading on and observing the opposition the writer has constructed. Fear of Yahweh is contrasted with the fool's haughty rejection of wisdom. Fear is knowing what to respect, knowing how to place oneself in a learning posture. Fools are not those who cannot learn but those who will not. Just as we will be reminded of the fear of Yahweh throughout the book of Proverbs, so we will meet its opposite in the figure of the fool again and again.[17]

---

15. Crenshaw, *Education in Ancient Israel*, 66–69.

16. J. Day, "Foreign Semitic Influence on the Wisdom of Israel and Its Appropriation in the Book of Proverbs," in *Wisdom in Ancient Israel: Essays in Honour of J. A. Emerton*, ed. J. Day, R. P. Gordon, and H. G. M. Williamson (Cambridge: Cambridge Univ. Press, 1995), 67. Fear of the deity, while not central to Babylonian wisdom literature, can be found in the "Counsels of Wisdom" and the "Babylonian Theodicy."

17. See the section "Fear of Yahweh" in the introduction.

Fear of Yahweh also speaks to the intended readers of the book of Proverbs. The book is written not for a general audience but for a particular people—those who fear the Lord. Anyone can join this community, but the prologue clearly creates insiders and outsiders. Outsiders may learn also, but they may not remain outside the learning community for long.[18] The prologue invites its readers to read on and decide.

WISDOM WAS THE central expression of intellectual life in the ancient Near East (see the introduction). We should also remember that nearly every culture in history has had its own wisdom tradition, each with a slightly different form and purpose.[19] Practical strategies for managing the demands of daily life often led to theoretical reflection on the nature of this world with the hope of finding some sense of order. Greek rhetoric and philosophy also grew out of a concern to discover and teach how one lives life well—rhetoric emphasizing the practical and philosophy the theoretical.[20]

Today, the self-help and inspirational sections of the bookstore offer many guides to the contemporary pursuit of wisdom. We must be careful, then, to grasp and teach a biblical vision of wisdom, appreciating that which is common to all wisdom traditions while holding up that which is unique to the Bible. From the prologue to Proverbs we learn that wisdom is something that can be taught and learned, that this teaching has something to do with the formation of character, and that wisdom is anchored in the fear of Yahweh. In other words, this book sets out for its readers three pursuits under the banner of wisdom: knowledge, character, and piety.[21]

Knowledge. We begin with a look at the acquisition of knowledge and the matter of education. Verse 2 tells us that wisdom and discipline can be

---

18. For this idea of a distinct readership, see C. Seitz, *World Without End: The Old Testament As Abiding Theological Witness* (Grand Rapids: Eerdmans, 1998), chs. 7, 10.

19. Kurt Rudolph, "Wisdom," in *The Encyclopedia of Religion*, ed. Mircea Eliade (New York: MacMillan, 1987), 15:393—401.

20. B. A. Kimball, *Orators and Philosophers: A History of the Idea of Liberal Education* (New York: College Entrance Examination Board, 1995). Some rhetoricians were known as "sophists" or "teachers of wisdom," G. A. Kennedy, *Classical Rhetoric and Its Christian and Secular Tradition from Ancient to Modern Times* (Chapel Hill: Univ. of North Carolina Press, 1980), 25—40.

21. R. J. Clifford speaks of three dimensions in wisdom: sapiential (a way of seeing reality), ethical (a way of conducting oneself), and religious (a way of relation to the order of God); see *The Wisdom Literature* (Nashville: Abingdon, 1998), 50, after L. Alonso-Schoekel, *Proverbios* (Madrid: Ediciones Christiandad, 1984).

attained; they can be learned. The terms for "knowledge" and "understanding" join with the literary forms of "words of insight," "proverbs and parables," and "sayings and riddles of the wise" to indicate that learning wisdom is an intellectual activity that requires study and reflection. It demands the use of the mind. So also contemporary believers are called to give attention to preaching and teaching on wisdom and Proverbs. We also have the ability and the privilege to read and study this book of Proverbs for ourselves. Reading, says one theologian, is a soul-making activity.[22] It changes us in ways we do not always expect.

Such reading can and should be done in private, but if I may be allowed a personal word, I would also hope that these texts would be read and discussed in groups. As I have taught and preached from the book of Proverbs in local churches, I am surprised to hear that few can remember when they last heard a sermon from Proverbs[23] or looked together at its chapters. While there is a bit of preaching to the choir in addressing those who are reading this book, I would urge pastors and church leaders to include study and reflection on biblical wisdom literature as part of the educational ministry of their churches.

In more general terms, this call to understand proverbs and the other literary forms found in this book of Scripture demands that Christians use their minds as they seek to live their faith. There is no excuse for a lack of diligence in thinking through the implications of scriptural teaching for the issues and problems facing individuals and societies in the third millennium. If anything, Proverbs wants us to study its wisdom to turn our attention to the world around us.[24]

Character. The educational dimension of wisdom is not a pursuit of academic study that remains detached from real-life issues. The teaching function of Proverbs should be understood as a work of formation that brings the demands of the intellectual life together with concerns for moral character and faithful relationship with God.[25] For the church, this means taking the

---

22. Stanley Hauerwas, *Wilderness Wanderings: Probing Twentieth Century Theology and Philosophy* (Boulder, Colo.: Westview, 1997), 171. "Good writers therefore try to force those of us who read them to attend to what we read, for in so doing, they demand of us the formation of new habits, which thereby changes our lives," 172.

23. For help in preaching from the book of Proverbs, E. Achtemeier, *Preaching from the Old Testament,* and D. Gowan, *Reclaiming the Old Testament for the Christian Pulpit,* have chapters on preaching from the wisdom literature. T. Long, *Preaching and the Literary Forms of the Bible,* and A. M. McKenzie, *Preaching Proverbs,* have chapters dedicated to the book of Proverbs.

24. R. Clapp, *A Peculiar People: The Church As Culture in a Post-Christian Society* (Downers Grove, Ill.: InterVarsity Press, 1996), offers some suggestions.

25. D. J. Estes, *Hear My Son: Teaching and Learning in Proverbs 1—9* (Grand Rapids: Eerdmans, 1997), 14.

---

educational task seriously. But does it not also speak to our primary educational system? We must listen to those educators who insist that there is no value-free education, no educational practice that teaches without having a formative effect on character.[26] Whether one believes that religion should be taught and practiced in public schools or not, both sides of the educational debate should be able to agree in principle on certain moral qualities we hope to instill in our children. No matter what we believe about prayer in school or how reading is taught, we should be aware that our educational practices shape moral and religious judgment.

Education, then, is never practiced separately from character formation. Wisdom and folly are moral terms. The untutored become wise or fools, depending on their acceptance or rejection of wisdom's teaching. Jesus likened the choice to locating the foundation for a house (Matt. 7:24–27). Moreover, the book of Proverbs views education and character formation as a matter of faith.[27] So also the development of character determines how the savvy skills of wisdom, prudence (Prov. 1:3), knowledge, and discretion (1:4) are used. They can be used for what is right and just and fair, and in so doing reflect the very character of God.

These human skills of discernment and shrewdness need not be used at the cost of healthy community. Fast thinkers and smooth talkers need not become business cheats and corrupt politicians. Kings and courtiers of the ancient world were charged with using their authority to guarantee just and fair dealing in their lands. So today, those who learn wisdom are marked by a passion for justice and doing what is right in their business and their personal lives. These human capabilities must be conscripted, corrected, and disciplined under the fear of Yahweh.

Fear of Yahweh. This pursuit is difficult to appreciate in our contemporary addiction to good feelings. Advertisers learned long ago that the merits of a particular product are not nearly as appealing as the emotions that can be associated with them. So also, one study of contemporary sermons concluded that much American preaching works from similar assumptions,

---

26. Ashely Woodwiss supports this point while arguing for another: "While the term *catechesis* may be off-putting to some Protestants (and invoke painful memories for some Catholics!) it points to the substantive differences that ought to exist between Christian educational practice and secularized public education. Education is always character formation. The question is, what kind of character and for what?" "What Is the Church Good For?" *Books and Culture* 3/6 (1997): 39.

27. J. R. Wilson, *Gospel Virtues: Practicing Faith, Hope, and Love in Uncertain Times* (Downers Grove, Ill.: InterVarsity Press, 1998), 72–88. Four features of faith apply to education in the book of Proverbs: It is all encompassing and does not fall into secularism, it is communal, it is a gift, and it makes personal demands.

stressing the themes of love and grace that promote good feelings at the expense of themes of rebellion, brokenness, and repentance.[28]

Yet fear of Yahweh is precisely about turning from rebellion to teachability before God. Good feeling comes by embracing all of reality, including our need to submit to authority greater than our own. The life of wisdom is not just good sense or a list of principles for a happy life (true as this may be); it is above all an attitude toward God that influences all of our decisions and actions. This attitude does not take away our privilege and responsibility to make choices and plans; it sets them in the light of God's claim on the world he made, as well as on our lives.

We often shy away from phrases like "the fear of the LORD" because we want to say that God is loving, like a father looking down the road for his lost son, or tender, like a mother nurturing her children. We are afraid that speaking of God's mighty reign and claim on our lives will be alienating, not attractive. Yet our enjoyment of that love takes on new meaning when we come to know the One who loves us in the way he wants to be known. As we will see, the fear of Yahweh goes hand and hand with the knowledge of God (1:7; 2:5).

What would the Lord have us know about himself? On the plains of Moab, Moses told the Israelites that the land they were about to enter was a gift, and that once they started to enjoy its vineyards and olive groves, they should not forget Yahweh, who brought them out of Egypt and slavery. They were to fear Yahweh by obeying the commands, decrees, and laws that Moses taught them (Deut. 6:10–19). He was the One who gave them their freedom and a land to live in. They had been liberated from the power of Egypt and its king to become citizens of a new land and to serve its Lord. Fear of Yahweh proved that the Israelites knew this God and understood their relationship with him.

We will see that this covenant history is never far away from the writer's mind in Proverbs. There is a strong difference between the emphasis on successful living we find in today's motivational literature and the Bible's emphasis on living in loving and obedient relationship with the Lord. In the first, honest and fair living is good business that increases the likelihood that one will lead a happy and prosperous life. In the Bible, these ideas are affirmed, but they are set in the larger scheme of honoring God by attaining the righteous character for which we were created.

---

28. M. G. Witten, *All Is Forgiven: The Secular Message in American Protestantism* (Princeton: Princeton Univ. Press, 1993).

THIS PROLOGUE TELLS us that the book of Proverbs is primarily concerned with the formation of character through the cultivation of wisdom. It describes three basic dispositions that those who would be wise ought to display: the humility of the learner (to learn wisdom and discipline), love for one's neighbor (to practice wisdom and virtue), and fear of Yahweh (to consistently return to the beginning). The prologue draws our attention to these dispositions so that readers may recognize them as they appear throughout the book.

Humility of the learner. Wisdom is not so much a goal to be attained as a posture of humility, a willingness to receive instruction. A wise person is a learning person, a person in process, not a finished product. The flurry of educational terms in the prologue cover both the means and ends for learning; they appear again and again throughout Proverbs. As we have seen, the word "discipline" is used three times in this prologue with the sense of the "discipline of instruction." This willingness to submit to teaching is what fools reject along with wisdom; in a later instruction the son is urged, "Do not despise the LORD's discipline and do not resent his rebuke, because the LORD disciplines those he loves, as a father the son he delights in" (3:11–12).

Teaching is not only for the untutored or the simple; even those who are wise add to their learning (1:4–5), for the need is never satisfied and the knowledge available is never depleted. Whether young or mature, simple or wise, all are called to heed the instruction of this book. It is a commonplace that the wise know what they do not know. May the attitude of humility it expresses be as common! Here is no call to false humility or self-abasement, a sort of "Well, I guess I don't know very much." Rather, it is an admission that we never lose the need to learn and grow in living life well. The book of Proverbs assumes that its readers are daily learning new ways to put into practice the teachings of wisdom.

Certainly this education in wisdom takes place as one studies Proverbs and uses it as a lens to aid in observing life's lessons and a guide to "lab practice" in the life of the church community. For leaders in the church, this means taking a learner's posture in meetings and team projects. Seminary teachers often say that courses in church leadership help fledgling pastors learn to pay close attention to the way a church body makes decisions and fulfills its mission. If pastors walk into churches believing they know how everything should function, they will quickly learn what they do not know! In the same way, board and committee members can practice humble teachability by listening to other points of view and by harnessing angry words.

The practice itself becomes part of the course of study. The emphasis on prudence and discretion in 1:4 suggests that it is not always possible to know how to respond to situations ahead of time but rather to be prepared with habits of attentiveness and openness that allow good decisions to rise and make themselves known. The humility of the learner allows life experience, illuminated by Scripture, to become one's teacher.

In addition, many church leaders have seen the need to seek out a mentor who can offer help and perspective in interpreting the strange beast we call the life of the Christian community. The Evangelical Covenant Church I serve has instituted a program of mentoring that pairs experienced pastors with those just beginning their ministries. Former seminary students have spoken of their appreciation for the listening ear and challenging feedback.

Mentoring also takes place in regular study. Pastors and parishioners alike would never say that they do not need the refreshment found in reading good books of biography and theology; instead, they say they are too busy, and they are right. Activities fill our calendars the way floodwater fills empty spaces, so scheduling regular time for study requires both an acknowledgment of the need and the discipline of saying no. Although that discipline can be taken to extremes, it is one way to practice the humility of the learner.

Love for neighbor. We have also seen that the thematic center of this introduction is the triad of virtues that are found in 1:3b. Righteousness, justice, and straight dealing cannot be understood in abstraction; they must be practiced. And they cannot be practiced in isolation; they show themselves in the way we treat others. In this way, the prologue introduces themes of justice and neighbor love that appear again and again in Proverbs. For example, we can show neighbor love in the way we talk with and about one another: "A man who lacks judgment derides his neighbor, but a man of understanding holds his tongue. A gossip betrays a confidence, but a trustworthy man keeps a secret" (11:12–13). This book has much to say about the use of our speech, and so one way of practicing neighbor love is to watch the way we use our words.[29]

The concern for fair dealing with one's neighbors extends to the use of wealth and resources: "The rich rules over the poor, and the borrower is servant to the lender. He who sows wickedness reaps trouble, and the rod of his fury will be destroyed. A generous man will himself be blessed, for he shares his bread with the poor" (22:7–9). These three brief sayings work together

---

29. W. R. Baker, *Sticks and Stones: The Discipleship of Our Speech* (Downers Grove, Ill.: Inter-Varsity Press, 1996). Baker expounds the biblical teaching of speech ethics with frequent reference to ancient Near Eastern wisdom, Greek philosophy and rhetoric, and the rabbinic tradition.

to acknowledge the advantages of wealth and warn that they must be used justly and compassionately. As one avoids acts of injustice and embraces a giving spirit, righteous character grows within that person.

For Americans this means taking seriously the claim that we have the means but lack the political will to virtually bring an end to world hunger. A number of presidential studies in the 1970s concluded with Jimmy Carter's commission on hunger that "if decisions and actions well within the capability of nations and people working together were implemented, it would be possible to eliminate the worst aspects of hunger and malnutrition by the year 2000."[30] Sadly, we know that the challenge was not heeded and that the numbers of the hungry in the United States and around the world has increased disproportionately with the growth of world population. Christians who choose the neighbor love of Proverbs will both give and seek to bring an end to unjust economic practices on a local and national level.

At other times, neighbor love will show itself in support and help in time of need. After a youth was killed in a drive-by shooting in Chicago, a pastor told his congregation: "We have to do something to help this young man's church care for the family. They can't do it—they are in too much pain and grief. It's up to us. We have to do something. We are their neighbors." In the book of Proverbs, wisdom is revealed in action, especially in loving action toward one's neighbor. The wise person practices what is learned out of loving reverence for the Lord.

Fear of Yahweh. The fear of Yahweh is that first principle of knowledge rejected by the fool, who despises wisdom and discipline. To submit to instruction is to acknowledge an authority higher than the fool's own. Therefore the fool, wishing to be his own authority, does not know whom he should fear. Yet without that fear, that acknowledgment of God's gracious authority, there can be no knowledge of the sort that is described in Proverbs. The phrase "fear of the LORD" recurs throughout the entire book of Proverbs and concludes its final chapter: "Charm is deceptive, and beauty is fleeting; but a woman who fears the LORD is to be praised" (31:30). She is no fool, and as the description of Proverbs 31 shows, in her practice of all that has been said in Proverbs, she is an example of the character of wisdom.

Humility of the learner and the love for neighbor alone will not lead one to this kind of wisdom. Here is no mere course in self-improvement; the

---

30. Cited in D. Beckmann and A. Simon, *Grace at the Table: Ending Hunger in God's World* (Downers Grove, Ill.: InterVarsity Press, 1999), 4. The authors, leaders in Bread for the World, a Christian citizen's movement, recommend political action to accompany the work of feeding hungry people. Changing national policies, they argue, will bring about long-term results.

search for the life of wisdom finds its beginning and end in the fear of God. Every pithy saying, every astute observation, every moral exhortation in the book of Proverbs is meant to lead us to awe-filled knowledge of God. The instructions of chapters 1–9 and the sayings of chapters 10–31 not only seek to show how wisdom works in the world, they are out to reveal the glory of God in the sort of wisdom that holds the world together. The fitting response for us is awe and worship.

But what kind of worship, some will ask. Certainly no one wants to rush into the conflict over styles of worship that segregates people into separate services so that everyone's preferences can be honored. One answer to the question instructs us to look to worship that exists for itself and no other purpose, worship focused on contemplation of the God of Israel and world history, worship intended first and foremost to promote the knowledge of God with human responses as a natural result. In other words, worship that seeks to communicate the person and work of God will lead to honest and heartfelt human responses, fear of Yahweh chief among them. Knowledge apart from worship can be lifeless and sterile, and worship without knowledge can be empty, but worship that is founded on knowledge of God stands a good chance of expressing praise that is reverent and real.

Still, we read that the fear of Yahweh is the beginning of this knowledge, and we observed that the triad of knowledge, wisdom, and discipline in 1:7 repeats the same Hebrew words used in 1:2 to open the prologue. The verse actually takes the reader back to the beginning to start over, to begin again, knowing what is expected and knowing the first principle, the fear of Yahweh. The book of Proverbs is not about developing moral character as an end in itself. It is about the character-forming work of the fear of God, the basic disposition that returns us again and again to humble teachability and neighbor love. We who know the fear of Yahweh do not return to first principles as a sign of failure but as a sign of growth. The more we learn, the more wise we become, the more we see how great is our need for God. The end is the beginning.

Proverbs 1:8–19

8 LISTEN, MY SON, to your father's instruction
    and do not forsake your mother's teaching.
9 They will be a garland to grace your head
    and a chain to adorn your neck.

10 My son, if sinners entice you,
    do not give in to them.
11 If they say, "Come along with us;
    let's lie in wait for someone's blood,
    let's waylay some harmless soul;
12 let's swallow them alive, like the grave,
    and whole, like those who go down to the pit;
13 we will get all sorts of valuable things
    and fill our houses with plunder;
14 throw in your lot with us,
    and we will share a common purse"—
15 my son, do not go along with them,
    do not set foot on their paths;
16 for their feet rush into sin,
    they are swift to shed blood.
17 How useless to spread a net
    in full view of all the birds!
18 These men lie in wait for their own blood;
    they waylay only themselves!
19 Such is the end of all who go after ill-gotten gain;
    it takes away the lives of those who get it.

Original Meaning

THE LITERARY SETTING for the instruction in chapters 1–9 is the home schooling of a young man coming of age. The education depicted here is not an example of home schooling as we know it today, with lessons in literature, science, and math, yet its life lessons have a similar goal of preparing a young person for adult life. The refrain "my son"[1] that appears throughout chapters 1–7 (1:8; 2:1; 3:1; 4:1; 4:10, 4:20; 5:1;

---

1. See the introduction for a discussion of how young women can appropriate teaching that is not addressed to them. Although everyone faces this problem as readers of an ancient text, it is especially acute for female readers.

6:1; 6:20; 7:1; 7:24) marks a call to attention, a common feature of ancient Near Eastern instructions. The parallel verse structure of 1:8 indicates that both father and mother participate in the education of this young man. This address to a "son" may refer to a parental relation or the relation between teacher and pupil,[2] but the teaching of Lemuel's mother in 31:1 suggests that mothers were also commonly seen as teachers of their sons. Still, the parents' teaching seems to be spoken mostly by the father. Later in the instruction the father recalls when his own father introduced him to wisdom (4:1–9), making the same promises of garlands and crowns (cf. 1:9).

Three invitations appear in Proverbs 1. The young listener is told to pay attention to the teaching of his parents (1:8) and the correction of Woman Wisdom (1:33), but to ignore the offer to join violent men (1:10, 15). In essence, each invitation is a call to join or identify with a way of life. The motif of competing voices and invitations, calls and seductions runs throughout Proverbs 1–9, and the repetition urges the reader to consider the ends or consequences of these crucial life decisions.

If the prologue of 1:1–7 presents the purposes of the book and the benefits that can be gained from its study, the sections that immediately follow offer two vivid examples of wisdom instruction. The invitation to join violent men (1:8–19) and the first speech of personified Wisdom (1:20–33) are lessons in learning how to discern true speech from false. Said another way, if the prologue is about learning, with synonyms for knowledge and understanding scattered throughout, the instruction that follows teaches that knowledge is gained by paying careful attention to the speech one hears. One must attend to words, their outcomes, and the character of the persons who speak them. This concern for the right use of speech also appears in the collection of proverbs and sentences (15:1–7; 26:22–28).

1:8–9. It is important to notice that the first lessons of parental instruction do not teach directly; they quote. The parents direct attention away from themselves, turning the young man's attention to the voices he will hear when he leaves them to make his way in the world. This sort of simulation training is designed to show where the different invitations will ultimately lead those who speak them as well as those who accept them. Politicians and other public persuaders know how to use the inoculation effect to answer objections and counterarguments before listeners encounter

---

2. T. A. Hildebrandt, "Proverb," in *Cracking Old Testament Codes: A Guide to Interpreting the Literary Genres of the Old Testament*, ed. D. B. Sandy and R. L. Giese Jr. (Nashville: Broadman and Holman, 1995), 240. R. Murphy, *Wisdom Literature*, 55, finds similarities to the casuistic, "If you are . . ." in Ptahhotep, but there are no indications of the court context of Ptahhotep here.

them somewhere else. Here the parental teachers hope to do the same by quoting and then refuting the seductive messages that will inevitably try to undo their teaching.

In 1:8–9, the parents address the young man directly. The word they use for teaching (*musar*, "instruction") was used in the prologue that also spoke of young men receiving "instruction" and wise ones who "listen" (*šmᶜ*). The first line of verse 8, then, sums up the prologue and links it with the parental instruction that follows in chapters 1–9. The second line of verse 8, "do not forsake your mother's teaching," echoes the wisdom and discipline that fools despise in verse 7. Verse 8 not only summarizes the importance of heeding instruction, it also links the prologue with the issue of knowing whom to listen to. The lesson is deceptively simple. Listen to your parents. Do not listen to greedy men. More importantly, listen to wisdom, for it is wisdom that your parents teach you. Lesson number one in developing discernment about how to live is learning how to listen and to whom.

1:10–16. The writer does not use soft words to describe those who speak next. In 1:10, they are called "sinners," and their invitation is called "enticement" (using the same Heb. root used for the "simple" in 1:4). Their call not only appeals to the simple, it makes simple those who take it to heart. The parents' warning, "Do not give in to them," is literally, "Do not go!" Some see this invitation to street violence as a real danger for Israelite youth in the early monarchic era,[3] while others see it as symbolic and applicable to any sort of corporate violence.[4] Probably both levels would be heard by ancient listeners.

The parental instructor knows well what those men will say and gives the young listener a preview. They will declare their intent to lie in wait, to ambush the innocent, and to swallow them the way the underworld (*šᵉʾol*) swallows the dead. Perhaps this violence is planned for its own thrill, but the gang also hopes to gain valuable plunder. By quoting their hopes for easy riches, the gains of 1:13 are set in contrast with the rewards of 1:9. Unlike the garland and chain that are won through study and discipline, these goods come at bitter cost to the victims.

Therefore, there is a tragic irony as this gang of thieves proclaims loyalty to one another through the promise of a common purse. It is a promise of community, but what community can you have with people who are enemies of community? Others have to pay the price for your fellowship. Their community does not build, it destroys. It does not embrace, it eliminates. The promises of these violent men repeats first plural pronouns; "we" and "us"

---

3. Hubbard, *Proverbs*, 51.
4. Van Leeuwen, "Proverbs," 38.

seek to create a sense of comradery, but it is, as Kenneth Burke once described war, a "disease of cooperation."

Along with quick riches and a sense of belonging, another enticement may be the lure of excitement and power.[5] The quotation seems to end abruptly, but perhaps this is because enough has been heard, we know the purpose of this group of men. They promise the power of violence, the riches of stolen gain, and the fellowship of thieves.

Parental instruction resumes in 1:15, repeating terms from 1:10: "My son, do not go along with them."[6] Literally, the phrase reads, "do not walk in their way," a parallel to "do not set foot on their paths." Verse 16 adds that their feet rush along that path to sin and bloodshed, but it is not clear why the parents repeat what readers have already learned from verse 11. Genesis 9 warns against taking the blood of another human, and we know that bloodshed was a common metaphor for crime and injustice in the prophets, but why do the parents stress the matter of walking and running? It is because these men are rushing into a trap.

1:17–19. Verse 17 contains the first real proverb of the book of Proverbs. This lesson-in-a-saying departs from the typical instruction form in that it speaks no imperative and offers no reward. Yet this simple saying is difficult to understand, in part because it seems to intrude on its context. It does not seem to fit, and so it works like a riddle. Riddles use a cipher language that offers a clue at the same time that it conceals a trap.[7] Therefore, we read this proverb about a trap, watching for ways that it may work as a trap itself.

A net or trap often appears in the Bible as a metaphor for the violence of the wicked (Mic. 7:2) as well as their judgment (Job 18:8–10; Ps. 141:10; Hos. 7:12). Trapping is a form of hunting with a long history in the ancient Near East, and even today there are many varieties of birds in Palestine. The net used in ancient times was probably strewn with seeds, and birds were caught when the hunter pulled the drawstrings.[8]

Part of the difficulty of interpreting the proverb and its riddle is a problem of translation. The term for "useless" (*ḥinnam*) can also mean "for no reason" or "for nothing." It is also used in 1:11 of the "harmless soul," who has

---

5. Kidner, *Proverbs*, 60.

6. Note that outcomes are also compared. The "my son" of 1:8 and 15 are both followed by motive clauses marked by "for" (*ki*). T. Boys, *Tacita Sacra* (London: T. Hamilton, 1824), quoted in R. Meynet, *Rhetorical Analysis: An Introduction to Biblical Rhetoric* (Sheffield: Academic Press, 1998), 97.

7. Crenshaw, *Education in Ancient Israel*, 116.

8. O. Keel, *The Symbolism of the Biblical World: Ancient Near Eastern Iconography and the Book of Psalms*, trans. T. J. Hallett (New York: Seabury Press, 1978), 92.

done nothing to provoke attack.[9] Then there is the matter of how to interpret "in full view of all the birds." The phrase literally reads, "in the eyes of." Most take the saying as a jab at the foolishness of scattering seed on the net while the birds are watching, assuming that the birds see the would-be-trappers and stay away. How true to nature is this? Once the trappers have left, the birds head for the seed, because they do not understand the difference between food and bait. This is the whole idea of the trap; birds are caught unaware. Therefore, the phrase "in the eyes of" may refer to the bird's understanding (or lack of it). The saying could follow the Hebrew word order and read, "For nothing is the net spread in the eyes of every bird."[10] Whatever translation is chosen, the point of the proverb is that birds are only trapped when they are unaware that there is a trap.

Now we begin to see the connection between this saying about birds and traps and the invitation of this gang. Notice that the proverb is framed with blood in 1:16 and 18. Seeking the blood of others, the gang actually lies in wait for its own; it will fall into its own trap. Traps work when the prey does not know what is happening, and so the violent men do not know they will be caught themselves. They believe they lie in wait for someone's blood, for "no reason" (1:11), yet they lie in wait for their own (1:18 repeats the terms for "lie in wait" and "waylay"). Like the birds that see "no reason" to avoid a net strewn with seed, these men are caught unaware. A proverb (or riddle) about traps is used to demonstrate that the way of violent gain is a trap itself.

The afterword or coda in 1:19 adds focus to what has already been said in 1:18, repeating the word for life (*nepeš*) used there. Just as the violent people "waylay only themselves" (lit., "their own life"), so "ill-gotten gain ... takes away the lives of those who get it." The young man, hearing this last teaching of the parents, should also make a comparison between the deadly lure of ill-gotten gain and the garland and chain of instruction. The one reward leads to death, while the other, by implication, leads to life.

Thus, the first instruction ends by urging the young learner to consider the outcomes and consequences that follow from the way of life one chooses. The instruction reveals the self-deception at work in the gang's invitation and intends to teach the young student how to discern truth from falsehood. There is more here than learning to avoid trouble; it also means learning to listen to the words of others with wisdom. Only the simple believe everything they hear. One chooses a way in life, in large measure, by what one chooses to listen to and believe.

---

9. Clifford, *The Wisdom Literature,* 58, translates both occurrences with "senselessly."
10. While the translation is not Garrett's, the insight is his; *Proverbs,* 70.

Bridging Contexts

THE READER'S ROLE. With this first encounter with the words "my son," readers are asked to identify with a boy coming of age and preparing to make his way in the world. Younger or older, male or female, this readerly role here is necessary, for all that follows in the book is cast in terms of the young man's education. We may find it strange that such a role is required of us as readers, but we will see that the concerns of Proverbs transcend the boundaries of gender and age as well as those of time and place.

The concerns of the young man ultimately are the concerns of all believers. So, for example, the parents' concern for listening carefully to the invitations that come one's way are not much different from those of parents today. One of the most important marks of wisdom is the ability to discern truth from error; one uses it to distinguish sincerity of character from motives less noble. While this lesson must be learned by the young, the work of critical listening is equally important for adults. It helps one learn the difference between wisdom and folly.

We have seen that the parents want their son to consider the character of those who speak as well as the outcomes of the words he will hear. Words reveal the intentions of the heart, but also, as we noted earlier, the direction of one's life, symbolized in the way or path one walks. The proverb of the net uses the images of bait and trap to argue that quick and easy stolen gain exacts its cost sooner or later. The timeless issues touched here are false and enticing speech, its indications of character, the deadly ends of violence and ill-gotten gain, and the self-deception necessary to walk this path of life.

Why begin with theft and violence? Gangs succeed because they promise to meet needs for security and identity that are neglected in families and homes. One inner-city principal recommends the three R's of recognition, respect, and routine, a balance of affection and discipline. When these are lacking, children and adolescents turn to the gang that uses the language of family to express loyalty to one another. Recruiters make promises that the gang will provide and look out for these kids while downplaying the threats and violence that come to any who want to leave.[11]

In seeking to bridge contexts, readers may ask why this ancient picture of theft and violence comes first in the instruction of the young man. While there are many parents today who are afraid that their sons and daughters

---

11. M. L. Taylor, "Local Perspective: The Principal of Albany Park Multicultural Academy Speaks Out on Gangs," *Hands-On* 9/4 (1999): 4.

---

will join gangs, most readers of this commentary would probably say that their children do not find the invitation attractive. When I preach and teach from Proverbs in churches, I jokingly ask if anyone there has been tempted to join the Mob. No one ever answers yes, and then I observe that it is strange to begin a book of teaching by warning against a way of life that few readers find tempting.

As Scripture, the book of Proverbs must be read and studied in the context of the Hebrew canon, and so we should look for similar themes and references to other biblical texts. Thus, for example, the old cartoon plot of the coyote who falls into the trap he set for the roadrunner can be found in the Psalms. Prayers for deliverance often ask for this form of poetic justice: "Keep me, O LORD, from the hands of the wicked; protect me from men of violence who plan to trip my feet. Proud men have hidden a snare for me; they have spread out the cords of their net and have set traps for me along my path. . . . May disaster hunt down men of violence" (Ps. 140:4–5, 11b; see also 35:5–8; 64:1–10).

In addition, certain words and phrases of this first instruction lead the reader to other biblical pictures of violence. Joseph's brothers overpowered him and sold him into slavery for twenty shekels of silver (Gen. 37:19–28). Many of the words used by the brothers are echoed in the words of the gang here—most notably "blood" (*dam*), "pit" (*bor*), "profit or gain" (*baṣaᶜ*), and "life" (*nepeš*).[12] Furthermore, Proverbs 1:16 uses virtually the same Hebrew words as Isaiah 59:7, "their feet rush into sin; they are swift to shed innocent blood."[13] The larger context of the chapter calls a wayward Israel to account for its sins against its citizens, repeating the absence of justice (Isa. 59:6, 8, 9, 14). Bloodshed and betrayal are stressed.[14]

These two quotations from Israel's biblical tradition suggest that from beginning to end, Israel's story included violence for the sake of gain. The ideal of justice and neighbor love mandated in Proverbs 1:3 was perverted into abuse of sibling and neighbor. Prophets pronounced their judgment on a society that went after "ill-gotten gain" (1:19). Jeremiah 6:13 and 8:10 use the term, not as a synonym for violence but as its possible motivation, "greedy for gain."

---

12. See also Mic. 7:2, "All men lie in wait to shed blood; each hunts his brother with a net."

13. Many commentators view this as a gloss, a quote inserted from Isa. 59:7 to explain the enigmatic proverb in Prov. 1:17. R. J. Clifford, "The Text and Versions of Proverbs," in *Wisdom, You Are My Sister* (CBQMS 29; Washington, D. C.: Catholic Biblical Assocation of America, 1997), 48. The reference to Isaiah does seem intentional, but for a different purpose as explained above.

14. Harris, *Proverbs 1–9*, 43, 52–61.

These intertextual references[15] in particular portray Israel at its worst, selling and betraying brothers for gain. By directing the reader to the beginning and end of Israel's history, this text in Proverbs suggests that the violence and greed of a marauding band is a picture of what Israel (and Judah in particular) had become. Joseph's brothers become a symbolic type of later Israel, whose violence of greed and injustice Isaiah laments (Isa. 59:6–14).

In sum, the references to texts from the Torah and the Prophets suggest that violence like that practiced by the gang has been present in Israel's history from inception to the Exile. Could it be that readers were to see in this warning against gang violence the consequences of Israel's own story, in particular, Israel's own entrapment in the net of greed? If we are to hear the message of this parental instruction in its biblical context, we will recognize the potential to be greedy for gain in ourselves and will also acknowledge the temptation to ill-gotten gain, even though temptations to violence are rarer.

GREED AS A TRAP. We are now in a better position to suggest a reason that the instruction begins with a warning against violent gangs. Even as we join with the parental teachers in deploring this way of life, we should be careful about equating this gang with modern gang life, especially if it leads us to see gang members as anything other than humans who need love, correction, and redemption. One volunteer in a college one-on-one program spoke of the lessons she learned in trying to befriend an eighth-grade girl struggling to stay in school and avoid the gangs: "How can we dissuade young people from such an appealing and welcoming option when there are no favorable alternatives? It is unfair to criticize gang members for poorly choosing their path in life if we are unwilling to give them some favorable choices."[16] Gang members themselves say that they are seduced by the promises of wealth, power, and belonging because they see little hope in meeting any of their needs for security any other way. Churches can and should support those ministries that attempt to offer "favorable choices," remembering that for many, the temptation is real.

Still, the warning seems extreme: Who of us reading this book is tempted by violent crime? Tempted to join the Mob or a street gang? Who of us would say, "Yes, that's what I want"? So we read along, ready to pass by the words of the gang and go on to whatever else the text has for us. We read

---

15. Ibid., 52–65. Harris argues that the citations are intentional, reinforcing the parent's instructions with teaching from the Torah and Prophets.

16. B. Anderson, "Musings: Being Taught While Serving," *Hands-On* 9/4 (1999): 21, 30.

on and find a proverb. As we look more closely at it, we see the folly of the gang compared with birds trapped in a net. But we aren't ready for what comes next. This is the end of all who are greedy for gain, ill-gotten and otherwise, for greed takes the life of its possessors (1:19)! Now we see that violence is a symptom, an end result of greed, desire that has gone out of bounds. To hear the prophets tell it, greed for gain leads to violence and bloodshed. To hear James tell it, evil desire entices, conceives, and gives birth to sin. Desires that battle within lead to battles and quarrels without (James 1:13–15; 4:1). Finally, adds the proverb, violence becomes its own trap.

Perhaps we have walked into a trap. The trap of the proverb is that we believe we would reject violence, but then few are enticed by violence. We would reject ill-gotten gain, although we might understand the temptation to cut corners to come out ahead. We read on, perhaps even past the proverb, and miss its point about greed. Greed can be defined as desire that knows no bounds, desire so strong that it does not care what is done to satisfy it or what harm it does to others. There's a trap that can catch us unaware. If we put this truth in our minds and then listen to the media barrage for a week, we may well be surprised at the desire, if not blatant greed, that we find, not only in the commercials but also in the programming itself.

Birds unaware, caught in a trap. While we may distance ourselves from greed and violence, most who will read this are Americans, people whose set of expectations of what we need is probably higher than much of the rest of the world. Juliet B. Schor, in her book *The Overworked American*,[17] argues that Americans over the last fifty years have always chosen higher pay over time off; we work more so we can have more. Expectations of what we need have risen and so have expectations of how long we need to work for it, leading to an ever escalating cycle of "work and spend."

In a sequel, *The Overspent American*,[18] Schor uses her own research to tell us what we may wish we didn't already know: We are still keeping up with the Jonses, but the Joneses are no longer the people who live next door (we hardly know them). Rather, the "reference groups" that we form at work and play tell us what we should acquire to show that we are successful. Schor claims that even children's play groups and preschools can whet the appetite for designer clothes and expensive shoes. Add television and other media examples to the picture, and our reference groups expand to two or three economic levels above us.

---

17. J. B. Schor, *The Overworked American: The Unexpected Decline of Leisure* (New York: Basic Books, 1991).

18. J. B. Schor, *The Overspent American: Upscaling, Downshifting, and the New Consumer* (New York: Basic Books, 1998).

After surveying a telecommunications corporation with 85,000 employees, Schor found that each hour of weekly TV viewing reduced annual savings by $208. Those surveyed reported that it was not the commercials but the lifestyles portrayed in the programs that had the greatest effect on their attitudes toward spending. Lest we think that television viewing is the only factor that increases spending and reduces savings, note that Schor also found that each additional level of education beyond high school reduces annual savings by $1,148. She also gives some examples of people who have "downshifted," either out of choice or as victims of corporate downsizing. Over half of those she surveyed told her the change enhanced their lives so much that they hoped to make it permanent.

Now this is not a putdown of hard work or the realization that simply making it these days is not easy; it takes work and it takes time. But the proverb asks that we always examine the results of our choices and that we keep vigilant watch on our desires. Desires are not bad, but they become greedy desires when loved ones are given second place and relationships suffer—family and friends, churches and communities. Given that we live and breathe in a culture of consumerism, it is not too much to ask that we keep watch over our response to it.[19] Greed is a trap, and traps only work when they are not seen for what they are. The proverb keeps us from walking on blindly—the point of birds trapped unaware. It is a warning that the power of greed can sneak up on us. Greed can crowd out the more important parts of our lives, such as community, virtue, and integrity.[20]

Thus, the proverb is like a trap for us. If we rush by and say, "That does not tempt me," the proverb reminds us that birds are trapped because they are unaware of the danger. But we are caught by a merciful trapper. Can you imagine anyone who would go through all the trouble to bait a net, catch the bird, and then let it go? Yet that is what the Lord is doing here. We are caught so that we can go free. We are caught in this trap of a proverb so we might be spared the real one, the larger one of getting caught up in greed unawares. We then become aware of the dangers that might ensnare us and take the warning.

We might generalize one step further. The proverb is about being aware, having the ability to see the trap, and therefore having the ability to choose another way. If the proverb is designed to make us aware of the trap of greed,

---

19. Schor's book is reviewed, along with Robert Frank's *Luxury Fever*, in "No Satisfaction: The Trials of the Shopping Nation," *The New Yorker* 74/43 (Jan. 25, 1999): 88–92.

20. Some help in understanding the problem can be found in R. Clapp, ed., *The Consuming Passion: Christianity and the Consumer Culture* (Downers Grove, Ill.: InterVarsity, 1998). Clapp observes that the "consumptive ethos is exceedingly complex," 12.

the larger context of this passage also instructs us to learn wisdom by practicing discernment. Just as the young learner was urged to recognize the enticements of the gang for what they were, we are being taught to listen critically to persuasive messages that come at us daily. Certainly we can point to advertising, but as Schor has shown, the ethos of consumerism permeates our culture. Careful and critical listening is one way that Christians can practice discernment in weighing the promises and claims set before us.

According to many, our standard of living is derived at great cost to the rest of the world. How, then, do we listen to voices all around telling us to improve our lot when the voice of Jesus tells us to look out for the least of his brothers and sisters? Jesus warns us about the dangers of greed, also asking us to watch the birds. They don't work too many hours; they don't gather too much and then have garage sales; they don't even have barns. What are you worried about? What do you think you lack that you need all these things? Aren't you more valuable than these birds that God cares for? Two are sold for a penny, yet not one falls to the ground that God does not see! Don't be afraid, you are worth more than many sparrows (Matt. 6:25–34; 10:29–31; Luke 12:22–34).

In sum, the parent's first lesson in wisdom asks its readers, both ancient and contemporary, to practice discernment in listening, to pay attention to outcomes, and especially to do these while watching out for temptations to greed. This first lesson in wisdom, then, asks each of us to think about the messages we hear. Can we tell the difference between truth and deception, between promise and seduction? It asks us to think about the consequences that will come if we follow the urgings of those messages. Do they bring life to ourselves and our communities, or do they take it away? It asks us to think about what we really want in life. Finally it urges us to consider the choices we make to fulfill our desires, mindful of the danger that those desires can get hijacked by greed. Wisdom offers to guide us in asking those questions, as we will see in the following section.

Proverbs 1:20–33

20 WISDOM CALLS ALOUD in the street,
    she raises her voice in the public squares;
21 at the head of the noisy streets she cries out,
    in the gateways of the city she makes her speech:

22 "How long will you simple ones love your simple ways?
    How long will mockers delight in mockery
    and fools hate knowledge?
23 If you had responded to my rebuke,
    I would have poured out my heart to you
    and made my thoughts known to you.
24 But since you rejected me when I called
    and no one gave heed when I stretched out my hand,
25 since you ignored all my advice
    and would not accept my rebuke,
26 I in turn will laugh at your disaster;
    I will mock when calamity overtakes you—
27 when calamity overtakes you like a storm,
    when disaster sweeps over you like a whirlwind,
    when distress and trouble overwhelm you.

28 "Then they will call to me but I will not answer;
    they will look for me but will not find me.
29 Since they hated knowledge
    and did not choose to fear the LORD,
30 since they would not accept my advice
    and spurned my rebuke,
31 they will eat the fruit of their ways
    and be filled with the fruit of their schemes.
32 For the waywardness of the simple will kill them,
    and the complacency of fools will destroy them;
33 but whoever listens to me will live in safety
    and be at ease, without fear of harm."

HERE WE HAVE our first encounter with the personified voice of Wisdom. She appears as an orator, speaking to the crowds passing by in the public squares, a role that appears again in chapters 8 and 9. These speeches form a frame or inclusio around the instructional literature of Proverbs 1–9, marking a major unit but also stressing what is important. Because writers tend to place matters of greatest significance at the beginnings and endings of works, we notice that Wisdom's offers to give instruction come to all. Those with ears to hear will receive it. The speeches are also unusual. There is no other instance of Wisdom speaking in public settings apart from the apocryphal book of Sirach.[1]

Biblical scholarship has tried to establish the historical origins of this personification but has not reached a consensus.[2] While some see similarities to the Egyptian principle of universal order (*ma²at*), others find resemblance in goddess figures.[3] Whatever resemblances we can find to other ancient Near Eastern figures (noting that there are significant differences as well), we must remember that the speeches of Wisdom are literary creations, spoken as instruction by the parental teacher of Proverbs 1–9. We would expect that so important and multidimensional an entity as wisdom would require the use of figurative language to do it justice.

Personification is a literary device used throughout Scripture, often used to describe the Lord's attributes. His throne is founded on justice and judgment (Ps. 97:2), and the heralds that go before him are kindness and truth (89:14); kindness meets truth, and justice and peace kiss (85:10).[4] Yet nowhere else but here in Proverbs do we find an attribute or an abstract entity personified as a speaking character. While this figure speaks authoritatively and calls attention to herself, Wisdom also directs her listeners to "fear the LORD" (Prov. 1:29). This main character of the instructions is a mysterious figure, appearing as both teacher and intermediary, so we will watch her words carefully.

---

1. Murphy, *Wisdom Literature*, 55.

2. See the survey of views in C. V. Camp, *Wisdom and the Feminine in the Book of Proverbs* (Sheffield: Almond Press, 1985), 23–46; and J. Day, "Foreign Semitic Influence on the Wisdom of Israel and its Appropriation in the Book of Proverbs," in *Wisdom in Ancient Israel: Essays in Honour of J. A. Emerton*, ed. J. Day, R. P. Gordon, and H. G. M. Williamson (Cambridge: Cambridge Univ. Press, 1995), 68–70.

3. See the Akkadian Oracles and Prophecies spoken by women and goddesses, *ANET*, 449–51. Unlike Wisdom, these goddesses direct worship to themselves: "I am Ishtar of Arbela. ... When you were small, I sustained you. Fear not, praise me!"

4. R. Murphy, *The Tree of Life: An Exploration of Biblical Wisdom Literature*, 2d ed. (Grand Rapids: Eerdmans, 1996), 133–34.

As we examine the speech of personified Wisdom, we learn that the main emphasis of the entire first chapter is the fate of those who reject wisdom. Therefore, one can read this chapter as an extended illustration of 1:7: "Fools despise wisdom and discipline." Wisdom's speech also continues the first lesson of discernment and listening that began with the parent's instruction in 1:8. The young man is to learn how to discern who is worthy of his trust and who is not.

When we compare these speeches of the parental teachers, the gang, and Wisdom, a number of similarities and differences appear. (1) The literary context presents this speech of Wisdom as quoted speech, spoken by the parents to the son in the same way that the parents quoted the enticement of the violent men. Both examples of quoted speech illustrate the deadly direction of a life that rejects Yahweh and his wisdom (1:18–19, 25–28). The parents offer Wisdom's speech as another word of warning.

(2) There are a number of similarities between the instruction of the parents and Wisdom's speech. Both urge the young man to listen (1:8, 33). This call to listen and obey (Heb. šmᶜ frequently carries both senses) frames this subsection and offers another indication that the speeches are to be read in light of each other. Both promise rewards: The parents liken their teaching to a garland and necklace (1:9), while Wisdom offers safety and security (1:33). The gang also promises rewards (1:13–14), but the parents and Wisdom join their voices to show that those rewards are false and short-lived. Both speak of a "way" that ends in disaster (1:19, 31), and both use negative motive clauses that begin with "for" (*ki* in 1:16, 32). In this way the disaster of the bird in the net and the danger of waywardness and complacency are linked hook and eye.

(3) Finally, the key words of the prologue ("wisdom," "simple," "fools") are in Wisdom's speech but not in the words of the gang. To summarize, the similarities show Wisdom's speech to be an extension of the prologue and the parent's teaching. The parents quote Wisdom's words as a counter to the speech of the gang; her words are presented as testimony that the teaching of the parents is true.

The first image that the listening son receives of Wisdom is startling: a woman, raising her voice to speak in the town square! Certainly the picture sets Wisdom apart in a set of roles distinct from those expected of women at the time. Unlike other persuasive women such as Abigail (1 Sam. 25:23–35) or the wise woman of Tekoa (2 Sam. 14:1–21), Wisdom does not appeal and does not take a subservient role. She speaks with strong authority, setting herself over and against her audience. Like Deborah the prophetess (Judg. 4:4–5:31), she leads and challenges. Yet no woman ever spoke to crowds in the city the way Wisdom does, and this calls readers to attention.

Both elements of this picture, her voice and the public setting, are repeated four times. If the streets are noisy, she must be heard above them, and so we imagine a voice that is loud and insistent. Does anyone stop to listen? One often sees street preachers with a bullhorn in cities, but they rarely draw a crowd. So Wisdom cries out to anyone who will listen but then turns to address those who will not. As we look closely at this speech, we should remember that Wisdom's negative message in this chapter is matched with the positive messages of chapters 8 and 9.[5] However, because her speech comes right after the words of the gang, we should not be surprised that her negative message comes first. Her words of coming disaster answer the words of violence spoken by the gang.

Wisdom's speech can be divided into three sections following the use of the key word "call" (Heb. *qr²*, 1:21, 24, 28).

"Wisdom calls aloud in the street" (1:20–23)
"You rejected me when I called" (1:24–27)
"Then they will call to me but I will not answer" (1:28–33)

Each section addresses a different audience, and each makes use of a different verbal tense. Whereas Wisdom calls to all in a present tense, she addresses the simple and fools, who rejected her calls in the past. She then turns away from them to say that they will call on her in the future to no avail.

Wisdom's Call to All (1:20–23)

THE FIRST OF Wisdom's addresses calls out to anyone who will hear. Her question, "How long?" pleads and threatens judgment at the same time, just as it did for Jeremiah (Jer. 4:14, 21; 12:4; 31:22; 47:5).[6] It is this rejected prophet who comes closest to the picture we have here of someone warning and calling for repentance in a public setting (Jer. 7:1–29).[7] Wisdom's first address also uses terms from the prologue (Prov. 1:4, 7); the "simple" (1:4) can learn if they leave their simple ways behind (the Heb. root for "entice" in 1:10 is *pt²*, "simple"), but if they love those ways and hate knowledge, they become fools who hate wisdom and discipline (1:7). Mockers

---

5. Hubbard, *Proverbs*, 55, rightly observes that this address is the negative antithesis of the speech in ch. 8.

6. See also Ex. 10:3; 1 Sam. 1:14; 2 Sam. 2:26; Hos. 6:5.

7. Harris, *Proverbs 1–9*, 93–95. In the early days of this country, women speakers such as Harriet Livermore, who preached before Congress, claimed that like the prophets, they received their authority to speak from God. See M. W. Casey, "The First Female Public Speakers in America (1630–1840): Searching for Egalitarian Christian Primitivism," *JCR* 23/1 (March 2000): 1–28.

do not merely choose to ignore, their rejection is active; they scoff and ridicule (cf. Ps. 1:1).

Whether one reads the Hebrew of 1:23 in the past tense as the NIV does or in the present conditional sense as does the NRSV,[8] the point is still clear. Wisdom's rebuke is correction, an offer of instruction that is personal and direct. If listeners respond (lit., "turn"), she promises to share her thoughts using phrases and terms that are used elsewhere of the Lord (lit., "my spirit [*ruaḥ*] and my words [*dabar*]").[9] To reject this instruction is to reject Wisdom herself, who calls and stretches out her hand. Yet her teaching is so out of step with the bustle of business as usual that her words go unheard.

Wisdom's Call Rejected (1:24–27)

A SECOND ADDRESS begins in 1:24 with a second use of the word "call." Wisdom says she has called and called, just as she is doing now, but she has been speaking to deaf ears. The results of this rejection, introduced in 1:26, are "disaster" and "calamity," and this brings laughter to Wisdom. Just as the gang's evil was repaid with evil in the parent's earlier instruction, so it will be for those who ignored Wisdom's rebuke. As they mocked, so will she. She will laugh the way Yahweh laughs over the defeat of his enemies (Ps. 2:4; 37:13; 59:8). The next verse (Prov. 1:27) pictures a storm of ruin overtaking these detractors. The source of the calamity is not named; Wisdom does not bring it about, she only rejoices at its coming.

Wisdom's Refusal to Answer a Call (1:28–33)

WISDOM'S THIRD ADDRESS begins in 1:28 with an echo of her own calls (*qr'*, 1:20, 24). Just as she called and was refused, now she will not answer when they call. They can look for her, but she will not be found (Yahweh says the same about himself in Mic. 3:4). Perhaps this is why Wisdom no longer addresses them directly but uses third-person pronouns and verbs. Instead, her words seem to be directed to the larger public (including the learning son, and the reader who identifies with the son).

If we imagine a crowd gathered to hear Wisdom, the first speech makes her typical offer of correction to those who haven't been listening, the second singles out the fools who have rejected her, and the third turns from them to address the larger crowd. Jesus often did the same when, after contro-

---

8. "Give heed to my reproof; I will pour out my thoughts to you. . . ."

9. R. Murphy translates the first phrase as yet another rejection of Wisdom, "turn from my reproof," but this move toward consistency is unnecessary ("Wisdom's Song: Proverbs 1:20–23," *CBQ* 48 [1986]: 456–60).

versy with the Pharisees or his disciples, he spoke to the larger crowd, hoping someone who had been listening in would turn to hear more (Mark 7:14–23; 8:31–37).

The charges of 1:22–23 are revisited in 1:29–30, but so is the equation of 1:7, this time in the negative. If "fear of the LORD is the beginning of knowledge," Wisdom's unresponsive audience has shown that it wants nothing to do with either. Their rejection of Wisdom is now revealed for what it really is, a rejection of the Lord. Wisdom stresses that this rejection has not been done out of ignorance but out of choice.

Just as the picture of a bird and a net was used earlier (1:17) to create an ancient version of "what goes around comes around," so Wisdom says that their ways and their schemes will become the bitter fruit with which they will be gorged (1:31). The connection between verses 30 and 31 is especially significant. If the fools will not accept Wisdom's "advice" (from ʿṣh, 1:25, 30), then their own "schemes" (also from ʿṣh, 1:31) will be their reward.

The image of bitter fruit is followed by the plain talk of 1:32–33: The ways of the fools will prove fatal. Wisdom's speech is not followed by any teaching from the parental instructor. Instead, she gets the last word, but that word still repeats what the parents said earlier: death—for the simple and fools (1:22, 32). The Hebrew word used for "complacency" can be used for peace (17:1) and security (Ps. 122:7), but here it is ironic; the security is false, contrasted with the peace and safety she promises (cf. Dan. 8:25; 11:21, 24). Wisdom adds a positive word to end her speech and in doing so calls out once again to be heard. She echoes the parents as she urges her listeners to attend to her own teaching (cf. Prov. 1:8 and 33).

We have seen that a number of terms are repeated in a way that connects the verses in which they appear. This use of repetition suggests that Wisdom's speech can also be diagrammed in a chiastic pattern, in which the second half revisits the topics of the first in reverse order.[10] The beginning and ending correspond as contrasts. As Wisdom calls out to all in 1:21, only those who listen to her in 1:33 will find safety (Heb. "the one"). The center and most important part of the structure is Wisdom's chilling promise to those who did not listen to her; she will laugh, mock, and refuse to answer them when their trouble comes (1:26–28).[11]

The chiastic or mirror structure can also be diagrammed to highlight the change from second to third person in the address to the simple and fools:

---

10. P. Trible, "Wisdom Builds a Poem: The Architecture of Proverbs 1:20–33," *JBL* 94 (1975): 509–18. D. Garrett, *Proverbs*, 71, and Fox, *Proverbs 1–9*, 101–4, propose different arrangements.

11. Garrett, *Proverbs*, 71.

A 1:20–21 - Wisdom calls out to all
  B 1:22–23b - Appeal to simple and fools—"you"
    C 1:24–27 - Wisdom rejects those who reject her—"you"
  B' 1:28–32 - Fate of simple and fools—"they"
A' 1:33 - Final call to listen and promise of safety to those who hear

The change to third person "they" in 1:28 signals that Wisdom's words of rejection are final. She no longer addresses the simple, scoffers, and fools directly but turns to explain her reaction to anyone who will listen, especially the young learner and the reader. The final call also promises safety to those who will listen; it offers a confirmation to those who have already chosen to walk along Wisdom's path. Like the prologue, it encourages the reader to continue reading the book and to walk in the ways of wisdom.

Bridging Contexts

PERSONIFIED WISDOM. In moving from ancient days to our own, we need to look closely at this figure of personified Wisdom and learn what she has to tell us about God and human nature, since both remain the same over time. The first task, therefore, is to come to a better understanding of the character of Wisdom and the roles she takes. Note that here for the first time, Wisdom is written in Hebrew plural (*hokmot*), not singular. The change has intrigued some interpreters, who take it as a sign of fullness or majesty (like the plural *ʾlohim*), but we note here that it distinguishes this speaking voice of personified Wisdom from the voiceless and faceless wisdom that was mentioned earlier (the same plural form is used in 9:1 but not in 8:1–36).[12]

Earlier we noted that Wisdom enacts three roles in her speech: She offers the counsel of a wisdom teacher, she calls for repentance like a prophet, and she identifies herself with the words and actions of the Lord.[13] (1) As a wisdom teacher, she offers advice (*ʿesah*) and rebuke (*tokahat*).[14] She calls the simple away from their simple ways (1:22, 25, 30) by offering preventative counsel and correction.

(2) Like a prophet she calls them to pay attention and to repent (Heb. *šwb*; "turn" is translated "responded" in 1:23)[15] and warns of coming disaster. She

---

12. Abstracts of quality often take feminine plural (B. K. Waltke and M. O' Connor, *An Introduction to Biblical Hebrew Syntax* [Winona Lake, Ind.: Eisenbrauns, 1990], 121, sec. 7.4.2).

13. Trible reviews scholarly opinion and derives four roles: preacher of repentance, prophet, teacher, and counselor, "Wisdom Builds a Poem," 509.

14. See McKane, *Proverbs*, 274–76.

15. Fox, *Proverbs 1–9*, 99, understands the verb as only a call to attention, but the larger context supports a sense of turning to repent or "respond."

understands their rejection of her as a rejection of God (1:29–30; see also 1 Sam. 8:7–8).

(3) However, we should notice that she identifies herself with the Lord in words and ways that wisdom teachers and prophets do not. For example, she does not use the prophetic formula "This is what the LORD says," but seems to speak for herself. Whereas the prophets quoted Yahweh as saying, "I called and you did not answer" (Jer. 7:13), and "I held out my hands" (Isa. 65:2), Wisdom says these things about herself. Her listeners are to show their fear of the Lord by turning to her for correction and counsel (Prov. 1:29–30). If they do, she promises to pour out her heart and thoughts in words that resemble the words of Yahweh in Joel 2:28.[16] In sum, Wisdom identifies herself with Yahweh by using words and describing actions that normally come from God alone. Yet the identification is not complete, because she calls her hearers "to fear the LORD," not her. Although, like Yahweh, she threatens to be unreachable when the day of trouble comes, she does not say that she will bring the trouble; she only knows that it will come.

It is important to keep all three roles in mind when trying to understand this portrait of Wisdom in the book of Proverbs. Wisdom teaches, corrects, and seeks to bring her listeners into relationship with God. In this personification, wisdom as a gift to humanity and wisdom as a characteristic of Yahweh are brought together in poetic (and therefore somewhat ambiguous) language. The portrait is developed more fully in Proverbs 3, 8, and 9, but for now we note that Wisdom is to be understood as a personification, not another form of deity, and that her calls are made to offer guidance, not to receive obedience or worship. Some claim that prayers and praises offered to Sophia (the Greek word for wisdom) are not offered to a goddess but to the Lord, who is wisdom, yet this passage gives us good reasons to question the practice.[17]

Like the wisdom teacher and the prophet, the persona of Wisdom is a means by which the thoughts and desires of Yahweh are communicated to a wayward humanity. By keeping the three roles together, the emphasis can remain on the act of communication and the role of a servant and messenger.

---

16. B. Waltke, "Lady Wisdom as Mediatrix: An Exposition of Proverbs 1:20–33," *Presbyterion: Covenant Seminary Review* 14 (Spring 1988): 1–15. Waltke understands her role as that of a mediator who speaks to humans with the authority of divine revelation.

17. Rosemary Reuther expressed surprise that the idea of prayer to Sophia or Divine Wisdom would provoke criticism, since she understands it as one of the many biblical images for God ("Divine Wisdom and Christian Fear: The Controversy over Female God-Images in the Churches Today," 30 *Good Minutes: The Chicago Sunday Evening Club*, broadcast January 1, 1995).

Just as it would be a mistake to worship a wisdom teacher, a prophet, or any of God's messengers (see the example of Paul and Barnabas in Acts 14:8—18), so it would be wrong to speak of Wisdom's identification with Yahweh as a feminine manifestation of deity. While it is true that a literary personification is not the same kind of figure as a historical prophet, it is important to remember that Yahweh has also given Wisdom the task to teach, to guide, to correct, and to warn in much the same way as human figures do.

The character of God. We thus learn something about the character of God, the giver of this gift of wisdom. Warnings, even threats of destruction, are signs of grace when they are given to keep those whom God loves from destruction. The picture of Wisdom calling out to those who walk beyond the sound of her voice bears a striking resemblance to Paul's chilling picture of humanity in Romans 1:18—32. The repeated phrase, "God gave them over" (Rom. 1:24, 26, 28), points to the same truth: Those who want no part of God will get their wish. Yet Wisdom's desire to reach out to willful humanity also reminds us of Paul's words about the gospel: "Through him and for his name's sake, we received grace and apostleship to call people from among all the Gentiles to the obedience that comes from faith" (Rom. 1:5).

Even as we come to discover God's grace in this portrait of Wisdom, we also come to understand ourselves as people who need that grace. While we may not find ourselves in the portrait of the mocker and the fool who spurn Wisdom's call, we may be more like the simple than we care to admit. Remembering that the simple are those who are open to a fault, susceptible to influences both good and bad, we can see in ourselves the tendency to wander away after false promises and deceptive desires (such as the enticements described in Prov. 1:8—19). We can also appreciate how slow we are to listen, especially to a word of correction. The mocker and fool represent those who take that unwillingness to listen to its fateful end. We do not need to follow their way to appreciate our own stubbornness. In Matthew 11:19, Jesus tells those who refused to listen to John or to him that "wisdom is proved right by her actions."

Teaching style. Finally, it is important to remember that the warnings of Wisdom are part and parcel of the parental teaching that continues throughout chapters 1—9. The parents are teaching through the voice of personified Wisdom in the same way they quote other voices, such as the gang (1:8—18) and the future words of the young man himself (5:12—13). For this reason, parents today can learn much by attending to the teaching style of these ancient parents and their use of quotation and description. In the voice of Wisdom, they have given their teaching a voice that calls, corrects, and warns. It not only brings their teaching to life, it plugs that teaching into something greater than themselves.

Wisdom speaks with the authority of God, but it does so by pointing to the calamity that comes to those who ignore her, saying, "This too is part of God's world." Prophets like Moses and Jeremiah make similar warnings about taking the wrong path, but unlike their appeal to a revealed message from God, Wisdom appeals to the experience of fools. They will need her help at some future time when they do not know how to get out of the trouble they have created for themselves. Wisdom uses the trouble that comes to fools as the proof that she (and the parents she speaks for) are right.

WE HAVE SEEN that the three sections of chapter 1 work together to create a warning that also makes an invitation to Wisdom's teaching. Wisdom calls and reaches out to every reader with an offer to instruct and correct, while her warnings point to the general human tendency to walk away and stray from her path. In making contemporary application, three aspects of Wisdom's calls are important: They tell us the truth about human nature, they tell us of God's love and care for wayward humans, and they tell us that the time to respond to this truth and love has its limits.

The truth about human nature. Wisdom's warning and correction tell us the truth about human nature. In a word, we can easily be led astray. As the old hymn puts it, "Prone to wander, Lord I feel it, prone to leave the God I love." While the book of Proverbs is addressed to those standing at a crossroads ready to choose a path in life, most readers today hear Wisdom's words as people who have chosen the Christian way. We want to follow the way of Jesus. As we follow him on that way, we also learn that we are at a new crossroads every day, and every day must choose to follow Jesus again. And every day, the other path that leads away from him beckons. As we grow, we are sometimes amazed at the ways it exerts its influence over us. We may not abandon his way completely like those addressed by Wisdom, but if we are honest, we recognize that we also wander.

We may wonder why this book of wisdom begins with such a negative picture. Without it, the instruction in wisdom could be misunderstood as having little that makes it different from the shelves of self-help literature we find in our bookstores today. Without it, we might get the mistaken notion that the goal of wisdom teaching is to prepare Christians for a successful and happy life. Not so. Tony Campolo tells college students and their parents that they do not need to worry about paying attention to self-fulfillment; that comes as natural as breathing. Rather, they need a sense of mission.

I mean, you ask an American mother, "What do you want your child to be when he grows up?" You get one standard answer: "I just want my children to be—[Audience says, "Happy."] ... Happy—it's the American creed. You don't know the whole Declaration of Independence, but you do know this line, that all of us are entitled to life, liberty, and—? [Audience says, "Happiness."] No wonder we're messed up! ... You should stay in school and you should get an education, but the purpose of an education is not to get a good job and make a lot of money. The purpose of a job, the purpose of an education is this: An education is to train you to serve other people in the name of Jesus Christ![18]

Campolo's words also apply to education in wisdom. Wisdom does offer success and happiness as rewards and by-products of the life lived under her guidance, but Wisdom's teaching will never set us on a course of irresponsible self-fulfillment. Her warnings prevent us from thinking too highly of ourselves and too little of God.

God's love and care for wayward humans. The warnings are also a sign of God's love and care for us. When I was a boy, I had a Superman suit that actually had printed on the part of the shirt that was tucked in, "This suit does not give you the power to fly. Only Superman can fly." I did not believe the warning that was written to keep me from hurting myself. I kept looking for higher things to jump from in the hope that some miraculous wind would carry me off to the clouds. When my Dad caught me jumping from the fender of his new car, he gave me a warning I did believe—good thing he got to me before I headed for the roof!

Likewise, parents today warn their children about choosing friends and activities wisely because they want to keep them from harm. So, as we saw in an earlier section, few today would find themselves tempted by invitations to join violent gangs, but temptations to unjust gain (and perhaps even the violence that is justified by it; see 1:8–19) are never that far away from us. Wisdom's warnings not only expose the violent way for what it is, they also warn us against the harm that will come to us if we choose to live without correction and instruction. Her speech seems to answer the invitation of the violent men, but more important, it speaks to all who wish to live apart from Wisdom's teaching. The dangers of greed and violence are always present; they only vary in degrees of intensity and expression. If violence only returns to the hand that produces it, Wisdom pleads and threatens so that we might

---

18. A. Campolo, "The Faith Equation," in *Ten Great Preachers: Messages and Interviews*, ed. B. Turpie (Grand Rapids: Baker, 2000), 29–31.

not harm others, but also that we might suffer no harm ourselves. Her warnings are a communication of God's love.

Therefore, Wisdom's speech sums up all that has gone before and offers a second lesson in listening and discernment. Like the parental wisdom teachers, she urges us to learn how to listen with discernment and to use that discernment to decide who is worthy of our trust. If we are to ignore the temptations of gain and their false promises, we are also to recognize her words as true (she will have much more to say about this in 8:6–14). In her correction, she will tell us the truth about ourselves as well as the truth about the way to walk in this world.

Wisdom teaches her listeners to discern truth from false promises by paying attention to long-term outcomes. Look at the results over time, she seems to say, and you will know whose words are sound. She will laugh last and best when trouble comes, when those who reject her "eat the fruit of their ways." Yet like a prophet, she also ends her speech with an invitation to turn and find safety and security. Parents often speak of the difficulty they have in helping their sons and daughters think about long-term consequences. The pleasures and rewards of "now" are immediate, strong, and hard to resist. It may be that parents can earn a hearing by following Wisdom's example, pointing out how some do live to regret their choices. They can also invite their children to a life that is free from fear, lived in the love and care of the Lord.

Limitation in the time to respond. Finally, Wisdom's words help us to recognize that in God's way of doing things, the time for second chances is long but limited. Wisdom's urgency should move us to more, not less, concern to call others from going their own way. Our efforts in evangelism can use Wisdom's roles as teacher and corrector to reach out to others with practical hope. We can offer warnings as well as teaching in life skills so that lives can change for the better. Although the saying has become commonplace, it is worth repeating: God loves us just the way we are, but also loves us too much to let us stay the way we are.

Wisdom's offer of counsel and correction give us new insight into the love of the Lord that we can share with others, and this insight has its implications for preaching. Some like sermons that "make it practical" with specific guidance in what to do in concrete situations. Others find this overly simplistic and want to hear sermons that offer theological principles that listeners can apply on their own. Of course there should be plenty of both in preaching, but Wisdom's street sermon reminds me that at least some of my sermons should give practical instruction and talk with listeners about consequences and outcomes, both negative and positive.[19]

---

19. I argued this point in "Preaching Lawfully," *Ex Auditu* 11 (1995): 145–52.

Although Wisdom's speech makes clear that there comes a time when it is too late to change one's mind, her invitation at the end of her speech reminds us that the times in which we are casting pearls before swine are few. Knowing that time is limited, Christians ought to be known as the people who give second chances and more. One church joined with the city of Chicago to start some alternative schools geared to give dropouts a chance to pick up their education where they left it off. The school is strict, but the students know they are valued.[20] Wisdom offers second chances and more. She also offers a course in prevention, teaching a way that prepares for the future. Instead of reading her words as unrestrained condemnation, we can receive them as the strong invitation of one who hopes that the tragedy of some will become a lesson for many.

---

20. "School Gives Teens Another Chance," *Chicago Tribune*, Friday, Aug. 23, 1998.

Proverbs 2:1–22

¹ MY SON, IF YOU accept my words
  and store up my commands within you,
² turning your ear to wisdom
  and applying your heart to understanding,
³ and if you call out for insight
  and cry aloud for understanding,
⁴ and if you look for it as for silver
  and search for it as for hidden treasure,
⁵ then you will understand the fear of the LORD
  and find the knowledge of God.
⁶ For the LORD gives wisdom,
  and from his mouth come knowledge and
    understanding.
⁷ He holds victory in store for the upright,
  he is a shield to those whose walk is blameless,
⁸ for he guards the course of the just
  and protects the way of his faithful ones.

⁹ Then you will understand what is right and just
  and fair—every good path.
¹⁰ For wisdom will enter your heart,
  and knowledge will be pleasant to your soul.
¹¹ Discretion will protect you,
  and understanding will guard you.

¹² Wisdom will save you from the ways of
    wicked men,
  from men whose words are perverse,
¹³ who leave the straight paths
  to walk in dark ways,
¹⁴ who delight in doing wrong
  and rejoice in the perverseness of evil,
¹⁵ whose paths are crooked
  and who are devious in their ways.

¹⁶ It will save you also from the adulteress,
  from the wayward wife with her seductive words,
¹⁷ who has left the partner of her youth
  and ignored the covenant she made before God.

¹⁸For her house leads down to death
  and her paths to the spirits of the dead.
¹⁹None who go to her return
  or attain the paths of life.

²⁰Thus you will walk in the ways of good men
  and keep to the paths of the righteous.
²¹For the upright will live in the land,
  and the blameless will remain in it;
²²but the wicked will be cut off from the land,
  and the unfaithful will be torn from it.

HAVING EXAMINED THE prologue (1:1–7) and the two warnings that follow (1:8–19, 20–33), we now enter into the first of the parents' teachings on God's gift of wisdom. Whereas chapter 1 opens with the invitation to study and adds warnings to those who refuse, chapter 2 calls the "son" to begin the study, followed by promises of finding wisdom and enjoying its protection. As was common in the ancient Near East, each section of teaching has a predictable pattern or *form*. An address ("My son") is followed by a charge or condition ("if you accept my words"), which is followed in turn by a series of motivations or rewards ("then you will understand the fear of the LORD"). Often there is also a mention of final outcomes. The first chapter of the Egyptian *Instruction of Amenemope* shows a similar form in its first section after the prologue:

> Give your ears, hear the sayings,
> Give your heart to understand them;
> It profits to put them in your heart,
> Woe to him who neglects them!
> Let them rest in the casket of your belly,
> May they be bolted in your heart,
> You will find it a success;
> You will find my words a storehouse for life,
> Your being will prosper on the earth.¹

While all of chapter 2 follows this pattern,² other instructions use the pattern as an introduction to further teaching (see 7:1–5), and some develop

---

1. *AEL*, 2:149; see also *ANET*, 421–22.
2. McKane, *Proverbs*, 278–81, claims that strictly speaking, the typical components of ancient Near Eastern instructions (imperatives, motives, and conclusions: "Do this . . . for

variations on the pattern (see 3:1–10; 4:1–9; 5:1–6; 6:1–5). In this way, ancient teachers framed their instructions with relationship and rewards. Our attention to form can help us discern the approach they used.

Understanding the *structure* of this chapter is also essential to understanding its content and rhetorical purpose. (1) We should notice that the poem is compacted into twenty-two lines, the number of letters in the Hebrew alphabet. However, each verse does not begin with a different letter from the alphabet as do, for example, the acrostic poems in Proverbs 31, Lamentations 1–4, or Psalm 119. This use of a nonalphabetic acrostic format shows up again in chapter 5; some even think it appears at the conclusion of the instructions (Prov. 8:32–9:18).[3] Clearly Proverbs concludes with an alphabetic acrostic in chapter 31, highlighting the importance of beginning and ending sections.[4] The acrostic structure may highlight the idea of completion or comphrehensiveness as does our saying, "Everything from A to Z." If so, the structure of this chapter may itself be a way of stating that everything that needs to be said about this topic is said here in this book.

(2) The six subsections of chapter 2 form an extended conditional statement, the protasis ("if") of verses 1–4 followed by five apodoses: "then" in verses 5–8, 9–11, "in order to" in verses 12–14, 16–19, and 20–22.[5] Interestingly, the first three of these six sections begin with the letter *aleph* ("A," vv. 4, 5, 9) and the last three begin with the letter *lamed* ("L," vv. 12, 16, 20). Readers should note that *lamed*, the first letter of the second half of the Hebrew alphabet, is used in the second half of the poem.[6] Based on these clues we can suggest the following outline:

Aleph stanza (2:1–4), "If you" (three times, vv. 1, 3, 4)
Aleph stanza (2:5–8), "Then you will understand" ("guard," v. 8)

. . . so that . . . ") are not in this text. However, if one takes the whole chapter as a literary unit, all three can be found: imperative ("turn your ear to wisdom," 2:1–4), motive ("he guards the course of the just," 2:8–19), and conclusion ("thus you will walk in the ways of good men," 2:20–22).

3. See D. N. Freedman, "Acrostic Poems in the Hebrew Bible: Alphabetic and Otherwise," *CBQ* 48 (1986): 408–31; "Acrostics and Metrics in Hebrew Poetry," *HTR* 65 (1972): 367–92, for examples in Lam. 5, Ps. 33 and 94, and Proverbs.

4. D. N. Freedman, "Proverbs 2 and 31: A Study in Structural Complementarity," in *Tehillah le-Moshe: Biblical and Judaic Studies in Honor of Moshe Greenberg*, ed. M. Cogan, B. L. Eichler, and J. H. Tigay (Winona Lake, Ind.: Eisenbrauns, 1997), 47–55. Both acrostics, having nearly identical counts of syllables, serve as a set of bookends, a structure echoed in Sirach.

5. After Scott, *Proverbs*, 43–43.

6. Murphy, *Proverbs*, 14, after P. Skehan, "The Seven Columns of Wisdom's House in Proverbs 1–9," in *Studies in Israelite Poetry and Wisdom* (CBQMS 1; Washington, D. C.: Catholic Biblical Association, 1971), 9.

Aleph stanza (2:9–11), "Then you will understand" ("protect," v. 11)
Lamed stanza (2:12–15), "to be saved" from evil men
Lamed stanza (2:16–19), "to be saved" from the adulteress
Lamed stanza (2:20–22), "in order to walk" safe in the land

This outline helps us observe the repetition of terms for understanding and protection, the dominant themes of the passage. Other interpreters see a progression that moves from knowledge of God to the resulting right behavior.[7] The repetition of "save you" in 2:12 and 16, however, puts the stress on protection or deliverance from seduction. Wisdom protects by enabling its possessor to say no to sinful behavior.

Aleph Stanza, "If You" (2:1–4)

THE THREE "IF'S" that make up the protasis here equate accepting the parental teacher's words with the quest for wisdom. Recalling the reference to that teaching in 1:8, the parent draws attention to "my words" and "my commands," perhaps in contrast to the words of the gang in 1:10–14. The first imperative verb ("accept") is the same Hebrew word used for "acquiring" in 1:3 (*lqḥ*); the second urges the son to "store up" the commands. This process of learning, accepting, and keeping is equated with attentiveness to wisdom and understanding (2:2), calling out for insight and understanding (2:3) and searching for them as for treasure of silver (2:4).[8]

Whereas wisdom "raises her voice" (1:20), here it is the young man who must cry aloud (2:3, both use the same Heb. expression for "lift the voice"), perhaps as a response. The stress is on the active role the young man must play in his education, calling out as if his life depends on it, searching as if the wealth of the world will be his, turning his ear and leaning his heart (often associated in the Old Testament with what one desires and chooses).[9] The three "if you" phrases work together to portray this search for wisdom as strenuous, requiring all the strength one has. An instruction from the Egyptian twelfth dynasty (1940–1750 B.C.) urges the son to take on the life of the scribe and learn writing because it is superior to farming, fishing, and other types of hard and dirty labor. The pragmatic lecture then gives way to

---

7. Garrett, *Proverbs*, 75, argues that the section on God emphasizes understanding God and his ways, the second on wisdom emphasizes "proper and careful behavior in life."

8. See the connection between mining and wisdom in Job 28.

9. M. V. Fox, "The Pedagogy of Proverbs 2," *JBL* 113 (1994): 237. Fox argues that "incline the heart" denotes more than paying attention but actually desiring and choosing, as in Judg. 9:3; 1 Kings 11:3; and Ps. 119:36, encompassing both attention and the action that results.

a more transcendent outlook: "A day in the school-room is excellent for you; it is for eternity, its works are (like) stone. . . . I shall tell you other things, to teach you wisdom."[10] Here too the rewards make the work worthwhile.

Aleph Stanza, "Then You Will Understand" (2:5–8)

THE FIRST OF the apodoses (beginning with "then" in v. 5 and followed by "for" in v. 6) presents the student with the first reward of such diligence. It is not wisdom, as we might expect, but God. The quest for wisdom, understanding, and insight (2:3) brings one to "the fear of the LORD" (2:5), the beginning of knowledge (cf. 1:7)—here set in parallel with "the knowledge of God."[11] This twofold foundation for wisdom study is repeated in 9:10 near the conclusion of the first major section of Proverbs. "Fear of the LORD" and "find" in 2:5 hark back to wisdom's refusal to be found because her hearers did not choose to fear the Lord in 1:28–29. Knowledge such as this is more than intellectual apprehension; it is a way of knowing that permeates one's entire being, touching the emotions and will. It requires the commitment of the whole person.

In contrast to "you will understand . . . and find" in 2:5, the Lord is the grammatical subject of all the statements that follow. It may come as no surprise that wisdom is in the final accounting a gift of God (2:6), but what a contrast that gift makes with the sweaty, fervent, and even desperate work of study just described! Fear of the Lord in Proverbs is often associated with human limits. Here the tension between human effort and divine grace does not "put us in our place," it lifts us up and encourages success. The "knowledge" of 2:6 stands alone and takes on a more general meaning than "knowledge of God" in 2:5. "From his mouth" most likely depicts God as the great teacher working through the parent's wisdom, teaching rather than giving direct revelation.

"Victory" or competence[12] leads the list of benefits that follow (2:7–8), although the arena of that success is not mentioned (it most likely refers to success in life, esp. the ability to live life well).[13] The three benefits that

---

10. "The Teaching of Duaf's son Khety," in R. B. Parkinson, *Voices from Ancient Egypt: An Anthology of Middle Kingdom Writings* (Norman: Univ. of Oklahoma Press, 1991), 75–76.

11. Fear and knowledge are "the two classic Old Testament terms for true religion—the twin poles of awe and intimacy" (Kidner, *Proverbs*, 61).

12. Clifford, *Proverbs*, 44, has "resourcefulness" in agreement with M. V. Fox, "Words for Wisdom," *ZAH* 6 (1993): 149–69, who stresses the attribute or "ability to devise plans and stratagems of a sort that give one power, particularly in conflicts," over the outcome it brings.

13. A. Ross, "Proverbs," 912, says that "the term includes the ideas of both sound wisdom and its effect: viz., abiding success, i.e., achievement and deliverance."

---

follow all mention Yahweh's protection ("shield," "guard"), the image of the way ("walk," "course"), and the character of the way and its travelers ("upright," "blameless," "just," "faithful"). Four descriptions of the traveler in verses 7–8 put responsibility on right living—that traveler is upright, blameless, just, and faithful. In sum, the search for wisdom brings the wonderful gifts of knowledge, especially knowledge of God, and as a result, the protection one needs to walk on the way. At least part of that knowledge is that of God as our guardian. Psalm 84:11 says, "For the LORD God is a sun and shield; the LORD bestows favor and honor; no good thing does he withhold from those whose walk is blameless" (cf. Ps. 28:7).

Aleph Stanza, "Then You Will Understand" (2:9–11)

THE EMPHASIS ON PATH, character, and protection extends into this next section. Like the first apodosis (2:5–8), the second also begins with "then you will understand" and is followed by a "for," which explains the opening claim. Here, instead of understanding "fear of the LORD," the son understands "what is right, just and fair" (nouns in Heb.), repeating the central virtues of 1:3 associated with the "good path." Knowledge of God is inseparable from ethical knowledge.

"Wisdom" and "knowledge" (paired again) are internalized in 2:10, entering the diligent heart and forming a character that seeks to do right by others. It is not clear whether we are to continue to view wisdom as a personification; it/she does not speak, wisdom acts (or is active), but so do the related terms of knowledge, discretion, and understanding. Discretion and understanding (terms associated with wisdom and knowledge), thus internalized, offer protection, but it is still not stated why the protection is needed.

Lamed Stanza, "To Be Saved" from
Evil Men (2:12–15)

THE NEXT TWO SECTIONS describing "wicked men" (2:12–15) and the other woman (NIV "adulteress," 2:16–19) are similar in a number of aspects: Both continue to use the image of the path, both place stress on the misuse of words, and most important, the young man needs to be protected from both. Notice that the young man is to be saved from the "ways" of the wicked men. The danger lies not in what the men will do to the young man but in their invitation to join them on their evil way (cf. 1:10–19; 4:14–19). Their "perverse" or twisted words (2:12) either lie or stir up evil—the latter is more likely, though the former is always present. The six descriptions of their way not only repeat the idea of leaving the straight path to walk the crooked, they stress the fact that they love doing it.[14] By implication, internalized wisdom leaves the young man rejoicing in what is just, right, and fair; wisdom provides protection from seduction.

Lamed Stanza, "To Be Saved" from the Adulteress (2:16–19)

IF THERE IS DANGER to the young man from the influence of wicked men, a similar danger is represented by the woman who, like the wicked men, misuses words (2:16; lit., "smooth words"; cf. the "perverse words" of 2:12) and departs from right behavior (2:17; cf. 2:13); from her the young man needs to be saved (2:16, "to deliver you from"; cf. 2:12). Once again the problem is influence. Like the wicked men, she has left the good path and wants to take the young man along. She has not only left her husband (lit., "companion of her youth"),[15] but she has also "ignored [lit., forgotten]"[16] the covenant of her God."

While this use of the term "covenant" (the only one in Proverbs) refers to the covenant of marriage and not the covenant God made with Israel, one cannot help but remember that when Israel broke its covenant with God, the prophets likened Israel to an unfaithful wife (Jer. 3:6; Hos. 2:1–13). The abandonment of marriage became a symbol for faithlessness of all kinds.[17] Unlike 2 Kings 17:35–38, the use of "covenant" here does not mention other

---

14. C. C. Maier, "Conflicting Attractions: Parental Wisdom and the 'Strange Woman' in Proverbs 1–9," in *Wisdom and Psalms: A Feminist Companion to the Bible (Second Series)*, ed. A. Brenner and C. R. Fontaine (Sheffield: Sheffield Academic Press, 1998), 104. Maier suggests that the symbol of the wicked men possibly reflects a historical group of "upper-class males who gain their riches not through inherited wealth but by taking part in international trade and usury." Such a view allegorizes the violence and thievery, ignores the evidence for symbolism of prophetic concerns for covenant faithfulness, and overlooks the possibility that an upper class male can be led astray by petty thieving and womanizing. The biblical image of violent men is applicable to a wide range of situations without an appeal to historical speculation. Shakespeare's Falstaff and the wild Prince Hal from *Henry IV* are examples of wild living done for its own sake.

15. See Mal. 2:14; all adultery involves some form of abandonment. Note that "partner of her youth" is restated as "wife of your youth" in Prov. 5:18; the theme of adultery applies to men and women alike.

16. See also Gen. 40:23 and Jer. 2:32 for forgetting in general. Other texts use the word for forgetting God (Deut. 8:14; Jer. 3:21) and God's law (Hos. 4:6). Jer. 13:21–25 associates forgetting with adultery (13:27).

17. Warnings against adultery as a form of faithlessness against one's neighbor are common in ancient wisdom literature, esp. in Egypt. "The Instruction of Ptahhotep" reads, "Beware of approaching the women! ... A thousand men are turned away from their good; a short moment like a dream, then death comes for having known them" (*AEL*, 1:68).

gods, but in abandoning the covenant of marriage, this Israelite woman has in effect also severed covenant relationship with God.

While her actions are adulterous, the terms used to describe her in 2:16 are translations of Hebrew words that describe what is "strange" (*nokriyyah*, "foreign, strange, alien"; *zarah*, "foreign, other," the latter used for strange or "unauthorized" fire in Lev. 10:1). Some scholarly discussion has argued that the strange woman symbolizes non-Israelite groups and influences toward idolatry, but this is unlikely.[18] She is "strange" or "other" in the sense that her actions place her outside the norms of the Israelite community, even though she comes from within it.[19] As with the wicked men, her choices are symbolic of a way of life, not of a nationality. She is estranged and a stranger to the way of Yahweh, but this is seen in her wayward behavior, not in any idolatry.

The strange or adulterous woman appears four times in Proverbs 1–9 (2:16–22; 5:1–23; 6:20–35; 7:1–27). Each description highlights the false and seductive nature of her words (2:16; 5:3; 6:24; 7:5) and the deadly end of her way (2:18; 5:5; 6:26; 7:26–27); these are repeated of Woman Folly in 9:17–18. Just as the violent men will meet a violent end, so the path of adultery is a path of folly that leads to death. Again, wisdom that is "stored up" and internalized (2:1) provides the needed protection against invitations to a path that only goes one way (2:19).

Lamed Stanza, "In Order to Walk" Safe in the Land (2:20–22)

THE FINAL REWARD for seeking wisdom is *good* company, walking together on the paths of the righteous.[20] We can say that righteousness is its own reward and we would be right, but the conclusion of this long instruction also men-

---

18. J. Blenkinsopp, "The Social Context of the 'Outsider Woman' in Proverbs 1–9," *Bib* 72 (1991): 457–73. C. C. Maier, *Die "Fremde Frau" in Proverbien 1–9* (OBO 144; Göttingen: Vandenhoeck & Ruprecht, 1995), 99, argues that the mention of "covenant" names her as a member of Israelite society who has departed from its norms. Her loyalties are "other," but her origin is not.

19. There is a good case that the terms make reference to the woman's relation to another man. Whybray, *Proverbs*, 55, argues that the Bible uses *zarah* for persons outside the family or tribe, or even for a person other than oneself (Job 19:27; Prov. 14:10; 27:2). Therefore, the "other woman" could be "the wife of another man" and *nokriyah* a reference to another family (see Gen. 31:15).

20. Righteousness becomes the source or capstone for all other virtues, originating in the God who is "righteous in all his ways" (Ps. 145:17) and who "is our righteousness" (Jer. 33:16). Persons created in the image of God are to bear witness to this righteousness in their lives (Isa. 42:6). M. Ish-Horowicz, "Righteousness (*sedek*) in the Bible and Its Rabbinic Interpretations," in *The Interpretation of the Bible: The International Symposium in Slovenia*, ed. J. Krašovec (JSOTSup 289; Sheffield: Sheffield Academic Press, 1998), 577–87.

tions the reward of life in the land. For ancient Israel, land was not considered a possession as much as a privilege. Its inhabitants lived on the land not as overlords but as stewards, enjoying the fruits of obedient relationship with God (Deut. 4:31–35; 8:1; Jer. 7:1–15). The wicked and the faithless (Deut. 8:19–20; 30:15–20; Isa. 24:6; Jer. 3:8, 20) enjoyed no such benefit.

The phrase "torn from it" echoes the threat of Yahweh in Deuteronomy 28:63: "Just as it pleased the LORD to make you prosper and increase in number, so it will please him to ruin and destroy you. You will be uprooted from the land you are entering to possess." Psalm 37 (esp. vv. 3, 9, 10–11, 22, 27–29, 34) depicts life lived in the land as true life and life outside the land as being "cut off," a kind of death (see also Zech. 13:2, 8).[21] This conclusion helps us appreciate the persuasive purpose of this whole chapter. In its original context, this instruction would be heard as an invitation to seek wisdom as a way of life—*way* emphasizing that wisdom is more than intellectual pursuit, *life* emphasizing its rewards of deliverance from removal from the land and death. It is God who accomplishes that deliverance and protection, and the means by which he accomplishes it is the gift of wisdom.

THEME WORDS. When we ask how we are to understand this invitation to wisdom in our day, we begin by looking for the themes that stand out in the chapter and by asking what principles uphold those themes; the principles we find communicate what God is like and what God wills for us to be and do. One key to uncovering the main themes of a passage is the repetition of key words or clusters of words, a mainstay of biblical rhetoric. So we have seen that "wisdom" and "understanding" are not only the most repeated, they are also closely associated, sometimes set in parallel (2:2, 6, 10–11). These and other repeated words such as "upright" (2:7, 9, 13, 21 and its related terms), "protects" (2:7–8, 11–12, 16 and related terms including "save"), and the various words for "way" (2:8–9, 12–15, 18–20) function as *theme words*. In them, God's gifts of wisdom and understanding are depicted as guardians to keep one walking in right relationship with God and humans. The image of the guardian extends the theme of accepting the parents' teaching in order to withstand calls to take the wrong path.

Words and images repeated from earlier chapters are also important. Thus if, as we read, the book and its collection of proverbs and sayings are for attaining wisdom and discipline, these words from 1:1–7 and others are

---

21. Maier, *Fremde Frau*, 100–101.

echoed in 2:1–2, where the appeal becomes more personal. In both chapters, the exhortation to heed the parents' teaching is followed by teaching about the words of men and women. The two speeches of chapter 1 correspond to the twofold promise of protection from their enticements in chapter 2.

Chapter 1		Chapter 2	
1–2	Proverbs for gaining wisdom	1–8	Cry out and search for wisdom
3	Right, just, and fair	9	Right, just, and fair
7	Fear of LORD is beginning of knowledge	5	Fear of LORD and knowledge of God[22]
10–19	Wicked men invite (paths)	12–15	Protection from wicked men (paths)
20–31	Wisdom abandons	16–19	Wisdom protects from strange woman
32–33	Death and life (live, škn, 33)	20–22	Life (live, škn, 21) and death

Whereas chapter 1 begins with a description of the study followed by warnings of what happens to those who refuse, chapter 2 begins with a call to study followed by promises of finding wisdom and enjoying its protection. Just as chapter 1 ends with a promise of safety that seems out of place with all the warning that has gone before, so chapter 2 jolts the reader by following its promises of safety with a grave warning. Even as this text looks back to the preceding chapter, it also offers a preview of what is to come. Friendship with Yahweh (2:5–8) is the topic of 3:1–12; love of wisdom (2:9–11) is treated in 3:13–18 and 4:1–9, the seduction of evil men (2:12–15) appears again in 4:14–19, and the warning against adultery (2:16–19) is repeated in 5:1–20.[23]

In sum, this chapter functions within the literary context of Proverbs 1–9 to repeat the warnings and admonitions that come before it and present an overview of topics to come. When we ask what themes and underlying principles of this text speak to the life of the church today, we note that *understanding* the fear of Yahweh and *protection* from seductive influences both act as motivations that foster the *desire* for wisdom.

---

22. If 1:7 marks the beginning of wisdom, 2:5 notes its culmination (see M. V. Fox, "Ideas of Wisdom in Proverbs 1–9," *JBL* 116 [1997]: 620).

23. Skehan, "The Seven Columns of Wisdom's House," 9–10.

As we examine these themes, we can also ask what is new here. Repeated terms can also expand on ideas that have come before, so the word "understanding" and its cognates (2:2, 3, 5, 9, 11) develop important themes from chapter 1. In particular, the phrase "then you will understand" accompanies and introduces the exposition of two important topics from the prologue: fear of Yahweh (1:7) and communal virtues (what is right, just, and fair, 1:3). The parallel structure suggests that they are inseparable; right relation with God (based in fear and knowledge) and right relation with the community are two sides of the one coin of wisdom.

Understanding fear of the Lord and knowledge of God. (1) The statements about God that were only implied in chapter 1 (esp. 1:7) are made explicit in chapter 2: God is the One who gives wisdom, and it begins in a relationship with him. The quest for wisdom encouraged in 2:1—4 leads to its source. The knowledge of 1:7 is now filled out as knowledge of God. Although not stated outright, there is some indication that all true knowledge begins with knowledge of God.

The book of Proverbs is practical in its emphasis, but this does not mean that it is unconcerned about matters of theology and worship. The short but frequent references to "the LORD" (*yhwh*, i.e., Yahweh) are meant to be appreciated as precious, even as we view gold and jewels. Stated another way, the references to Yahweh in the book carry more weight, are more dense, and rightly receive an extra measure of our attention, for it is here that the writers lay out what they hold to be most basic and primary. If repetition is one way of placing emphasis on important themes, rare and infrequent use of significant, highly charged terms is another.

With this in mind, we can ask ourselves what it means to "understand the fear of the LORD" or to "find the knowledge of God" (2:6). If the Lord gives wisdom, knowledge, and understanding, even "directly from his mouth," the close association with "fear" and "knowledge of God" suggests that wisdom is not just practical teaching or life lessons, it has something to do with relating to God. Conversely, theological study—study done with the intention to know God more fully—cannot be separated from the way one lives one's life.[24]

In her book *By the Renewing of Your Minds*, Ellen Charry argues that modern and even postmodern theological discourse overlooks, as a function of its operational method, the pastoral intention of premodern theologians.

---

24. F. M. Wilson, "Sacred and Profane? The Yahwistic Redaction of Proverbs Reconsidered," in *The Listening Heart: Essays in Wisdom and the Psalms in Honor of Roland E. Murphy, O. Carm.*, ed. K. G. Hoglund et al. (Sheffield: JSOT Press, 1987), 313—34. See also W. G. Jeanrond, "The Significance of Revelation for Biblical Theology," *BibInt* 5 (April 1998): 243—57.

Those thinkers sought, in her view, to inculcate the knowledge of God with the result that persons should love God "with all their heart, soul, mind and strength." A statement from her preface reports on her experience of reading Athanasius, Augustine, Anselm, and Aquinas (among others):

> They were striving not only to articulate the meaning of the doctrines but also their pastoral value or salutarity—how they are good for us. I also noticed that they understood human happiness to be tied to virtuous character, which in turn comes from knowing God. Becoming an excellent person is predicated on knowing God. For these theologians, beauty, truth, and goodness—the foundation of human happiness—come from knowing and loving God and nowhere else.[25]

Charry quotes Paul's "renewing of your minds" (her version of Eph. 4:23), but can we not say that the book of Proverbs also spurs us on to doctrinal study? We are mistaken if we make a distinction between the practical teaching of wisdom and the more explicit theological teaching of other parts of Scripture. As practical as wisdom can be, it is no less theocentric in its orientation.

(2) We affirm that knowing and loving God are ends in themselves, but the Scriptures do not separate that knowledge of God from virtue, and communal virtue at that. The famous statement of the *Shema* ("Hear . . . ," Deut. 6:4) is followed immediately with a reference to the commands, the majority of which are about good treatment of one's neighbor. Jesus linked his restatement of the *Shema* with the Levitical teaching that "you shall love your neighbor as yourself" (Lev. 19:18; Matt. 22:34–40). So here in Proverbs 2 understanding the fear of Yahweh is set in parallel structure with understanding "what is right and just and fair—every good path."

A path is in itself a symbol of community, because in walking a path, one walks where others have and continue to walk.[26] The important issue is the companions one chooses, and this matter comes up again in 2:20, "You will walk in the ways of good men." So the young man is told to avoid the ways of the perverse man and the wayward woman because they not only mean death for him, they mean destruction for the life of the community. Thus, the

---

25. E. T. Charry, *By the Renewing of Your Minds: The Pastoral Function of Christian Doctrine* (New York: Oxford Univ. Press, 1997), vii. Charry dedicated her book to a young man who is serving a life-sentence in prison for following the way of violent men outlined here; she reports that she speaks with him every week on the phone.

26. W. P. Brown, *Character in Crisis: A Fresh Approach to the Wisdom Literature of the Old Testament* (Grand Rapids: Eerdmans, 1996), 40, after C. Newsom, "Women and the Discourse of Patriarchal Wisdom: A Study of Proverbs 1–9," in *Gender and Difference in Ancient Israel*, ed. P. Day (Minneapolis: Augsburg Fortress, 1989), 156.

themes of right relation with God and neighbor from the prologue (1:1–7) are restated and expanded in chapter 2 with new insight and examples.

Righteousness, justice, and equity are theological terms that speak of right relation with God as the basis for right relation with one's neighbor. I once heard Bruce Waltke explain that the football that broke his neighbor's window not only affected his neighbor but his standing with his mother, who had told him not to kick the ball in the street. In wisdom terms, straying from the path of that wisdom teaching set before us damages our relationship with both God and neighbor.

Protection. What is also new in this chapter is the idea of protection. Wisdom and its accompanying virtues are God's means to protect one assailed by wicked men (cf. 1:9–19) and wicked women (the antitype of wisdom, 1:20–33). Therefore, the warnings of danger voiced by the parents who quote the wicked men and Woman Wisdom in chapter 1 are followed by promises of protection from such dangers. "Whoever listens to me will live in safety and be at ease, without fear of harm" (1:33). Wisdom that warned and threatened in chapter 1 now becomes a gift that protects from waywardness.

Wisdom, knowledge, discretion, and understanding protect the young man by keeping him on good and safe paths (2:9–11). The word "good" in 2:9, 20 frames a section that repeats the image of leaving the good path to walk on the dark, crooked, and deadly ways (2:13–15, 18–19; if one includes verbs of motion, there is a mention of path in every verse). The path of these feet is matched with words that twist truth and smooth over deception; "perverse" words are "crooked" (2:12) and "seductive" words are "smooth" (2:16). In other words, wisdom protects the one who learns it from the dangerous consequences of lies.

The lies of the wicked men promise ill-gotten wealth without punishment, as we have seen in chapter 1. The lies of the strange woman are not yet stated but are heard in her other three appearances (5:1–6; 6:20–35; 7:1–27), lies that one can have what one wants without acknowledging any boundaries or suffering any consequences. No wonder Wisdom says, "Whoever listens to me will live in safety and be at ease, without fear of harm" (1:33).

Therefore, the second principle we learn from this chapter is that knowledge of God and God's way provides protection against the lies that will ultimately cause our downfall. In the view of Proverbs, there are no "harmless lies" spoken by these evil characters. In seeking to bring the wisdom of Proverbs into our time, we must look for similar messages that might deceive and lead us along dangerous paths and look for ways that wisdom helps its possessor expose those lies. Wisdom enters the disciple's heart and protects in the end, not only from the harm that might come to us if we depart from true and good pathways but also from the unrighteous, unjust, and uncaring lives that drag our communities down with us (2:9; cf. 1:3). After all, this is what these men and women will do to any who will listen.

Wisdom saves us not only from the lies of others but also from ourselves and what we might become if we heeded them. From this text we learn that without such protection, we can easily be led astray. Humility motivates one to hold back from claiming moral competence too quickly. Wisdom is not innate, it must be learned. At the same time, wisdom will help one learn to discern good from evil, to recognize it when it is coming. When we see the wicked men and strange woman as symbols of evil, then evil becomes real to us, an enemy of wisdom that the wise learn to avoid (14:16; cf. Job 28:8). One might even speak of a fear of evil that corresponds to the fear of Yahweh (Prov. 3:7; 16:6; cf. 8:13). We become good not only by learning what is right but by avoiding what is evil.[27]

Desire. The third theme that is emphasized and new in this chapter is the theme of desire, presented in the words of teacher about the son's role in his education. All students have to do their homework, but more is implied here. The urgency with which the young man is told to seek wisdom suggests that education in wisdom begins with a desire to have it. It may be that words like yearning and longing are not strong enough to describe this desire that cries out and searches intently. Desire can be misdirected and step out of bounds, becoming irresponsible and destructive, as shown in chapter 1. The greedy men desired wealth and valued that more than the persons they would hurt to get it. In the fervent teaching of this chapter, desire is to be directed toward wisdom and carried out with the single-minded purpose of the treasure hunter.

Today's readers may well ask: How does one teach about having desire? Put another way, how does one communicate it? This is the rhetorical problem the teacher tries to solve here, and the problem is no less acute in our own time. In fact, it may be worse. The peoples of Egypt and Mesopotamia left us wisdom writings, funeral inscriptions, and other literature that again and again affirmed the essential goodness of right dealing and justice. Those themes were emphasized over and over, right alongside descriptions of the good life (wealth, status, health, and longevity).

This is not to say, of course, that such aspirations were always followed by the citizens or their king (ask the enslaved Hebrews!), but they were woven into the literary culture of the time. If an archaeologist were to sift through the literature, films, and music of our time, I wonder if that future

---

27. P. J. Nel, *The Structure and Ethos of the Wisdom Admonitions in Proverbs* (BZAW 158; Berlin: Walter de Gruyter, 1982), 120–27. "The motivation and starting point of wisdom's ethos is the recognition of evil," 126.

scholar would be puzzled by the flood of communication about desire in popular culture and the relative absence of any mention of virtue and responsibility. At the time of this writing, television game shows such as *Who Wants to Be a Millionaire?* enjoy great popularity. Would a show called *Who Wants to be Good?* draw the same audience?[28] Moreover, the book of Proverbs sets all virtue in the context of the knowledge of God, and we must admit that the desires of our time and even our own desires have not consistently been directed toward knowledge of God.

The teacher must persuade the young learner that it is good to desire wisdom, and he does so in a way that at first seems artless. The teacher simply associates the search for wisdom with the search for other desirables, such as silver or hidden treasure, and then makes the surprising move of substituting fear and knowledge of God! There are no appeals or proofs that wisdom and knowledge of God are superior; rather, it is assumed. Someone might observe that in our day a teacher cannot make the same assumption, because the ancients did not divide life into sacred and secular realms the way we do. However, I believe that the parental teacher's attempt to shape the young man's desires is more likely to be successful in our day for that very reason, because it also does not make the mistake of separating the good life from the virtuous life (and its theological foundations).

We do make that separation, not by denying that virtue is good but by simply focusing on what we want and need, neglecting all else. I also have a hunch that the same process was at work many years ago and prompted the wisdom writings. Why would they have been created if there were not a need to teach and remember that desire and responsibility cannot be separated? The teacher of Proverbs believes that desires can be shaped, the good life kept in union with the wise life. As we move on to discuss the contemporary significance of this wisdom teaching, we will need to examine how the principles that shape the teacher's views on desire, understanding, and protection work themselves out in our day.

EDUCATION IN THE **contemporary** home. As I teach and preach from the book of Proverbs in local churches, parents often come up to talk after class or worship service, asking, "How can I get my kids to listen to this?" They then tell their stories of teenage children who are learning to say "no" to their guidance, just as they did when they were

---

28. Many will agree with David Gill: "We are living today in an ethical wilderness" (*Being Good: Building Moral Character*, 11).

learning to talk. These parents are worried that their kids will not listen to them, but they are more concerned that their kids are listening to messages likely to lead them to harm.

In Martin Scorcese's film *Cape Fear*, a released convict wants to take his revenge on the lawyer who fudged facts and flaunted procedures to send this wrongly accused man to prison. The ex-con makes the lawyer suffer, not by physically attacking him or his family but by making them afraid. He pretends to befriend his daughter and turns her against her parents, telling her that they set limits on her freedom to keep her from growing up; he tells her there is a world to explore where she can test out her own ideas and make her own choices.

Sadly, much of what the ex-con says about the parents is true, and as they become more and more afraid, they try to exert more and more control, telling their daughter not to have anything to do with him. This, of course, alienates her even more. Yet the daughter cannot see that parents must set limits as she learns how to handle her freedom, while the parents cannot see that they have failed to encourage her in that growth. The tender balance of restraint and freedom has been upset, and the crisis of the vengeful ex-con and his seductive words only make it worse.

In this chapter of Proverbs, the parental teachers are well aware that their son is susceptible to voices that call him to cast off the restraints of their teaching. They also know that those voices call at a time in life when desires for sexual experience and peer pressure are strong. But these teachers do not say "no" for the young man; instead, they give him reasons and resources to enable him to say "no" for himself. In addition, they teach him to say "yes" to the way that leads to life instead of death.

We can look at their approach to learn what we might practice for ourselves, but we should also remember that their world was not our world, so their practices cannot be applied in our day without some reflection about the differences. Also, following the approach of Proverbs will not guarantee that kids will listen, nor does it mean that something was done wrong if they do not. As we will see many times in the study of this book, Proverbs and biblical wisdom observe how life *usually* works, knowing full well that barking dogs do bite sometimes.[29]

The teaching of this chapter urges parents to take seriously the task of wisdom education in the home. This is not to say that churches can afford to ignore this portion of the Scriptures; rather, families must give it attention since parents are, as part of their task, the primary teachers. Education is

---

29. Holmgren, "Barking Dogs Never Bite, Except Now and Then: Proverbs and Job," 341–53.

taking place all the time in home, some intentional and much that is unaware, and so it seems reasonable to ensure that teaching in biblical wisdom be included in the process.

If we can draw a model of pedagogy out of this chapter, it is above all else grounded in God's desire to be known and loved by young and old alike. The simple but profound thought that God delights to be in relationship with us is encouraging and motivating. Education in the ancient Near East could be harsh and demanding with a heavy emphasis on the authority of the teacher. Many have seen Israelite wisdom teaching as similar, quoting the "spare the rod and spoil the child" texts (13:24; 19:25; 22:15; 29:15, 17). Yet when we remember that God not only loves us but wants to be known and loved, we notice two things about this parental instruction.

(1) It not only urges the learner to listen, it encourages him or her to become active in acquiring learning, storing up, turning the ear, inclining the heart, crying aloud, and searching relentlessly. In a word, wisdom is a gift, but wisdom requires work. We must not only tell our children and young adults that they have the responsibility and right to determine the course of their learning, we must teach in a way that says that we believe it. We can encourage questions and critical reflection. We can ask learners to talk and write about what they see as important, and we can ask them to formulate their own questions about the subject under study. I often ask students in college and seminary classes, "What do you want to learn from this course?" I tell them that I have some content I want to teach and they need to learn, but I also do not want their concerns to go overlooked.

Moreover, young learners must be reminded that God has made sure that the search for wisdom always leads to him. God wants to be found, and while sin often has us looking for God the way a mouse looks for a cat, sin need not have the final say. I like to remind myself when I teach and preach that God is doing something in the lives of these people and that my job is to show them from Scripture how that works. I am grieved when friends tell me that they grew up hearing that God knows and watches everything they do, and that it was said in a way that brought needless shame. Let us be sure that our teaching brings out the other side, that God wants us to know him in all his goodness, splendor, and love.

(2) We can appreciate that teaching involves some learning that is not self-directed but rather approaches more of what we would call a lecture. The teacher urges the son to "accept" the words spoken and "store up" the commands (2:1) in a manner Fox likens to "rote learning." In this way, the tradition of hard-won wisdom is passed on from generation to generation. While the son is encouraged to work at his learning, observing outcomes and discerning the truthfulness of the words he will hear, he is also to store up that

which has been handed over to him, even if it is not seen as relevant or useful at the time.[30]

As any teacher and many a student know, study does not always pay its rewards right away. If wisdom is not only a work but a gift, we can encourage patience, recognizing that the fruit of wisdom must come in their season. We can honestly share how many of life's lessons did not come to us until late, and we can also bear witness to the long, steady growth of knowledge of God in our lives. Perhaps also as teachers we may demonstrate the same patience ourselves as we wait and trust God to be at work in our children's lives.

It is this combination of active learning and patient waiting that characterizes the educational approach at work here. If the son is told to store up the commands "within you" in 2:1 as a first step, he then awaits the time when wisdom enters the heart and becomes his own (2:10). The learner is not only asked to listen but to take initiative and ownership, to explore on his own, with the goal of becoming wise and knowing God, not simply conforming to parental norms. The son is also asked to make his own discerning choices of companionship, choosing good company over bad (2:20)— again, as in chapter 1, based on the ability to identify and avoid seductive speech. A process of receiving, responding, and finally assimilating or integrating wisdom into one's life aims at the goal of independent moral and spiritual judgment.[31]

While directions about behavior are part of the parents' teaching, they do not seem to nag the son about behavior but rather hold out the goal of becoming wise and free, able to decide what is right for one's self. Knowing that God through wisdom protects the son, they learn to let go in trust and confidence that inspires us to do the same.

Education for all. Parents, then, also learn in this process of educating the next generation. If parents, or better all adults, want to become effective teachers, they too will take the lessons of chapter 2 to heart and not make the mistake of only directing them at the young. The matters of desire, understanding, and protection are just as central to the life of wisdom when one is past adolescence—perhaps even more so, because the seductions become more subtle. Kids may stray outside of the norms governing their exploration of desire, sexual and otherwise, but it is the adult population that dishonors marriage with adultery and destroys community with ruthless self-advancement. The film *Cape Fear*, mentioned earlier, shows the outwardly

---

30. Fox, "Pedagogy," 241–43. Fox makes reference to medieval rabbinic commentators who thought that spiritual enlightenment must be awaited patiently.

31. Estes, *Hear My Son: Teaching and Learning in Proverbs 1–9*, 135–49.

respectable lawyer admitting to a friend that he had bent the rules to gain a conviction, then cheating on his wife, then taking more and more illegal steps to eliminate the ex-con. The audience is left asking: Who is the evil one here, the man consumed with hate and revenge or the hypocritical representative of the law? The answer is, of course, both.

Therefore, we must ask ourselves what our actions reveal about our true desires. Are our greatest efforts directed toward acquiring wisdom? If so, what kind of wisdom do we seek, that which enables us to succeed or that which enables us to be good *and* do well? If we believe we have to choose between being good and doing well, we may have our answer. What goals do we have for learning wisdom? Do we value knowledge of God above all else, making time for the study, prayer, and meditation it needs to grow? Is loving God the result for which we long, hope, and pray?

In our churches, I am concerned that we ignore the wisdom writings, but also that we may teach them without highlighting that the goal of wisdom is knowing God. If Ellen Charry is right, then we study because we love God, and that study leads us to greater love. Certainly this is a motivation for study, as I remember that my favorite teachers in seminary were the ones who showed the love of God in their lives and showed the rest of us how to come to where they were.

Protection. Finally, we might ask ourselves how that knowledge and love of God protects us from the seductions urging us to chase after irresponsible wealth and pleasure. The power of this protection seems to lie in the ability to say no, to refuse to join the voices that would lead us astray into folly. For this reason, the protection of which we speak begins to sound more like resistance, and images of Paul's armor-clad believer come to mind (Eph. 6:10–18).

Tucked between advertising for designer clothing and articles on children's fashion, a feature in the *New York Times Magazine* described the life of a conservative Christian family.[32] The parents have decided to build a home and family that participates as little as possible in a culture they believe has taken a wrong turn. They home-school their seven children, buy clothing at consignment stores to avoid going to shopping malls, and celebrate a simple Christmas with a single shared family gift. Why? Because they believe that in order to teach their children to live wisely, they need to eliminate outside influences as much as possible.

The author of the article responded with a mixture of admiration and bewilderment, writing that the "way they practice their faith puts them so sharply and purposefully at odds with the larger culture that it is hard not to

---

32. M. Talbot, "A Mighty Fortress," in *The New York Times Magazine* (Feb. 27, 2000).

see the Scheibners, conservative and law-abiding as they are, as rebels." After reading the article, a professor at a divinity school wrote about his wonder at their ability to shape their own counterculture in a way that few Christian churches seem capable.[33] The point to be made here is not for home-schooling versus public education, or even dropping out versus engagement, but rather for the education in wisdom that leads to resistance. If we fear for our children, we'd better fear for ourselves as well.

---

33. M. Volf, "Floating Along?" in *The Gospel and Our Culture* 12/1 (March 2000): 1–2, reproduced from the April 5, 2000, issue of the *Christian Century*, 114.

Proverbs 3:1–35

❦

¹ MY SON, DO NOT forget my teaching,
    but keep my commands in your heart,
² for they will prolong your life many years
    and bring you prosperity.
³ Let love and faithfulness never leave you;
    bind them around your neck,
    write them on the tablet of your heart.
⁴ Then you will win favor and a good name
    in the sight of God and man.

⁵ Trust in the LORD with all your heart
    and lean not on your own understanding;
⁶ in all your ways acknowledge him,
    and he will make your paths straight.

⁷ Do not be wise in your own eyes;
    fear the LORD and shun evil.
⁸ This will bring health to your body
    and nourishment to your bones.

⁹ Honor the LORD with your wealth,
    with the firstfruits of all your crops;
¹⁰ then your barns will be filled to overflowing,
    and your vats will brim over with new wine.

¹¹ My son, do not despise the LORD's discipline
    and do not resent his rebuke,
¹² because the LORD disciplines those he loves,
    as a father the son he delights in.

¹³ Blessed is the man who finds wisdom,
    the man who gains understanding,
¹⁴ for she is more profitable than silver
    and yields better returns than gold.
¹⁵ She is more precious than rubies;
    nothing you desire can compare with her.
¹⁶ Long life is in her right hand;
    in her left hand are riches and honor.
¹⁷ Her ways are pleasant ways,
    and all her paths are peace.

¹⁸ She is a tree of life to those who embrace her;
    those who lay hold of her will be blessed.

¹⁹ By wisdom the LORD laid the earth's foundations,
    by understanding he set the heavens in place;
²⁰ by his knowledge the deeps were divided,
    and the clouds let drop the dew.

²¹ My son, preserve sound judgment and discernment,
    do not let them out of your sight;
²² they will be life for you,
    an ornament to grace your neck.
²³ Then you will go on your way in safety,
    and your foot will not stumble;
²⁴ when you lie down, you will not be afraid;
    when you lie down, your sleep will be sweet.
²⁵ Have no fear of sudden disaster
    or of the ruin that overtakes the wicked,
²⁶ for the LORD will be your confidence
    and will keep your foot from being snared.

²⁷ Do not withhold good from those who deserve it,
    when it is in your power to act.
²⁸ Do not say to your neighbor,
    "Come back later; I'll give it tomorrow"—
    when you now have it with you.

²⁹ Do not plot harm against your neighbor,
    who lives trustfully near you.
³⁰ Do not accuse a man for no reason—
    when he has done you no harm.

³¹ Do not envy a violent man
    or choose any of his ways,
³² for the LORD detests a perverse man
    but takes the upright into his confidence.

³³ The LORD's curse is on the house of the wicked,
    but he blesses the home of the righteous.
³⁴ He mocks proud mockers
    but gives grace to the humble.
³⁵ The wise inherit honor,
    but fools he holds up to shame.

Original Meaning

THE BENEFITS OF acquiring wisdom again take center stage in Proverbs 3, especially in the famous verse 5, "Trust in the LORD with all your heart and lean not on your own understanding; in all your ways acknowledge him, and he will make your paths straight." This verse is often understood as a promise of guidance and sometimes even as a warrant for making choices that go against one's own judgment. "It seemed crazy, but I felt the Lord's leading. . . ." However true it may be that God's guidance can lead us in unexpected directions, a study of this verse in its context will both enrich and challenge this understanding. In short, the teaching of this chapter urges its readers and hearers to give up their fantasies of self-determination and self-sufficiency and turn to wisdom, a guide and protector from the real danger of self-destruction. This theme of chapter 2 is repeated and developed, adding the benefits of long life, wealth, and honor (see, e.g., 3:16); wisdom alone leads to life and šalom.

Proverbs 3 is constructed as a series of three instructions, each marked by the address "my son" (3:1, 11, 21). The most outstanding feature of these instructions is the list of five admonitions in the first (3:1–10) and the list of five prohibitions in the last (3:27–31). For this reason, many commentators find only two instructions, setting 3:13–20 apart as a hymn or interlude.[1] In my judgment, the distinctive character of the texts featuring personified Wisdom does not necessarily determine rhetorical structure. While it is true that "my son" does not always mark a new section in Proverbs, there are other indicators that a three-part division is the intended design here. Each address is followed by an admonition beginning with "do not." Moreover, the name of "the LORD" (Yahweh) occurs nine times in this chapter, three times in each of the divisions.[2] An outline of the chapter based on a threefold division looks like this:

Five Admonitions: "Do not forget my teaching" (3:1–10)
Blessings of Wisdom: "Do not despise the LORD's discipline" (3:11–20)
Five Prohibitions: "Do not let sound judgment and discernment out of your sight" (3:21–35)

---

1. M. V. Fox, "The Pedagogy of Proverbs 2," 235, and *Proverbs 1–9*, 141–71, recognizes only two "lectures" (3:1–12, 21–35) with an "interlude" in 3:13–20. Also, McKane, *Proverbs*, 289; Meinhold, *Die Sprüche I*, 72–82; Scott, *Proverbs*, 46. R. C. Van Leeuwen, "Proverbs," 47, sees a similar alternation between instruction and hymn at work in Prov. 8–9. P. Overland, "Did the Sage Draw from the Shema?" *CBQ* 62 (July 2000): 424–40, claims that correspondence with Deut. 6:4–9 establishes the coherence of Prov. 3:1–12.

2. Kidner also divides this way, *Proverbs*, 63–66.

This structure directs the reader to pay close attention to the prominence given to the name of Yahweh. Yahweh is to be trusted, feared, and honored (3:1–10), Yahweh disciplines and creates (3:11–20), and Yahweh looks after those who walk in his way, opposing the wicked (3:21–35). In the first section, the admonitions to trust, fear, and honor Yahweh come in direct succession (3:5, 7, 9). In the second and third sections, the name of Yahweh creates a frame around the connected teachings: wisdom's benefits (3:11–12, 19) and the five teachings of neighbor love (3:26, 32–33).

This outline also helps us observe that the teaching of the parents and the discipline of Yahweh together offer the sound judgment and discernment the young learner will use to relate to the community. Given the focus on right relationship to God in 3:1–10 and right relation to members of the community in 3:21–35, one can see the themes of piety and righteousness from chapter 2 developed here (cf. 3:4, "favor and good name" before God and humans) as well as the theme of "finding" wisdom (2:1–6).[3]

Five Admonitions (3:1–10)

THE THREE BENEFITS of long life, prosperity, and good reputation appear at the very start of the first instruction (3:1–4). However, these objects of desire do not come as ends in themselves but as the result of effort in learning wisdom and living wisely. The teacher means to point out the difference. Five admonitions follow on one another, all taking the form of imperative, charge, and motivation. So, for example, following the typical address "my son," the first admonition charges the son to remember parental teaching by keeping the commands in the heart,[4] then presents the benefits of long life and prosperity (cf. 1:8; Ex. 20:2 may be in mind here). This admonition not only comes first, it serves as an introduction and summary of all that follows. Specific charges are linked to specific aspects of long life and prosperity as the list continues.

The four admonitions that follow each include some mention of God. The last three use the name Yahweh, making the claim that he is to be trusted, feared, and honored. Therefore, each admonition charges the son to give up a self-centered fantasy and replace it with a God-centered reality. Readers too

---

3. A. Meinhold, "Gott und Mensch in Proverbien III," *VT* 37 (1987): 468–77.

4. The heart is most likely the seat of intentions here, but in other contexts, the heart is said to experience distress (Ps. 13:3) and joy (Ps. 4:8; 13:6; 16:9). M. S. Smith, "The Heart and Innards in Israelite Emotional Expressions: Notes from Anthropology and Psychobiology," *JBL* 117 (1998): 429. See also Van Leeuwen, "Excursus: The Heart in the Old Testament," in "Proverbs," 60–61; the heart is used metaphorically for the "internal wellspring of the acting self."

are challenged to hand over the fantasies of callous independence (3:3–4), self-determination (3:5–6), freedom to make one's own moral rules (3:7–8), total ownership of goods (3:9–10), and freedom from correction (3:11–12). Taken together, their message is clear: "You cannot be masters of your own destiny; you cannot be your own gods."

Yet the charges do not stand alone, and the complete portrayal of God is not negative or harsh. The benefits of long life and "propsperity" (*šalom*, 3:2) become the key motivation for the entire section. Descriptions of a good name (3:4), straight paths (3: 6), bodily health (3:8), and overflowing barns and wine vats (3:10) are all variations on the theme of the good life. It is better to think of these benefits as results rather than rewards. Wisdom writers understood the life of *šalom* as a gift that Yahweh intends for the enjoyment of all. They also knew that some choose to depart from that path and therefore also pass up the fruits that grow along its way.[5]

Verses 1–4 may be read together, or at least in parallel, highlighting the trio of long life, prosperity, and good name. The charges to keep teaching and commands in the heart (3:1) correspond with love and faithfulness written on the heart and bound around the neck (3:3). So also the benefits of many years and prosperity (3:2) is matched with favor of God and the community (3:4). This parallel stresses that remembering this teaching brings about desired benefits, but the benefits are acquired through wise and righteous living, not by chasing after them.

The metaphor of writing highlights this work of memory. The learner is told to write love and faithfulness on the tablets of the heart (3:3; cf. 1:9; 6:21; 7:3; Deut. 6:8; Jer. 31:33). So also writing and placing the commandments on doorposts and binding them on forehead and arms (Deut. 6:8–9; 11:20) write not so much to make a record for accuracy as to make a reminder of the place this word has in our lives.[6]

Although the terms "teaching" (*torah*), "commands" (*miṣwot*), "love" (*ḥesed*), and "faithfulness" (*ʾemet*) are most often used with reference to God's own actions and attributes (and so highlight the intense presence of Yahweh in this passage), here they show how humans may learn to live life as God intended (Prov. 3:4; cf. Luke 2:52). The contrast here is not between sacred and secular wisdom as many interpreters claim, but between being wise in one's own eyes (Prov. 3:7; cf. Isa. 5:20–21) and having favor in the sight (lit., "eyes") of God and other humans.

---

5. So also Murphy, *Proverbs*, 24, speaks against the argument in favor of rewards presented by Whybray, *Proverbs*, 58–65.

6. S. Niditch, *Oral World and Written Word: Ancient Israelite Literature* (Louisville, Ky.: Westminster John Knox, 1996), 86–87. The charge to write commands and bind them around the neck plays on the iconic value of writing.

The two admonitions in 3:5–8 go together like the pair in 3:1–4; the negative imperatives in both warn against trust in one's own understanding (v. 5) and wisdom (v. 7). The positive imperatives come first, however; "trust in the LORD" and "fear the LORD" bring their welcome benefits of security and health. Just as in 3:1, 3 where the teaching is to be written on the heart, so here one is to "trust in the LORD with all your heart" (3:5). The parallel with "lean not on your own understanding" indicates that "trust" is trust in the goodness of God's ways, communicated in covenantal teaching like that of Deuteronomy, but also here in wisdom teaching. Therefore, those who choose the way of wisdom as their own (3:6) trust that God knows how things ought to go and are willing to stake their lives on it.

Thus, 3:5 should not be used to support the notion that this confidence is a sort of blind trust that suspends critical judgment. Rather, the student of wisdom learns to have confidence that living for God is the most reasonable thing to do, and this will be proved as Yahweh makes straight the path (3:6). The Hebrew word for "straight" denotes travel made safe by clearing and leveling the road.[7] Making a straight path is also a form of guidance, as, for example, when one creates a path for water (cf. NIV text note). In short, 3:5–6 speak more about guidance in ethical behavior than particular choices such as career or mate. Leaning on one's own understanding is more than failing to pray about decisions. It is more like being wise in one's own eyes (3:7), that is, believing that one can determine what is right and wrong without guidance from God and his gift of wisdom.

The last admonitions (3:9–10) stand out from the others; not only are they more specific, but they can also be traced to the rules for worship in Israel in the giving of firstfruits (Ex. 23:19; Num. 28:26–31; Deut. 26:1–11). The practice of offering a portion of one's means to God acknowledges God as the source and provider. If there is any area in which people in every age are tempted to be wise in their own eyes, it is in the fantasy that wealth is a product of their own competence and nothing more. The teaching answers such a fantasy by pointing to barns of grain and vats of grapes, agricultural products of human labor that in the end are beyond human control. These blessings of overflowing containers completes the list of benefits enjoyed in the life of šalom (cf. Prov. 3:2).

In sum, the first instruction of chapter 3 sets its sights on the heart and its relation to God. In so doing, it looks ahead to the teaching of 4:20–27 that the heart is the wellspring of life. It is the heart that gives direction to a life by making the primary choice between arrogant self-reliance and trust. The heart that trusts Yahweh, fears Yahweh, and honors Yahweh under-

---

7. Kidner, *Proverbs*, 64, notes the parallel with Cyrus, Isa. 45:13; cf. 40:3.

stands and knows that life can only be found in paths that lead straight toward him, not away.

Blessings of Wisdom (3:11–20)

THE "MY SON" and "do not" of 3:11 mark the beginning of a new section, just as they do for 3:1 and 21. In this section there is only one admonition (to welcome Yahweh's discipline), which is followed by a poem in praise of wisdom's great worth. The admonition advises the young man to neither despise nor resent Yahweh's "discipline" (*musar*) and "rebuke" (*tokaḥat*), for they are signs of fatherly love. The potential for the son to "despise" and "resent" such teaching stands in stark contrast with the "love" and "delight" with which it is given. Unlike the more tangible motivations of 3:1–10, this one holds out God's love as a motive in itself. Taken in context with all of the parental instructions of chapters 1–9, the statement becomes a strong reminder that this parental teaching originates in the parental love of Yahweh. His discipline sets in motion a chain of teaching that extends from generation to generation (cf. 4:1–4).

The "discipline" (*musar*) spoken of here is primarily that of teaching and correction. It is not equivalent to punishment, although Proverbs uses the word in a few contexts where the translation "punishment" is warranted, usually in association with folly (13:24; 16:22; 22:15; 23:13). Discipline may use punishment as a teaching method to supplement verbal correction, but it is not clear that physical punishment is in view in this context.[8]

The parent's verbal corrections of 3:1, 3, 5, 7 set the stage for the comparison with Yahweh's fatherly chastening. The use of the word "rebuke" (*tokaḥat*) recalls the verbal correction offered by Wisdom (1:23, 25, 30), whose threats of coming disaster do not use the word "discipline" or "punishment." Also, the emphasis on teaching and correction in this context does not include the idea of hardship or suffering,[9] as it does in Job 5:17–18 or Hebrews 12:5–6 (which quotes this saying in a discussion of persecution). Other contexts use the motif of fatherly discipline for testing (Deut. 8:5) and punishment (2 Sam. 7:14; Ps. 89:32–33), but not these here. Verbal discipline both teaches and corrects.

The admonition is followed by a hymn-like poem in Proverbs 3:13–18. "Blessed," the first word of verse 13 and the last word of verse 18, frames a

---

8. The LXX translates "and he punishes" in the second line of 3:12. The word *mastigoi*, "beats," reads the Heb. *k*ᵇ as an imperfect verb instead of a noun (based on its use in Job 5:18), but the emendation to the Heb. required to read that way is unnecessary; the text makes sense as it stands.

9. In disagreement with Kidner, *Proverbs*, 64, and Scott, *Proverbs*, 47.

section that extols the supreme worth of Woman Wisdom. This word also reminds readers that the Psalms describe the happiness of one who follows the teaching (*torah*) of Yahweh, to be desired "more than gold, more than pure gold" (Ps. 119:126–127; cf. 19:7–10). Personified Wisdom makes her second appearance in Proverbs, although she does not speak as she did in chapter 1. To "find wisdom" recalls the vocabulary of Proverbs 1:28: "They will look for me but will not find me," and its echo in 8:17: "I love those who love me, and those who seek me find me."

Two sets of images follow the blessing of the one who finds wisdom and gains understanding; in the first, images of silver, gold, and rubies compare her worth and profit to the world's greatest wealth (3:14–15) of precious metals and jewels[10] (and what they can buy). If their glitter fades next to her radiant worth, what becomes of all other dreams and desires? The last line reaches a climax with its answer: more than silver, more than gold, more than rubies, nothing you can think of compares!

A second series of images complements the offer of long life and prosperity from 3:2. Like a patron, Wisdom offers long life in her right hand, riches and honor in her left (3:16).[11] Her ways are "pleasant" or perhaps kindly (*no'am*), and her paths are "peace" (*šalom*). The repetition of *šalom* from 3:2 (NIV "prosperity") once again identifies Wisdom with the parent's teaching, just as her speech followed that of the parents in chapter 1.

As used throughout the book of Proverbs and indeed throughout the Bible, *šalom* is a term rich with meaning. It can variously be defined as peace, abundance, and well-being—all signs of the good life lived in harmony with God and God's creation. Thus, this poem uses a number of images to get across its picture of *šalom*. The "tree of life" is a widespread symbol of goodness and blessing in the ancient world. Goddesses were often depicted as trees, sometimes flanked by worshipers.[12] Here in Proverbs, the phrase that wisdom "is a tree of life" is most likely modeled after Genesis 3:22, but inter-

---

10. The term may refer to red corals, but since they are not as valuable in our day, the translation of "rubies" works well.

11. C. Kayatz, *Studien zu Proverbien 1–9* (Neukirchener-Vluyn: Neukirchener Verlag, 1966), 104–5, claims to have found an Egyptian precursor to this image. A drawing portrays a feminine personification of Ma'at, the Egyptian principle of order, holding a sign of life in her right hand and a scepter signifying rule and honor in the other. However, determination of influence is difficult and precarious; one should look first to the biblical context to determine the meaning of the image and acknowledge that a number of variations on a common image were widespread in the ancient world.

12. O. Keel and C. Uehlinger, *Gods, Goddesses and Images of God in Ancient Israel*, trans. T. Trapp (Minneapolis: Fortress, 1998), 393–405.

preters have also claimed influence from other ancient Near Eastern texts, such as the Epic of Gilgamesh.[13]

In seeking to understand this image, we do well to examine other scriptural contexts first before casting a larger net into ancient Near Eastern literatures. In the book of Proverbs, the fruit of the righteous is a tree of life (11:30); so is a longing fulfilled (13:12), the teaching of the wise (13:14), and a tongue that brings healing (15:4). Thus wisdom as the tree of life inspires behaviors that are also life-giving. In Genesis, the tree of life and the tree of knowledge of good and evil are both in the middle of the garden (Gen. 2:9). Yet after the first couple ate from the tree of knowledge in hopes of becoming "like God, knowing good and evil" (3:5), God held the first couple back from the tree of life to save them from becoming like God again and living forever (3:22–24).[14] The everlasting trees in Ezekiel 47:12 bear fruit for food and leaves for healing. Both the Genesis and Ezekiel images appear in Revelation: The tree of life at last becomes accessible in Revelation 2:7 and Ezekiel's tree bears its fruit in Revelation 22:2.

In sum, in the Old Testament the specific phrase "tree of life" is limited to Genesis and Proverbs, but the tree in Proverbs does not carry the narrow meaning of everlasting life; it appears as more of a source of good life and health than of eternal life.[15] Yet readers of long ago may have been reminded of the account in Genesis and noted that now they are encouraged to take hold of the tree of life—here in Proverbs a metaphor for acquiring and following wisdom (the same word for "take hold" is used of the father's words in Prov. 4:4).

A similar appeal is found in Psalm 1, where the one whose delight is in the law of Yahweh is compared to a flourishing tree. In both texts, the blessings of life follow on obedience to Yahweh's teaching.[16] It seems best,

---

13. R. E. Clements, "Wisdom," in *It Is Written: Scripture Citing Scripture: Essays in Honour of Barnabas Lindars*, ed. D. A. Carson and H. G. M. Williamson (Cambridge: Cambridge Univ. Press, 1988), 68–69, suggests that associations from both traditions may have been in the mind of the wisdom writer.

14. W. Vogels, "'Like One of Us, Knowing *tob* and *raᶜ* ' (Gen. 3:22)," *Semeia* 81 (1998): 145–57.

15. R. Marcus, "The Tree of Life in Proverbs," *JBL* 62 (1943): 117–20, argues that the phrase in Proverbs carries with it a connotation of health and healing that carried over into Jewish tradition. Modeled after the book of Proverbs, the book of Sirach has Wisdom describing herself as a number of desirable trees with blossoms, "a harvest of honor and wealth" (Sir. 24:17).

16. On the use of the tree and its association with happiness and reward in Ps. 1:3–5, see Y. Gitay, "Psalm 1 and the Rhetoric of Religious Argumentation," in *Literary Structure and Rhetorical Strategies in the Hebrew Bible*, ed. L. J. de Regt, J. de Waard, and J. P. Fokkelman (Winona Lake, Ind.: Eisenbrauns), 237–38.

then, to understand the phrase "tree of life" in Proverbs 3:16–17 as summarizing the ways and benefits of wisdom. With this biblical usage as a base, references to ancient Near Eastern literature and iconography can enrich our understanding of this ancient imagery without requiring theories of direct influence.

In 3:19–20, a depiction similar to the creation account from Genesis 1 makes a surprising appearance, almost as if the tree of life triggers other thoughts about creation. Here "wisdom," "understanding," and "knowledge" are the guiding principles. The same wisdom that made a place for life by dividing the waters above from the waters below also lets down from above only enough water at a time to allow life to flourish. The blessing of water falling from the heavens may echo the blessing of Deuteronomy 28:12, "The LORD will open the heavens, the storehouse of his bounty, to send rain on your land in season and to bless all the work of your hands. You will lend to many nations but will borrow from none," and its reversal in 28:23: "The sky over your head will be bronze, the ground beneath you iron" (neither can be split to let water out).

If the admonitions in Proverbs 3:1–10 challenge the reader to remember that life and its goodness are gifts of Yahweh, this picture of creation does the same through poetic imagery. Moreover, if wisdom is the principle by which the Lord gives life, it makes sense that those who find it and lay hold of it (3:13, 18) are called "blessed." Wisdom's role in creation is merely sketched here, but it will be developed when she speaks for herself in chapter 8, using many of the terms found here.[17] For now it is enough to notice that references to creation undergird the good life and *šalom* offered by wisdom through the parents' teaching. If Woman Wisdom was involved in the creation of a place for life to thrive, then, metaphorically speaking, she surely can bestow God's gift of life through her teaching.

Five Prohibitions (3:21–35)

THIS FINAL SECTION presents the typical elements of the instruction form in a different order: a charge to keep wisdom teaching (3:21), descriptions of benefits (3:22–26), and a series of ethical teachings (3:27–31). Departure from the form is also significant. Whereas the first of the instructions in this chapter came from the parent (3:1) and the second names "the LORD" (3:11–12), the third begins with a charge to keep "sound judgment and discernment"

---

17. "Blessed" in 3:13 and 8:32, 34; "silver and gold" in 3:14 and 8:10; "rubies" in 3:15 and 8:11; "riches" in 3:16 and 8:20–21; "heavens," "clouds," and "foundations" in 3:19–20 and 8:27–29. See also the terms for worth in 31:10–12 and "blessed" in 31:28.

(3:21). This is the first of the addresses that does not refer to teaching external to the son, whether from the parents, Wisdom, or Yahweh. Instead, these acquired capacities for thinking and living in accordance with wisdom teaching will direct the young man on his way, keeping him safe.

The goal of wisdom teaching is the formation of a person of discernment. "Sound judgment" uses the same word as does 2:7 for "victory" (*tušiyya*) and denotes clear thinking in practical matters. "Discernment" ("discretion" in 1:7 and 2:11, *mᵉzimmah*) refers to the capacity for internal thinking and planning.[18] Thus planning and acting come together, using the terms the parents used earlier as they urged the son to accept their teaching. The gifts of wisdom's skills promised in chapter 2 have now been acquired, and the father now urges the son to hold onto them: "Do not let them out of your sight" (3:21). The son hears his father tell him to keep them "before your eyes" to prevent becoming "wise in your own eyes" (3:7). The teachers of Proverbs (parents, Wisdom, Yahweh) do their work with the goal of imparting this ability so that students can use discernment and decide for themselves; a major theme of Proverbs is learning how to live wisely by internalizing teachings and using them to develop the skills of living.

As in chapter 2, "sound judgment and discernment" are associated with images of safety and security (2:7, 11), a reversal of the terrors of 1:22–32. Yahweh will keep the wise son safe; he will also keep his foot from being snared ("safety" [*beṭaḥ*] uses the same Heb. root as "trust" in 3:5). Most travel in the ancient world was by foot, so a safe road was a clear and smooth road, one free of stones and briars.[19] Safe passage by day is paired with peaceful rest at night, confident that someone is standing guard (cf. Ps. 91:5; 127:2). The pairing of day and night is a merism, a figure of speech stressing that Yahweh protects all the time. The assurance that he will be the son's confidence comes again in Proverbs 3:31–32, restating the disaster of the wicked in 3:25.

The list of five prohibitions against bad treatment of neighbors in 3:27–32 stands in structural symmetry with the five admonitions to honor Yahweh in 3:1–10. The structure seems to say that right relationship with God moves one to right dealings with one's neighbors. Each prohibition begins with the Hebrew negative *ʾal* and concludes with a warrant or reason for the prohibition. The list can be best understood if these six verses are read as a sequence of three pairs (vv. 27–28, 29–30, 31–32).

---

18. Fox, "Words for Wisdom," 159–65.

19. D. Dorsey, *The Roads and Highways of Ancient Israel* (Baltimore: Johns Hopkins Univ. Press, 1991), 30–33. See also idem, "Travel; Transportation," *ISBE*, 4:891–97.

The warning of 3:27, "Do not withhold good," sounds like an odd way to recommend doing good, but the second line reads literally, "when it is in your hand to do," leading readers from the general maxim in verse 27 to the particular case of one who pays what is owed in 3:28. Whether "it" refers to payment of a debt or wage or to making a gift or loan to help in time of need, the point is clear. Saying "tomorrow" is a way of putting off both neighbor and the opportunity to do a good deed. Employers in Israel were warned against taking advantage of the poor by withholding daily wages (Deut. 24:14—15; Lev. 19:13). Timely follow-through of one's promises and commitments is also a good principle. "The positive aspect of the maxim is *bis dat qui cito dat*: 'he gives twice who gives promptly.'"[20] An ancient version of our "talk is cheap" comes from Sumer: "What comes out of someone's mouth is not in his hand."[21]

The next pair of prohibitions moves from the sin of withholding good to the greater wrong of planning and doing harm to a neighbor (Prov. 3:29—30; the term "neighbor" makes a link with vv. 27—28). Both withholding good and planning harm speak of damage done to an innocent neighbor who "lives trustfully" nearby ("trust" translating the same Heb. word as in 3:5 and "safety" in 3:23).[22] As in the case of withholding payment, here again an innocent neighbor's expectations are thwarted, this time by a false accusation (most likely in a legal dispute). Trust is repaid with treachery. Ahab and Jezebel's theft of Naboth's vineyard is the Bible's most vivid example of a false accusation used for illegal gain (2 Kings 21:1—29).

A single prohibition and its supporting argument form the final pair of prohibitions (Prov. 3:31—32). Ways of violence stand in contrast with ways that acknowledge Yahweh (3:6) and wisdom's paths of peace (3:17). The terms "no reason" (*ḥinnam*, v. 30) and "violent men" (*ʾîš ḥamas*, v. 31) recall the bandits of 1:10—19 and the wicked men of 2:12—15, men whose ways are not to be taken (1:15; 2:12). They are not to be "envied" because Yahweh "detests" them—"detests" designating that which he finds an abomination (*tôʿabat yhwh*). This phrase is found only in Deuteronomy[23] and Proverbs. While some argue for Proverbs' dependence on Deuteronomy, we simply note the use of the term to express God's intense hatred of evil

---

20. Kidner, *Proverbs*, 66.

21. B. Alster, *Proverbs of Ancient Sumer*, 1:319 (UET 6/2 322).

22. Hubbard, *Proverbs*, 77, translates 3:29, "for he dwells with you for safety's sake," adding that neighborhood watch signs of today show that we also look to our neighbors for security.

23. *Tôʿabat* is used in Deuteronomy with idols and the gold and silver used to make them (Deut. 7:25), blemished sacrifices (17:1), cross-dressing (22:5), and dishonesty in trade (25:16). Blessings and cursings come in 11:26—28 and 27:14—28:68.

and leave questions of literary influence aside.[24] "Confidence" (*sod*) repeats the Hebrew term for "foundations" in 3:19; here it is most likely a term for God's secret counsel (cf. Amos 3:7).

The final three verses continue the series of contrasts that began in Proverbs 3:32, each comparing Yahweh's dealings with the righteous and the wicked. If the earlier section of admonitions (3:3–11) put Yahweh at the center of the disciplined life, these contrasts add to the earlier list of benefits, stressing God's friendship with the wise. "Grace" (*ḥen*) recalls the favor of 3:4 and 22 (cf. James 4:6; 1 Peter 5:5). "Honor" (*kabod*, Prov. 3:35) looks back to the honor given to God in 3:9. God's opposition to the wicked takes on a social dimension, mockers being mocked in return and fools held up to shame in the community.

Verse 35 reverses the order of the previous contrasts so that the wise come first and fools come in dead last. In all, this third instruction juxtaposes the safety of the righteous with good done to the trusting neighbor. Threats of ruin to the wicked (3:25, 33) frame the teaching about doing good, not harm (3:27–31). Blessing comes to the righteous (cf. 10:6–7, 22). Keeping one's neighbor safe results in safe protection from Yahweh. This chapter, like the two before it, ends with a vision of trouble for the wicked and safety for the righteous.

In sum, the three instructions of chapter 3 work together to present the benefits of acquiring wisdom by appealing to human desires for the good life in all of its dimensions, spiritual and social. The good life of *šalom* only comes about when we seek it for others instead of for ourselves only. Love and faithfulness (3:3) not only embody God's way of doing things; they win favor and a good name, with God and with those who benefit from our commitment to that way. Fear of Yahweh (3:7) leads one to turn away from doing evil to others. Honoring Yahweh with wealth (3:9) certainly involves fair treatment of neighbors and care for the poor. Finally, trust in Yahweh is more than trust for our own well-being; it is for that of others. The straight path of 3:5 is echoed in 3:25, 31–33 as safety from the ruin of the wicked.

---

24. Murphy, *Proverbs*, 23, calls the similarities, "cultic associations." But R. E. Clements, "Abomination in the Book of Proverbs," in *Texts, Temples and Traditions: A Tribute to Menachem Haran*, ed. M. V. Fox et. al. (Winona Lake, Ind.: Eisenbrauns, 1996), 211–25, argues that wisdom writers used the phrase for something that is wrong in and of itself. McKane, *Proverbs*, 301, insists that the common vocabulary is not an indication of interdependence but rather a general antipathy to injustice in the ancient Near East.

As we bring the insights of this chapter into our own time, we must remember that "trust in the Lord" in the context of this chapter also carries with it the idea of following the Lord's way of wisdom in order to enjoy its benefits. Believers today can make the mistake of taking the rich imagery of blessing in these instructions as promises rather than as motivations to learn and live by wisdom. These instructions do not promise that those who trust the Lord will find the right career or life partner or always enjoy success and prosperity. Rather, they urge their readers to let wisdom guide them in the way they go about enjoying the gifts of this life and to keep them from making the error of setting their own good life above that of others.

Consumerism. As contemporary culture is saturated with the ethos of consumerism, so the culture of ancient Israel had its own perils of making the gifts of health, reputation, and prosperity into the highest goals in life, bypassing the virtues of humble worship and neighbor love. The biblical stories of wily Jacob meeting his match in his greedy uncle Laban (Gen. 27:1–31:55) show that this danger has always been with us, though today's marketing strategies present the undisciplined pursuit of our desires as a virtue. Magazine racks filled with advice on how to pursue *Money* and *Healthy Living* set out smiling examples for us to follow, and Christians can mistakenly transfer the advice and promises of those teachers over to the biblical text, perhaps without realizing what they are doing. This is not to say that believers should not desire life's good things, that we should not manage our finances or quit exercising, but rather that we were created to desire more than that.

The parental wisdom teachers of Proverbs set out to correct the human tendency to pursue the fruits of wisdom as ends in themselves. They knew the dangers of putting the blessings of life, possessions, and status before all else, even in the place of God, and of making them into idols. They saw that without fear of Yahweh and the love of wisdom, the quest for the good life can go terribly wrong. They offered their instruction and correction to show us how to put first things first, to keep us from putting the cart of the good life before the horse of wise and godly living. Again, remember that the portraits of wickedness in these chapters are extreme examples of what can happen in yielding to the same temptations that assault us. While we may not live like those examples of evil, we may give in to those seductions to lesser degrees.

Šalom. The sages who gave us the book of Proverbs drew their insights from observation of the way life works and from the traditions of Israel we know today as the Old Testament. Twice in this chapter the word *šalom* is used to describe Wisdom's benefits ("prosperity," 3:2) and the paths by which they are attained (wisdom's paths are "peace," 3:17). Thus the term *šalom* can be used for well-being (Gen. 29:6; 43:27; Ps. 28:3; Isa. 7:18; Jer. 6:14) as well as for friendly relationships (Gen. 34:21; Judg. 4:17; 1 Kings 4:24; Zech. 6:13) and peace.

There is a wordplay on Solomon's name (*šᵉlomoh*) and peace (*šalom*) in 1 Chronicles 22:9–10.[25] This meaning corresponds to the only other use of the word *šalom* in Proverbs: "There is deceit in the hearts of those who plot evil, but joy for those who promote peace" (Prov. 12:20). Faithful use of words and actions promotes *šalom* in relationships and demonstrates that God is present there. "Our creator does not want us to live in broken relationships, hurting each other with words and images that destroy our joy and delight and spread hatred and despair."[26] As two of the three occurrences in Proverbs of *šalom* are here in this chapter, we must pay special attention to that theme.

Key terms for the benefits of *šalom* in the first section recur in the second and third, joining them together as links in a chain. In the first instruction, the Hebrew terms for "prolong your life"(*ʾorek yamim*) and "prosperity" (*šalom*) in 3:2 are used again in the second instruction as "long life" (3:16) and "peace" (3:17). Thus the rewards for attending to the parental teaching are identified with wisdom and its benefits. The "honor" (root *kbd*) of the firstfruits in 3:9 is answered with honor from wisdom (3:9) and Yahweh (3:35).

Love of God and neighbor. We have seen that just as chapter 2 used the literary form of the acrostic to define itself as a unit, so chapter 3 uses the rhetorical device of inclusio or framing. The parallels between the first instruction with its list of five admonitions and the third with its list of five prohibitions are key to understanding the message of the chapter. We have also seen that the one list describes right relation to God and the other right relation to neighbor, yet the teaching makes use of common vocabulary and imagery. Just as the young learner is never to let love and faithfulness "leave" (3:3), so he must preserve (lit., "not leave") sound judgment and discernment (3:21). In each case the reward is "life" (*hayyim*, 3:2, 22). The word "favor" (*hen*, 3:4), coming as a reward for keeping love and faithfulness tied around the "neck," appears again in the third instruction as "grace" for the neck (3:22). The "trust" in Yahweh who makes paths straight (3:5) is echoed in the "safety" on the way (root *bth*, 3:5, 23).

---

25. P. Nel, "שלם," *NIDOTTE*, 4:131.

26. Q. J. Schultze, *Communicating for Life: Christian Stewardship in Community and Media* (Grand Rapids: Baker, 2000), 26.

Moreover, insofar as we have noted some correspondence between the first instruction and the charge to love God in Deuteronomy 6,[27] we also observe that it extends to the third instruction about fair dealings with neighbors.[28] In this way the twin concerns in Deuteronomy of love of God and love of neighbor resonate with the teaching of Proverbs 3. Thus, the one concrete teaching in the first teaching is the offer of the firstfruits (3:9; cf. Deut. 26:1–11), and this is answered in the third section with the teaching that can be read, "do not withhold good from its owner" (Prov. 3:27; cf. Deut. 24:12–15; cf. 15:9).

When Jesus brought together the commands to love God and one's neighbor (Mark 12:28; cf. Deut. 6:5 and Lev. 19:18), he drew from an old biblical tradition, one common to Deuteronomic teaching and Proverbs' wisdom. This tradition knew how easy it is to forget to trust, fear, and honor Yahweh, and they knew that those who forget God start to forget their neighbors as well. Idolatry and injustice are never far away from each other. These terms seem strong for our own day, because they are so definitive. Who would answer yes to the questions: "Are you an idolater? Do you practice injustice?" But we know, as did the sages of old, that these dangers do not announce themselves when they come on the scene, they simply appeal to our desires and tempt us to put those desires above all else (cf. James 1:14–15).

The direct teaching of the first and third instructions urges us to examine our lives, mixture of good intentions and weaknesses that they are, and to strive for consistency. We may not conduct our lives the way the teacher says the wicked do, but that teacher also knows we are subject to the same temptations. As we seek to bring the teaching of this chapter into our own day, we will also take care to not separate love of God from love of neighbor, whether they be neighbors in our church, community, or human race.

Woman Wisdom. Sandwiched between the direct teaching of two instructions on right relations with God and with neighbors is the indirect or poetic instruction on Yahweh's discipline. It moves from the address and charge into the motivation of God's love for those he teaches and his poem in praise

---

27. A correlation between Prov. 3:1–10 and Deut. 6 highlights the following echoes: "Bind" and "write" love and faithfulness (3:3; cf. Deut. 6:8–9), "all your heart" (Prov. 3:5; cf. Deut. 6:5), health and nourishment to body and bones (Prov. 3:7–8; cf. Deut. 6:5, "all your soul), "wealth" and "crops" (Prov. 3:9–10; cf. Deut. 6:5, "all your strength" or abundance, Heb. *meʿod*) (see Overland, "Did the Sage Draw from the Shema?" 427–33). Also the commands "do not forget" (Prov. 3:1; cf. Deut. 6:12) and "fear of the LORD" (Prov. 3:7; cf. Deut. 6:13) share common vocabulary.

28. Deut. 6:4–9: "sit," "walk on the road [*derek*]," and "lie down" (cf. Prov. 3:24). Clifford, *Proverbs*, 52, does not conclude that Proverbs is talking about law, but "that there was a common tradition of exhoratory rhetoric among the scribes of Jerusalem."

of wisdom. Women in churches and classes have told me that they appreciate the positive association of this personification of Wisdom with teaching and the tree of life, since the association of Eve and the tree of life in Genesis is often the only image that is heard in church teaching. The neglect can support the error that extends the error of Eve's action to all women, assuming that somehow they are weaker or more susceptible to sin. Students of church history know that this misinterpretation has a long tradition behind it. The picture of Woman Wisdom as a teacher and source of life is a welcome corrective and should be lifted up.

What shall we say about the story of Eve and the fruit that she saw was "good for food and pleasing to the eye, and also desirable for gaining wisdom?" (Gen. 3:6). This is not the place to do justice to the extensive history of interpretation of this foundational passage, but we may wonder if it was the third quality, "desirable for gaining wisdom," that must have been especially appealing since all the trees of the garden were pleasing to the eye and good for food (Gen. 2:9). Reading the story with Proverbs 3 in mind, we might ask, Did the first couple fail to trust in Yahweh? Did they seek to become wise in their own eyes? Was their rejection of Yahweh's instruction not to eat from the tree a way of despising his discipline and correction?

Whatever the answers to those questions may be, I suggest that the sages' positive use of images reminds us of the painful Genesis story in order to tell a new story, in which instruction is received and life with its blessing is granted.[29] It directs our attention past the grief that drives Psalm 90 with its images of dust and brevity and toward the joy of life that comes in Psalm 1, a poem that uses the words and images also used here: obedience, openness to God, blessedness, trees that thrive. Here in Proverbs as in Psalm 1, God watches over the way of the righteous but not the way of the wicked (Ps. 1:6). In bringing this teaching into our own time, we must allow God's discipline to teach us the difference between grasping for forbidden fruit to make us wise in our own eyes and holding on to the tree of life, that is, wisdom that has learned to trust.

Trust. In the teaching of Proverbs, trust is the antidote to worry, not because it means we will have all we desire but because trust will keep us from taking matters into our own hands—that is, to turn from God's way to life and its blessings in order to grab the fruit for ourselves that we may well have been given in time. The problem is the human inclination to put well-being and possessions above everything else, even neighbor and God. This

---

29. See also Vogels, "'Like One of Us,'" 145–57. If Vogels is right that holding Adam and Eve back from the tree of life was the first act of salvation, we find another here in Proverbs: God's correction offering another chance at life as it was meant to be.

being the danger, we can see why the teacher is at such pains to tell us that wisdom is worth more than silver, gold, jewels, or anything else we might imagine. Wisdom here is the symbol for the obedient life sketched out in the rest of the chapter. To hold her is to hold everything; to miss her is to miss life.

Perhaps the greatest illusion of all time is that there is nothing of more value than certain pieces of metal or stone. So Jesus taught his followers, "Do not store up for yourselves treasures on earth, where moth and rust destroy, and where thieves break in and steal. . . . For where your treasure is, there your heart will be also. . . . No one can serve two masters. Either he will hate the one and love the other, or he will be devoted to the one and despise the other. You cannot serve both God and Money. Therefore, I tell you, do not worry . . ." (Matt. 6:19–25). Thus, the teacher's comparison of wisdom's worth with silver, gold, and precious stones is not only meant to increase our estimation of her but also to make us aware of the need to put those valuables in their proper place. If we put them first, then there is no life, no *šalom*. If wisdom is devalued, so is God's discipline, and as a result, so are other persons.

Trust in Yahweh is more a matter of yielding to the wisdom of his ways than in expecting provision; trust is the antidote toward the self-rule of autonomy.[30] Having said this, Proverbs 3 also reminds us that by putting obedience over the concern for the goods of this world, we do find that we have been provided for. Furthermore, trust in Yahweh implies that he is trustworthy; to give him the reins means he knows what is good for us better than we do ourselves. This is not to say that trusting God means we no longer are responsible for figuring out the best course of action, but that we put God's desires at the center of our decision-making. The parent's instruction, "Do not forget my teaching," seeks to nurture a heart that trusts Yahweh and abandons the fantasies of autonomy, untutored self-rule.

Discipline and correction. In this chapter there is the good news that through the parents' teaching in wisdom, God disciplines and corrects. Moreover, that discipline is the sign of love, love like a father for his son. Of course, it is the love of parent for child that is expressed in the language of the time and the ancient genre of wisdom instruction. This is not the preferential love that Jacob showed to Joseph, the "son of his old age" (Gen. 37:3), or that of the father who buys a baseball glove for his child yet to be born. This parental love seeks to shape character. The repeated prohibitions

---

30. The point is made very well in the final chapter of B. Hybels, *Making Life Work: Putting God's Wisdom into Action* (Downers Grove, Ill.: InterVarsity Press, 1998), 192–206, a series of lessons from the book of Proverbs.

("do not") use the binary approach[31] of "not this, but that" to correct learners, just as a violin teacher takes hold of the hand of the student to say, "Stop doing that and do it this way." Correction is as important to teaching as positive instruction.

It is good news that God remains willing to correct instead of writing off those who err. As we read the contrasts between the righteous and the wicked, we should remember that it is not Yahweh who has given up on the wicked but the wicked who have given up on Yahweh and his correction. It is that corrective aspect of instruction that protects and keeps us safe from "the ruin of the wicked." In other words, the safety described again and again in Proverbs is not primarily that of angels who keep us from stepping in front of speeding trucks (although I believe this does happen). Rather, the correction of the Lord keeps us from stepping onto paths that inevitably lead to destruction. Again, this is said, not to make less of divine protection but rather to understand the original intention of this text. We err when we interpret instruction as a promise.

We also misunderstand 3:11–12 when we set them in the context of suffering, a context foreign to Proverbs. I do not deny, of course, that suffering can be a great teacher; many persons who have suffered illness or great loss will testify that it is. Suffering as a means of God's discipline is part of the argument of Job's comforters in Job 5:17–18 and 33:15–30. Striking and wounding are specified in Job 5:17–18 in parallel with binding and healing, but there is no such reference to striking in Proverbs 3:11–12 and no indication that the discipline and rebuke mentioned there are anything other than verbal instruction and correction.

Inasmuch as it is presumptuous and dangerous to counsel that suffering is sent to teach (remember that the counsel of Job's friends was finally rejected by God), I believe it is also mistaken to use this text from Proverbs to counsel those who are experiencing great pain. Jesus, like Job, refused to connect physical misfortune and suffering to sin, as in the case of the man born blind (John 9:1–5). Except for clear cases when consequences follow from wrongdoing, when we presume to know what has brought on the suffering of another, we are in danger of inflicting great hurt and dishonoring God.

But what of Hebrews 12:5–6 and its quotation of this text? Note first of all that Proverbs 3:11–12 is applied to the suffering of persecution, not personal suffering. Note too that Hebrews stresses the point of sonship, as expounded in Hebrews 12:7–10, probably quoting the LXX of Proverbs and

---

31. On the use of binary opposites in teaching, see K. Egan, *Teaching As Storytelling: An Alternative Approach to Teaching and the Curriculum* (London: Routledge, 1988), 27–31.

its translation of "punish"[32] to demonstrate that the hardship of persecution is not a sign of God's abandonment but of God's love. Hebrews was written to encourage the perseverance of Christians suffering the hardship of persecution, not illness or personal loss.

Moreover, I maintain that this understanding of hardship as discipline comes from the wider biblical tradition, not this text of Proverbs. The stress in Proverbs 3 is on protection and freedom from evil's consequences, not on coping with pain and suffering. If we find ourselves ready to say something like, "Perhaps this misfortune happened because the LORD wants to teach you . . ." we should hold our tongues, practicing another teaching of the book of Proverbs.

We might be able to better appreciate the rhetorical strategy of 3:11–12 and their context by looking at Deuteronomy 8:1–9:5, a text with concerns and terms similar to those of Proverbs 3. There we read a charge to follow Moses' command with a reward of life (Deut. 8:1), followed by a review of Yahweh's leading and teaching in the desert: "Know then in your heart that as a man disciplines his son, so the LORD your God disciplines you" (8:5). The Israelites are to walk in his ways and fear him (8:6) as he leads them into a land of lush provision (8:7–13), never forgetting Yahweh or trusting their own ability (8:14–18). They are not to trust in their own righteousness but to recognize that the wickedness of the nations drove them out (9:4–5).

They are also to remember that Yahweh led them into the desert to humble them and test them, and to teach them that persons "[do] not live on bread alone but on every word that comes from the mouth of the LORD" (Deut. 8:3). In other words, the emphasis is on provision; God led them into a place where there was no water or food and gave it to them (8:15–16), and this was done to "discipline" (or "instruct," *musar* [8:5]) them and give them something to remember (8:17). If they forgot, then they were not to be disciplined but destroyed like the other nations (8:19–20). The focus is not on punishment but provision. Israel was brought to a place of need to learn that there is more to life than the satisfaction of need; there is trusting relationship with God. Israel failed to learn the lesson as Zephaniah 3:2 reports. Speaking of Jerusalem, he says: "She obeys no one, she accepts no correction [*musar*]. She does not trust [*betah*] in the LORD, she does not draw near to her God."

I believe something similar is going on in Proverbs 3: God disciplines (3:11–12) and directs the student's attention to Wisdom and her provision (3:3–18). Wisdom is involved in the creation of a place with just enough

---

32. See the discussion of 3:11–12 in "Original Meaning" section, esp. the argument for translating "father" rather than "punish."

water for life to thrive (3:19–20), and provision comes from God's hand, not our own. The lesson is taught by means of blessing, not punishment. Disaster comes to the wicked (3:25, 31–35), not as instruction but as judgment.

To sum up, Proverbs 3 is about trust and about how trust can discipline our desires in the direction of God and the gift of wisdom. Desires can move us to greed or, as the teaching of this chapter shows, toward contentment. The chapter urges us to honor God, find wisdom, and do good to our neighbors—all three touching on the way we think about and handle our wealth. Central to the chapter is the image of creation; by wisdom and understanding, a life-sustaining environment was established, life-threatening flood waters were held back, and life-giving dew was allowed to fall. These poetic images of wisdom reinforce the directives to love God and neighbor by inserting a picture of God making a place for life. They support the claim that trust in Yahweh does bring the šalom of security, health, and plenty. They also provide a model for a life lived in harmony with one's neighbors, illustrating another dimension of šalom.

In short, the hymn-like praise of wisdom links together the instructions on relating to God and neighbor in a way that underscores aspects of life in each (cf. "life" in 3:2, 18, 22). As we have looked at the three instructions and their interaction with one another, we have seen that teaching about wisdom (3:7, 13–19, 35) appears in each as well as the benefits of life, plenty, and honor. However, most important is the chapter's insistence that wisdom is the means God uses to sustain and nurture life. If Wisdom was instrumental in God's bringing order and life to this created world, then she can surely do the same for those who find her.

 AS WE LISTEN to hear the message these principles have for our contemporary situation, we must also take care to understand these principles in the intention they were given. They are not sure-fire promises of success, as if Yahweh were bound to provide a healthy and prosperous life to all who turn to him. We know better, and so did the people of long ago. They knew that there is no formula that will give us mastery over our future or mastery over God. In fact, the motive clauses in these admonitions are not promises at all; they are descriptions of how life generally turns out for those who understand its principles. They offer no guarantees against sickness or poverty, but they do suggest how we can avoid bringing them on ourselves.

The big message. As teachers and preachers work at communicating the message of these three instructions, it is my hope that the larger message of the whole will shape the teaching of any one part. Here's how it goes: Do not be wise in your own eyes so that you fail to trust that God's ways are best (3:1—10). Do not reject the Lord's teaching so that you miss the life-giving riches of wisdom (3:11—20). Do not lose your sense of judgment and discernment so that you take what belongs to your neighbors (3:21—32). If you remember these things, you will preserve life and *šalom* for others and for yourselves.

Preachers and teachers may want to focus on the main point of each of the three instructions separately, but they should do so with the rhetorical strategy of the whole chapter in view. Although there are directives at the beginning and end of the chapter, the primary rhetorical strategy is to make changes in attitude that will lead to changes in actions. In other words, directives about tithing firstfruits and paying what is owed to others all point to one's inner responses toward God, toward others, and toward wealth.

To say this is not to imply that actions are not important, but rather the contrary, that actions reveal attitudes because they are motivated by attitudes. Kenneth Burke called attitude an incipient action, or as I like to say, an action waiting to happen. He understood that the most effective rhetoric seeks to make changes in how people think and feel about the world around them, believing that changes made there will influence the choices they make. The rhetoric of this chapter, setting a poetic teaching on the value of wisdom between two sets of practical teachings, was shaped to influence our attitudes toward persons and things, to teach us how to respond to each.

I once received a gift of a unique calendar. Instead of pictures, each month posted a different quote from C. S. Lewis. The one I remember (but have yet to track down) said that only two things last forever: God and human persons. As I reflect on that statement, I realize how easy it is to try to use God and people in our love of things, instead of working the other way around. The sages who preserved and passed down Proverbs 3 believed that this deadly reversal of priorities can itself be turned around. They saw the dangers of living life under one's own rule, so they placed teaching about loving Yahweh first. They saw that in our worry over our security, we can all too easily value riches above anything or anyone, so they put images of wisdom and creation next. Finally, they knew how easy it is to hold back or even to take what is not ours, so they offered their teaching on right treatment of neighbors.

Here is the rhetorical strategy behind those famous words, "Trust in the LORD with all your heart." Trust is the antidote to autonomy, worry, and a preoccupation with holding and taking. Put another way, this chapter sets out trust as a way to learn how to love God, how to love the things of this world, and how to love other persons, keeping each in its proper place.

The novels of Wallace Stegner tell stories of people who, to greater or lesser degrees, failed to learn the lessons of this chapter. His first, *The Big*

Rock Candy Mountain, was based on the life of his family, his father a figure of all that was foolhardy about the early twentieth-century expansion of the American West. Reflecting on that experience years later, he wrote:

> Ordinary people . . . are just as susceptible to dreams as the ambitious and greedy, and respond as excitedly to the adventure, the freedom, the apparently inexhaustible richness of the West. . . . I know that historical hope, energy, carelessness, and self-deception. I knew it before I could talk. Father practically invented it, though he qualified more as sucker than as booster, and profited accordingly.[33]

Stegner's father moved his family continually around the West, always in search of the big payoff—sometimes farming, sometimes speculating, sometimes running illegal liquor. His last get-rich-quick scheme moved him to buy land and cut down acres of two-hundred-year old oak trees and sell them for firewood. Stegner remembers, "He died broke and friendless in a fleabag hotel, having done more human and environmental damage than he could have repaired in a second lifetime."[34] He took the name for *The Big Rock Candy Mountain* from the hobo song his father used to sing about a land where everyone can get something for nothing. In a television interview, Stegner said, "I was trying to write my father out of my life," for in the father's search for the big windfall, his family became the losers.

Practicing *šalom*. In Proverbs we find a father and mother who hope to write themselves into their son's life for good, and a Lord who, like a father, wants to do the same. Their images of good life and *šalom* are more than some version of the legendary *Schlarafenland*, where rivers flow wine and roasted chickens run by with fork and knife sticking out. Their instructions do not promise something for nothing but rather the hard-won fruits of learning that transform a person from the inside out. There are really only two commands in this chapter. The first, said in many ways, is "find wisdom," with its implications of learning the teachings so we learn to love. The second is "keep a close watch on your hand," making sure it does not hold back or grasp what is not ours in the first place. Notice these are not far from Jesus' command to love God and one's neighbor. Believers cannot separate the two. Put another way using terms central to this chapter, believers cannot enjoy *šalom* without practicing *šalom*.

We could say that following the directives and transforming our perspective by means of the three instructions in this chapter leads to a life of

---

33. W. Stegner, *Where the Bluebird Sings to the Lemonade Springs: Living and Writing in the West* (New York: Random House, 1992), xix—xx.
34. Ibid., xxi.

virtue, which is an acquired character that makes choices based on what is good in the practice itself, beyond whatever positive outcomes are the result. The reward is ultimately the reward of doing what is right for its own sake. Some business ethicists believe that the possession of virtue, not a foolproof set of rules or guidelines, best explains positive ethical decisions that are made in business.[35] Moral codes and company credos give words to what is expected of corporations because they focus not so much on what to do in every case but on what kind of people and corporation the credo envisions.

Today's corporate business world is vastly different from the family-owned agrarian business of ancient times; one main difference is that responsibility for the corporation's actions is often diffused. Employees at all levels feel that they have little impact on the practices of the organization, but a group of theologians and business executives met to discuss ethical codes to guide individual and company actions. They developed the "Ten Commandments for the Marketplace," which sound as if they were inspired by the teaching of the sages:

1. *Treat individuals as sacred.* People are more than means to another's end.
2. *Be generous.* The benefits will exceed the cost in the long term.
3. *Practice moderation.* Obsession with winning is dehumanizing and idolatrous.
4. *Disclose mistakes.* Confession and restitution are necessary means to restoring ethical character.
5. *Arrange priorities.* Have long-range goals and principles in mind.
6. *Keep promises.* Trust, confidence, and authenticity are built over a period of time.
7. *Tell the truth.* Falsifying information destroys credibility.
8. *Exercise a more inclusive sense of stewardship.* Charity does not stop at home but extends throughout our global-oriented society.
9. *Insist on being well informed.* Judgment without knowledge is dangerous.
10. *Be profitable without losing your soul in the process.* Evaluate your Profit and Loss Statement in light of your trade-offs—a business audit is much more than an accounting of dollars and cents.[36]

---

35. O. F. Williams and P. E. Murphy, "The Ethics of Virtue: A Moral Theory for Business," in *A Virtuous Life in Business: Stories of Courage and Integrity in the Corporate World,* ed. O. F. Williams and J. W. Houck, (Lanham, Md.: Rowan & Littlefield, 1992), 13. The project was inspired by A. MacIntyre, *After Virtue,* 2d ed. (Notre Dame, Ind.: Univ. of Notre Dame Press, 1984).

36. C. S. Calian, "Religious Roots and Business Practices: Vignettes from Life," in *A Virtuous Life in Business,* 85.

Racial reconciliation. Perhaps there is no greater opportunity for the practice of šalom in the American church than the work of racial reconciliation, since it is here that the church is given the chance to heal and restore what has been held back for so long. Here's what I mean. As I write, the nation is celebrating the birthday of Martin Luther King, and the familiar cadences of "I have a dream" are sounding on radio and television. King began his speech with another metaphor, the check returned for "insufficient funds." Stating that the authors of the Constitution and Declaration of Independence signed a "promissory note" to guarantee all citizens "the unalienable rights to life, liberty, and the pursuit of happiness," King went on:

> It is obvious today that America has defaulted on this promissory note insofar as her citizens of color are concerned. Instead of honoring this sacred obligation, America has given the Negro people a bad check, a check which has come back marked "insufficient funds." But we refuse to believe that the bank of justice is bankrupt. We refuse to believe that there are insufficient funds in the great vaults of opportunity of this nation. So we've come to cash this check—a check that will give us upon demand the riches of freedom and the security of justice. We have also come to this hallowed spot to remind America of the fierce urgency of now.[37]

King may or may not have known that he was making a paraphrase of the instruction, "Do not say to your neighbor, 'Come back later; I'll give it tomorrow,'" but he knew that his concern for fairness came from the Bible.

A pastor I know was making plans to attend a denominational conference on the theme of ethnic diversity. When he talked about it with some members of the congregation, they responded with bewilderment. "Why would you need to go to that?" they asked. "We don't have any diversity in our community or our church. We're all white here." The pastor explained that this was just the problem in our nation and our churches, citing the adage that the most segregated hour of the week is 11 o'clock on Sunday morning.

The pastor went to the conference and heard preachers of all colors speak powerfully to the topic, one quoting Cornelius Plantinga Jr.'s definition of sin as the "vandalization of *shalom*."[38] The preacher explained that šalom is not a

---

37. M. L. King Jr., "I Have a Dream," in *Three Centuries of American Rhetorical Discourse: An Anthology and Review*, ed. R. F. Reid (Prospect Heights, Ill.: Waveland Press, 1988), 724. On King's use of the Bible in his speeches and sermons, see R. Lischer, *The Preacher King: Martin Luther King Jr. and the Word That Moved America* (New York: Oxford University Press, 1995), 197–220.

38. C. Plantinga Jr., *Not the Way It's Supposed to Be: A Breviary of Sin* (Grand Rapids: Eerdmans, 1995), 7–23. The preacher was my seminary teacher, Dr. C. John Weborg.

passive blessing but an active participation with God in nurturing well-being for individuals and communities. Because it can be either dismantled or built up, "peace" is often too mild a translation that can misinterpret *šalom*. Many believe that peace is a passive experience, the absence of war, but peace requires much hard work. The preacher went on to talk about economics and opportunity, adding that the biblical vision of *šalom* is a fruit of justice that addresses who gets what and when.

The pastor then went back and talked with the congregation about ways they might work to practice *šalom* to counteract the ways it is vandalized in our churches and communities. As they talked, attitudes began to change. Contacts were made with a neighboring congregation from a different ethnic background, and the relationship has grown. The various efforts of churches and parachurch organizations toward racial reconciliation take steps forward that are welcome. We will argue over means, but we must not ignore the need to reach the goal.

A story of *šalom*. Trust in the Lord brings about a *šalom* that is a result of the obedient life and a gift of God. A few years back I received a letter that seemed so much in accord with the images of wisdom and *šalom* that I asked permission to share its story. The letter came from an old college friend who started his studies with a strong determination to become a doctor. He was a Christian, but sometime during that year he made a shift in priorities and put a sign on the door of his dorm room to mark the change. After his name he wrote, MAJOR: GOD. MINOR: Biology. He finished college and ROTC, joined the Army, and went to medical school. He became a pediatrician, and, after his time of service, went career, turning down more lucrative offers in the belief that the Army was where God had called him to be.

He and his wife had five kids while they moved all over the country for various Army assignments. They did not want to take a call to Hawaii because it was so far from family and living conditions would be crowded. But after prayer and careful consideration they went, and they began to take foster children into their tiny home. One day my friend and his wife heard about twin babies, born premature with multiple problems, back in the hospital with bruises and broken bones just three months after going home. One had congenital heart problems; the other had a fractured neck. No foster home could be found to take both babies, so they brought them home and put their resources to work. My friend arranged for numerous surgeries for the neck, spinal cord, and heart. His wife, a social worker, stayed with them at a number of hospitals on the island and mainland; one trip separated them for a month. When the court terminated parental rights, they adopted the twins the day they turned three.

In their letter, my friend, the pediatrician, said that these were the most difficult and emotionally disturbed kids he had ever seen but added that they could not think of giving them up. The letter went on to list the activities of the other five kids, each in turn: sports, music, dance, and help with the care of the twins. I finished reading the letter, wondering what those children think as they watch their parents' faith in action, making a space for life in their home and lives. This story is told, not to say that everyone is called or able to reach out like this, for situations and resources differ. But it is offered as an example of parents who hope to write themselves, their love of God and his wisdom, into their children's lives, who have ordered their priorities so that life and šalom come first, hoping that their children will take hold of the tree of life and learn to make a place for others to live. Let their story be our encouragement, and let wisdom be our teacher.

Proverbs 4:1–27

❦

¹ LISTEN, MY SONS, to a father's instruction;
  pay attention and gain understanding.
² I give you sound learning,
  so do not forsake my teaching.
³ When I was a boy in my father's house,
  still tender, and an only child of my mother,
⁴ he taught me and said,
  "Lay hold of my words with all your heart;
  keep my commands and you will live.
⁵ Get wisdom, get understanding;
  do not forget my words or swerve from them.
⁶ Do not forsake wisdom, and she will protect you;
  love her, and she will watch over you.
⁷ Wisdom is supreme; therefore get wisdom.
  Though it cost all you have, get understanding.
⁸ Esteem her, and she will exalt you;
  embrace her, and she will honor you.
⁹ She will set a garland of grace on your head
  and present you with a crown of splendor."

¹⁰ Listen, my son, accept what I say,
  and the years of your life will be many.
¹¹ I guide you in the way of wisdom
  and lead you along straight paths.
¹² When you walk, your steps will not be hampered;
  when you run, you will not stumble.
¹³ Hold on to instruction, do not let it go;
  guard it well, for it is your life.
¹⁴ Do not set foot on the path of the wicked
  or walk in the way of evil men.
¹⁵ Avoid it, do not travel on it;
  turn from it and go on your way.
¹⁶ For they cannot sleep till they do evil;
  they are robbed of slumber till they make someone fall.
¹⁷ They eat the bread of wickedness
  and drink the wine of violence.

¹⁸ The path of the righteous is like the first gleam of dawn,
  shining ever brighter till the full light of day.

¹⁹ But the way of the wicked is like deep darkness;
   they do not know what makes them stumble.

²⁰ My son, pay attention to what I say;
   listen closely to my words.
²¹ Do not let them out of your sight,
   keep them within your heart;
²² for they are life to those who find them
   and health to a man's whole body.
²³ Above all else, guard your heart,
   for it is the wellspring of life.
²⁴ Put away perversity from your mouth;
   keep corrupt talk far from your lips.
²⁵ Let your eyes look straight ahead,
   fix your gaze directly before you.
²⁶ Make level paths for your feet
   and take only ways that are firm.
²⁷ Do not swerve to the right or the left;
   keep your foot from evil.

Original Meaning

AT FIRST READING, it appears that there is little new in this chapter; references to wisdom and the metaphors of path, heart, and treasure have all appeared before. The goal of the interpreter, then, is to discern how these metaphors are used in this literary context and how they relate to the sections that come before and after. It is noteworthy that in contrast with chapter 3, there are no references to the presence or teaching of Yahweh, but this does not indicate that an earlier, nonreligious form of wisdom instruction has been preserved here.[1] If anything, the verbal link between the father's "instruction" (4:1, *musar*) and the Yahweh's "discipline" (3:11, also *musar*) indicates a tradition of teaching that begins with God[2] and is passed from generation to generation.

A series of additional verbal links suggests that the first half of this chapter is to be read in relation to the last half of the preceding chapter. Here is a chart that compares the discipline of Yahweh (3:12) with the instruction of the two fathers (4:1, 4, 10).

---

1. McKane, *Proverbs*, 302–3; see also N. C. Habel, "The Symbolism of Wisdom in Proverbs 1–9," *Int* 26 (April 1972): 131–57.

2. Plaut, *Proverbs*, 67: "The father speaks as if he were in the place of divine authority, and indeed Jewish tradition compares the parent to God."

Proverbs 3		Proverbs 4	
12:	Yahweh's *musar* like a father's	1—3:	The father's *musar*
13:	Wisdom and understanding	5—7:	Wisdom and understanding
22:	Life and grace	9—10:	Grace and life
23:	Safe way, not stumble	11—12:	Straight way, not stumble
24:	Sweet sleep	16:	No sleep for the wicked
25:	Ruin of wicked	19:	Path of wicked darkness
26:	Yahweh your confidence	18:	Path of righteous bright
31:	Do not envy violent man	17:	They drink wine of violence
31:	Do not choose his ways	14—15:	Do not walk in way of evil men

The significance of the comparison becomes clear when we observe that there is no mention of Yahweh in chapter 4 whereas he takes center stage in chapter 3. In chapter 3 we have the view from above; Yahweh is the one who teaches and disciplines, looks out and protects, and blesses the righteous. Chapter 4 gives us the view from below, in which fathers teach sons to observe the ways of both the righteous and wicked. It is a signal that this teaching comes from God. By placing chapters 3 and 4 next to one another, the sages who gave us these instructions meant to show that it would be a mistake to separate the wisdom instruction of the home from the wisdom teaching of the Lord.

The picture of Yahweh teaching and correcting as a loving father (3:12) makes a theological statement that is key to all of the instructions in Proverbs 1–9, revealing the larger picture of what the parents are doing as they teach their son(s). They pass on what they have received from Yahweh, the source, the beginning of wisdom teaching. Therefore, the stress in this chapter is on the transmission of wisdom.

Chapter 4 consists of three lessons, each beginning with an address to the next generation. Key words and images define the theme of each section.

Grandfather's Teaching: "Get wisdom" (4:1–9)
Key words: Get/acquire
Key image: Wisdom is like a good wife

Paths of Righteousness and Wickedness (4:10–19)
Key words: Path/way
Key image: Wisdom is like a clear and well-lit path

Anatomy of Righteousness (4:20–27)
Key word: Heart
Key image: Wisdom is like a sound and healthy body

In this chapter, the young learners are urged to acquire wisdom, walk in its pathways, and put all their members in its service. The key word "life" and its cognates appears in all three sections (4:10, 13, 22, 23).

Grandfather's Teaching (4:1–9)

HERE WE FIND the most detailed depiction of wisdom instruction in the book of Proverbs. The father, representing both father and mother, describes his own training. He quotes the words his father spoke to him, and in so doing, he also passes on the same teaching to his son. While it is difficult to determine a precise setting in life from this literary picture of home-schooling in wisdom, we can infer that without some semblance to life in ancient Israel, the teaching of this text would carry little authority.[3] In other words, while evidence for schools in ancient Israel is sketchy at best,[4] it is likely that a tradition of wisdom education in the home was passed on from generation to generation.

The instruction begins with the plural "my sons" instead of the typical singular (cf. 5:7; 7:24; 8:32). It is striking that the plural is used to introduce the remembered example of one-to-one instruction. Shifts between singular and plural are common in Proverbs, so we cannot say for sure if the shift is a symbolic nod to the larger reading public. If so, it may signal to the reading public that they are privileged to listen in on an early example of home-schooling, or they may signify that this teaching will pass through successive generations. Does this remembrance come from Solomon, recalling the teaching of David his father? Although the attribution of 1:1 allows for the association,[5] it does not require it (see date and authorship in the introduction). Therefore, one can imagine the instruction taking place in any Israelite home, especially since the issues it touches are universal.

The connection between "a father's instruction" (4:1) and the teaching of past generations comes through the father's quotation of words he first heard long ago. The words are not his own, they have come from his father and presumably from his father before him. We have noted the previous chapter's reminder that Yahweh disciplines those he loves the way fathers do (3:11–12;

---

3. G. Baumann, "A Figure with Many Facets: The Literary and Theological Functions of Personified Wisdom in Proverbs 1–9," in *Wisdom and Psalms: A Feminist Companion to the Bible*, 2d series, ed. A. Brenner and C. R. Fontaine (Sheffield: Sheffield Academic Press, 1998), 46–52.

4. Whybray, *The Book of Proverbs*, 22–25.

5. Clifford, *Proverbs*, 61, proposes an association with 1 Kings 3:7 and Solomon's claim that he is "only a child." See also Sir. 51:13–50; Wisd. Sol. 7:1–14, where the young person seeks wisdom directly from the Lord.

also Deut. 8:5), a reminder that this activity of passing on teaching and discipline begins in God. There are other links as well. Just as the *musar* of Yahweh was followed by the happiness of those who find wisdom (Prov. 3:13–18), so here the father's *musar* points the learner toward her benefits (4:6–9). The repetition of "life" and "heart" (3:1, 22; 4:4) also links the teaching of both generations. Tradition is not handed down for its own sake but for the sake of "life."

It is not certain why the father describes himself as "still tender," using the word for the "gentle tongue" of 25:15, though the word also carries the idea of weakness. In this case, the boy is too young or not strong enough to take care of himself. The word for "only child" is the same as used of Isaac in Genesis 22:2; it may be a sign of fatherly devotion as in Genesis or an indication that the son is very young and has no siblings yet. Either way, the description points to the parents' diligence in teaching the next generation.

The remembered teachings of the father's father are short and direct: "Get wisdom! Get understanding!" Twice these short expressions are followed by pictures of love given and returned (4:5–6, 7–9). Wisdom not only repays love with protection, she returns honor for honor, symbolized by a garland or crown. The language used for acquiring wisdom carries overtones of courtship.[6] The terms "love," "embrace," and "not forsaking" (4:6, 8) suggest a marriage, as does the word "get" (*qnh*), which can be used for marriage (Ruth 4:8, 10) but also for purchase (Gen. 25:10, where Abraham acquires a cave). In any case, terms typically used of marriage suggest that wisdom is to be found just as a young man finds a good wife (Prov. 18:22; 8:35; 31:10). Just as the young man is not to forsake his father's teaching (4:2), so he is not to forsake wisdom (4:6).

The translation of 4:7 is a subject of scholarly debate; the LXX omits the verse entirely, but that is not a solution if we wish to follow the Hebrew text. The NIV translation ("Wisdom is supreme") comes closest to capturing the intention of the expression *re'šit ḥokmah*, that wisdom is of supreme value; nothing is worth more (cf. 3:13–18; 16:16; 17:16). But given the appearance of *re'šit* in 1:7 and 8:22, it is possible to read, "The *beginning* of wisdom: Get wisdom!"[7] It may be that a primary reading with secondary overtones is intended.[8]

In other words, a double meaning may stress that wisdom is of supreme worth; therefore, she comes first in value and first in time (see comments on

---

6. R. Murphy, "Wisdom and Eros in Proverbs 1–9," *CBQ* 50 (1988): 600–603; *Proverbs*, 27–29.

7. Garrett, *Proverbs*, 87; Kidner *Proverbs*, 67; Kidner observes that the phrase calls for the decision to pursue wisdom more than intelligence.

8. D. Grossberg, "Multiple Meaning: Part of a Compound Literary Device in the Hebrew Bible," *East Asia Journal of Theology* 4 (1986): 77–86.

1:7). The point is that many generations have proved the worth of wisdom, and this also puts the father to the test. The sons can ask if experience has proven his claims, and what is more, sons can observe their fathers to see whether what they say is true. One wonders whether the son might ask if his father has received the garland of grace and crown of splendor (4:9).

The second line of 4:7 is difficult to translate as well. The Hebrew word for "acquire" or "get" (*qnb*) is used twice in a phrase that literally reads, "And in all you acquire, acquire understanding." Thus, the NIV footnote suggests, "Whatever else you get. . . ." If "all you acquire" is understood as "possess," the line would read, "With all you possess, get understanding,"[9] similar to the NIV's "Though it cost all you have. . . ." I favor the footnote because it is consistent with the many comparisons of wisdom and wealth. But whatever the reading, the point is that wisdom is the most valuable of possessions, just as Jesus spoke of the kingdom of God as a great treasure and costly pearl (Matt. 13:44–46).

Continuing the personification of Wisdom as a woman of great worth (cf. 31:10; cf. Ruth 3:11), the remembered words of the grandfather again urge the son to love wisdom because she is worthy. The returns of protection (Prov. 4:6) and honor (4:8) are, therefore, secondary motivations. "Garland" and "crown" in 4:9 are symbols for honor as in 12:4, "A wife of noble character is her husband's crown, but a disgraceful wife is like decay in his bones."[10]

In summary, while the benefits of life, protection, and honor have already been set out in chapter 3, the first instruction of chapter 4 sets those benefits within the scene of a father instructing his son. In this vivid retelling, readers learn that each generation has been instructed to find a good life partner who will bring the one who finds her "good, not harm, all the days of her life" (31:12). While such teaching finds its origin in Yahweh, it also comes down from father to son, generation after generation. Each generation's teachers associate the supreme good of wisdom with the desire to find a mate, adding that the young man would do well to seek out a *good* mate; a good woman will do him good in turn. This teaching will continue with warnings against adultery in chapter 5.

Paths of Righteousness and Wickedness (4:10–19)

THE SECOND INSTRUCTION begins like the first, with a call to attention, "Listen my son" (this time in the singular). Having recalled his father's teaching

---

9. Fox, *Proverbs 1–9*, 171.

10. On the garland and crown, see also 16:31; Isa. 62:3; Jer. 13:18; Ezek. 16:12. Recall that "the wise inherit honor," Prov. 3:35.

about wisdom's benefits, the father now turns his attention to his own teaching: "I guide you in the way of wisdom and lead you along straight paths" (4:11; cf. 3:6, where Yahweh does this). The repeated words "path" and "way" contrast the clear and well-lit path of the righteous with the dark and treacherous way of the wicked. A play on the key word *kšl* (NIV "stumble" in 4:12, 19; "fall" in 4:16) shows how each path leads to a different end. If the son will follow the way of wisdom, he will not stumble, but evil men try to make others stumble, only to find that they stumble in darkness themselves.

The verse that does not use the metaphor of the path is 4:13, where the imagery shifts to guarding a treasure, perhaps a glance back at wisdom's supreme worth (4:1—9). "Hold on to instruction" uses the same word for those who "embrace" the tree of life (3:18); here the son is urged to "guard" this treasure because it is his life (cf. 4:4, 10). Set in the context of the journey on the path, the image portrays a traveler who watches his coin purse, keeping it closely hidden.

In 4:14—15 we have six different ways of saying, "Don't go there" (four in v. 15 alone!). The word for "turn" occurs in Proverbs only here and in 7:25, where it advises the son to turn from the "ways" of the adulteress. Here also, the son is told to avoid the path of the wicked and "go on your own *way*," that is, the way of wisdom (cf. 4:11).

Two sets of reasons are put forward in 4:16—17, each introduced by *ki* ("for"): The mischief of the wicked keeps them from sleep and becomes their substitute for food and drink. The travelers on this path will not stop to rest until they have reached their goal of doing someone harm; the metaphor may also extend to the wayside meal of violence they will have before they sleep, since eating and sleeping are often mentioned as the rewards for completing a day's journey. It is not clear whether the young man avoids becoming the victim whom they make stumble (4:11) or one of the violent men who stumbles in the dark (4:19), though context points to the latter.

The climactic contrast of light and dark in 4:18—19 reminds readers of the wicked men's preference for evil over sleep (4:16) as well as the safe path and sweet sleep of the wise (3:23—24). The path of the righteous offers only faint light at first, but as its light increases, it offers safe passage (4:17; cf. 2:20). Yet while the righteous travel paths of ever-increasing light, the wicked walk in enveloping darkness that eventually prevents sight, and this causes them to stumble (cf. 2:13, "dark ways"; also Ex. 10:22; Jer. 23:12).[11]

---

11. The contrast of light and dark has been called an "archetypal metaphor" because it is readily understood, applicable to a wide range of situations and able to evoke intense emotions. M. Osborne, "Archetypal Metaphor in Rhetoric: the Light-Dark Family," *Quarterly Journal of Speech* 53 (1967): 115—26.

In a payback reminiscent of the scene in chapter 1, those who want to make others stumble now stumble themselves, because of the darkness they have both sought and created. Just as the men of chapter 1 were caught like birds unaware, these men "do not know" what they stumble over.[12] Not knowing or understanding the consequences of one's actions is an essential component of sin and folly.[13] Once again the reader learns to avoid the way of wickedness, not only for the harm it does to others but for the harm that comes back on those who walk it. In summary, this section of instruction contrasts the benefits that come to the righteous and the woes of the wicked (for other examples, see 1:32–33; 2:20–22; 3:33–35). The contrast foreshadows the collection of righteous/wicked proverbs of contrast in chapters 10–15, but it is also basic to the theological outlook of the entire book.

Anatomy of Righteousness (4:20–27)

A NEW INSTRUCTION begins with a singular "my son" (4:20) and a charge to pay attention in which the son is told literally to "turn your ear" to the words (cf. 2:2). An anatomy of righteousness follows, urging the son to keep the father's words before his eyes and in his heart so they can direct the action of his mouth, lips, and feet. The heart, earlier commanded to lay hold of the grandfather's words (4:4), is mentioned again, this time as a spring of life that is to be guarded so that the teachings that guide a person's life are kept intact (4:23).[14] While the instruction seems to mix metaphors by moving from a stored treasure to a flowing spring, both insist that the heart that holds onto teaching is a source of life.

Thus, the word "life" (*ḥayyim*) comes at the beginning of 4:22 and the end of 4:23, closely connected to the heart. Just as wisdom holds life in her hands and is a tree of life to those who hold onto her (3:16–18), so here life flows from the heart that holds onto the teaching it receives. In the view of the teachers, this source of life was maintained not by keeping bad things out of it but by putting good teachings in and keeping them there (4:20–21). The heart, the seat of intentions, thoughts, and emotions, served as the control

---

12. This description of the two paths does not speak in the imperative voice of the instruction, but that does not mean it is to be separated from it as Whybray, *Composition*, 13, suggests. Rather, the metaphor of the path links it to the instruction (cf. 3:17) and serves as its climax (see Fox, *Proverbs 1–9*, 182).

13. Van Leeuwen, "Proverbs," 59, points out that the adulteress does not know her paths are crooked (5:6), the simple young man goes to his death "not knowing" (7:23), and those who go to Folly's house "do not know" that the dead are there (9:18).

14. Heart can refer to mind (3:3; 6:32; 7:7), emotions (15:3, 15), will (11:20; 14:14), or one's whole inner being (3:5) (see Kidner, *Proverbs*, 68).

center for the rest of human anatomy, especially the organs of speech. A guarded heart and straight speech go together (4:23–24).

If we compare these verses with the Egyptian instructions, we see that control of what comes out of the heart goes with (and perhaps begins with) control of what comes out of the mouth. The first instruction of Amenemope says that the teachings stored in the heart will guide the tongue:

> Give your ears, hear the sayings,
> Give your heart to understand them;
> It profits to put them in your heart,
> Woe to him who neglects them!
> Let them rest in the casket of your belly.
> May they be bolted in your heart;
> When there rises a whirlwind of words,
> They'll be a mooring post for your tongue.
> If you make your life with these in your heart,
> You will find it a success;
> You will find my words a storehouse for life,
> Your being will prosper on earth.[15]

Other instructions teach that one guards the heart by not saying everything that is in it. So Ptahotep says: "Conceal your heart, control your mouth, then you will be known among the officials"; and Papyrus Insinger: "He who guards his heart and tongue will sleep without an enemy."[16] A proverb from Sumer puts the stress on watching one's words: "A heart never created hatred, speech created hatred."[17] The close association of the mouth and heart in these texts implies that one conceals both heart and speech to avoid trouble, though the stress in Proverbs is on the total rejection of perverse and corrupt talk. In fact, the next set of body images shows the outflow of a heart that is guarded; perversity and corrupt talk are placed far from the mouth and lips, eyes look straight ahead, and the feet do not turn right or left from level and sure paths (4:24–26). The Hebrew terms contrast what is straight and crooked in all three.

The whole body is dedicated to the straight and narrow way, even as a villain dedicates his body parts to evil (cf. 6:16–19). Using overstatement to illustrate this point, Jesus taught his followers to rid themselves of sin by removing erring members (Matt. 5:27–30). In seeking to hear the message directed at

---

15. *AEL*, 2:149.

16. *AEL*, 1:75; 3:202.

17. B. Alster, *Proverbs of Ancient Sumer: The World's Earliest Proverb Collections*, 2 vols. (Bethesda, Md.: CDL Press, 1997), 1:24.

original hearers, we should remember the strong association of a guarded heart, straight paths, and straight talk. So also crooked paths and perverse words go together, just as violence and corrupt talk (i.e., the violence of dishonesty) are closely associated (Prov. 4:17, 24; cf. 2:12–15). The association of the heart and speech in 4:22–23 also anticipates the deceptive speech of the adulterous woman in 5:1–6 (where crooked paths reveal her intentions).

The father ends this instruction by repeating his father's charge to not swerve either to right or left (4:27; "swerve" repeats the same Heb. term used in 4:5).[18] In the view of the teachers, one "turns" to do evil. Keeping straight also means making "level paths" for the feet, a metaphor for keeping one's way safe through wise and moral living. The NIV footnote shows that the verb may also be read "consider the paths," the way it is translated in 5:5 for the woman who does not consider her way of life, and in 5:21 for Yahweh, who considers all a person's ways. Some commentators prefer to be consistent, translating all three as "pay attention" or "take heed."[19] However, since the verb is used of leveling a road in some other contexts, a metaphoric use of this concrete action may be part of a wordplay that alludes to the other meaning. There is more connection between considering one's ways and acting accordingly than first appears (to appreciate the full force of the wordplay, see comments in ch. 5).

In summary, the last lesson (4:20–27) begins with the father's instructions and ends by going back to the student's own journey. Not only is the learner to keep the father's instructions in the heart (4:23), he is to guard that heart as a wellspring. The movement from receiving parental instruction to walking in one's own way is true to the life process of maturation, but it also observes the difference between remembering a parent's teaching and developing one's own way of living. The ethical life is not only an inheritance, it is a life work. For this reason, the father appeals to the son to take his teaching with him on the journey, here symbolized as choosing a good mate, a good path, and a good heart.

LEGACY AND TRADITIONS. By recalling the teaching of his own father, the teacher in this chapter invites his son to enter into a legacy and a tradition of wisdom. A legacy is a gift received from an ancestor, while a tradition is that which is handed onto descendants. The

---

18. Using another Heb. word for "turn" (*swr*), the metaphor of right and left was well established (Deut. 5:32; 17:11; 28:14; Josh. 23:6).

19. McKane, *Proverbs*, 311; Kidner, *Proverbs*, 68.

father calls on the son to receive this gift; in fact, he is urged to "get" it. But this father looks forward to the day when he will see his son teach his own son. Religious and ethnic communities pass on their customs, traditions, and celebrations to keep them alive and bring comforting memories, but more important, to shape the outlook and character of those who carry them. Older members of those communities often mourn the loss of the old ways because they believe that they are good ways to live. Teaching is another way that tradition is passed on, as Charles Kraft argues:

> The father teaches, communicates with the son, because he wants the son to value what he values, and maintain the character that he maintains. He wants the son to share in his inner likeness, just as he sees that the son bears his genetic image. So Jesus modeled what our relationship with the father is supposed to be like. He is the second Adam who came to reflect God's glory in his life. Therefore, this teaching about fathers and sons points to the desire of God to have children (sons and daughters) who seek to please him and reflect his glory.[20]

Certainly this desire was the reason that Yahweh instructed Israel not only to keep his commands on their hearts but also to teach them to their children at home, on the road, at all times (Deut. 6:6–7). God thought of Israel as his son and longed to have that son resemble him through godly character formed through teaching (8:5). So this chapter links God's desire to teach and shape character (Prov. 3:11–12) to the tradition of parents teaching their children.

Importance of literary context. As we begin the process of translating the message of this chapter for the contemporary church, we first remember that the rhetoric of Proverbs directs us to pay close attention to literary context. This rhetoric typically reuses vocabulary and images from the previous instruction in a hook-and-eye structure that can be easily noticed by attentive readers. Such repetition with variation works from the same mindset as poetic parallelism, encouraging the reader to examine words and images that stand side by side as new insights emerge. We noted above that links with chapter 3 use the images of paths and protection to bring a long-standing tradition of fathers teaching their sons into the larger picture of God's disciplining as a father disciplines a son. By juxtaposing chapters 3 and 4, the sages who brought these instructions together identify the chain of teaching as beginning and ending with God.

---

20. C. H. Kraft, *Communication Theory for Christian Witness*, rev. ed. (Maryknoll, N.Y.: Orbis, 1991), 4–10.

This rhetorical association implies that God himself is teaching when parents teach their children. We misread the chapter if we fail to acknowledge the presence of Yahweh even in those chapters that do not name him. Wisdom writings often help us see God at work in ways that seem hidden. Noting the absence of God's name, voice, or direct action in the books of Ruth and Esther, the rabbis of old asked, "Where is God's hand?" The answer: "Nowhere and everywhere. God's hand is never absent, but it is sometimes gloved." The genius of the book of Proverbs is its ability to speak the language of ancient Near Eastern wisdom and the human quest for knowledge at the same time that it pulls back the curtain to show God working behind the scenes in the order of creation and the teaching of the wise. It is not always easy to see God's hand at work in the teaching of a Sunday school or confirmation class, but it is there.

It is also important to set each instruction or each chapter within the larger context of Proverbs 1–9, for each chapter adds new information to the extended metaphor of choosing a path for life developed in chapter 2: Learn from your parents, don't listen to evil men, and choose the company of wisdom over that of the adulteress. Like ripples moving out in concentric circles from a stone dropped in the lake, these themes will play out again and again as the basic relationships of one's life (neighbors/friends and marriage partner) are either honored or abandoned. Again and again the choice is shown to be a choice between life and death.

Along with repeated words and images, the chapter also repeats themes from earlier chapters as it states themes that will be touched again in later chapters. Like the warp and woof of a tapestry, these themes hold the book together in a coherent whole. So, for example, in the first instruction of this chapter (4:1–9), the charge to search for wisdom in 2:1–11 is brought together with the praise of wisdom's great worth in 3:13–18 as wisdom is called supreme or "first." The previous teachings are repeated and enriched. The emphasis of the latter instruction is on getting wisdom and keeping her by loving and honoring her, the way one would a spouse—a theme that appears again in chapters 8 and 31.

Recalling the preview of the instructions in chapter 2, readers will remember that when anyone heeds the advice to "get wisdom" (4:5, 7; cf. 2:1–4), they also find the knowledge of God (2:5). Therefore, the efforts to "get wisdom" are also efforts to know and love God. Chapter 4 develops two themes from the preview of chapter 2, the theme of loving wisdom (compare 4:1–9 with 2:1–11) as well as the theme of avoiding wicked men (4:14–19 with 2:12–15). We will see that the theme of avoiding adultery (2:16–20) is picked up in chapter 5, which has a number of significant links with the last instruction in chapter 4 (4:20–27; see comments in ch. 5). The point of this review of the literary context is that as preachers and teachers work with chapters that are comprised of individual instructions, they may want to draw them together, or they may choose to keep the larger context in view as they work with each instruction separately.

Guarding heart and teachings. The father quotes his father as saying the same of his teaching: *"Lay hold* of my words with all your heart; *keep* my commands and you will live" (4:4). In fact, the charge to "get" and "keep" is key to all three instructions in chapter 4. In the second unit, the son is to listen and accept the father's sayings (4:10), but also to hold onto instruction, to not let it go, and to guard it (4:13). In the third, the son is to pay attention to the words (4:20), but also to keep them in the heart (4:21), and in so doing, to *guard* that heart (4:23). While the idea of acquiring and storing up teaching has been heard in 2:1 and 3:1—4, new in this chapter is the emphasis on guarding (4:13), especially guarding the heart (4:23). To guard these teachings and the heart that holds them is to guard one's life; this enriches the image of wisdom as protector. As the young man guards his heart, wisdom watches over his way and guards him (4:6).

We misunderstand this metaphor if we assume that this watching brings protection from all life's ills, as if Wisdom were some guardian angel. Rather, Wisdom protects her charges from stumbling into ways of life that bring harm to self and others. We also misunderstand the idea of guarding if we limit it to keeping harmful things out of the heart. I have heard many a teaching urging me to be careful about the content of the books I read, the films I see, and the music I hear, asking me to consider what I want to keep in my heart. There is truth here, of course. Certainly the parents hope that wisdom, not folly, will become the guiding principle of their son's life. However, the idea of guarding here seems to be more like protecting a treasure, a keeping of what is important, neither losing it nor abandoning it. In Proverbs, wise people guard their hearts, not only by keeping harmful influences out but, more important, by putting wise teachings in and keeping them there.

How are they "kept?" (1) The teachings are stored in the learner's memory. Charges to not forget (4:5) the father's words nor let them out of sight (4:21) urge the son to commit them to memory, where they can be called on at a later time. We have seen that this view of storing teaching in the heart was widespread in the ancient Near East. Memory as an aid to learning is contested in our age; many teachers want their students to do more than simply memorize information, they want them to be able to interact with it and create new syntheses with acquired knowledge. However, the work of committing teachings to memory need not be merely an exercise in rote learning. One scholar of medieval literature has argued that memorized words and images were meant to help with original thinking, to create new thoughts and shape character.[21] While we do not see a theory like this explicitly stated in the parent's teachings, we can appreciate that their emphasis on memory work had similar goals in mind. Certainly their use of vivid images was meant to make their teaching memorable.

(2) The teachings are kept as they are translated into action. The three instructions work together to urge the son to get wisdom, choose the right path, and put the members of his body in line with that goal. Avoiding evil and choosing good not only shows that the teachings have been internalized, they reinforce them. Finally, the teachings are closely associated with life. As we have seen, each charge to receive and hold onto the teachings is followed by a motivating word about life: "Keep my commands and you will live" (4:4); "accept what I say, and the years of your life will be many" (4:10); "guard it well, for it is your life" (4:13); "for they are life to those who find them" (4:22).

The father does not say "Live by them"; rather, he says "They *are* your life." As the son keeps and guards the teachings of his father, he also keeps and guards his very life. No wonder they are so valuable! While we may be inclined to see life as a reward for following wisdom's way, it is more in line with the view of the sages that life here is a gift that can either flourish or be lost. The repetitive emphasis on protection drives home the fragility of life, which is easily lost, robbed, or (to repeat what was said about *šalom* in ch. 3) vandalized. Life is not a reward but a gift that must be preserved, nurtured, and cared for. Any carelessness can lead to a wrong turn onto the path of evil and its life-destroying force. Therefore, as violent men seek the harm of others and cause their own in the process (4:14–19), the work of God in giving life is undone.

To summarize, the contribution of this chapter is its emphasis on keeping and guarding the teachings, symbolized as the good partner of wisdom, the good way of the straight path, and the good person with a protected and guarded heart. When reading Proverbs, it is important to remember that in the symbolic world of the teachers, wisdom "keeps," while folly and its manifestations of evil steal, drain, vandalize, and disturb the balance of life as God has ordered it.

In a sense, the teachers have what we might call an ecological view of the created order. God, who created this world and brought into it the gift of life, has set up an order and a *šalom*, which are easily (though not finally) disturbed—a balance that can be upset. When the sages made their observations

---

21. M. Carruthers, *The Craft of Thought: Meditation, Rhetoric, and the Making of Images, 400–1200* (Cambridge: Cambridge Univ. Press, 1998), 105–7.

about the way the world works, noting its order and making predictions, they saw the intimate connection between that order and the life it holds.

Perhaps more than metaphor is at work as their instruction compares the path of the righteous to the first gleam of dawn and the way of wickedness to deep darkness that makes them stumble. Nature's order is reflected in the moral cosmos as well, and the sages frequently reminded their readers that Yahweh is no distant deist's God, letting consequences work themselves out, but is intimately involved in people's lives. Part of that involvement is handing out just rewards to the righteous and wicked (3:33–35), and part is starting a tradition of wisdom teaching that turns its students away from death.

God's created order, its gift of life, and wisdom teachings recommend a response that all must be protected so that the precious gift of life will not be lost. As we will see, the plots of wicked men, the lure of the seductress, and all other manifestations of folly and wickedness work to disturb order and ultimately to steal life. Because "life" is such an all-embracing term and a central concept to the outlook of Proverbs, it is easy to become jaded to its frequent appearance. Yet it is a necessary foundation for understanding the process of teaching (10:17) and its intended outcome, righteousness (12:28).

THE TRADITION CARRIED ON. Not too long ago I attended a worship service that included the dedication of a new baby, a joyful event for both the family and the congregation. In this service, the child's grandparents also stood up as witnesses, and as I watched, I wondered if their thoughts went back to the time they brought their own daughter forward in dedication. When they did, they were, in a sense, hoping for the day when their daughter would initiate her own child into the Christian tradition. Their work of parenting had come to fruition as their daughter and her husband did what they had done years before, promising to raise the child in the knowledge of God's love, teaching the child what had been taught to them. The rite of dedication also gave witness to the call of God that initiated this tradition.

What happens in between the time of these dedications, these markers of a new generation, and what influences each generation of parents to bring their children forward and use word and symbol to give them over to the Lord? We see some of that process in the opening scene of the chapter, as a father remembers what it was like to learn from his own father. Now, fully grown, he sees through his father's eyes. In between comes teaching and love.

As part of the worship service, the minister went to the parents to take the child, and of course, the parents became a little nervous, hoping the baby would not fuss or cry. There is always some nervousness about letting go of a child and placing it in the hands of another, but that dedication is the first of many acts of letting go. Teaching is another. It is the way the vows parents make before God work themselves out as new lives are encouraged to choose the direction they will take. As those grandparents once taught their child, they were in a sense teaching their grandchildren and all who would come after.

The teaching parents of Proverbs seem to understand that their teaching will in some ways lead their son away from them to a life partner and course of life, but they also want the son to take with him what they have found to be most valuable and life-giving. They know that he will be responsible for making his own decisions once he sets out on the path, but they can ask him to remember them as he walks toward life.

Passing on life learning. We use the word "life" in a number of different senses. Sometimes we mean that which breathes and grows, as when we speak of a plant, an animal, or a person. At other times, we mean a lifetime and its meaning, as in the question, "What is life, and why do I live it?"[22] At still others, especially if we attend to the teaching of Proverbs, we use the word "life" in its fullest sense of living in accord with the purpose that first moved God to shape a world and breathe into a pair of nostrils. So this teaching that passes endlessly from parents to children sets its focus on life choices, made early on, that determine the final outcomes that fulfill or frustrate that purpose for life.

The images of wisdom as a life partner, a path for life, and a guard to the wellspring of life are symbols of lifelong commitments that direct everyday choices, just as a sailor sets out for a distant point and makes small-scale adjustments to keep the ship on course. The recurrence of the image of the way in all three instructions also suggests the image of the journey. A person heading out on a long journey on foot, as people did in Bible times, would always choose a good traveling companion, one who watches out for you. You would choose a well-traveled and safe path, and you would take care to watch how you use your body members, keeping eyes on the goal and feet on that path.

---

22. J. E. Loader, *The Logic of the Spirit: Human Development in Theological Perspective* (San Francisco: Jossey-Bass, 1998), 5. Loader views the question as a cry of the human spirit "to someone or someplace beyond the self." "The human spirit, for all its creative energy, will wander aimlessly through time without any sense of its true center of gravity unless it is seized by the Spirit of God. Then it may beg on its knees to be transformed and thereby be conformed to what God is doing in the world to make persons human the way Jesus was human" (54–55).

At a workshop for pastors, the facilitator began the time of introductions by sharing some of the struggles he was having with his teenage son, particularly with behaviors of missing school and shoplifting. As the introductions moved around the circle, a majority of the pastors said that they could identify with the leader's struggles, because they had similar struggles with their own sons and daughters. It must have been a relief for these people to hear that they were not alone, but at the same time I thought I heard their consternation that the option of the bad way seems so strong for so many. In a sense, these pastors were giving testimony to their own awareness that they could not exert control over the lives of their children, that they could not determine their choices and keep them from harm.

In the view of many young men and women, teaching and control are the same thing. Unfortunately, many parents make the same mistake. The parental teachers of Proverbs show us how to avoid that mistake by viewing their teaching and our own as a legacy, a gift that can be accepted or rejected, heeded or ignored. This is not to say that parents will abdicate their responsibility to watch out for their child's well-being and safety, nor that parents will offer their teaching in a laissez-faire manner. The effort at persuasion in this text is too intense to allow us to think that. But it does mean that teaching looks forward to a time when the journey begins and the final stages of leaving take place, and it makes both parents and children aware that it is coming. It does not say to the children, "Stay under my authority and protection forever," but instead, "Take some of me with you when you go; that will protect you."

Parents can acknowledge that the process moves along too quickly for them; for the children, it often moves too slowly. The chapter's invitation to watch a tradition of parents teaching their children can also encourage today's parents to share openly about how the tradition has been good for them, how it has been a source of protection and honor, how it has given them something that has become more valuable to them over time, and how it gives them something to pass on to their children. The emphasis on testimony may also encourage parents to share their own mistakes and mishaps when appropriate; it can be a sign that wisdom does not arrive in one single package.

The image of the tradition also repeats the emphasis on the son as an active learner first seen in chapter 2 and developed in chapter 3. We must acknowledge that as far as we can tell, ancient wisdom education was not a model of the Socratic method; examples of dialogue between teacher and pupil are rare in wisdom literature.[23] Still, the parental teachers of Proverbs

---

23. J. Crenshaw, "The Missing Voice," in *A Biblical Itinerary: In Search of Method, Form and Content: Essays in Honor of George W. Coats*, ed. E. E. Carpenter (JSOTSup 240; Sheffield: Sheffield Academic Press, 1997), 133–43.

recognized that learning is not a passive activity; it requires desire and effort on the part of the learner. In more contemporary terms, "there is no true learning if someone is not searching."[24] One educator has written:

> Proverbs is *the* Bible book about education.... But ironically, the book talks more about learning than it does about teaching. Notice how Proverbs constantly addresses learners with these pieces of advice:
>
> * Learn (e.g., 7:1–3)
> * Learn the right thing (e.g., 16:16–24)
> * Learn from the right teachers (e.g., 13:20)
>
> The whole of the book makes no sense without keeping in mind that the learner is responsible for his or her own learning. The learner has choices. The learner has options. The learner decides.[25]

Both the responsibility to learn and the responsibility to live with the outcomes are signs that teaching is a process of letting go; it answers the young person's perception that parents only want to control by stressing the responsibility of that young learner to choose.

Tradition of wisdom. Does this chapter and its emphasis on tradition offer anything to those who are not raising children? Going back once again to that service of dedication, I remember a moment when the congregation stood up and vowed to love, guide, and teach the child as part of their responsibility as the family of God. In a sense, belonging to a church means that every member is involved in raising the children in some way, taking opportunities to love them as a Sunday school teacher or a volunteer youth worker. One way to value the Christian tradition is to love the children of the church (or any child who needs love for that matter), perhaps taking extra interest in one young person's growth. Sometimes parents are bothered that their children find it easier to talk openly with other adults, but this is easy to understand, since none of the issues that cause tension in the home are on the line. Parents can also appreciate the importance that another listening ear offers to a young person's sense of worth.

Entering into the tradition of wisdom teaching is akin to the apostle Paul's vision of discipleship in 2 Timothy 2:1–2: "You then, my son, be strong in

---

24. J. Westerhoff, *Spiritual Life: The Foundation for Preaching and Teaching* (Knoxville: Westminster John Knox, 1994), 42. Westerhoff believes that the best teachers are those who know how to make a place for the learner to ask questions and search for answers.

25. A. Peetoom, "One Christian's Defense of Whole Language," *Christian Educators Journal* (December 1993): 23–25. I'm grateful to David Lindberg for giving me a copy of this article.

the grace that is in Christ Jesus. And the things you have heard me say in the presence of many witnesses entrust to reliable men who will also be qualified to teach others." If we are to teach, we are also to practice what we teach. Specific instructions are few in this chapter as compared with the concrete directions in chapter 3. Instead, the images of chapter 4 work together to influence the larger life choices that determine the smaller ones.

Just as the image of a tradition of teaching carried from generation to generation speaks of something that must be guarded, protected, and maintained, so the images of life that is guarded challenge our view of discipleship. We are challenged to give up the idea that life in its fullness is a reward, an end that results from following the ways of wisdom, and to think instead of life as the gift of God (even mediated through wisdom teachings) that can be violated or lost. Discipline is not so much a matter of doing the right things to bring good results, found in so much contemporary self-help wisdom writing, as it is maintaining the gift of life for one's self and others.

While it is certainly true that consequences follow out of the choices one makes, wise living does not bring about the good life. Rather, it keeps one from getting lost. It points out the folly of choosing evil as though it were some path to gain and instead reveals it for what it is, a true loss of life and character. The wisdom of Proverbs would have us follow the ways of the Lord, not because we are empty but because we are full. It seems to me that we often live in the poverty of riches, knowing that we have a lot but believing we are poor because we don't have as much as someone else. Wisdom wants us to follow the ways of the Lord because we have been richly blessed and are in danger of giving it away through folly, like Esau's birthright, sold for a pot of stew (Gen. 25:27–34), or like the prodigal son's lost inheritance (Luke 15:13–14).

The teaching of this chapter challenges us to a life of discipline, both in being open to correction but also in practicing self-discipline that guards what one thinks, says, and does, because guarding these things guards life. At first look, the motivations of this chapter seem to appeal only to the young man's self-interest. But with a closer look at the topics of violence and perverse speech it becomes clear that the life that is guarded belongs to the young man and his family and his community. We need never think that we seek wisdom solely for the good she brings to us. Rather, Wisdom gives her blessings to our families and churches through us.

Proverbs 5:1–23

❦

¹ MY SON, PAY attention to my wisdom,
   listen well to my words of insight,
² that you may maintain discretion
   and your lips may preserve knowledge.
³ For the lips of an adulteress drip honey,
   and her speech is smoother than oil;
⁴ but in the end she is bitter as gall,
   sharp as a double-edged sword.
⁵ Her feet go down to death;
   her steps lead straight to the grave.
⁶ She gives no thought to the way of life;
   her paths are crooked, but she knows it not.

⁷ Now then, my sons, listen to me;
   do not turn aside from what I say.
⁸ Keep to a path far from her,
   do not go near the door of her house,
⁹ lest you give your best strength to others
   and your years to one who is cruel,
¹⁰ lest strangers feast on your wealth
   and your toil enrich another man's house.
¹⁰ At the end of your life you will groan,
   when your flesh and body are spent.
¹² You will say, "How I hated discipline!
   How my heart spurned correction!
¹³ I would not obey my teachers
   or listen to my instructors.
¹⁴ I have come to the brink of utter ruin
   in the midst of the whole assembly."

¹⁵ Drink water from your own cistern,
   running water from your own well.
¹⁶ Should your springs overflow in the streets,
   your streams of water in the public squares?
¹⁷ Let them be yours alone,
   never to be shared with strangers.
¹⁸ May your fountain be blessed,
   and may you rejoice in the wife of your youth.

¹⁹ A loving doe, a graceful deer—
  may her breasts satisfy you always,
  may you ever be captivated by her love.
²⁰ Why be captivated, my son, by an adulteress?
  Why embrace the bosom of another man's wife?

²¹ For a man's ways are in full view of the LORD,
  and he examines all his paths.
²² The evil deeds of a wicked man ensnare him;
  the cords of his sin hold him fast.
²³ He will die for lack of discipline,
  led astray by his own great folly.

MORE THAN ANY of the other instructions in chapters 1–9, the lectures of chapter 5 address the perennial issue of marital faithfulness and describe the disastrous results of its compromise. The warning against the "strange woman," the second of four,[1] is the only one to include a positive description of marital fidelity. Although the teaching seeks to discipline the awakening sexual awareness of young males, it is a concern for all, young and old, male and female, just as it has been since ancient days.

Warnings against promiscuous women were common in the ancient Near Eastern instructions directed to young males. Still, original audiences for the book of Proverbs would most likely also be familiar with the prohibitions of the Ten Commandments and prophetic descriptions of adultery as symbols of covenantal unfaithfulness. The teaching about the wisdom of faithfulness in marriage also symbolizes faithfulness to the Lord. By stressing faithfulness to the "wife of one's youth" (5:18), the parents also make sure that the young man hears that his relationship with wisdom is to be like a lifelong marriage.

Warnings against extramarital sex and adultery also come to the forefront in the next two chapters, occupying more and more of the parental teachers' attention. Following the basic structure outlined in chapter 2, the theme of adultery and the strange woman in chapters 5–7 follows the top-

---

1. The four descriptions of the strange woman (NIV "adulteress") are in 2:16–19; 5:1–14; 6:24–35; 7:5–27. Each adds its details to the composite picture of the strange woman. The warning in this chapter is filled with images of loss and dissipation, a contrast between keeping what is one's own and losing it to others (waters and wife). Ch. 6 lays out the problem of the wrathful husband, ch. 7 on the words of the strange woman and their deadly lure. Each description begins with nearly identical words for her seductive speech.

ics of friendship with Yahweh (2:5–8; cf. 3:1–12), love of wisdom (2:9–11; cf. 3:13–18; 4:1–9), and the enticement of evil men (2:12–15; cf. 4:14–27).[2] Another way of looking at the progression of these chapters is to focus on relationships. If the emphasis of chapter 4 was placed on the relationship of a father with his son, chapter 5 turns to the relationship of husband and wife. Chapter 6 will focus on the neighbor; even the warning about adultery there brings in the wronged husband. Finally, chapters 4–5 seem especially interrelated, as shown by the repetition of key terms that appear in a mirror reflection:

A (4:1–9) Lay *hold* of my words (*temak*, 4:4)
Get Wisdom and *love* her as one would a wife (4:6)
Embrace her (4:8)
Garland of *grace* (*ḥen*, 4:9)

  B (4:10–19) *Years of life* will be many (4:10)
  Safety: if you hold on to *instruction* (*musar*, 4:13)
  Wicked *eat* (4:17)

    C (4:20–27) *Pay attention; listen well* (4:20)
    Keep words within your heart (*šemor*, 4:21)
    Truthful *lips* (4:24)
    Straight and *considered paths* (4:26)

    C' (5:1–6) *Pay attention; listen well* (5:1)
    To *maintain* discretion (*šemor*, 5:2)
    Knowledgeable and lying *lips* (5:2–3)
    Crooked *paths* that are not *considered* (5:6)

  B' (5:7–14) *Years of your life* given to one who is cruel (5:9)
  Ruin, not safety: "I hated *discipline*" (*musar*, 5:12)
  Others *eat* (5:10)

A' (5:15–23) Be captivated by your wife's *love* (5:19)
A *graceful* deer (*ḥen*, 5:19)
Why *embrace* another man's wife? (5:20)
Cords of sin *hold him fast* (*tamek*, 5:22)

The A sections associate faithfulness to wisdom with faithfulness to one's spouse, while the B sections contrast the results of receiving or rejecting wisdom. The C sections contrast the way of integrity with the way of the adulteress, a way characterized by false and ruinous speech.

---

2. Skehan, "The Seven Columns of Wisdom's House in Proverbs 1–9," 9–14.

Looking more closely, we see that chapter 5 contains three addresses ("my son[s]," 5:1, 7, 20), but the consistent focus on the theme of fidelity in marriage unifies the chapter into one larger instruction.[3] Correspondence of some key terms suggests a chiastic or mirror pattern that overlays the larger structure of chapters 4–5, modifying it slightly by breaking 5:15–23 into two sections.

> A (5:1–6) Avoid the adulteress—the *strange woman*
> > B (5:7–14) Do not give what is yours to others—lest *strangers* feast on wealth
> > B′ (5:15–19) Drink from your own well—do not share with *strangers*
> A′ (5:20–23) Why be captive of the adulteress—the *strange woman?*

The repetition of terms at the beginning and end of the chapter create a frame or inclusio that links the two A sections. Death and dying as a result of ignoring wisdom teaching appear in 5:5 and 23. The Hebrew terms for "lead" in 5:5 and "hold him fast" in 5:22 come from the same root (*tmk*), creating a link between being led away to the grave and being held fast in sin. The frame also pairs the words for the woman who "gives no thought" to her "way" (5:6) and the "way" that Yahweh "examines" (5:21). The word "strangers" (5:10, 17) links the two B sections. Other key terms repeat throughout the chapter as well. The other woman is mentioned in three sections (5:3, 17, and 20), and there are recurrences of "end" (5:4, 11), and "discipline" (5:12, 23). Verses 12–14 and 23 both conclude with a lack of discipline that leads to ruin.

Avoid the Adulteress (5:1–6)

THE TEACHER REPEATS the anatomy of wisdom from the previous chapter: The son is to turn his ear (5:1; cf. 4:20), to let his lips preserve knowledge (5:2; cf. 4:24), and to keep his feet from following the path of the other woman, whose feet go down to death (5:5; cf. 4:26). Just as discretion will keep its possessor (cf. 2:11), so here the young man is to "maintain discretion" and "preserve knowledge" (5:2). Discretion and knowledge are paired only here and in 8:12 in all of the Hebrew Bible. In both contexts, it is discretion that enables the young man to choose wisely. In a sense, he keeps and preserves what wisdom possesses and gives.

As always, the teacher places responsibility squarely on the shoulders of the son. He is to maintain discretion and preserve knowledge via speech

---

3. Clifford, *Proverbs*, 69, points out the contrast between the dangers of the forbidden woman (vv. 1–14) and the joys of loving one's own wife (vv. 15–23).

(5:2); he is to guard and protect it as he lives by it and as he passes it on to the next generation. He is to *listen* to the teaching (with his ears), *live* it (by choosing good paths with his feet), and *leave* it with the generation to come (with his lips).

The teacher then warns that single-minded faithfulness to this goal can be compromised by the temptations of adultery (5:3–6). The description of the adulteress (lit., the "strange woman," *zarah*, 5:3) pits her words against the words of the teacher, raising the issue of trust. If the character of a person's words is measured by the end they bring about, then her end (and potentially his), is bitter. It is not surprising that the teacher's second call to attention follows a description of her path to the grave (Heb. *šᵉʾol*, the home of the dead[4]; cf. 2:18–19; 9:18). Verse 7 literally reads, "do not turn aside from the speech of *my mouth*."

The warnings against sexual involvement with the "other woman" are earthy, the motivations imaged here as bitter gall and sharp sword. The name of Yahweh does not appear, nor does the prohibition against adultery (Ex. 20:14), although both can be assumed in the background that is made more explicit in Proverbs 5:21. If adultery is an offense to Yahweh, it is also ruinous to the naive person who believes that one can escape unscathed. The young man is challenged to look around to see that experience proves the truthfulness and authority of the wisdom teacher and Yahweh, whom he represents.

The deceptions of adultery are communicated via images of eating and drinking. Just as the wicked eat wickedness and drink violence (4:17), the words of the strange woman are like honey and oil—at first (5:3). Her lips "drip with honey," an image possibly meant to carry overtones of her kisses (Song 4:11; 7:9).[5] Then they become bitter and sharp, just as a false friend's words can seem "smooth as butter" and "more soothing than oil," but are in reality "drawn swords" (Ps. 55:21). Gall, sometimes called wormwood, is the bitter juice derived from leaves and buds of the plant Artemesia, often used in the treatment of worms (Lam. 3:19; Amos 6:12). The two-edged sword has two "mouths" in Hebrew, so that "the sword devours one, as well as another" (2 Sam. 11:25). Readers should keep watch to see that images of eating and drinking continue throughout the chapter.[6]

---

4. R. L. Harris, "Why Hebrew *Sheʾol* Was Translated 'Grave,'" in *The NIV: The Making of a Contemporary Translation*, ed. K. L. Barker (Grand Rapids: Zondervan, 1986), 58–71. See also E. Merrill's observation that *šᵉʾol* is both a place and power ("שְׁאוֹל," *NIDOTTE*, 4:6–7). The emphasis here is likely on place, the end of the woman's path.

5. Scott, *Proverbs*, 54.

6. The young man is to drink from his own cistern, not hers (5:15), and we might even look to the intoxication in 5:19, 20, and 23 as part of the eating and drinking motif.

The principal contrast here is drawn between the deceptively sweet and smooth lips of the other woman and the lips of the young man that are to preserve knowledge and wisdom. We can infer that the father has preserved wisdom and knowledge with his lips and hopes to continue the preservation on the lips of his son. He is to keep knowledge and not lose it, considering his paths and keeping them straight (compare 4:26 and 5:6). If the young man takes her crooked path and misses the path of life, the tradition of knowledge and wisdom is lost. We do well to pay attention to the symbolic significance of this picture. The strange or loose woman is not identified, so we cannot say whether she is a foreigner, wife of another, or prostitute (cultic or otherwise). What is clear is that the young male is to avoid her at all costs. She represents both the folly of adultery and all that is foreign to the way of wisdom.

The translation of 5:6 seeks to clarify a difficult Hebrew phrase (lit., "lest she consider the way of life"; cf. "lest" in 5:9–10). Two of the verbs in the verse can also be translated second-person masculine, and so the rabbis of old took it to read: "You cannot weigh the path of life, for its ways wander and you do not know how." They concluded that one should keep all the commands because we cannot know how God weighs life and its rewards.[7] But context indicates that it is the woman who does not know, just as the wicked "do not know" in 4:19.[8] She gives no thought to her way of life, recalling 4:26, a sentence that uses the same Hebrew word to urge the learner to consider the paths of his feet. "She does not know" in 5:6 also recalls the wicked who do not know what makes them stumble (4:19).

The symbol of the way links the end of chapter 4 and beginning of chapter 5, comparing evildoers who do not see where they are going with the young man who should. In sum, if this young man does not keep discretion and knowledge on his lips, he will be led astray by the lips of another, and the tradition of wisdom and life will be lost to that family line. He will also lose his life (5:5). We read on to see what that loss of life entails.

Do Not Give What Is Yours to Others (5:7–14)

A RENEWED CHARGE to listen in 5:7 seems to say, "Now this is important. Be sure to get this." The plural "sons" suggests that the teaching is directed to a wide audience (cf. 4:1; 7:24). Directing attention away from the strange

---

7. Plaut, *Proverbs*, 75.

8. Garrett, *Proverbs*, 91–92, translates, "her ways wander and you do not know it," arguing that the death of the young man is at issue. The masculine second person "you" is consistent with 5:9, but the third person feminine is consistent with the verbs of 5:3–6. I take it as decisive that "her paths are crooked," the clear reading, is in parallel with the person who does not consider *her* paths (so also Fox, *Proverbs 1–9*, 193).

woman and her deceptive charms, the teacher says, "listen to me" and "do not *turn* from what I say," keeping attention on the metaphor of the path. The son is told to make his path *far* from the woman, to not go *near* her door of her house (for "door," cf. 8:34; 9:14); one sure way to avoid trouble is to stay clear of it.

The motivations or reasons for the charge in 5:9–14 are all negative; each involves some sort of loss, whether it be loss of strength, years, wealth, or honor. Even the tradition of instruction can be lost if it is rejected (5:12–13). This woman has a house that is to be avoided (5:8; cf. 2:18; 7:8); if it is not, one's wealth and toil go to another man's house (5:10).

· Because the teacher draws such a vivid picture of adultery and its outcomes in a community setting, interpreters have struggled with the historical and social background of the imagery, mostly because of lack of agreement about the historical basis for the strange woman and the masculine "strangers."[9] We have said in chapter 2 that the woman is strange, not because she represents foreign peoples or religions[10] but because she is not one's own wife; she belongs to another or, simply put, is "other." Whatever symbolic significance the woman carries, interpretation must begin with the actual consequences of adultery.

Yet if we agree that the teacher speaks of adultery and its costs, it is still not clear how the adulterer loses strength, years, and wealth to others. Commentators' suggestions include damages paid to a betrayed husband (5:10; cf. 6:35), money given to a mistress, payment for blackmail, and venereal disease (5:9, 11). The wide range of interpretation points up the difficulties, but the loss of one's wealth, then honor to another family is the simplest and most likely.[11]

If we cannot determine the social situation with precision, we can look at the symbolism of the teacher's scenario and see that death (5:5–6) is here defined as loss of strength, years, substance, and reputation, the reverse of wisdom's benefits of long life, riches, and honor (3:16). While it would be useful to know the historical referents that original hearers may have known, the

---

9. See Perdue, *Proverbs*, 120–21, for a summary of the view that "strangers" represent foreign religions, and McKane, *Proverbs*, 311–20, for the argument against it.

10. Blenkinsopp, "The Social Context of the 'Outsider Woman' in Proverbs 1–9," 457–73. See also Camp, *Wisdom and the Feminine in the Book of Proverbs*, 269. Camp sees the intermarriage of the exiles in Ezra 10:2–11 as a possible background, particularly the forfeiture of property described in 10:8. However, the similarities do not by themselves establish a historical connection. While a canonical reading can better understand the significance of the teaching in Proverbs by reading Ezra, using Ezra as the historical referent is not warranted when reading a text that only makes historical references to Solomon and Hezekiah.

11. See Whybray, *Proverbs*, 88.

cumulative strength of the many images does tell us that the teacher means to scare the son, primarily by showing him that a foolish choice would mean the loss of everything he holds dear. The poetic justice at work shows that in going after a strange woman, one that is not his own, the son could lose all that is his own to strangers.[12] It may be that a sidelong glance at the cost of acquiring wisdom ("all you have," 4:7) is intended.

The teacher then fast-forwards this fictional narrative to the end of the son's life, the time when "flesh and body are spent." He tells the young man he "will groan" the way a heart groans in anguish from a sick and wasted body (cf. Ps. 38:3–9). Elsewhere in Proverbs this groan is used to describe a lion's roar and a king's wrath (19:12; 20:2; 28:15). The sound of this groan and the words that follow is heart-wrenching, but they are really the teacher's words; the son never actually speaks in Proverbs. Instead of reporting the recrimination of the assembly, the teacher puts words of remorse in the mouth of the son, perhaps to increase the shock effect. This is the second time negative consequences and regret have followed rejection of discipline and correction (cf. 1:29–31). There may be an intended irony that words of regret speak with discretion and knowledge that come too late (5:1–2).

Perhaps the most potent source of regret is the shame that comes to light in the last few words of 5:14, "in the midst of the whole assembly." The teacher concludes the story by showing how adultery that begins in private becomes public, not only with loss of wealth but also loss of standing, so that the whole family is shamed (cf. Sir. 23:21–26 for shame of adultery in the community). The public stoning of Deuteronomy 22:22 is probably not in view here, but that text does give us a sense of the abhorrence the community was taught to feel about adultery. For them it was a public matter. Loss of everything included public reputation.

In sum, the instruction of Proverbs 5:7–14 warns that if the young man chooses the words of the adulteress over the instruction of the teachers, he will lose all that he might have kept: strength, wealth, and social standing. In this way, the choice to love folly instead of wisdom is symbolized as a rejection of wisdom and her gifts of life, riches, and reputation. The parental teacher imagines what the young man will say when the truth is known, hoping that the young man's own voice will prove to be persuasive. The son's regrets clearly state the sages' view: Adultery is not only a sin that exacts payment, it is the ultimate symbol of the fool's pathway.

---

12. Fox, *Proverbs 1–9*, 194–97. Fox rightly suggests that "strength" in 5:9 points to the productivity of procreation and agriculture, both of which produce a kind of wealth and strength. One has offspring to help one build up one's substance. To lose these would be to lose one's legacy.

Drink from Your Own Well (5:15–23)

HAVING MADE HIS scenario on adultery as frightening as possible, the teacher now turns to admonition, using images of flowing water to recommend marital faithfulness. Just as the speech of the adulteress tasted like honey and oil that turned to bitter gall, so here drinking water becomes a metaphor for faithful sexual expression with one's spouse. The contrast is striking; the Hebrew word for "in the midst" appears in both 5:14 and 15, comparing the public shame "in the midst" of the assembly with water drunk "from the midst" of one's own cistern. "Your own," repeated in 5:15, introduces the emphasis on privacy and possession that runs throughout the exhortation. Just as the narrative scenario on adultery depicted loss and regret, here the teacher uses poetic imagery to offer an alternative, an example of keeping and preserving.

Interpreters wrestle with the use of water metaphors in 5:15–20. Is the water from the well a wife? Are the springs in the streets the love of the wife or the husband? Before solutions are considered, some observations should guide the discussion. (1) It is important to remember that the idea of "your own" is repeated throughout the chapter, and it is especially emphasized in 5:15 and 17 (the Heb. suffix for "your" is used throughout). The contrasting idea is repeated in 5:16–17; the water should not overflow in streets or public squares, it should not be shared with "strangers."

(2) The instruction must be set in the larger context of Proverbs 1–9. So, for example, the key word "embrace" is used for wisdom (3:18; 4:8) and the adulteress (5:20) to construct a contrast between wisdom and folly.

(3) It is especially important to appreciate that the experience of reading or hearing the poem is also a part of its persuasive strategy. By likening the sexual intimacy of marriage with sensual images of drinking and swooning, the teacher here means to create a scene that is as inviting as the scene of loss was meant to be frightening. In other words, the poem appeals to the young man's senses to render marital faithfulness attractive.[13] These guidelines may help us discern the writer's overall message and purpose, even if the referents of the water imagery may be difficult to determine.

What do these various symbols of water and drinking stand for? The suggestions made by interpreters include: the pleasures of physical love, the production of offspring, the squandered seed that does not produce offspring, or the wife herself.[14] We may take a clue from Song of Songs 4:12–15, in which the man tells his beloved, "You are a garden locked up, my sister,

---

13. R. Alter, *The Art of Biblical Poetry* (New York: Basic Books, 1985), 179–84.
14. See Fox, *Proverbs 1–9*, 200–201, for a brief history of interpretation.

my bride; you are a spring enclosed, a sealed fountain. . . . You are a garden fountain, a well of flowing water streaming down from Lebanon."[15] Note that "fountain" and "wife of your youth" are in parallel lines (Prov. 5:18), suggesting they are synonymous, but it is even more important to take the verse as a whole. It directs the son to have physical relations with his wife alone.

If this is key to understanding the passage,[16] it can also be argued that all of the water imagery in the poem speaks of the marriage relationship, itself a source of delight, refreshment, offspring, and ongoing life.[17] It is this relationship that should not overflow into the streets, and loving attention should not be shared with strangers.[18] The Hebrew words for "streets" and "public squares" are both in 7:12 for the adulteress who is there, and it is stolen water that folly pronounces sweet in 9:17. In sum, reading the images as making primary reference to sexual relationship is consistent with the guidelines of context and sensual imagery outlined above. Hubbard put it well: "The contrast between the harlot's honey that goes bitter (vv. 3–4) and the wife's water that stays sweet ('running') is the point of the whole chapter."[19]

The metaphor of drinking from one's own cistern and well may mark the saying of 5:15 as a proverb.[20] The actions of 5:16 are clear enough: Springs overflow or disperse in the streets, and streams of water do the same in the public squares. However, the LXX adds a negative, which commentators take as a clue to read "lest" or "let not." The NIV correctly reads the Hebrew text in the form of a question, designed to be answered in the negative. A similar use of rhetorical questions appears in 6:27–29.

---

15. For physical love described as drinking wine, see Song 1:4; 4:10; 5:1; 7:9; 8:2.

16. P. A. Kruger, "Promiscuity or Marriage Fidelity? A Note on Prov. 5:15–18," *JNSL* 13 (1987): 61–68.

17. W. C. Kaiser Jr., "True Marital Love in Proverbs 5:15–23 and the Interpretation of the Song of Songs," in *The Way of Wisdom: Essays in Honor of Bruce K. Waltke*, ed. J. I. Packer and S. K. Soderlund (Grand Rapids: Zondervan, 2000), 106–16. Kaiser concludes that the water satisfies a husband's desire. It is best not to look for distinctions in the five water metaphors (cistern, well, springs, streams, fountain), for they all point to the refreshing and life-giving qualities of water. Because it is scarce and precious in the Middle East, water spilled in the streets is like loss of life.

18. For cisterns privately owned, see 2 Kings 18:31; Isa. 36:16; Jer. 38:6. Kruger views the waters of the cistern and springs in the streets as symbols for one's wife and the strange woman respectively, but the word for "strangers" in Prov. 5:17 is the masculine *zarim*, which cannot refer to the strange woman. If, however, the metaphor itself is "fluid," then we have a hint that others, "strangers," will ultimately possess what is the man's own if he takes his own loving attentions and brings them to the street.

19. Hubbard, *Proverbs*, 93.

20. Scott, *Proverbs*, 55, translates, "As the saying is. . . ."

Gazelles and does (5:19) are associated with awakening love in Song of Songs 2:7 and 3:5. The Hebrew for "may her breasts satisfy you always" is similar to the invitation of the adulteress, "Let's drink deep of love," in Proverbs 7:18. "Captivated," restated in 5:20 and 23 ("led astray"; Heb. ʾśgb) is key to understanding the chapter, as the commentary on those verses will show.

In sum, the teacher implores the son to be faithful to his wife. In the larger context of Proverbs 1–9, the exhortation also symbolizes the son's relationship with wisdom, for she is to be found just as one finds a good wife (18:22; 31:10; cf. 8:35).[21] Given that the metaphor of the well can be applied to the love of one's own wife or a foreign/strange woman (23:27b), we can observe that this love, associated with springs and wells, is also associated with wisdom. "The spring/well is a trope for his relations with his wife, wisdom, and God."[22] In other words, the sexual metaphors always point in some way to relations both human and divine.

Why Be Captive of the Adulteress? (5:20–23)

THE CONCLUSION OF this parental teaching begins with a rhetorical question "Why?" providing a strong antidote to folly even as it highlights it. Verse 20 is connected with 5:19 by the word "captivated" (ʾśgb; cf. 5:23).[23] The teacher restates the problem of adultery, this time drawing attention to the ever-present eyes of Yahweh (5:21). The instruction concludes, as did that of chapter 3, with a motivation based on Yahweh's supervision of life; "he examines" every person's "paths" (cf. the same Heb. term in 4:26; 5:6, pls). The warning to the son to consider his paths (4:26) and the example of the adulteress who does not (5:6) is now brought full circle with a reminder that Yahweh considers everyone's path.[24]

But this is not the only motivation for avoiding adultery. Piling up terms for sin, 5:22 envisions evil as a trap, cords that will trip up those who do wrong and hold them there until a hunter comes to end their lives (cf. to the birds in 1:17). But the loss of life is not so much due to the choice of evil as

---

21. R. Murphy, "Wisdom and Eros in Proverbs 1–9," *CBQ* 50 (1988): 600–603.

22. L. Lyke, "The Song of Songs, Proverbs, and the Theology of Love," in *Theological Exegesis: Essays in Honor of Brevard S. Childs*, ed. C. Seitz and K. Greene-McCreight (Grand Rapids: Eerdmans, 1999), 210–11. Lyke contends that the metaphors for sexuality have human and divine registers that are "inseparable," 222–23.

23. J. Goldingay, "Proverbs V and IX," *RB* 84 (1977): 80–93, sees no relation between 5:20 and 5:21–23 and relocates verse 20 between 5:2 and 3, but this is unnecessary. Apart from the catchword that connects the three verses, one can also see the strategy for placement in the mirror structure of chs. 4 and 5.

24. Paths can refer to wagon tracks or as a metaphor for "habits" (Kidner, *Proverbs*, 71).

the earlier rejection of discipline (*musar;* cf. 5:12). In other words, it is the choice of an extramarital sexual partner that traps and kills, yet that is only the result of refusing instruction and fear of God. "The wicked are always running with death at their heels. That death is most likely the reverse of Shalom, life that is short, deprived, and alienated. Death involves corruption, a cutting off from all that has value, including God."[25]

The meaning of the phrase "led astray" (5:23) must be appreciated in the light of the play on this word in 5:19–20.[26] For example, the New Jewish Version uses "infatuated" in all three instances, so that 5:23 reads, "He will die for lack of discipline, infatuated by his great folly," stressing that both Eros and folly have the power to fascinate and deceive. Of all the terms that might be used to translate the three occurrences, "lost" may come the closest to capturing the sense of the Hebrew. If one can stagger, be intoxicated, swoon, be captivated with passion, become "lost in love," one can also be "lost" by one's own folly, "led astray" with judgment, dulled in a kind of drunkenness, "lost" in the sense of reaping a disastrous result. Allen Ross prefers the word *captivated:* "If the young man is not *captivated* by his wife but becomes *captivated* with a stranger in sinful acts, then his own iniquities will *captivate* him; and he will be led to ruin."[27]

In sum, chapter 5 develops the idea of keeping the heart (4:21–23) by urging the son to preserve knowledge (5:1–2), that is, to keep hold of wisdom in the face of temptations to lose or reject it. In the economy of the sages, one keeps wisdom and keeps all that one has as a result (4:1–9). To lose or forsake wisdom is to lose everything else as well (5:7–14). The example in this chapter is the marriage relationship. To take one's intimacy to strangers is to risk losing all to strangers; to drink from one's own well is to keep all that is one's own, including one's life.

Bridging Contexts

MARRIAGE IMAGERY. One way to find what is timeless and enduring in a text is to look for the overarching theme that ties its teachings together. At first reading, this chapter appears to be about faithful marriage and the threat of adultery—and so it is, claiming eighteen

25. R. Murphy, "The Kerygma of the Book of Proverbs," *Int* 20 (1966): 3–14.

26. Basic meaning is "to stray" (Ezek. 34:6), perhaps from drink (Isa. 28:7). One should not lead astray (Deut. 27:18; Prov. 28:10). The term can also stand for unintended error (Gen. 43:12; Ps. 119:67; Prov. 20:1; Eccl. 10:5; Isa. 28:7), but one may not excuse self (Eccl. 5:6) (E. Jenni and C. Westermann, eds., *Theological Lexicon of the Old Testament,* trans. M. E. Biddle, 3 vols. [Peabody Mass.: Hendrickson, 1997], 3:1302–4).

27. Ross, "Proverbs," 931.

of the twenty-three verses.[28] However, the chapter opens and closes with more general exhortations to accept parental instruction in the way of wisdom. Those exhortations set out the purpose for all that comes in between: "that you may maintain discretion and your lips may preserve knowledge" (5:2). The ultimate goal of the wise life is illustrated here as faithfulness to one's spouse. Going one step farther, we also observe that this theme of wise living points beyond love of wife and love of wisdom to love of God. Here, as in so many of the prophets' speeches, the marriage metaphor points to a relationship with God.

In order to appreciate the significance of the main theme, contemporary readers must pay attention to the writer's literary strategy of contrasting images. By holding out vivid pictures of what is desirable in life and placing them alongside images of death, the teachers of Proverbs make their rhetorical appeals. Like visitors to an art museum, readers today can view these pictures created for ancient audiences and learn from their message.

Three contrasts in characterization coalesce into one overall comparison between keeping what is one's own and taking what belongs to others. (1) The first is the contrast between the honeyed lips and smooth words of adultery and the lips that preserve wisdom and knowledge (5:2–3). The reader recalls that in chapter 4, the father sought to pass on the tradition of wisdom to his son, who in turn will pass it on to others. In the father's view, wisdom is preserved or "kept" by internalizing it and teaching it. Neither happens if one chooses to listen instead to the lies of adultery.

One of the main contrasts to observe, then, is between what the young man is to become and what the other/outsider woman already is. His lips are to preserve knowledge, and he must consider the paths of his feet (5:2; 4:26–27). Her lips drip deceptive honey and oil; she does not consider the way of life, apparently unconcerned that Yahweh does (5:6, 21). In this way, adultery and rejection of the way of wisdom are closely related. For this reason, the teacher warns the son that if he chooses adultery, he will say, "How I hated discipline! How my heart spurned correction" (5:12; cf. 1:7).

(2) A second contrast is the difference between the long-lasting joy of marital faithfulness and the temporary and stolen pleasures of adultery. Therefore, a scenario of a relationship with the other woman is developed as a contrast with a loyal covenantal relationship with one's own wife. The contrast is symbolized in the waters contained and enjoyed at home and the waters that are poured out in the streets. Faithfulness is a form of keeping;

---

28. After the introduction of the theme in 2:16–19, sixty-five verses deal with sexual conduct. There are more verses devoted to the strange woman than to Woman Wisdom! (see Murphy, "Wisdom and Eros in Proverbs 1–9").

unfaithfulness, a form of losing. The ironic turn of the contrast says to the son, "When you take what is not yours, you can end up losing what is"—a message that is applicable today.

(3) The third set of images contrasts being lost in love with being lost in folly. There is a profound difference between ecstasy and stupor, and this is the difference between the joys of marital love and the pleasures of adultery. One sharpens judgment, the other dulls it. One supports and nurtures the covenantal relationship, the other destroys that relationship and the one who wanders away from it.

On a symbolic level, then, the overall contrast is between going to folly, personified as an "other woman," who is not one's own, and staying faithful to wisdom, who is personified as a virtuous woman and good wife. The contrast is developed more fully in chapters 7—9, and this larger context instructs us to read what is said about the other woman as an antitype to wisdom. In other words, whenever we read a description of her behaviors, we can look at their opposite and learn more about the qualities of wisdom (and vice versa when wisdom is described). If the other woman lies, Wisdom tells the truth (8:6—8); if the other woman's path leads to death, Wisdom's path leads to life (3:16—17); if the other woman leads astray, then Wisdom is a good guide that leads along good and safe paths (2:10—22). Thus the contrast between personified Wisdom and Folly in chapters 1—9 appears here as adultery and marital faithfulness are compared.

In sum, each of the contrasts illustrates the irony of adultery and all other related follies to say, "If you take what does not belong to you, you wind up losing what does." The prophet Nathan used a parable to get this truth across to a king who had become so entangled in sin's folly that he hoped to cover up adultery with murder. The prophet broke through his self-deluding defenses with a story of a man who had flocks of sheep but stole the only lamb his neighbor had. Enraged, King David pronounced his own sentence: "The man who did this should die!" Shaken out of his stupor, he saw that what he had done was sin against God, he repented, and he suffered the loss of the child that had been conceived, the first of many losses (2 Sam. 12:1—25). His own life had been spared, but he would later say, "If only I had died instead of you—O Absalom, my son, my son!" (2 Sam. 18:33).

Eros and wisdom in marriage. With the theme of keeping and losing in mind, we may make the bridge from ancient times to today by looking at both the concrete experience of marital love and its symbolic representation of a lifelong relationship with wisdom. We cannot divide our interpretation into literal and symbolic senses, because faithfulness is an expression of wisdom, adultery a form of folly. If we talk about wisdom, we must talk about faithfulness; if we talk about folly, we must talk about the foolishness of adultery.

To begin with the concrete experience of marital love, the teachers of Proverbs not only acknowledge the power of eros in the son's life, they give it their blessing. We should observe that, unlike so many of the erotic images that compete for our attention in contemporary media, the most vivid images of sexual ecstasy here describe the joys of marriage. To state the obvious in order to develop the point, the instruction to find these joys at home in marriage contradicts a great deal of popular thinking on the subject.

The transition from an institutional to a companionship view of marriage in the twentieth century has placed increasingly high expectations on marriage, including strong romantic feelings and great sex.[29] Lewis Smedes has observed that our culture typically tells us to define our lives in terms of present needs and future possibilities, not commitments we have made in the past. The question, Smedes says, is what kind of people we want to be, covenant keepers or self-maximizers. The first thinks of marriage in terms of faithfulness, the second in terms of romance and fulfillment, and both coexist within each of us. Yet to focus only on the latter is to give way to folly: "Only a fool would claim to know all that marriage is for. But perhaps our culture has made fools of us all by getting us to believe that marriage is only for making people happy and that successful sex is its dream come true."[30]

For this reason, seeking fulfillment outside of a relationship that has gone flat seems justifiable to a person who feels so deprived. Many a Hollywood movie justifies the start of a new relationship with a quick glimpse of an unhappy marriage. While we must recognize the reality of troubled marriages and that some are broken beyond repair, we should also refuse to be taken in to believe that convenient plot devices describe the way life works in the real world. We also refuse to accept that unhappiness in a present relationship is reason enough to begin another.

The admonition to rejoice in the wife of one's youth speaks to the fact that the power of eros can drive in two directions. It can lead toward or away from lifelong commitment. The Song of Songs also shows how the detailed descriptions of ancient love poetry evoke a longing for exclusive relationship, describing an eros given by God as means of bonding (5:19; Song 2:16—17; 4:5). The lush and erotic poetry quotes the lovers saying, "You and no other." When the woman warns, "Do not arouse or awaken love until it so desires!" (2:7; 3:5; 8:4), she speaks with wisdom about the appropriate use of its power. For that reason, she tells her lover to "place me like a seal over your heart,

---

29. K. Kayser, *When Love Dies: The Process of Marital Disaffection* (New York and London: Guilford Press, 1993), 1—3.

30. L. B. Smedes, *Mere Morality: What God Expects from Ordinary People* (Grand Rapids: Eerdmans, 1983), 160—67.

---

like a seal on your arm; for love is as strong as death, its jealousy unyielding as the grave" (8:6). Both the teachers of Proverbs and the unnamed lovers of the Song of Songs claim that human eros is meant to create bonds that last, but they also know that the same eros can draw one away if nothing else in the relationship supports and strengthens that bond.

The discipline of saying no to inappropriate desire, then, should find its counterpart in saying yes to building a strong marriage. Eros alone is not enough to keep a relationship together, but wisdom in its reflective and loving capacities can. The difference between waters poured in the streets and waters gathered in cisterns and wells speaks to the wisdom of enjoying the delights of erotic pleasure within the bounds of faithfulness and promise. Wisdom also helps a person discern the lies in false promises of pleasure that call from beyond those boundaries. The sages' imagery of instruction not only dares to talk about the physical pleasures of marriage, it does so to encourage readers to understand that they are designed to be *enjoyed*, and enjoyed within boundaries.

The church needs to do the same, explaining how saying no to that which is out of bounds is not an end in itself but a way of saying yes to God's gift of sexual pleasure. Moreover, it is a way of keeping and not losing, that is, keeping this gift of sexuality within proper boundaries so that its intent of creating bonds is not lost.

God's faithful love. We have also seen that these instructions about marriage and adultery are symbolic of the young man's relationship with wisdom who, as wife and teacher, protects her spouse from the seductive words of the other woman (2:16–19; 7:4–5). The instructions juxtapose charges to maintain both discretion (5:2) and the marriage relationship (5:15–19), to preserve knowledge as well as waters. As we have seen above, this "keeping" of passion is similar to the way the Song of Songs uses the "Nuptial Metaphor"[31] to speak to our faith commitments *and* our human relationships. Each helps us understand the other, and the sages would remind us that life's experiences have many lessons to teach if we pay attention to them. In his memoirs, Malcolm Muggeridge wrote about the experience of meeting his wife at the train station:

> There is always a dread on such occasions that somehow the rendezvous will not be kept; that arrangements which seemed so precise will somehow have gone awry. So one studies the gathering faces with mounting anxiety; every sort of face showing up expect the particu-

---

31. P. Ricouer, "The Nuptial Metaphor," in A. La Cocque and P. Ricouer, *Thinking Biblically: Exegetical and Hermeneutical Studies,* trans. D. Pellauer (Chicago and London: Univ. of Chicago Press, 1998), 266–303.

lar one in question, until, at last, there it is; unmistakable, unique, infinitely dear. . . . What is love but a face, instantly recognizable in a sea of faces? A spotlight rather than a panning shot? This in contradistinction to power, which is a matter of numbers, of crowd scenes. I heard of an inscription on a stone set up in North Africa which reads: "I the captain of a Legion of Rome, have learnt and pondered this truth, that there are in life but two things, love and power, and no man can have both." Some twenty centuries later, I append my own amen.[32]

In presenting the joys of exclusive, committed love, the sages of Proverbs appeal to the human experiences of love, asking us to see them as windows for understanding God's exclusive, even jealous love for us. God's exclusive love—"you and no other"—is the foundation of God's covenant with Israel, as Deuteronomy 7:7—8 signifies:

> The LORD did not set his affection on you and choose you because you were more numerous than other peoples, for you were the fewest of all peoples. But it was because the LORD loved you and kept the oath he swore to your forefathers that he brought you out with a mighty hand and redeemed you from the land of slavery, from the power of Pharaoh king of Egypt.

And the response is just as singular in devotion (Deut. 6:4):

> Hear, O Israel: The LORD our God, the LORD is one. Love the LORD your God with all your heart and with all your soul and with all your strength.

Jeremiah 3:19—20 combines metaphors of sonship and marriage to make a similar point:

> "I myself said,
>
> > 'How gladly would I treat you like sons
> >   and give you a desirable land,
> >   the most beautiful inheritance of any nation.'
> > I thought you would call me 'Father'
> >   and not turn away from following me.
> > But like a woman unfaithful to her husband,
> >   so you have been unfaithful to me, O house of Israel,"
> >   declares the LORD.

---

32. M. Muggeridge, *Chronicles of Wasted Time I: The Green Stick* (New York: W. Morrow and Co., 1973), 269.

If the covenant and the prophets help us understand the love of God through this nuptial metaphor, a God who is jealous yet faithful even in the face of betrayal, then the wisdom writings of Proverbs and the Song of Songs help us understand the sanctity of human love that is as strong as death— *because it is like God's love* (or should be) in its focus on the one. When humans commit to one another saying, "You and no other," they reflect God's exclusive love for us that evokes a similar response in return. Therefore, just as adultery is the ultimate picture of folly, so faithful married love can be a picture of divine love, God's grace revealed in human faithfulness.

Yahweh's role in the end of the wicked. If God's love is reflected in the discipline and joy of faithful marital sexual love, the final scene of the chapter, the end of the wicked, points to another aspect of God's character. Does 5:21–23 picture God's judgment? The only mention of "the LORD" in this entire chapter states simply that he sees all, that a person's ways are in "full view" and Yahweh "examines" every path. Nothing more is said, and we may conclude that the picture of God here is passive, for he does nothing to judge. Yet 5:22–23 speaks of a disastrous end, namely, the wicked caught in the cords of sin, forfeiting life itself because of folly.

One of the puzzles of Proverbs is the tension created between texts that speak of God's active supervision of human affairs and those that portray God as an observer, not passive but involved in watching. Here again, we recognize that the sages saw no contradiction between sin's earthly consequences and God's final judgment of human character. Again, Paul's repeated phrase that God "gave them over" (Rom. 1:24, 26, 28) to sinful ways is incorporated in God's wrath (1:18). Here in Proverbs Yahweh is not so much an active judge who dispenses rewards as an overseer who makes sure that everything works as it should. "Folly," then, comes not only in rejecting discipline (Prov. 5:23) but also in believing that God does not see or does not care. Both couldn't be more mistaken. As Plantinga puts it:

> Sin is folly. No matter what images they choose, the Bible writers say this again and again. Sin is missing the target; sin is choosing the *wrong* target. Sin is wandering from the path or rebelling against someone too strong for us or neglecting a good inheritance.... To rebel against God is to saw off the branch that supports us.[33]

Here the instruction that began in chapter 4 has come full circle. Just as the teacher promised, "Do not forsake wisdom, and she will protect you" (4:6), so here the wicked who have taken the other road (4:14–17) come to their awful end, their way is a "deep darkness" that makes them stumble (4:19).

---

33. Plantinga, *Not the Way It's Supposed to Be*, 123.

Refusing to keep the words of instruction (4:20–5:2) and rejecting wisdom, they have lost all to death. The conclusion of 5:21–23 shows how the folly of human adultery is but one species of the folly of rejecting wisdom.

LIES. In the film *Presumed Innocent*, a successful middle-aged lawyer gets involved with a coworker whose seduction is, in part, accomplished with words. "It's going to be so good," she says, and it seems to be—for a time. Later, when the woman has been murdered and he is charged with the crime, the lawyer comes to his senses. Recounting the details to his lawyer, he remembers how he felt out of control, like a fool: "I used to phone her just to hear her voice and then hang up—like a kid." He is acquitted of the crime only to find out that it was his wife who killed his lover. Like King David, he is released from one penalty only to suffer another.

While most cases of marital unfaithfulness are not as dramatic, the film, like the portrayal of adultery in this chapter, highlights not only the losses that follow this reaching out of bounds, but the lies that come before. It is no accident that the description of the other woman centers on her words, not her beauty, because she represents the lie that sexual pleasure can be enjoyed in ways it was never designed for. The film suggests that the teachers of Proverbs are not alone but rather join their voices with the voice of experience.

To take another example, many people write off blues music because it sometimes brags about extramarital sex, but a great many of the songs lament the pain of betrayal. The Texas bluesman B. K. Turner sounded as though he had taken this chapter for inspiration in his song "No Good Woman." And Robert Cray, in "Strong Persuader," is the masculine seducer who comes to remorse.

The lyrics of these songs remind us that the problem of the "No Good Woman" can just as likely be a problem of a "No Good Man." We would be mistaken to understand the symbolism of the other woman as communicating a negative view of women; no, the other woman personifies the falsehoods that either male or female can speak. While the teachers of Proverbs were probably not the first to observe that adultery takes root in the soil of deception, they take special pains to speak directly to the son (and indirectly to Scripture readers) to make sure that this principle is heard and heeded.

One lesson for the church in this chapter, then, is the charge to reject the lies that swell in our culture and seep into our consciousness by degrees. (1) The first lie is that the power of eros is the reason and basis for the marriage relationship. Taken to the extreme, this view claims that a marriage is only as good as its sexual relationship. If eros is present, the marriage is good; if not, something is wrong. Similarly, the myth of romance that plays out in so many movies celebrates the magic of love that is both irresistible and above any accountability.

(2) The second lie is that self-fulfillment, including sexual fulfillment, is the primary goal of human life, all others secondary in importance. The teachers of Proverbs do not condemn joy and fulfillment, for as we have seen, they celebrate the pleasures of married love. But neither do they force issues of character and faith to bow before that throne.

(3) The third falsehood is that sex can be enjoyed outside of a lifelong relationship. In this view, the sexual relationship is seen as more of an object to be acquired than as a bond between persons. Sexual delight is affirmed by the chapter, but when enjoyed apart from a relationship of faithfulness, it is treated as a thing, separate unto itself, "to be indulged in, played around with, and enjoyed quite separately from a faithful relation of love and responsibility...."[34] While Christians would readily reject the last of these lies, they may still find themselves vulnerable to the first two, just because they are more subtle. Because they are harder to identify, Christians may be tempted to rationalize unfaithfulness, forgetting that the one who looks outside of marriage is deceived, just as the deceiver of Proverbs 5:6 is herself deceived.

Instructions. In place of the lies, the sages offer three instructions to Christians today, each built on the images of drinking in the chapter. (1) They want us to recognize the honeyed lips of invitation for what they are, a deception. The "end" reveals what is real, a crooked path that leads to death. The images of loss, loss of strength, years, wealth, and toil once again urge the contemporary readers to consider the outcomes and consequences of their actions.

(2) The sages tell those of us who are married or will be to "drink from your own well" (5:15), that is, to practice faithfulness with intention and effort. Faithfulness first requires a decision to say no to adultery no matter what the circumstances or possible justifications. Adultery is always wrong; it is never right. Faithfulness also requires the work that it takes to build marriages.

Psychologist John Gottman has become well known for asking the question: Given that so many marriages fail, what is it that contributes to those that are a success? He and his colleagues have watched happy couples interact and created a list of characteristics that build marriages: pleasure, intimacy, admiration with respect, passion, and commitment to a shared view of the future. They also list some destructive characteristics: criticism, contempt,

---

34. Aitken, *Proverbs*, 66.

defensiveness, withdrawal.[35] Their work has fostered a number of educational workshops for couples, many of which are sponsored by local churches. One pair of psychologists I know run weekend sessions to teach the skills of communication that build marriages. They often ask, "Given what we spend so much on so many things in a year, doesn't an investment of time and money in learning to build marriages seem worthwhile?"[36]

(3) "Rejoice in the wife of your youth" (5:18) actually contains two commands. To rejoice is to praise, to encourage, to appreciate, to value the other enough to work at marriage. To rejoice is also to reserve these things for one's spouse alone, the wife (or husband) of one's youth. The accent of the water imagery that follows is on the second person pronoun: *your* cistern, *your* well, *your* springs, *your* streams, *your* fountain. The repetition is not to be taken as a right of possession but rather a call to exclusive partnership.

This call to exclusive relationship is also a call to joy; it is the discipline that brings pleasure. "Love is a virtue. Perhaps love always begins as a feeling, but certainly it must be continued as a virtue if it is to continue indeed. Feelings come and go; virtue is skill and strength that persist, an aspect of character."[37] And it is virtue that keeps feeling alive. Certainly a relationship of commitment brings with it its own joys. Although the word is not used here, one can speak of a marriage covenant, something more than a contract that can be broken.[38]

Spiritual applications. We should not leave this chapter without some word that the warnings against adultery in particular are also warnings against folly in general. Even as we recognize the seductions of the other woman as a challenge to the marriage covenant, we also recognize that the seductions of this world lead us away from faithfulness to God. Just as someone might imagine that it is possible to have a spouse and someone else at the same time, so it is folly to believe that one can be in relationship with God and have our own way, making decisions that undermine that commitment. Sin is both seductive

---

35. J. M. Gottman and L. J. Krokoff, "Marital Interaction and Satisfaction: A Longitudinal View," *Journal of Consulting and Clinical Psychology* 57/1 (1989): 47–52.

36. Karen Kayser observes that couples who view marriage as a lifelong commitment do stay together in greater numbers, in part because of their intention to make it work. She also recommends that couples invest in learning marriage building skills and not wait until there are problems to seek help (*When Love Dies*, 122–26; 140–47).

37. J. W. McClendon Jr., *Ethics: Systematic Theology* (Nashville: Abingdon, 1986), 1:154. Following Jonathan Edwards, McClendon distinguishes grace-love (that loves for the good of the other) and delight-love (that brings good to the lover). Both are at work in this picture of married love.

38. M. L. Stackhouse, *Covenant and Commitments: Faith, Family, and Economic Life* (Louisville: Westminster John Knox, 1997), looks to the biblical covenant to guide discussions on marriage and family issues.

and deceptive. Sin is a folly trying to convince any who would listen that it is possible to reach out and take what is not ours to have. The sages shake us into awareness with the maxim: Take what is not yours; lose all that is yours.

The sages' teaching can also be summed up in a more positive maxim: Guard the heart to live well; live well to guard the heart. Here is a way of saying that good practice shapes good character, which in turn leads to more good practice. One becomes good by doing good. Good persons do good deeds, and good deeds shape good persons. It is the practice of faithfulness that dispels the illusions and self-deceptions of folly.

In the novel *Straight Man*, Hank Deveraux is a man with more problems than any chair of a college English department should have. He's in full-blown mid-life crisis, wondering if it is worth refereeing fights between faculty who take themselves and their careers too seriously and teaching students who don't take anything seriously. He is aware that a number of his colleagues are involved in extramarital affairs, and he realizes that he is tempted also, especially by the attractive young adjunct who has been flirting with him. Hank is also afraid his wife is having an affair, although he has no evidence to back up his imaginations. She has gone out of town for a job interview, and Hank wonders if it has anything to do with the fact that his friend the dean has also gone on a trip. In the middle of a very bad day, Hank slips away to a phone booth in the basement of the English building and calls her.

> "Hank," she says. . . . "It feels like a week." "My thought exactly," I confess, and that's not all I'm thinking. Because it's both wonderful and oddly sad to hear the familiar voice of this woman who shares my life, to feel how much I've missed it. By what magic does she softly say my name and in so doing restore me to myself? More important, why am I so often ungrateful for this gift? Is it because her magic also dispels magic? Is it because her voice, even disembodied as it is now, renders lunatic the fantasies that have been visiting me of late? "Lilly . . . ," I say, allowing my voice to trail off and wondering if, when I say her name, it has for my wife any of these same magical properties.[39]

Human love, claimed the sages, is itself an expression of wisdom, a practice that dispels the deceptions of folly, even the self-deceptions, and in so doing reflects the love that calls us back to our true selves.

---

39. R. Russo, *Straight Man* (New York: Random House, 1997), 196.

Proverbs 6:1–35

¹ MY SON, IF YOU have put up security for your neighbor,
    if you have struck hands in pledge for another,
² if you have been trapped by what you said,
    ensnared by the words of your mouth,
³ then do this, my son, to free yourself,
    since you have fallen into your neighbor's hands:
  Go and humble yourself;
    press your plea with your neighbor!
⁴ Allow no sleep to your eyes,
    no slumber to your eyelids.
⁵ Free yourself, like a gazelle from the hand of the hunter,
    like a bird from the snare of the fowler.

⁶ Go to the ant, you sluggard;
    consider its ways and be wise!
⁷ It has no commander,
    no overseer or ruler,
⁸ yet it stores its provisions in summer
    and gathers its food at harvest.

⁹ How long will you lie there, you sluggard?
    When will you get up from your sleep?
¹⁰ A little sleep, a little slumber,
    a little folding of the hands to rest—
¹¹ and poverty will come on you like a bandit
    and scarcity like an armed man.

¹² A scoundrel and villain,
    who goes about with a corrupt mouth,
¹³   who winks with his eye,
    signals with his feet
    and motions with his fingers,
¹⁴   who plots evil with deceit in his heart—
    he always stirs up dissension.
¹⁵ Therefore disaster will overtake him in an instant;
    he will suddenly be destroyed—without remedy.

¹⁶ There are six things the LORD hates,
    seven that are detestable to him:

17   haughty eyes,
       a lying tongue,
       hands that shed innocent blood,
18   a heart that devises wicked schemes,
       feet that are quick to rush into evil,
19   a false witness who pours out lies
       and a man who stirs up dissension among brothers.

20 My son, keep your father's commands
     and do not forsake your mother's teaching.
21 Bind them upon your heart forever;
     fasten them around your neck.
22 When you walk, they will guide you;
     when you sleep, they will watch over you;
     when you awake, they will speak to you.
23 For these commands are a lamp,
     this teaching is a light,
   and the corrections of discipline
     are the way to life,
24 keeping you from the immoral woman,
     from the smooth tongue of the wayward wife.
25 Do not lust in your heart after her beauty
     or let her captivate you with her eyes,
26 for the prostitute reduces you to a loaf of bread,
     and the adulteress preys upon your very life.
27 Can a man scoop fire into his lap
     without his clothes being burned?
28 Can a man walk on hot coals
     without his feet being scorched?
29 So is he who sleeps with another man's wife;
     no one who touches her will go unpunished.

30 Men do not despise a thief if he steals
     to satisfy his hunger when he is starving.
31 Yet if he is caught, he must pay sevenfold,
     though it costs him all the wealth of his house.
32 But a man who commits adultery lacks judgment;
     whoever does so destroys himself.
33 Blows and disgrace are his lot,
     and his shame will never be wiped away;
34 for jealousy arouses a husband's fury,
     and he will show no mercy when he takes revenge.

³⁵ He will not accept any compensation;
    he will refuse the bribe, however great it is.

THE CHAPTER BRINGS together two instructions, both concerning behaviors and associations that the wise person avoids. The first set of teachings tells how one deals with other men, here described as brothers and neighbors (6:1–19); the second returns to the subject of the strange/other woman (6:20–35).

Avoid the Way of Pledges, Sluggards, and Scoundrels (6:1–19)
    Get free from pledges (6:1–5)
    Go learn from the ant (6:6–11)
    Watch out for the scoundrel (6:12–15)
    Hate the seven things Yahweh hates (6:16–19)

Avoid the Way of Adultery (6:20–35)
    The commands are a guide for life (6:20–24)
    The adulteress preys on your life (6:25–29)
    The husband will show no mercy (6:30–35)

Avoid the Way of Pledges, Sluggards, and Scoundrels (6:1–19)

THE FOUR WARNINGS of 6:1–19 are separate from the instructions on adultery; without this section, that theme would continue uninterrupted in chapters 5–7.[1] Remembering that evil deeds ensnare the wicked (5:22), we might read 6:1–19 as an exposition of that theme. The excursus also reminds the reader that not all enticements to folly come from women. Even so, this first set of teachings seems as out of place as the form in which it is presented.

The instruction begins with the customary "my son," but the typical call to attention is omitted, as are the motivational clauses. Only four sets of imperatives and character descriptions remain (6:1–5, 6–11, 12–15, 16–19); the descriptions use figurative language to create interest and drive the point home. Analogies from the animal kingdom urge the son to learn from gazelles, birds, and ants, while two inventories of human anatomy tell the learner what to avoid. The four sections are related, the first two linking

---

1. Many interpreters have noted the interruption as well as the apparent lack of coherence in 6:1–19. For a summary, see Harris, *Proverbs 1–9: A Study of Inner-Biblical Interpretation*, 112–15.

pledges and laziness, the second two linking the specific example of the scoundrel's behavior with a more general description of wickedness.[2]

The four sections, though distinct, are linked to one another by catchwords. Common throughout are references to body members: heart (6:14, 18), eyes (6:4, 13, 17), hands (6:1, 3, 5, 10, 17, and perhaps 13b), mouth and tongue (6:2, 12, 17), and feet (6:13, 18). An emphasis on speaking, words, and nonverbal communication also links the sections together. The four teachings of the section serve as warnings of dangerous outcomes, each pointing to those examples the son should avoid. Three different men with three different faults are depicted: the speculator who becomes trapped in unwise pledges (6:1–5), the sluggard who becomes prey to poverty (6:6–11), and the scoundrel who stirs up dissension and is destroyed (6:12–15). The words to the speculator and the sluggard are in a second-person imperative, the description of the scoundrel is in the third person. Finally, a list of seven behaviors Yahweh hates extends the portrait of the scoundrel (6:16–19).

Get free from pledges (6:1–5). In verses 1–5, a warning against a potential danger of pledging security presents another instance in which the young man is in danger of losing his livelihood to strangers, for "another" in 6:1 is *zar* (lit., "stranger"; cf. 5:10), masculine of the same root used for the other/strange woman ("adulteress" of 5:3). If the wicked are caught by their own sin (5:22), here one can be caught in a hasty pledge.[3] While we are not certain about the practice in view, most likely the teacher speaks against the guarantee of security for someone else's loan. The teachers of Proverbs took a dim view of such pledging; each mention of the practice in the book (11:15; 17:18; 20:16; 22:26; 27:13) warns against getting involved.

The parallel structure of 6:1 sets taking a pledge for a "neighbor" alongside striking hands for "another." While some interpreters name one as the creditor and the other as the debtor, the parallel structure and use of the same preposition in both couplets indicate that the young man is to steer clear of making pledges for anyone, whether close friend or someone less familiar. Strictly speaking, the admonition is not to avoid such entanglements, although that is implied, but to get out of them as soon as possible. The

---

2. Whybray, *The Composition of the Book of Proverbs*, 51, supports those commentators who find a common theme of folly in 6:1–11 and a theme of wickedness in 6:12–19.

3. In Israel, borrowing and lending was to be done in a spirit of charity, without charging interest (Ex. 22:25; Lev. 25:35–37; Ps. 15:5). Debts were to be canceled if one could not pay (Deut. 15:2), and lenders were not to take a millstone necessary for work or a coat necessary for warmth as security against the debt (Deut. 24:6, 10–13). The Bible includes many reports of creditors who were harsh (2 Kings 4:1; Neh. 5:1–12) and charged exorbitant interest (Ezek. 18:8; 22:12).

command "humble yourself" can also mean "go quickly," and the double sense may be intentional.

The most significant key word in these first five verses is "hand," which in the Hebrew Bible is often a symbol for power. So one strikes hands in pledge (*kap*, 6:1), and thus plays into the neighbor's hand (*kap*, 6:3), but one can get free the way gazelles and birds escape the hand of the hunter (*yad*, twice in 6:5). Striking the hand commits one to a pledge (11:15; 17:18; 22:26), but the one who makes the pledge is ensnared by words, just like the evil man (12:13), the fool (18:7), and one who makes a rash vow (20:25). When I study this passage with church groups, someone always asks why one might guarantee a pledge for a stranger, and the suggestion of some sort of percentage cut is probably correct. Financial speculation can be dangerous, especially when it can lead to the loss of all one has.[4] Therefore, pledges made for a neighbor or a stranger are equally dangerous.

Go learn from the ant (6:6—11). Having just used the analogy of the survival instinct of a bird from a trap (6:5), this second warning concentrates on the ant's foresight and hard work (6:6).[5] Such analogies taken from the animal kingdom were common in the ancient Near East[6]; Solomon taught about plants and animals as a sign of his wisdom and learning (1 Kings 4:33).

The term translated "sluggard" (*ʿaṣel*) occurs fourteen times in Proverbs and nowhere else in the Old Testament. If we look at the appearances of this figure in Proverbs, we learn that the sluggard exemplifies folly (Prov. 19:15; 21:24—26; 26:12—16), particularly in matters of food production. Therefore, the sluggard must look to a lowly creature to learn wisdom, one of the topsy-turvy motifs of wisdom literature.[7] The ant has no ruler, yet it works to provide for itself, gathering and storing. It is self-governed and self-directed, it does not need to be told what it should do; moreover, it does not need to learn, it teaches. To drive home the point on diligence, the LXX adds material about the hard-working bee and its benefits to humans.

Imperative gives way to sarcasm as the teacher asks, "How long will you lie there?" (6:9), and adds a mock quotation, in effect saying, "Oh, you say, 'Just

---

4. Fox, *Proverbs 1—9*, 213—14, cites Sir. 29:14—20: "Give surety for your neighbor (only) in accordance with your ability, and keep yourself from collapse" (cf. Sir. 8:13).

5. The ant appears again in 30:25 as one of four small but wise creatures; the second line recalls 6:8b ("they gather their food in summer").

6. A letter from an Akkadian ruler also argues from the ant's behavior: "Further, when (even) ants are smitten, they do not accept it (passively), but they bite the hand of the man who smites them. How could I hesitate this day when two of my towns are taken?" *ANET*, 486.

7. The motif is not limited to wisdom writings; the Bible often compares the knowledge of animals with the stubborn foolishness of humans (Job 12:7; Isa. 1:3; Jer. 8:7).

a few more minutes and I'll get up,' but I know you." Three "little" things (sleep, slumber, and the folding of hands, 6:10) add up to the big trouble of poverty, the third reminding the reader of the hands foolishly struck in pledge. Hands folded when they should be working are the ultimate sign of sloth.

The metaphors for poverty of 6:11 are difficult to translate; literally, "bandit" is "one who goes about traveling" and the "armed man" is a "man of the shield." Most interpreters extend the meaning of the first to refer to one who goes about like a vagabond (thus the NIV footnote, "like a vagrant") or a roaming bandit. Translation suggestions for the "man of the shield" include the "beggar" (so the NIV footnote, after a Ugaritic cognate) and a "bold or insistent man" (after an Arabic cognate). Whatever the precise referent of the metaphors, their central meaning that the sluggard will be surprised and overtaken by poverty is clear.

The example of the ant's diligence and planning challenges avoidance of one's duties and responsibilities. It urges the young man to prevent being caught in the position of needing a loan and a guarantor. Taken together, the first two teachings resemble our proverb, "Neither a lender nor a borrower be," for efforts to help others are counterproductive if they allow irresponsibility to go unchecked. The teachings also show that laziness is, at its root, a failure of love. While others work to provide for self and family, caring for others, the loafer wants to be carried.[8] In sum, the theme common to the first and second teachings may well be that of laziness, a willful negligence that looks to others to bear the burdens that should be one's own. Just as it is wrong to take what is not one's own, so it is wrong to shirk responsibility for what is.

"Sleep" (6:4, 9–10) and "hand" are the terms that link these first warnings. To the one who would strike hands in a pledge, the teacher says, "Save yourself, free yourself! Do not sleep, or you will become the prey of a hunter." To the one who would fold hands in rest, the teacher says, "Rouse yourself! Do not sleep, or you will become the prey of that robber poverty." In both cases, sleep, a form of negligence, puts one under another's power and risks the danger of losing one's material wealth to others, a theme first introduced in chapter 5.

The two warnings work together to present a lesson on responsibility. The young man is told not to take responsibility for someone else's finances and to make sure that he never needs others to take responsibility for him.[9] Of course, this call to responsibility does not rule out lending to the poor and caring for their needs. Note 19:17: "He who is kind to the poor lends to the

---

8. Hubbard, *Proverbs*, 99.

9. Perhaps this is why Jeremiah could complain, "I have neither lent nor borrowed, yet everyone curses me" (Jer. 15:10).

LORD, and he will reward him for what he has done" (cf. 14:21, 31; 17:5; 22:22–23). But one ought not to borrow for purposes of speculation, and one ought not be a beggar out of laziness.

Watch out for the scoundrel (6:12–15). The next two warnings (6:12–19) have a number of common features that should be read in light of one another. Most striking are the parallels between the physical/moral description of the scoundrel and the list of seven actions that are detestable to Yahweh. Both name the body parts of mouth, eye, feet, hands, and heart, showing how each can be used in ways other than what God intended and wisdom counsels.

Second-person address suddenly shifts to third-person description in 6:12. The "scoundrel" (lit., "man of *beliyyaʿal*"; i.e., worthless man), a recurring figure in Proverbs, uses hatred as a weapon (10:12), scorching speech and gossip to separate close friends (16:27–28), and false witness to mock at justice (19:28).[10] Like the bandit who "goes about" (*mehallek*, 6:11), he "goes about" (*holek*, 6:12) with a corrupt or crooked mouth (cf. 4:24).

Here in this first description, mouth, eye, feet, and fingers are all used to communicate false and damaging messages. For example, the wink (6:13) is malicious in 10:10 and a sign of perversity in 16:30. It is not clear whether these signals are secret and seen only by some, or made openly as an accusation, insult, or even a curse.[11] What is clear is the evil intent with which they are presented. They are outward expressions of internal plotting and deceit (6:14).

"Deceit in his heart" can be translated "perversity of his heart" or "trickery in his heart" (NJB). The word for "perversity" (*tahpukot*) is almost never used outside of Proverbs, where it is typically associated with speech that is crooked or turned upside down (2:12; 8:13; 10:31–32; 16:28, 30). Such speaking literally plows evil and sows discord, the latter a problem that appears again in 6:19. Perverse to the core, this person's deceit overturns what is wise and good.

The disaster that pursues the scoundrel will come suddenly, making its appearance all the more frightening (6:15; cf. 3:25; 29:1b). Yahweh is not named as the judge who brings this destruction. As is typical in Proverbs, the trouble simply comes and leaves this man ruined like a city beyond repair.

Hate the seven things Yahweh hates (6:16–19). Similar in its description of body parts dedicated to evil, this section presents a list of six, no seven, practices Yahweh hates. The numerical saying x, x+1 is not unique to

---

10. Fox, *Proverbs 1–9*, 219, observes that in Judg. 19:22 and 1 Kings 21:10, such men have reputations that precede them.

11. Hubbard, *Proverbs*, 101, views them as "hexes, spells, evil eyes, harmful omens," and other acts of magic or witchcraft (cf. Deut. 18:9–14).

the book of Proverbs (cf. 30:15–31)[12] or even the Bible.[13] Although numerical sayings are found in various ancient cultures, their precise function is not known. It may be that these catalogs and inventories evoked a sense of order that was then ascribed to the order of creation. The numerical pattern not only has the feel of a riddle, it places emphasis on the final statement as a kind of climax.

In this case, the last two items in the list are not body parts at all but persons recognized by their actions: the "false witness" and the "man who stirs up dissension." The false witness suggests a legal setting, perhaps a property dispute,[14] which may also be the source of the dissension between brothers. Thus, the climax to this section brings together the parts into one hideous whole, rephrasing and intensifying the description of the scoundrel in 6:12–15. Evil plotting and scheming of the heart is common to both (6:14, 18). The new twist on this anatomy of evil is that the entire body is not only dedicated to wicked speech and signals but to all forms of arrogance and falsehood, even bloodshed.

The seven items listed are detestable to Yahweh; that is, they are abominations (*to'ebah*) that provoke loathing. In Proverbs, the perverse are an abomination to Yahweh (3:32; 11:20), as wickedness is an abomination to Woman Wisdom (8:7). Other abominations in Proverbs include dishonest scales (11:1; 20:10, 23), lying lips (12:22; 26:25), the sacrifice of the wicked (15:8–9; 21:27), evil thoughts (15:26), the arrogant (16:5), false judges (17:15), and scoffers (24:9). Often named in covenantal contexts, abominations were morally offensive, as in the case of false weights (Deut. 25:16; cf. Prov. 20:10) or perversions of worship (Isa. 1:13; cf. Prov. 21:27).

The descriptions of the scoundrel and the seven things that Yahweh finds abominable remind the reader of the story of Naboth's vineyard in 1 Kings 21. Ahab offered to buy the property, but Naboth refused, and Ahab went home sullen and angry. Jezebel conspired against Naboth, sending letters in Ahab's name. Scoundrels (21:10, 13) were brought in to bear false witness, and as a result, innocent blood was shed. Ahab was remembered as the worst of the evil kings of Israel, who "behaved in the vilest manner by going after idols" (*t'b*, "did abomination," 1 Kings 21:26). He rejected God and God's ways, but still Yahweh sent the prophet Elijah to confront him (21:17–29). Sadly, the king and queen who were charged with protecting justice were caught perverting it.

---

12. Whybray, *Proverbs*, 99–100, points to a similar form in Amos 1:3, 6, 9, 11, 13; 2:1, 4, 6.

13. W. M. W. Roth, *Numerical Sayings in the Old Testament: A Form Critical Study* (VTSup 13; Leiden: Brill, 1965); "The Numerical Sequence x/x+1 in the Old Testament," *VT* 12 (1962): 300–311.

14. Hubbard, *Proverbs*, 102–3, sets all of 6:1–19 in the context of legal entanglements.

In sum, the four teachings of Proverbs 6:1—19 work together to create a portrait of folly in its various forms. The young man here is warned about what he might lose in bad deals and neglect and about wicked men who "go about," scheming to take what is not theirs. Each of the four sections concludes with a negative outcome: The one who pledges is caught in a trap, the sluggard will be ambushed by poverty, the scoundrel will be overtaken by disaster, and the one who stirs up dissension provokes Yahweh's loathing—no more threat need be said. The one who pledges can get out of the trap and the sluggard can get up and learn from the ant, but the scoundrel will be destroyed without remedy (6:15).

There are good indications, then, that the insertion of these four warnings is not haphazard. We have seen that the teachings on pledges and laziness are related by the call to action (no sleep for the eyes or rest for the hands) and the freedom of self-discipline (free from the power of a neighbor's hand and free from the need of an overseer). Likewise, the separate but similar teachings on the wicked person and the actions hated by Yahweh are related by the misuse of body parts for evil and its recompense. Yahweh hates these evils, and those who do them will be destroyed.

Taken together, the teaching of the four warnings may be paraphrased: Do not allow your members to become passive so that you are under another's power, and do not let your members become active for evil so that you imagine you are a power over others. Both extremes ignore the reality of Yahweh's righteous rule. If the first two have a message about earning and protecting one's own substance from loss, the last two warn about those who would take it from others.

The teachings of 6:1—19 also build on the motifs set out at the conclusion of chapter 5. Yahweh looks on the ways of humans (5:21 and 6:16—19); the lack of discipline and folly of 5:23 is illustrated in 6:1—11, and the deeds of the wicked one of 5:22 are outlined in 6:12—19.[15] The insertion of these four warnings also looks ahead to the warnings on adultery, for the first description in 6:20—35 defines adultery as taking another man's wife, a cause of dissension (cf. 6:12—19), while 7:10—27 portrays it as a trap that will catch the unsuspecting (cf. 6:1—11). Just as this section harks back to the preview in 2:16—19,[16] it also looks ahead, alerting the reader to pay attention to these similarities.

---

15. Whybray, *Composition*, 49.

16. Skehan, "The Seven Columns of Wisdom's House in Proverbs 1—9," in *Studies in Israelite Poetry and Wisdom* (CBQMS 1; Washington, D.C.: Catholic Biblical Association, 1971), 9—14, believes that 6:1—19 correspond to the introduction in ch. 2, particularly the mention of wicked men in 2:12—15. While those men also appear in 4:10—27 and possibly 3:29—35, the juxtaposition of evil men and the other/strange woman in ch. 6 is most like that of 2:12—19.

Avoid the Way of Adultery (6:20–35)

THREATS AND WARNINGS continue as the teacher reminds the son that no one who touches another man's wife will go unpunished (6:29; this third teaching on adultery continues into ch. 7; cf. 2:16–19; 5:1–20). The familiar form of the instruction reappears: There is an address and call to attention (6:20–21), followed by motivations (6:22–24). Three metaphors recommend the parents' instruction. The father's commands and mother's teachings are to be tied to the son's heart and around his neck (6:20–21; cf. 3:1–3; 7:1–3).[17] Next, the teachings are likened to a guide who will not only stand guard while the son sleeps but will give direction in the daylight (6:22). Finally, the commands and corrections are likened to a lamp that keeps feet from stumbling in the dark and onto a path to life (6:23; cf. Ps. 119:105).

The need for reminders and protecting guides becomes clear in Proverbs 6:24, namely, to keep the son from the immoral woman and her smooth tongue. The Hebrew text reads "evil woman," so the NIV translates "immoral woman," but the LXX reads the same Hebrew consonants as "the neighbor's woman" (cf. 6:29). The parallel line in 6:24 does not call her the "other woman" (*zarah*) but the "wayward wife" (lit., "stranger," *nokriyyah*). As in prior teachings, the teacher warns the son about her "smooth tongue" (cf. 2:16; 5:3; 7:21) but here adds a description of her beauty, particularly her eyes or seductive glances (6:25; cf. Song 4:9).

Three arguments from analogy then drive home the prohibition of Proverbs 6:25. The parents compare (1) payments due the prostitute and adulteress (6:26), (2) adultery and the fire that burns lap and feet (6:27–29), and (3) the fates of the hungry thief and the adulterer (6:31–32). Three negative outcomes are named, respectively: loss of life, punishment like burning, and the combination of public disgrace and a husband's angry vengeance.

(1) The first analogy comes in the form of a proverb, literally: "for a prostitute, as much as a loaf of bread, but the wife of a man hunts a life" (6:26). The adulteress is not called a prostitute but is compared to one to show that the price of a prostitute is low compared with the price of adultery. The wife of another man preys on human lives (*nepeš*), an image repeated in 7:21–27; yet it is also true that the man who commits adultery destroys himself (lit., "his life," *nepeš*, 6:32). We may be surprised by this casual observation about the price of a prostitute, for the practice was neither condoned nor outlawed

---

17. Murphy, *Proverbs*, 38, sees a reference to the Shema ("Hear O Israel"), Deut. 6:6–9 and 11:18–21, after Maier, *Die Fremde Frau in Proverbien 1–9* (OBO 144; Göttingen: Vandenhoeck und Ruprecht, 1995), 153–58. Murphy goes on to suggest that parental teaching is placed on a level with that of Moses. Their teaching actualizes the commands, moving from matters of moral legislation to moral character.

in Israel. For example, the story of Genesis 38 is more concerned with Judah's wrong against Tamar than with his hiring a prostitute.

(2) Sexual passion is often likened to fire that cannot be quenched, but here the negative side of the comparison is driven home. Fire must be handled with respect and be contained. You cannot hold fire in your hand or touch it without experiencing searing pain; likewise, you cannot touch another's wife without experiencing punishment. Fire contained in a lamp can light a road, but no one wants to have fire in the lap or under the feet. It is debatable whether the lap and feet are euphemistic for sexual organs, but the comparison of remorse with burning pain is clear.

(3) The third comparison is a variation on the first; no one despises the thief who steals because he is hungry (stealing perhaps a loaf of bread? cf. 6:26), but even that crime has its payment. Legislation in ancient Israel decreed that the thief must pay back two to five times what was taken (Ex. 22:1–8). If the thief could not pay, he was to be sold to pay the debt. Seven times seems severe, yet even that price is small compared to the costs of adultery, for it claims a man's life (*nepeš*, cf. 6:26). One who would do such a thing is a fool (lit., "lacking in heart"). This loss of life may or may not involve sudden death (see the death penalty for adultery in Lev. 20:10 and Deut. 22:22), but this fool is certainly on the path to death, marked by blows and social shame (cf. Prov. 5:14). What began in secret eventually will come out into the open.

The text does not specify whether the offense comes before the legal assembly, for the focus turns to the offended husband, who seeks his own vengeance. Jealousy enrages a man's fury, a formidable enemy (cf. 27:4), and here "husband" is a *geber*, the Hebrew word for a warrior. The link with the previous comparisons is the matter of payment. The prostitute takes a loaf of bread, the thief must pay back sevenfold, but the husband will take no compensation. He will decide the terms of the punishment, and they will be severe.[18]

Divine judgment receives no mention here apart from the possible association between seven things Yahweh hates and the sevenfold repayment, but this is not obvious. Again, the negative consequences of reaching out of bounds come more from the way life works than from God's direct intervention. Three comparisons, all painful, once again direct the young man to consider the costs before turning away from his parents' teaching.

---

18. Note that the woman assures the young man that her husband is on a distant journey in 7:19–20. Fear of meeting the wronged husband shows up in ancient Near Eastern texts as well.

AVOIDING RISK. Because the collected warnings of this chapter are as puzzling as they are vivid, we begin by asking right away what is similar and different about these characters and those we might meet today. The person who makes an unwise pledge certainly brings to mind the contemporary practice of cosigning loans for a home or business or even making such loans. While many people may regret having made personal loans that were never repaid, the teachers do not warn against loaning to another but against pledging security for another, as we will hear again throughout the book (11:15; 17:18; 20:16; 22:26; 27:13). The problem was endangering one's household, pledging what one cannot afford to do without.

The principle to be carried over into contemporary life is that one should remain free of entanglements, especially those entered with the idea of quick and easy gain. In this way, gambling all of one's savings on a "sure thing" in the stock market, or even borrowing to go after it, can be just as greedy and foolish. Therefore, because it is both wise and good to "lend . . . without expecting to get anything back" (Luke 6:35), lending freely without thought of gain (Deut. 15:8; Ps. 37:26), we see that the teaching here does not warn against loans and gifts to those in need but against shaky business ventures. The warnings against falling into the power of another speak to our ability to manage our affairs; it should not feed contemporary notions of individualism and self-reliance that show no concern for the community.

Diligence. Just as the sages recommended diligence in avoiding risky business entanglements, so they encouraged diligence in working to earn one's living. However, it would also be a mistake to read the teacher's warnings about poverty as proof that no one who is willing to work will be poor. Hard work pays its rewards for many but not for everyone. Since the mid-twentieth century, those who have documented the experience of the poor have shown that unemployment and the need for assistance are rarely matters of choice; things are never as simple as they seem.[19] One pastor writes:

> All too often, talk about personal responsibility serves subtly or not so subtly to deflect attention from structural injustice. That need

---

19. E. Liebow, *Tally's Corner: A Study of Negro Streetcorner Men* (Boston: Little, Brown & Co., 1967) is the classic study of urban poverty. More recently, B. Ehrenreich, *Nickel and Dimed: On Not Getting by in America* (New York: Metropolitan Books, 2001), documents the author's experience of working at a series of minimum wage jobs.

not follow from an emphasis on spiritual transformation, but in practice it often does. I believe, as I've said, that the gospel is good news for the poor, dramatically changing lives and communities from the bottom up. Yet I want to take issue with the notion that the personal sins and failures of inner-city residents are at the center of inner-city poverty. From 1986 until a few years ago, I lived as a pastor and neighbor in Sandtown (Baltimore). As I reflect on my neighborhood and the struggles for life which people there face every day, I see no way around recognizing racial oppression and economic exclusion as key factors in inner-city dislocation. In fact, I believe they are among the most prominent causes.[20]

Each time we meet the figure of the sluggard in Proverbs, we will hear the teachers warn that laziness will make one poor, but we will never hear them claim that the poor are lazy (cf. 24:30–33). We dare not use this text to point the finger at the unemployed and underclass and forget the opportunities and privileges that many who read this enjoy without much of a thought. Proverbs never allows for an attitude of superiority but rather encourages kindness, mercy, and most of all doing what is right and just and fair (1:3). The lesson to be drawn from the lecture to the sluggard is a warning that we who have means might turn out to be lazy in failing to shoulder responsibilities that are ours to bear.

Greed and falsehood. The sage's passion for justice and fair dealing continues with the description of the scoundrel, the antitype of all that they wish to instill in their young charges. Who is the scoundrel? Anyone who promotes one's own good at the expense of others, thus disturbing the good of the community. We will meet this figure and his practice of stirring up discord again (10:12; 16:27–30). In seeking to find a contemporary analogy for the dissension he causes in our time, we must ask to what use this evil behavior of lies and schemes are put.

The list of things odious to Yahweh in 6:16–19 continues the imagery of body members dedicated to evil, and so this anatomy of wickedness may offer more clues. The list concludes with the specific sin of false witness and a second mention of dissension, this time "among brothers" (6:19). Some interpreters see a verbal connection between these behaviors and the story of Joseph and his family (Gen. 37–50),[21] but the closer parallel is with Isaiah 59:7

---

20. M. R. Gornik, "Practicing Faith in the Inner City," *Books and Culture* 7/3 (May/June 2001): 10–12.

21. Harris, *Proverbs 1–9: A Study of Inner-Biblical Interpretation*, 112–15, looks to the conflict and Judah's taking of a pledge on behalf of Benjamin, but the connection is tenuous.

(common words in italics): *"Their feet rush into sin,* they are swift to *shed innocent blood.* Their *thoughts are evil thoughts,* ruin and destruction mark their ways." We also remember that images of feet and blood appeared in Proverbs 1:10–19 as a warning against violence born of greed.

Therefore, the wicked man is a symbol of wanting and taking what is not one's to have, similar to the figure of the other/strange woman. Like the other woman, his way is both dangerous and seductive; the wicked man is what any of us could become. Although the teachers do not offer their correction to him, suggesting that this man is too far gone to receive correction (cf. 1:24–31; 9:7–8), his way is still a danger to us.

We have seen the devastating effects of taking what belongs to another in the stories of Ahab and Jezebel's theft and murder of Naboth, and of David's adultery with Bathsheba and murder of Uriah. As is true in many cultures, the lives of the monarchs became lessons for the people. While most Christians today may not have the power to do such things as these, we read and tell their stories because we are prone to the same temptations of desire. I once heard the filmmaker Oliver Stone claim that the same identification that sparks our fascination with Shakespeare's kings also draws us to the fall of Richard Nixon. For all their power, leaders are flesh and blood, like ourselves, who must come to terms with desire. Perhaps this is the strategy of the sages in setting these warnings against greed and falsehood in the midst of the warnings about adultery, for they all grow from the same root.

Similarly, Psalm 50 brings these sins together. In the psalm God upbraids the wicked:

> You hate my instruction
>   and cast my words behind you.
> When you see a thief, you join with him;
>   you throw in your lot with adulterers.
> You use your mouth for evil
>   and harness your tongue to deceit.
> You speak continually against your brother
>   and slander your own mother's son. (Ps. 50:17–20; cf. 52:2–4;
>   55:20–23)

It is no accident that such inventories of sin in Scripture correspond to the Ten Commandments. It is striking, therefore, that this chapter of Proverbs reports violations of the last five commandments of murder, adultery, theft, false witness, and coveting (Ex. 20:13–17). The last sums up those that come before; it is covetousness, desire that knows no boundaries, that motivates the other sins against neighbor and God. "You shall not covet your neighbor's house. You shall not covet your neighbor's wife, or his manservant or maid-servant, his ox or donkey, or anything that belongs to your neighbor" (Ex. 20:17).[22] Ezekiel, wrestling with the question of whether the guilt of parents is visited on their children, lists the wrongs of a "violent son" who looks a lot like the wicked man of Proverbs in his coveting and taking (Ezek. 18:11–13):

> He defiles his neighbor's wife.
> He oppresses the poor and needy.
> He commits robbery.
> He does not return what he took in pledge.
> He looks to the idols.
> He does detestable things.
> He lends at usury and takes excessive interest.

Will such a man live? He will not! Because he has done all these detestable things, he will surely be put to death and his blood will be on his own head.

To summarize the discussion so far, we have seen that the follies and evils of chapter 6 are brought together under the covetousness that can motivate sins as diverse as taking another man's wife and scheming to take another man's rightful property or due. Both cause dissension, both damage the well-being of the community.

Positive and negative inventories. But what of the warnings against unwise pledges and short-sighted laziness? By juxtaposing these vignettes with the seductions of extramarital relations, it shows adultery to be both naive and evil. Like the traps and ambushes of laziness, it will catch one unaware (cf. 7:1–27), and like the schemes of wickedness and falsehood, adultery steals, lies, and stirs up dissension (cf. 6:24–35). Moreover, common to all of the warnings of chapter 6 are the payments exacted, so the theme of unnecessary loss continues. In each case, the teachers point out the irony we have observed throughout the instructions: Those that take from others end up having others take from them.

The portrait of the scoundrel and the list of abominations in 6:12–19 also direct the reader to the more positive description of human anatomy in 4:20–27, where perversity and corrupt talk are put away, where eyes look straight ahead and are not haughty (or "lifted," 6:17), and feet walk only on

---

22. In Israel and the ancient Near East, adultery was a crime against the wronged husband, not the wife. See L. Purdue, J. Blenkinsopp, J. J. Collins, C. Meyers, *Families in Ancient Israel* (Louisville: Westminster John Knox, 1997), 183–85.

level and firm paths, far from evil. Most important, the heart is guarded as the wellspring of life (4:23); it is not allowed to plot evil and devise wicked schemes (6:14, 18). The heart is the control center of human thought and action, so it is not surprising that it is central to these positive and negative inventories and mentioned throughout the warnings that come in between (5:12; 6:14). The heart directs the use of the various body parts; thus, we see the predominance of the mouth in chapter 5 and the repeated use of the word "hand" in chapter 6.

Therefore, before we go on to explore the contemporary significance of the teachings, we should note that the character sketches of chapter 6 also relate to the larger teaching strategy of Proverbs. As we have seen, the teachings on security, sluggards, and scoundrels appear throughout the collection of individual sayings.[23] Because these figures appear again and again throughout the book, the reader is signaled to pay special attention to them as reverse images of the virtuous life. We might speak of laziness and wickedness as the passive and active dimensions of sin, and the sages would have us attend to both. Their answer to sloth is diligence, that is, extending the effort it takes to learn wisdom and to live wisely. Their answer to wickedness is righteousness; more than the rejection of evil grasping, righteousness is the desire to do what is right and good for one's neighbor.

Preachers and teachers may wish to use the arrangement of chapters 4–6 to inform their comments, comparing the uses of the body imagery and their warnings against the painful consequences of active and passive sin. More important, teachers and preachers will seek to show that the problems of sloth, villainy, and adultery are not only disastrous to self but stir up trouble for others as well. They are sins against the community and disturb the well-being of all. While self-interest may come first in these warnings, the social pressure of the community is always in view.

Finally, teachers and preachers will show that the ethical appeal of the sages is directed toward Israel's standard of life before its God. It is of interest that the instruction only states that God hates certain behaviors, yet does not speak of his vengeance. Readers are called to shape their hearts in such a way that they begin to hate what God hates and love what God loves. The miscellaneous instructions of this chapter are more than practical advice about loans and laziness, they offer theological insight into Yahweh's desire for a just and harmonious life together.

---

23. For example, the lazy and the wicked are juxtaposed in 10:3–4, 25–26. The scoundrel appears again in 16:27–30. Both chs. 10 and 16 mark the beginning of new sections; see the outline in the introduction.

THE WAY OF RESPONSIBILITY. Although the miscellaneous warnings that comprise this chapter appear out of place and unrelated to their literary context, by taking a closer look, we have seen that the binary opposites that characterize much of Proverbs' teaching appear here as well. The outline presented earlier summed up 6:1–19 as the ways of the sluggard and the scoundrel. We observed that the warnings against pledges and laziness are linked together by images of misused hands and costly sleep, both a form of sloth. Likewise, the two lists of body parts both depict evil that is conceived in the heart and stirs dissension among brothers. If the sluggard does not want to earn his own way, neither does the scoundrel, who wants to take what is his neighbor's.

Standing at the crossroads of choice, the teachers of Proverbs point to the way of diligence and righteousness as an alternative route. In many ways, their work is not much different from the many television judges who hear case after case of conflicts over money, relationships, and responsibility, except that these teachers also urge their charges to remember what God hates and loves.

The teachers of Proverbs see that both pledges and laziness are forms of shirking responsibility for one's self and livelihood. Their message is deceptively simple: Take responsibility for what is yours, and do not take responsibility for what is not. Both use animal images to urge the use of our survival skills; trapped animals struggle to get free and ants model foresight, self-initiative, and industry. In fact, both recommend learning wisdom to be able to see negative outcomes before they arrive.[24] The warning against pledges tells us to avoid bad commitments or to get out of them as soon as possible, while the picture of the sluggard tells us to keep commitments that are good. The knack for learning how to decide which is which is the mark of godly wisdom, for the problem facing many if not most Christians today is not idleness but overcommitment.

Bill Hybels tells the story of a father who was so committed to his work and community that he decided he would sleep in on Sundays instead of taking his young daughter to the Sunday school she loved dearly. Diligent in so many areas of life, he had overcommitted himself and ignored what was important to her. We can understand his way of thinking because many of us feel like busy ants already, scurrying around and carrying heavy loads, or like birds caught in the traps of our schedules, but Hybels calls this kind of busyness "selective sluggardliness."[25]

---

24. Van Leeuwen, "Proverbs," 74, particularly in realizing when one has made a mistake.
25. B. Hybels, *Making Life Work: Putting God's Wisdom into Action* (Downers Grove, Ill.: InterVarsity Press, 1998), 36–38.

We can test our commitments by asking whether they give us excuse to neglect what is most important in life. For some, that most important area may be caring for loved ones, for others it may be the discipline of self-care, getting enough rest, and recreation. The principle of avoiding bad commitments will lead us to take stock of how we have apportioned our time, money, and other resources, so that we can make and keep good ones. The lesson to be learned here is to avoid those responsibilities that are not ours so we can be free for those that are.

The ant is a model of making an appropriate commitment and sticking with it. It is her wisdom that is praised (cf. 30:25; the Heb. word for ant is feminine), for she not only works with great energy, she directs it toward the right goal. The irony of contemporary life is that we are lazy about a great number of things in the midst of frantic activity. For us, good commitments might include the rest and worship of Sabbath-keeping, unhurried time with family and friends to build strong relationships, and schedules planned far enough in advance to ensure that what we do, we do well. Too often I find that I take on too much and then end up doing a half-baked job at my personal and professional commitments. We know we have made bad choices when someone else loses because we have chosen poorly. In sum, while the warnings about pledges and laziness certainly advise diligence in financial matters, they especially warn against all forms of "sluggardliness."

The way of righteousness. Even as the sages recommended diligence as a way of taking care of one's own responsibilities, they looked to righteousness as the way one learns to take care of others. Righteousness, the capacity for just and fair relationships, detours its possessors from the path of the wicked scoundrel. The teachers of Proverbs knew that social life is based on confidence in character and trustworthiness, a desire to do good without its being required.

Thus, we have seen that the enemy of righteousness, typified by the scoundrel and list of abominations, is covetousness, that shadow side of desire that is directed to what a neighbor has. Covetous desires are never satisfied; there is no brim of the cup, no lip to the bottle. Coveting does not know what it means to wait, it lives only in the present. It is not only shortsighted but narrow in scope, for it looks out for one's own, and only one's own. It sets up the individual as the only standard; it only asks what is good for the self, not what is good for the family, community, or in our ever-shrinking global economy, the world. If we are honest, we will acknowledge that we live in a culture that runs on desire the way a rocket uses up its fuel, but we also know that we ourselves struggle to be responsive to those in need. We alternate back and forth between contradictory impulses with the dangers of covetousness always near at hand.

The sages set out these two ways of thinking in stark contrast, but they were not alone. Take time to read Psalms 14 and 15 together at one sitting. Notice that the fool who says there is no God devours others as if they were bread, while the one whose walk is blameless does what is righteous; no slander is on his tongue and does his neighbor no wrong. The scoundrel, like the fool of Psalm 14, is a picture of desire gone amuck with coveting and with lies, bloodshed, and discord following in his wake. The portrait is so startling, we are inclined to avert our eyes from it, but the sages present it twice, insisting the second time that Yahweh hates every last detail.

These ancient teachers were not satisfied to offer practical advice for living well, for they knew that even that could become self-serving. Instead, they held up their portraits of evil at its worst so that their audiences could view it, like Psalm 14, as a mirror image of the righteous persons they might become. If the scoundrel would take what is his neighbor's, we can learn to bless our neighbors in good times and assist them in bad. If this villain uses his body members against others, we can learn to use them for serving, speaking truth, and striving for peace. And if his scheming heart is filled with covetousness, we can learn to fill ours with contentment.

Contentment and commitment. Contentment is that virtue that knows what it means to be satisfied, to say "enough." If covetousness begins with a sense of lack, contentment knows a sense of gratitude. It refuses to believe that life's goals are achieved in an accumulation of things, but rather appreciates that the material goods of this world are to be enjoyed, not hoarded and stockpiled. Too much of contemporary communication would have us become people who consume, not people of character.

In the city where I live, busses did not always have advertisements posted on their sides, but now one for an Internet stock trading site advised, "Maybe you need to get a bigger wallet." I could not help but think of the story Jesus told about the man who would build bigger barns, the man God called a "fool" (Luke 12:20). I also was surprised at the setting of the story: Jesus told it when two brothers came with a dispute over their inheritance. Jesus concluded the parable by warning, "This is how it will be with anyone who stores up things for himself but is not rich toward God" (Luke 12:13–21). We don't need bigger wallets; we need bigger hearts.

Perhaps, then, the temptations of adultery are the test case of these matters of commitment and contentment. As we observed throughout this study, adultery destroys not only the one who practices it but the partners who are wronged. Saying no to its seductions demonstrates the virtues of diligence and righteousness: diligence, because the person who says no is careful to consider costs and maintain commitments; righteousness, because the decision to say no not only respects one's neighbor, it displays a contentment that does not need to look over the fence to see what the neighbor has. The teacher's warnings are fierce, but they should be, for the costs of heading in the wrong direction are high. Here is Bill Hybels again:

> After being a pastor for more than two decades, I have lost count of the number of times I have sat with wayward husbands or wives who have wept in a cathartic, heart-wrenching way that you have to hear to appreciate. Almost every time they have said, "I have wrecked everything because of what I have done. If only I could turn the clock back. If only I could make a different choice."[26]

Wise persons can take the long view, look at the end of the road, and visualize positive and negative outcomes, not only for ourselves but for those around us.

In sum, the various warnings about disaster ask three things of its listeners: (1) to practice self-discipline of our desires with the *diligence* and wisdom of hard working ants; (2) to recognize the *righteousness* of neighbor love, replacing covetousness with contentment; (3) to begin to hate what God hates so that we can love the way God loves. Thus, here the teachers of Proverbs begin with an appeal to self-interest in order to teach us to love God and neighbor as we are prone to love ourselves.

---

26. Ibid., 144.

Proverbs 7:1–27

1 MY SON, KEEP my words
   and store up my commands within you.
2 Keep my commands and you will live;
   guard my teachings as the apple of your eye.
3 Bind them on your fingers;
   write them on the tablet of your heart.
4 Say to wisdom, "You are my sister,"
   and call understanding your kinsman;
5 they will keep you from the adulteress,
   from the wayward wife with her seductive words.

6 At the window of my house
   I looked out through the lattice.
7 I saw among the simple,
   I noticed among the young men,
   a youth who lacked judgment.
8 He was going down the street near her corner,
   walking along in the direction of her house
9 at twilight, as the day was fading,
   as the dark of night set in.

10 Then out came a woman to meet him,
   dressed like a prostitute and with crafty intent.
11 (She is loud and defiant,
   her feet never stay at home;
12 now in the street, now in the squares,
   at every corner she lurks.)
13 She took hold of him and kissed him
   and with a brazen face she said:

14 I have fellowship offerings at home;
   today I fulfilled my vows.
15 So I came out to meet you;
   I looked for you and have found you!
16 I have covered my bed
   with colored linens from Egypt.
17 I have perfumed my bed
   with myrrh, aloes and cinnamon.

¹⁸ Come, let's drink deep of love till morning;
   let's enjoy ourselves with love!
¹⁹ My husband is not at home;
   he has gone on a long journey.
²⁰ He took his purse filled with money
   and will not be home till full moon."

²¹ With persuasive words she led him astray;
   she seduced him with her smooth talk.
²² All at once he followed her
   like an ox going to the slaughter,
 like a deer stepping into a noose
²³   till an arrow pierces his liver,
   like a bird darting into a snare,
   little knowing it will cost him his life.

²⁴ Now then, my sons, listen to me;
   pay attention to what I say.
²⁵ Do not let your heart turn to her ways
   or stray into her paths.
²⁶ Many are the victims she has brought down;
   her slain are a mighty throng.
²⁷ Her house is a highway to the grave,
   leading down to the chambers of death.

Original
Meaning

THE PARENTAL TEACHERS have saved their most vivid images and warnings about the strange/other woman for last. The fourth appearance of this woman is the longest, the most descriptive, and most important, a narrative in which the smooth speech mentioned in every appearance is finally heard (7:14–20; cf. 2:16; 5:3; 6:24). The report of her words recalls terms used in the parents' teaching of 6:20–35. Her smooth tongue and persuasive words (6:24; 7:5, 21) deceive the young man who lacks judgment (6:32; 7:7; he is, lit., "without heart"), convincing him that her husband will not know or retaliate (6:34–35; 7:19–20). Only when it is too late does this young man realize that these words have made him prey and taken his life (6:26; 7:21–23). The fault is his own, for had he heeded his parents' instructions and called to wisdom, he would have been protected (6:20–24; 7:1–5).

The woman's false speech also relates to what follows in a chiastic structure that includes speeches of personified Wisdom and Folly.

A Speech of the adulteress (7:14–20)
  B Speech of Woman Wisdom at the gates (8:4–36)
  B' Speech of Woman Wisdom at her house (9:4–12)
A' Speech of Woman Folly (9:16–17)[1]

This organization brings together the words of adultery and folly as a common foil for the words of Wisdom. Just as every description of the other woman mentions her smooth words and ways that lead to death (2:16–18; 5:3–5; 6:24–26; 7:5, 26–27), so Woman Folly is both deceitful and deadly (9:17–18).[2] So we see that in the context of the instructions of chapters 1–9, the final three chapters present extended speeches of females who call out to men. The overall intent is to convince the young man to choose a lifelong relationship with Wisdom.

Is this a story about an actual event? Like most of the instructions and sayings, the story is the distillation of an event that happens time and time again, often enough to serve as a symbol for the seductive appeal of folly. The motif of the unknown woman appears in the wisdom instructions of Egypt and Mesopotamia:

Beware of a woman who is a stranger,
One not known in her town;
Don't stare at her when she goes by,
Do not know her carnally.
A deep water whose course is unknown,
Such is a woman away from her husband.
"I am pretty," she tells you daily,
When she has no witnesses;
She is ready to ensnare you,
A deadly crime when it is heard.[3]

Therefore, this figure of the strange/other woman presents both a concrete warning about the dangers of adultery and, in its literary context of chapters 1–9, a symbolic inducement to listen to Wisdom instead of Folly. Problems of identification abound, insofar as deceit is associated with a woman and female readers today confront a teaching that seems to be directed to men only (see comments in Bridging Contexts section). For now, note that chapter 7 tells a story of a deception similar to that of the gang of

---

1. G. A. Yee, "'I Have Perfumed My Bed with Myrrh': The Foreign Woman (ʾiššâ zārâ) in Proverbs 1–9," *JSOT* 43 (1989): 53–68.

2. The viewpoint is extended into the individual sayings as well. The speech of the strange woman is a pit (22:14), and the prostitute is a pit that lies in wait (23:27–28).

3. *The Instruction of Any*, in AEL, 2:137. See also Lambert, *Babylonian Wisdom Literature*, 102–3.

bandits in chapter 1. There the teacher quotes the male gang's invitation to walk the way of violence, using words that appear again in this chapter: "come," "lie in wait," "find," and "grave."[4] Just as these men did not know that they would become like birds trapped in a net, so the young man, believing that he is heading for a celebration of sensual delights, finds himself tricked and snared. Walking away from wisdom's path either for violent gain or unlawful delight is a fatal mistake.

The story of the chapter unfolds in a mirror-like fashion:

A 7:1–5 Call to attention—protected from the woman
  B 7:6–9 A simple young man wanders
    C 7:10–20 The woman described and quoted
  B' 7:21–23 A simple young man is slain
A' 7:24–27 Second call to attention—an image of the woman's slain victims

Call to Attention—Protected from the Woman (7:1–5)

THE FIRST CALL to listen (7:1) once again urges the young man to keep and store the words and commands of his parents, using words similar to the previous instruction (cf. 6:20–21). "Keep" is repeated in the first lines of 7:1 and 2, and the parallel lines add "store up" and "guard" to impress the importance of remembering the commands (*miṣwot*) and the teachings (*torot*). Again, the learning of wisdom is the way to live. The whole person—eye, hand, and heart—is to be dedicated to the task (cf. Deut. 6:5–9). The "apple of the eye" (7:2) is the pupil or dark part; the same word used for "dark of night" in 7:9 and "pitch darkness" in 20:20. One Jewish tradition says that it is the place where the whole person is reflected in the eye of another. Israel is the apple of God's eye (Deut. 32:10), as is the psalmist (Ps. 17:9).[5]

Binding on the fingers (7:3; cf. 3:3; 6:21) continues the idea of remembering, just as Israel was commanded to tie the commands to hand and forehead (Deut. 6:8). Writing them on the tablet of the heart reminds readers of the doorframes and gates (Deut. 6:9), but here they are internalized, written on the heart. So also a lover can be set as a seal on the heart (Song 6:8). This keeping and remembering is a way of proving faithful to Wisdom, as faithful as calling her a sister and a kin (perhaps as a spouse; Song 4:9, 10, 12; 5:1–2). Here is another sort of binding; keeping (*šmr*) the teachings, symbolized as a relationship with Wisdom, will keep (*šmr*) the young man from the other woman and her seductive words (Prov. 7:2, 5). Those words are literally

---

4. Yee, "The Foreign Woman," 56.
5. Plaut, *Proverbs*, 99.

smooth or slippery (cf. 2:16; 5:3) and lead astray (7:21). Smooth talk is always dangerous in Proverbs, for it leads one off the path of wisdom and onto the path of death.

A Simple Young Man Wanders (7:6–9)

WE CANNOT SAY for certain who the speaker of chapter 7 is, for the text does not tell us. It may be the father, but it could be the mother. Warnings against spending strength on women come from King Lemuel's mother, as does praise of a good woman (31:2–3, 10–31). The woman at the window is a narrative type scene in the Bible (Sisera's mother, Judg. 5:28; Michal, 2 Sam. 6:16; Jezebel, 2 Kings 9:30–33) and in ancient iconography.[6] Some interpreters believe that the speaker may be a female because the teaching itself would help women who had much to gain from monogamous relationships with males and much to lose if the males were promiscuous.[7] However, it must be remembered that while the speaker *may* be female, we cannot be certain; the arguments cannot prove what the text places beyond our grasp. Moreover, the viewer at the window is not always female; Abimelech also looked out the window at Isaac and Rebekah (Gen. 26:8). What is clear from reading the other biblical pictures of the viewer at the window is a foreshadowing that trouble is on its way.

Watching those who are passing by, the speaker notes that among the "simple" and "young men" (lit., "sons") is one who "lacked judgment," most likely the teacher's preview of the way the story will unfold. This particular young man is "lacking heart," a problem worse than simple naiveté, for the teacher has used this expression to describe the one who commits adultery and destroys himself (6:32). Woman Wisdom will use the term in her invitation (9:4), as will Woman Folly (9:16). Later in Proverbs, it describes a man of bad speech, one who makes rash pledges, and a sluggard (10:13; 11:12; 12:11; 17:18; 24:30; cf. 6:1–19). To "lack heart" is to do the opposite of what parents and Wisdom teach; it is no innocent ignorance.

The teacher also observes the direction of the young man's wanderings and the time of day. He is walking in the direction of the woman's house, although

---

6. O. Keel and C. Uehlinger, *Gods, Goddesses, and Images of God in Ancient Israel*, trans. T. Trapp (Minneapolis: Fortress, 1998), 210. An ivory plaque from Samaria has a picture of a woman in a series of frames that appears to be a woman looking out a window, but the authors add that it is not clear if it depicts a goddess, a cult prostitute, or someone else.

7. For a summary of the position, see A. Ogden Bellis, "The Gender and Motives of the Wisdom Teacher in Proverbs 7," in *Wisdom and Psalms: The Feminist Companion to the Bible, Second Series*, ed. A. Brenner and C. R. Fontaine, (Sheffield: Sheffield Academic Press, 1998), 84–86.

we cannot determine whether it is in hope of finding her.[8] We are more concerned that it is twilight, just as the dark of night is falling, the same dark as the apple of the eye in 7:2 (*ʾîšôn*). The repetition signals the wrong choice. There may be another play on words with Hebrew *yôšan*, sleep: "Instead of being out in the black night, the young man should have been in bed."[9]

The Woman Described and Quoted (7:10–20)

THE HEBREW TEXT uses *hinneh* (7:10; lit., "look now!") to create a "you are there" experience and signal the sudden appearance of a woman, heading in his direction to meet him. Before we hear her, we see her. She is "dressed like a prostitute," perhaps a reference to the veil that Tamar used to pose as a prostitute (Gen. 38:14–15), though the word for the veil is not used. No cultic references are implicit in the term "prostitute" (*zonah*); it applies to anyone who engages in promiscuous behavior and endures social shame.[10] Perhaps the description is also a reminder that a prostitute is not as dangerous as an adulteress (Prov. 7:26). In any case, her attire signals her intent.

Along with the outward description comes a revelation of character. Her "crafty intent" is literally a kept or guarded heart; ironically, the same expression is used positively throughout the instructions for guarding the teachings for the protection they provide (3:1, 21; 4:6, 13, 23; 5:2; 6:20). Here the idiom betrays her secretive demeanor that conceals thoughts and attentions.[11]

However secretive she may be, she is anything but quiet. Like Woman Folly she is noisy (7:11; cf. 9:13). In Proverbs, a wise person practices restraint, often silent but when appropriate, what comes out of the mouth is honest and straight. This woman is just the opposite, duplicitous and loud. She is "defiant" or rebellious; her feet never stay at home (do they rush to evil like those of 6:18?). Instead of staying home, she takes to the streets and squares, ironically the same places Wisdom offered her teaching (1:20). We will see that where Wisdom goes, folly is never far away (9:3, 14).

Unlike Wisdom, however, this woman makes no public invitation but rather lurks at the corner in the dark, near the street where the young man wanders (7:8). Suddenly the scene takes on the character of a hunt (cf. the

---

8. The apocryphal Sir. 9:7 includes in its warnings about prostitution and adultery, "Do not look around in the streets of a city, or wander about in its deserted sections."

9. Plaut, *Proverbs*, 101.

10. P. Bird, "'To Play the Harlot': An Inquiry into an Old Testament Metaphor," in *Gender and Difference in Ancient Israel*, ed. P. L. Day (Minneapolis: Fortress, 1989), 75–94. Texts like Hosea use the metaphor to name Israel as the despised *zonah*.

11. Clifford, *Proverbs*, 83, observes a wordplay on the prostitute's clothing, so that "the woman may cover her breast (= heart) with a shawl while at the same time covering her heart (= mind, intent)."

wicked men in 1:11). Like a hunting animal, she grabs the unsuspecting youth and kisses him. Her brazen face is literally made strong and hard, a sign of stubborn defiance of social custom.[12] So Jeremiah told Israel, "You have the brazen look of a prostitute; you refuse to blush with shame" (Jer. 3:3; nearly half of the chapters in Jeremiah use the word for shame).[13]

The woman finally speaks words that should bring her to shame.[14] She says she has been busy making preparations at home. Three enticements follow: the sacrifices at home offer the delicacy of meat to eat (7:14), the bed at home offers the pleasures of love (7:16–17), and the husband *not* at home promises a sense of security (7:19–20). Having touched his lips with a kiss, all her other seductions come from her words. She is able to appeal to all his senses and make it sound as if her home is a place of paradise. What the young man does not know is that these words are the bait of a trap. The contrast between her many words and his silence is telling.

(1) The first enticement claims that a lavish meal of a freshly slaughtered offering is waiting at her house. "Fellowship offerings" (sometimes called peace or *šalom* offerings) were of three kinds: thanks or declaration, votive, and free will (Lev. 3:1–17; 7:12–16). Offerings made of one's freewill or in fulfillment of a vow were to be eaten on the day of the sacrifice, with any leftovers eaten the next day. The blood sacrifice allowed the worshiper to draw near to God,[15] and the supply of meat provided an opportunity for communal sharing and celebration.

Apart from the invitation to join her in feasting, it is not clear why these are her first words. Some have suggested other motivations behind the sacrifice. One theory suggests that the woman resorts to prostitution to get the money for payment of a vow, but sufficient evidence is lacking. Equally unlikely is the older proposal that the woman belongs to a foreign cult and pledges the goddess of love that she will find someone to join her in lovemaking.[16] The simplest explanation is that she wants the young man to join

---

12. Garrett, *Proverbs*, 106, and D. A. Garrett, "Votive Prostitution Again: A Comparison of Proverbs 7:13–14 and 21:28–29," *JBL* (1990): 681–82. In both instances, the brazen face indicates a "bold faced lie."

13. B. A. Musk, "Honour and Shame," *Evangelical Review of Theology* 20 (1996): 164.

14. R. Alter, *The Art of Biblical Poetry* (New York: Basic Books, 1985), 57. Alter suggests that in this narrative (rare among biblical poetic texts), reported speech reveals character as it does in prose texts.

15. N. Kiuchi, "Spirituality in Offering a Peace Offering," *TynBul* 50 (1999): 23–31.

16. K. Van Der Toorn, "Female Prostitution in Payment of Vows in Ancient Israel," *JBL* 108 (1989): 193–205; G. Boström, *Proverbia Studien: Die Weisheit und das fremde Weib in Spr. 1–9* (Lund: Gleerup, 1935), 120–34. Boström's association with the goddess Astarte has been revived by J. B. Burns, "Proverbs 7:6–27: Vignettes from the Cycle of Astarte and Adonis," *SJOT* 9 (1995): 20–36.

her in a feast because she has just presented a sacrifice; the irony, of course, is that he is the next victim.[17]

A discerning youth might ask why she is making this communal offering alone, without husband and without neighbors, and so readers conclude that this young man may understand the sexual overtones of her invitation but not the consequences. She would have the young man believe she is acting alone, but chapters 5 and 6 remind us that the community and her man are never far away—they will come around, and the shame and blows will be real.

(2) She promises not only a feast but the pleasures of a bed made delightful to the eyes and perfumed with sweet-smelling spices. Both the linens and spices are costly items, suggesting that her husband has provided well for her, but she has not purchased them for him.[18] Myrrh, aloes, and cinnamon are included in the garden of fragrances used to describe the woman of Song of Songs 4:14. Myrrh and aloes perfume the king's robe at his wedding in Psalm 45:8, and myrrh and cinnamon were used in sacred anointing oil (Ex. 30:23; 25:6).

Having spoken of the preparations she has made by herself, she goes on to describe the pleasures that await the two of them. Using the only first person plural in the speech, she says, "Let's drink deep of love till morning; let's enjoy ourselves with love" (7:18). Drinking reminds the reader of the water metaphors of chapter 5 and the streams that spill out into the streets where the two of them now stand, a contrast to the "satisfaction" of a wife (5:19; cf. Ps. 36:8). "Till morning" is meant to be a sign of the delights they will enjoy throughout the night, but it also suggests that it will only be that long. It is an impoverished definition of love—sensual pleasure without emotional attachment and commitment.

(3) The woman reports that her husband has gone away for a long time, probably to assure the young man that they will not be caught. While this may direct the reader back to the husband's fury in 6:33–34, readers already know that she is the real danger; she stalks one's very life (6:26). The sense of distance has already been suggested with the linens from the south and spices from the east. "We get an image of the cuckolded husband, a man of

---

17. T. W. Carledge, *Vows in the Hebrew Bible and the Ancient Near East* (Sheffield: JSOT Press, 1993), 55, 140. Clifford, *Proverbs*, 88–89, draws an interesting parallel with Judg. 11:30–31. The common vocabulary of "vow," "come out," and "meet," suggests that the young man, like Jepthah's daughter, will become a sacrifice that fulfills a vow, but this connection is tenuous.

18. However, linens and spices on a bed can also signify death and burial (2 Chron. 16:14; Matt. 27:59; Mark 15:46; Luke 23:53; John 11:44b; 19:40; 20:7). See R. H. O'Connell, "Proverbs VII 6–17: A Case of Fatal Deception in a 'Woman and the Window' Type-Scene," *VT* 41 (1991): 235–41.

affairs traveling to distant parts to accumulate the wealth his wife lavishes on imported linens and scents."[19]

The woman does not even call him "husband" or "my man." He is literally "the man, not in his house." The use of the keyword "house" (7:6, 8, 11, 19, 20, 27) suggests that the trouble comes because no one is at home where each should be. The young man is out walking, she does not stay at her house, and the husband is not at his home but away, taking care of business.

A Simple Young Man Is Slain (7:21–23)

"WITH PERSUASIVE WORDS she led him astray" (7:21). The persuasive words are literally "much teaching," making a play on the Hebrew root *lqh*, which can mean "take" or "receive teaching," that is, to learn (4:2; 9:9). The same root is used in 6:25: "Do not lust in your heart after her beauty or let her *captivate* [take] you with her eyes."[20] The persuasive words lead the young man astray to his death, which the narrator likens to animal slaughter.

The teacher's comparison shows that these domestic and wild animals (ox, deer, bird) alike do not know the fate that will befall them because they cannot recognize the danger. So also Jeremiah complained, "I had been like a gentle lamb led to the slaughter; I did not realize that they had plotted against me" (Jer. 11:19). All three animals make a death march, not knowing they will step toward their deaths.[21] In the same way goes the young man, just like a dumb beast, for he has allowed empty words to deceive and "take" him.

Second Call to Attention—An Image of the Woman's Slain Victims (7:24–27)

THIS SECOND CALL to attention is directed at "my sons," the plural probably directed to the larger readership, particularly since this is the last of the parents' formal instructions. After this, Wisdom will become the primary speaker. Coming at the heels of the woman's smooth talk, one can hear an emphasis in the words, "Listen to *me* ... pay attention to what *I* say" (7:24).

The teacher again directs his teaching at the "heart," the seat of intentions, warning that it should not turn or stray to the other woman's paths. If the heart stays fixed on the right path, the feet will follow. Repeating the bloody images of the previous section, the teacher adds that the young man is not

---

19. Alter, *Art of Biblical Poetry*, 59.

20. The word appears a third time when she says that her husband has "taken" a bag of money (7:20), even as his wife "takes" the young man with her "teaching."

21. The NIV footnote follows the versions in reconstructing the Heb. to read, "like a fool to the stocks for punishment" (TNK).

a single casualty, for *"many* are her victims," and those killed are a "mighty throng," mixing military and hunting metaphors. Assyrian kings had their exploits in hunting depicted on stone reliefs to prove their strength and courage in battle.

Because the narrator's description of this seduction is typical of many like it, we take it not so much of a sign of one woman's conquests but as deceptions that have brought down many a man. Certainly the final image the parental teachers wish to leave in their son's mind is that of the highway to *šᵉ'ol* ("grave"), again mixing metaphors to liken her house to that way. It was the house and its awaiting pleasures that seemed so alluring, yet it became a home of the dead (an image that reappears in chs. 8 and 9).

To summarize, this narrative poem introduces the adulteress as a speaking character (preparing the way for Woman Folly in ch. 9 and contrasting with Wisdom in chs. 8 and 9), bringing together metaphors of house, way, darkness, and most important, the trap. In chapter 1, the net that catches birds works because the men do not recognize it; the same idea is repeated here. In chapter 1 the young man is told to observe the fate of the violent men who entice with promises but are caught like birds in their own trap; here, the victim is also seduced with promises. But this time, the fate falls on him, not the seducer! Moreover, as in chapter 1, Wisdom's voice follows with words of truth. Finally, a house can become a way of darkness, for deception can be practiced there, and seductions can conceal knowledge. But the learner/reader must be prepared for such deception and should be able to recognize traps in words that sound too good to be true.

THE TEACHER'S FINAL lecture presents a worst-case scenario of folly to the young man. Having heard of other/strange woman, he now hears and sees her. If, like the simpleton of the story, he succumbs to her deceptive charms, he will have failed this course of wisdom. The genius of this narrative metaphor lies in using a particular case of folly (adultery) to teach lessons about wisdom in general. Readers are led to make this move from particular case to general truth as the teacher points to that lifelong relationship: "Say to wisdom, 'You are my sister'" (7:4).

Understanding the feminine symbolism. The task for the contemporary reader is to follow the direction of the symbolism, discerning how its timeless truths apply to particular situations today. The question is not whether the lectures on adultery are symbolic, but how and of what. An appreciation for both original and contemporary contexts requires that we combine reading the Bible as canon (received theological document) with retelling the

Scriptures as an imaginative work (literary art), putting hands, feet, flesh, and bones of real people to the text. The interpreter's task is to reimagine the text through study of the lives of people in the pews.[22]

Again the issue is not whether the narrative poem is symbolic but of what. Those who study the ancient social context find correspondence with the return from exile reported in Ezra and Nehemiah. So, for example, some see the strange woman as a symbol for marriage with foreign women, whose alien worship brought a threat to land ownership.[23] Others extend the symbol of the other/strange woman to include all that Israel's sages and priests find abhorrent—ritual defilement from mixing sacrifice, sex (Lev. 7:19–20), and idolatry.[24]

However, one reading that stays close to the literary context of Proverbs argues that the case at issue is "adultery or sexual intercourse with unfamiliar women, which are challenges to family integrity."[25] Adultery in this context threatens social status and property because the injured husband may go to court (6:34–35) or seek financial compensation (5:9–10). Because there is no clue to the reader that the seduction scene is an allegory for sociopolitical events,[26] we take the other/strange woman to mean "not one's own" and adultery as the taking of a sex partner who is not one's own as well.

A more prevalent view understands the strange/other woman to be symbolic of the folly of evil in all its seductive power. For this reason, it is here in this chapter more than any other that we should consider the wealth of scholarship produced by women concerned with the portrayal of the feminine (or positive and negative portraits of feminine figures) in the discourses of Proverbs 1–9. We should listen carefully when writers like Gail Yee tell us that the reader's identification with the concerns of a young male is more difficult and complicated for women, as is the use of a female figure as an

---

22. N. S. Murrell, "Hermeneutics as Interpretation Part 2: Contextual Truths in Sub-Version Preaching," *Caribbean Journal of Evangelical Theology* 3 (1999): 53–57.

23. Blenkinsopp, "The Social Context of the 'Outsider Woman' in Proverbs 1–9," 457–73; H. C. Washington, "The Strange Woman (ʾissa zara/nokriya) of Proverbs 1–9 and Post-Exilic Judaean Society," in *Second Temple Studies 2: Temple and Community in the Persian Period*, ed. T. C. Eskenazi and K. H. Richards (Sheffield: JSOT Press, 1994), 217–42. The translators of the LXX took the other/strange woman as a symbol of foreign wisdom, particularly Greek philosophy; see J. Cook, "ʾishah zarah (Proverbs 1–9 Septuagint): A Metaphor for Foreign Wisdom?" *ZAW* 106 (1994): 458–76.

24. See, e.g., C. V. Camp, "What's So Strange About the Strange Woman?" in *The Bible and the Politics of Exegesis*, ed. D. Jobling et. al. (Cleveland: Pilgrim, 1991), 17–31.

25. C. Maier, "Conflicting Attractions: Parental Wisdom and the 'Strange Woman' in Proverbs 1–9," in *Wisdom and Psalms: A Feminist Companion to the Bible (Second Series)*, ed. A. Brenner and C. R. Fontaine (Sheffield: Sheffield Academic Press, 1998), 102.

26. An example of a clearly identified allegory is the parable of the trees in Judg. 9:7–21.

embodiment of evil.[27] Women in the study groups I lead say the same. They have heard women unfairly blamed for cases of adultery and are sensitive to how literary symbols can be misused. They also ask how women are to respond to feminine portraits, both negative and positive, that speak primarily in terms that appeal to the interests of men?[28] How can they be understood so as to prevent the possibility of their being misunderstood?

(1) Interpreters must reflect carefully on the nature of a literary symbol. Carol Newsom rightly points out that the practical advice about avoiding adultery and the symbolic reference to wisdom are never separated; they are never simply one or the other. They are metaphoric extensions of concrete descriptions, metaphors that are socially constructed. The difference between the depictions of adultery in the film *Fatal Attraction* and in Proverbs 1–9 is that the latter claims that these conflicts are ultimately about whose words we choose to believe and the choice of Folly over Wisdom. However, the depiction in Proverbs does not challenge the fact that its discourse was most likely written by males for males and that this text makes the strange woman marginal and dangerous.[29]

For this reason some hope to recover a woman teacher in Proverbs 7, while others deconstruct what seems to be an overly simple portrayal of an innocent man and a wicked woman.[30] We have seen, however, that the text does not name the teacher, so we can surmise but not prove that the speaker is female. We have also seen that the young man is held responsible for his actions and that the contrast between the saintly figure of Wisdom and sinner Folly makes no claim to speak about the nature of the sexes. Both men and women can be seduced by evil or become instruments of seduction, as the invitation of the men of violence shows (cf. 1:10–19). In our preaching and teaching on this text, we must show that there is no innocent party to adultery, male or female, just as there is no innocent folly in Proverbs.

---

27. Yee, "The Foreign Woman," 53–68. C. L. Seow, "Dangerous Seductress or Elusive Lover? The Woman of Ecclesiastes 7," in *Women, Gender, and Christian Community*, ed. J. D. Douglass and J. F. Kay (Louisville: Westminster John Knox, 1997), 23–33. Seow adds to the list of seductresses the woman who is a snare in Eccl. 7:25–29.

28. J. Cheryl Exum suggests that we always ask the question of a text, "Whose interests are being served?" J. C. Exum, "Feminist Criticism: Whose Interests Are Being Served?" in *Judges and Method: New Approaches in Biblical Studies*, ed. G. A. Yee (Minneapolis: Fortress Press), 65–90.

29. C. A. Newsom, "Woman and the Discourse of Patriarchal Wisdom: A Study of Proverbs 1–9," in *Gender and Difference in Ancient Israel*, ed. P. L. Day (Minneapolis: Fortress, 1989), 142–60.

30. A. Brenner "Proverbs 1–9: an F Voice?" and F. van Dijk-Hemmes, "Traces of Women's Texts in the Hebrew Bible," in *On Gendering Texts: Female and Male Voices in the Hebrew Bible*, ed. A. Brenner and F. Van Dijk-Hemmes (Leiden: Brill, 1993), 113–30.

(2) We must translate the imagery in ways that are faithful to both the original context and our contemporary experience. Much contemporary scholarship places its emphasis on male control of female sexuality, claiming that the narrative represents a masculine fear of women who refuse to yield control of their lives. In response, Alice Ogden Bellis points out that the direct teaching of the text speaks to the need for control, or better self-control, of *male* sexual behavior, for there are many more stories in the Hebrew Bible of men raping women than there are of women seducing men.[31] Women readers, then, are called to identify with the concerns of the parental teachers for their son's pursuit of wisdom and his rejection of invitations to evil. Although it requires the work of translation, it is possible to reverse roles and cast seduction in a male voice, as Bellis did in a letter to her daughters:

> You know that I love you more than anything else in the world. I want you to be happy, but as you know, life is tough, life is real. It takes more than being an excellent student, world-class athlete or prizewinning dancer or musician to lead a happy life. These things are important and you are on your way to achieving some of these goals, but it takes more to be happy. And so I ask you to try to discover what is true and just and wise....
>
> Make truth your lover, justice your muse. Truth will stand by you if you lose your friends or your job because you refused to do something unethical. Justice will encircle you with warmth more real than a fire when people shun you for standing up for the dignity and worth of every person regardless of their personal characteristics, or when you blow the whistle on wrongdoing....
>
> Truth and justice are elusive. They present themselves to those who seek them persistently and seriously. They hide from everyone else. Do not be misled by handsome faces, by beautiful bodies, by the right clothes, or by correct manners. Especially do not be deluded by flatterers who tell you that you are beautiful (of course you are!) and then ask you to give them your body or your soul. The pretty boys and jocks will beckon to you. They will ask you to go out. Soon, they will ask you to bed. It's a dangerous world. Their ways lead to death, not just moral death, but physical death as well. Drugs and alcohol and cigarettes are some of the ways of those who want to show off, but inside are little boys. They want easy sex with no responsibility. Do not cavort with folly. Do not consort with the frivolous. Rather spend

---

31. Bellis, "Gender and Motives," 79–91. Bellis reminds readers that this concern for sexual freedom in particular and women's freedom in general is both Western and contemporary; it was most likely not part of the cultural understanding of the original audience.

your time with men of substance and worth. A good man is hard to find, but he is more precious than jewels.[32]

Bellis has listened carefully to the literary symbolism, and that work has guided her in creating this contemporary paraphrase. We who teach and preach need to do the same, attending the symbols of relationship. With a careful and subtle use of irony, the descriptions of marital faithfulness and adultery use a common vocabulary to show that the same actions can build or destroy intimacy. Thus, the young man is to embrace Wisdom (4:8), not the strange woman (5:20). The other/strange woman will take hold of him (7:13), but he should take hold of Wisdom (3:18; 4:13).

(3) We should also remember that the words of this adulteress are seductive because they are, to a large measure, true to human experience. Spouses can leave their mates alone more than they should, and the immediate pleasures of strange beds are real. There is a sense in which both Wisdom and Folly speak to lived experience,[33] even while the purposes to which their words are directed are broader concerns for one's life direction.

In seeking to build a bridge between this ancient symbolism of adultery and our own understanding of what happens in an extramarital affair, we might think of levels of otherness or outsideness. The other/strange woman in Proverbs may have been created to represent someone outside of the national or tribal family, and she is certainly outside the marital family unit. But perhaps most important, she stands outside the value system taught in the book of Proverbs. The symbolism of evil in the strange/other woman should be understood in terms of evil behavior (speech and deed), just as it is for the gang of wicked men. Evil behavior should not be identified with gender, for neither has a corner on initiating marital unfaithfulness.

Preventing misunderstanding. Because the point of the narrative is the danger of adultery in particular and folly in general, preachers and teachers should take two corrective steps to prevent misunderstanding. (1) They should make clear that the woman's behavior in this chapter is a symbol of sinful folly, reminding their hearers that the narrative makes no negative comments about women or female sexuality. It is one thing to be aware of the overwhelming power of one's sexuality, it is another to blame it on someone else.[34] Because there is a long history of ascribing temptation and even

---

32. Ibid., 90–91.

33. C. Camp, "Wise and Strange: An Interpretation of the Female Imagery in Proverbs in Light of Trickster Mythology," in *A Feminist Companion to Wisdom Literature*, ed. A. Brenner (Sheffield: Sheffield Academic Press, 1995), 150; originally published in *Semeia* 42 (1988): 14–26.

34. For this reason, teachers of past generations, such as Richard Rolle, also warned young Christians to steer clear of women: "For nothing so harms a novice, nor is there any

evil to women (often making misguided reference to Eve's offer of the forbidden fruit), we must be counteractive in teaching a biblical view.

(2) Preachers and teachers should remember to talk about the temptations of adultery and folly in terms that can apply to both sexes, choosing general terms or balancing the use of images and examples between those that speak to females and those that speak to males.

The best approach we can take will recognize the symbolism of folly in this portrait of a predatory sexual encounter, and like the teachers of Proverbs, name it and face it. It is a mistake to allegorize the story so it becomes just a statement about folly and does not speak to the issue of sexuality out of control. At the same time, it is a mistake to so focus on the sin of adultery as to miss the larger point about the folly of sin. Certainly speaking to the matter of marital infidelity is in line with the teacher's strategy, and today's teachers and preachers should also address the confused thinking about sex that permeates our general culture and perhaps even our churches. We teach to counteract those confusions and clarify that our misunderstandings about sex can take the forms of idolatry and seduction.

Sex in contemporary society. Thus, we must find ways to talk about the goodness of sex *and* the essential goodness of boundaries in a culture that makes too much of sex and too little of boundaries. It is even appropriate to suggest that our culture has made sex into an idol. We have not only worshiped it with our attention and dollars, we expect it to serve and fulfill our most basic physical and emotional needs for esteem and intimacy. Yet ironically, such a view of sex trivializes it because it isolates it from the essential dimensions of commitment and transparency that mark honest and committed relationships.

Sex is both *less* than we think and, at the same time, *more* than we think.[35] Our culture overstates its capacity to make our lives complete and so understates its true purpose, to bond humans together in joyful and mutual commitment. If we listen to the woman's speech and hold the immediate experience of passion higher than commitment (7:18), we will most likely hear echoes of what many today think and feel. Of course our culture believes such things, but are we who name the name of Christ doing any better? Might one factor behind the prevalence of affairs and divorce in the church be that the we have bought into the myth as well?

---

thing that so quickly draws the one sitting in prayer away from the heavenly symphony ... like the pleasing beauty of a beautiful woman." Quoted in A. W. Astell, *The Song of Songs in the Middle Ages* (Ithaca, N.Y.: Cornell Univ. Press, 1990), 113.

35. G. Spencer, *A Heart for Truth: Taking Your Faith to College* (Grand Rapids: Baker, 1992), 115–33.

Some interpreters have suggested that the woman's invitation makes a parody of the relationship between lovers in the Song of Songs, a poem that depicts a woman who goes out at night to find her lover (Song 3:1–4) and whose friends bless them with "drink your fill, O lovers" (5:1). Both Scriptures use the motifs of ancient love poetry, Song of Songs extolling a love that is exclusive and respectful.[36] The descriptions of physical beauty and the delights of physical embrace praise the loved one; they do not leer. Moreover, the man and woman both speak to one another in turn, their praises and words of longing a sign of a relationship between equals that they intend to last forever. By contrast, in Proverbs only the woman speaks, she does not praise the young man (although there is some flattery involved in "I sought you"), but instead praises the experience of sex. Could it be that our culture lives by an understanding of sexual expression more like the woman's seduction than the lover's invitations?

It may be that while Christians reject the sin of adultery, we embrace the view of sexual experience that motivates the woman's enticement to adultery. The mistake comes in elevating that experience above all the other aspects of marriage, making it the test of the marriage. In sum, the text speaks directly about the dangers of adultery in terms of a culture in which adultery was defined as taking another man's wife. But it may also reveal attitudes toward sex in general that are very much like our own and equally dangerous. Moreover, when this exaggerated view of sex is isolated from relationship, when it does not matter who the partner is, when it ignores boundaries, sexual expression can backfire in dangerous ways.

Yet, as we have seen, the story of this not-so-secret case of adultery also points beyond itself to the larger error of choosing the wrong partner, a woman who looks and sounds a lot like Folly instead of Wisdom. Instead of speaking to Wisdom words of intimate relationship (7:4), the simple young man lets the woman and the folly of her proposal speak to him (7:5). There is a sense in which adultery as a particular case of the folly of sin also illustrates the seductions of sin. Just as the sin of idolatry sets anything related to self, its wants, and its desires in place of God, so sin, the seducer, believes lies and tells lies in its effort to get what it wants. Thus, the woman's invitation, a trap concealed and baited, is not much different from the gang's invitation to easy gain. Both lead astray to "other" paths (1:15; 7:25), and both are deadly.

We have seen that Proverbs begins with an invitation to violent crime that most readers would find easy to reject, only to be surprised that the invita-

36. Clifford, *Proverbs*, 86–87, after D. Grossberg, "Two Kinds of Sexual Relationships in the Hebrew Bible," *HS* 35 (1994): 7–25.

tion is an extreme case of the seductions of greed and covetousness to which all are prone (cf. the comments on ch. 1). Likewise, not many may be approached by an aggressive wife (I know of only one other instance in the Bible, the story of Joseph, Gen. 39), but the seductions of pleasure without promise reach us all. For this reason, the series of instructions offered by the parental teachers begins and ends with voices that can lead the young man astray.[37] Both voices promise pleasures that hide the fact that death waits at the end. If there is any difference, it is that the violent men of chapter 1 are caught while this story is about a young man who is himself caught, and readers can easily put themselves in his place.

 PREACHING THIS PASSAGE. I don't think I've ever heard a sermon on this chapter of the book of Proverbs, perhaps because its message seems so clear and direct that preachers conclude that no work of interpretation and application is needed. It may also be the case that the topic is one preachers would rather avoid, for how does one preach about this scene of seduction and infidelity without sounding judgmental, sexist, or both? It is understandable, then, if some avoid the topic of adultery among Christians by spiritualizing the message about sin and folly, the way the Song of Song's message about faithful committed love is spiritualized into an allegory of Christ and the church (or for Jews, Yahweh and Israel).

However, we have seen that the symbolism of this story sums up the real human experience of sexual seduction to make a point about all kinds of seduction, especially those that lead away from the Lord and his wisdom. We have also seen that the story is not an allegory of historical circumstances concerning intermarriage with foreign women among returning exiles. The narrative art of the teacher's story spoke to an original audience in which young men needed caution about their awakening sexuality, and to a community that needed counsel about the seductions of sin. In this way the story spoke *to* a historical situation, not *about* it.

This portion of Proverbs was written as a warning against those actions and the enticements that precede them, and it should be used to make a similar warning. Our preaching and teaching should follow the rhetorical purpose for which the text was written. Turning first to the particular issue of sexual sin, the church can acknowledge that we rightly speak to our teenagers about their emerging sexuality, but mistakenly assume that we do not need

---

37. The teacher's voice continues into chs. 8 and 9 as it quotes Wisdom and then Folly, but the direct address of "my son" disappears.

to teach adults about relationships and sex. Certainly it is appropriate to use discretion in speaking about matters of sexual behavior, but our embarrassment over the issue should never promote silence. Instead, we must help young adults understand their sexual desires and their needs to enter into a whole relationship with a life partner.

Fulfillment in marriage. At different times, single young men have told me that they envy those who are married because they are no longer subject to sexual temptations. I remind them that the number of cases of infidelity and divorce among Christians argues otherwise. A psychologist friend suggests that evangelical Christians have the highest rate of divorce for two reasons: (1) The commitment to save sex for marriage inevitably encourages young Christians to marry for sex; (2) many of these young Christians believe that the one they marry has been chosen by God. As right as it is to save sex for marriage, these beliefs also can lead youth to neglect or downplay their own assessment of whether the person makes a good life partner. In other words, the exaltation of feelings of love join with these Christian beliefs to lead young believers to ignore the larger matters of dealing with a real person for a lifetime. Romantic notions of love and marriage must be tempered with wise counsel about mate selection.

It may be that myths about marriage have contributed to these misunderstandings. In his classic *The Road Less Traveled*, M. Scott Peck expresses his astonishment when a group of married adults shared that they believed that marriage was intended to fulfil their personal needs. Not a word was said about the joint effort at helping one another grow into mature persons! Too many believe that marital joy comes without the discipline of nurturing a relationship with a real person. Perhaps the enticements of adultery are the shadow side of the marriage myths among us. Perhaps prevalent among believers is a mindset that believes that marriage brings all the joys of the Song of Songs without the mutual commitment and work that such a love requires.

When this fails, the similar descriptions of a married woman's bed in the story of Proverbs 7 can be appealing. Along with warnings about the temptations of infidelity, positive teaching on ways relationships are nurtured is essential. It is one way to call wisdom sister (7:4). We can also encourage healthy marriages by asking single and married persons alike to examine their sexual desires and submit them to careful reflection. Psychologists tell us that extramarital affairs are not primarily about sex but about personal issues that are swept under the rug; affairs are often motivated by problems that do not receive the attention they require. For some, the exhilaration of an affair compensates for a sense of inadequacy in other areas of life. For others, it is a means to avoid honest relationship with one's spouse. Whatever its motivating cause, misunderstandings of sex and marriage as well as the temptations to extramarital relationship should be addressed through preaching, Christian education, and pastoral care.

Dangers of sexual fantasies. Unfortunately, contemporary life presents more opportunities to engage in fantasy than in honest reflection. The woman's description of her bed appeals to the senses, hoping the anticipation of its pleasures will move the young man. She cultivates desire, not to serve the growth of a relationship but to serve her own ends. In our time, we see a similar misuse of such sensuous appeal in the commercialization of sex, not only in mainstream advertising, television, and films but also in the burgeoning pornography industry.

Just across the mountains of Hollywood in the San Fernando Valley, video and internet production of pornography accounts for somewhere between ten and fourteen billion dollars in sales per year, more than the money people spent on movie tickets and more than the money spent on professional baseball, football, and basketball combined. One producer said, "We realized that when there are 700 million porn rentals a year, it can't just be a million perverts renting 700 videos each."[38] The privacy of home video and pay per view has made porn more popular than ever, for it allows people to indulge without anyone ever knowing. Because of its availability and secrecy, it becomes a snare for many, and it too should earn a warning.

Along with positive teaching about relationships, warnings should also teach about the necessity of setting limits, similar to the teacher's warning "do not stray into her paths" (7:25), for opening one's mind to the images and allure of pornography is like opening one's ears to her invitations. Porn is never harmless, and I say this in part because I see it has become the source of laughs on TV sitcoms. Porn is not harmless even if it never leads to violence against women; it harms one's view of sex and one's view of other persons as objects to be used. Finally, it humiliates and degrades those who use it, as many have testified. Public preaching and teaching on the passage can both point out porn's dangers and compassionately offer help in confronting the underlying conflicts that motivate its use.

Forms of temptation. Finally, the church should also unmask the different forms these temptations take. Characterization in this story presents both a wandering young man and a predatory wife, and the church's teaching should in turn acknowledge the reality of both forms of behavior, even among Christian believers. Although the number of predators may be small, this story in Proverbs presents the opportunity to talk about such behavior and offer warnings of its signs. Charm, flattery, and extravagant promises

---

38. F. Rich, "Naked Capitalists," *New York Times Magazine* (May 20, 2001), 51.

have been used by many men and women to prey on the vulnerable. If the predator is actively intent, the wanderer is inattentive. He or she simply does not pay attention to the need to stay vigilant and set boundaries that would screen out such attempts at seduction.

Too many pastors and counselors hear that an inappropriate relationship "just happened." But a psychologist friend tells me that most often, the person who says that was either actively looking or at least had been open to the possibility of an affair, putting himself or herself in a compromising situation in hope that something might happen. Such openness to enticement is encouraged by any number of factors, usually connected with some unmet emotional need. Solid teaching can encourage careful planning to avoid those compromising situations. In their book *Meditations for the Road Warrior*, editors Mark Sanborn and Terry Paulson offer a list of "ways to avoid temptation" for those who do a lot of traveling on business. The list includes asking the hotel desk to turn off adult movies, having friends to call when feeling lonely and vulnerable, and avoiding travel with anyone with whom one is tempted to cross boundaries.[39]

It should be added that predators and wanderers include Christian pastors and staff ministers as well. One journalist who has reported on a number of stories of clergy misconduct concluded, "My work as a reporter has been one part of my learning about boundaries. . . . I quickly calculated that neither I nor my personal clergy and clergy friends were predators. Wanderers, however, sounded like a continuum broad enough to include millions of people. My education continues."[40] While the number of cases of sexual misconduct is relatively small compared to the great majority of ministers who do their work with integrity and care, even one case is too many. The church can do its part by teaching about proper conduct and dealing openly and honestly with misconduct when it happens. Ministers and laypeople alike can do their part by recognizing wandering for the widespread problem that it is.

Preaching and teaching on this chapter should explain that the narrative about adultery, with its seduction and lies, is symbolic of the lies of folly in general. In other words, this scene is a symbol of adultery, which is a symbol of folly. As we have discussed sexual sin, we have seen that it is one

---

39. M. Sanborn and T. Paulson, eds., *Meditations for the Road Warrior* (Grand Rapids: Baker, 1998), cited in C. Crosby, "Advice for the Road Warrior," *Life@Work Journal* 1/3 (August, 1998): 10–11.

40. R. M. Saucier, "One Reporter's Story," in *Restoring the Soul of a Church: Healing Congregations Wounded by Clergy Sexual Misconduct*, ed. N. M. Hopkins, and M. Laaser (Collegeville: Minn.: Liturgical Press, 1995), 191.

species of seduction. A more general definition of seduction includes anything that promises fulfillment without mention of commitments or costs. Seduction speaks of gains and pleasures without responsibility and work. Real fulfillment requires the price of work, but the lies of folly exacts payments much more costly and final. Folly offers something for nothing. Like snake oil, it promises to cure every ill and enhance our lives with no side effects. We may laugh and ask how people in the past could be so gullible and buy snake oil, but as the ploys become more sophisticated, we find ourselves duped in more ways than we recognize.[41]

Thus, with bitter irony, the teaching parent calls the woman's seductive words "teaching" (lqḥ), reminding the son that he must learn how to discern good speech from bad. It may be that the writer intended readers and hearers to learn from this perversion of teaching, for this woman's bad teaching becomes a test case in recognizing snake oil for what it is. We will see that just as Wisdom's true and faithful speech answered the gang's enticement to evil (1:10–33), so Wisdom's instruction answers the bad teaching of the other woman (8:7–10).

---

41. The image is Spencer's, *A Heart for Truth*, 115–16.

Proverbs 8:1–21

¹ DOES NOT WISDOM call out?
  Does not understanding raise her voice?
² On the heights along the way,
  where the paths meet, she takes her stand;
³ beside the gates leading into the city,
  at the entrances, she cries aloud:
⁴ "To you, O men, I call out;
  I raise my voice to all mankind.
⁵ You who are simple, gain prudence;
  you who are foolish, gain understanding.
⁶ Listen, for I have worthy things to say;
  I open my lips to speak what is right.
⁷ My mouth speaks what is true,
  for my lips detest wickedness.
⁸ All the words of my mouth are just;
  none of them is crooked or perverse.
⁹ To the discerning all of them are right;
  they are faultless to those who have knowledge.
¹⁰ Choose my instruction instead of silver,
  knowledge rather than choice gold,
¹¹ for wisdom is more precious than rubies,
  and nothing you desire can compare with her.

¹² "I, wisdom, dwell together with prudence;
  I possess knowledge and discretion.
¹³ To fear the LORD is to hate evil;
  I hate pride and arrogance,
  evil behavior and perverse speech.
¹⁴ Counsel and sound judgment are mine;
  I have understanding and power.
¹⁵ By me kings reign
  and rulers make laws that are just;
¹⁶ by me princes govern,
  and all nobles who rule on earth.
¹⁷ I love those who love me,
  and those who seek me find me.
¹⁸ With me are riches and honor,
  enduring wealth and prosperity.

¹⁹ My fruit is better than fine gold;
   what I yield surpasses choice silver.
²⁰ I walk in the way of righteousness,
   along the paths of justice,
²¹ bestowing wealth on those who love me
   and making their treasuries full.

ALONG WITH THE ode to the woman of strength in chapter 31, the speech of Woman Wisdom in chapter 8 is one of the best-known portions of the book of Proverbs. Here for the second time in the book personified Wisdom calls out like a street preacher, seeking hearers and followers.[1] She describes herself, her qualities, and her gifts and speaks of her existence at the dawn of creation. Her words not only contribute to our understanding of that creation but also to our understanding of the Word, who was with God in the beginning (John 1:1).

As in chapter 1, Wisdom's public address comes after a foolish invitation to live outside the boundaries of God's ways, an invitation that promises the good life but conceals a deadly trap (cf. comments on 1:8–19 and 7:1–27). Again, we find Wisdom calling out in the public square. Four different descriptions—the heights, the meeting of the paths, the gates, and the entrances—show that she has chosen to stand where she can be heard by the greatest number (as in 1:20–21). She makes clear that she calls out to all (as in 1:33), but especially to the simple and the foolish (as in 1:22).[2] Coming at the beginning and near the end of the section of instruction (chs. 1–9), Wisdom's speeches in chapters 8–9, in a way, have the first and last word. Her promise of life comes after and before the images of death that frame the instructions (1:19; 9:18). It is interesting to note that among all the wisdom writings, only in Proverbs does the LXX use the verb "to proclaim" (*kerysso*): in 1:21 ("she cries out") and in 8:1 ("Does not wisdom call out?").[3]

There is one important difference between the speech of chapter 1 and the speech here in chapter 8. In a strange reversal, Wisdom's earlier speech

---

1. See the discussion on personification in 1:20–33.

2. Meinhold, *Die Sprüche*, 1:135–37, sees a structure similar to the speech in ch. 1: Introduction (8:1–3; cf. 1:20–31), Wisdom's Speech (8:4–36; cf. 1:22–33), Invitation (8:32–36; cf. 1:32–33). He notes that in 8:4–11, four lines speak to her addressees (vv. 4–5), eight to the quality of her speech (vv. 6–9), and four to the comparison of wisdom with treasures (vv. 10–11).

3. R. Murphy, "The Kerygma of the Book of Proverbs," *Int* 20 (1966): 5.

marked the end of her appeal—her words of judgment were final: "You will call, but I will not answer" (1:28). Like a movie that begins with the ending to explain how the story got there, so here Wisdom's first speech starts at the end of the story to show how such a tragic ending comes about. Here at the conclusion of the instructions, she sounds like she is beginning her appeal; the call to "listen" that closed her first speech (1:33) comes near the beginning of her second (8:6).

The speech of Wisdom in chapter 8 stands alone as a work of art but also as a strategic answer to all that has come to the reader's attention since her last appearance. In chapters 7—9, the juxtaposed speeches of Folly and Wisdom follow a chiastic pattern.

    A 7:14—20   Speech of the other/strange woman
     B 8:4—36   Speech of Wisdom
     B' 9:5—6   Speech of Wisdom
    A' 9:16—17   Speech of foolish woman[4]

Unlike the strange woman, Woman Wisdom offers good teaching (cf. the "teaching" of the adulteress's persuasive words in 7:21). Because so much attention is devoted to Wisdom's startling claims about herself in 8:22—36, we will treat those verses separately in order to devote adequate attention to 8:1—21, the section that precedes.

    8:1—5   Wisdom speaks to all humankind
    8:6—11   Wisdom speaks what is noble and precious
    8:12—16 Wisdom gives righteous counsel to rulers
    8:17—21 Wisdom gives love, honor, and wealth to those who love her

Wisdom Speaks to All Humankind (8:1–5)

WHO IS THE speaker who asks, "Does not wisdom call out? Does not understanding raise her voice?" (8:1). While it may be an unnamed narrator who introduces wisdom in chapter 1, in this text and again in chapter 9, it is more likely meant to be taken as the voice of the teaching parent, here drawing a contrast between Wisdom's words and those of the other/strange woman in 7:24—27. If it is indeed one of the parents, this teacher continues the identification between the parent's teaching and Wisdom that was woven throughout the instructions of chapters 1—7.

4. G. A. Yee, "The Theology of Creation in Proverbs 8:22—31," in *Creation in the Biblical Traditions*, ed. R. J. Clifford and J. J. Collins (CBQMS 24; Washington, D.C.: Catholic Biblical Association, 1992), 86.

Verses 2–3 draw a comparison between the other woman, who lurks in streets and squares in the dark of night (7:12), and Wisdom, who publicly takes her stand at the heights, crossroads, and gates, calling out in the bustle of broad daylight. The heights provide a spot where all can see and hear; one must work hard to ignore her, for Wisdom will speak there again, as will Folly (9:3, 14). The place where the paths meet (lit., "between the paths") assures that many will be walking by. The gates are the place of civic business; archaeologists have uncovered within the city gate structure side rooms that may have been used for such meetings.[5]

Wisdom stands at the entrances to speak to all who come and go, much like Jeremiah stood at the entrance to the temple (Jer. 7:2). Here Absalom addressed individuals as they came to see the king, but for wicked purposes (2 Sam. 15:1–2). The four terms of Proverbs 8:2 do not all describe the same place, but each is a prominent and public spot, near the place where public decisions were made and where speakers were heard.[6]

Like the teacher who views the events of chapter 7 from above the street, Wisdom places herself above the crowd to speak to them, a strong contrast to the actions of the other/strange woman, who brings her lovers down to death and Sheol. Every line suggests that her speech is public and offered to all; unlike the adulterous woman who speaks to one young man, Wisdom calls out to everyone, at the gates where many are coming and going, and she states her purpose (cf. 1:20–21). Whereas the adulteress was loud and defiant (7:11), Wisdom raises her voice to call out to all humankind (lit., all the "sons of Adam [ʾadam]"; 8:4—ʾadam perhaps referring to humankind and the first man at the same time).

Yet like the other/strange woman, Wisdom also narrows her sights on the simple and those lacking judgment (lit., "lacking heart"; cf. 7:7) so they might "gain" (lit., "understand") prudence and "gain understanding [lit., heart]." In other words, Wisdom makes clear that her listeners are to be active in responding. There is no passive listening, only learning or ignoring, gaining or losing. Everyone is included in the fourfold address that goes out to all humankind but especially to the simple (just as the simple need prudence, cf. 1:4).

Wisdom Speaks What Is Noble and Precious (8:6–11)

"LISTEN" (8:6) ECHOES the words of the teacher (1:5; 1:8; 4:1, 10; 5:7; 7:24) and Wisdom herself (1:33). Like the teacher, she has confidence in her sound

---

5. E. Scheffer, "Archaeology and Wisdom," *OTE* 10 (1997): 459–73.

6. Fox, *Proverbs 1–9*, 267, sees Woman Wisdom moving between places within and without the city walls.

words (4:2): They are "worthy" and "right." "Worthy" translates a word that could refer to "princely things,"[7] certainly that which is noble and honorable. "Right" might better be rendered "upright," a key word of the speech (*mĕšarim*, 8:6—9; cf. 1:3; 2:9).[8]

To summarize, in each of the eight lines of 8:6—9, Wisdom makes her claim to speak rightly. Starting with 8:6b, four consecutive lines assert that her lips or mouth speak right words, a contrast to the honey-dripping lips of the other woman (5:3) and the corrupt mouth of the scoundrel (5:12, 17). Her words are "true" (*ʾemet*, 8:7a) and "just" ("righteous," *sedeq*, 8:8a); her lips find wickedness detestable ("abominable," *toʿebah*, 8:7b; cf. 6:16; 12:22; 16:13), and her mouth rejects crookedness and perversity (8:8b; cf. 2:15; 4:24; 6:12).

However, Wisdom adds that she is not the only one who recognizes the quality of her speech, for they are also faultless (*yošarim*, 8:9; "straight," not "crooked," as in 8:8) to those who have found knowledge; those who are discerning or understanding (*mebin*, cf. same root as "gain [understanding]" in 8:5) know they are right. By implication, the simple and foolish are to trust the testimony of those who recognize this quality; if they do, they will have made the first step toward discernment and knowledge.

There is some rhetorical appeal to the character of the audience in this claim, for readers who have taken the time to attend to the message of the book will certainly wish to be counted among the wise.[9] Knowing that one needs wisdom is the first sign of having it. If the words are right and faultless to them, what are they to fools—insufficient, false, worthless? Most likely, fools see her message as no use to them and reject it (cf. 1:24). But Wisdom begins her appeal, not with benefits to the listener, but simply by declaring the quality of her words. Because they are true and right, they are precious and valuable.

Based on this quality, the invitation of 8:10—11 makes a fourfold comparison between her teaching and this world's treasures. The first two lines press for decision with the imperative "choose" (lit., "take," using *lqḥ*, the root used for teaching and learning) "instruction" (*musar*, teaching and correction) rather than silver, knowledge rather than choice gold. The second two lines

---

7. Some commentators emend the word *negidim* (lit. "nobles" or "princes") to read "straight things," but Kidner, *Proverbs*, 77, disagrees. Perhaps here is a pun that looks ahead to wisdom's assistance of kings and governors in vv. 15 and 16. Garrett, *Proverbs*, 107, suggests emending to "discerning" (*mebin*) after v. 9.

8. Murphy, *Proverbs*, 50.

9. T. B. Farrell, *Norms of Rhetorical Culture* (New Haven and London: Yale Univ. Press, 1993), 94—99, contends that establishing good character is not the task of the speaker alone but audience and communicator together. See 1:5 and 9:9 for a similar strategy of appeal to the character of the listener.

present the motivation: Wisdom is better than rubies or anything else one may desire; nothing "can compare with her." The change of speaker from "me" to the third person "her" interrupts Wisdom's speech but perhaps it alludes to 3:15, which is repeated nearly verbatim, and the similar phrasing to describe the woman of 31:10. Wisdom is so valuable that nothing compares with it, a statement also true for the person who lives by wisdom.

Wisdom Gives Righteous Counsel to Rulers (8:12–16)

CONTEMPORARY READERS MAY find it strange that Wisdom, who claims to hate pride and arrogance, speaks so highly of herself. But it is one thing to boast and set oneself as better than others and another to speak truthfully about what one can do to serve them. Wisdom portrays herself here as counselor to kings and a principle of social order.[10] So an Egyptian stele on display in the University of Chicago's Oriental Institute shows a king presenting the gods with a figure of Ma'at, the personification of world order, tradition, and truth—a sign that he will uphold divine standards of just rule.[11] In the ancient world, rulers claimed divine sanction and guidance in maintaining a just society in which all could live in peace and prosperity.[12] Because this need for divine guidance and help was widely recognized, it is not unusual that Wisdom as spokesperson for Yahweh claims to offer counsel to kings after the model of female counselors.

Verses 12 and 17 both begin with the Hebrew pronoun "I" (*'ani*) to introduce speech that uses first person forms throughout.[13] The trio of wisdom terms, "prudence," "knowledge," and "discretion," are familiar from the prologue (1:1–7). The verbs draw the reader's attention, for she "dwells together" with prudence and "finds" knowledge and discretion, just as humans are to do. So also the prologue stated that "the fear of the LORD is the beginning of wisdom" (1:7), even as all three of wisdom's speeches mention "fear of the

---

10. Comparable to the woman of Tekoa (2 Sam. 14), Abigail (1 Sam. 25), and Bathsheba (1 Kings 1); S. Schroer, "Wise and Counseling Women in Ancient Israel: Literary and Historical Ideals of the Personified *HOKMA*," in A. Brenner, ed., *A Feminist Companion to Wisdom Literature* (Sheffield: Sheffield Academic Press, 1995), 67–84.

11. E. Teeter, *The Presentation of MAAT: Ritual and Legitimacy in Ancient Egypt* (SAOC 57; Chicago: The Oriental Institute, 1997). Teeter understands the scene as a legitimation of the king's competence and authority to govern.

12. So, e.g., The Code of Hammurabi begins, "At that time Anum and Enlil named me to promote the welfare of the people, me, Hammurabi, the devout, god-fearing prince, to cause justice to prevail in the land. Hammurabi, the shepherd, called by Enlil am I, the one who makes affluence and plenty abound" (*ANET*, 164).

13. Murphy, *Proverbs*, 49. Clifford, *Proverbs*, 93, adds that the use of the first-person "I" sound unites the Heb. text of 8:12–21.

LORD" (1:29; 8:13; 9:10). So here in verse 13, the parallelism suggests that wisdom herself practices this fear. Finally, wisdom also rejects evil, even as she encourages her listeners to follow her example. Two times in 8:13, evil is specified as "pride," "arrogance," (lit.) "way of evil," and "mouth of perversity" (cf. 7:16–19).

Verse 14 lists the possessions Wisdom offers to kings in 8:15: "counsel" (cf. 2 Sam. 17:7; 1 Kings 1:12), "sound judgment," "understanding," and "power." Readers may be surprised at the inclusion of power with typical wisdom terms, but the combination suggests that wisdom and power cannot be separated. So Proverbs 20:18 warns, "Make plans by seeking advice; if you wage war, obtain guidance" (cf. 21:22).

Verses 15–16 are parallel in Hebrew, both beginning with "by me" (*bi*) and both ending with *ṣedeq*, the word for "righteous" or "just." The NIV footnote reports that the translators have followed the LXX in translating "all nobles who rule on earth" instead of "and nobles—all righteous rulers," but this translation disturbs the parallelism of the two verses and its echo of the pairing of righteousness and justice in 8:20. The second line of verse 15 expands the introduction of royal rule, adding that wisdom's counsel enables rulers to enact laws (*ḥqq*) that are just. This Hebrew word depicts a line or circle drawn as a boundary, similar to those boundaries set by Yahweh at creation (8:27, 29).[14]

This first mention of just government sums up all that has been said about right and just behavior, even as it looks ahead to the topic of kings and just government in the individual sayings of chapters 10–22. While many suggest that Proverbs was designed to train princes and courtiers, like other ancient Near Eastern instructions, there is no evidence in the speech that this feature of Wisdom's activity is limited to court personnel. Wisdom stands in the public places, and her message goes out to all. She offers the same guidance to kings and commoners so that readers of the instructions can put the principles of good government into practice with one's neighbor, doing justice, coveting neither goods nor spouse. Likewise, the pride, evil ways, and crooked speech that became the downfall of so many kings is rejected by the citizens as well.

Wisdom Gives Love, Honor, and Wealth to Those Who Love Her (8:17–21)

THE END OF the first half of Wisdom's speech brings together terms for love and wealth and associates them with righteousness. As with the previous

---

14. R. Van Leeuwen, "Proverbs," 90, and "Liminality and Worldview in Proverbs 1–9," *Semeia* 50 (1990): 111–44.

section (8:12–16), this one begins with the pronoun "I." Terms from the previous section are revisited as Wisdom now reports on her love. While she hates evil in all its manifestations (8:13), she loves those who love her (8:17, 21). "Love" frames 8:17–21 and may be another use of erotic language to describe the seeker's relation to wisdom (cf. 8:31). "Finding" (*ms*²; cf. "possess" [*ms*²] in 8:12; see also 8:35–36) echoes wisdom's earlier refusal to be found (1:28), the other/strange woman's finding her young victim (7:15), and later sayings about finding a wife (18:22; 31:10; cf. Song 3:1–4; 5:6). Common to all is the symbolic overlap of choosing wisdom and choosing a good life partner (Prov. 3:15; 4:5–6; 7:4; 8:34). However, it is also the case that Woman Wisdom offers her patrons gifts and blessings as if she were an ancient goddess, although no claim to divinity is made.[15]

Whereas wisdom is to be chosen over riches (8:19; cf. 8:10–11), wisdom also promises the good things of this life to those who love her. Like the good wife of chapter 31, she brings profit of riches and honor, long lasting wealth and prosperity (8:18). The last of the terms, "prosperity," translates *ṣᵉdeqah*, typically rendered "righteousness," but for the sake of parallelism a derivation is used in the NIV. The overlap of meanings is intentional, for the way of righteousness will appear in 8:20, where *ṣᵉdeqah* is clearly the typical meaning. Righteousness is the "fruit" that is better than fine gold (8:19); one could craft silver apples and pomegranates, but the intangibles of righteousness and honor are what last (cf. Isa. 5:7 for righteousness as fruit).

The association of wisdom's virtues with wealth occurs again in 8:20–21. Righteousness and justice take the reader back to the programmatic statement of the prologue and its trio of righteousness, justice, and upright dealing (1:3). Wisdom claims that she walks in the paths that were recommended throughout the parents' lectures. To walk on these paths is to walk with her. These virtues are the way to wealth, for they lead to wisdom, who bestows wealth to those who *love* her, repeating the key term (8:21; cf. 8:17). Shortcuts that lead away from her may bring wealth also, but by implication, it will not endure (8:18). Choose wealth over wisdom, and at best, you will have it for a time. Choose wisdom over wealth and one will have riches enough, along with the honor that comes from having walked in righteousness and justice.

As we review our findings about this first part of Wisdom's speech, we notice that terms and themes reappear in a parallel pattern:

8:5	gain *prudence*	8:12	I wisdom dwell with *prudence*

---

15. Clifford, *Proverbs*, 95.

8:6–7	*my lips detest wickedness*	8:13	I *hate* pride, arrogance, evil, and *perverse speech*
8:8–9	*righteousness*	8:14–17	*righteousness*
8:10–11	instruction *better than gold*	8:17–20	fruit *better than fine gold*

If readers are meant to discern a parallel structure between the two parts of the speech, or at least a similar flow in theme, the second half may be seen as the practical outworking of the truths of the first. In other words, if the simple are to gain prudence (cf. 1:4), then wisdom knows how to find it, for she lives with it. If her lips detest wickedness, she also hates it in humans. If her instruction is better than gold, we see that choosing it not only brings what is right, but it also brings health, riches, and honor. But most important, comparing the two halves of the speech and the repetition of the term "righteous" in both suggests that rulers who make just laws are those who are discerning enough to recognize the worth of her words; or in reverse, if one recognizes the righteousness of her words, then that one will rule in righteousness (8:15–16).

THE FUNCTION OF **the speech.** In seeking to build a bridge between the ancient and contemporary worlds, we must spend time with this first part of Woman Wisdom's speech before going on to the more famous second part. Much can be learned if we pay attention to the speech itself and hold onto the questions of personification and identity, first asking about the function of the speech. The two parts of the speech in chapter 8 work together, but by looking at the first part separately, we have seen that it echoes many features of Wisdom's presentation in chapters 1–7: the public stand and call to the simple and fools (1:20–22), *finding* wisdom (1:28), an invitation to *listen* to her counsel (1:32), value greater than silver, gold, rubies, or any desire (3:15), ways and paths (3:16), the call to love her and her rewards (4:6–9), and, most important, "fear of the LORD" (1:29).

In literary terms, these words of Wisdom are a personification of the invitation to study, a continuation of the teacher's personification that began in chapter 1. One advantage of personification is a reduction of focus, a capacity to make complicated concepts or issues more manageable and easier to understand.[16] Moreover, personification not only teaches, its artistry delights,

---

16. B. Brummett, *Rhetoric in Popular Culture* (New York: St. Martins, 1994), 63–66, 157–59, calls this a metonymic function of artistic works: "Metonymy occurs when something

echoing the mood of celebration that runs through the entire chapter.[17] Most important, this personification is best understood as a communication of God's will to humankind, designed to move us to respond with faith and obedience.[18]

When we compare Wisdom's speech to the words of the other/strange woman, we notice that wisdom promises to bless her companions, especially rulers. She does not offer stolen pleasures but what is needed for righteous and just rule. Wisdom loves truth, and we have seen that the other woman is a liar; her words are smooth, seductive, and deadly.[19] Therefore, before taking on the matters of wisdom's presence at creation, we do well to turn our focus toward the main features of the first part of the speech, for it is here that Wisdom establishes her credibility, or rhetorical *ethos*.

Although the idea of *ethos* (character) was developed by classical rhetoricians to describe the relationship a speaker builds with a listening audience, speakers today also wish to appear competent, honest, and caring.[20] As Wisdom speaks of her love of truth and sound speech, she not only enhances her credibility to speak and be believed, she treats themes that are sounded throughout the book: true speech, good government, and enduring wealth. Common to all three is Wisdom's concern for righteousness, so we will begin there.

Righteousness. The importance of righteousness is introduced in the first part of the speech, where the Hebrew root *ṣdq* is translated "just" (8:8, 15, 16), "prosperity" (8:18), and "righteousness" (8:20; see comments in Original Meaning section). The translation obscures the emphasis of the speech, a

---

complex is reduced to a more manageable sign of complex things, as when the complexities of British government are reduced into the public figures of the Prime Minister, or of the reigning monarch."

17. H. C. Brichto, *Toward a Grammar of Biblical Poetics: Tales of the Prophets* (New York: Oxford, 1992), 258. "Biblical Hebrew, to the best of my knowledge, has no word for the abstraction expressed in our word *art*. And even in modern Hebrew there is no alternative to the loan word *humor*. Artistry, however, is one of the meanings of *hokma* (wisdom), and the closest approximation to the humorous is the root *ṣḥq* (smile, jeer, laugh)."

18. R. Murphy, *The Tree of Life*, 147, says: "The best one can say is that Lady Wisdom is a divine communication: God's communication, extension, of self to human beings. And that is no small insight the biblical wisdom literature bequeaths to us."

19. C. Fontaine, "The Social Roles of Women in the World of Wisdom," in *A Feminist Companion to Wisdom Literature*, ed. A. Brenner (Sheffield: Sheffield Academic Press, 1995), 33–34, observes that the speech of the other woman is a reverse image of the wifely virtues of ch. 31 and a perverse use of Woman Wisdom's power of speech in chs. 1, 8, and 9.

20. Aristotle, *On Rhetoric*, trans. G. A. Kennedy (New York/Oxford: Oxford Univ. Press, 1991), 2.1 (120–21). Kennedy uses the terms "practical wisdom" (*phronesis*), "virtue" (*arete*), and "good will" (*eunoia*).

summary of all that has gone before in the instructions; the character sketches and advice of the previous chapters were about righteousness and justice, not simply the good that will come to the young man, although it is included. In reality, right choosing is motivated by benefits to self, consequences to others, and loyalty to a greater principle or code, in this case, the fear of Yahweh. The emphasis on justice also looks ahead to the contrasts between righteousness and wickedness in the individual sayings.

We might think of righteousness as an aspect of wisdom in that it involves knowing what is right to do in a situation. In contrast with the first speech, where the key terms were correction and reproof (1:23–25, 30), here the emphasis is on virtue, knowing what faithfulness requires. Earlier Woman Wisdom spoke of those who would not listen; here she holds up examples of those who do, and they discern the truth (8:9) and rule accordingly (8:15–16).

The two speeches are two sides of a coin, each stressing essential features of wisdom. By linking righteous words with righteous action, Wisdom's rhetoric resembles those theories of communication that understand speech as a form of action that impacts others. Words are not inert transfers of ideas but real actions with real effects. Common wisdom would affirm that as one speaks, so one acts, even as Jesus argued that the two were intimately linked. As we have seen, righteousness is a social virtue that describes actions that are done with the good of one's community in mind.

Themes of Wisdom's speech. (1) Wisdom wants hearers that will to listen to her and understand that her words bring prudence and understanding (8:4–5). Whereas in her first speech she refers to her words as rebuke and advice (1:23–25), here she stresses their value as truth. Each of the terms she uses to describe her speech stresses the dimensions of righteousness, justice, and fair dealing that were central to the prologue (1:3). Speech that is true is speech that is faithful; the word *ʾemet* in 8:7 speaks not of truth in the abstract but truth that is "true" to a relationship with another—so also for "right" (*mešarim*, 8:6) and "just" (*sedeq*, 8:8). Similarly, Moses characterized the ways of God as faithful and just (Deut. 32:4).

While Wisdom is certainly speaking of her instruction (*musar*, 8:10), her lips and mouth that speak what is right also stand in stark contrast with the scoundrel of 6:12. The contrast suggests that her instruction is also faithful to her hearers the way this evil person's speech is not. She sets her commitment to her hearer's good, and that should be true of all kinds of speech, whether teaching or everyday dealing. She hints that her right teaching should be passed on from parent to child and also practiced in everyday speech that is right, just, and fair. Right teaching produces righteous social interaction.

Wisdom asks her hearers to practice what she herself does, so the more she establishes her trustworthiness and credibility, the more she also provides a model. She not only wants to be seen as trustworthy and believable but also worthy of emulation. This emphasis on right relation should draw our attention to the creative energy our words carry. Nothing builds confidence and community like truth, and nothing destroys them like lies. In our emphasis on rhetorical persuasion, we should keep in mind that Wisdom's first concern is for the ethical component of her speech (*ethos*), not whether her words are persuasive or effective. Advertisers, politicians, and preachers alike would do well to follow her model. Too often, what the world wants is wealth and power, when what it needs is truth.

(2) A second theme of Wisdom's speech is her concern for good government. The first mention of kings in the book of Proverbs (8:15) reminds the reader of Solomon's request for wisdom (1 Kings 3:4—15). Yahweh, appearing in a dream, urged Solomon to ask for whatever he wished. The king remembered the kindness shown to David and his son, asking for "a discerning heart [lit., a heart that hears] to govern your people and to distinguish [lit., discern] between right and wrong." Yahweh granted the wish plus all that he did not ask for, namely, riches, honor, and a long life—the trio of motivators in Proverbs. Readers of Wisdom's speech can also recall that wisdom characterized Solomon's rule (1 Kings 4:29—34).

However, the earlier chapters of 1 Kings show a different side of Solomon, the son whom David charged to repay his enemies: "Deal with him [Joab] in your wisdom, but do not let his gray head go down to the grave in peace" (1 Kings 2:6), and, "Do not consider him [Shimei] innocent. You are a man of wisdom; you will know what to do to him. Bring his gray head down to the grave in blood" (2:9). Solomon secured his rule by eliminating Joab and Shimei as well as his half-brother Adonijah, demonstrating another sort of "wisdom" that makes power, not truth, the ultimate standard (2:13—46).[21] The request for the wisdom of God marks a turn in Solomon's thinking, a turn more in line with the thinking of Job, who recognizes that "to God belong wisdom and power; counsel and understanding are his" (Job 12:13; cf. 12:10—25).

Moreover, the narrative points out that David was also prone to this worldly wisdom and was himself counseled by women who turned him away from potentially unjust and destructive actions. Abigail, intelligent and beautiful, was a woman of *ṭobat śekel* (lit., "good understanding," 1 Sam. 25:3),

---

21. I. W. Provan, "On 'Seeing' the Trees While Missing the Forest: The Wisdom of Characters and Readers in 2 Samuel and 1 Kings," in *In Search of Wisdom: Essays in Old Testament Interpretation in Honour of Ronald E. Clements*, ed. E. Ball (JSOTSup 300; Sheffield: Sheffield Academic Press, 1999), 153–73. Provan argues that every mention of wisdom prior to Solomon's requests illustrates the limitations of human wisdom and its machinations.

who used persuasive speech to keep David from destroying that fool Nabal and all his men.[22] More ambiguously, the wise woman of Tekoa (2 Sam. 14:2), coached by Joab, uses a parable to persuade the king to bring back the exiled Absalom. Her praise of David's wisdom, "like that of an angel of God," may have more to do with flattery than truth, for Absalom did not return as a reconciled son. Instead, he led a rebellion against David and was killed by Joab, the very man who had worked to bring him home.[23]

These narratives illustrate by negative and positive examples the intimate relationship of wisdom and rule. While it would be false, of course, to say that all kings govern wisely, this chapter assures us that righteous rule is a sign that wisdom is present. As we seek to relate the teaching of this passage to our own day, we will note that Wisdom is not only concerned with individual well-being but also with good government that rules in fairness. Christian readers of Wisdom's words must ask themselves how they are contributing to good government, both by supporting just rule and practicing fairness in areas in which they exercise authority.

(3) A third theme of Wisdom's speech concerns the wise person's attitude toward wealth. Yahweh was pleased that Solomon did not ask for wealth and honor but for wisdom to rule the people, and so he gave Solomon that wisdom plus wealth and honor (2 Kings 3:12). In the same way, Wisdom is glad to provide riches and honor to those who choose her above them. Twice, readers are advised to choose her fruit above that of any glittering treasure (Prov. 8:10—11, 18—21; cf. 3:13—15), and reading these words, we acknowledge that all too often, we are influenced by what our eyes see instead of what we hear from wisdom. Is it not the desire for wealth that frequently tempts one away from wisdom and obedience?

If we were to live by bread alone and not by every word that comes from the mouth of God, then any means to get bread, even stealing (cf. ch. 6), would be acceptable. So also, if we live only for the goods of this world, we might be convinced that greater accumulations of wealth are good also. While wisdom is not opposed to one's securing wealth and honor, she resists it when it is done for its own sake.

In other words, to seek the goods of this world as the ultimate goal of life is not only to miss the greater goods for which we were created but also to

---

22. W. Janzen, *Old Testament Ethics: A Paradigmatic Approach* (Grand Rapids: Eerdmans, 1995), 17—19, calls the account a "wisdom model story" after P. K. McCarter Jr., *I Samuel: A New Translation with Introduction, Notes and Commentary* (AB8; Garden City, N.Y.: Doubleday, 1980), 401. McCarter saw it as "a story about the education of a future king. David is like the young man to whom much of the Book of Proverbs is addressed. . . ."

23. See also Provan, "On 'Seeing' the Trees," 165—71.

make ourselves open to two great dangers. (a) The first is to squander our love on objects that cannot love us back. A financial magazine once ran an article about a couple that put pictures of the cars, boats, and homes they hoped to acquire on their refrigerator as motivational inspiration. As I read about that, I thought of the pictures I had seen on refrigerators in other homes, pictures of relatives, missionaries, and children's artwork. Psalm 49 quotes a poet claiming to speak "words of wisdom ... an utterance of understanding ... a proverb ... a riddle" about riches. One who has riches without understanding will not endure, but is "like the beasts that perish" (Ps. 49:12, 20).[24] Similarly, Jesus taught that no one can serve two masters to show that when our loyalties try to include both God and money, they are never equally divided (Matt. 6:19–24).

(b) The danger of putting wealth first can become the ground of wrong treatment of others. Jesus also echoed Wisdom's words in his parables of the treasure hidden in the field and the pearl of great value, both worth selling everything to acquire them (Matt 13:44–45). Whereas Jesus used the pearl as a figure for the kingdom of heaven, John Steinbeck imagined what would happen if a poor man found such a real pearl. The fictional character of his story *The Pearl* became the victim of traders who first conspired to offer a low price for the treasure and then hunted him down to take the pearl, ready to take his life if necessary. Steinbeck's bitter tale reverses Jesus' wise order of priorities to show the disastrous outcomes of folly. Certainly in our day of ever-encroaching commercialism (is there anywhere we do not see or hear advertising?), we must take care to silence the din of acquisitiveness to hear Wisdom's words.

In sum, we see that Wisdom offers to all (8:1–11) what she gives to kings (8:12–21). Even as her words about righteousness in speech, rule, and wealth intertwine to weave a tapestry picture of a just society, we see that righteousness necessarily shows itself when the citizens of that kingdom/community speak honestly, observe righteous and just laws, and refuse to make wealth the ultimate goal of life. In so doing, they live as their rulers ought to live, taking their cues from them. Therefore, just as the story of Israel reports on the successes and failures of its kings, so Wisdom reports her instruction of kings so that common people may learn to follow their example. In this way, social and personal righteousness come together, for the incentives to just living apply equally to citizens and kings. Readers can keep this in mind when they read that like wisdom, kings love righteousness and honest speech (note the similarities in 16:11–16, where wisdom again is better than gold).

---

24. Meinhold, *Die Sprüche*, 1:139.

HONESTY AND INTEGRITY. Wisdom's call to all who will listen extends to readers in the twenty-first century, directing us to consider the nature of her words and the decisions it requires of us. We have seen that the rhetorical strategy of the first half of Wisdom's speech emphasizes reference to her own righteousness in speech and action, to establish her credibility and to serve as a model for rulers and citizens alike. Moreover, we have seen that Wisdom rejects what Yahweh hates (8:7–8, 13; cf. 6:16–19), the only such negative reference in the speech. This association not only further enhances Wisdom's credibility as speaking the mind of Yahweh, it serves as a model for what believers might practice today. Therefore, although the proverbs and other wisdom writings have been compared with popular literature and called instruction for success, it is better to say that it is instruction for success in righteousness.

Here truth is true to another person; the opposite of such faithfulness is the wicked, crooked, and perverse speech of a person found unworthy of trust. Americans who have become cynical after learning that their presidents have lied about war, wiretapping, and womanizing now listen with a critical ear. They will not tolerate speech that distorts or traffics in half-truths, presenting only what serves the speaker's purposes. Therefore, righteous speech is ethical; it speaks the truth out of concern for another and rejects self-serving distortions.

Wisdom's use of persuasion tells us that she respects the right of her listeners to choose and recognizes that coercion will not win long-lasting friends anyway. Therefore, her call is a call for evangelicals to practice honesty about their faith, neither painting discipleship in rosy colors that ignore the costs of discipleship nor condemning the practices of the world without acknowledging that Christians are equally tempted to them. If we believe the Christian way is the right way to live, then we will seek to be winsome and persuasive, not combative about eroding morals. Like Jesus, we will seek those with ears to hear or those who discern that Wisdom's words are right (8:9). Such an approach also leaves room for questions, honoring and receiving them as signs of interest.

For years, evangelist Cliff Knechtle has been visiting college campuses, setting himself in a public space and taking just a few minutes to speak about the claims of Jesus. He then turns to the crowd and says, "I'll bet you have questions you would like to ask someone who believes that Jesus Christ is worth following and living for." And because there always are questions, the real work of witness starts in earnest as Cliff listens carefully and offers thoughtful responses.[25] His hearers are testing his words to discern if they are right.

So also, the church will work to earn the right to speak to the social and ethical issues of our day by speaking forthrightly and with respect for those who differ. It is easy to attack persons and positions from the safety of a pulpit; it is much more difficult to enter into public debate by means of open-ended writings and public forums. Blessings on those churches who are not only faithful in the work of catechism (i.e., instructing its own in the faith) but also in taking on the important issues of the day and inviting the community to an exchange of views. When incidents of racially motivated violence started appearing in one of our Chicago neighborhoods, the local clergy association gathered to plan a special service to proclaim the message of racial reconciliation and went around the neighborhood to invite households to attend. Mindful of Wisdom's love of faithful speech, Christians will strive to practice it.

Concern for righteous rule. Similarly, Christians will also identify themselves with Wisdom's concern for righteous rule, for they are certainly concerned with freedom to worship and witness as well as righteousness, justice, and fair dealing in their communities and their nation. All too often, however, the church has fallen into one of the two extremes of withdrawal or imposition. *Withdrawal* from public life is often motivated by a false dichotomy between faith and works, so that evangelism becomes a gospel activity, but caring for the poor or calling out for just treatment of immigrants and minorities is not.

Imposition of a Christian viewpoint engages society, but only on its own terms. I recall conversations with those who were angry at Christians who ran for positions in local government and school boards but who were not forthcoming about their positions until they had been elected. By the reports I heard, they relied on garnering enough votes to force their positions through rather than using persuasion to make long-lasting changes. I contend that it is not for lack of voices that we have not been heard, but for lack of persuasiveness born of integrity, a concern to demonstrate good will, good character, and good sense in our speaking.

Wealth. Wisdom's offer of enduring wealth will encourage Christians to assess their own beliefs and attitudes toward the material goods of life. Recalling Jesus' teaching on the kingdom pearl that was worth more than any treasure, believers will hear in wisdom's words a call to make relative comparisons, that is, to reflect on the relative values of wealth and wisdom. Wisdom has

---

25. C. Knechtle, *Give Me an Answer That Satisfies My Heart and Mind* (Downers Grove, Ill.: InterVarsity Press, 1986).

something to say about the way wealth is gained and distributed. Her love of truth and faithfulness points to the other teachings in Proverbs about unjust paths to wealth. If you have to choose, choose the wise way over wealth, integrity before gain.

However, it is also true that integrity brings its own wealth, and it is long-lasting. Wisdom also speaks against the unreflective rejection of wealth. The simple lifestyle of frugality and freedom in giving is admirable, but simple living is not a value in and of itself. It is not the refusal to acquire or spend that marks the righteous person, but the desire to do right by self, neighbor, and God. Here is a vision of wealth that has not compromised. The intertwining of terms offers a vision rarely seen, but all the more attractive for that reason.

The parallel references to gold and righteousness present the hearer/reader with a choice. "Choose my instruction instead of silver, knowledge rather than choice gold" (8:10) highlights the basic decision that confronts every person, every day. Silver and gold are more than metaphors for the supreme value of wisdom's teaching, they also represent the real choice we often face between that which has integrity and that which sells. This is not to say that one must always choose between the two or that doing right always means rejecting profit. In fact, wisdom says the opposite; she not only "walks the way of righteousness along paths of justice," but she also bestows "wealth on those who love me and [makes] their treasuries full" (8:20–21). Likewise Jesus taught that in seeking first the kingdom, all other needs are met, if not with wealth, at least with provision. In this way, provision and even wealth are seen as gifts. When we think we can achieve them, we are in danger of becoming lost in our own sufficiency.[26]

Therefore, the church (members and leaders alike) must confront the temptation to commercialize its work, asking if their choices are made on the basis of what is true, right, and just or on what fills parking lots and offering plates. To say this is not to downplay the importance of evangelism and church growth, only to question some of its practices. If we are ever tempted to downplay Wisdom's words on truth and justice to make our message more attractive, we can let those words call us back. Twice Wisdom links noble speech with true wealth. She takes the chance that the discerning will know the worth of her words (8:9); she makes the audacious claim that truth is worth something, worth more than anything else (8:10–11)! If she is confident that her truth will be recognized and honored, we should be too.

Power. Finally, Wisdom introduces the topic of power (8:14). We have heard references to the three motivators of health, wealth, and honor

---

26. J. Ellul, *Money and Power*, trans. L. Neff (Downers Grove, Ill.: InterVarsity Press, 1984), 35–72.

throughout the instructions, but here Wisdom begins to speak of power and authority. In a sense, speech and wealth are vehicles of power as much as any official capacity to govern, for by all three we are influenced and moved. For that reason, Christians should make themselves aware of the subtle and not-so-subtle forms of power that arise in our interactions.

"Power profoundly impacts our interpersonal relationships, our social relationships and our relationship with God. Nothing touches us more profoundly for good or for ill than power."[27] With these words, Richard Foster tells us that power is not limited to rulers alone but is relevant to all persons, great or humble. Therefore, contemporary readers will not set aside Wisdom's words to kings and rulers but will study them closely for their insight into the responsibilities of power, for it can be used to create or to destroy.

(1) We must admit that we can be seduced by power as much as by health, wealth, or honor, setting it above all other commitments. As the popular saying goes, "Everyone wants to rule the world." As a boy, I remember going to the county fair and watching a pen full of billy goats play king of the mountain on a series of wooden ramps. How symbolic of so many of our interactions! We clamor and strive for position and face the temptation of using underhanded means to get there.

(2) We must use whatever power we possess to build others up instead of trampling them down. Managers can take care to work for the good of the company *and* those placed under their authority. Church leaders can commit themselves always to consider people more important than any problem they are facing.[28] Parents and teachers should seek to use encouragement more often than coercion. Foster recommends a "vow of service," a commitment to reject the power games of modern society, to say yes to true power harnessed for the good of all, to discern and confront powers that enslave, and to lead through servanthood in little things, seeking neither titles nor honors, only the joy of helping.[29]

Wisdom herself offers her counsel and teaching as a form of power, but she is careful to point to the responsibilities of that power, responsibilities that are learned by placing a higher value on righteousness and setting the gifts of wealth and power in their proper places.

27. R. J. Foster, *Money, Sex, and Power: The Challenge of the Disciplined Life* (San Francisco: Harper and Row, 1985), 175. Foster's discussion of power is essential reading.
28. The phrase is borrowed from R. Fisher and W. Ury, *Getting to Yes: Negotiating Agreement Without Giving In* (New York: Penguin, 1981).
29. Foster, *Money, Sex, and Power*, 228–48.

Proverbs 8:22–36

²² "THE LORD BROUGHT me forth as the first of his works,
    before his deeds of old;
²³ I was appointed from eternity,
    from the beginning, before the world began.
²⁴ When there were no oceans, I was given birth,
    when there were no springs abounding with water;
²⁵ before the mountains were settled in place,
    before the hills, I was given birth,
²⁶ before he made the earth or its fields
    or any of the dust of the world.
²⁷ I was there when he set the heavens in place,
    when he marked out the horizon on the face of
        the deep,
²⁸ when he established the clouds above
    and fixed securely the fountains of the deep,
²⁹ when he gave the sea its boundary
    so the waters would not overstep his command,
and when he marked out the foundations of the earth.
³⁰   Then I was the craftsman at his side.
  I was filled with delight day after day,
    rejoicing always in his presence,
³¹ rejoicing in his whole world
    and delighting in mankind.

³² "Now then, my sons, listen to me;
    blessed are those who keep my ways.
³³ Listen to my instruction and be wise;
    do not ignore it.
³⁴ Blessed is the man who listens to me,
    watching daily at my doors,
    waiting at my doorway.
³⁵ For whoever finds me finds life
    and receives favor from the LORD.
³⁶ But whoever fails to find me harms himself;
    all who hate me love death."

PERHAPS THE MOST famous portion of the book of Proverbs is the speech personified Wisdom makes in praise of her own antiquity. Although age was more of a sign of wisdom in ancient times than it is now, more than wisdom of years is communicated here. Wisdom's presence at creation suggests that she knows how the world was put together and therefore knows how it works, inspiring the poetry of later wisdom writers like the son of Sirach. The scene also inspired certain New Testament writers, who found fitting language to describe the exalted Christ, risen from the grave and ascended to the heavens.

Even the most casual reader will notice a shift in topic that marks the second half of Wisdom's speech in 8:22. (1) It is the only verse in the whole speech to begin with the Hebrew *yhwh*, placing special emphasis on "the LORD," who is the main actor in all that follows. Wisdom is happy to say only that *she was there* when Yahweh made the heavens and the earth.

(2) The scene changes from a description of the present to a recollection of the primeval past. The LXX adds a verse that reads, "If I declare to you the things that daily happen, I will remember also to recount the things of old." Wisdom takes her listeners back to the dawn of creation to claim that she was a witness to God's great work of setting out the boundaries of the world. In asserting that she was there first, before any other part of creation, Wisdom continues to establish her credibility; that is, she enhances her authority to speak on behalf of God.[1]

It is important to keep in mind that the speech moves toward the call to listen in 8:32. More than a recap of 8:6, that final call defines the purpose of the entire speech. Wisdom speaks about her role in the founding and administration of the world *so that* she can make a claim that sounds like Jesus' words, "No one comes to the Father except through me" (John 14:6). She states that she should not be ignored, certainly not by those who would reject Yahweh's way, nor by those who call themselves believers.

The second half of Wisdom's speech is organized chronologically:

Wisdom was there *before* anything else (8:22–26)
Wisdom was present *when* the orders of creation were set in place (8:27–31)
Wisdom is *now* the one to whom we must listen (8:32–36)

---

1. The concerns for speaker credibility, or rhetorical *ethos*, were discussed in 8:1–21. We might say with only a little exaggeration that the concerns of *ethos* shape the whole speech. The three qualities of the trustworthy speaker are: good character (integrity) 8:1–11; good will (love) 8:12–21; good sense (competence) 8:22–31.

This structure highlights the authority of her ways and words (8:32–33). To ignore them is to hate them, and to hate her is to love death (8:36). Thus both chapters 7 and 8 end with the word "death" (*mawet*), a bitter frame surrounding the images of creation and life. This second half of Wisdom's speech also repeats and develops images and themes from 3:13–19. If the first half of that earlier text extolled Wisdom's worth and rewards (3:13–17; cf. 8:1–21), the second uses images of creation and life (3:18–20; cf. 8:22–36).

Wisdom Was There Before Anything Else (8:22–26)

THE FIRST CHALLENGE to the interpreter is establishing a translation of 8:22, as the NIV footnotes indicate. The first note on 8:22 tells us that "his works" translates literally as "his way," that is, a course of action, consistent with the use of "way" in Proverbs, which may have the derived sense of divine "dominion."[2] The second note on this verse reflects the decision to translate Hebrew *qanani* as "brought me forth," echoing Eve's words in giving birth to Cain (whose name makes a pun on the word, Gen. 4:1). But the word can also mean "create" (NRSV; cf. Gen. 14:19, 22; Deut. 32:6; Ps. 139:15) or "acquire" (Gen. 25:10; 33:19; Prov. 20:14); this latter meaning is used throughout Proverbs, particularly with reference to acquiring wisdom (4:5, 7; 15:32; 16:16; 17:16; 18:15; 19:8; 23:23).[3]

By itself, "acquired" can imply that Yahweh acquires Wisdom like a wife or as a preexistent being, neither of which fits the context of creation or later references to Wisdom's being born. Many interpreters find it theologically problematic that Yahweh would have a consort or that there are other uncreated eternal beings beside him. Readings that take "acquire" in this way press the imagery into service for which it was not designed; the repetition of birth images speaks against the marriage view. Most likely, some association with Proverbs' use of "acquire wisdom" is intended, so that Yahweh himself acquires her before setting out to do anything else, a course Wisdom recommends to her human pupils. This understanding of "acquire" need not imply that Wisdom is an eternal presence, only that some association with creation and birthing imagery is intended (8:24–23).

---

2. Habel, "The Symbolism of Wisdom in Proverbs 1–9," 131–57, argues that the primary symbol of the book is *derek*, the *way* of wisdom. Personified Wisdom is first a guide and protector, then the wayside counselor, then the cosmic, primordial force, who is "the beginning, impetus and source of Yahweh's own way."

3. Aitkin, *Proverbs*, 82, helpfully points out that the root meaning of "acquire" can be used for the acts of purchasing (Gen. 47:20), creating (Gen. 14:19), or begetting (Gen. 4:1). See also B. Vawter, "Proverbs 8:22: Wisdom and Creation," *JBL* 99 (1980): 205–16, who would retain the meaning "acquire."

The "first of his works" can also be translated "beginning," for the Hebrew *reʾšit* appears here as it does in 1:7, but also in 4:7, as first in importance: "Wisdom is supreme [*reʾšit*]; therefore get [*qnh*] wisdom. Though it cost all you have, get understanding."

Two other terms describe Wisdom's origins in 8:23–26, each set in the context of the time before creation. (1) Wisdom says in 8:23, "I was *appointed* [*nsk*] from eternity, before the world began," using a word that in some contexts describes the casting of a mold (thus the NIV footnote "fashioned"); this verse also repeats *reʾšit* ("beginning") and *qedem* ("before") from 8:22. (2) Continuing the thought in 8:24, she speaks of a time when there were no oceans or gushing springs, saying that then she was "given birth" (*ḥyl*).[4] Similarly, before the mountains, before the hills, before the earth or fields or any of the dust of the earth, she was "given birth" (again, *ḥyl*). The birthing, of course, is figurative, for the same word is used of bringing forth or birthing weather in 25:23: "As a north wind *brings* rain, so a sly tongue *brings* angry looks."

Coming through every one of Wisdom's statements is the claim that "I was here first"; Wisdom comes on the scene at the beginning, before Yahweh did anything else. This observation should guide our reading of all that follows, for the stress here is on Wisdom's coming forth as a work of Yahweh, not on the work she herself does. Nowhere in this text does it say that Yahweh did these things by her, although this is the message of 3:19–20. Later wisdom writings such as Sirach will also make the claim, but it is not to be found in this text.

Moreover, the text apparently makes no fine distinction between Wisdom's being created or birthed, both images ending up at the same destination of "first." The challenge for Christian readers is to avoid overreading this text on the basis of later biblical and theological distinctions. To pre-Christian readers and hearers, the birthing image was repeated to emphasize that before doing anything else to give form to heaven and earth, Yahweh first brought forth Wisdom.

Is Wisdom who speaks here the gift to humans of skill and insight (personified as a teacher and guide), or is she a personification of divine wisdom that put the world into order, or both? Immediate context does not grant many clues, but the larger context of the speech favors the former, that the Wisdom who speaks is she who can be both acquired and passed on from generation to generation, even as she herself teaches. With the claim that she

---

4. J. A. Foster, "The Motherhood of God: The Use of God-Language in the Hebrew Scriptures," in *Uncovering Ancient Stones: Essays in Memory of H. Neil Richardson*, ed. L. M. Hope (Winona Lake, Ind.: Eisenbrauns, 1994): 93–102. After examining the four uses of the term for birthing (here and Deut. 32:18; Ps. 90:1–2; Isa. 45:9–11), Foster concludes that the point is not so much the motherhood of God as the imagery of creation having a beginning like a birth, so she translates "to bring forth in pain" or to "writhe in labor."

was there before the waters were gathered and hills settled, Wisdom can claim access to the knowledge she offers to teach. If she were asked the question God asked of Job, "Were you there when I laid the earth's foundation?" (Job 38:4),[5] she would answer "Yes!"

In other words, here Wisdom enhances her authority and credibility by means of an ancient motif of knowledge. Only the one who knows how the world came to be and how it works is able to claim real knowledge; all else is limited at best, puffery at worst. To summarize, in this first section of the speech, Wisdom is the focus of all the action, although the action is accomplished by "the LORD" (Yahweh), whose name is the first Hebrew word in 8:22. Yahweh is the one who brought forth Wisdom before all else, making her appearance unique.

Wisdom Was Present When the Orders of Creation Were Set in Place (8:27–31)

WISDOM NOW MOVES from her own "coming forth" in 8:22–26 to her presence as the heavens and waters were divided (cf. Gen. 1:1–13), from a time when "there was not" to the time when the waters were gathered.[6] This, her second reminder to readers that "I was there," leads them to her celebration of creation in Proverbs 8:30–31. Each line of her report turns the spotlight on Yahweh's handiwork, a structured place for all that lives to dwell safely and thrive. The emphasis on place omits any mention of organic life apart from a side reference to humanity in 8:31. In stark contrast to the Genesis account, Wisdom's description of creation makes no mention of the lights, the plants, or any creatures of land or sea. Instead, she focuses on the physical environment and the proper location of its component parts. Readers will also notice that the terms she uses for God's work are assembled to create a picture of stability and order, even fixity.

Verses 27–28 move from the heights where Yahweh has set the heavens up in place and fixed the clouds to the depths where the seas are "marked."[7] The term for that marking (*ḥqq*) is used twice in 8:29, "when he gave the sea its *boundary* . . . and when he *marked out* the foundations of the earth," drawing a circle the way one uses a compass, setting boundaries so that the waters

---

5. Murphy, *Proverbs*, 52, sees a similar motif at work in Eliphaz's taunts to Job (Job 15:7–8).

6. Each line begins with Hebrew *bᵉ*, which the NIV translates "when."

7. So we recall that the creation is a separating of waters above and below by means of a sky-firmament and a separation of dry land and seas by boundaries (back to Gen. 1 and 9). Job asked who possessed the wisdom to count the clouds and tip over the water jars of the heavens, and the answer to his rhetorical question is Yahweh (Job 38:37). Note Ps. 78:23: "Yet he gave a command to the skies above and opened the doors of the heavens."

do not move past his command (lit., "pass over his mouth"). So Isaiah spoke of Yahweh who sits above the circle of the earth (Isa. 40:22). As we noted previously, the same term for that marking is used in Proverbs 8:15 for the enactment of just laws; as Yahweh sets boundaries for the seas that they dare not cross, so rulers enact boundaries of life that give it order and security.[8]

In other words, Wisdom, who watched Yahweh set the boundaries of creation, shows kings how to do the same for the social order. By fixing of heavens and drawing a circle on the deep, Yahweh puts a limit on the waters, stopping what in times of flood seems unstoppable. This sign of orderly creation echoes what was said in 3:19–20 about making a place for life to thrive. As the heavens are fixed above the skies and the seas fixed at their boundaries, so this place of life is stable and secure.

After the long series of "when's" comes the climax: "Then I was the craftsman at his side" (8:30), the double use of the Hebrew verb of being ("I was") adding emphasis. Gender considerations aside, the term "craftsman" is not the only plausible translation of Hebrew *ʾamon*. Scholarly debate has presented three renderings ("artisan," "counselor," or "child/nursling"); we will first consider the larger context and then return to discuss this contested term. What is clear in 8:30–31 is that Wisdom recalls the joy of those days, for she reports having been filled with delight daily, rejoicing before Yahweh at all times and rejoicing in the whole world; the human creation (8:31; lit., "the sons of *ʾadam*"; cf. 8:4) is her special delight. The two terms of joy are repeated in reverse order:

A *delighting* day after day
  B *rejoicing* at all times before the LORD
  B′ *rejoicing* in the world of his earth
A′ *delighting* in the children of Adam[9]

The word "delight" (*šaʿašuʿim*) is rare, the root used most often in Psalm 119 for the delights of the *torah* (119:16, 24, 77, 92, 143, 174). The prophets Isaiah and Jeremiah use this word for Yahweh's delight in his children in spite of their waywardness (Isa. 5:7; Jer. 31:20). Here in Wisdom's speech, there is some question over who takes delight. The LXX and some contemporary interpreters would translate that Wisdom is "his delight."[10] If so, Wisdom's

---

8. Van Leeuwen, "Proverbs," 93–94; although the symbolic connection he sees between the waters here and the waters of sexuality in 5:15–20 is not as obvious. The link between boundaries of the sea and human behavior in Jer. 5:21–29 is much closer to the imagery set out here. On the boundaries of the sea, see Job 38:8–11; Ps. 104:6–9; 148:4–6.

9. G. A. Yee, "An Analysis of Prov. 8:22–31 According to Style and Structure," *ZAW* 94 (1982): 58–66.

10. Fox, *Proverbs 1–9*, 287.

words might be paraphrased, "His delight was in me, my delight in his [creation of] humanity." Either way, the central meaning of the text, delight that culminates in Wisdom's pleasure in the "sons of ʾadam," remains constant.[11]

Wisdom also rejoices (8:30–31, *mᵉśaḥeqet*), the parallel lines noting her joy in God's presence and the new world he has made. Some take the Hebrew term to mean that Wisdom is playing or frolicking like a child. In this view, Wisdom first reports her metaphoric birth and then speaks of her childhood, playing while Yahweh works on setting up the world.[12] Play fits the hypothetical context of a child's development, but simple rejoicing before the works of Yahweh is more consistent with the extended description of the creation.

Thus, the primary sense of *mᵉśaḥeqet* shows Wisdom rejoicing before Yahweh, with possible secondary overtones of childhood play as a kind of wordplay. But it should also be noted that the same Hebrew verb appears in 1:26, where Wisdom "laughs" (root *śḥq*) at the calamity of the wicked. Just as Wisdom rejoices and celebrates the new and orderly world in chapter 8, she laughs at wicked scoundrels who disturb the social order.[13] In sum, while the translation of 8:30–31 is difficult, it is clear that when the world and humankind came into being, Wisdom was beside the One who brought it about, rejoicing and taking delight in what she saw.

So is the ʾamon of 8:30 an artisan (cf. Song 7:1),[14] a counselor,[15] or a nursing child (cf. Lam. 4:5)?[16] The strongest images of the poem show God's set-

---

11. Van Leeuwen, "Proverbs," 94–95, notes the delight and celebration at the completion of a construction project (1 Kings 8:62–66; Job 38:7; Jer. 30:18–19; 31:4; Zech. 8:5). Use of the verb for dancing and rejoicing at victory can be found at 1 Sam. 18:7; 2 Sam. 6:5, 21; 1 Chron. 13:8; 15:29; Jer. 30:19; 31:4.

12. Fox, *Proverbs 1–9*, 288–89, suggests that she plays before God, enjoying her study of the wonders of his work in the world, just as study in the Jewish tradition is considered a joy. See also Yee, "Theology of Creation" 85–96.

13. Perhaps this laughter plays on the mocking laughter of Wisdom's detractors (*śḥq* italicized): fools *find pleasure* in evil conduct (10:23), a wicked person can deceive a neighbor and claim to have been *joking* (26:19), and a fool can go to court and *scoff/mock* (29:9), bringing misery.

14. C. L. Rogers III, "The Meaning and Significance of the Hebrew Word ʾamon in Proverbs 8:30," *ZAW* 109 (1997): 208–20, argues that the words are in apposition, translating, "I was beside him, who is an ʾamon," naming Yahweh, not Wisdom, as artisan. Murphy, *Proverbs*, 47, seeks to preserve the ambiguity with "Then I was with him, as artisan."

15. Clifford, *Proverbs*, 23–28, 100–101, follows the tradition that takes ʾamon as a loanword from Akkadian *ummānu*, the scribe or sage who brought the arts to the world. She is therefore not a counselor to Yahweh but to humankind. See also Van Leeuwen, "Proverbs," 94–95, who argues that the *ummānu* does represent an "architect-adviser."

16. V. Hurowitz, "Nursling, Advisor, Architect? ʾamon and the Role of Wisdom in Proverbs 8:22–31," *Bib* 80 (1999): 391–400; M. Fox, "ʾamon Again," *JBL* 115 (1996): 699–702, argues for "being raised, growing up" (cf. Est. 2:20).

ting up the boundaries of creation's waters; this work is framed by his bringing forth Wisdom like a birth (8:24–25) and her rejoicing at Yahweh's creation of the world and humankind (8:30–31). If she were an artisan, it would be the only case in Proverbs in which she functions as an agent of creation, for "by wisdom" at 3:20 presents her as an instrument at most; again the focus is on Yahweh's activity. And while it is true that she speaks of her birth and that "rejoicing" can refer to play, this is slight evidence that we are watching a child busy at games or frolicking as Yahweh creates.[17] But we have seen that she teaches rulers to do what Yahweh does, that is, to set out boundaries and their order for the sake of life on earth (8:14–16; cf. 3:13–20 and the repetition of "life"). We also know she rejoices in the "sons of ʾadam" (8:31) and turns to address them as "my sons" (8:33).

Therefore, the image of a sage or counselor to humankind stands out as the most fitting in the context, even while there may sound overtones of an artisan or a child who grows up to build her own house (cf. 9:1). For this reason, our comments will focus on her claims that she was there first as a counselor, expressing delight. To summarize, in this section of the speech, Yahweh is the only actor until Wisdom forcefully states "I was" twice in 8:30, artistically turning the spotlight to her role of counsel and her celebration of God's work of creation. Because she delights in the way the world was ordered, she offers her counsel concerning that order to the humans she also finds delightful.

Wisdom Is Now the One to Whom We Must Listen (8:32–36)

WISDOM THE COUNSELOR and teacher now returns to the present. As she does, she begins to speak like the parental teachers: "Now then, my sons, listen to me" (cf. 5:7; 7:24), issuing a call to attention followed by charges and motivations. Reprising terms from the opening of her own speech, Wisdom once again calls out to the "sons of ʾadam" (cf. 8:4, 31), charging them to "listen" (šmʿ, repeated in 8:33 and 34; cf. 8:6).

Wisdom then adds that those who listen are "blessed" or happy (ʾašre, 8:32, 34; cf. 3:13; Ps. 1:1), and she explains what she means by listening. (1) It means keeping her ways (Prov. 8:32), practicing the ways that are pleasant and šalom (3:17). (2) It means listening to her instruction, just as in her first speech, Wisdom made special reference to those who ignored her counsel (8:33; cf. 1:25; 13:18; 15:32). (3) Those who listen watch daily at her doors, just as she daily took delight in Yahweh's work (8:34; cf. 8:30). They are

---

17. The images of building are clear in the poem, but it is not clear to me how this is creating a safe place for Wisdom to play as Yee, "Theology of Creation" 85–96, argues.

blessed as they wait (lit., "keep"; cf. 8:32) at the posts of her doorway, perhaps a wordplay on the door or opening of her lips in 8:6 (root *ptḥ*).

So we notice that while Wisdom begins by going to the entrance to the city to find hearers, she ends by inviting her hearers to come to *her* door, staying clear of the other woman's door (5:8). In each of the three verses (8:32–34), the word "listen" reminds the reader of the activity that comes first and foremost in wisdom instruction and the life of faith.

The motivations of 8:35 and 36 begin, as most do, with the linking word "for" (*ki*), and the motivations also revisit words used earlier in this speech and throughout the instructions. "Whoever finds me finds life" not only recalls the seeking and finding of 8:17, it adds the cherished treasure of "life," reminding the reader of the life she holds in her hand (3:13–18; esp. 3:13). To find Wisdom is not only to find life but favor from Yahweh. A good person finds such favor (12:2), but so does one who finds a wife (18:22)! God is pleased with all actions inspired by Wisdom, taking the same delight that Wisdom herself takes in humankind.

However, the one who fails to find her or "misses" her (*ḥṭʾ*, the word for sin as missing the mark) does violence to himself, reminding the reader of the violent men whom Yahweh hates (3:31–32; cf. 4:17; 10:6, 11). Violence is a term used most often by the psalmists and prophets for the one who harms another to do himself good. That violence is a form of self-hatred, and so to hate Wisdom is to hate oneself. Even as she loves those who love her (8:17), to hate her is to have another love, and that love is death. So in surprise to our ears, Wisdom ends her speech, not with an inspirational story or uplifting metaphor but with the clear and cold reality of death, using the same word that concluded the story of the other woman (*mawet*, 7:27) and the same image that will conclude the teaching of the next chapter and first portion of this book (9:18). Thus, the speech that traveled back in time to the origins of life also holds up the sad irony that many will choose to miss the one who makes that life available to all.

In sum, all of Wisdom's self-description has led to this moment when Wisdom calls for a hearing, repeating many of the terms the parents used in teaching about her. In a sense, the entire speech of chapter 8 is both a recap of the parents' exhortation to get wisdom and an introduction to the sayings of the community in chapters 10–22. As readers read the instructions that came before her speech and the collected proverbs that come after, they are hearing Wisdom's voice through the voice of family and community. In the sages' symbolism, the content of Proverbs is not simply shared bits of life's lessons, it is instruction in the workings of the world from the one who watched it come into being. Together, the two parts of the speech in chapter 8 say to their readers, "Seek Wisdom, and find wealth and life as well. Seek wealth or life apart from her, and you will miss Wisdom and find death." In many ways, the message of this speech resembles the teaching of Jesus in Mark 8:35–38 (TNIV; cf. Matt. 10:39; Luke 17:33; John 12:25).

> For those who want to save their life will lose it, but those who lose their life for me and for the gospel will save it. What good is it for you to gain the whole world, yet forfeit your soul? Or what can you give in exchange for your soul? If any of you are ashamed of me and my words in this adulterous and sinful generation, the Son of Man will be ashamed of you when he comes in his Father's glory with the holy angels.

TO REVIEW OUR findings so far, we have seen that Wisdom first speaks of the time *before* anything was made, claiming, "I was there first" (8:22–26), asserting the right to speak authoritatively. She then speaks of the time *when* the boundaries of creation were drawn and says, "I was there rejoicing," demonstrating that her knowledge of the world and its order is comprehensive (8:27–31). Finally, she turns to speak of *now*, saying, "I am here, speaking and teaching," adding that her instruction is the way to life and the favor of Yahweh, that her knowledge of Yahweh is intimate (8:32–36). In all, her speech looks to God, the giver of life, and argues that she has been given the authority to offer it.

The challenge of this portion of the book of Proverbs and its presentation of personified Wisdom is the sheer volume of discussion that has been written concerning it. The task of wading through the various interpretations can leave the reader feeling lost and confused. Moreover, Christians have a special interest in the image of Wisdom present at the dawn of creation, for it was appropriated by the New Testament writers as they sought to give expression to what they saw and heard in the person of Jesus. In our own day, the scene of a female figure at God's side, watching the earth and heavens set into place, has been of interest to those with feminist and ecological concerns. Many contemporary readers of Proverbs want to know if this text foreshadows the coming of Jesus and whether this feminine portrait has significance for our understanding of the Lord we worship.

Literary character of the speech. The place to begin in order to hear the message of this text to the church today is the literary character of the speech. In the context of Proverbs, personified Wisdom's words are presented as quotations of one of the parental teachers, spoken as an argument for undertaking the study of wisdom. In this way the voice of the parents symbolically makes the tradition of wisdom, given by God and passed on from generation to generation, their son's teacher. Moreover, in the context of Proverbs, Wisdom's words of persuasion counter the manipulative invitations of the strange/other woman in chapter 7 and Folly in chapter 9.[18] We must remember that the speech is part of the teacher's strategy of quoting discourse in order to make comparisons with rival views, evaluating their claims.

We must also remember that Wisdom is a personification of the wisdom that originates in the fear of God (cf. 1:7); therefore, we continue to ask about our response to God who gave this gift. He made her first so she could watch God set boundaries in creation and teach us how to set similar boundaries, so that we, the children of *'adam*, might live in the world God made. He originated this gift of Wisdom so that she might teach us. To listen to her is to listen to Yahweh and find his favor. The prominence of creation images in this part of the speech can draw attention away from the conclusion and its clear indication of the speech's purpose. First and foremost, then, we must understand the speech as a call to learn wisdom and view the details of creation imagery in that light.[19]

We must seek to understand the personification of Wisdom in terms of its primary setting, for the unnamed speaker describes her as a street preacher, a town crier, a herald of the king, who not only claims to have much to give (8:1–21) but strengthens her credibility by highlighting her experience and competence (8:22–26). The link between the two parts of the speech is the act of giving. Just as Yahweh set up an orderly world (holding back the waters) and gave it to humankind, so Wisdom speaks and "creates" an orderly world through her good teaching, a world to inhabit[20] that she offers to humankind.

We also see that the two parts of Wisdom's speech work in tandem, the testimony of her true words matched by her testimony that she witnessed Yahweh's activity of building the ordered world. Finally, in both parts of the speech she calls hearers to "listen" (8:6, 33–34). Wisdom's true and just speech is worth more than anything else in creation, just as she came before anything else in creation (8:10–11, 19, 22–26). She loves those who love her and seek her, just as she delights in the humans whom she invites to wait at her doors (8:17, 31–34).

---

18. C. V. Camp, *Wise, Strange, and Holy* (JSOTSup 320; Sheffield: Sheffield Academic Press, 2000), uses the symbols of Wisdom and the strange woman as a lens for the conflict in the Bible between that which is holy and that which is not.

19. While Wisdom may serve as a symbol of created order, as von Rad observed, she is more than the "self-revelation of creation." G. von Rad, *Wisdom in Israel* (Nashville: Abingdon, 1972), 144–76. Murphy, *Proverbs*, 54–55, adds that she is the "revelation of God."

20. So W. P. Brown, *The Ethos of the Cosmos: The Genesis of Moral Imagination in the Bible* (Grand Rapids: Eerdmans, 1999), 10–11, speaks of character using the original meaning of *ethos* as "stall" or "dwelling." "At base, it designates a *place* or habitation."

In sum, what we find in the speech is a two-part invitation to learn and study wisdom, based primarily on the *ethos* (character) of this teacher who is older than all worlds and, by implication, the first teacher of the tradition. The parental teachers did not speak so highly of their own experience, even while they were conscious of passing on this tradition.

In chapter 4, the father looked back on his own experience of study but also remembered that his father urged him to get (*qnh*) wisdom and get (*qnh*) understanding (4:5; cf. 8:22). He realized that his father spoke of his words and Wisdom as though they were one, calling the son to choose her (and therefore, his words) over anything else he might acquire (*qnh*, 4:7). Each generation is in a sense taught directly by one's forebears, yet they are also taught by the one who was present at the ordering of the world (cf. 3:20). Moreover, in contrast to the angry words of chapter 1, we see here that Wisdom delights in humankind and loves those who love her, so readers are encouraged to find her the way a man "finds" a wife (18:22; 31:10).

Wisdom's relationship to creation. There is a sense in which each section of this second half of Wisdom's speech makes a different association with creation, each one highlighting the rhetorical purpose. (1) The *before* section of the speech (8:21–26) makes an association between Wisdom and creation by establishing her presence as a witness. Like Genesis 1, the subject of the verbs is God; Wisdom does not claim to be cocreator with Yahweh,[21] for throughout Proverbs he is creator of all people (14:31; 17:5; 20:12; 22:2; 29:13). We have observed that Wisdom has the answers to Yahweh's questions that Job did not. Yahweh asked Job where he was when the earth's foundations were set and the stars sang and the angels shouted (Job 38:1–7); Wisdom tells her listeners that she was there, rejoicing (Prov. 8:30–31). Thus, we read these statements of her presence at creation and believe her claim to speak with knowledge and authority.

(2) The *when* portion of the speech (8:27–32) associates the separation and binding of waters with her celebration of its order. Yahweh asked Job if he knew who put the sea behind doors and "fixed limits for it" (*ḥqq*, Job 38:10); Wisdom claims that she saw how the work was done, how the "boundaries" were "marked out" (*ḥqq*, Prov. 8:29; cf. Ps. 104:6–9; 148:4–6; Jer. 5:21–29). A key connection appears between the rulers of earth who

---

21. G. M. Landes, "Creation Tradition in Proverbs 8:22–31 and Genesis 1," in *A Light Unto My Path: Old Testament Studies in Honor of Jacob M. Myers*, ed. H. N. Bream, R. D. Heim, C. A. Moore (Philadelphia: Temple University Press, 1974), 279–93. Both texts included the presence of primordial waters and the motif of priority in creation, but Prov. 8 uses ten different words for creation whereas Gen. 1 uses three or four. See also M. Bauks and G. Baumann, "Im Angang war . . . ? Gen. 1:1ff und Prov. 8:22–31 im Vergleich," *Biblische Notizen* 71 (1994): 24–52.

enact (*ḥqq*) righteousness and Yahweh, who sets limit for the sea and marks the foundation of the earth (also *ḥqq*). Just as Wisdom's activity of teaching what is right and just comes to expression in just rule (Prov. 8:15—16), so Yahweh's act of ordering the cosmos comes to climax in the setting of stable foundations and flood wall boundaries (8:27—29). Both Wisdom's speech and the world are marked by the inscribing (*ḥqq*) of boundaries.

In other contexts these boundaries are called decrees: "Keep falsehood and lies far from me; give me neither poverty nor riches, but give me only my daily bread [lit., "bread that is *decreed*," 30:8] ... lest they drink and forget *what the law decrees*, and deprive all the oppressed of their rights" (31:5; cf. 10:1). Certainly the association with Wisdom implies that she helps earthly rulers rule in righteousness based on the way Yahweh established the bounds of creation. Limits or boundaries, whether physical or social, are the foundations of rule and authority. As Wisdom rejoiced with Yahweh in the order of the world, so she is with rulers, helping them establish the same sort of order in the social world. Just as Yahweh set a limit for the waters, dividing them in making a space for life (Gen. 1) and setting them loose in judgment (Gen. 9), so the chaos of human sin needs limits.[22] Earthly rulers set similar boundaries that make a place for life to thrive.[23] So this mention of order and rule sets the stage for the individual sayings about the king (14:28, 35; 16:10—15; 20:2, 8, 26, 28; 25:2—6; 30:22—31; 31:1—4).[24]

(3) Wisdom's witness to creation allows her to say, "*Now* then, my sons, listen to me" (8:32), associating Yahweh's "way" of creation with her "way." Yahweh asked Job, "Who endowed the heart with wisdom or gave understanding to the mind?" (Job 38:36). Wisdom offers instruction that claims to make its students wise (Prov. 8:33; cf. 8:14). Moreover, she claims that those who find her find life and Yahweh's favor (8:35), thus fulfilling the purposes for which the orderly world was made. In so doing, she offers to share her close knowledge of God with those who seek her. Therefore, the speech, as an integral part of Proverbs, is best understood as the rhetoric of the wisdom tradition, a summons to a life of study and the knowledge of God (2:1—6).

Any discussion of Wisdom's call must be set in this original context, and its purpose as a summons must come before any other discussion of its sig-

---

22. So also the "twin pillars" of creation and covenant are woven throughout wisdom theology. R. L. Schultz, "Unity or Diversity in Wisdom Theology? A Canonical and Covenantal Perspective," *TynBul* 48/2 (1997): 271—306.

23. Brown, *Ethos of the Cosmos*, 12—27, reminds us that ancient Near Eastern creation accounts often stood as symbols of the ideal social order.

24. C. V. Camp, *Wisdom and the Feminine in the Book of Proverbs* (BLS 11; Sheffield: Almond Press, 1985), suggests that the symbol of Wisdom was a strategic response to the loss of the monarchy in postexilic Judaism.

nificance. But we cannot stop there if we wish to let Wisdom's words speak to our contemporary situation. It is her claim to offer counsel to kings, instruction to all, and life to those who seek her that moved the first Christians to understand the life and ministry of Jesus in terms of this literary figure. Just as she claimed to have had her existence before creation and the authority to teach on behalf of Yahweh, so Jesus, the firstborn of creation, also taught and brought his followers into relationship with God (Col. 1:15–23). It is this portrait of Wisdom's antiquity and authority to teach, even to reveal God's will to humankind, that drew New Testament writers to the personification of Wisdom as a way of describing the life and work of Jesus. Therefore, our consideration of contemporary responses will work in reverse, beginning with the biblical teaching about Jesus, the wisdom of God (1 Cor. 1:24, 30), then considering our responses to the voice of Wisdom herself.

FEMALE WISDOM? When I teach in churches, I am often asked about the connection between the voice of personified Wisdom and Sophia Christology, for many local congregations and the church bodies to which they belong wrestle with the claims that Sophia is an overlooked feminine aspect of God and the person of Jesus (*sophia* is the Greek translation of ḥokmah, "wisdom"). While some recommend combining Jesus and Sophia in worship or even substituting Sophia for the name of Jesus in traditional hymns,[25] others question the need to "regender" the gospel and image of God for believers today.[26]

Feminist appropriation of Wisdom's words here in chapter 8 take a variety of forms. For some, the image of a female counselor presents a model of wisdom and justice as a resource for women's faith.[27] Others find an identification of Wisdom with God, so that Wisdom is herself a divine

---

25. S. Cole, M. Ronan, H. Taussig, *Wisdom's Feast: Sophia in Study and Celebration*, new ed. (Kansas City, Mo.: Sheed and Ward, 1996). Included in this new edition is a report of the Sophia movement in the 1980s and early 1990s.

26. K. H. Jobes, "Sophia Christology: The Way of Wisdom?" *The Way of Wisdom: Essays in Honor of Bruce K. Waltke*, ed. J. I. Packer and S. K. Soderlund (Grand Rapids: Zondervan, 2000), 226–50, examines the claims of the Sophia movement in detail before concluding that the regendering is both anachronistic to the time of the Bible and inappropriate for our own. See also the discussions of personified Wisdom in 1:20–33 in this commentary.

27. S. Schroer, "Wise and Counseling Women in Ancient Israel: Literary and Historical Ideals of the Personified HOKMA," in A. Brenner ed., *A Feminist Companion to Wisdom Literature* (Sheffield: Sheffield Academic Press, 1995), 195. Schroer believes that Wisdom's picture of a counseling woman who can challenge, rejoice, and become angry is true to women's experience.

being.[28] The discussion is extensive and properly belongs in the field of New Testament studies. Therefore our brief discussion here can at best arrive at some sense of the afterlife of this famous text and point to references for further exploration.

The question of Sophia in contemporary theology and worship is raised by the New Testament writers' use of creation imagery:

> In the beginning was the Word, and the Word was with God, and the Word was God. He was with God in the beginning. Through him all things were made; without him nothing was made that has been made. (John 1:1–2)

> He is the image of the invisible God, the firstborn over all creation. For by him all things were created: things in heaven and on earth, visible and invisible, whether thrones or powers or rulers or authorities; all things were created by him and for him. He is before all things, and in him all things hold together. And he is the head of the body, the church; he is the beginning and the firstborn from among the dead, so that in everything he might have the supremacy. (Col. 1:15–18)

> In the past God spoke to our forefathers through the prophets at many times and in various ways, but in these last days he has spoken to us by his Son, whom he appointed heir of all things, and through whom he made the universe. (Heb. 1:1–2)

It appears that these texts were inspired by the personified Wisdom of Proverbs, but we also know that these portraits were not informed by the Proverbs texts alone but on citations from the additional books that were included in the LXX, the Apocrypha. In these books, the portrait of Wisdom in Proverbs was developed.

Wisdom praises herself
    and tells of her glory in the midst of her people.
In the assembly of the Most High she opens her mouth,
    and in the presence of his hosts she tells of her glory:

---

28. See K. M. O'Connor, "Wisdom Literature and Experience of the Divine," in *Biblical Theology: Problems and Perspectives* (Nashville: Abingdon, 1995), 183–95, who writes: "In contemporary rereadings of the text, Wisdom offers biblical theology a symbol of God who breaks the boundaries of gender and nationality, who relates to humans in intimacy and mutuality, and who joins them to the earth and to one another at her banquet of life." O'Connor goes on to argue that the speech is an example of ancient Near Eastern aretology, in which a goddess praises herself. "Hence Proverbs 8:1–21 and the poems that follow (8:22–32, 32–36) by their very genre, cast Wisdom as a divine being."

"I came forth from the mouth of the Most High,
  and covered the earth like a mist.
I dwelt in the highest heavens,
  and my throne was in a pillar of cloud.
Alone I compassed the vault of heaven
  and traversed the depths of the abyss.
Over waves of the sea, over all the earth,
  and over every people and nation I have held sway.
Among all these I sought a resting place;
  in whose territory should I abide?
Then the Creator of all things gave me a command,
  and my Creator chose the place for my tent.
He said, 'Make your dwelling in Jacob,
  and in Israel receive your inheritance.'
Before the ages, in the beginning, he created me,
  and for all the ages I shall not cease to be." (Sir. 24:1–9 NRSV)

I learned both what is secret and what is manifest,
for wisdom, the fashioner of all things, taught me. . . .
For wisdom is more mobile than any motion;
because of her pureness she pervades and penetrates all things.
For she is a breath of the power of God,
and a pure emanation of the glory of the Almighty;
therefore nothing defiled gains entrance into her.
For she is a reflection of eternal light,
a spotless mirror of the working of God,
and an image of his goodness.
Although she is but one, she can do all things,
and while remaining in herself, she renews all things;
in every generation she passes into holy souls
and makes them friends of God, and prophets;
for God loves nothing so much as the person who lives with wisdom.
  (Wisd. 7:21–28 NRSV)

God did not choose them,
  or give them the way to knowledge;
so they perished because they had no wisdom,
  they perished through their folly.
Who has gone up into heaven, and taken her,
  and brought her down from the clouds?
Who has gone over the sea, and found her,
  and will buy her for pure gold?

No one knows the way to her,
    or is concerned about the path to her.
But the one who knows all things knows her,
    he found her by his understanding.
The one who prepared the earth for all time
    filled it with four-footed creatures;
the one who sends forth the light, and it goes;
    he called it, and it obeyed him, trembling;
the stars shone in their watches, and were glad;
    he called them, and they said, "Here we are!"
    They shone with gladness for him who made them.
This is our God;
    no other can be compared to him.
He found the whole way to knowledge,
    and gave her to his servant Jacob
    and to Israel, whom he loved.
Afterward she appeared on earth
    and lived with humankind. (Bar. 3:27–37 NRSV)

Analogies, typology, and later identification. The New Testament portraits of Jesus who was present and instrumental in creation did not claim one-to-one identification with these portraits of Wisdom but rather used the principle of analogy to say that Jesus, the wisdom of God, is *like* these various earlier portraits. Just as the writers of these Old Testament and apocryphal books did not intend to create a portrait of a coming messenger of God, neither did the New Testament writers claim that Jesus was that figure. Rather Jesus, present and instrumental at creation, was identified as sharing features in common with that literary personification of the wisdom tradition.

In other words, as we read Old Testament and New Testament texts together, we do not see that Wisdom's speech points forward to Jesus (a concern that would have surprised the writers and those who passed it down) but that the New Testament writers looked back for analogies.[29] Just as John the Baptist spoke of Jesus as the "Lamb of God," alluding to the sacrificial texts, so Paul spoke of Jesus as the "wisdom of God" (1 Cor. 1:24), using this Old Testament text to help his readers understand aspects of his person and work.

In other words, the writer of Proverbs did not intend to describe a messiah or the person of Jesus; rather, later inspired writers (such as Paul) saw a correspondence and used a form of typology to make it clear to their read-

---

29. T. Longman III, *How to Read Proverbs* (Downers Grove, Ill.: InterVarsity Press, 2002), 109–10, reminds us that personification is a metaphor, a poetic device. Therefore, we must treat the analogy as a response to this poetic description of wisdom.

ers. Typology is a form of identification that points out similarities and correspondences to show how one person or event in Scripture is like another, also pointing to the same God at work in both. As still later generations of Christians grappled to understand the person and nature of Jesus the Christ, however, they looked to these Old Testament and apocryphal texts for further light on the New Testament teaching.

The Christological controversies of the early church used Proverbs 8 according to the practice of the time. Old Testament texts were not read according to their historical context but for Christological significance, using a typological method. Greek apologists such as Athenagoras (*On Defense of the Faith* 10) and Justin (*Dialogue with Trypho* 61) sought to prove the divinity and eternal nature of the Son. They reasoned that God was never without his wisdom, but that wisdom was begotten before all else came into being. As support they read the Latin and Greek versions of Proverbs 8:22, "the LORD created me." Later, Athanasius claimed that the term "created" refers to Christ's incarnation, not preexistence, contrary to Arius, who held that "created" implied inferiority.[30] Thus an identification with Jesus as that person depicted in Proverbs 8 led the disputants to look to a text that did not refer to Jesus, read in languages other than the original, to draw conclusions about his nature.

In my judgment, a similar identification of Jesus with the composite picture of the Old Testament and apocryphal portraits of Wisdom is at the heart of the present controversy over the use of Sophia as an appropriate term of worship. Readers in our congregations today will ask: Is the Woman Wisdom of Proverbs an Old Testament picture of Jesus? As we interpret today, we must remember that the New Testament writers, inspired by the Holy Spirit, looked back to the Old Testament to understand what had taken place in their own time. The fact that later generations used that typology in ways it was never intended (e.g., using the poetic depiction of Wisdom's origins to defend a position on the nature of Christ) does not give us permission to make the identification that Jesus was or is Woman Wisdom of Proverbs. We can instead affirm the New Testament writers' claim that Jesus is like Wisdom in significant ways.

In sum, it is one thing to claim that the New Testament writers used the image of a person, present at creation and a teacher of humankind, to describe Jesus; it is quite another to claim that this personification is to be identified as Jesus. Sophia was never meant to become a term of worship; rather, Wisdom was personified to direct our worship to the Father who gives

---

30. This discussion is indebted to D. H. Williams, "Proverbs 8:22–31," *Int* 48 (1994): 275–79; and F. C. Holmgren, *The Old Testament and the Significance of Jesus: Embracing Change, Maintaining Identity* (Grand Rapids: Eerdmans, 1999), 139–91.

wisdom, Christ who teaches and embodies the wisdom of God, and the Spirit who grants wisdom. Therefore, in seeking to appropriate the significance of Wisdom's self-declarations, we must focus on her purposes of exhortation and invitation and take great care in making statements about the origins and nature of this literary figure for the wisdom tradition.

Example of worship. Following the intention of this Old Testament text, the church should honor the authority of Wisdom, but only as a personified voice of the wisdom tradition that teaches us how to live and love God. We should not appropriate the language of Sophia as an accolade of worship, especially when it addresses her as a real person, even a goddess,[31] or so identifies her with Jesus that the identities are collapsed. Rather, the figure of Wisdom offers an *example* of worship; she teaches us how to offer praise to God that rejoices in the creation of physical order and humankind. Woman Wisdom is not an object of worship; rather, Wisdom is a *leader* of worship, and her example of worship emphasizes the creative action of God's wisdom.

Music and liturgy that celebrates creation along with Wisdom is appropriate, as is thanksgiving for the gift of wisdom that informs us about this life-giving order. Praise to God for the gift of wisdom is always appropriate, and the personification can be used to describe the wisdom that loves truth, speaks fairly, and is worth more than silver or gold. In a word, such worship celebrates the vision of life as God created it to be, balanced and whole.

Yet that same love for truth and fair speaking will also rage like a prophet when the powers of the earth and its rulers do not follow her example. Prayers and shouts of protest are also appropriate in a worship service that cites Wisdom's threats to those who have rejected her, even as we cite the prophets who railed against irresponsible Israel. Injustice is every bit a violation of wisdom as it is a violation of the covenant stipulations about matters of fairness and justice. The church can honor the authority of Wisdom as she leads the church in worship and directs the congregation's attention to God, but also as she teaches[32] the church

---

31. E. Achtemeier, *Preaching Hard Texts of the Old Testament* (Peabody, Mass.: Hendrickson, 1998), 111–15, reminds us that "personified wisdom is not divine or a hypostatsis or an incarnation of God: The monotheistic Hebrew Scriptures would never accept such a doctrine. She reveals the ways of God—of love and righteousness and life—that are built into the structure of the universe. Indeed we would not go wrong if we characterized wisdom as the plan of God, whereby he has ordered all the natural world and directed the course of human history," 112.

32. Does this picture of a teaching woman speak to the issue of women's leadership in the church's ministry? Even if we grant that Wisdom is a personified literary figure and not a real teaching woman, she also embodies the roles of counseling women in the Old Testament, including Lemuel's mother in Prov. 31. This image in itself does not establish a

concerning her ways of life and directs the church's attention toward our responsibilities.[33]

Ecology. Although the depiction of creation is presented to argue for Wisdom's authority and the authority of the social order she teaches, Wisdom's offer of life also directs our attention to matters of justice and order with regard to the physical environment. If Wisdom rejoices in the order and beauty of creation, then we may conclude that creation is worth preserving, every bit as much as the social order it represents.

Christians will differ over how best to manage the physical resources that have been placed in our care. Some may believe the position of others is too extreme, for some will advocate use and development while others will think of preservation and limits on that development.[34] My own experience of seeing abandoned bauxite minepits in Jamaica has convinced me that business organizations are not always careful to clean up after themselves. The biologist Calvin DeWitt has been a vocal proponent of preservation, arguing that there need to be untouched places where the earth and heavens can sing forth the glory of God.[35] It is not coincidental that Wisdom's offer to teach the ways of life is authenticated by her presence at the time the earth was organized into a home for living beings.

In summary, Wisdom's offer of life is predicated on acceptance of the counsel she offers to kings and commoners, the instruction she holds out to all. To the wisdom writers who gave us her words, life can either be cut short and emptied, or it can be enriched, lived to the fullest. This gift of life can either be joined to Wisdom, she who knows the structure and plan of its Creator, or suffer the consequences of doing without it.

---

warrant, but it points toward a picture of women active in ministry, not away from it. See R. T. France, *Women in the Church's Ministry: A Test Case for Biblical Interpretation* (Grand Rapids: Eerdmans, 1995), for a discussion of approaches to the question and a position favoring women in ministry.

33. R. Murphy, "The Kerygma of the Book of Proverbs," *Int* 20 (1966): 3–14. "Only wisdom personified is said to proclaim (*kerusso*) in the LXX. What is the message? It is the message of life."

34. P. A. Olson, *The Journey to Wisdom: Self-Education in Patristic and Medieval Literature* (Lincoln and London: Univ. of Nebraska Press, 1995), contends that the early and medieval Christians did not foster a cavalier attitude toward the environment, as some have charged, but rather that their understanding of the wisdom tradition encouraged reverence toward the created world. D. Edwards, *Jesus the Wisdom of God: An Ecological Theology* (Maryknoll, N.Y.: Orbis, 1995), overreads the connection of Wisdom and Jesus but makes important points about environmental stewardship that are supported by the general teaching of Proverbs.

35. For a description of DeWitt's work, see Q. J. Schultze, *Communicating for Life: Christian Stewardship in Community and Media* (Grand Rapids: Baker, 2000), 1–4.

Proverbs 9:1–18

¹ WISDOM HAS BUILT her house;
   she has hewn out its seven pillars.
² She has prepared her meat and mixed her wine;
   she has also set her table.
³ She has sent out her maids, and she calls
   from the highest point of the city.
⁴ "Let all who are simple come in here!"
   she says to those who lack judgment.
⁵ "Come, eat my food
   and drink the wine I have mixed.
⁶ Leave your simple ways and you will live;
   walk in the way of understanding.

⁷ "Whoever corrects a mocker invites insult;
   whoever rebukes a wicked man incurs abuse.
⁸ Do not rebuke a mocker or he will hate you;
   rebuke a wise man and he will love you.
⁹ Instruct a wise man and he will be wiser still;
   teach a righteous man and he will add to his learning.

¹⁰ "The fear of the LORD is the beginning of wisdom,
   and knowledge of the Holy One is understanding.
¹¹ For through me your days will be many,
   and years will be added to your life.
¹² If you are wise, your wisdom will reward you;
   if you are a mocker, you alone will suffer."

¹³ The woman Folly is loud;
   she is undisciplined and without knowledge.
¹⁴ She sits at the door of her house,
   on a seat at the highest point of the city,
¹⁵ calling out to those who pass by,
   who go straight on their way.
¹⁶ "Let all who are simple come in here!"
   she says to those who lack judgment.
¹⁷ "Stolen water is sweet;
   food eaten in secret is delicious!"
¹⁸ But little do they know that the dead are there,
   that her guests are in the depths of the grave.

COMING ON THE HEELS of Wisdom's majestic speech of chapter 8, the conclusion of the instructions in chapter 9 sums up all that has been said before with a final appeal to study wisdom, here depicted as an able and generous host. The most outstanding feature of this finale is the juxtaposition of speeches from Wisdom and her nemesis, Folly. We have noted that chapter 8 departed from the typical instruction form of ancient Near Eastern wisdom literature (call to attention, charge, and motivation).[1] Instead, Wisdom called from the heights to any and all who would listen; so here also, Wisdom calls out to all, particularly the simple, but her words now echo back in a mocking parody from personified Folly.

Therefore, like the two speeches of chapters 7–8, these two speeches in chapter 9 contrast the ways of wisdom and waywardness. As readers study this contest of words and ideas, they can also imagine the parents getting ready to send their son out to make his way in the world, once again urging him to remember all they have taught him. It remains to be seen whether he will remember his parents' instruction.

These descriptions and quotations of Wisdom and Folly are a study in similarities and contrasts. Both Wisdom and Folly call out from a house situated in the highest place. Both begin with the same invitation: "Let all who are simple come in here," adding an invitation to a meal. Both Wisdom and Folly use proverbs; Wisdom's speech concludes with a series of proverbs, ending with, "If you are wise, your wisdom will reward you; if you are a mocker, you alone will suffer" (9:12). Folly has only one proverb, but it is revealing: "Stolen water is sweet; food [bread] eaten in secret is delicious" (9:17).

However, the teacher shows these similarities only to point out the glaring differences. Wisdom works at building and preparing in order to have a sumptuous banquet to offer her guests while Folly sits at her door, loud, undisciplined, and without knowledge. The meals are different, Wisdom offering wine and meat, Folly offering only bread and water. There are the differences in outcome. Wisdom offers a future, a call to maturity, and in a word, life. Folly only offers the immediate pleasure of good things enjoyed outside their intended boundaries, hiding the fact that such pleasure brings death.

---

1. M. Odell Gilchrist, "Proverbs 1–9: Instruction or Riddle?" *Proceedings of the Eastern Great Lakes and Midwest Biblical Societies* 4 (1984): 131–45, believes that the instruction genre does not fit this chapter and that chs. 1–9 together form a riddle to expound the thematic statement of 1:1–7. McKane, *Proverbs, 1–10*, acknowledges that less than half of chs. 1–9 conforms to this definition of instruction. Moreover, the antithesis between avoiding the other woman and embracing Wisdom is not seen in Egyptian charges to avoid adultery.

A series of concentric ring structures shape this chapter, contrasting Wisdom and Folly's invitations as well as the responses and fates of mockers and wise ones. The structure also sets "the fear of the LORD" at the center of its reflections on learning (9:10).[2] This central section includes a number of terms from the prologue and chapter 1, but those terms appear also in the two invitations that frame it.[3]

Wisdom's Invitation (9:1–6)
    Description and location (9:1–3)
    Invitation to the simple—"life" (9:4–6)
Learning Wisdom (9:7–12)
    Responses of mockers and wise persons (9:7–9)
        "Fear of the Lord is the beginning of wisdom" (9:10)
    Final outcomes of mockers and wise persons (9:11–12)
Folly's Invitation (9:13–18)
    Description and location (9:13–15)
    Invitation to the simple—"death" (9:16–18)

The structure of the chapter reveals that this debate by Wisdom and Folly is not only about choosing one host/teacher over the other but about what kind of person the hearer will become. Decision demonstrates character, so that one becomes either a mocker or a wise one.

Wisdom's Invitation (9:1–6)

THE SPEAKER, MOST likely one of the parental teachers of chapters 1–8, again introduces Wisdom's speech, setting it at the highest place in the city (cf. 1:20–21; 8:1–3). From this visible and central location, she invites her hearers to the house she has constructed and the feast she has made ready. The picture of Wisdom building a house reminds the reader of the cosmos building of 8:27–31 and the doors of 8:34, suggesting that this house is symbolic in some way of her teaching. Just as Yahweh ordered the universe and its boundaries,[4] so Wisdom builds a house in which she dwells and offers her teaching, symbolized

---

2. Meinhold, *Die Sprüche*, 1:156.

3. Whybray argues that the prologue of Proverbs provides the hermeneutical lens for the rest of the book and should be consulted as a touchstone for interpretation, but not as a clue to a "grand structural scheme" (*Reading the Psalms as a Book* [JSOTSup 222; Sheffield: Sheffield Academic Press, 1996], 84).

4. R. C. Van Leeuwen, "Building God's House: An Exploration in Wisdom," in *The Way of Wisdom: Essays in Honor of Bruce K. Waltke*, ed. J. I. Packer and S. K. Soderlund (Grand Rapids: Zondervan, 2000), 204–11, shows the parallel between God's founding the earth by wisdom, understanding, and knowledge (3:10–20) and building a house (24:3–4).

in the lavish banquet. In interpreting the symbolism of this picture, however, readers should not allegorize the details so that meat and wine represent two different kinds of teaching or the maidservants teachers of wisdom.[5]

What, for example, does the house represent? The wide range of suggestions is evidence that clear indications are lacking; proposals include: a palace, a temple, a school, and even the universe itself. Michael Fox suggests it is an ancient symposium.[6] Most likely, the house is like a mansion, representing security and splendor.[7]

The seven pillars are "hewn," possibly the way a stone cutter shapes rough stone (though the LXX reads they were "set up"). The pillars may be supports (Judg. 16:25, 26, 29),[8] decoration (as in Solomon's temple, 1 Kings 7:2–22), or symbols of the pillars of the earth (Ps. 75:3; cf. 1 Sam. 2:8; Job 9:6; 26:11).[9] Interpreters have looked outside the book for analogies in ancient Near Eastern imagery as well as within the book itself, such as the seven Hebrew poems in chapters 2–7.[10] However, the seven superscriptions in the book may just as likely be a candidate (1:1; 10:1; 22:17; 24:23; 25:1; 30:1; 31:1). No clear direction is given, but we will not go far afield if we remember that the number *seven* is often associated with seven days of creation and completion. If Wisdom has built her house, it is finished and it is good—nothing else is needed.

Not only does Wisdom demonstrate her positive character through her hard work of building (cf. 14:1), she also knows how to throw a great party (perhaps as a celebration of the building's completion, cf. Solomon's temple, 1 Kings 8:62–66).[11] It must be remembered, however, that in the context of the poem, Wisdom builds the house so that she can invite her guests to enjoy the banquet, symbolic of her instruction (as she makes clear). The meal is luxurious, for wine and meat were not daily fare for the commoner. The slaughter of

---

5. K. G. Sandelin, *Wisdom as Nourisher: A Study of An Old Testament Theme, Its Development Within Early Judaism and its Impact on Early Christianity* (Åbo: Åbo Akademi, 1986), 19–26. Sandelin shows how early Jewish and Christian communities did such allegorical reading.

6. M. V. Fox, "Ideas of Wisdom in Proverbs 1–9," *JBL* 116 (1997): 626. See also Sir. 32:1–13.

7. Estes, *Hear My Son*, 122; Aitken, *Proverbs*, 90; Whybray, *Proverbs*, 142–43.

8. Clifford, *Proverbs*, 106.

9. Van Leeuwen, "Proverbs," 102.

10. Skehan, "The Seven Columns of Wisdom's House in Proverbs 1–9," 9–14. Again, allegorical fancy has derived every sort of referent for the seven pillars, including the seven days of creation, the seven planets, the seven liberal arts, and the seven fruits of the spirit (see Fox, *Proverbs 1–9*, 297–98).

11. Susan Niditch suggests that it is a victory-enthronement banquet on the analogy of Isa. 55 (*Oral World and Written Word*, 22). Clifford, *Proverbs*, 104, notes that Isa. 55 requires turning from evil before eating the sacred meal; he also thinks that Folly's call resembles the goddess Anat's deceptive and dangerous invitation to Aqhat.

meat says more about the richness of the meal than any religious rite; the word for ritual sacrifice is not used. Wine mixed with spices appears in Song of Songs 8:2, but Wisdom may just be preparing her wine for drinking by mixing it with water. The preparations ready, she sends out her maids, who call out the invitation on behalf of their mistress from the high places of the city.

Wisdom's speech is less public address than public invitation to her table, but as in chapter 8, she addresses the simple, those who "lack judgment [lit., heart]." The structure, however, pairs two addresses with two recipients; the simple are invited to literally "turn in here," and those who lack heart are called to come and eat her food (lit., bread) and to drink that mixed wine. The hospitality is her teaching, as confirmed by the prologue and its promise to give "prudence to the simple" (1:4). In contrast to the other woman, her meat and drink will bring life, not death (9:6; cf. 7:14–18; 21–27). But to come to her is to leave those simple ways behind (*peta'im*, cf. 9:4) and to walk in a new way, the way of understanding.

The invitation makes clear that not to decide is to decide; one gives up something, either simple ways or life. At the beginning of her first speech Wisdom asked, "How long will you simple ones love your simple ways?" (1:22); so here she speaks of those ways as rivals, incompatible with what she will provide. To turn aside (*swr*, 9:4) to her house is to abandon the paths of purposeful ignorance and foolishness. Wisdom holds her potential guests responsible to turn aside from a dead-end path and to walk in the way of understanding. The shift in metaphor makes the young learner a traveler once again, stressing the importance of choosing the right way. As Wisdom stated at the end of her first speech, "the waywardness of the simple will kill them" (1:32), and so here she offers to direct them on a straight path that leads to life (cf. 9:11).

In sum, the images and words of personified Wisdom together create a picture of a woman who is self-sufficient, industrious, wealthy, and concerned for the welfare of others, particularly the hungry, simple youth.[12] She is the embodiment of the wise person of Proverbs, a person who is careful to learn wise ways and teach them to others. This picture of Wisdom will take many forms throughout the book, male and female, but will reappear as a competent female provider once again in chapter 31.[13]

---

12. The picture extends the images of the tree of life (3:18), the protector (4:6–9), and a "sister" (7:4). In a sense, all three of the intervening images can be interpreted as metaphors for a good wife.

13. R. C. Stallman, "Divine Hospitality and Wisdom's Banquet in Proverbs 9:1–6," in *The Way of Wisdom: Essays in Honor of Bruce K. Waltke*, ed. J. I. Packer and S. K. Soderlund (Grand Rapids: Zondervan, 2000), 117–33. However, I do not agree with Stallman that Wisdom represents God, who is the host. Rather, she resembles him, and her feast resembles his provision of the wisdom tradition, which will teach and nourish those who accept the call.

Learning Wisdom (9:7–12)

THE SECTION THAT follows Wisdom's invitation appears to intrude, interrupting the contrast with the invitation of Folly. While most interpreters conclude that the section is secondary and therefore unrelated, it is possible to observe an intention behind the inclusion of this discourse. This section not only repeats significant terms from the prologue, it also summarizes the theme of receiving or rejecting instruction that carries throughout the rest of the book (13:1; 15:5, 12; 16:20; 17:16; 18:15; 19:8, 25; 23:9; 27:22).[14]

The structure of the section begins with the responses of the mocker and the wise person (9:7–9) and ends with their rewards (9:11–12). In the central position of this frame, "the fear of the LORD" links response and outcome, explaining the difference as fear of Yahweh (9:10). Therefore, juxtaposition of elements that appear dissimilar on the surface need not be taken as a sign of patchwork; the chapter is more like a skillfully sewn quilt, beautiful in its assembly of varied pieces.

The shift from second-person public invitation to third-person counsel about the mocker (9:7) leaves the reader wondering who is speaking and who is being addressed. However, "you" resumes in 9:8 and "me" occurs in 9:11. While it is possible that the speaker is the unnamed teacher, perhaps the parents addressing other teachers, it is also possible to hear the words as part of Wisdom's larger address. The counsel is directed to "whoever" will correct, rebuke (three times in 9:7–8), and instruct (9:9), suggesting that the intended listener is either a teacher or a person who is expected to become one.

Recalling the father's remembrance that he in turn was taught by his father before him (4:3–4), we can surmise that Wisdom also intends for those who accept her learning to teach it to others. A learner by definition is one who becomes a bearer of the tradition. Joubert's saying, "The one who teaches learns twice," is fitting here. Each of the three sayings about teaching in 9:7–9 can stand independently as proverbs. Read together as a group, they shape a teacher's expectations while at the same time making teaching appealing, for who does not want to be counted among the wise?

Wisdom's invitation included a word of correction in 9:6, and that correction is carried into 9:7–9, gathering together synonyms for correcting and instructing. These sayings distinguish the responses of the wicked and the wise. While the mocker and wicked reject correction, the wise one not only welcomes correction but receives instruction. The twofold aspect of teaching, including both the negative and positive, runs throughout the instructions. The threefold rebuke of 9:7–8 is central to Wisdom's first speech

---

14. Meinhold, *Die Sprüche*, 1:155–58.

(1:23, 25, 30); those she castigates as mockers do not receive it (1:22), and so no mention is made of any teaching in chapter 1.

In Wisdom's view, people show their character by their response to correction, mockers by rejecting correction or the wise by receiving it. However, the rejection mentioned here is more than the deaf ear of chapter 1. The mocker actually turns back to insult and do harm as a sign of hatred, similar to the hatred that shows itself in 1:29: "They hated knowledge and did not choose to fear the LORD" (cf. 1:7, "fools despise wisdom and discipline.").[15] By contrast, the wise person loves those who give rebuke and learns from those who offer instruction. The wise become wiser and the righteous add to their learning (9:9), echoing the goal of the prologue in 1:5: "Let the wise listen and add to their learning."[16]

Verse 10 also echoes the keynote of 1:7 in the prologue by reminding the reader that "the fear of the LORD is the beginning of wisdom, and knowledge of the Holy One is understanding." Thus, Wisdom brings her own invitation to a climax by citing this programmatic statement of piety, knowledge, and character. In the context of the instructions of Proverbs 1–9, "fear of the LORD" creates a frame around all that comes in between. Inviting the simple to her feast, she also intends to point her learners to the fear of Yahweh. The last word of 9:10, "understanding," repeats the last word of 9:6, underscoring its importance.

Like 8:13–14, this discourse places a "fear of the LORD" saying just before Wisdom goes on to describe what she offers. The next two verses (9:11–12) offer the motivation of rewards, continuing the focus on the wise person that began with 9:9 and carried through 9:10. Second-person address resumes as Wisdom speaks of herself, "For through me your days will be many, and years will be added to your *life*," repeating the key term from 9:6. The promise of life has been consistent with Wisdom's appearances (1:32–33; 3:18; 8:35); she protects her charges from early death, unlike her enemy (9:18), and offers them long and satisfying life. What follows in 9:12 is a new turn, literally: "If you are wise, you are wise for you, but if you mock, you alone will bear it." This final proverb causes the reader to stop and reflect.[17]

---

15. The righteous person has appeared before (2:20; 3:33; 4:18), but for the first time such a one is associated with wisdom, perhaps a foreshadow of the contrast between the righteous and wicked central to chs. 10–15.

16. In the ancient Near East, teachers recognized that everyone can be taught, but some will not learn. The problem was not a lack of intelligence but will. M. V. Fox, "Who Can Learn? A Dispute in Ancient Pedagogy," in *Wisdom You Are My Sister* (CBQMS 29; Washington, D.C.: Catholic Biblical Assocation of America, 1997), 62–77.

17. The LXX adds some exposition: "Son, if you are wise for yourself, you shall also be wise for your neighbors; and if you should prove wicked, you alone will bear the evil. He

Taking the proverb as Wisdom's last words, we see that she puts responsibility squarely on the shoulders of the listener, making it clear that one "reaps what one sows." She tells each of her listeners to decide whether they will be a wise one or a mocker. Once you hear the call of Wisdom, she warns, you are no longer simple or unlearned. You are either on your way to becoming wise or you are a scoffer; it all depends on your response. And if you are wise, you are not only learning for yourself, you are learning for others, for you will become a teacher. Wisdom's feast, then—her instruction and her correction—is a first course in the fear of Yahweh. Her call is not an invitation to some school of manners or moral self-improvement. Rather, it is an invitation to know the Holy One.

Folly's Invitation (9:13–18)

WHEN WISDOM SPEAKS in Proverbs, it is typically in answer to the voice of wickedness and folly. Wisdom's first speech in chapter 1 is preceded by the invitation of the violent men, and her great speech in chapter 8 is preceded by the smooth words of the other woman. Now, her banquet invitation is followed by a nearly identical call from Folly.

The differences are significant. Whereas Wisdom was portrayed as hardworking and generous, Folly is loud and boisterous (like the other woman of 7:11), "undisciplined" (*p^etayyut*, uses the same root letters as "simple"), and without knowledge. Just as Wisdom calls from the highest places, Folly takes a seat at the high places and, adds the teacher, calls to those who pass by, going straight on their way (the root *yšr*, "straight," is often used for "upright"; cf. 22:3=27:12, where the "simple pass by [lit.]"). Folly's identical call to the simple to "turn in here" (lit., 9:16; cf. 9:4) takes on a new meaning in this context. She calls away those who want to walk a straight path.

Like Wisdom, Folly offers something to eat, but the fare is meager. The Hebrew follows the same word order in both lines of 9:17: "Water stolen—sweet; food (bread) in secret—delicious" (lit., "pleasant," perhaps mocking the description of wisdom in 2:10; 3:17). Put this way, readers can identify with the enticement, for they know that there is a pleasure in doing what is wrong, a thrill from going out of bounds. Yet they also see how ridiculous these words are, for they offer bread and water as better than meat and wine! Compared with the other woman's invitation to a feast of meat in chapter 7, these words reveal such foolish seductions for what they are:

that stays himself upon falsehoods, attempts to rule the winds, and the same will pursue birds in their flight: for he has forsaken the ways of his own vineyard, and he has caused the axles of his own husbandry to go astray; and he goes through a dry desert, and a land appointed to drought, and he gathers barrenness with his hands."

ridiculous, laughable, deceptive, and cheap. One might even say that Folly has no food to offer, for to taste her food requires stealing. There is no real offer of nourishment for life here, only lust that leads to death, even as she tries to make it appear better.

The "stolen water" reminds the reader of the waters of sexual intimacy that can either be contained at home or poured out in the streets (5:15−18). So too, the "[bread] eaten in secret" is most likely another description of infidelity, for the adulteress comes out in the dark to tell the young man that the husband is gone, the coast is clear, no one will know (7:6−20). Like the strange woman's invitation to feasting in chapter 7, Folly separates deed from consequence, offering pleasures but hiding the trap of death. Woman Wisdom, by contrast, does point out the difference, stating that she has life and Folly has death (9:11−12; cf. 8:35−36).[18] So here, Folly is not given the last word, but the teacher reminds us that those she calls "do not know"[19] about the dead who forever remain in her house, a highway to Sheol (cf.7:23−27; 5:5−6).

Folly's use of the very same words as Wisdom (9:4, 16) sounds like mocking, proving her to be one of the mockers who will not receive correction but rather does harm (9:7−8). The figure of Folly is both laughable and tragic; her brief appearance draws together all that has been said about the other woman and wicked men, for both misuse the power of speaking and lead all who believe their lies to violence and death. Therefore, even while Wisdom's previous speeches answered the enticements of the gang and the seductions of the other woman, here the teacher gives Folly one last chance to speak with "smooth words," but they have lost their power, having been exposed for what they are in the previous instructions.

Because readers now know how false words can cover up rotting graves, they will not be taken in. However, danger still lurks, for the young man has not yet chosen Wisdom.[20] In fact, readers never see him make that choice; rather, they are put in the same position as that young man, faced with making the choice between two calls. If readers choose Wisdom, they will continue to read and learn to interpret more difficult sayings. If they refuse, it is not because they haven't heard Wisdom's side of the story.

---

18. C. V. Camp, "Woman Wisdom as Root Metaphor: A Theological Consideration," in *The Listening Heart: Essays in Wisdom and the Psalms in Honor of Roland E. Murphy*, ed. K. Hoglund et al. (JSOTSup 58; Sheffield: JSOT Press, 1987), 45−76.

19. The word "guests" comes from *qr²*, "to call." The LXX does not present a tragic ending in 9:18: "But he knows that mighty men die by her, and he falls in with a snare of hell. But hasten away, delay not in the place, neither fix your eye upon her: for thus you shall go through strange water; but abstain from strange water, and drink not of a strange fountain, that you may live long, and years of life may be added to you."

20. Gilchrist, "Proverbs 1−9: Instruction or Riddle?" 131−45.

Bridging Contexts

AS WE HAVE made our way through chapters 7–9 and its portraits of women wise and foolish, we have seen that their appeals bring out either foolishness or wisdom in the men who listen to one or the other. We have seen that the "simple" young man was mentioned three times in the first chapter (1:4, 22, 32) but has not been seen again until he wanders near the home of the adulteress (7:5). For this reason, Wisdom directs her words to all who are simple (8:5; 9:4, 6), to counteract the deadly seductions of all such Folly (9:16–18). We have also seen that those who heed Wisdom's invitation are themselves called "wise" (8:33; 9:8–12), while those who refuse her are called "mockers," a term that appears only once between chapters 1 and 9 (3:34).

Recapitulation. The point of this review is that chapters 7–9 recapitulate the terms and themes of the opening chapter, answering some of the questions that were raised there. If we wondered why the parents chose to begin their teaching with warnings about violent predators (1:10–19), we now see that at root, there is much that violence has in common with the sin of adultery. Both involve seductions of unrestrained desire, and both do harm to a neighbor. If we wondered why Wisdom was so strident in her first speech, we now see that it is because previous invitations to her banquet of instruction have been rejected.

Like a movie that begins with a foreshadow of the end, so Proverbs begins with her final words to mockers who have spurned her correction and hated fear of Yahweh (1:22–33). Moreover, those mockers have not learned the ways of understanding that Wisdom promised to teach (9:6, 10). Just as Wisdom pronounced their suffering in chapter 1, so here she places it on the shoulders of the listener: "If you are a mocker, you alone will suffer" (9:12). Close reading of this recapitulation draws our attention to the important but often overlooked middle section of 9:7–12. It is here that "the fear of the LORD . . . the beginning of wisdom" (cf. 1:7; 2:5; 8:13) is sounded once again as the all-important focus of learning and decision-making.

Wisdom's offer. The symbolism of Wisdom and her banquet is the embodiment of both divine summons and human response.[21] In attending to the metaphor, readers "move from being spectators to participants, from

---

21. R. Murphy, "The Faces of Wisdom in the Book of Proverbs," in *Mélanges bibliques et orientaux en l'honneur de M. Henri Cazelles*, ed. A. Caquot and M. Delcor (Neukirchen-Vluyn: Neukirchener Verlag, 1981), 337–45. Murphy proposes that the inaccessibility of wisdom in Job and limits on human attainment in Ecclesiastes distanced wisdom so that Woman Wisdom and her call developed as a integration of divine call and human response.

mere students to disciples."[22] And, as we have seen, Proverbs 1–9 presents a metaphoric system that integrates images of creation, stressing the importance of boundaries and the wisdom to recognize them, the "way the world works," and the wisdom to cooperate with its order. The symbol of Woman Wisdom boldly proclaims that there is a moral grain in the universe and that "to follow her precepts is to go with this grain rather than rub up against it for it is essentially a moral grain. There is a moral order at the heart of all creation and Wisdom leads people to it."[23] In sum, then, the call of Wisdom symbolizes both the created moral order and the need to choose one's response to it. Therefore, Wisdom's offer of instruction includes a call to correction/rebuke, fear of Yahweh, and discernment.

(1) Wisdom offers *correction*, or, as she says three times, *rebuke*. Readers may not find this aspect of instruction appealing and may ask, "What kind of a feast is that? You invite me to a dinner and then tell me it's going to be a lecture on good behavior, served with a dessert of 'you'll thank me for this someday' speeches?" Hearing this, we can understand why Wisdom does not get as many takers as we might imagine. Wisdom demands a decision to grow, a change of direction, whereas Folly doesn't demand anything.

Perhaps that is why Wisdom continues to talk about correction, seeking to make it more attractive. Correction (*yoser*) comes from the same Hebrew root as "discipline" in 1:2–3, and the word encompasses both teaching the right way and pointing out the wrong. Its appearance here also foreshadows the various proverbs that will speak of teaching offspring and servants (19:18; 22:6; 29:17; 29:19), as well as the teaching of Lemuel's mother (another teaching woman, 31:1). To receive correction is to submit to wisdom that is external to one's self, whether it comes from a teacher like Lemuel's mother or a book like Proverbs. Rebuke, Wisdom goes on to say, reveals character. Mockers refuse it and scorn the source, while the wise love the one who brings the opportunity to learn. In the sayings, the one who brings rebuke is held in esteem (25:12; 28:23). In fact, it is a sign of love, just as Yahweh disciplines like a loving father (3:11–12).

In our day, there seems to be a move away from correction in education (both Christian and public) in part, I think, because too often it has been given without love. We don't like to hear preachers who "judge" and prefer those who accentuate the positive. Likewise, there is much debate over whether public education should promote values of openness and inclusion, and that valid concern sometimes rules out any discussion of what it means

---

22. Stallman, "Divine Hospitality," 120.

23. R. Mason, *Old Testament Pictures of God* (Oxford: Regents Park College, 1993), 201–2. Mason adds that the personification also shows a breakthrough of the feminine part of God.

to be ethical persons. Of course, no one likes to have someone tell us that our words or behavior are offensive or even sinful. But if we have the attitude of the wise person, one who is teachable, we will get over the pain, listen to what others have to say, and weigh their words against the standards of Scripture.

Teaching on correction appears throughout the book. While Wisdom upbraids those who have rejected her correction (1:23, 25, 30), the parents warn their son not to reject Yahweh's loving correction (3:11–12), quoting words he might say one day if he does (5:12). Positively, corrections are the way to life (6:23). The warnings against rejecting correction are scattered among the sayings (10:17; 12:1; 13:18; 15:5, 10, 31, 32; 27:5; 29:1, 15). Certainly the correction and rebuke named here is wisdom teaching that steers its students away from proud and unloving attitudes and behaviors. To receive the correction is, therefore, to admit that one does not always choose humble and loving paths, but it is also to acknowledge that those paths are hurtful to ourselves as well (5:12; 6:23; 10:17; 12:1, where correction is paired with discipline).

(2) One of the first lessons Wisdom's correction provides is instruction in *"the fear of the* LORD*."*[24] In one sense, fear of Yahweh is assumed if one is to be open to Wisdom's teaching, but it never ceases to be the "beginning of wisdom." Wisdom knows that this is the first and primary correction, because humans, even believers, are inclined to leave the Lord out of their plans and considerations. For some that inclination is powerful, having wandered far away, and as a result, their behaviors are a danger to self and others. But for the majority, it is easy to slip into a comfortable assurance that the Lord is our friend and therefore does not want to bring up any issues of correction for us to face. If fear and knowledge of the Holy One are wisdom and understanding (1:10), then we learn here that the most important knowledge is personal and that without it, all other learning is inadequate.

Fear of Yahweh tells us that God wants to be known. That is not what immediately comes to mind when we hear the phrase "fear of the LORD," probably because it conjures up a one-dimensional idea of fear and a one-dimensional view of God. Therefore, Wisdom corrects the view of God as only a judge who meets us once at the end to pronounce sentence, or the cosmic cop who hides in a squad car along the highway to catch those who scoff

---

24. "Fear of the LORD" frames the instructions of chs. 1–2 and 8–9 (1:7, 29; 2:5; 8:13; 9:10; the phrase also appears in 10:27; 14:27; 15:33; 19:23; 22:4; 31:30). Themes appear in mirror fashion. In the first and last, "the fear of the LORD is the beginning" (1:7; 9:10), in the second and fourth it leads one to shun evil (1:29; 8:13), and the middle appearance urges seeking and finding Wisdom (8:13).

life's traffic laws. We may know people who are investigating, inquiring, and considering a relationship with God in Christ but yet are weighed down by this misunderstanding, or we may carry it within ourselves. Thankfully, we can say to our friends that God wants to be known in God's fullness and that the loving power that would save us and lead us is also fearsome.

We might wish there was a better word to use in place of "fear," but there isn't. In the Hebrew Bible, this word is used when people are in terror for their lives, and it is the same word used for awe and respect. The word "fear" is used for the decision to turn from evil, and it is used to communicate comfort in the prophetic oracle, "Do not fear." It is important to understand and teach that the same God who inspires fear tells us not to fear.

We can then understand why Jesus often had to say "Don't be afraid" so many times, even after some danger had passed. Read Mark 4:35–41 and notice that the disciples were afraid, perhaps more afraid, *after* the seas had become calm. Read Mark 5:1–15 and see that the townspeople were afraid *after* the storm within the demoniac had subsided. Read Habakkuk 3:16 and see how a vision of deliverance can make one's heart pound and knees tremble. The One who saves is fearsome, and our conversations with seekers can stress the salvation side of the equation, even as we do justice to God's justice. God wants to be known, and he wants to be known for who he is.

Do we need Wisdom's correction about the fear of God as well? Perhaps so, because it is easy to become jaded and, dare I say, bored in our knowledge of God, either because it is partial and inaccurate or because it is distant and detached. I once heard a comedian talk about taking his kids to the zoo. When they came home, their mother asked, "What did you see?" and they answered, "We saw a lion," in a voice that sounded as though it wasn't very exciting. The comedian then joked that he wanted to take them back to the zoo, throw them in the cage, let the lion chase them around, let them run and scream, and then at the last minute, just as the lion is about to pounce, pull them out of the cage and say, "Now you've seen a lion!" Of course the father would never do such a thing, but his scenario points out the difference between detached knowledge and knowledge that is "up close and personal."

The analogy is incomplete, however, because the Lion of Judah is as loving as he is fearsome, and the children in C. S. Lewis's Narnia tales rode on the back of the great Aslan, fearsome and good. God wants to be known, and Wisdom wants to bring us to deep knowledge of the One who set the heavens and earth in their places (8:22–31). To know God in God's fullness is to experience some sense of fear, yet Wisdom also wants us to share the joy she had at God's side (8:30–31). When we cry out for Wisdom, we also cry out for deep and personal knowledge of the wisdom of God—the God who inspires both fear and love.

(3) Wisdom's correction teaches us *discernment*, even though the word "discernment" is not used in the translation of Proverbs 9. The juxtaposition of Wisdom and Folly's competing claims, both beginning with an identical invitation, makes discernment a matter of choice—the learner must decide whose words to believe, whom to trust. After I preached on this chapter, one of the listeners in the congregation told me that he was struck that Wisdom and Folly can use similar words to send different messages. He was concerned that so many of the competing messages that bombard us in media can all sound very much like Wisdom. He was right that part of Folly's deception is to disguise herself and mimic Wisdom, but it is also true that Folly reveals herself eventually as a mocker. Just as her message of stolen water loses its sheen upon closer examination, so contemporary forms of wisdom that turn its hearers away from the Lord will in time show themselves for what they are.

In fact, the teacher relies on the power of knowledge to lead its bearer to right choices. In Wisdom's speech, the root word for "know" appears in 9:9 as "teach" (lit., to cause one to know) and in 9:10 as "knowledge of the Holy One." Folly, on the other hand, speaks without knowledge (9:13) and traps her victims who "do not know" about the death that awaits them (9:18).[25] As we observed in chapter 1, the teachers quote voices of Wisdom and Folly side by side so that the learner can learn the difference between promises that are too good to be true and a commitment to teach, correct, and love. The teacher brings the learner to a recognition of issues and consequences, but ultimately, the learner decides.[26] Therefore, the teaching that begins with correction (i.e., teaching that exercises authority) intends to lead its students to the point where they can decide for themselves, having internalized what the teacher knows. External authority gives way to authority that comes from within, so that the student has learned through practice how one makes wise choices.

In my judgment, it is important that both sides of the teaching strategy be honored in all forms of education, whether it takes place at home or in school. Radicals may stress the student's choice in education, and conservatives may stress the exercise of authority, yet both are present in Wisdom's

---

25. So also with the acquisition of "understanding" (*binah*). The proverbs promise to teach how one understands words of insight (1:2); the father urges the son to acquire understanding (4:1, 5, 7); Wisdom claims to possess understanding (8:14) and to be able to help others acquire it (9:6), directing them to the fear of the Lord and knowledge of the Holy One that is understanding (9:10).

26. Estes, *Hear My Son*, 123.

example. Receive correction, she says, so you can learn what it means to practice discernment. Our goal in education, whether practical, moral, or religious (if they can be divided at all), is to keep this ultimate goal in view. Before the learner can become a teacher, he or she must be able to tell the difference between truth and lies, and it is Wisdom's hope that this will lead one to desire the truth. Therefore, even the invitation to learn wisdom assumes some measure of discernment on the part of the learner.

In sum, just as Moses called the Israelites to become a wise and understanding people (Deut. 4:6) and one of its greatest kings asked for wisdom to discern between good and evil (1 Kings 3:9), so the reader of Proverbs is called to join with the young man in making a decision about Wisdom's instruction. Should the reader make that decision, simple ways are left behind, and one makes the first steps toward receiving correction: learning the fear of Yahweh and practicing discernment.

LEARNING DISCERNMENT. "No TV until you've done your homework!" We often pit education and entertainment against each other, just as this chapter pits Wisdom against Folly. We say that the first is good and brings long-lasting rewards, while the second makes false promises of pleasure without cost or consequences. And don't we believe that the same is true of study versus entertainment?

What lies underneath our fears is the suspicion that media and its use as entertainment is a more effective teacher. When I was a boy, John Lennon said that the Beatles were probably more popular than Jesus, and churches gathered to smash and burn their records. Underneath this reaction, I think, was the fear and recognition that he was right, that for many, the Beatles were more popular and influential. I also remember a segment on the Mickey Mouse Club when the "cubmaster" took his guitar and sang a song about the wisdom of Proverbs, then recited a lesson for the day. Who then would have believed that in years to come, churches would boycott Disney studios? Arguing that journalists and media reporters have become "more powerful than ministers, novelists, professors, and politicians," Harvard researcher Peter H. Gibbon has argued that our wired world is a world without heroes, with no one left to admire. Speaking of our concerns for children, he writes:

> As parents, we need to realize that there are dangers that come with too many choices and too few guides. We need to remind ourselves that their well-being depends not only on nutrition, sunlight, and exercise; on friendship, work, and love; but also on how they see the

world. Subtly and powerfully, the media helps shape their world view.[27]

Many parents I know are concerned about the effects of media on their children's beliefs, attitudes, and choices. Knowing the fear of the Lord helps us with our fears about bad influences. In other words, it is better to fear the Lord than to have too great a fear of negative influences. Let's be clear—there are choices to be made in life, and we want our children to make them well. Those choices lead us toward life or toward death, for ourselves and for others. The wrong decisions bring death to the spirit, the soul, and in some cases, even death to the body. That is why we're so concerned. But I notice that this chapter puts the stress on the power of persuasion and decision, not the power of the influences. Wisdom recognizes that positive and negative influences are out there, but instead of attempting to shut negative messages out, she tries to help the reader learn to discern and decide.

Listen to the offer of Wisdom as she says, "Come to this feast, taste of my teaching, my correction, my wisdom, and you will be prepared. You'll be able to make good decisions; you'll have maturity and insight, and, as a result, you'll enjoy long life." Wisdom recognizes that good and bad influences are out there, but she also knows that the real power is not in the influences but in the power to discern and choose.

Therefore, I agree with Romanowski in *Pop Culture Wars*[28] that discussion and criticism form a better strategy than either regulation or boycott control. The book asks believers to recognize that pop culture is both a business and a form of art (having deconstructed the lowbrow/highbrow distinction). Romanowski also describes the evangelical Christian culture as a combination of Victorian piety and the American myth of rugged individualism. In particular, we buy into a narrative in which good always triumphs, and good and evil are clearly defined. Yet we know that life does not present itself that way, so we may ask ourselves why we so often reject the options of critical listening and the practice of discernment in favor of such unrealistic guides for life.[29]

Ironically, we hold onto a view of Christian life shaped to a large degree by popular entertainment even while we worry over its negative influences.

---

27. P. H. Gibbon, "The End of Admiration: The Media and the Loss of Heroes," *Vital Speeches of the Day* 65 (June 15, 1999): 523.

28. W. D. Romanowski, *Pop Culture Wars: Religion and the Role of Entertainment in American Life* (Downers Grove, Ill.: InterVarsity Press, 1996). See also Romanowski's *Eyes Wide Open: Looking for God in Popular Culture* (Grand Rapids: Brazos, 2001).

29. N. Gabler, *Life the Movie: How Entertainment Conquered Reality* (New York: Vintage Books, 2000), argues that our understanding of life has been profoundly shaped by the "reality" of the movies.

Is a film or story really better just because it only presents immorality when it can be punished and made an example? Wisdom acknowledges that evil sometimes wins, which in fact makes her rhetoric all the more urgent. Because so much is at stake, she asks those she calls to listen to her, *so that* they can also learn to listen carefully to the voices around them and make appropriate choices.

Knowledge and fear of God. Those decisions are based on an ever-deepening knowledge of God, on the fear of the Lord. Knowing God becomes a basis for knowing how to live, how to choose. To say this is not to claim that there is never a time for advice. Proverbs 10−22 are full of maxims on how to live and get along with others. But we might say that Wisdom is not concerned with the many day-to-day choices we make, at least at the start, because to her, it is more important to get the big decision right. So there is a way of living that begins with the knowledge of God, knowing what pleases him and what grieves and angers him. This knowledge begins to shape behavior as it is guided by commandments (*torah*) and wisdom (*ḥokmah*). However, the reverse is also true; study of the commandments and wisdom writings is not only meant to teach us how to live but also to bring us into the presence of God.

Here is the fear of God: knowing the God who so badly wants to be known by us. Every appealing aspect of Wisdom's person and benefits is designed to help us understand God's desire to be known in all of his fearful majesty and in all of his life-giving love. To say "the fear of the LORD is the beginning of wisdom" is to say that God wants to be known. He wants us to know what it is like to be like Moses, both afraid to look at God (Ex. 3:6) and bold, saying, "Show me your glory" (33:17−34:7), hearing all the time that God is gracious and merciful. God wants us to stand with Job, wondering if God is a monster and then hearing that God is even bigger, mightier, and kinder than he knew. And I contend that this is the correction we need most, because it is the easiest thing to let slide.

The presence of God. If we will let the chapter teach us, it will convince us that moral examples and proverbial advice alone will not bring us into the presence of God; in fact, sometimes morality has the opposite effect of inducing pride. Fear of the Lord, by contrast, is the first step toward humble knowledge of God. It will also assure us that seductive images need not lead inevitably down Folly's path to death. Instead, we can set our confidence in the capacity for decision that lies within those who walk by the banquets of Wisdom and Folly. This teaching knows that temptations are out there and that they are seductive, but it also believes in the power of holy persuasion and therefore sets out Wisdom's feast, the fear of the Lord—that is, the many dimensioned knowledge of the Holy One.

When Israel and Judah were exiled to the kingdoms of Assyria and Babylon, they were surrounded by images of power and empire. They saw great statues of winged bulls with human heads and stone relief pictures of kings conquering wild beasts and nations, including the Israelite city of Lachish. Without words these ancient media said, "These are the powers, O Israel, that brought you out of your land and will keep you here." Those exiled Israelites were supposed to learn the fear of wealth and power, not with a trembling terror but with a dull, throbbing ache that they were outgunned and overwhelmed. But with the help of prophets like Isaiah, they began to put things in perspective. Those who lived in the shadow and fear of great powers heard the Lord say to those powers, "You're not so tough."

> Who has measured the waters in the hollow of his hand,
>   or with the breadth of his hand marked off the heavens?
> Who has held the dust of the earth in a basket,
>   or weighed the mountains on the scales
>   and the hills in a balance?
> Who has understood the mind of the LORD,
>   or instructed him as his counselor?
> Whom did the LORD consult to enlighten him,
>   and who taught him the right way?
> Who was it that taught him knowledge
>   or showed him the path of understanding?
>
> Surely the nations are like a drop in a bucket;
>   they are regarded as dust on the scales;
>   he weighs the islands as though they were fine dust.
> Lebanon is not sufficient for altar fires,
>   nor its animals enough for burnt offerings.
> Before him all the nations are as nothing;
>   they are regarded by him as worthless
>   and less than nothing.
>
> To whom, then, will you compare God?
>   What image will you compare him to? (Isa. 40:12—18)

While we are using another sense of the word "empire" when we speak of media conglomerates, for many of us they become a symbol of being outnumbered and overwhelmed by influences, and we fear for ourselves and our children. But Wisdom calls us to fear the Lord, not the powers of media seduction to loose behavior, superficial consumer living, or any other aspect of contemporary popular culture. In its face we too can say, "You are not so tough. We are not afraid of you and what you can do to our kids—we fear the Lord."

But how can we expect our children to want to come to a banquet if we never attend ourselves? Jesus' parable about refusals to attend the great banquet show how easily distracted we can become (Luke 14:16–24). Wisdom will not speak again, or at least not directly, in this book of Proverbs. Yet, the invitation to her feast suggests that the proverbs and riddles that follow ultimately come from her voice of teaching. They will teach the understanding and discernment she promises. They will present glimpses of life and examples of responses wise and foolish, righteous and wicked. Each saying is in a sense an invitation to her banquet, always followed closely by the cheap imitation of Folly.

Proverbs 10:1–32

THE PROVERBS OF SOLOMON:

A wise son brings joy to his father,
  but a foolish son grief to his mother.
2 Ill-gotten treasures are of no value,
  but righteousness delivers from death.
3 The LORD does not let the righteous go hungry
  but he thwarts the craving of the wicked.
4 Lazy hands make a man poor,
  but diligent hands bring wealth.
5 He who gathers crops in summer is a wise son,
  but he who sleeps during harvest is a disgraceful son.
6 Blessings crown the head of the righteous,
  but violence overwhelms the mouth of the wicked.
7 The memory of the righteous will be a blessing,
  but the name of the wicked will rot.
8 The wise in heart accept commands,
  but a chattering fool comes to ruin.
9 The man of integrity walks securely,
  but he who takes crooked paths will be found out.
10 He who winks maliciously causes grief,
  and a chattering fool comes to ruin.
11 The mouth of the righteous is a fountain of life,
  but violence overwhelms the mouth of the wicked.
12 Hatred stirs up dissension,
  but love covers over all wrongs.
13 Wisdom is found on the lips of the discerning,
  but a rod is for the back of him who lacks judgment.
14 Wise men store up knowledge,
  but the mouth of a fool invites ruin.
15 The wealth of the rich is their fortified city,
  but poverty is the ruin of the poor.
16 The wages of the righteous bring them life,
  but the income of the wicked brings them punishment.
17 He who heeds discipline shows the way to life,
  but whoever ignores correction leads others astray.

¹⁸ He who conceals his hatred has lying lips,
  and whoever spreads slander is a fool.
¹⁹ When words are many, sin is not absent,
  but he who holds his tongue is wise.
²⁰ The tongue of the righteous is choice silver,
  but the heart of the wicked is of little value.
²¹ The lips of the righteous nourish many,
  but fools die for lack of judgment.
²² The blessing of the LORD brings wealth,
  and he adds no trouble to it.
²³ A fool finds pleasure in evil conduct,
  but a man of understanding delights in wisdom.
²⁴ What the wicked dreads will overtake him;
  what the righteous desire will be granted.
²⁵ When the storm has swept by, the wicked are gone,
  but the righteous stand firm forever.
²⁶ As vinegar to the teeth and smoke to the eyes,
  so is a sluggard to those who send him.
²⁷ The fear of the LORD adds length to life,
  but the years of the wicked are cut short.
²⁸ The prospect of the righteous is joy,
  but the hopes of the wicked come to nothing.
²⁹ The way of the LORD is a refuge for the righteous,
  but it is the ruin of those who do evil.
³⁰ The righteous will never be uprooted,
  but the wicked will not remain in the land.
³¹ The mouth of the righteous brings forth wisdom,
  but a perverse tongue will be cut out.
³² The lips of the righteous know what is fitting,
  but the mouth of the wicked only what is perverse.

BEGINNING WITH THE comparison of wise and foolish sons in 10:1, the collection of proverbs in chapters 10–15 brings together contrast after contrast, challenging readers to look closely at the many variations of opposition between the "righteous" and the "wicked." The righteous and wicked contrasts are clustered in 10:1–11:13, thus placing ethical concerns at the forefront of this larger section of individual sayings (10:1—22:16). This section is the second part of the book's three-part teaching strategy.[1]

In this first collection of sentence proverbs (see the second collection at 25:1—29:27), two smaller sections appear. In chapters 10—15, antithetic parallelism dominates, so that each two-line saying demonstrates a contrast, often between the righteous and the wicked. Chapters 16—22 (up to 22:16) use more synonymous parallelism, though some contrasts are drawn between the foolish and the wise. While often the foolish and wise are identified with the wicked and the righteous respectively, this identification does not mean they are equivalent expressions. Finally, in chapters 15 and 16 themselves, a concentration of Yahweh proverbs establishes a theological center to the larger collection of individual sayings in 10:1—22:16.

Proverbs 10 does appear to have an organizational scheme, although not every proverb neatly fits its themes. Following a prologue on wise and foolish sons, two larger sections, each beginning with the word "blessing," can be marked.

Prologue: Wise and foolish sons and the watching Yahweh (10:1—5)
Blessing and the life of the community (10:6—21)
Blessing of Yahweh and the ends of the righteous and wicked (10:22—32)

The first and last sections name "the LORD" (Yahweh), while the middle one does not. Each of the two larger sections end with a proverb pair about righteous and sinful speech (10:20—21 and 31—32). There is also some pairing of bicola through 10:20—21 (vv. 2—3, 4—5, 6—7, etc.),[2] but the proverbs are also related by catchwords and themes to those that come before and after (Prov. 10:8 and 10 both use identical second lines, as do 10:6 and 11).[3] The connections "suggest that a collection of proverbs is not merely a compilation of random observations but a synthetic compendium of insights from a coherent world and throwing light on a coherent world."[4] Not all interpreters are convinced that such arrangements represent the writer's intention, since not all proverbs of a proposed section are related to its theme. In my reading, the sections mark the way a critical mass of similar proverbs gathers together, interacting as readers make comparisons, while maintaining their character as independent sayings.

---

1. J. Goldingay, "The Arrangement of Sayings in Proverbs 10—15," *JSOT* 61 (1994): 75—83. See also the outline of the book of Proverbs in the introduction.

2. Clifford, *Proverbs*, 111.

3. T. Hildebrandt, "Proverbial Strings: Cohesion in Proverbs 10," *GTJ* 11 (1990): 171—85, divides into vv. 1—5, 6—11, 12—21, 22—30 (vv. 31—32 start a new string that continues into ch. 11).

4. Goldingay, "The Arrangement of Sayings in Proverbs 10—15," 79.

READING THE SENTENCE PROVERBS

Because this commentary will treat the individual (or sentence) proverbs as independent sayings and as part of a collection assembled by the sages, some explanation of my interpretive method may help readers use it in teaching and preaching (see also "What Is a Proverb" in the introduction). In the Original Meaning section, I will comment on each proverb as a saying in its own right, sometimes suggesting how it may have been used in ancient culture. I will also note where catchwords and similar links with other proverbs appear, but only stating where they may be found and possible groupings. In the Bridging Contexts section, I will make interpretive comments on the links, suggesting themes and theological insights that draw sections together. In the Contemporary Significance section, I will try to show how those themes might speak to our lives today, hoping that these general comments will apply to a number of different proverbs.

How does one study the proverbs as individual sayings? The most basic and fruitful practice compares the two parallel lines, looking for the ways in which the two lines are similar and looking for the ways in which they are different. Thus, for example, in 10:29, "The way of the Lord" is stated in the first line and implied in the second, yet that same way is both "a refuge for the righteous" and "ruin for those who do evil." The juxtaposition of the two lines often has an element of surprise that closer inspection uncovers. So here, the "way of the Lord" might be understood as the way one walks in life, a recurring image in the instructions of chapters 1−9. However, this way is a ruin for those who have never walked on it, so the second line defines "the way of the Lord" as a reference to God's way of dealing with the world. The comparison also clarifies the use of the metaphor "way."[5]

Whereas many of these individual sayings most likely had their origin in oral culture,[6] they now reside in collections where they are read and deciphered. We will see that a number of proverbs speak to common themes like money, friendship, or honest speaking. One can learn a great deal by bringing these proverbs together and summarizing their teaching.[7] But this is not the way these sayings are presented to the reader. Instead, proverbs on

---

5. A. Berlin, "On Reading Biblical Poetry: The Role of Metaphor," VTSup 66 (1997): 25−36: "The basic form of metaphor is parallelism, in the sense of the contiguous or syntagmatic arrangement of paradigmatic elements such that unlikes become alike. The inevitable conclusion is that both parallelism and metaphor are the defining characteristics of biblical poetry."

6. See the comments on "What Is a Proverb" in the introduction.

7. As recommended by T. Longman III, *How to Read Proverbs*, 117−44. See also the commentaries by Kidner, Hubbard, and Farmer.

a similar topic are scattered throughout the collection, yet often a catch-word or recurring image will lead the reader to interpret one proverb in the light of the other. Just as the two lines relate to one another, so repeated and contrasting words, images, and themes of the individual sentence proverbs "speak" to one another.

The fact that these proverbs are brought together in complementary or contrasting relationships suggests that this is an intentional arrangement. So, for example, the famous pair at 26:4–5 recommends two different responses for handling the fool. Interpreters have surmised that readers discern which approach is right by taking account of the situation. Sometimes one should "answer a fool according to his folly," but at other times one should not. Hildebrandt finds sixty-two examples of proverbial pairing (124 verses out of 595 in Prov. 10–29). He finds pairs that are related by semantics, syntax, and theme (and distinct from their neighbors).[8]

Therefore, this commentary will also attend to repetitions and contrasts that link the proverbs in their literary context.[9] The proverbs seem to start one theme only to leave it off while taking on another that is related in some more or less obvious way. The theme will be picked up again, restated with variation of both vocabulary and content. For example, themes and images of final outcomes, blessing, but also dread and annihilation, intertwine in 10:22–32, although not every saying in this section treats that theme.

This technique reminds me of the interweaving of multiple stories in television dramas and soap operas. D. W. Griffith, one of the first great film directors, kept audiences on the edge of their seats when he brought together four related stories of Intolerance. Griffith's intent was to show how the different stories related to a common truth; in a similar way, proverbs present various viewpoints of that common truth. Therefore, sections of these collected sentence proverbs do not address a single theme or present a monologue but rather use similarity and contrast in the way impressionist painters used strokes of color. For Claude Monet, splashes of light brown, when mixed with other strokes of blue or even green, could become a picture of a haystack at morning, noon, or sunset. So also in the writings of the ancient Near East, bringing disparate texts together by means of a perceived commonality can be seen in the Gilgamesh Epic and in Psalms 19, 83, and 89.[10]

---

8. T. Hildebrandt, "Proverbial Pairs: Compositional Units in Proverbs 1–29," *JBL* 10 (1988): 207–24.

9. See Hildebrandt, "Proverbial Strings," 171–85. Proverb sentences are bonded by catchwords, rhetorical devices, themes, sound echoes, and shared syntactic construction.

10. N. Sarna, "Psalm 89: A Study in Inner-Biblical Exegesis," in *Biblical and Other Studies*, ed. A. Altmann (Cambridge, Mass.: Harvard Univ. Press, 1963), 29–46.

Integration can take place by means of vocabulary. Whybray suggests that criteria for discerning larger or smaller collections of sayings look for frequency of sound or sense. If a collection shows much use of a sound or word and the sense or theme seems also to be repeated, the greater the likelihood that the sayings were intended to be read together. The likelihood is even greater when sound and sense work together.[11] Heim believes that related proverbs were gathered together into clusters, like the clusters of grapes on a vine.[12] His determination of clusters does not allow for overlap or hinging; a proverb belongs to either one group or another, but this oversimplifies the complex network of relationships one can observe. Sometimes clusters span two chapters, but the commentary will follow the traditional chapter divisions and point out the links.

To summarize, readers can look for the following relations between individual proverbs: pairs, catchword clusters, links that may begin or end a section, and concentrations of Yahweh sayings. The connections highlight the concentrations of related proverbs and may point to an intended literary structure. The most general statement we can make, and probably the safest, is that the sayings began as folk proverbs and were later collected and arranged by an editor or editors. While it is clear that some proverb pairs and concentrations of Yahweh proverbs are the products of an editor's design, it is less certain that all of the relationships readers find between individual sayings are also by design. The lack of agreement about groupings among interpreters shows these proposals are somewhat subjective. Rather than saying that the proverbs are gathered into discrete sections, the outlines presented here are intended to point out concentrations of proverbs on a common theme. No outline will capture the organizational strategy of the collection, but suggestions about clusters can alert the reader to relationships and interaction.

Because the proverbs are arranged in sequence, this commentary assumes that reading the sayings in relation to one another can yield greater insights. Some that are generated may be the products of reader's intuitions, but in the sage's strategy of comparing and contrasting, that is not so bad. It may be that the sages who collected and arranged these proverbs said, "These are the relationships we see—if you see others, then you are using your learning to discover new truths." As individual sayings, the proverbs not only name a situation but suggest a strategy for coping with it. As sayings in a collection, they interact, amplifying each other, qualifying one another, and teasing the

---

11. Whybray, *The Composition of the Book of Proverbs*, 66–68.

12. K. M. Heim, *Like Grapes of Gold Set in Silver: An Interpretation of Proverbial Clusters in Proverbs 10:1–22:6* (BZAW 273; Berlin/New York: Walter de Gruyter, 2001).

reader to find the connections and draw readerly conclusions. Both interpretive approaches rely on the perceptiveness of the reader and the willingness to take time to reflect and probe beneath the surface.

Finally, we can ask: Who is the speaker in this series of comparisons? Proverbial sayings are typically the property of the community that uses them, and so the nameless voice that teaches by provocation can be thought of as the community that seeks to bring its members into conformity. The sayings pass on the accumulated wisdom of those who have gone before and those who keep the tradition alive. The proverbs are a means of socialization.[13]

In any case, what is more significant is that the voice of the parent recedes. The reference to father and mother in the opening verses of chapter 10 is made in third person—they no longer speak to the son, as though the young man has been turned out into the world, or to the teaching of the community. Once the instructions of chapters 1–9 have been heeded (or mastered), the reader/student is ready to learn from the larger pool of wisdom from the community. However, it is also conceivable that parents used the community's teaching.[14] Moreover, given that the sayings come immediately after the invitation to Wisdom's banquet of learning, we can also say that this omnipresent teacher is the voice of Wisdom herself, calling young men ("sons") to walk in her straight paths. Ultimately, we may also say that the voice of the teacher is that of Yahweh, who gives wisdom as a gift to those who cry out for it (2:1–6).

Prologue: Wise and Foolish Sons and the Watching Yahweh (10:1–5)

THE SECTION IS framed with contrasts between wise and dishonorable sons in verses 1 and 5; terms for material substance and wealth are woven throughout.

10:1. "Proverbs of Solomon" recalls the opening words of the book as it marks a new major section. We might ask why the superscription is necessary; a first and obvious answer is the change in form from extended instruction in chapters 1–9 to the individual saying or sentence.

Each line of the saying in 10:1 begins with Hebrew *ben* ("son"), reminding the reader of the many instructions that began with the address, "my son." Unlike the instructions of chapters 1–9, the speaker is not identified as a parent teaching a young son, yet this unidentified voice describes the

---

13. Crenshaw, *Education in Ancient Israel: Across the Deadening Silence,* 133.
14. Ibid., 279.

contrast between the wise and fools in terms of the joy or grief it brings to parents. In ancient times as now in the Middle East, children grew up to be a family's honor or shame. Even today men in Arab cultures are addressed by the name of their oldest son. When my father-in-law worked in Amman, Jordan, he was called "Abu Steve" ("father of Steve").

The intended contrast, then, is not between joyful fathers and grieving mothers but between the honor or shame that comes to both parents based on their son's choices. Therefore, this first proverb supplements the instruction of 9:12 that one is wise for one's own sake, adding that life choices also cause others to rejoice or grieve. The rejoice/grief pair is found only in 14:13 and the strong parallel of 17:21.[15] The appearance of a "wise son" and his parents marks the middle and end points of the contrasting proverbs (10:1; 15:20).[16] The mention of family also connects with the larger theme of establishing a household, which runs throughout Proverbs.[17]

10:2. This contrast is (lit.) between the "treasures of wickedness" that are no profit when compared with "righteousness that delivers from death." "Death," the last word in the saying, determines its meaning. For anyone who takes moral shortcuts in acquiring wealth, those riches will not offer security or long life, the opposite of death in Proverbs (cf. 15:16; 21:6). "Righteousness" implies the presence of Yahweh, who is named in the next verse.

10:3. The truth of 10:2 can be attributed to the general order of the world, but in the final analysis it is Yahweh who sees to the care of the righteous (cf. also Ps. 37:19, 25; Prov. 13:21). Here is no promise that righteousness will shield its bearer from all troubles and cares. Rather, the righteous will not suffer the hunger that comes from thwarted craving, the trouble that comes to those who get caught in their ways (cf. the gang of ch. 1). The contrast of 10:3 lies between the life or desire of the righteous ("life," *nepeš*, can also mean "throat") and the desire or craving of the wicked. Thus, desire brings life or death, depending on the intention that guides it.

Verses 2–3 form a couplet, each beginning with the Hebrew negative *lo* ("not"), so they should be compared. The first and second lines of each match up well: Treasures of wickedness do not profit (v. 2a), but Yahweh does not allow the righteous to go hungry (v. 3a). That stress on Yahweh's care for the righteous explains why righteousness delivers from death (v. 2b). So we also see that the terms for righteousness and wickedness correspond, with wickedness going first and last, righteousness going in between. We will note a similar pairing as we look at verses 4–5.

---

15. A. Niccacci, "Analyzing Biblical Hebrew Poetry," *JSOT* 74 (1997): 82.

16. R. Scoralick, *Einzelspruch und Sammlung* (BZAW 232; Berlin: de Gruyter, 1995), 174.

17. Clifford, *Proverbs*, 111.

10:4. This verse in Hebrew is structured chiastically, with terms for poverty and wealth coming at beginning and end, the contrast between slack and diligent hands adjacent to one another in the middle. The statement grows richer in meaning when set alongside its adjacent verses and in its larger context of 10:1—5. Its general truth about the value of hard work should not be taken as a promise that God is constrained to fulfill but as a description of what generally happens in life. Murphy reminds us that "no proverb says it all."[18]

10:5. The contrast between industry and idleness in verse 4 is here enriched with a twist: The one who gathers is wise, but the one who sleeps is not called a fool as we would expect; instead, he is a shameful son. Substitutions like this are a kind of association,[19] and here it links folly with disgrace. The picture of harvest in the book of Ruth shows everyone involved in the strenuous work; when the crop is ready, it cannot wait, it must come in. The idea of someone sleeping during this time is not only a symbol of laziness (cf. 10:4) but also of disregard for the concerns of family and village. No wonder the word "fool" is not strong enough!

Verses 4–5 also relate to one another in chiastic or mirror fashion—the laziness, poverty, and shame of 10:4a and 10:5b contrasted with the diligence, wealth, and wisdom of 10:4b and 10:5a. The theme of laziness reappears in 10:26, and so we will watch to see how it is used there.

In sum, the individual lines of 10:1—5 are sewn together in pairs and quartets to assemble a complex quilt of values and admonitions. The beauty of the picture that results is diminished when the pieces are only viewed in isolation. In other words, these sayings are meant to be read as individual parts but then integrated into larger wholes. What is gained are the insights into interaction between pairs, each enriching the meaning of the other "as iron sharpens iron."

Larger structures of arrangement can be noted as well. A chiastic structure of 10:1—5 is defined by the use of keywords and recurrent themes. The keyword "son" and the theme of parental joy and honor link verses 1 and 5. The words "righteous" and "wicked" and the theme of riches create a compound truth in verses 2 and 4; diligence and wealth are better than laziness and poverty, but ill-gotten treasures will not profit. The center of the structure (v. 3) sets the situation of wealth and poverty in the larger context of God's care for the righteous and his frustration of craving greed.[20]

---

18. Murphy, *Proverbs*, 77.

19. K. Burke, *A Grammar of Motives* (Berkeley: Univ. of California Press, 1945).

20. See Hildebrandt, "Proverbial Strings," 173–74; Whybray, *Composition*, 84, 86–87, 94, notes the relationships between the proverbs but not the concentric structure.

> A Wise son makes parents glad, foolish son brings grief (v. 1)
>   B Treasures of wickedness do not profit (v. 2)
>   C Yahweh satisfies and thwarts (v. 3)
>   B' Riches of the diligent (v. 4)
> A' Wise son gathers, sleeping son brings shame (v. 5)[21]

What new insight is added by reading the first five verses together? They recommend wise attitudes toward both wealth and family. Verse 2, following on verse 1, offers wisdom as the antidote for folly, defined as a wicked craving for treasures. Verses 4–5 together speak of a wealth gained through wisdom's diligence, defining folly as sloth, not grasping. Both forms of folly bring negative consequences to the family. Yahweh's oversight of human affairs makes sure that life is lived in a balance between active acquiring and passive receiving. There is to be no grasping in wickedness, no slacking in laziness. Both have a common root in irresponsibility—a failure to work for one's own. Both, in a sense, are forms of stealing. There is a circular movement of the section that associates the lazy son of verse 5 with the grieved parents of verse 1, but it includes the reminder that diligence without righteousness is worthless.

In my view, the most significant feature of this structure compares the importance of these decisions about wealth and community with the ever-present justice of Yahweh. However we allow structure to guide our reading of 10:1–5, it is clear that this section serves both to introduce the collection of sayings that follows and to look back at the concerns of the first prologue and the instructions of chapters 1–9. Just as the section links what comes before and after, so the concerns of wisdom, righteousness, and fear of Yahweh are linked and inseparable.

Blessing and the Life of the Community (10:6–21)

IN THIS SECTION, proverbs about speaking and listening are intertwined with proverbs that touch on the matters of wealth, income, and rewards.

10:6. "Blessings," the first word of the saying, has no referent; it is not stated what the blessings are or who gives them. The context of verses 5 and 7 speak of honor in family and community, but verse 22 names blessings

---

21. However, the many overlapping links allow for different perceptions of structure. Van Leeuwen, "Proverbs," 106–7, sets out a chiastic structure framed by the terms "wise" and "fool" in verses 1 and 8. T. A. Perry, *Wisdom Literature and the Structure of Proverbs* (University Park: Pennsylvania State Univ. Press, 1993), 73, believes that the negative and positive statements of vv. 1–2 and 3–4 relate to one another chiastically, thus setting vv. 1–4 apart. Neither takes account of the repetition of "son" or the shift to metaphors for speech that begins in v. 6.

of wealth from Yahweh (see also 10:6, 7, 22; 11:11, 26; 24:25; 28:20). The ambiguity leaves open both possibilities, so we look to the parallel line for help. In contrast to blessings that come on the head is violence that overwhelms the mouth of the wicked (cf. second line of 10:22, that Yahweh adds no trouble to his blessing). Honor and wealth are so intimately related in Proverbs that it is impossible to separate them, and so we look to a primary sense of honor with a secondary sense of wealth that often brings honor to those who practice diligence (10:4–5) and righteousness (10:6–7).

The second line can be read forward or backward in Hebrew, reversing the subject and object, so the footnote in the NIV reads, "but the mouth of the wicked conceals violence." The word translated "overwhelms" (*y^ekasseh*) basically means "cover," so the second line can read, "violence covers the mouth."[22] The rest of the Old Testament uses the word in two ways: "conceal" (as in Job 16:18 and Prov. 10:8; so NRSV and NIV footnote) and "fill" (as in Isa. 60:2; Ezek. 30:18; Jer. 3:25, yielding "violence fills the mouth," as if to overwhelm it; cf. Hab. 2:17).[23] The ambiguity in this verse seems to be intentional: A wicked person's mouth can conceal violence, but ultimately, that violence will come back to overwhelm it.

The Hebrew phrase is repeated in the second line of Proverbs 10:11, yet the LXX translates the two lines differently. This variation has led many commentators to conclude that the text has been corrupted. However, the second lines of verses 8 and 10 are also identical, so we take the repetition as intentional and read the Hebrew text as it stands.[24]

10:7. The righteous/wicked contrast carries over from 10:6. Just as the first line of verse 6 begins with the word "blessing," so the first line of verse 7 ends with it. Again, the referent is not stated, so we are not sure what the blessing is, who gives it, or who it is for, but the second line fills in more of the picture. Instead of the expected opposite "curse," the "blessing" of the first colon is contrasted with a name that rots, a vivid description of social shame. Like the human body, reputations can putrefy and then disappear.

10:8. The contrast between the "wise in heart" and the "chattering fool" (lit., "fool's lips") is really a contrast of attitudes toward speaking and listening; the wise are silent and learn from commands, while the fool's lips are too busy prattling to learn what would prevent ruin. So Hosea warned that "a people without understanding will come to ruin!" (Hos. 4:14). Failure to listen

---

22. As preferred by Kidner, *Proverbs*, 85.

23. Clifford, *Proverbs*, 113, who also argues that a chiastic pattern in the verse argues for reading the "mouth of the wicked" as subject.

24. Garrett, *Proverbs*, 118, takes the repetition as intentional rhetorical device that marks off a section.

also characterizes the mocker and wicked man (Prov. 9:7–9). Wisdom that begins in the heart listens; it is open to teaching, while the heart that lacks wisdom shows itself in folly on the lips. The second line of 10:8 is identical with the second line of 10:10.

10:9. The Hebrew wordplay can be translated literally, "Who walks right walks safe," reminding the reader of wisdom's promises of protection (1:33; 4:6; cf. 3:23–26). The contrast between a walk of integrity and ways that are crooked reminds the reader of the two roads seen so often throughout chapters 1–9. The contrast of final destinations warns against loss of reputation, not the physical danger that a reader might expect. This exposure to social disapproval echoes the judgments of 10:5 and 7. The Hebrew word for "integrity" (*tom*) is repeated in 10:29, translated as "righteous."

10:10. Unlike the nine previous proverbs, this saying presents not a contrast but a twofold picture of wickedness, comparing the pain inflicted on others with the ruin that comes to the "chattering fool." A wink is typically a secret signal associated with the evil and deceptive person in Proverbs. That person also comes to disaster (6:12–15), but it may be that the contrast intended here juxtaposes the grief caused to others and the grief brought on oneself. The comparison may also link the sly and smug wink that thinks it has put one over and the fool that is too busy babbling to learn; both come to a grievous end.

The second line of the verse is identical with 10:8, and this second repetition of a line (cf. 10:6b, 11b) suggests an intentional arrangement. The LXX has a different second line that reads "but the one who rebukes boldly makes peace" (adopted by NRSV, Clifford, and Murphy). However, the change is not required to make sense of the Hebrew text, and so the TNK translates it: "He whose speech is foolish comes to grief."

10:11. The contrast between the righteous and wicked resumes with this verse, but it will not appear again until 10:16. "Violence overwhelms the mouth of the wicked" (cf. 10:6) may speak of the violence that comes from a wicked mouth, the way that "guilt was all over his face" points to the irony of deception that reveals more than it hides. If so, then its second appearance here, set in contrast with the mouth from which life springs like a fountain, adds nuance and color. In both verses 6 and 11 the righteous are associated with blessing and life, the wicked with violence that cuts life short.[25] The repetition of lines suggests a mirror arrangement that matches the righteous/wicked sayings of verses 6–7 with 11 and the chattering fools of

---

25. Goldingay, "The Arrangement of Sayings in Proverbs 10–15," 79–80, argues that the translation, "the mouth of the wicked covers violence," highlights the sages' desire to repeat terms and phrases with different meanings.

verses 8 and 10. The structure draws our attention to the importance of speech. "Fountain of life" is introduced here for the first of four times in Proverbs (cf. 13:14; 14:27; 16:22); here it is used for righteous speech that refreshes and maintains life.

10:12. The catchword "covers" links with neighboring verse 11, where "overwhelms" translates the same Hebrew word (cf. comments on 10:6 and 11). Here the term signifies neither deceitful concealing nor overwhelming violence,[26] but the covering that promotes healed relationships, the way that a bandage covers a wound. Hatred stirs up, love smoothes over. Discord and dissension spring from hatred, but harmony is nurtured by love (cf. James 5:20; 1 Peter 4:8). Without naming the human faculty of speech, this verse not only offers guidance in using it but praise for its beauty when used rightly.

10:13. There are two contrasts in this saying, the first between the wisdom that is found on the lips and the punishment that falls on the back, the second between the person who has discernment and the one who lacks judgment (lit., "lacks heart"; cf. 9:4). The proverb joins with those that have come before to point out the pipeline that connects heart and lips (10:6, 8, 10, 11). The person of discernment has wisdom to give from a heart that has stored up knowledge (cf. 2:1–2; 3:1; 4:20–21); the person lacking in heart has nothing to give but only receives punishment. Perhaps the contrast also means to show that the wise understand sound speech while fools only understand punishment (cf. 9:12).[27]

10:14. A contrast similar to that of verse 13 sets the good possession of the wise against the bad consequences that come to the fool; the catchword *ḥkm* (wisdom, wise) also links the two verses. The wise in their knowledge know when to share it and when it is best to keep it in reserve; fools, lacking such discretion and self-control, speak in ways that eventually will come back to harm them.[28]

10:15. This proverb is linked with verse 14 by the catchword "ruin" (*mᵉḥittah*) and by the comparison of the wise who store up knowledge with the rich who store up wealth as fortification. Here the contrast lies in the security wealth provides for the rich with the assault of poverty on the needy. One protects, the other attacks (cf. "ruins" in Ps. 89:40–41); the same is true of wisdom and folly. The point centers in the metaphor that one stores knowledge for protection, not in any virtue of storing up wealth and not in any blame

---

26. "Covers" is also used in v. 18 in relation to "hatred."
27. Murphy, *Proverbs*, 74.
28. So Kidner, *Proverbs*, 87, who sees the wise "storing up for the right occasion . . . it refers to discretion, not erudition." See also Clifford, *Proverbs*, 114, "The wise feel no need to express all their knowledge in words."

for poverty on folly. The proverbs warn that lazy fools become poor and vulnerable (cf. Prov. 6:11), but they never claim that all who are poor are lazy.

10:16. It is the topic of economics that links verses 15 and 16 thematically, moving from general terms for economic status to more specific terms for wages and income.[29] Taken together, these two verses make the point seen earlier (10:2–5) that righteousness can offer some sense of security that ill-gotten wealth cannot; in fact, the income of the wicked leads to disaster. While wealth can protect, that protection becomes a metaphor for the results of righteous action. Only the wages of righteousness can give final security. The righteous/wicked contrast does not appear again until 10:20.

10:17. "Life," the catchword in verses 16 and 17 (cf. 10:2, 11), is abundant life in the sense of wisdom's offer of health, security, and prosperity. Its contrast is not with death but with "punishment," a word usually translated "sin," a falling short of the mark. The idea of falling short may be used for inadequate income, the opposite of a reward.[30] The Hebrew is difficult and could be translated, "A path to life, whoever observes instruction, but whoever rejects reprimand goes astray."[31] The point is not so much whether one goes down a right path or leads another that way, for both usually go together. Rather, the main contrast observes that a person either heeds (*šmr*; lit., "keeps") discipline and correction or abandons it; the choice determines whether one walks the path of life or wanders. Walking and wandering recount the major themes of chapters 1–9 (esp. 9:7–8). The contrast with "life" is similar to that in 10:16; one expects to read "death" but instead finds wandering or erring, a kind of "sin."

10:18. Each of the proverbs in 10:18–21 is connected to the theme of right speaking. The main contrast in 10:18 is not as clear, since both lines name a sin of speech. The difference between hiding hatred and spreading it through slander is one of action, not intent; both forms of deceit have the potential to be equally destructive. Some believe that the verse should be emended to agree with the LXX, "The one who forgives hatred has righteous lips."[32] Others argue that "lying lips" should be the subject (so NRSV), and still others suggest that both lines take the predicate "is a fool." The difficulties in translation should not obscure the wordplay on "cover" (*ksh*; cf. 10:6, 11, 12), especially in combination with "hatred" here and in 10:12. Love may cover wrongs, including hatred's dissension, but concealed hatred is deadly.

10:19. This proverb warns against the dangers of slander from another angle. The second line literally reads, "The one who restrains lips. . . ." The

---

29. Hildebrandt, "Proverbial Pairs," 214.
30. Clifford, *Proverbs*, 115, translates *ḥaṭṭaʾt* as "want" (cf. 21:4; Job 14:16; also Rom. 6:21).
31. Murphy, *Proverbs*, 70–71.
32. Garrett, *Proverbs*, 120.

connection with "lying lips" in verse 18 points to a time when concealing or holding back speech can be a good thing. Words are like sheep; the more there are, the better the chances that some will go astray. The same word for wise (*maśkil*) is used of the wise son in 10:5.

10:20. The contrast of worth ("choice silver" versus "little value") traces the outflow of the tongue to its source, the heart. "Choice silver" reminds the reader of the promised yield of wisdom that is even greater than silver (3:14). Here "heart" is indicative of the source and intention, a theme continued in 10:21. To be lacking in heart is to lack judgment and character (10:13; cf. 4:23).

10:21. "Lack of judgment" is literally to "lack heart" (cf. v. 13). Here, as in verse 20, the heart stands in parallel with that which speaks. Readers would expect a contrast between wise lips that nourish others and a foolish heart that does not, but as is often the case in these proverbs, the second line highlights the negative consequences that fall back on the fool. The word "nourish" comes with the image of the shepherd who feeds the sheep, contrasted with the fool who cannot even feed himself. The wise speak in a way that benefits others; the fool speaks in a way that leads to his own ruin (cf. 10:10).

In sum, this section ends with a pair of proverbs that stress the value of wise speech, contrasting it with the trouble that comes to the wicked and fools. The proverbs of the section describe the contrasting outcomes in terms of outcomes in this life; they support the idea that "what goes around comes around" more than "vengeance is mine, says the LORD." We will read on to see that the proverbs in 10:22–32 do describe the fate of the wicked in terms commonly associated with the judgment of Yahweh.

Blessing of Yahweh and the Ends of the Righteous and Wicked (10:22–32)

THIS SECTION IS marked out by three proverbs that name "the LORD" (10:22, 27, 29), each with its own description of "trouble" that comes on the foolish and wicked. The righteous/wicked contrast appears in most of these proverbs.

10:22. This saying on the blessings of wealth calls for extra attention. First, we look inside the proverb and note the contrast between two related actions of Yahweh; his blessing brings wealth and he adds no trouble to it. The second line sounds strange to our ears, though not when we learn that "trouble" is in store for the wicked, as the following verses make clear. The Hebrew word for "trouble" (*ʿeṣeb*) in Proverbs can also be used for harshness (cf. 15:1), sorrow, or hard labor (5:10; 14:23). So a footnote in the NRSV offers an alternate translation, "and toil adds nothing to it."

At face value this alternate reading appears to contradict the sages' approval of hard work stated in 10:4, but it reminds readers that work done with an attitude of self-sufficiency runs counter to Israel's faith and wisdom. So Psalm 127:1, credited to wise Solomon, states: "Unless the LORD builds the house, its builders labor in vain. Unless the LORD watches over the city, the watchmen stand guard in vain." Next, we look at other proverbs in the chapter with similar vocabulary and theme. Proverbs 10:6–7 have said that blessings come to the righteous, not violence or dishonor; a similar view of final accounting runs throughout 10:22–32. Taken together, 10:6–7 and 22 name the typical wisdom trio of substance, longevity, and honor. Therefore, in this present verse, the blessing of Yahweh brings wealth that does not come with the trouble that comes with the wealth the wicked obtain.

10:23. The contrast between the fool's evil and the love of wisdom highlights different tastes in what brings pleasure and delight. The second line sounds tautological; we would expect a man of understanding to take delight in wisdom, or perhaps in this context, wise conduct. The contrast is with the irony of the shortsighted fool, who finds pleasure in what will destroy him (cf. 10:21). Note the link with desire and fear in 10:24. The word for "delight" is used twice in 8:30–31 for the mutual affection that Wisdom and people of understanding have for each other.

10:24. The unwanted dread of the wicked will still come, while that which the righteous desires will be given. The similarity is the certainty of reward, the contrast in whether the outcomes are welcome. Compared with verse 23, we might observe that the pleasure of evil conduct mentioned there is followed here by the horror of its final consequences. A similar statement comes from Psalm 37:4: "Delight yourself in the LORD and he will give you the desires of your heart." The converse is treated in Psalm 37:10: "A little while, and the wicked will be no more; though you look for them, they will not be found."

10:25. The comparison is similar to that of verse 24, this time using the metaphor of a sweeping storm that carries away anything not secured fast. Read together, 10:24 and 25 suggest that the righteous desire and are given long life. The Hebrew for "forever" (ʿolam) is repeated in 10:30: "The righteous will never [lit., forever . . . not] be uprooted." A similar picture to the one in this proverb pair was presented by Wisdom in 1:26–27.

10:26. This vivid saying not only interrupts the sequence of righteous/wicked proverbs, it seems to change the subject abruptly. Moreover, instead of the expected two-part comparison, there are three. Van Leeuwen calls this a saying about "the incongruous or unfitting,"[33] and its appearance here seems out of place as well. Taken together, the three irritants suggest that

---

33. Van Leeuwen, "Proverbs," 112. Other proverbs on the incongruous: 25:20; 26:1; 27:14. On the sluggard, see 6:6; 13:4; 15:19; 19:24; 20:4; 21:25; 22:13; 24:30–34; 26:14–16.

the sluggard who will not work for his own benefit also will not work for the benefit of others. Presumably, the "one who sends him" hopes that he will represent him well, probably in carrying a message. The employer's disappointment is even more extreme in 26:6: "Like cutting off one's feet or drinking violence is the sending of a message by the hand of a fool." Still, the opposite, refreshment like the cool of snow on a hot day, comes from a trustworthy messenger (25:13; cf. 13:17). The proverb may recommend getting rid of the sluggard like one who spits out vinegar or moves out of a smoky place.

Read from two different points of view, the proverb sends two slightly different messages. From the perspective of the one sending, wisdom suggests that the sender should consider what is fitting and weigh outcomes when choosing a representative. But the one who is sent should also consider outcomes and determine what kind of messenger one will be. Who, the proverb asks, would choose a sluggard to be a messenger? So diligence in learning wisdom is recommended via a negative example.

10:27. The contrast between long life and years cut short also pits fear of Yahweh against wickedness. The theme returns to the respective futures of the righteous and wicked, reminding the reader of 10:16. Wisdom and long life are linked in 3:2, 16; 19:23. Fear of Yahweh will appear again throughout the sayings in 14:26–27; 15:16, 33; 16:6; 19:23; 22:4, but it especially directs the reader back to the prologue and its development in chapters 1–9.

10:28. Having seen what lies ahead for the righteous and wicked in 10:27, this second saying of a pair is a variation on the theme of 10:24, that only the righteous receive what they hope for. The wicked not only fail to get what they desire (10:28), they do receive what they fear (10:24). We may observe a mirror pattern in the framing of two proverb pairs about future outcomes (10:24–25 and 27–28) around the incongruous proverb about vinegar, smoke, and sluggards. Is there a connection? Certainly the one sending gets an unexpected result from choosing the sluggard, perhaps like tasting vinegar when one expects wine. Likewise, hoping for good, all the sender gets from the sluggard is irritation.

10:29. The last of the three proverbs about Yahweh in this section is also in construct/genitive form like the others: having considered the *blessing* of Yahweh and the *fear* of Yahweh, the proverb now recommends the *way* of Yahweh. Here is the only direct association of "the way" with Yahweh in the book of Proverbs (cf. 3:17; 4:11; 8:20); it is a refuge for those who walk in it. A similar image, using the same Hebrew word, comes from Psalm 37:39, "The salvation of the righteous comes from the LORD; he is their *stronghold* in time of trouble."

The Hebrew for "righteous" in this proverb is the same word used in 10:9 for the person of "integrity" (*tom*) who walks securely, and the "ruin" (*mᵉḥittah*) of evildoers is the same as that of 10:14–15. "The way" in this proverb creates some overlap between the way as a path for humans to walk and the way of God's dealings with humans. Both are based on God's righteousness.

10:30. The metaphor of the land follows the motif of two ways in 2:20–22 and its echoes of the threats in 1:26–32. The wicked are threatened with dispersion as in 10:25, but here the image is of a plant pulled up by its roots (cf. Jer. 1:10). The Hebrew for "forever" (*ᶜolam*) is repeated from Proverbs 10:25 to read, "the righteous are forever, not to be moved." It is not clear whether the principle is for all landowners or just for the covenant people of Israel. The motif of living in the land is central to Psalm 37 (vv. 22, 27, 29, 34).

10:31. The last two proverbs of chapter 10 deal with the topic of speech. This final proverb pair in the chapter should be read together, since the second lines of both describe misuse of the tongue and mouth as "perverse" (2:12, 14; 6:14; 8:13; 10:31–32; 16:28, 30). Notice also the contrast between the mouth of the righteous and the mouth of the wicked in 10:31a, 32b.

The mouth of the righteous literally "bears the fruit of wisdom" (cf. 12:14; 13:2; 18:20). The image of a tongue cut out of the mouth in 10:31b is gruesome, yet such things were done in the ancient Near East. There may also be a metaphoric nod to the line before, so as to say that every tree that does not bear good fruit is cut down. So Jesus reminds us that we will know false prophets by their fruit since it is from the heart that the mouth speaks (cf. Matt. 7:15–21; Luke 6:43–45). Just as the wicked are removed from the land (Prov. 10:30), so Psalm 37 repeats the picture of the wicked who are "cut off" (Ps. 37:9, 22, 34, 38).

10:32. The word used for "fitting" (*raṣon*) in Proverbs 10:32 is typically used for favor, particularly the favor of Yahweh (11:1, 20, 27; 12:2, 22; 15:8; 18:22). So Wisdom says, "For whoever finds me finds life and receives favor from the LORD" (8:35; cf. 3:12, "delights"). Note the contrast of favor and perversity—the latter on the nature of the speech, the former on the response it brings.

This final proverb pair puts the stress on speech that bears fruit of wisdom and knows what is fitting and favorable, just like the pair that closed the last section (10:20–21). The two proverb pairs on proper use of speech frame the outer edges of a chiasm.

A On the tongue (10:19–21)

B On personal security (10:22–25)

C On laziness (10:26)

B′ On personal security (10:27–30)

A′ On the tongue (10:31–32)[34]

Highlighting this structure can help us interpret 10:26 as a call to diligence in cultivating wisdom, especially the wisdom of speech that knows how to build up and teach others. Most important, the righteous know how to speak with wisdom (bringing forth its fruit) and how to say what is fitting ("the righteous know favor"). In contrast to the lazy messenger of 10:26, the righteous deliver what is expected.

In sum, in this last section, three proverbs about the gifts of Yahweh—wealth, long life, and refuge—are followed by proverbs about the fate of the wicked, who know no such security. Instead, they are "like chaff that the wind blows away" (Ps. 1:4). More than a collective statement that "you reap what you sow" (cf. Prov. 10:6–21), these sayings point instead to Yahweh's oversight of human affairs.

Bridging Contexts

OVERVIEW AND EMPHASES. As we have seen in our study of chapter 10 so far, the arrangement of the individual sayings, the "Proverbs of Solomon," is far from random. Signs of relationship between verses and sections lead us to look for themes that tie larger portions together. So, for example, this chapter begins with the contrast between a wise and lazy son (10:5) and finishes with a picture of a lazy messenger (10:26); the lazy son grieves his parents while the lazy messenger irritates the one who sent him. This placement of the only two proverbs on this theme suggests that we are to pay special attention to them as guides for understanding the chapter. In particular, the repeated images of laziness reinforce Wisdom's call to diligent study in chapter 9 as they direct that diligence to the practice of wise speech, a theme clustered in 10:6–21 (see vv. 13, 19; also v. 31), and wise conduct, clustered in 10:22–32 (see v. 23).

This first chapter of a new major section (10:1–22:16) extends the themes of chapters 1–9 by placing them in a new setting. Whereas relation to parents was primary, the focus now turns to relation to the community. We might imagine how the young man learns from the wisdom of the community as collected in its proverbs, sayings that both repeat and extend the parents' teaching. Relationship with Yahweh, one of the main emphases of the

---

34. Garrett, *Proverbs*, 121.

parents' instructions (along with learning and character), is sounded three times in the last part of this chapter.[35] We might also say that personified Wisdom has now become a teacher as well. Having made her initial appeals about the worth of her teaching in chapters 1–9, she now makes her instruction known through the collective wisdom of the sayings.

Themes. We begin by identifying major themes and then look to see how they work together. Themes and their key terms are like colors in stage lighting that blend to give light and color to the scene. They are also like photo-mosaic pictures that bring together smaller pictures to make one larger one. The individual proverbs work together like sticks in a bundle or a threefold cord that cannot be broken (Eccl. 4:12). The themes of this chapter form as a series of contrasts:

- laziness versus diligence
- shame versus honor
- poverty versus wealth
- wise speech versus destructive speech
- righteousness versus wickedness

Diligence. Continuing the major motif from chapters 1–9, this chapter asks the question, "What is a wise son?" The sayings of 10:1–5 answer that a wise son pursues righteousness instead of craving and diligence instead of sleep. He is concerned about honor—honor for oneself, but more important, honor for the family, that it not be shamed. In the ancient world, sons were responsible for keeping up the family holdings in order to care for parents in their old age; they could either build up the estate or squander it in the manner of the prodigal son of Luke 15. Economic care for the family, concern for its well-being, is clearly associated with honor and shame.[36]

It may be hard to appreciate this expectation in our time when most people work for some sort of company instead of the family business. Sons and daughters move away to advance careers, sometimes taking spouse and grandchildren, while parents look forward to retirement, sometimes relocating in pleasant climes far away from their children. Today, parents try to build up their estates with a wish to place "no burden on the children," but as a result, no one talks about the needs of extended care until those needs are inescapable.[37] The principle behind the ancient picture carries over into our

---

35. Clifford, *Proverbs*, 112, finds the three main concerns of Proverbs in vv. 1–3: v. 1, sapiential; v. 2, ethical; v. 3, religious. These inseparable concerns recall the prologue of 1:1–7. So also Goldingay, "The Arrangement of Sayings in Proverbs 10–15," 81–82.

36. Garrett, *Proverbs*, 117.

37. V. Stem Owens, "What Shall We Do with Mother?" *Books and Culture* 5/4 (July/August 1999): 16–19.

day. Wise sons and daughters are diligent workers who provide for themselves but also recognize that they will be called on to care for the needs of their larger families, especially their parents. The teaching of the proverbs is not against mobility but is for loving responsibility.

Honor and shame. In 10:6–21, the portrait of the wise son is developed around the theme of honor and shame. The word "righteousness" is used for the opposite of wicked craving and grasping in 10:2–3. Verses 6 and 7 associate that righteousness with honor; the blessings for the head may be that memory that endures instead of decaying in shame. In ancient times, communities were too small and tightly knit to allow one's reputation to slide. Today, networks of communication and business relationships allow for one to earn favor with one community by earning dishonor in another. I was shocked to learn that the producer of a reality television show demanded that the cameras be kept rolling as one of the participants writhed in pain from an accident. It was only after the report of the producer's decision aired on an entertainment news program that I realized that this bad reputation made for "good television" as well. Who cares if the producer is reviled as long as it creates interest and makes the ratings soar? Shame may be in short supply these days, but that scarcity makes it all the more valuable.

Wealth and poverty. A cluster of proverbs in 10:1–22 are gathered around a related theme of wealth and poverty. The wise son gathers grain in summer (v. 5) but also stores up knowledge (v. 14). The surplus of wealth can offer the protection of a fortified city (v. 15), but its value is qualified as terms for wealth are associated with both dishonesty (v. 2) and righteousness (v. 16). Finally, wealth is qualified as it is credited to the blessing of Yahweh (v. 22); it is not a product of hard work and diligence alone. The sages' view of wealth itself was neutral, but they were also aware that it could present temptations to set wisdom's humility and fair dealing aside.

In the nineteenth century, preacher Russell Conwell presented his popular motivational talk, "Acres of Diamonds," six thousand times all across America. Conwell told his hearers that they were like the man who traveled the world to search for diamonds, not knowing that a diamond mine lay buried in his back yard! He added that they should look for a way to get rich as so many other Americans had done. Think of all the good one could do with money! To his credit, Conwell did a lot of good with the money he earned through his speaking, starting the first urban community college (today's Temple University) and promoting many programs to give the poor an opportunity to earn a living.[38]

---

38. R. Conwell, "Acres of Diamonds," in *Three Centuries of American Rhetorical Discourse: An Anthology and Review*, ed. R. F. Reid (Prospect Heights, Ill.: Waveland, 1988), 573–86. His is the second name in Gordon-Conwell Theological Seminary.

However, "Acres of Diamonds" also appealed to the bootstraps ethic of men like Andrew Carnegie, whose book *The Gospel of Wealth*[39] argued that anyone could make a better life for self and society if one were willing to work. While there may be some truth to his observations, Carnegie failed to mention that his wealth was gained in part by paying unfair wages and crushing strikes and protests with force. As Tom Skinner used to say, "It is hard to lift yourself by the bootstraps when someone keeps cutting the straps." The proverbs may link wisdom with diligence and wealth, but the sages also knew that it is possible to pervert that truth in a way that brings hardship to others. Diligence in acquiring wealth must be matched by diligence in fair dealing and honest speaking (10:9–11).

Today, preachers can gather an audience by proclaiming a gospel of health and wealth. Their message echoes the themes of wisdom's call to hard work and prudence, but it errs when it overlooks wisdom's call to social responsibility. One cannot seek health, wealth, and honor by practicing a personal righteousness that ignores the responsible care for family and community. As we watch the sages' attitude toward wealth, we will keep in mind that its acquisition and use can reflect either righteousness or its opposite, but not both.

Wise speech and righteousness. Proverbs scattered throughout the chapter show that the wise son knows how to use the gift of communication for the benefit of others. The bad news comes first; chapter 10 introduces the topic with repeated descriptions of speech overwhelmed by violence (vv. 6 and 11) and of chattering lips that come to ruin (vv. 8 and 10). Such talk stirs up discord (v. 12), brings trouble (v. 14), and spreads lies and slander (v. 18); the more words, the more sin (v. 19). By contrast, the mouth of the righteous is a spring of life (v. 11) and a source of wisdom (v. 13), characterized by restraint and propriety (v. 19). Two proverb pairs stress the value of righteous speech: It is choice silver and a source of nourishment to others (vv. 20–21); it bears the fruit of wisdom; it knows what is fitting and favorable (vv. 31–32).

While most of the proverbs on speech are gathered in clusters, especially in groups of four (10:10–14, 18–21), they are also intertwined with proverbs on work and its returns of wealth. The pair at 10:20–21 overlap images of bounty and sharing. Not only is the tongue of the righteous like silver, their lips bring nourishment to others, just as the wise son gathers in summer to provide for himself and his family. Even as goods and wealth are earned to

---

39. A. Carnegie, *The Gospel of Wealth and Other Timely Essays* (New York: The Century Co., 1900). See also M. Marty, *Pilgrims in Their Own Land* (Boston and Toronto: Little, Brown, & Co., 1984), 307–11.

care for others, so wisdom is stored so that it may be shared. As wealth should be shared, so should wisdom be shared in wise speaking. Just as diligence in making a living is rewarded, so is diligence in allowing wisdom to inform one's words. Taken together, the proverbs gathered here create a mosaic of one who is diligent in caring for others—food enough for family, wisdom to nourish the community.

How is wise speaking beneficial to the community? Truth promotes trust; honesty in speaking shows real concern for the other, while speech that hides hatred only pretends and in time will be revealed for what it is (10:9–10). Wise speaking points to that which promotes life. It lifts up the value of honesty, fair dealing, and peacemaking (10:11–12), teaching by word and example. It also lifts up the values of restraint and propriety, knowing that there are times when it is wise to hold back to avoid the danger of slander or of saying words that will later bring regret (10:18–19). A wise person knows when to spend words and when to save them (10:31–32).

It may be that here is a shift in emphasis from learning wisdom (as laid out in chs. 1–9) to sharing wisdom in the community, primarily through honest speaking and fair dealing but perhaps also through teaching. Just as fathers and mothers teach sons, so here right speaking is a kind of teaching. As we study the proverbs of chapters 10–22, we will watch to see what is added to enrich this picture of wise speaking. For now, we note that these proverbs on wise speaking are introduced by a proverb pair about "blessing" (10:6–7). The blessing appears to be that of the community, who honors the wise son with a good name, one that does not rot.

The wisdom of Jesus. The picture of the wise son reminds Christian readers of Jesus, who as a boy sat in the temple, listening to the teachers and asking questions. Luke's story is framed with two statements: "The child grew and became strong; he was filled with wisdom, and the grace of God was upon him" (Luke 2:40), and "Jesus grew in wisdom and stature, and in favor with God and men" (Luke 2:52). The emphasis on relationships with family, community, and God echoes the wisdom themes of this chapter of Proverbs. That Jesus speaks well in the temple and grows up to "proclaim the year of the Lord's favor" in the synagogue (Luke 4:19; cf. Isa. 61:2) confirms that this wise son's words will bring sustenance and life to many (Prov. 10:20–21, 31–32).

While it was probably not Luke's intention to preserve this story as an example of education in wisdom, it does mark the point at which Jesus demonstrated his growth in wisdom, and the story marks his transition into the life of the adult community. We might say that here, as in Proverbs, family education was supplemented by the teaching of the larger community. In the same way, the course of study that is the book of Proverbs here moves out of parental teaching to the teaching of the community. As readers identify with the figure of the wise son, they see the issues in new and different ways, ways that the instructions of chapters 1–9 do not communicate. These sayings are memorable and cumulative. They stick and gather in the mind to assemble a picture of wise adult living. The chapter sets out its portrait of the wise son as one who knows how to work and speak in the ways that bring the blessing of the community.

Blessing from above. Another concern of the chapter is the blessing from above, as stated in the "LORD" proverbs that are clustered in 10:22–32. Just as diligence in work and in speaking leads to life, so the sages understood that this diligence reflects God's lordship over life. God's work in overseeing the actions of the righteous and wicked brings the same life-giving order to the community that hard work and disciplined speech do. The contrasts between the blessings and terrors in 10:22–32 show how Yahweh restores order to a community life that has been disturbed through unrighteous deeds and words. Such a view is central to the wisdom psalms,[40] and their perspective will offer help in interpreting these proverbs.

As we have seen, 10:22–32 include three sayings about Yahweh that take a construct or genitive form: "the *blessing* of the LORD" (v. 22), "the *fear* of the LORD" (v. 27), and "the *way* of the LORD" (v. 29). Each describes a choice that a wise son or daughter makes, a choice to seek God and his ways over one's own. Each of the three sayings expounds the theme of 10:3, Yahweh's care for the righteous and his frustration of the schemes of the wicked. Nearly all the proverbs that follow predict a bright future for the righteous and an early end to the wicked.

The long view. The bold statements of these proverbs sound like promises that are too good to be true, and for that reason, they seem to assume a readership that knows that life does not always look this way. Readers throughout the centuries have asked whether it is always the case that the righteous are fed and the wicked go hungry (10:3), or whether the wicked experience terrors while the righteous receive their desires (v. 24).

The question is at least as old as the Psalms. Of the wisdom psalms, Psalm 37 stands as an especially pointed response to the apparent prosperity of the wicked. It is striking that the psalm focuses attention on the lived experience and doubts of the observer: "Do not fret because of evil men or be envious of those who do wrong; for like the grass they will soon wither, like green plants they will soon die away" (Ps. 37:1–2). "Do not fret when men succeed in their ways, when they carry out their wicked schemes. Refrain

---

40. See A. R. Ceresko, "The Sage in the Psalms," in *The Sage in Israel and the Ancient Near East*, ed. J. G. Gammie and L. G. Perdue (Winona Lake, Ind.: Eisenbrauns, 1990), 217–30.

from anger and turn from wrath; do not fret—it leads only to evil" (37:7–8). The psalm looks ahead, beyond present circumstances, to a future reckoning at the same time that it looks back for assurance: "I was young and now I am old, yet I have never seen the righteous forsaken or their children begging bread. They are always generous and lend freely; their children will be blessed" (37:25–26). The psalm is aware that Yahweh's care and provision are a real hope, yet it is a hope that must be appreciated from the long view that looks to the past and the future.

In addition to the similarities in theme and image, every proverb in 10:22–32 shares some vocabulary with Psalm 37: *blessing* (Prov. 10:22; Ps. 37:22, 26), *wisdom* (Prov. 10:23; Ps. 37:30), *desire* (Prov. 10:24; Ps. 37:4), *wicked no more* (Prov. 10:25; Ps. 37:10), *forever* (Prov. 10:25, 30; Ps. 37:28), *smoke* (Prov. 10:26; Ps. 37:20), *perish/come to nothing* (ʾbd, Prov. 10:28; Ps. 37:20), *refuge* (maʿoz, Prov. 10:29; Ps. 37:28 ["stronghold"]), *the land* (Prov. 10:30; Ps. 37:3, 9, 22, 27, 29, 34), *cut off* (Prov. 10:31; Ps. 37:9, 22, 28, 34), and *mouth of the righteous* (Prov. 10:31; Ps. 37:30). While we cannot determine whether this section of Proverbs was modeled after the psalm or vice versa, we can say with confidence that the common images, vocabulary, and theme mark a common intention to affirm God's righteous rule of the world's moral order when observers may be inclined to doubt it.

Both texts of Proverbs and Psalms challenge us to affirm that care when present circumstances seem to deny it. J. C. McCann adds that it is unfair to the book of Proverbs to turn the reality of divine retribution into a "religion machine."[41] In such a view,

> every event or experience must be understood directly and unambiguously as the reward or punishment of God. If a person is wealthy, for instance, his or her wealth is to be interpreted as a reward from God. And, if a person is poor, then poverty is to be viewed as punishment from God.[42]

However, Proverbs does not support such a rigid interpretation of life; in fact, proverbs that stress the equality of rich and poor (22:2) argue against it. So does the arrangement of the book of Psalms, placing the confident psalms of retribution (Ps. 1–2) against the loud wail of lament (Ps. 3). Like Job, they understand that suffering is not necessarily a divine punishment, or conversely, that wealth and ease are necessarily signs of favor. Such is the

---

41. J. C. McCann, "Wisdom's Dilemma: The Book of Job, the Final Form of the Book of Psalms, and the Entire Bible," in *Wisdom, You Are My Sister*, ed. M. L. Barre (CBQMS 29; Washington, D.C.: Catholic Biblical Association of America, 1997), 18–30.

42. Ibid., 19.

eschatological perspective of wisdom that affirms God's presence and rule when it is hard to see.

In seeking to apply 10:22−32 to our own day, Christians must avoid mechanistic understandings of God's moral order and remember that the long view calls them to affirm God's care even when present circumstances do not appear to show it. The collection of proverbs in chapter 10 encourages the reader to integrate the view from below (i.e., the limited human perspective) with the view from above (i.e., God's perspective on final outcomes).

The introduction of 10:1−5 presents the view from above and the view from below at the same time. A diligent hand makes wealth (v. 4), but Yahweh makes sure the righteous are fed (v. 3). So 10:6−21 offer the view from below, noting the consequences of wisdom and folly, just as 10:22−32 describe the view from above in which Yahweh blesses the righteous and removes the wicked from the land. The blessing of Yahweh mentioned in 10:22 reminds readers that all efforts to gather the rewards of wisdom are set within God's sovereign rule. Work makes wealth, but not without the blessing of God. Thus, we arrive at two complementary understandings of blessing: The first is a matter of act and consequence, the second a matter of grace. The blessing of a good reputation is a matter of choice over which one has some control, but the blessing of Yahweh that makes wealth and adds no trouble (in contrast to treasures of wickedness) is beyond human power to determine. Still, that blessing will come to those who chose God's way.

The sluggard. Finally, what shall we say about the sluggard (10:26), who seems to be neither righteous nor wicked but somewhere in between, a rather laughable figure? His portrait woven throughout Proverbs satirizes him as a man of immense appetite and minuscule ambition. Probably the most memorable picture is the combination of the two characteristics in 19:24 and 26:15: The sluggard buries his hand in the dish but is too lazy to lift it back to his mouth! His appearance early in the collected proverbs provokes curiosity, particularly amidst such serious proverbs about Yahweh's blessing and the frustrated end of the wicked.

Moreover, this buffoon who sets teeth on edge and makes eyes smart harks back to the one description of the sluggard in 6:9−11,[43] which is also tucked away among more serious matters of bad business and adultery. In fact, the sluggard's portrait in chapter 6 is juxtaposed to that of the wicked, who communicates evil, is overtaken by disaster (6:12−15), and angers Yahweh (6:16−19)—just as in chapter 10, where the sluggard (10:26) is juxtaposed

---

43. Outside of the sluggard sayings in the collected proverbs (10:26; 13:4; 15:19; 19:24; 20:4; 21:25; 22:13), there are three extended portraits (6:6−11; 24:30−33; 26:12−16).

with the wicked who use speech to stir up dissension (10:10–12, 18–19) and anger Yahweh (10:22–32).

We might then rephrase our question to ask: How are we to understand the relationship between the wicked and the sluggard? Put another way, why did the sages decide to put this proverb about the sluggardly messenger smack in the middle of all this winnowing of righteous and wicked? We observed earlier that the proverb about the poor fit of messenger and sender does not fit its context, but perhaps it fits better than we first realized. The wicked are easy to spot, and perhaps their way is easy to avoid. But the way of the sluggard, now there is a danger! We can be lazy in failing to learn wisdom and practice disciplined speaking. If this warning against sloth in learning wisdom is the intended message, then the juxtaposition of sluggards among the wicked is meant to jolt the reader into awareness, as is the humor of incongruity set among the serious tone of the contrasts. As we saw in chapter 1, it is possible to walk by active and obvious wickedness and say, "No problem here," only to find that there are other more insidious forms that will catch us unaware.

Therefore, the sluggard not only warns us against a way of life that will eventually bring displeasure to others, it also uses the humor of incongruity to draw a larger lesson about diligence in cultivating our own life of wisdom and faith. Because it does not seem to fit, it attracts our attention and highlights the problem of the lazy son we first observed in 10:5. It comes at the center of a concentric structure about final ends and the importance of wise speaking that nourishes others. Laziness in this area can slip by just because it is so sneaky; it does not fit the pattern, and it is more funny than terrifying. But it is dangerous, and perhaps this is why the proverbs use humor to catch us off guard, the way Shakespeare used his wise fool to speak truth to King Lear. It is also striking that the two proverbs about laziness in 10:5 and 26 are set in proximity to sayings about Yahweh's care and justice. Perhaps this is another way of setting the seriousness of sin alongside the humorous folly of the sluggard in order to jolt us into awareness.[44]

To zoom in on one aspect of sluggardly behavior, we see that laziness in speech is especially dangerous when we realize that we can say things that we shouldn't or fail to speak when we should. I keep a Sumerian proverb posted by my desk that says, "The one who knows but does not speak is a fool." While it is true that the one who speaks and does not know is also a fool, I find I am more challenged by the need to speak out when the needs and rights of others are at stake. In that way, my speech can begin to nourish

---

44. "What is fitting" in 10:32 can also be translated "favor" (*raṣon*), that which is pleasing to others; the word is used in Isa. 42:1 to describe the delight of Yahweh in his servant.

others. The last two verses of chapter 10 reinforce the themes of wisdom and right speaking. Our speech either helps and nourishes others, or it leads to our own downfall!

ON CHILDREN GROWING UP. The image of the wise son that frames the first section of this chapter resonates with the concern that parents have for their children today, even while circumstances are vastly different. Whereas in ancient times, almost all males grew up to work for the family business, today it is more typical for young men and women to work for a company with little connection to the family. Although the home schooling movement is growing, education for most children now takes place outside the home and is extended into teenage and young adult years.

This extended period of adolescence and delay of adult responsibilities can leave both parents and kids confused, each not knowing what to expect of the other. Parents joke among themselves and get knowing smiles. I heard one say, "My teenager thinks his job is to lounge in his room and my job is to come home with food." One Baby Boom comedian asked, "Can it be possible that our kids are even lazier than we were?" and went on to present the details of the case to a laughing audience. The humor arises from hearing ourselves say things that our parents said to us about the conveniences they never had and the hard work they had to do. We are also surprised that we have grown up to value diligence and productivity over spontaneity and fun.

The proverbs on the wise son encourage parents to teach and model the value of diligence and righteousness for their sons and daughters. If we fail in this, we fall short of our duty as parents and as a church. However, we would make a mistake if we take these texts as proof that our kids need a kick in the pants and in so doing, only give them a message of rejection. The goal for our kids is growth in wisdom as the fountain source of all the virtues, including diligence. That being the case, we can be patient with our kids when we watch their ups and downs in making the transition from dependent children to responsible adults. We can expect that these lessons will not be learned right away, but take time.

At the same time, we must prepare our kids to take on adult responsibilities and hold them accountable when they do not. Oprah Winfrey's talk show is an interesting indicator of trends in society. On one program she brought in a psychologist to talk tough love to grown children who were living at home as if they were still teenagers, paying no rent and sponging. While some counseling might be appropriate to get at the apparent lack of motivation, his simple message of taking adult responsibility made good sense. One young man was camped out with cable TV in his mother's dining room and tried to use charm and humor to defuse her exasperation, saying he was in a time of transition and will find his life's direction in due time. The psychologist told him, "You don't need to find yourself; you need to find yourself a job."

Mentoring youth. An adult who lives like a dependent child is inappropriate and shameful, but we should not use these proverbs to club our kids. A youth worker told me of one young man who slept all the time because his body was in a growth spurt. Other adolescents may show a lack of motivation because they are truly confused about making their way into adult life. Another youth worker said, "For twenty-two years I have worked with and counseled teenagers and their families, and I can honestly say that I have never seen such a tidal wave of hopelessness as has hit this generation. As I talk with teenagers today, there is a sense of despair and disillusionment. The world makes no sense to them." He recommends making a difference with unconditional love: "When I was a child, I needed love most when I deserved it least. I've heard it said, 'Teenagers are the most unlovable when they need the most love.'"[45]

In sum, the wise and foolish sons in this passage succeed or fail to take on adult responsibilities, and for that reason it is not appropriate to use this text to criticize teenage laziness. Nevertheless, one can see that patterns are developed in youth that extend into adulthood. Parents encourage industry or sloth by either challenging or enabling. The biblical principle at issue in 10:1–5 is growth in wisdom that shows itself in shouldering adult responsibility, including care for one's family, and by extension, one's community. The joy of the parents in 10:1 can provide some guidelines for encouraging that growth in our children. The opposite of shame is pride, and parents can certainly foster character and behavior that brings pride by expressing it to them.

One way to apply the emphasis on joy (10:1) and honor (10:5) is to tell our kids when they have done us proud. Once, at home on college break, I was walking out of the kitchen to head for some activity that I don't remember, but I do remember my father looking across the table and saying, "Hey! I'm proud of you." There is a sense in which the positive message can also be communicated via the negative. One pastor told his teenager, "For better or worse, what you do reflects on me." Another said, "Tell me, what's your last name? Don't let them say, 'What kind of clown is his father?'"

45. C. Wysong, "Code Blue: An Urgent Call to Save Our Kids," *The Covenant Companion* (September 1999), 6–9.

A university professor who had been invited to speak at a conference was asked to send a resumé. Instead, he sent a list of all his students who had gone on to teach in his field with a note attached: "Everything important I've ever done is there." The principle of bringing joy to others who have taught us extends to the work of the church as well. Just as I hope I'm making my parents proud of me, so I want to honor those who taught and nurtured me in the Christian life. In the same way, I hope to receive honor through the successes and contributions of those I teach and mentor. The images of wisdom instruction in the home point to the larger chain of disciple-making by which we reproduce ourselves in the faithful lives of others.

It is good for us to remember that we have been mentored and can do the same for younger believers, and this may even help us put into perspective our thoughts about our own accomplishments. We may look with envy at those who go on to have great influence and notoriety in their ministries and view our own contributions as small. Yet those who reach high stand on the shoulders of those who taught them, and who knows who will stand on ours and what they will do? We may take encouragement that our faithfulness in teaching can live on long after us. One wonders if those teachers in the temple knew what they were doing when they were answering the questions of Joseph and Mary's wise son.

Wise speaking and wise living. The wise son of his parents grows up to become a wise son of the community, and the collected proverbs of 10:6–21 sketch a portrait of one who receives its blessings in life and death (vv. 6–7). The sayings contrast actions that either build or damage relationships of trust with neighbors. They frequently point to speaking body parts (the lips, tongue, and mouth) as well as their source, the heart, which is either teachable or worthless (vv. 8, 20). This picture of a responsible and compassionate member of the community moves us to take stock of our own participation in the life of church and society, particularly in the matter of wise speaking.

Recalling Luke's picture of Jesus the wise son who grows up to read and speak in the congregation, we note that his speech and his actions show concern for the well-being of the poor. Our understanding of Jesus' ministry is enriched when we understand the story of his life and teaching as instructive and redemptive, a source of good news in our preaching, just as weighty as his death and resurrection. Craig Loscalzo is concerned that our desire to preach the redemptive message of the cross and atonement may pass by the good news of Jesus' teaching and healing that makes up the greater portion of the Gospels. He writes, "Living within the province of God means learning how to be effective faithful citizens; we thrive on both *kerygma* and *didache*. The gospel makes foreigners into citizens and helps citizens remember the purpose of their citizenship."[46] This portrait of the wise son of the community helps us appreciate the life of Jesus as example of kingdom citizenship.

How is Jesus' life an example of wise living for us? We first notice that his words nourish many as they bring forth wisdom (cf. 10:21, 31). While we remember that the primary context of Proverbs is honest speaking and dealing in daily working relationships, we might also ask if some sense of teaching wisdom by practicing wise speech is in view also. Not all are called to become teachers of wisdom, but all can instruct through the practice of wise speaking, even as Jesus did. Many of the texts that we preach in sermons began as conversations between Jesus and tax collectors, adulterers, Pharisees, and disciples. Sometimes the outcome of these conversations was confrontation and sometimes the granting of forgiveness; in every case, the words became examples of wisdom and love. When Zacchaeus promised to give half of his riches to the poor and pay back anyone he had cheated four times over, Jesus said, "Today salvation has come to this house" (Luke 19:9). Zacchaeus had spoken wisely also.

Wise sons and daughters of their communities take their relationships seriously, recognizing that they are not independent persons. Their words are concerned with the profit to the other person more than the profit for themselves. Perhaps this is one reason why wise speaking is contrasted with violence and ill-gotten treasures. The speech of the wise is like gathering crops and sharing the wealth. Comparing the tongue of the righteous with choice silver forces us to ask what do we really count as worthwhile.

Borrowing Daniel Boorstein's conception of "consumption communities" to describe the pseudo-communities that join together around brand-name loyalty and contemporary visions of the good life, Quentin Schultze points out that mediated communication of films, television, radio, and magazines have replaced older community traditions. Schultze argues that these communities of consumption identify us primarily as people who buy and use consumer goods, to find identity in what we buy instead of how we use our resources for the kingdom of God. "Our gifts, talents and possessions should foster deeper communities of shalom."[47] Wise speaking values relationships of shalom over the competition and loneliness of consumption.

Wise speaking is concerned with its more immediate effects on others. The sages who collected these proverbs saw violence as an outcome of greedy desire for gain; they may have been surprised to learn that we also think of

---

46. C. Loscalzo, *Evangelistic Preaching That Connects: Guidance in Shaping Fresh and Appealing Sermons* (Downers Grove, Ill.: InterVarsity Press, 1995), 47.

47. Q. J. Schultze, *Communicating for Life: Christian Stewardship in Community and Media* (Grand Rapids: Baker, 2000), 116–17.

hurtful words as a form of violence. Still, they saw equal wrong in spreading slander and covering hatred with lies (10:18). The popular proverb, "Sticks and stones may break my bones, but words can never hurt me," is a defense that shows how badly words can hurt. One seminary student shared with her classmates:

> Every week I help at a children's program at a nearby church. We play games, have snacks, make crafts and talk about God. And, nearly every week, without fail, someone ends up in tears. I have spent more than a few afternoons drying tears and speaking soothing words. But, you see, the sad thing is that these tears are not from falls or bruises. They bounce back easily from those. The tears come from mean words said by other kids.[48]

What is true for kids is true of adults as well. Followers of Jesus practice wise speaking when they resist temptations to profit and power over others, speaking only that which nourishes and restores.

Praise and hope. The teaching of the chapter does not center on human relationships alone. The collection of Yahweh proverbs scattered throughout 10:22−32 inspires Christian readers to praise and hope. Praise celebrates the diligent God, who does not slumber like the foolish and careless son but rather watches to make sure that the righteous do not go hungry and that wicked grasping is frustrated (10:5). This God is the source of wisdom's benefits, wealth without trouble, long life, and refuge (10:22, 27, 29). We praise Yahweh who does not let evil go unchecked, even when circumstances may lead us to think otherwise. Hope comes to Christian readers as they hear that wicked deeds and those who do them will come to an end, while the righteous have a future (10:25, 30). Hope comes about from taking the long view that this collection of sayings offers; it hears the questions of doubt and answers them instead of dismissing them.

Reading these proverbs along with wisdom psalms in services of worship is itself a form of praise and an expression of hope, for it assumes that God is present and watching, even at those times when God appears absent. This form of praise is akin to praying psalms of lament that nearly always point ahead to the time when believers will praise.[49] They assume that God hears, even as psalmists ask if they have been abandoned. We may shy away from taking the words of lament on our lips in worship, for it can seem as though

---

48. K. Erickson, "Words, Words, Words," presented in Communication Skills for Ministry class at North Park Theological Seminary, March 29, 2001.
49. C. Westermann, *Praise and Lament in the Psalms* (Atlanta: John Knox), 1981.

we are doubting God's goodness to us. However, prayer is a sure sign of faith, for it refuses to walk away from God even when it asks whether God ever walks away from us. In a similar way, these proverbs not only inspire our faith, they give us permission to voice our doubts and questions. Reading the proverbs along with wisdom psalms allows them to speak to the congregation at the same time that they are potentially addressed to God.[50]

A final word. Finally, as we take the proverb about vinegar and smoke to heart (v. 26), we recall that laziness in those who should be caring for others as responsible adults is particularly shameful. We also saw that the chiastic structure of 10:20–32, framing the sluggard saying with teaching on speech and God's watchfulness, suggests that the one who sends messengers is the Lord. After all, the Yahweh proverbs all appear in the vicinity of proverbs about laziness! Further, the image of laziness that brings stinging pain to the eyes and teeth of another echoes the combined sense of the chiasm in 10:1–5, that a son's laziness brings grief and shame to his parents. The larger context of the chapter, then, indicates that the saying about sluggards teaches that diligence with speech—that is, becoming a wise one who labors hard to nourish others—is *the* goal of wisdom instruction. To become a person who speaks wisely and teaches others to do the same is to honor our parents, communities, and God.

It is significant, then, that at this turning point in the book of Proverbs, we observe a shift in emphasis. Whereas in chapters 1–9, the parents urge their son to *get* wisdom, here the collected wisdom of the community adds a call to *give* wisdom in the form of speech that nourishes others (10:21). As the son grows to take his place in the community as a responsible adult, he is to learn that care for others involves stewardship of the gifts of material resources and communication. Both require diligence and oversight. Just as humans need water and food to live, so life together requires speech that nourishes many as a spring of life and bears the fruit of wisdom. Proverbs would make teachers of us all!

---

50. R. K. Johnston, "Practicing the Presence of God: The Wisdom Psalms as Prayer," in *To Hear and Obey: Essays in Honor of Fredrick Carlson Holmgren*, ed. B. J. Bergfalk and P. E. Koptak (Chicago: Covenant Publications, 1997), 20–41, esp. 25: "What we have in the wisdom psalms is a joining of instruction with prayer, prayer with instruction."

Proverbs 11:1–31

❧

¹ THE LORD ABHORS dishonest scales,
   but accurate weights are his delight.
² When pride comes, then comes disgrace,
   but with humility comes wisdom.
³ The integrity of the upright guides them,
   but the unfaithful are destroyed by their duplicity.
⁴ Wealth is worthless in the day of wrath,
   but righteousness delivers from death.
⁵ The righteousness of the blameless makes a straight way
      for them,
   but the wicked are brought down by their own
      wickedness.
⁶ The righteousness of the upright delivers them,
   but the unfaithful are trapped by evil desires.
⁷ When a wicked man dies, his hope perishes;
   all he expected from his power comes to nothing.
⁸ The righteous man is rescued from trouble,
   and it comes on the wicked instead.
⁹ With his mouth the godless destroys his neighbor,
   but through knowledge the righteous escape.
¹⁰ When the righteous prosper, the city rejoices;
   when the wicked perish, there are shouts of joy.
¹¹ Through the blessing of the upright a city is exalted,
   but by the mouth of the wicked it is destroyed.
¹² A man who lacks judgment derides his neighbor,
   but a man of understanding holds his tongue.
¹³ A gossip betrays a confidence,
   but a trustworthy man keeps a secret.
¹⁴ For lack of guidance a nation falls,
   but many advisers make victory sure.
¹⁵ He who puts up security for another will surely suffer,
   but whoever refuses to strike hands in pledge is safe.
¹⁶ A kindhearted woman gains respect,
   but ruthless men gain only wealth.
¹⁷ A kind man benefits himself,
   but a cruel man brings trouble on himself.

¹⁸ The wicked man earns deceptive wages,
  but he who sows righteousness reaps a sure reward.
¹⁹ The truly righteous man attains life,
  but he who pursues evil goes to his death.
²⁰ The LORD detests men of perverse heart
  but he delights in those whose ways are blameless.
²¹ Be sure of this: The wicked will not go unpunished,
  but those who are righteous will go free.
²² Like a gold ring in a pig's snout
  is a beautiful woman who shows no discretion.
²³ The desire of the righteous ends only in good,
  but the hope of the wicked only in wrath.
²⁴ One man gives freely, yet gains even more;
  another withholds unduly, but comes to poverty.
²⁵ A generous man will prosper;
  he who refreshes others will himself be refreshed.
²⁶ People curse the man who hoards grain,
  but blessing crowns him who is willing to sell.
²⁷ He who seeks good finds goodwill,
  but evil comes to him who searches for it.
²⁸ Whoever trusts in his riches will fall,
  but the righteous will thrive like a green leaf.
²⁹ He who brings trouble on his family will inherit only wind,
  and the fool will be servant to the wise.
³⁰ The fruit of the righteous is a tree of life,
  and he who wins souls is wise.
³¹ If the righteous receive their due on earth,
  how much more the ungodly and the sinner!

Original Meaning

THE OPENING PROVERB of chapter 11 tells us that Yahweh hates dishonest scales; falseness links it with false speech in the verse before (10:32) and false assessment of self in 11:2. Again the wisdom theme says, consider the ends of the two ways. Wisdom and the wise are named at the start of the chapter (11:2) and at the end (11:29–30). Sayings about women appear in 11:16 and 22; directed to males, these proverbs about good and bad character in women look ahead to the finale of the book, the praise of the good wife in 31:10–31.

Following on the four proverbs about "the LORD" (*yhwh*) in 10:3, 22, 27, 29, Proverbs 11 has two. The proverbs of 11:1 and 20 are similar in vocabulary and theme, stating clearly what Yahweh abhors or detests (*toʿebah*) and what brings him delight (*raṣon*). While some believe that they mark an inclusio,[1] the proposed outline here takes the Yahweh proverbs as the beginning of two larger sections. There is no clear outline to this chapter,[2] yet similarities with neighboring proverbs suggest clusters of proverbs gathered around a theme.

Such outlines, of course, can at best point out some thematic clusters, though we must recognize that a few themes, such as perishing versus hope, appear in more than one cluster.[3] We should also remember that relationships between proverbs go in so many directions. Therefore, teachers and preachers can identify clusters and choose either to select a smaller section for discussion or to draw together similar proverbs in a chapter or larger section that bridges two chapters. In my view, the Yahweh proverbs at 11:1 and 20 suggest the following outline:

Yahweh Detests Dishonest Scales (11:1–19)
    Honesty, humility, and integrity (11:1–3)
    Fates of righteous and wicked compared (11:4–8)
    Right and wrong use of speech (11:9–14)
    Wages and outcomes (11:15–19)

Yahweh Detests Perverse Hearts (11:20–31)
    Desire and discretion (11:20–23)
    Giving and receiving (11:24–28)
    Gardens and houses (11:29–31)

The chapter opens and ends with the theme of just reward, which also runs throughout. Just as Yahweh hates dishonesty in the form of cheating weights (like the dishonest thumb on the grocery store scale), so both righteous and wicked receive their due on earth. What people give, they receive in turn, even as verse 1 emphasizes honesty and integrity in relationships.

---

1. Garrett, *Proverbs*, 124.
2. Interpreters have not reached any agreement on structure. A. Scherer, *Das weise Wort und seine Wirkung*, 88, divides vv. 1–2, 3–8, 9–13, 14–16, 17–23, 24–26, 27 (theme verse), 28–30. Meinhold, *Die Sprüche*, divides vv. 1–2, 3–8, 9–15, 16–22, 23–27, 28–30, 31. Scoralick, *Einzelspruch und Sammlung*, 196, divides larger sections according to framing verses, 10:28–11:7, 11:8–12:13 (with subsections 11:8–17 and 12:4–13).
3. Garrett, *Proverbs*, 48, observes that "random repetition" of certain themes uses the element of surprise to show emphasis, perhaps more effectively than placing them in single clusters (eg. 17:1, 9, 14, 19, 27–28).

Other related themes that are woven through the chapter include proper use of wealth (11:4, 15, 18, 22, 24–29) and speech (11:9–14). Recurring images of rescue, escape, and safety appear as well.

Yahweh Detests Dishonest Scales (11:1–19)

11:1. THE FIRST THREE proverbs of chapter 11 hold up honesty, humility, and integrity. Verse 1 probably comments on 10:32 by means of the linking word *raṣon*, pointing to that which is appropriate or delightful.[4] The link with 10:32 also yields a list of three forms of perverseness that contrast with the integrity of 11:3: false business practice, false assessment of self, and false use of the tongue. The negative rewards for such falseness are Yahweh's displeasure, disapproval of one's neighbors (shame), and destruction. Integrity guides and leads its bearer forward, while duplicity destroys and brings its bearer to an end.

The contrast between integrity and crookedness is also in 10:9. Ancient dealers sometimes kept two sets of weighing stones, one for buying and one for selling, as archaeologists have discovered (cf. Deut. 25:13–16; Amos 8:5). The practice, always condemned in Scripture, is here called (lit.) "an abomination to the LORD" (*toʿebat yhwh*; cf. Prov. 11:20).

11:2. Pride in the Old Testament is often different from our ideas of vanity and conceit (11:2). It points to the folly and arrogance of those who believe they can abuse others and not be brought to account. "See what they spew from their mouths—they spew out swords from their lips, and they say, 'Who can hear us?' But you, O LORD, laugh at them" (Ps. 59:7–8). Wisdom, its opposite, knows we have to give answer for our actions and therefore has a sense of boundaries.

11:3. This contrast in 11:3 is between guidance and destruction. It imagines roads filled with dangers or rushing white water rivers filled with treacherous rocks. One would be glad to have a guide in such situations, and integrity promises to be that companion. The duplicity (*selep*) of the unfaithful is twisted, just as a bribe twists the words of the righteous (Ex. 23:8; Deut. 16:19). The verbal form of this word appears in Proverbs 13:6: "Righteousness guards the man of integrity, but wickedness *overthrows* the sinner."

11:4. The next seven verses (11:4–10, except for v. 7) present variations on the word for righteousness (*ṣedeqah*) and its use in verse 4. Each verse describes either the bad consequences that come on the wicked, the rescue of the righteous, or both. There may be a chiasm; verses 6 and 8 seem to match regarding escape for the righteous, while verse 7 repeats the sad end of the wicked.

---

4. Whybray, *Proverbs*, 176.

After three juxtapositions in 11:1–3 (truth versus falsity, humility versus pride, integrity versus duplicity), the parallelism of 11:4 is striking since it places the "profit" of wealth in opposition with the profit of righteousness (what "delivers from death"). The opposition is surprising, yet the proverb shows how people put their trust in one or the other. More than a simple "you can't take it with you,"[5] the point is rather that one can use wealth in a righteous way, but wealth in itself offers no security. Hosea chastised those who cheated in business and then trusted in their wealth (Hos. 12:6–8). On the positive side, one might think of Jesus' parable of using wealth to make friends for eternity (Luke 16:1–15). Such creative use of money is an expression of righteousness. The vocabulary of the proverb reminds the reader of Proverbs 10:2: "Ill-gotten treasures are of no value, but righteousness delivers from death."

11:5. Verses 5–6 form a pair contrasting the fates of the righteous and the wicked, each beginning with the same word, "righteousness." "Righteousness of the blameless" (11:5) repeats in reverse the same Hebrew roots used for "integrity of the upright" in 11:3 and repeats the image of the straight and safe way.

11:6. So also, the "desire" of 11:6 uses the same word as "craving" in 10:3 (*bawwah*), so we might better speak of "inordinate desire" (i.e., desire that knows no boundaries). There is some wordplay between 11:5 and 6; the same Hebrew root (*yšr*) is used with the righteousness that "makes straight" and the righteousness of "the upright." The contrast in the two proverbs is clear; righteousness keeps its bearer safe and free while wickedness ensnares and destroys.

11:7. This proverb reflects on the experience of hope and rewards. Because the wicked have no desire for the enduring treasures of wisdom, their hopes and dreams die with them. The word for power can also refer to one's wealth, connecting this verse with those that came before.[6] The same Hebrew words for "hope perishes" and "expected" appear in 10:28 as "hope comes to nothing" and "prospect."

11:8. Like 11:6, the proverb in 11:8 contrasts the rescue of the righteous with the trouble that "comes on the wicked instead." Here, as in all the previous sayings, trouble is personified as a hunter that kills its prey, as the wicked often view themselves (cf. 1:10–12). The irony of the sages shows that the wicked bring their own trouble on themselves (cf. 1:18).

---

5. Murphy and Huwiler, *Proverbs, Ecclesiastes, Song of Songs*, 54.

6. Clifford, *Proverbs*, 122; cf. Ps. 49:12: "But man, despite his riches, does not endure; he is like the beasts that perish."

11:9. These next six proverbs are clustered around the theme of speech; all except verse 13 begins with the Hebrew letter *bet*. The first four are placed in a chiastic order according to key words: neighbor (11:9), wicked/city (11:10–11), neighbor (11:12).[7] The last two contrast the time to keep a secret quiet (11:13) and a time to make good counsel public (11:14). Perhaps readers are meant to read 11:12–14 together as they develop the theme of helpful and damaging use of speech set out in 11:9. If we take 11:9–14 as a section, the theme of speech that destroys is viewed from a number of angles and set in contrast with a number of virtues.[8]

The first line of 11:9 introduces its own surprise, for it is not with physical violence that the godless person destroys a neighbor but with words. Most likely this refers to a bad report or some other form of slander, but what do the righteous escape "through knowledge"? Do they escape such hostility, or are they free of the need to speak in this way? The context of the preceding verses (11:5–8) suggests that the righteous are delivered from the troubles that ungodly behaviors bring on those who do them. We may not be protected from the verbal assaults of others, but we will be rescued from the backlash that uncontrolled speech brings on itself.

11:10. Verses 10–11 are linked by the catchword "city," and they bring the series of righteous/wicked contrasts to a climax (the terms do not appear again until 11:18). "Joy" is the key to the contrast of 11:10; the city rejoices when the righteous do well (lit., "it is good") and when the wicked perish (cf. 11:7). It sounds as if the proverb both affirms the system of just rewards stated in the previous verses and acknowledges that it is not always the way life works. The sounds of rejoicing may come when outcomes are fitting because too often they are not.

11:11. We now see why the city rejoices as stated in the previous verse: The life of the city is affected for better or worse by the character of its citizens. The blessing of the upright is most likely the good (*ṭob*) that their ways bring about in 11:10. The righteous not only bring good on themselves but on others. Here is good news that may even have an element of surprise, even while the contrast is obvious; the destructive talk of the wicked does widespread damage.

11:12. The words of the wicked destroy by deriding others or by breaking confidence; thus, 11:12–13 go together. The discerning and trustworthy person keeps silent on both counts. The word "neighbor" links 11:9 with

---

7. A. Scherer, "Is the Selfish Man Wise?: Considerations of Context in Proverbs 10:1–22:16 with Special Regard to Surety, Bribery, and Friendship," *JSOT* 76 (1997): 82.

8. Whybray, *Proverbs*, 179.

11:12, the latter adding that such behavior demonstrates (lit.) "lack of heart." "Understanding," like "knowledge," helps one discern when it is right to remain silent; as a result this wisdom delivers a righteous person from trouble.

11:13. The first line of this proverb seems obvious—by definition, the gossip betrays confidences (cf. 20:19). But the term "gossip" is (lit.) "one who goes about," trading in either merchandise (Ezek. 27:3–11) or slander (Lev. 19:16; Jer. 6:28; 9:4; Ezek. 22:9). Therefore, some intention of gain, either in material goods or in status, seems the motivation. This proverb certainly applies to personal relationships, but business practices are included as well. Bad reports can ruin both a person's reputation and business.

11:14. As we saw in 11:10–11, the effects of speech are not only individual in scope but affect entire cities and even nations (11:14). The reference to "guidance" (*taḥbulot*) in this verse reminds the reader of the prologue (1:5). A negative picture of advice comes in 12:5: "The plans of the righteous are just, but the advice of the wicked is deceitful." The positive view is in 20:18: "Make plans by seeking advice; if you wage war, obtain guidance" (cf. 24:6). Wisdom promised to be such an adviser in 8:14. Just as negative words can tear persons and cities down, good counsel, the kind that wisdom offers, builds up and brings victory.

11:15. Verses 15–19 look at the topics of money and neighbors. In this collection of individual sayings, Proverbs contains three references to surety, that is, the practice of guaranteeing a loan, all of them against it (11:15; 17:18; 20:16). The warnings given in 22:26–27 are sober and funny at the same time; if you cannot pay, they will take your bed from under you! Is this a contradiction of the call to charity found throughout the sayings and instructions (14:21, 31; 17:5; 19:17; 22:22–23), or is it an example of doing the right thing at the right time? The surrounding verses suggest that both are true; it is better to give generously than make a pledge.[9] Proverbs 11:14 speaks of foolish actions without wisdom and discernment, while 11:17 praises the man of *ḥesed*.[10] "Another" in 11:15 uses the same Hebrew word as in the warning in 6:1 (*zar*, "stranger"), and we most likely have a recapitulation of that theme. Here, as there, the admonitions to neighbor love are qualified by this warning against surety.

---

9. A similar view comes from Sir. 29:14–20. "A good person will be surety for his neighbor, but the one who has lost all sense of shame will fail him. . . . Being surety has ruined many who were prosperous, and has tossed them about like waves of the sea; it has driven the influential into exile, and they have wandered among foreign nations. The sinner comes to grief through surety; his pursuit of gain involves him in lawsuits. Assist your neighbor to the best of your ability, but be careful not to fall yourself" (NRSV).

10. Scherer, "Is the Selfish Man Wise?" 62–63.

11:16. Verse 16 not only stands out from its context, but the meaning of the vocabulary is difficult to determine. As the NIV translates, the kind-heartedness of the woman wins her the favor of others while the ruthlessness or aggression of men wins wealth. By implication, the men gain no reputation, only material goods that will be lost at the end of life. The LXX has a fuller reading, which the NRSV incorporates as the original text: "A gracious woman gets honor, but she who hates virtue is covered with shame. The timid become destitute, but the aggressive gain riches."

However, the pithy saying can be read as it stands in the Hebrew text if *ḥen* ("gracious") is translated as "charm" (cf. 31:30) or "beauty."[11] In this reading, both beauty and violence are noted for the gain they bring, honor to the woman and wealth to the men. "Respect" (*kabod*) translates a term that can refer to wealth (Est. 5:11; Ps. 49:16), but in Proverbs, it typically refers to human honor (Prov. 3:35; 15:33; 18:12; 20:3; 25:27; 26:8; 29:23), the honor that Solomon did not request but was given (cf. 1 Kings 3:13). If this is the case, the saying is of a kind with Proverbs 11:22, setting beauty and character in contrast.

11:17. An argument in favor of reading 11:16 with the NIV is the similar parallel of a man of kindness (*ḥesed*) with the cruel one who harms (lit.) "his own flesh" (11:17). Kindness and cruelty done to others turn back on the doer, as the other verses of the chapter attest. So the worthy woman "brings him good, not harm, all the days of her life" (31:12). Conversely, one is not to do harm to one who has not dealt it to you (3:30).

11:18. The righteous/wicked contrast reappears, linked here with the contrast between "deceptive wages" and "sure reward." If one of the characteristics of the wicked is deception, once again they, like the righteous, reap what they sow. There is a wordplay on the Hebrew for "deceptive" (*šaqer*) and "reward" (*šeker*). "Sure" translates *ʾemet*, completing the typical pair with *ḥesed* in 11:17, often translated "love and faithfulness" (cf. Ps. 25:10; 61:7; 85:11).

11:19. "Life" and "death" complete each line of 11:19, which contrasts a person of true righteousness and one who pursues evil. The first word (*ken*) can be translated as "true" or "sure," but also as the simple particle "thus" or "so." Some resolve the confusion by emending *ken* to *tikkon* ("to be firm or established") to keep the contrast of steady leading with "frantic pursuit."[12] Again, the point is clear that immediate pursuits determine ultimate destinations.

---

11. Clifford, *Proverbs*, 124; Van Leeuwen, "Proverbs," 118–19.
12. Clifford, *Proverbs*, 124–25; also Murphy, *Proverbs*, 80.

Yahweh Detests Perverse Hearts (11:20−31)

11:20. A SMALL CLUSTER in these verses move from Yahweh's reaction to human hearts and ways to the punishment and wrath that come on the wicked. Nestled in between is a startling proverb about the beautiful woman; just as it seems out of place in its context, the proverb talks about that which is not fitting.

Like the dishonest scales of 11:1, perverse hearts are (lit.) "an abomination to the LORD" (*to'ebat ybwb*), an abhorrence that provokes his disgust. Here the point of 11:1 is made without the metaphor of the scales and weights; the heart directs one's way, and ways that are blameless or have integrity (*tam;* cf. 11:3) bring Yahweh delight (*raṣon;* cf. 11:1). In 11:1, the response was to actions; here it is to their intentions that motivate them. As is often the case in Proverbs, Yahweh's direct intervention in human affairs is not portrayed, but readers are given a view of what brings him pleasure (cf. 12:2).

11:21. As is also true of Proverbs, outcomes and rewards are not attributed to Yahweh directly but only by implication, as the juxtaposition of 11:20−21 shows. This open-ended view of punishment can see just deserts come in everyday events, yet the second line of 11:21 can be read, "the offspring of the righteous will go free," reminding the reader of Exodus 34:6−7 (cf. Num. 14:18). If this is the intent of the saying, the contrast is between sure punishment of the guilty and sure grace to the righteous. Again, such certainty is needed in a world in which the opposite appears to be the case. "Not go unpunished" throughout Proverbs covers the catalog of sins: adultery (6:29), wickedness (11:21), pride (16:5), mocking the poor (17:5), false witness (19:5, 9), and a hurry to get rich (28:20).

11:22. We must be careful to distinguish proverbs that are more direct or literal from those that are metaphorical. Thus, the metaphor in 11:22 may point to a truth already known and assimilated, or it may begin there and jolt us into new understanding.[13] The proverb stands out against the background of its context just the way the beauty of a gold ring stands out against the background of an ugly snout. The picture of a beautiful ornament placed where it will be covered in mud and swill suggests that physical beauty without character is also not fitting, out of place. "Shows no discretion" is (lit.) "turns away from discernment"; the root meaning of the verb *ṭ'm* is "to taste" (as in "taste and see that the LORD is good," Ps. 34:8). The meaning was extended to include "discernment," as in Psalm 119:66: "Teach me knowledge and *good judgment*, for I believe in your commands." Beauty and good judgment were both found in Abigail (1 Sam. 25:3, 33).

---

13. W. van Heerden, "Proverbial Wisdom, Metaphor and Inculturation," *OTE* 10 (1997): 518−19.

Proverbs 11:22 may be asking the wicked of 11:18, what is it you want? Gold? But is life only measured in terms of gold? And who would put a gold ring in a pig's snout? No one, yet we isolate beauty from discretion all the time, just as we want riches without wisdom. Neither is fitting. "Charm is deceptive, and beauty is fleeting; but a woman who fears the LORD is to be praised" (31:30). Again, these sayings are directed to men but overheard by women. The saying is less a putdown of beautiful and foolish women than of men who might prefer them. If readers can agree that beauty without discretion is of no value, then they should equally agree that wealth without wisdom has no value.

11:23. This proverb seems to be a rejoinder to 11:7; the "desire" (*tiqwah;* cf. 11:7; 10:28) of the righteous for good is contrasted with "the hope of the wicked." The terse phrasing of the Hebrew brings this out: "The desire of the righteous, only good; the hope of the wicked, wrath." The righteous desiring good, receive good; the wicked, hoping for gain, receive their own destruction in return. In this way, the hope or expectation of the wicked dies with them. This verse makes the connection of the verses in 11:20–23 clear, pitting good desires against wicked hope.

11:24. The proverbs of 11:24–28 form another series that seems to gather around the theme of how one handles desire and wealth. Hebrew participles dominate, translated as "one who does xxx," placing emphasis on actions as a sign of character. Verses 25–27 deal specifically with generosity.

Generosity is encouraged by comparing outcomes once again (11:24). The contrast is made between one who scatters freely (Ps. 112:9) and one who not only fails to give generously but withholds what is due to another—most likely in wages or payment of debt. Literally, that one withholds what is upright (*yšr*), repeating the term from Proverbs 11:3, 5, 6, 11. This theme of generosity versus withholding runs throughout this section (cf. Deut. 15:1–11).

11:25. Expounding the theme of 11:24, the proverb in 11:25 does not contrast outcomes but uses both lines to highlight the blessings of the righteous. The generous man is literally a "person of blessing" (*nepeš bʰrakah;* cf. "blessing" in 11:11 and 10:6–7, 22), who "becomes fat."[14] "Refreshment" is a term associated with water and giving drink. The one who nurtures others will be nurtured in turn.

11:26. "Blessings on the head of the one who sells grain" (lit. trans. of 11:26) repeats "blessings" (*bʰrakah*) from the previous verse (cf. 10:6–7). Its contrast is again withholding, this time the holding back of grain that would help others who are hungry, presumably for profit via price gouging. Blessings

---

14. Clifford, *Proverbs,* 125–26, suggests that *nepeš* be translated in its basic sense of "throat" or "neck," yielding "the throat of blessing will grow fat."

and curses point to public opinion. While the honor that comes from others is not the primary motivation for doing good, it is not discounted. The wise Joseph stored grain, but he did so to save the people.

11:27. Continuing the themes of public favor and rewards, 11:27 compares two seekers: one who seeks good and finds goodwill, the other who pursues evil for others only to have it "come to him." The goodwill or favor may be that of Yahweh (*raṣon;* cf. "delight" in 11:1, 20) or public approval ("what is fitting," 10:32). Again, such favor only comes as a benefit of seeking good; seeking the favor for its own sake without the good tempts one to present false appearances.

11:28. The term "righteous" reappears in 11:28, comparing such persons to a flourishing green leaf (cf. Ps. 1:3), a treasured thing in arid Palestine. No positive action is mentioned as in the previous sayings, only the negatively charged "whoever trust in his riches." A false sense of security in what one owns motivates the evil behaviors of withholding charity, withholding in speculation, and active pursuit of evil. If anyone believes that one's holdings are one's strength, then anything is justified. Sadly, the one who turns that belief into action falls dead like a dried-up leaf. Positive images of trees appear again in Proverbs 11:30.

11:29. The metaphors of comparison now center on the household. To "trouble the house" (lit. trans. of 11:29a) is to act in ways that bring harm on those closest to us. The reader thinks of the foolish son who does not care for the family (10:1, 5) but also Achar (1 Chron. 2:7). Thus, the negative recompense for evil even extends to one's family. Instead of inheriting family wealth, this sort of person inherits only wind, perhaps because it has been squandered in folly. This sort of fool will never be the head of the house but rather a servant in it, the thought that was in the mind of the prodigal son as he returned home (Luke 15:19, 21). Proverbs about the fool who serves the wise will appear again (e.g., Prov. 14:19; 17:2).

11:30. What appears to be a straightforward comparison (11:30) is actually an unresolved conundrum in biblical studies. The first line is clear enough in comparing a righteous person to a sturdy well-watered tree with good fruit (Ps. 1:3; 92:12; Isa. 58:11; Jer. 17:5-8); the fruit of the righteous is like the tree of life (with possible allusion to the tree of life in Gen. 2:9; 3:22-24).[15] As is the case in all the "tree of life" sayings in Proverbs, the fruit is not forbidden but offered to sustain and nourish life (Prov. 3:18; 13:12; 15:4). Not

---

15. G. T. Sheppard, *Wisdom As a Hermeneutical Construct: A Study in the Sapientialising of the Old Testament* (Berlin and New York: Walter de Gruyter, 1980), 53–54. See also Sir. 1:16–20; 6:19 and the motif of the exalted garden as new paradise (cf. Deut. 8:7–10; Ezek. 40:1–48:32).

only do the righteous thrive like green leaves (11:28), they bear fruit that feeds others.

The second line of 11:30 is not so easy to read, for the Hebrew *loqeaḥ nepašot* ("to take lives") usually means "to kill." Yet if the writer meant "kill," we are surprised to find a "wise" one as the subject of the verb.[16] Instead, we could translate *leqaḥ* as like the American idiom, "I get what you mean," and read, "One who comprehends souls is wise." The saying then corresponds to 1:3, which can be translated either "to receive instruction" or to "comprehend instruction."[17]

The metaphor of tree and its fruit recommends the translation, "and the wise gathers life/lives." To gather lives like fruit then denotes the wise one who plucks people from the power of death. The closeness of the Hebrew to the phrase "takes life" may be intentionally ironic, for this is action that gives life instead.[18] As in chapter 10, we have here an encouragement to become wise in order to save not only one's own life/soul (*nepeš*) but also the lives of others (10:11, 21, 31; cf. 24:11). In sum, while the Hebrew text is difficult, that in itself does not provide sufficient reason to emend; the wise promote life, they do not take it away.

11:31. The final saying of chapter 11 also presents a number of difficulties. It appears to be a summary of all that has gone before in the chapter, affirming that the righteous do receive their reward in full (the verb form *yᵉšal-lam*, "receive their due," is related to the root of *šalom*, "peace"), and the verb does double duty in the second line for the wicked. "On earth" is best read not as the here and now as opposed to the afterlife but as modifying righteous, "the righteous on the earth are rewarded in full." While some interpreters suggest that both the righteous and wicked are rewarded for their misdeeds,[19] in Proverbs the righteous are always rewarded for their good deeds and evildoers for their misdeeds (6:31; 13:13, 21; 19:17; 25:22).

Perhaps 11:31 speaks to readers who are inclined to doubt the latter (if not both). We may be somewhat convinced that righteousness pays its rewards, but too often we see the wicked going free and start to wonder. Job himself had such doubts (Job 21:19, 29–34; 34:9), and the psalmist seeks

---

16. Many interpreters attempt to solve the problem by reading the word for "wise" (*ḥakam*) as *ḥamas* ("violence"), after the LXX's "lawless"; thus, the REB and NRSV translate, "violence takes lives away."

17. D. C. Snell, "'Taking Souls' in Proverbs 11:30," *VT* (1983): 362–65. Snell quotes the medieval commentator Moses Qimhi, "Or again, one who 'takes' souls with his wisdom saves [them] from evil."

18. W. I. Irwin, "The Metaphor in Proverbs 11:30," *Bib* 65 (1984): 97–100.

19. Whybray, *Proverbs*, 188–89, cites Eccl. 7:20 in support: "There is not a righteous man on earth who does what is right and never sins."

to bring assurance to those who have them as well (see Ps. 37:21). Therefore, while certainty in translation is out of reach, it seems clear enough that a straightforward statement of just rewards both summarizes the theme of the chapter and lends its assurance that Yahweh hates perversity and loves righteousness; therefore, rewards will be forthcoming (cf. Prov. 11:21).

AS WE OBSERVED in chapter 10, the collection of independent sayings in chapters 10–22 is assembled in a way that invites the reader to look for relationships between them. Careful reading attends to clusters of proverbs gathered about a common theme as well as recurring key words and images that are woven throughout. Sometimes structures appear to link the parts together; sometimes a single outstanding metaphor will cause the reader to slow down, linger, and reflect.

Rewards. Proverbs that name "the LORD" (*yhwh*) provide the theological underpinning for the emphases that emerge. Wit and wisdom are required of the reader to pull out similar verses on a theme and show how they speak to each other, a sort of proto-midrash that shows skill in bringing texts together. The final rewards that come to the righteous and the wicked occupy center stage in chapters 10–15, and so readers must watch how successive proverbs add to the composite picture being assembled. Chapter 11 continues the series of contrasts begun in chapter 10, restating and enriching our understanding of the proper use of words and wealth, even as it includes two surprising proverbs on the beautiful woman.

In this chapter, the picture of persons who bring harm and ruin wherever they go is filled in with more details of the harm that comes back on them: They lose the wealth they so eagerly grasped, they lose honor in the eyes of the community, and finally they lose all hopes and expectations. The last four verses alternate images of fruit-bearing trees and failed inheritances, lush gardens, and scorching winds (11:28–31). Both the righteous and wicked are surprised: the righteous, because in seeking the good of others, they are themselves blessed; the wicked, because what they grasp so tenaciously is pried out of their hands.

Most likely, this flash forward to ends and outcomes is as much encouragement to the faithful as it is a warning to the learner, for it is this matter of just rewards that people of all ages have found hard to believe. The sages show their skill by assembling vignettes of life that demonstrate just how many experiences of life do confirm their claim. Observe, they say, how people praise the generous and curse the greedy, see how their deeds eventually catch up with them, and remember that Yahweh watches; he knows whether a weight stone or a heart is true.

Both the righteous and the wicked are inclined to doubt that goodness brings its own rewards and that there will be a final accounting for sin. That doubt leads some to greater sin, while others are tempted to despair. A cynical attitude can develop, as typified in the saying, "Only the good die young." As a reply, these proverbs say, look at how pride is followed by disgrace (11:2), how duplicity is discovered (11:3), and how money saves no one's life in the end (11:4). The signs are around us if we will look for them. Proverbs train the eyes to see.

The New Testament writers had their eyes trained by the Proverbs. Verse 30 and its image of gathering fruit reminds us of Paul's desire to gather some fruit among the Gentiles (Rom. 1:13) and Jesus' words about the harvest (John 4:36),[20] instructing us to value human lives over riches. Proverbs 11:31 is cited in 1 Peter 4:18 following the LXX's reading. Urging his hearers to undergo suffering for good deeds, the writer asks, "If it is hard for the righteous to be saved, what will become of the ungodly and the sinner?"

These writers knew that the rewards of wisdom do not eliminate suffering and disappointment, but they also knew that they had found a way to avoid the kind of trouble that boomerangs back to the one who causes it. They also knew that the difference between these two ways rests in an understanding of God's ways in the world, that it does make a difference whether one knows the fear of Yahweh or not. Those who have it seek to win his favor, not their own pleasures (11:1, 20). Bringing delight to God can become a primary motivation for seeking the good works of wisdom.

On words. The two most prominent works of wisdom in Proverbs 11 are the use of words and the use of wealth; in short, these proverbs are concerned about how we spend or save our currency in both. The cluster of proverbs on speaking in 11:9–14 adds to the insights collected in chapter 10. Lips of righteousness know what is fitting and nourish many (10:21, 32), and so good counsel also benefits the people (11:14). Lies, slander, and perverse speech do great damage (10:19, 31–32), as do godless corruption, derision, and gossip (11:9, 11–13). For this reason silence is itself a form of kindness that demonstrates knowledge and understanding (11:9, 12–13). This emphasis on self-control in speaking, this holding back from the sort of active evil that seeks the harm of neighbor, stands out in this cluster as an expansion of 10:19: "When words are many, sin is not absent, but he who holds his tongue is wise."

---

20. Irwin, "The Metaphor in Proverbs 11:30," 97–100.

Certainly the referent in these proverbs is the matter of reputation, and for that reason our stated opinions of others must be fair. Moreover, even when fairness warrants a negative judgment on a person, wisdom recommends withholding the bad report. It is the person lacking judgment who derides a neighbor (11:12); this proverb does not state whether that derision is fair, only that the person who speaks it understands little. We know enough of life to recognize that our knowledge of others is always partial at best and that we do not often know what the reasons and motivations behind the behavior of others may be. Therefore, it is best to reserve public comment and bring the matter before the neighbor in private.

Likewise, withholding words that preserve a confidence is a mark of loyalty to a friend, who has entrusted a part of himself or herself to another (11:13). Secrecy, says David F. Ford, has received a bad name because it is often associated with crimes and misdemeanors. "That is mainly because it is such a powerful and pervasive feature of life and is, therefore, like money or sex or communication skills, a prime target for corruption and manipulation."[21] However, the secrets of intimacy kept safe are gifts of discernment, bonds of trust that handle our knowledge of others with great care.

In ancient Israel, personal and business relationships were probably even more intertwined than is the case for us today. To slander a neighbor would most likely also ruin that neighbor's business reputation and standing in the community. Our networks of business and personal relationships may or may not overlap the way they did then, but the concern in Proverbs for preserving reputations applies to both. Therefore, the proverbs may be speaking directly to the economic issues involved in maintaining good relations, but there is also a sense in which the spending of words is symbolic of how we hold what others have placed in our trust. In this set of proverbs, withholding those words, perhaps for a time, perhaps forever, is a mark of wisdom, self-control, and friendship.

On wealth. The exact opposite is true of withholding wealth (see 11:24—29). The theme also appears in 11:4, where righteousness is worth more than wealth (cf. 10:2, 16). Riches by themselves will not pay the dues of character or save one from wrath. Generous giving, scattering like seed, yields a great crop; it is like the drink offered to others that will be returned (11:25). Business practices are included in such generosity. For example, it may be more profitable to withhold grain from sale until the price goes up, but the one who sells food at a fair price during a time of need has that blessing returned (11:26).

---

21. D. F. Ford, *The Shape of Living: Spiritual Directions for Everyday Life* (Grand Rapids: Baker, 1997), 103.

At root is one's attitude toward possessions. Trust in them, and you will learn how little they really can do for you (11:28). Hold them above relationships with family and friends, and you will learn what it means to lose both (11:29). The sages believed that the pursuit of wealth for its own sake had the dangerous tendency to push its seekers toward evil, not caring what means were used to obtain wealth. In their view, to seek evil was eventually to have it come upon oneself. In other words, the sages knew that the spiritual power of wealth was so great that those who believed they were in pursuit of wealth might find themselves pursuing evil in a tragic bait and switch.[22]

The twin concerns of speech and wealth tell us that one can spend bad words (11:9, 12, 13), hoard material goods (11:24, 26), and, in so doing, inherit the wind (11:29). But these proverbs also speak again and again of life, both in terms of individual lives lived to the full and as communal life lived in *šalom*. This *šalom* marks the reverse of folly's greedy economy; here neighbors hold back destructive words and share material blessing. When we are at our best, say the sages, the economy of wisdom prevails.

This idea of righteous spending develops the concerns of chapter 10 for wealth used for the sake of others and for speech that builds up and nourishes others through encouragement and teaching. Believers can model this economy in which one is enriched and refreshed, not by acquiring or hoarding but by giving. This is the wisdom that finds its place in Jesus' teaching: "Give, and it will be given to you. A good measure, pressed down, shaken together and running over, will be poured into your lap. For with the measure you use, it will be measured to you" (Luke 6:38; cf. Mark 4:24–25).

Startling images. Like the surprising proverb about vinegar and smoke in 10:26, Proverbs 11 has its startling images as well. The swine snout trimmed in gold stops readers in their tracks, making them laugh and ponder all that is being said with one ridiculous picture (11:22). The juxtaposition of beauty and ugliness also points to the clash of social expectations, for gold rings are found in fine homes, not in pigpens!

The placement of that proverb has something of the quality of a riddle, inviting readers to find the connection with the rest of the chapter. The first link appears to reach to the other proverb about a woman in 11:16, "A kindhearted woman gains respect, but ruthless men gain only wealth." As we have seen, "kindhearted" (*ḥen*) can also be translated as "charm" (cf. 31:30) or "beauty," and the woman who has this quality gains "glory." Whatever the translation of the first line, the second is clear in its depiction of a ruthless

22. J. Ellul, *Money and Power*, trans. L. Neff (Downers Grove, Ill.: InterVarsity Press, 1984), 73–99, speaks of the money as power that seeks human worship, even as Jesus used the Aramaic *Mammon* (Matt. 6:24; Luke 16:13) to personify it as "sort of a god."

grasp at wealth. The proverb may contrast kindhearted grace with such greed, or it may suggest that a woman of charming appearance grasps at glory for herself. If the latter, she would be like the woman who has beauty but no discretion. The contrast between beautiful appearance and good character is then like the contrast between the righteous and wicked. Character is more valuable than appearances (gold, beauty), at least to those who have let wisdom shape their deepest desires.

A similar comparison may connect this decorated hog with the tree of life in 11:30. The contrast between wealth that will not deliver in time of need and the righteousness that will (11:4, 16, 18, 28) is also important to 3:13–18. In that text, wisdom herself is worth more than silver and her profit is better than gold; she is the tree of life for those who hold her fast. So here in chapter 11 readers find a connection with the earlier theme of choosing wisdom as a life partner, seeking and valuing her over any misdirected pursuit of wealth and gain. If a man wants a woman simply for her beauty as an ornament to his life, he may learn that beauty is not enough. Here is more than a warning to women who live for appearances, for it confronts foolish men who do the same. Proverbs 3 reminds readers of the crucial choices before all of us: What do we love, wisdom or wealth? Appearances or substance? Seek "good sense" (11:22 NEB), not only for yourself but also in one you choose for a life partner.

In sum, the proverbs of chapter 11 take the basic contrast between wickedness and righteousness and use it to describe the way we handle our possessions and our words. Images make their points as well. The gold ring on a pig's nose adds a dose of humor to the matter of choosing what is fitting and appropriate, while the tree of life points to final outcomes. The first is a symbol of folly, the second of wisdom. The wise person, careful with comments and generous with possessions, uses both to build up and nurture others. Integrity that delights Yahweh and generosity that comes back to the giver point to those whose deeds and words bring the riches of wisdom to the community.

Preachers and teachers may wish to focus on one of the clusters concerning speech or wealth, or they may choose to use the pig's snout as a vivid picture of folly. Great care is required in speaking about the women of proverbs, for the assumptions these sayings speak against are still widespread in our own day; many in our churches believe that women need looks and men need money if they are to be attractive to one another. We might point out that folly can also appear as a handsome male or a wealthy woman. Whatever illustrations we choose, we must be careful to hold back words that will hurt and show that folly can take any number of poses. Certainly the first proverb about accurate scales can guide our teaching. Its metaphor of character in the balance offers a lens to examine all that follows and presents a number of strategies for communicating these sketches of righteousness and wickedness.

PERSONAL DESIRES AND OUTCOMES. How do we find the areas of life addressed by the theological and ethical principles we have discerned? Although any statement of a main theme is bound to leave out important details, we can begin with a look at the theme of desires and outcomes. "He who seeks good finds goodwill, but evil comes to him who searches for it" (11:27). Daily we are given countless opportunities to seek good instead of evil. The key is the way we "spend" our goods and our words. Withholding bad words is every bit as wise as selling good grain. Both actions rebuild the *šalom* ravaged by the evil deeds depicted in this chapter. In "seeking good" we are also seeking the kingdom of God and his righteousness, confident that all that we need will be given us as well (Matt. 6:25–34).

Let's face it. Too often we do worry over what we will eat and drink, what we will wear, and if we are honest, what these provisions say about our status when compared with others. We worry about what others will say about us. Rock bottom, we do believe that possessions and other forms of notoriety are positive signs of character, for they show that one is clever, assertive, and persistent—traits we favor. We may run after signs of status and success (how many members at that church?), hoping others will speak well of us; as a result, they become as valuable as nose rings for hogs.

It is a sad fact of life that too often, important choices are based on shiny appearances that may not reveal the true contents of the package. A short-lived media event was entitled *Who Wants to Marry a Millionaire?* Setting aside all pretense of any other motivations, a rich man was invited to choose from a group of beautiful women, all before the eyes of a television audience. Here were two people who really did not know much about each other except that the man had possessions and the woman had beauty. It was no surprise that the marriage did not last more than a few weeks, nor was anyone surprised to see the couple attempt to capitalize on their new found fame. Just as gold on a pig looks ridiculous, so beauty and wealth lose their appeal when they are not accompanied by the characteristics of wisdom.

Character pleasing to the Lord. The reversals of these proverbs and Jesus' teaching point out those acquisitions of character that are pleasing to the Lord, characteristics in which he delights. These proverbs continue to remind readers of God's presence and blessing in everyday life (cf. 10:3, 22,

27, 29), placing special emphasis on a God who delights in honest and fair dealing. Just as we are often both surprised and delighted when we encounter acts of honesty and integrity in others, so these proverbs remind us that these actions, however small and insignificant, bring joy to the One who created us for good works (Eph. 2:10).

I once spent a Christmas with some friends and their two children. As the presents were opened, my friends' eight-year-old daughter looked disappointed. She had received the gift of collectible stickers both kids had asked for, but they were stickers she already owned. "That's OK," her younger brother chimed, "I don't have those yet, and you don't have the ones I got. Let's trade!" The parents were delighted by the spontaneous show of thoughtfulness. So it is that acts of honest dealing, charitable giving, and genuine concern for the good of others pleases Yahweh in ways we can only begin to understand.

Straight dealing and generosity. Honest weights and blameless ways (11:1, 20) point us toward straight dealing and generosity. Straight dealing in speech should replace slander and gossip with silence, perhaps coupled with honest confrontation as Jesus presented in Matthew 18:15–18. Straight dealing with one's goods means making friends with wealth as Jesus taught in Luke 16. But here the idea common to both is looking out for the good of the neighbor and in so doing, seeking a good end. In an upside down gospel way, these proverbs show us that seeking the good of others is seeking good for ourselves (Prov. 11:27).

Generosity in speech does more than withhold harmful words, it also offers a gracious ear of listening, to hear those things kept secret for too long and offers a word of acceptance and forgiveness. A friend once said to me, "If we are to grow in our friendship, there are some things you need to know about me that I'm not proud of." After he shared his secrets, I thought it a privilege to be trusted in this way and thanked him for his honesty and openness. In the years that followed, I saw how that honesty encouraged me to share secrets of my own, confessing wrongs I had done and temptations I faced. My friend kept those secrets and continued to earn my admiration.

Many keep secrets out of pride or shame, however, and the results are devastating. In the English movie *Secrets and Lies*, a family is nearly torn apart by hiding from one another those things they think are unacceptable. A woman of color decides to find the birth mother she has never met, but that mother, a single white woman, has never told her other daughter or her brother about the birth and adoption. The brother has a wife who looks down on her sister-in-law for her past mistakes, but she also grieves that they cannot have children of their own. She swears her husband to secrecy, so her sister-in-law believes she is a selfish wife who doesn't want the sacrifices that come with having children. Mother and daughter meet and become close friends. When the mother invites her newly found daughter to a family barbecue, feelings explode, hidden thoughts and hurts are finally revealed, and the normally withdrawn brother finally lets loose, shouting "These secrets and lies are killing us!" The man, his wife, and his sister then begin the first steps toward reconciliation.

Generosity in speech also insists that the truth be spoken about others, correcting false reports when necessary. Born and raised in New Jersey, I once noticed a title in a bookstore, *The Ramapo Mountain People*. I knew the Ramapo area of my home state but had never heard of the mountain people, so I got the book and learned that they are a group of mixed ethnicity who live in the northern rural communities. Until the publication of the book, oral tradition and written reports told a story that brought together Hessians from the revolutionary war, prostitutes who had followed them over from England, black slaves, and Indians. In the course of his research, the author discovered that these people were actually the descendants of freed slaves who had become landowners and leaders in their community.

The writer also said that he had no intention of making a social statement when he began his study, but after it had been publicized in newspapers and television, a young woman of the community asked him to speak to a class in black history. She had been assigned reading that made reference to the legends about her own people. When the writer spoke and the true story was told, he said she beamed with pride. For this young woman, telling the truth about her heritage was a way of speaking rightly.[23]

Generosity with means is obvious enough, or at least it should be, for opportunities abound. This chapter offers us a reminder that "it is in giving that we receive." One way to counteract the power of wealth is to practice liberal, prodigal giving, giving when it does not make sense, when it does not fit the budget. John the Baptist not only told government employees to stop taking what was not theirs, he told all those who had two coats and food to share freely (Luke 3:7–14). Such acts of generosity demonstrate our trust in the One who holds the future in his hands, a trust that answers our fears and worries.

Perhaps the difference between stealing and hoarding is not as great as we might think. One takes what does not belong to us, the other keeps what

---

23. D. S. Cohen, *The Ramapo Mountain People* (New Brunswick, N.J.: Rutgers Univ. Press, 1974), 198–99. Another member of the community was quoted: "I'm glad to read the truth for once. The others who wrote about us just repeated the same old lies. . . . The kids are looked down upon in school because of the lies others have heard—that's why some of them don't want to finish school."

could belong to others. Our denominational magazine put out an issue that told the stories of persons who asked how God could use their lives to serve and bless others. Some became pastors in churches that served their communities, building schools and starting after-school programs. One mother affirmed her daughter's desire to work with the "Mission Year" program, living, working, and ministering in the city of Oakland. She spoke of her fears but also of her realization that she was being called to give what was most dear to her: "It was fine for someone else's child to risk the dangers and unknowns of the inner city for a year. But I preferred my firstborn stay in a more sheltered, gentler environment." This mother wrote about her fears to encourage other parents who might have the same feelings, quoting her daughter: "The safest place to be is in the will of God."[24]

Choices for good. Proverbs 11:1—3 brought together the problems of dishonesty, arrogance, and duplicity, recommending that they be countered with truthfulness, humility, and integrity. The contrasts of the proverbs may leave the impression that people are either one or the other, and the sages did recognize that there are some who give themselves to evil. However, they knew what we know from experience, that no one is completely righteous or completely evil. Yet they would teach us the choices we face every day, some of them very complicated, typically present themselves as choices between one or the other. Those choices set us on a trajectory toward good or trouble. Knowing that each receives its own rewards, these wise ones expect that we who read the deposit they passed down to us will bear fruit of righteousness, seeds of which will grow into the tree of life, to become one of those wise ones who will nourish and save lives.

In sum, these proverbs do not merely ask us to make changes in our habits of speaking and giving, they call us to look at our lives through the eyes of our neighbors, seeing the value of our lives in what they bring to others. Let the choices we make in our lives be blessed in a way that lifts up the city (or village, town, or suburb) instead of bringing it down (11:11).

In doing so, we can make it a practice to constantly evaluate our desires. What do we want from life? What do we consider most important, and what desires are secondary? Wealth in Proverbs is only a problem when it becomes a primary goal that replaces neighbor love. Wisdom teaches us to develop a holy freedom, one that allows us to keep a loose grip on our belongings and a generous embrace of those around us.

---

24. M. J. Morey, "Answering God's Call," *The Covenant Companion* (March 2000), 24—25.

Proverbs 12:1–28

¹ WHOEVER LOVES DISCIPLINE loves knowledge,
but he who hates correction is stupid.
² A good man obtains favor from the LORD,
but the LORD condemns a crafty man.
³ A man cannot be established through wickedness,
but the righteous cannot be uprooted.
⁴ A wife of noble character is her husband's crown,
but a disgraceful wife is like decay in his bones.
⁵ The plans of the righteous are just,
but the advice of the wicked is deceitful.
⁶ The words of the wicked lie in wait for blood,
but the speech of the upright rescues them.
⁷ Wicked men are overthrown and are no more,
but the house of the righteous stands firm.
⁸ A man is praised according to his wisdom,
but men with warped minds are despised.
⁹ Better to be a nobody and yet have a servant
than pretend to be somebody and have no food.
¹⁰ A righteous man cares for the needs of his animal,
but the kindest acts of the wicked are cruel.
¹¹ He who works his land will have abundant food,
but he who chases fantasies lacks judgment.
¹² The wicked desire the plunder of evil men,
but the root of the righteous flourishes.
¹³ An evil man is trapped by his sinful talk,
but a righteous man escapes trouble.
¹⁴ From the fruit of his lips a man is filled with good things
as surely as the work of his hands rewards him.
¹⁵ The way of a fool seems right to him,
but a wise man listens to advice.
¹⁶ A fool shows his annoyance at once,
but a prudent man overlooks an insult.
¹⁷ A truthful witness gives honest testimony,
but a false witness tells lies.
¹⁸ Reckless words pierce like a sword,
but the tongue of the wise brings healing.
¹⁹ Truthful lips endure forever,
but a lying tongue lasts only a moment.

²⁰There is deceit in the hearts of those who plot evil,
　　but joy for those who promote peace.
²¹No harm befalls the righteous,
　　but the wicked have their fill of trouble.
²²The LORD detests lying lips,
　　but he delights in men who are truthful.
²³A prudent man keeps his knowledge to himself,
　　but the heart of fools blurts out folly.
²⁴Diligent hands will rule,
　　but laziness ends in slave labor.
²⁵An anxious heart weighs a man down,
　　but a kind word cheers him up.
²⁶A righteous man is cautious in friendship,
　　but the way of the wicked leads them astray.
²⁷The lazy man does not roast his game,
　　but the diligent man prizes his possessions.
²⁸In the way of righteousness there is life;
　　along that path is immortality.

THE FAMILIAR METAPHOR of wisdom's way opens and closes the chapter; the way of discipline and correction is for those who love knowledge (12:1), the way of righteousness for those who desire life (12:28). That willingness to listen and learn leads to wise speaking and teaching so others may learn and live as well. One listens to learn to speak, one learns in order to teach. The following outline groups together proverbs according to recurring vocabulary and theme. Although all proverbs in a group do not speak to the theme, the contrast between righteousness and wickedness runs throughout.[1]

---

1. Perhaps 12:1–15 go together in a chiastic pattern, the first and last verses forming an inclusio on learning and listening.
　　A 12:1 Love discipline, love knowledge
　　　B 12:2 *Good* find favor
　　　　C 12:3 *Root of the righteous* endures
　　　　　D 12:4 Wives bring *honor and shame*
　　　　　　E 12:5–7 Wicked vanish, righteous stand
　　　　　D' 12:8–11 *Praise and blame* of workers
　　　　C' 12:12 *Root of the righteous* flourishes
　　　B' 12:13–14 Filled with *good* things
　　A' 12:15 Wise listens to counsel

The first and third groups stress the importance of good speech and listening to correction; they point to the activities of teaching and learning. The second and fourth groups talk about labor and fruits; the fourth incorporates sayings about counsel and encouraging words as a fruit of one's labor. The purpose in looking for such groupings is to recognize recurring elements. Like themes in a symphony or colored spotlights on a stage, the themes of proverbs appear and reappear, sometimes on their own, sometimes in combination with others.

All the proverbs of this chapter (except v. 14 and perhaps v. 28) make some sort of contrast. Yahweh is named only in 12:2, 22, both verses using the same Hebrew word for "favor" and "delight" (*raṣon*) in those who do good and deal truthfully. The key words "discipline," "prudent," and "snare" are applied to wise and foolish speaking, reminding readers of the invitations to wisdom and folly in chapter 1. Description of the "diligent" and "slack" recalls the lazy in chapter 6. Other proverbs link up with those that come before and after. Sayings about outcomes and women are clustered in 11:16–23 and 12:2–7. The word *musar* appears in 12:1 as "discipline" and in 13:1 as "instruction."

Learn and Stand (12:1–7)

THE PROVERBS OF this section link character and outcomes as summed up in verse 7; the righteous will stand while the wicked will vanish.

12:1. This proverb, like most, incorporates both similarity and difference. The obvious dissimilarity contrasts love of discipline, a sign that one loves knowledge, with hating correction, a sign that one is "stupid" (*baʿar*, "brutish" or "like a beast"; cf. 30:2; Ps. 73:22; 92:6). Thus, the opposite of knowledge is more than ignorance; it is allowing that lack of understanding to motivate and drive one's actions.

There is a difference between loving discipline—teaching and correction that warn of possible errors—and correction, which speaks to errors already

---

Likewise, 12:16–23 may form a subsection framed by the use of "prudent" in v. 16 and v. 23 and "truthful" in v. 17 and v. 22 (see the comments on vv. 13–23). The repetition of key words seems intentional.

2. Similar to A. Scherer, *Das weise Wort und seine Wirkung*, 109, who isolates 12:1 as an introduction, and K. M. Heim, *Like Grapes of Gold Set in Silver: An Interpretation of Proverbial Clusters in Proverbs 10:1–22:6* (BZAW 273; Berlin/New York: Walter de Gruyter, 2001), 155–57, who sets 12:25 with 12:16–23.

committed. "Discipline" (*musar*) has appeared in every previous chapter except chapters 2 and 11 and it will appear again in 13:1. The first line of 12:1 repeats "love" for emphasis, for readers know how rare that love is. Those who pride themselves on knowledge often avoid correction, yet those who love the truth want to learn when they are in the wrong.

12:2. The "crafty man" is (lit.) "one who schemes," using a word from the prologue (*m^ezimmah*, 1:4, where it is translated "discretion"). There, this skill of discernment means one can determine what is right; here the skill is used to devise wrong. Skills can be put to bad use if not tempered with correction and instruction. Perhaps the difference is that the one who is good shapes life according to values outside of the self while the one who schemes only looks within to one's own intentions; the proverb makes clear that such intentions can be other than good. Note the similarities with 11:27: "He who seeks good finds goodwill, but evil comes to him who searches for it." In 12:2, "the LORD" (*yhwh*) is named in both lines as the source of both outcomes. His "favor" (*rason*) links this proverb with "delight" (*rason*) in 11:1, 20.

12:3. The Hebrew phrase "root of the righteous" repeats in 12:12, where that root flourishes, another symbol of endurance. Here that root is (lit.) "never moved." Yahweh told the prophet Jeremiah that he would pull up the roots of those who wanted to establish themselves through wickedness (Jer. 1:9–10); those who would make themselves as strong as trees turn out to be nothing more than weeds. The presence of Yahweh named in Proverbs 12:2 lingers in this saying. It reminds the reader that no one lives independently, especially the wicked. In fact, the wicked can be sure they will perish, as has already been stated in 10:30.

12:4. The image of the worthy woman (*'eset hayil*) occurs at the end of Proverbs (31:10) and plays a significant role in the story of Ruth (3:11), which follows Proverbs in the Hebrew Bible. The image also takes the reader back to the sayings on women in Proverbs 11:16, 22. Those two sayings contrast a woman of grace (*hen*) with one who lacks sense. Here the connection with a husband's reputation and well-being is made explicit. As in previous proverbs about sluggards and pigs' noses (10:26; 11:22), this one stands out from its context, a series of four righteous/wicked contrasts (12:3, 5–7). The contrast with its background causes its readers and hearers to stop and reflect on such potent images as crowns (cf. 4:9) and rotten bones (cf. 10:7).

Once again, the focus is on the man's decisions about character. While we may rightly reject the thought that a woman only exists to do a man good, we do not have to reject the principle of choosing one's life partner wisely, true for both men and women. Directed toward men, this proverb urges its young readers to value character above beauty (cf. 31:29–30), but all readers are instructed to hold character as the most important quality to seek in a mate.

12:5. The contrast between "plans" and "advice" focuses attention on the intentions of persons, their deliberations on what they will and will not do. "Righteousness" makes the difference between intentions that deceive and those that are "just" (*mišpaṭ;* cf. 8:20; 13:23). While "advice" is typically good and beneficial in Proverbs (*taḥbulot;* cf. 1:5; 11:14; 12:5; 20:18; 24:6), this wicked counsel will certainly do harm. The Hebrew word for "deceitful" (*mirmah*) appears in 12:17 and 20 (i.e., three times in this chapter).

12:6. The first of a number of sayings on speech, the personification of words that "lie in wait" recalls the invitation of the violent men at the beginning of the book (1:11). Their downfall was clearly stated; here it is implied by contrasting their words with the "speech" (lit., "mouth") that delivers. The wit of the proverb has the upright delivered by the very means the wicked meant to do harm.

12:7. The theme of permanence first stated in 12:3 is echoed here. The first line can be read as an imperative: "Overthrow the wicked and they are gone." The image of a "house ... [that] stands" may refer to a family that endures, or it may serve as an independent metaphor for one's property. Either way, the principle that outcomes follow choices "stands firm" also.

Praise and Blame (12:8–12)

THE PROVERBS OF this section not only comment on character, they observe how human communities do the same when they assign praise and blame. Yet these concerns of shame and honor are blended with the basic needs of sustenance in the juxtaposition of 12:8–9. The person of intelligence earns honor, the one of perverse heart, shame. Yet it is better to be of small reputation if you have means (a servant) than to give yourself honors and lack bread.

Verses 9–11 work together also. The Hebrew words "lack" and "bread" from verse 9 appear in verse 11, but separately and with a twist. In verse 11, those who work the soil will have bread (*leḥem*), but those who go after empty fantasies lack sense (and by implication, bread).[3] In between, a saying that compares the compassion of the righteous and the wicked (12:10) hints at the inseparable qualities of wisdom, humility, and kindness. These qualities lead to the satisfaction of basic human needs.

12:8. Literally, the first line reads, "according to the mouth of his intelligence a man is praised," repeating the word "mouth" (*peh*) from 12:6, where it is used for speech. The perverse heart is not praised but despised and dishonored. The proverb reminds us of the importance of shame and honor as motivators for many cultures.

---

3. The phrases "lack bread" and "lack sense" may form an inclusio (Garrett, *Proverbs*, 131).

12:9. The "better...than" saying is a typical form of proverb (*ṭob...min*; see also 15:16–17; 16:8, 19, 32; 17:1; 19:1; 21:9, 19; 25:24; 27:5, 10; 28:6; see also 16:16; 22:1; 25:7). The strategy of comparison, however, has already been used; for example, wisdom is worth more than gold or jewels (3:13–15; 8:19). Although one would not wish to be despised for having a warped mind (12:8), a humble or small reputation in the eyes of others is not so bad. In fact, it is better than empty pretense. The comparison is heightened by juxtaposing the humble person who has a servant with the braggart who does not even have his daily bread.

12:10. Humility is also the theme of this proverb, setting the righteous person whose care extends outside the self with the wicked person whose attempts to show compassion are cruel. One cares for the lowest creatures, while the best the other has to offer is still hurtful. Better to be the righteous person's horse than the wicked person's neighbor!

12:11. A proverb about the rewards of labor moves the imagery from the stable to the field. "Works" uses the same Hebrew root as "servant" in verse 9 (*ᶜbd*), both in positive senses, and "lacks judgment" echoes the phrase "lacks food." This verse is nearly identical with 28:19.

12:12. This verse restates and summarizes the theme of the section, this time comparing the life and work of the righteous to a root, that part of the plant that goes deep into the earth to find water and nourish the plant and its good fruit. Righteousness bears fruit, but wickedness only desires what others have caught in their snare. In other words, the righteous work for what they own, but the wicked want what belongs to others, a theme that first appeared in chapter 1. "Root" echoes the "root of the righteous" in 12:3.

Speech and Silence (12:13–23)

VERSES 13–23 GATHER around the topics of speech and silence, but there are other relationships among the sayings. Just as there may be a chiastic structure for 12:1–15 as proposed earlier (see footnote 1), 12:16–23 may also be arranged in a modified chiasm.[4]

The vocabulary in 12:16–17 is repeated in 12:22–23. The prudent overlooks and keeps knowledge in 12:16, 23 (lit., "conceals," *ᶜarum koseh*), truth-

---

4. A 12:16 *Prudent* overlooks an insult
    B 12:17 *Truthful* witness/false (*mirmah*) witness
        C 12:18 Tongue of wise—healing
           D 12:19–20 *Truthful* lips, deceitful (*mirmah*) hearts
        C' 12:21 No harm to righteous
    B' 12:22 *Truthful* lips—Yahweh's delight
  A' 12:23 *Prudent* keeps knowledge to self

ful witness and lips (*ᵃmunah*), and false witness (*šaqer*) appears in 12:17, 22. In addition, the vocabulary in 12:20–21 appears in 12:25–26 (heart/joy and cheer; righteous/wicked). In between the two sets of linking pairs, 12:18–19 form a pair on the theme of speaking.[5] Likewise, catchwords link 12:24 and 27 by the repetition of "laziness" and "diligence" and 12:26 and 28 with a repetition of "way."[6]

Verses 18–21 are loosely linked by the themes of speech and *šalom*. One kind of speech brings healing, the other deep wounds (12:18). One lasts forever, one is gone in an instant (12:19). One is fueled by evil and deceit, the other a desire for peace and its accompanying joy (12:20); each is repaid in kind (12:21). The association of truthful speech and silent knowledge as seen in 12:16–17 appears in 12:22–23. Verse 22 reminds readers that Yahweh finds false lips detestable, a thought similar to the condemnation of 12:2.

We must remind ourselves that our desire to find an outline or rhetorical structure may not catch the spirit of discovery and gamesmanship that the sages required of their readers. We suggest outlines and arrangements to appreciate the recurrence of catchwords and themes, but many of the associations do not fit as easily within our orderly arrangements. Proverbs are often linked together by catchwords, so 12:12a and 13a may be linked by the imagery of the trap or snare as well as the righteous/wicked contrast. Verse 14 is connected to 12:11 by the theme of labor and may comment on 12:12, the flourishing root of the righteous producing good fruit.[7]

However, it is the emphasis on the use of lips and mouth that becomes the major linking device. In Hebrew, the "sinful talk" (lit., "trespass of lips") that ensnares in 12:13 contrasts with the "fruit" that fills the mouth in 12:14. In sum, my purpose in proposing groups and clusters is to point out connections; while the structures are speculative, they are intended to point out links between similar or contrasting proverbs.

12:13. Here is an ancient version of "what a wicked web we weave, when first we speak to deceive." Continuing the imagery of trapping from 12:12, this proverb contrasts the snare of the evil person's words with the escape of

---

5. R. Scoralick, *Einzelspruch und Sammlung*, 196–203. Scolarlick links 12:1–13 with 11:8–11 and 12:14–28 with 13:1–2. While 12:14 and 13:2 both use the phrase "fruit of the mouth" in association with "good," it is not immediately apparent to me that the repetition forms an inclusio.

6. Garrett, *Proverbs*, 133, links 12:24–28 in an ABCABC order according to theme. But v. 25 most closely resembles v. 20, and the repetition of "way" in vv. 26 and 28 suggests a pattern of ABCAC.

7. Garrett, *Proverbs*, 131, marks vv. 12–14 as a thematic grouping.

the righteous, echoing the theme of 12:6. This proverb explicitly shows the trap of evil words. The righteous, who do not lay such traps, never get caught in them, and the proverb suggests that they also escape the traps set by others. But those who use their words to "lie in wait" (12:6) end up being ensnared by them.

12:14. This verse does not present a contrast but compares the "fruit of the lips" with the "work of the hands" (cf. 13:2; 18:20). The metaphor likens the rewards of hard work (cf. 12:11) with the fruit of good speaking, linking hands and mouth (*peh*). Just as speaking is a form of doing, so both hands and mouth can be put to purposes good or evil.

12:15. The first of two proverbs about fools contrasts two counselors. The fool listens only to himself while the wise one "hears" (*šmᶜ*) advice or counsel (cf. Wisdom's counsel in 8:14). Proverbs 12:14 and 15 are a wonderful pair. The first stresses good speaking, the second careful listening. Along with use of ears, one can also find the images of mouth, hands, and eyes (Heb. "right in his own eyes") in 12:13–15 (cf. 4:20–27; 6:12–19).

12:16. Verses 15 and 16 are linked by the catchword "fool." The contrast in both verses is between the loud fool, blindly self-directed and easily provoked, and the silent sage, who listens to counsel and conceals an insult. The prudent person appears again in 12:23, where again silence demonstrates understanding and builds up relationships instead of breaking them down.

12:17. Silence is not required in every situation, however, for there are times in which an honest witness must make a report to counteract the lies of the false witness. The honest testimony is "righteous" (*sedeq*), while the false witness spreads "deceit" (*mirmah*; cf. 12:5, 20). Most likely the situation depicted is the settlement of a business dispute, though other settings are possible (cf. Deut. 19:15–18).

12:18. The first line can be read, "There is one who speaks rashly like the thrusts of a sword." The contrast with the healing tongue of the wise reminds the reader that words are rarely neutral, and they usually leave their mark for good or bad. It is not stated how the wise might come along to undo the damage of the reckless; perhaps it comes through countertestimony (12:17), or perhaps it is simply through compassionate care that brings healing. Similarly, a trustworthy messenger brings healing instead of trouble (13:17).

12:19. "Truthful lips" remind the reader of 12:17 and look ahead to 12:22. "Endure" translates the same word used in 12:3 for "established" (*yikkon*). The contrast is again between the brief and fleeting existence of the wicked and the staying power of the righteous. Lies may look as though they can feather one's nest and bring security, but in fact, they build the nest on a precarious branch. It sometimes takes time for truth to show itself strong, but as Van

Leeuwen observes, "What goes counter to reality is shattered by it in a moment, like a ship on the rocks."[8]

12:20. "Deceit" (12:5, 17) lives in the heart of those who devise evil, always looking for its chance to do harm. By contrast "joy" dwells in the heart of one who (lit.) "counsels peace" (*yoᶜaṣe šalom*). The word for "promote" is related to the "advice"(ᶜeṣah) of 12:15, suggesting that the wise one absorbs what is heard so it can be offered to others and the joy shared.

12:21. The joy of šalom described in 12:20 also brings with it freedom from fear. "No harm befalls the righteous," but the wicked get their fill. This proverb seems straightforward, and it may be that the interaction with 12:22 is intended. In the sayings, contrasts in rewards and outcomes are often juxtaposed with simple statements of Yahweh's reactions to evil and good. Yahweh is almost never depicted as active judge but as the one who watches his intentions and desires work themselves out on the stage of human action.

12:22. As in the previous three proverbs that name "the LORD," the focus is on that which brings him delight (*raṣon*, 11:1, 20; 12:2). That delight is in (lit.) "those who act in faithfulness" (*ᵉmunah*), repeating the root used for "truthful" in 12:17 and 19. That which Yahweh "detests" is an abomination, an action that provokes God's loathing and disgust (cf. 11:1, 20).

12:23. Just as the "prudent" person covers over an insult (12:16), so that person also keeps knowledge covered as well (*koseh* in both verses). The link with the earlier verse not only marks a frame or inclusio, it points up a particular virtue of prudence, the wisdom of knowing when to be silent and when to speak. As in 12:16, the fool simply blurts out what is inside without any consideration of its effects on others. The mention of "heart" points to the connection the ancients made between the contents of the heart and its gateway through the mouth and lips. This proverb provides a humorous explanation for why knowledge so often seems in short supply! It may also warn against talking too much.

Diligence and Laziness (12:24—28)

THESE LAST FIVE VERSES contrast diligence and laziness (12:24, 27) as well as the distinct ways of righteousness and wickedness (12:26, 28). This parallel structure is interrupted by an unusual proverb about fear and worry (12:25) that commands our attention.

12:24. The theme of work and its fruits from 12:9—14 reappears in 12:24 and 27, both using the same Hebrew word for "lazy" (*rᵉmiyyah*; cf. 10:4; 19:15). Together, these verses say that slackers are too lazy to even take care

---

8. Van Leeuwen, "Proverbs," 127.

for their own food, so they will certainly not have wealth. Ironically, if the lazy will not work for themselves, they will eventually be forced to work for another. The contrast between hands that work like a servant yet rule like a king shows the same kind of reversal of expectations as the hands that seek rest but wind up working in forced or conscripted labor (cf. Judg. 1:28; 1 Kings 5:13–14). There may be a wordplay in using *r*miyyah, for it comes from the same root as "deceit" (cf. Prov. 12:20). Thus, a slack or loose bow that fails is called "treacherous" (Ps. 78:57; Hos. 7:16), a metaphor for faithless Israel who promised to obey but did not, slacking in doing Yahweh's work (Jer. 48:10).

12:25. A proverb about worries and encouraging words seems out of place in the sequence, but the saying does relate to the larger context. The double use of "heart" and "joy" in 12:25 and 20 suggest they must be read together as a statement and development of a theme. The thread common to both is the positive result of good speaking; it brings "joy" to the speaker in 12:20 and "joy" to the listener in 12:25. Anxiety, by contrast, causes the heart (lit.) "to bow down" like prisoners before their captors (cf. Isa. 51:23).[9] Speech to oneself from within, from the anxious heart, is contrasted with the external word that brings joy (Prov. 14:13; 15:23). Again, as in 12:20, the work of a good person bears good fruit. The translation preserves some of the wordplay in the contrast between "weighs down" (*yašḥennah*) and "cheers up" (*y*ʿ*samm*ʿ*hennah*):

12:26. This proverb is not easily translated, so the NIV footnote shows the alternate reading for the first line, "is a guide to his neighbor." The second line is clear that "the way of the wicked leads them astray," a contrast to the way of righteousness and life in 12:28. Whereas no persuasive solution for the first line has been proposed,[10] I think it best to choose the alternate for its focus on travel and guidance. For example, if we translate "the righteous point the way to a neighbor," a contrast is drawn between a righteous one who is able to help others and a wicked one who cannot even take care of self (cf. 10:17; 11:24–27). The way of the wicked is no way at all, for it leads nowhere, and those who take it become lost.

12:27. The way to translate the first line of this proverb is somewhat unclear as well. Does the lazy person refuse to "roast" game, or does that person simply fail to "go after" it? Whatever the signs of laziness here, that slacking is contrasted with diligence (as in 12:24). If the hand of the diligent

---

9. The Greek Septuagint calls that anxiety a "fearful word."

10. J. A. Emerton, "A Note on Proverbs 12:26," *ZAW* 76 (1964): 191–93, vocalizes the Heb. *yater* as Hophal of *ntr* and translates "The righteous is delivered from harm, but the way of the wicked leads them astray."

---

rules in 12:24, here it holds its earnings as precious. Humorous proverbs about the sluggard typically make a serious point; like the wicked, lazy people have nothing to give others, for they cannot even take care of themselves!

12:28. The image of "the way," seen previously in the negative portrait of the fool and wicked person (12:15, 26), reappears here. "Way" and "path" are clear parallels, as are "life" and "death" (note that "immortality" is lit., "not death"), suggesting that the two lines contrast the way of life with the path of evil. In Proverbs, life is "not death"—that is, many years lived in health and security—rather than life eternal. Note that the life and death contrast is only used here in the last verse in this chapter. While the themes of life and death run throughout, this statement of the obvious stands alone and sums up all that has gone before, highlighting the image of the way. This last saying, more than any other, connects the themes of this chapter with the instructions of chapters 1–9 and the recurring motif of the two ways, life and death.

 IN CHAPTER 12, the contrast between the way of the righteous and the way of the wicked that dominates chapters 10–15 extends and develops the theme of outcomes and rewards. The righteous are rooted (12:3, 12) and will therefore live (12:28), while the wicked will not be established but overthrown (12:3, 7). This chapter also continues to probe the choices that bring about the two outcomes, examining intentions of the heart that direct the hands and lips.

This mosaic of individual sayings creates a series of pictures on the self-disciplines of speaking, the nature of public honor and shame, and Yahweh's reaction to these character choices. In all, the basic choice between listening only to one's own thoughts and desires or listening to the teaching of others is set out in stark contrast. As we draw together these proverbs we are reminded again and again that we need the teaching, correction, and counsel of others (12:1, 15), but we also need their encouragement (12:25) and approval (12:8). Most of all, we need to live in communities where truthfulness is prized (12:19, 22).

Listening. New to this chapter is the emphasis on reasons to refrain from speaking. The proverbs collected here make a connection between listening to correction (12:1, 15) and concealing both insults and knowledge by declining to speak of them (12:16, 23). One never learns wisdom if one never stops talking. The chapter includes a number of negative illustrations to suggest when one should be silent, avoiding such speech sins as bragging (12:9), rash words of anger (12:16), and reckless attack (12:18). Taking these proverbs to heart, we will learn to be "quick to listen, slow to speak and slow to become angry, because our anger does not produce the righteousness that God desires" (James 1:19–20, TNIV).

But more is at stake here, as valuable and necessary as this counsel is. The prudence that conceals insult and knowledge in Proverbs 12:16, 23 exercises discernment; it weighs the potential effects of words before releasing them, because like birds set free, they cannot be taken back. The heart that lacks such discernment lets folly fly (12:23). Therefore, the quality of the words we speak and the silences we keep reveal how well we have learned to consider the outcomes of our choices and actions. Heart and lips are every bit the actors that our hands and feet are.

Thus, the silence and reserve that listens to instruction and withholds insult is quite different from the emphasis on listening skills we find in contemporary marriage counseling and success literature, as valuable as these insights are.[11] The ancient sages did not speak about the value of feeling understood as we do, but they did understand that respect for others requires that we be quiet at times.

Such silence itself is a form of eloquence, for listening silence speaks a message of respect to those who would teach us, and knowledge kept hidden is the opposite of knowledge that puffs up (12:23; cf. 1 Cor. 8:1). Just as refusing to display knowledge is a sign of humility, so is refusing to respond to the insult. Thus, Moses refused to defend himself against the insults of his brother and sister (Prov. 12:16; cf. Num. 12:1–6). However, this humility does not mean that we never speak, only that we speak to build up and defend others, not ourselves. The one who listens to correction earns the right to teach and give correction, but the fool loses that right both by refusing to listen and by speaking words that harm.

Truth telling and *šalom*. A second emphasis of the chapter contrasts the deceit that hides in the heart (12:20) with the truthful lips that promote peace and endure (12:19; cf. 12:5, 17, 19, 22). Truth never requires silence or modesty, not in legal disputes or in personal relationships, for truth's desire is for good. Lies are conceived in the desire to gain some-

---

11. There are three books that I often recommend or assign in classes: R. L. Randall, *Let's Talk: Helping Couples, Groups, and Individuals Communicate* (Cleveland, Ohio: United Church Press, 1997), recommends attending to the purpose or frame of mind from which another speaks. M. P. Nichols, *The Lost Art of Listening: How Learning to Listen Can Improve Relationships* (New York: Guilford, 1995), urges readers to set aside internal responses so they can be free to listen. S. R. Covey, *The Seven Habits of Highly Effective People: Restoring the Character Ethic* (New York: Simon & Schuster, 1989), 236–60, made famous the aphorism "seek first to understand, then to be understood" in order to introduce skills of empathic listening.

thing unjustly, whether that gain be material possession or social standing (12:8–9).

As we have seen in earlier chapters, the history of Israel is replete with examples of lying and false witness for gain, including Ahab and Jezebel's theft of Naboth's reputation and vineyard, but other forms of deceit may be in mind here as well. Wisdom's counter to such damaging lies is a truthful witness, and its fruit benefits not only the witness (12:14, 19) but the entire community that enjoys its *šalom* (12:20). "But the wisdom that comes from heaven is first of all pure; then peace-loving, considerate, submissive, full of mercy and good fruit, impartial and sincere. Peacemakers who sow in peace raise a harvest of righteousness" (James 3:17–18). Truth builds trusting relationships and brings healing; therefore, we can say that truth brings life. Here is a specific example of righteousness in which Yahweh delights (Prov. 12:22).

The fruits of *šalom* are noticed by Yahweh but also by the community that benefits (12:20 and 22). Our behavior is being watched more often than we like to think, for the observers are either interacting with us or watching from a distance. Because our choices are under public scrutiny, wisdom is praised and perverse hearts are despised (12:8). But readers may still wonder why we so often see reputations made by wealth, power, and especially these days, by fame itself. Perhaps celebrity as fostered by mass media creates a different set of standards that would never be allowed in smaller communities.

In face-to-face relationships, it is intention for good that brings about praise. A wife that has a noble character of her own is no mere ornament for her husband but a partner in a loving community, a model for the community at large. So also the man who knows the needs of his animals and friends, providing food and a good word (12:10, 25), models the character of love that receives its reward of praise.[12] Maslow was right: In addition to air, water, food, and safety, we need to belong and we need the positive opinion of others. We can seek to gain it through false and hollow means of pretense or through sincere care. Righteousness is social in every respect, for it means we care how we are perceived by others. We need the positive regard of our communities, and the qualities listed here are the means to obtain them.

However, a look around at contemporary society might conclude that many people feel oppressed by their communities (or at least in competition with them), for they see that virtues often go unrecognized and that we often are held in judgment for deficiencies in lesser things. Doing the right

---

12. Van Leeuwen, "Proverbs," 129.

thing is not always repaid with honor, and we all know the stories of rewards in life going to the beautiful and talented, sometimes because they flaunt being "bad." Self-assertive and self-congratulating words and actions have won the good life for many.

Looking a little more closely, we can see that some of this reversal stems from our culture's tendency to misname the virtues that are acceptable. For example, one study of common conceptions of masculinity lists the following traits: (1) Be unlike females; (2) be successful; (3) be aggressive; (4) be sexual; and (5) be self-reliant.[13] Turning to the proverbs, one searches in vain for ostentatious display of wealth, machismo celebration of sexuality, or any value that, at root, is competitive. The sage's awareness of our interconnectedness goes against the grain of such competition, for in their view, we were created to build others up and be built up in turn (cf. Eph. 4:25–32). Here is another dimension of righteousness that brings Yahweh delight.

Yahweh's delight. In addition to the human virtues of listening and truth telling, we should also attend to the two sayings that speak of Yahweh's delight in them. When we reflect on what a chapter of Proverbs says about God, we should first observe what is said directly and then what is implied or can be inferred from those proverbs and their literary context. The first is primary and guides the latter. In chapter 12, the two verses that name "the LORD" (*yhwh*; 12:2, 22) identify what pleases him: a good person who deals and speaks truthfully. He condemns one who schemes and abhors one who speaks falsely. The first verse speaks of intention, the second of action; Yahweh observes and judges both.

Careful readers can draw implications from the interaction between these two sayings and the rest of the chapter. Therefore, as readers find themselves in agreement with the values of truth and straight dealing held up throughout the series of proverbs, they may also be pleased to read that Yahweh shares their reactions to these behaviors. But this chapter has also emphasized the social outcomes of praise and contempt based on one's reputation for speaking and acting. The community discerns what it finds favorable and unacceptable (cf. *raṣon*, favor or delight in 10:32; 11:27)—perhaps, we may say, after the example of "the LORD," who "delights" (*raṣon*, "favor" in 8:35) in those who find wisdom.

These proverbs describe Yahweh's purposes for the creation. In other words, while the outcomes of the contrasting proverbs do not speak of Yah-

---

13. J. A. Doyle, *The Male Experience* (Dubuque, Ia.: W. C. Brown, 1989); J. T. Wood, *Gendered Lives: Communication, Gender, and Culture* (Belmont, Calif.: Wadsworth, 1994), cited in D. J. A. Clines, "*Ecce Vir*, or Gendering the Son of Man," in *Biblical Studies/Cultural Studies: The Third Sheffield Colloquium* (JSOTSup 266; Sheffield: Sheffield Academic Press, 1998), 352–75.

weh's direct intervention in human affairs, they do correspond with what pleases him and what he detests. But it may also be that the strategy behind this collection of proverbs uses the reader's reaction to good and evil to show that Yahweh also loves what builds up and hates what tears down. In other words, the reader's reaction to the proverbs becomes a strong argument that Yahweh's way is the good way.

Implied in these proverbs may also be one answer to the question: "If God is so good, why is there evil in our world?" While we know there is no final answer to this question, we do learn from these sayings that God's displeasure at evil often takes the form of allowing events to run their course. So the prophet Habakkuk learned that God would deal with Israel's sin by raising up proud and ruthless Babylon against them (Hab. 1:1–11). Even as the wicked brought violence and injustice against the righteous, so the Babylonians would bring their evil on them.

While this is no final answer to the atrocities of violence that we and our parents have seen in our own days, we do learn a working principle that God's hatred of evil does not always intervene but often allows evil to boomerang back on itself. This principle probably makes more sense in a small community of face-to-face relationships than it does in larger matters of warfare and social domination. Learning to appreciate where in life a principle applies is one of the skills of discernment.

Those who teach and preach from this chapter may wish to use the two Yahweh proverbs to shape a message about intent and actions, pointing out the contrasts between deceit in the heart and truthful lips. Another strategy may choose a cluster, such as the trio on status (12:8–10) or the larger section on speech (12:13–23), and use one or two proverbs as examples of the theme.

THE WAY WE SPEAK **determines how others speak of us.** There is good news in this chapter, for even though words can lie in wait for blood and pierce like a sword (12:6, 18), there is life in the way of righteousness (12:28), life not only for the wise but also for those who benefit from the fruit of their lips (12:14, 17). The wicked are trapped in their own words, and fools are exposed. The order and boundaries set out by God at creation hold strong, even though they are often assailed, and so the wisdom of these proverbs advises joining the side of the winner. To do so is to invite instruction; ironically, the one who loves knowledge also loves correction, for only the fool has nothing to learn (12:1, 15). The proverbs of this chapter continue to encourage such openness to instruction by reminding its readers that wisdom and folly will make themselves known. Neither remains hidden for long.

The choice of wisdom over folly shows itself in choices that begin in the heart and manifest themselves in actions of hands and tongue. These choices accumulate into a portrait of character, for as Aristotle reminded us, virtue is a series of habitual choices. Stephen Fowl believes that construing a person's character is a "narrative achievement. That is, to render a character, one must fit that character into a narrative sequence of actions."[14] Each person, as it were, is in the process of writing a life story that demonstrates how well one has lived. That rendering of character is not done by the individual alone, however, but also by the church.[15]

If this is the case, then one renders self or renders the character of others based on the account of actions, a reflection on intentions, and an assessment of the outcomes or results. Proverbs asserts that we can determine how others will assess our characters. We are told that the community does and will make its judgments, even as stories about a person's actions are told in families and towns. Gossip tends to evaluate, sometimes fairly, sometimes not, but the stories are always framed in negative and positive judgments of character.

Jesus "welcomed Zacchaeus gladly," and this provoked a response from the people present who had made their evaluation: "He has gone to be the guest of a 'sinner.'" But Zacchaeus decided to change that assessment and start a new story of his life, giving half of his ill-gotten gain to the poor and returning what he had obtained by cheating four times over (Luke 19:1–10). The change was motivated by Jesus' radical acceptance of a sinner, but it could also be said that Zacchaeus began to rewrite his story when he took extraordinary steps to see Jesus, climbing the tree and risking ridicule. Jesus announced to the whole crowd that salvation had come to his house, and so "a good man obtains favor from the LORD, but the LORD condemns a crafty man" (Prov. 12:2). Intentions that begin in the heart show themselves in deeds and words, and the Lord who watches both sometimes overturns the judgment of the community.

The majority of sayings in Proverbs 12 center on how one uses the human capacity to influence others through speech. Verses 17–19 in particular note the possibilities of damage and blessing: "Words [that] pierce like a sword"

14. S. Fowl, "Learning to Narrate Our Lives in Christ," in *Theological Exegesis: Essays in Honor of Brevard S. Childs*, ed. C. Seitz and K. Greene-McCreight (Grand Rapids: Eerdmans, 1999), 351.

15. D. S. Cunningham, *Faithful Persuasion: In Aid of a Rhetoric of Christian Theology* (Notre Dame and London: Univ. of Notre Dame Press, 1990), 253.

can be reckless (12:18), but the tongue can cut in other ways that are more intentional. In the fifth century Romanos the Melodist preached a sermon in poetry, chanting that Judas "sharpened his tongue" to betray "Jesus, kissed in treachery—Christ, sold through jealousy—God, voluntarily seized."[16] The sermon warned against words used for evil, while other sermons sought to move others toward virtue.

In 1630, John Winthrop preached about the "city set on a hill," an image that inspired the rhetorical visions of John F. Kennedy, Martin Luther King, and Ronald Reagan. Winthrop's hope for this new model society lay with showing "more enlargement towards others and less respect for ourselves. . . . There are two rules whereby we are to walk one towards another: justice and mercy."[17] Both these preachers modeled in their speaking a view of a personal and social life guided by biblical virtues of these proverbs.

We take their message to heart, reminding ourselves that words can hurt or heal and asking ourselves how it might apply to leaders in the church: pastors, church leaders, and teachers in seminaries and Sunday schools. We know from experience that people can be vain and petty, but those same persons can also be just and compassionate. No one we know is, as we sometimes joke, "pure evil." We may find ourselves asking, How do these sayings portray human nature when they set one boldly against the other, and how do we read them, knowing that we have potential for both? My answer is to view the two characters of righteousness and wickedness and their two ways as symbols of the many daily choices we make.

Those daily choices assemble themselves into a character that then weighs in on one side of the scales or the other. We may be called upon to make momentous choices that influence many or we may not, but all of us face daily opportunities to speak truth, deal fairly, and receive correction when necessary. Fred Craddock, hearing many sermons in his childhood about heroic Christians, grew up believing that to give one's life meant making one great sacrifice to save someone else.

> I was sincere then, as I have been these forty-five years. I give my life, but nobody warned me that I could not write one big check. I've had to write forty-five years of little checks—eighty-seven cents, twenty-one cents, nibbled away this giving of life. Are you able to drink the cup? I can drink the cup in one giant quaff and let my life

16. St. Romanos, *Kontakia of Romanos, Byzantine Melodist—On the Person of Christ*, trans. M. Carpenter (Columbia: Univ. of Missouri Press, 1970), 169–70; cited in J. R. Jeter Jr., "The Development of Poetic Preaching: A Slice of History," *Homiletic* 15/2 (Winter 1990): 8.

17. P. Gomes, "The Best Sermon of the Millennium," *Pulpit Digest* 81/1 (Jan.–March 2000): 143–46.

be given. No, no, no. My life is one of drinking a sip here, a sip there, and soon you reach retirement and did anybody notice that you gave your life and drank the cup?[18]

A character is not narrated by one story but many. The binary opposition of the Proverbs asks us to decide which summary of our stories we would like to have characterize our lives. If popular opinion decides we are wise, our follies are not held against us the way they are if we choose the opposite. Then, even our wise acts and words go unnoticed. Just or unjust, I believe this kind of categorizing goes on, and the sayings may be telling us to get used to it and choose accordingly.

Choices made in favor of speaking the uplifting word (12:25) or the truthful word (12:17) can be the "way" of our lives. We may think without speaking, and we often speak without thinking. Proverbs would have us become persons who know when to speak and when to keep silent. Good speech results in the combination of both thinking and speaking. To speak is to act, so we are called to consider the effects of our words.

Truth is best spoken when the good of another person is at stake, and while this does not rule out times when we must speak the truth for ourselves, we always ought to ask who we are more anxious to defend. I know that my most frequent tendency is to speak in defense of myself and less often in defense of others. Certainly this means that bad reports about another's behavior in the church should not be swept under the rug, but neither should they be broadcast in gossip. Rather, testimony is heard, remembering that conflicting accounts may be inevitable (12:17).

Even though unfair gossip can circulate, these proverbs encourage us to trust that wisdom and folly will eventually be revealed and that we can even join in the process by choosing to speak words that are truthful and fair. In our business lives and social lives and in those times when the two intersect, we can refuse to speak in ways that bring us honor or profit when we don't deserve it, and we can speak up when the rights and reputations of others are on the line. Such truth telling is recognized by the community, because folly fools no one for long, and more important, it is always noticed by the Lord of truth.

---

18. F. Craddock, "Enduring the Small Stuff (Hebrews 12:1–2)," in *Ten Great Preachers: Messages and Interviews*, ed. B. Turpie (Grand Rapids: Baker, 2000), 42–50.

Proverbs 13:1–25

¹ A WISE SON heeds his father's instruction,
  but a mocker does not listen to rebuke.
² From the fruit of his lips a man enjoys good things,
  but the unfaithful have a craving for violence.
³ He who guards his lips guards his life,
  but he who speaks rashly will come to ruin.
⁴ The sluggard craves and gets nothing,
  but the desires of the diligent are fully satisfied.
⁵ The righteous hate what is false,
  but the wicked bring shame and disgrace.
⁶ Righteousness guards the man of integrity,
  but wickedness overthrows the sinner.
⁷ One man pretends to be rich, yet has nothing;
  another pretends to be poor, yet has great wealth.
⁸ A man's riches may ransom his life,
  but a poor man hears no threat.
⁹ The light of the righteous shines brightly,
  but the lamp of the wicked is snuffed out.
¹⁰ Pride only breeds quarrels,
  but wisdom is found in those who take advice.
¹¹ Dishonest money dwindles away,
  but he who gathers money little by little makes it grow.
¹² Hope deferred makes the heart sick,
  but a longing fulfilled is a tree of life.
¹³ He who scorns instruction will pay for it,
  but he who respects a command is rewarded.
¹⁴ The teaching of the wise is a fountain of life,
  turning a man from the snares of death.
¹⁵ Good understanding wins favor,
  but the way of the unfaithful is hard.
¹⁶ Every prudent man acts out of knowledge,
  but a fool exposes his folly.
¹⁷ A wicked messenger falls into trouble,
  but a trustworthy envoy brings healing.
¹⁸ He who ignores discipline comes to poverty and shame,
  but whoever heeds correction is honored.
¹⁹ A longing fulfilled is sweet to the soul,
  but fools detest turning from evil.

²⁰He who walks with the wise grows wise,
  but a companion of fools suffers harm.
²¹Misfortune pursues the sinner,
  but prosperity is the reward of the righteous.
²²A good man leaves an inheritance for his children's
    children,
  but a sinner's wealth is stored up for the righteous.
²³A poor man's field may produce abundant food,
  but injustice sweeps it away.
²⁴He who spares the rod hates his son,
  but he who loves him is careful to discipline him.
²⁵The righteous eat to their hearts' content,
  but the stomach of the wicked goes hungry.

Original Meaning

THIS CHAPTER BEGINS with another statement about parental teachers and their pupils (cf. "son" and "father" in 10:1 and *musar*, "discipline," in 12:1), but it contains fewer contrasts between the righteous and the wicked and no mention of God's involvement in human affairs.[1] The arrangement of the proverbs weaves together the themes of desire and discipline, and so we might call the theme "disciplined appetite" or "disciplined desires." Other key words (e.g., *tob*, "good" in 13:2, 15, 21, 22; the various translations of *nepeš*, "life," "desire" in 13:2, 3, 4, 8, 19, 25) appear with unusual frequency.

The chapter appears to be framed by key words, especially the *musar* of father to son ("instruction" in 13:1; "discipline" in 13:18, 24) and "eat" (13:2, 25). This inclusio links discipline and eating, but the repetition of "longing fulfilled" (13:12, 19) extends the metaphor so that eating becomes a concrete example of all sorts of desires. The chapter can be divided into two somewhat equal parts: Verses 1–16 focus on results that come to the individual, verses 17–25 on the effect of one's actions on others, particularly the inheritance one leaves.

More certain than any proposed outline are the clear connections made by catchwords, encouraging readers to identify pairs or small groups that highlight themes. Verses 12 and 19 repeat the phrase "longing fulfilled," and the verses in between seem to fall out in a mirror or chiastic pattern (vv. 13

---

1. J. Goldingay, "The Arrangement of Sayings in Proverbs 10–15," *JSOT* 61 (1994): 75–83.

and 18 paired on the topic of refusing instruction, vv. 14 and 17 the life-giving effects of good speaking, and vv. 15 and 16 terms for knowledge). In general, the chapter follows the pattern:

Discipline and eating (13:1–6)
Riches and virtues (13:7–11)
Desire fulfilled (13:12–19)
Prosperity and inheritance (13:20–23)
Discipline and eating (13:24–25)

Repetition of word and theme matches the first and last sections as well as the second and fourth. The verbal repetitions are so varied that we must recognize that one arrangement based on word repetitions leaves out other verbal links. For example, this arrangement splits up the link of the catch-word "fools" in 13:19–20. It is unlikely that those who wrote and gathered these proverbs thought in terms of outline; rather, they focused on recurrences and analogies that gave the general sense of traveling "there and back again." When travelers use landmarks to find the path home, there is no need to draw a map.

Discipline and Eating (13:1–6)

THE KEY WORD *nepeš* appears four times in this section, twice in verse 4 as "craving" and "desire," once in verse 2 as "craving," and once in verse 3 as "life." This word for "throat" or "neck" is used throughout Scripture to speak of life or its desires, depending on the context in which it is used. In this grouping, the term is used with images of eating and speaking to create picturesque lessons about both. Verses 5–6 contrast the righteous and the wicked.

13:1. The Hebrew word *musar* ("instruction, discipline") occurs three times in this chapter (13:1, 18, 24), a frequency second only to the four occurrences in chapter 15. Throughout the contrasting proverbs in chapters 10–15, instruction is frequently paired with correction, itself a contrast that says, "this way, not that way." The juxtaposition of the Hebrew in the first line can read, "A wise son, a father's discipline."[2] That is, if you see a wise son, then look for a father's teaching.

If, however, the son is a fool, do we blame the father? No, the word used in parallel to "son" is "mocker," a scoffer, one who does not listen to correction or rebuke. While responsibility is set squarely on the learner (cf. 12:1), the parent's responsibility to teach is upheld here and echoed in 13:24. In

---

2. The occurrences of "wise son" in 10:1; 13:1; 15:20 may mark the beginning, middle, and end of the contrasting proverbs in chs. 10–15 (Scoralick, *Einzelspruch und Sammlung*, 198–99).

Hebrew, the second line of 13:1 is nearly identical to 13:8; "rebuke" or "threat" (*ge'arah*) is a shout or stern word that deters someone from a course of action (cf. 17:10). So Jacob rebuked the young Joseph for his proud dreams (Gen. 37:10). Typically, God's rebuke is a loud shout that sets limits on waters or war (Job 26:10–11; Isa. 17:13).

13:2. This proverb contrasts the "fruit of the mouth" (*peri pi*) by which a person "eats good"[3] with hunger for violence, implying that the treacherous person both speaks and eats this dangerous fruit (cf. 10:11); the pairing of "good" (*tob*) and "unfaithful" (*boge'dim*) appears again in 13:15. The verb "eats" can be translated "may eat," heightening the sense that if a mouth produces good, it will eat good things in turn.[4] The contrast in the second line adds that good does not come to everyone who desires it (*nepeš*) without regard for their behavior. A similar contrast is intensified in 13:3, where the contrast is between "life" and "ruin" or destruction.

13:3. Two catchwords link verses 2 and 3: *pi* (NIV "lips/mouth") appears in the first line of each, and the double-duty *nepeš* is used for "craving"(v. 2) and for "life" (v. 3). Therefore, if the first lines of each verse are compared, a wise mouth produces good fruits to eat but also knows when to keep bad from coming out. The second lines work together to portray a greedy desire (*nepeš*) that leads to loss of life (*nepeš*) and ruin. A double meaning may be intended for "speaks rashly" (lit., "opens wide the lips"), a reference to hasty speech, but it may also refer to the greedy appetite for violence of 13:2. These two sayings caution us to watch what our mouths put out in speech as well as what they take in to satisfy their desires.

13:4. A proverb about the sluggard (cf. 6:6–9; 10:26; 21:25; 26:13–16) completes this cluster of sayings about appetite and desire. Here "desire" (*nepeš*) by itself brings nothing; it must be accompanied by industry, which (lit.) "fattens" or fills one's desire. The person who eschews violence and sloth in word and deed is rewarded accordingly.

13:5. Two righteous/wicked contrasts are juxtaposed in 13:5–6. The contrast in verse 5 pits falsehood against its result of shame and disgrace, with the implication that one leads to the other and the wicked bring both with them wherever they go. "What is false" is *debar-šeqer*, a false word or deed. The word for shame can be translated as "smell" or "stink."[5]

---

3. The NIV translates the more idiomatic "fruit of his lips," as in 12:14: "From the fruit of his lips a man is filled with good things." Scoralick, *Einzelspruch und Sammlung*, 198–215, believes that the repetition of similar first lines in 12:14 and 13:2 frames a section. It is not clear why this repetition should take priority over others.

4. J. Emerton, "The Meaning of Proverbs 13:2," *JTS* 35 (1984): 91–95.

5. McKane, *Proverbs*, 460.

13:6. This second contrasting saying personifies righteousness and wickedness as protector and destroyer. "Overthrow" (*slp*) can be translated "mislead" (cf. 11:3, where it is translated "duplicity"). This proverb and 13:18 depict the world as taking the side of the righteous against the wicked, "where the world is self-righting ... active, rewarding and punishing people."[6] The word for "guards" (*nṣr*) brings the reader back to 13:3 and the guarding of lips for life.

Riches and Virtues (13:7–11)

SAYINGS ABOUT RICH and poor people are juxtaposed with sayings about righteousness and pride. Verses 9–11 are linked by a triad of virtues: righteousness, wisdom (understood in this chapter as teachability), and industry.

13:7. Verses 7 and 8 are linked by the catchwords "poor" and "rich" to show that riches are not as clear an indication of status and worth as we often believe (though we do not often admit it). In both cases, the "poor" come off better than those who have riches or desire them. Appearances can be deceiving, as verse 7 shows, and riches are no guarantee of safety, a concern of verse 8. "Has nothing" recalls the sluggard of 13:4, but here the error is not laziness but the effort that goes into acting like someone of wealth and status (cf. 12:9). Just as one person can pretend to be important, another person may have wealth yet never show it off; the latter seems to be the better choice.

13:8. This verse allows that riches can get one out of trouble, but only as it reminds us that it is better to hear no threat of trouble at all. The source of this security is not stated, perhaps because the poor have nothing to covet or steal or because the poor are protected along with the righteous (13:6). The word for "ransom" is the same one used for "compensation" of the jealous husband in 6:35 and should therefore be understood as payment for damages or trouble, a release from obligation rather than a release from bondage (but see 21:18).

In any case, the poor do not have money to buy their way out of legal entanglements and other difficulties, but they may not need to as often as those with money do. The last three Hebrew words of 13:8 are identical

---

6. R. J. Clifford, "Proverbs as a Source for Wisdom of Solomon," in *Treasures of Wisdom: Studies in Ben Sira and the Book of Wisdom, Festschrift M. Gilbert*, ed. N. Calduch-Benages and J. Vermeylen (Leuven: Leuven University Press, 1999), 255–63. Clifford lists five themes from the book of Proverbs that influenced the Wisdom of Solomon: (1) Righteous person as the locus where divine action becomes visible, (2) God as a father who teaches his son by a process involving correction, (3) The wise king, (4) Life and death as more-than biological realities, (5) The world protects the righteous and punishes the wicked.

with those of 13:1 (lit., "does not hear a shout"), but the NIV rightly translates them differently. If there is any overlap of meaning, it is that scoffers refuse the threats of "rebuke" (13:1), whereas the poor here are depicted as not hearing any type of threat of insecurity (but see 10:15, where "poverty is the ruin of the poor").

13:9. This contrast between the righteous and the wicked is one of four in the chapter (13:5, 6, 9, 25), and the placement of the first three place a frame around the poor/rich sayings of 13:7–8. Translations differ between light that "shines brightly" (NIV) or light that "rejoices" (NRSV); 10:1 and 15:20 use the same Hebrew root (*śmḥ*) for the joy that a wise son brings to his parents. The image of the lamp signifies a long and happy life, a promise made throughout the book; the snuffed-out lamp of the wicked appears in Job 18:5–6; 21:17. The saying is repeated in Proverbs 24:20.

13:10. The main contrast between pride and wisdom is shown in one's attitude toward advice (cf. 11:2). By extension, quarrels come about when one refuses to listen to good counsel. We have met the man who stirs things up before (6:12–19). Here the source of his contention ("pride") is defined as an unwillingness to listen and learn, reminding the reader of 13:1.

13:11. The second proverb to use the word wealth (*hon*; cf. 13:7) contrasts the one who increases wealth little by little with one whose wealth dwindles away until there is little left. A translation difficulty lies in the word *hebel* (NIV "dishonest"; lit., "breath, breeze," Isa. 57:13), a word used in Ecclesiastes to signify what is both ephemeral and elusive (e.g., Eccl. 1:2–3).[7] Thus, the first line can read "meaningless wealth," echoing that use, but some would read "wealth from haste."[8] The contrast with the second line suggests that it is wealth gained from nothing, that is, from no labor—perhaps theft or speculation. The NIV's "dishonest" fits well with the context of pride and wickedness.

Desire Fulfilled (13:12–19)

THIS SECTION IS framed by the repetition of "longing fulfilled" (*taʾăwah*) in 13:12 and 19,[9] associating human hopes and dreams with the benefits of wisdom.

13:12. This proverb looks at the more basic and general topic of desire and hope, a larger category that includes our desire of material goods. The

---

7. I. W. Provan, *Ecclesiastes and Song of Songs* (NIVAC; Grand Rapids: Zondervan, 2001), 52.

8. The NRSV has "wealth hastily gotten." Clifford, *Proverbs*, 135–36, emends to read "hastily acquired," in comparison to 20:21 and 28:22, sayings that deal with hastily acquired wealth and its loss. So also Murphy, *Proverbs*, 93–94.

9. After Garrett, *Proverbs*, 137, who sees an inclusio here.

sages were not ascetics, but neither were they acquisitive. Verses 11 and 12 seem to be linked in a way similar to comparison between the tree of life and material wealth in chapter 3. The tree of life in Proverbs is associated with wisdom herself (3:18) and the speech of the righteous (11:30; 15:4). Here it speaks to the goodness of our longings (*ta²ʷwah*; cf. 13:19) that can be distorted by laziness and greed (13:4).

Although this proverb contrasts hope deferred and longing fulfilled, it does not admonish behavior but simply makes the contrasts and observes its effects. Note the link with "fountain of life" in 13:14. A similar reflection on the interior life of the heart, the seat of will and intention, occurs in 14:10: "Each heart knows its own bitterness, and no one else can share its joy."

13:13. The contrast between one who pays and one who is paid is in view here, as is the contrast between scorning instruction and respecting (lit., "fearing") a command. It is interesting that the tree of life and the Hebrew root of *šalom* both occur in 3:17–18 and in 13:12–13, where *šlm* is used as a verb meaning "reward." The LXX adds: "To a crafty son there shall be nothing good; but a wise servant shall have prosperous doings, and his way shall be directed aright."

13:14. The key word "life" (*ḥayyim*) here describes a fountain (cf. "tree of life" in 13:12). Both trees and fountains were signs of life in the arid climate of the ancient Near East. The presence of trees signaled that waters were near (Ps. 1; Jer. 17:8), and here the waters spring forth in a fountain. The fountain of life appears in Proverbs 10:11; 13:14; 14:27; 16:22, where it is associated with righteous speech, the fear of Yahweh, and understanding.

The saying in 13:14 is nearly identical with 14:27.[10] The images are striking; one can find a fountain of life giving waters or one can find a deadly snare, depending on where and how one looks. Readers recall that married intimacy was likened to a fountain and spring (5:15–18) while the intimacy of adultery was compared to the deadly trap (7:21–26). The reference to wise teaching directs the reader back to 13:1 and the willingness to receive advice, and it looks forward to the wisdom of keeping wise companions (13:20).

13:15. Verses 15–16 are linked by the use of terms from the beginning of the book: "favor," "prudence," "knowledge," "fools," and "folly" (1:1–7); "understanding" (*sekel*) in 13:15 appears as "prudent living" in 1:3. The use of "good" (*tob*) and "unfaithful" (*bogᵉdim*) in 13:15 is similar to 13:2; both proverbs make clear the outcomes that come to those who choose treachery. This saying compares "good understanding" that can be acquired with the "way"

---

10. Scoralick, *Einzelspruch und Sammlung*, 218–19, believes that similarities with 14:27 mark another section, with 13:14–19 set off as a subsection.

or actions of those who reject it. It is not clear whose favor is won, so the general favor of God and community is probably intended (cf. 3:4). The last word of the saying is difficult to translate. The NIV note reads "does not endure," and NRSV reads "ruin" with the LXX. The latter is more in keeping with the context of the chapter, but in either case, the negative outcome is clear.

13:16. Demonstration of learning, or lack of it, is at the heart of this proverb, which uses the Hebrew roots for "prudent" and "knowledge" from 1:4. "Prudent" is paired with the Hebrew for "fool" or "foolishness" in 12:16, 23; 13:16; 14:8, and with "simple" in 22:3 and 27:12 to create a common motif. The contrast illustrates the truth that we display either knowledge or ignorance when we act, and so we receive either favor or shame (cf. 13:15). The public nature of a person's actions is echoed in 13:17–18.

13:17. Proof that one's actions have their effects on others comes in the case of a messenger, where character counts for everything. Long ago, rulers and nobles trusted messengers to speak on their behalf, and so they chose carefully to make sure that the person sent represented them faithfully. Messengers like this bring healing; there is a reference to healing or health in every chapter from chapters 12–15 (12:18; 13:17; 14:30; 15:4). Closest in meaning to this proverb are 12:18 ("the tongue of the wise brings healing") and 15:4 ("the tongue that brings healing is a tree of life"). In these proverbs, healing is often contrasted with "trouble." Given that the basic meaning of *marpeʾ* is to restore, even to soothe and calm (Eccl. 10:4), it may be that faithful messengers do more than avoid causing trouble; they smooth it over. If you sent someone into a conflict situation, you would want one who would make it better, not worse.

13:18. The key word "discipline" (*musar*) appears, marking the beginning, middle, and end of this chapter (cf. 13:1, 24). As with the other occurrences, the word is paired with one for "correction." The word "honor" sends the reader back to the similar word "favor" (13:15), noting that the prudent and the trustworthy envoy receive praise, not blame (13:16–17). All are linked to the theme of receiving or ignoring teaching (see 13:19). The Hebrew roots for "shame" (*qln*) and "honor" (*kbd*) contrast what is light and insubstantial with what is weighty and important.

13:19. With the phrase "longing fulfilled," this saying marks the end of a frame with 13:12, but it is also linked with 13:20 by the catchword "fools." What is implied in 13:12 is explicit here as desires are fulfilled or frustrated, depending on one's response to instruction and correction. Fools who refuse to turn from evil will certainly not enjoy the sweetness of fulfilled desire; their actions will bear their fruits, but will they be sweet? According to 20:17, they will taste like gravel. Only a fool would fail to appreciate this truth after so many repetitions! The point is reinforced by the assonance between the

Hebrew for "desire" (*ta²wah*) and "detest"(*to⁶bah*; the *w* and *b* are both sounded as *v* in Hebrew), making the rhyme a strong component of the rhetoric.

Prosperity and Inheritance (13:20–23)

SAYINGS ABOUT WEALTH and inheritance (13:21–23) are juxtaposed with a profound proverb about the company one keeps (13:20), again contrasting wisdom and its rewards with the results that come when it is ignored.

13:20. Fools not only refuse to turn from evil, they also fail to choose good company. The first line shows the result in character; the second, the result in outcome. The truth that even one's choice of companions has its consequences is harder to see for those making the decision, as both parents and their children know. Together, 13:19 and 20 connect wisdom and longing, encouraging the learner that having desires is not bad but good, yet those desires must be pursued in wise ways.

13:21. The theme of rewards links 13:21–22 through their double use of the word "good" (*tob*)—as reward of prosperity in verse 21 and as a description of the good person in verse 22. Fools and sinners not only find trouble; here trouble is personified as seeking them. In contrast, the righteous are (lit.) "rewarded with good things." The words used in the phrase remind the reader of 13:13 (*šlm*, "reward") and 13:2, 15 (*tob*).

13:22. The Hebrew word for "good" (*tob*) comes first in the proverb here and last in 13:21 to show that the reward of verse 21 can be passed on to one's children and grandchildren. The "good" person keeps the "good" reward and passes it on, but sinners lose their wealth to the righteous and are left with nothing.[11] The term "stored up" underscores the frustrated plans, while "sinner," the last Hebrew word in this proverb and the first word of 13:21, creates a frame. The topic of gain appears again in 13:23, that of generations in 13:24.

13:23. The blessings of God and nature may favor the poor, but an astute observer will also note that their gain can be taken by injustice. The pessimism of this saying stands out from its context, yet its realistic outlook provides a counterbalance to the optimism of 13:22. We may say that verse 22 looks at the ultimate outcome while verse 23 looks at situations we often encounter in life. Proverbs describe what usually happens, not what always *must* happen. Said another way, it is true that we often see situations that look like verse 23, yet the unseen resolution of verse 22 is the one to bet on. Once again, learners are challenged to practice foresight, patience, and faith while maintaining a strong sense of justice.

---

11. Cf. Ps. 37:25–29; 49:10.

Discipline and Eating (13:24–25)

THESE LAST TWO VERSES repeat key words from 13:1–6: *musar* ("discipline"), *ʾokel* ("eat"), and *nepeš* ("life, soul," here "heart's content"), creating a frame around what lies between.

13:24. Whereas most proverbs that use *musar* ("instruction," "discipline") put the burden of learning on the student, this verse holds the parents responsible for administering the instruction of correction, an echo of 13:1. This is not the proverb we usually cite to warn children that they will be "spoiled" if the rod is spared (a saying not found in Proverbs); rather, this saying contrasts fathers who "hate" their children and those who "love" them by teaching them. The difference is "discipline," the accent falling on loving correction rather than a particular form of it. This verse can never be taken as support for corporal punishment. The various uses of *musar* throughout this chapter and the similar sayings make it clear that the issue is one of instruction, not the means used to bring it about (cf. 17:10; 19:18).[12]

13:25. This final saying contrasts satiation with hunger, but not without some ambiguity. Does the hunger of the wicked (lit., the "belly that goes wanting") point to their greedy appetites or the payback for them? The contrast of this proverb and the emphasis on outcomes in this collection suggest that this hunger is indeed a reward, but given what we have seen of the wicked and their undisciplined desires, it is a just one. In this chapter's final pairing of "eat" (*ʾokel*) and "stomach" (or "desire," *nepeš*), the disciplined person eats to satisfaction, experiencing neither gluttony nor worry. Such is the picture of *šalom* drawn by this grouping of proverbs.

MORE THAN ANYTHING ELSE, the collected proverbs of chapter 13 interweave sayings and images about *desire* and *discipline*, affirming that both are good and nonnegotiable elements of the world's created order. Life lived wisely honors desire and discipline, for to

---

12. This association of discipline with corporal punishment is the first of a few occurrences (cf. 22:15; 23:13–14; cf. 29:15). Ancient Near Eastern texts testify to its use in the education of young men, not children, so it may be that correction and beating were seen as synonymous, esp. when the teaching encountered resistance. Still, we cannot be sure that this was true in Israel, since there are other sayings that associate the word "discipline" with teaching, not with a rod. We then should put the emphasis on the goal of correction, not the means of physical punishment. Moreover, such discipline is to be enacted as a sign of parental love, for Yahweh disciplines (teaches and corrects) like a loving father (3:12; cf. 12:1). For other proverbs about the rod and *adult* folly, see 10:13; 22:8; 26:3.

deny that we have human desires and longings is to live a dishonest form of self-denial, while to ignore our need for discipline is to indulge a self-interest that is ultimately destructive. In other words, as we appropriate the message of these proverbs for our own day, we must remember the creative tension that holds together our appetites and longings with our willingness to learn and receive correction.

Desire. The first and last pair of proverbs in the chapter link sayings about parental instruction with contrasts between righteous and wicked desires. The interplay of these observations sparks insight, so the task of interpreting these proverbs includes attending to links and comparisons. One teaching strategy simply brings these two pairs together in conversation, while another explores their function as a frame for what goes between. Either way, abstract terms like "desire" and "discipline" must be made real by sticking closely to the concrete images that make the sayings so lively and evocative. For example, the "fruit of the lips" (good speech) is contrasted with a "craving for violence" (13:2). The one who guards lips guards life, but the one who opens those lips wide will come to ruin (13:3); the oral image can refer to either eating or speaking, both of which require discipline.

Because the collected proverbs in chapters 10—24 appear to be repetitive, scattering similar thoughts and pictures throughout the chapters with no apparent strategy, readers and commentaries often collect and compare proverbs on a certain topic.[13] However, this topical approach draws our attention away from the distinctive character of a cluster's themes and symbols. In this chapter, the topic of desire and its images of eating lead the reader to look more closely at proverbs about wealth and inheritance; symbols of the rod and friendship speak of the values of discipline. The composite picture presents a reflection on the legacy one leaves to future generations.

As we have seen, reflections on desire come together in the repetition of the word "eat" (ʾokel) in 13:2 and 25. The sage's confidence in just desserts for the righteous and the wicked was most likely as hard to believe then as it is today. The satisfaction that comes from hard work, honest dealing, and saving (13:4—5, 11) often seems naive when compared to the easy gains of the proud and powerful. The unfair loss of what little the poor have goes down hard (13:23). It must have been that way in Jesus' time also, for Mary glorified the Lord who scattered the proud, lifted the humble, filled the hungry with good things, and sent the rich away empty (Luke 1:46—55; cf. Prov. 13:7—10, 25). God is not named in this chapter of Proverbs, but the order

---

13. In my opinion, the best are by Hubbard and Farmer. Kidner's introduction also takes this approach; see the bibliography. See also Longman, 117—55, for guidance in doing topical study.

that leaves no righteous person to go hungry is his, even if believers often need reassurance that this is so.

Therefore, we too can see God's hand in the rewards of work and its prosperity, yet we will refuse to trust in them for status or security (13:7–8). Then as now, riches served as validation of one's efforts and merits, even as they appeared to promise hope and safety for future days. The sages affirmed having enough, even enough to leave to one's children (13:22, 25), but they also saw the dangers of stockpiling riches, hoping to buy what God alone provides. Worse off in their view are those who, following this misunderstanding of wealth, crave riches and end up with nothing (13:4, 7). The final proverb suggests that the righteous not only eat until their stomachs are filled, but literally to the satisfaction of their souls/appetites (*nepeš*, 13:25). Again, our desires are not evil but an aspect of this creation God has called good, especially when they include a desire for wisdom and righteousness.

However, there is also a desire that is not informed by wisdom, as Jesus warned, "Watch out! Be on your guard against all kinds of greed; life does not consist in an abundance of possessions" (Luke 12:15, TNIV) The Greek word for that greed (*pleonexia*) has been described as a "passion for more ... an insatiability for more of what I already experience or have. If I just had a little bit more, I would be happy.... 'Avoid *pleonexia* in all its forms.'"[14] Even as Jesus warned against greedy desires that could never be fulfilled, these proverbs affirm that there are longings that are fulfilled and should be (Prov. 13:12, 19).

I can't help but believe that the sages intended to pass on an attitude toward wealth and good things that enjoys them without compromising their integrity and, for that matter, our own. That attitude sees the goods of life as happy by-products, perhaps even rewards, for the primary goods of virtue. The sages watched outcomes and listened to opinions, noting that the outlook of those who live for gain is very different from those who live for integrity. They paid attention to results and said, "This is wisdom; this is our observation on the way life works." They remind us that so much trouble in life is the failure to look down the road at long-term results. Excessive craving is incomplete, for it falls short of desiring all that God has set out for us.

Discipline. The threefold emphasis on instruction and discipline (*musar*, 13:1, 18, 24) speaks to the human need for correction, honor, and love. Such input can come from parents or from one's companions. In both cases, the

---

14. J. C. Haughey, *Virtue and Affluence: The Challenge of Wealth* (Kansas City: Sheed & Ward, 1997), 19.

learner (here, the "son") exercises choice, first in attending to wisdom teaching at home, then in choosing wise teachers and friends (13:14, 20).

According to the sages, these choices turn one from death and keep one from suffering the harm that comes to fools. They understand the power of influence and make it clear that we not only select a path, but we also choose persons to walk that path with us. Wisdom never exists in the abstract realm; it most often comes to us in the form of a wise person. Moreover, we become those wise persons as we learn to avoid prideful disputes and humbly receive advice (13:10, 18). The sayings of this chapter assume that wisdom walks and talks in human form and that we learn wisdom so that we can become counselor friends and teachers ourselves.

Therefore, the discipline of desire taught in this chapter was never intended to be practiced in isolation but rather in partnership with those whose pathway is clear. This does not mean that one looks for faultless friends and teachers, for, of course, none exists. Rather, we learn to discern the direction of their lives as we listen to their words and watch their actions. We can ask whether this person's desires are informed by the larger picture these proverbs present. Is there a sense of struggle in seeking to put their principles into practice? We may even look for the kind of honesty that sometimes wonders out loud if these principles really do work. A person honest in this way is kin to the psalmists, who often wrote about justice before God and the community of believers; a person like that is more likely to show honesty in other areas of life as well. In sum, the sages urge their learners to practice wisdom in the choice of wise companions and mentors.

Leaving a legacy. The reward of 13:13 is followed by a proverb about teaching others, and the reward of prosperity in 13:21 is followed by an observation on who gets to leave that prosperity to the next generation in the end. As parents and children alike are encouraged to enter into the transfer of wisdom from one generation to the next, they are also shown that wisdom's rewards of life, wealth, and honor are passed on as an inheritance. Those who only hope to leave wealth and who discount the greater value of wisdom will end up disappointed.

We joke when we say, "The one who dies with the most toys wins," but I suspect such joking often reveals a lack of attention to the matter of legacy. What would happen if children were raised with the idea that they are receiving a way of life that has come down through the generations, tested and sure, and that they are being taught not only how to live it but how to pass it on? This thought redirects our efforts to provide both materially and spiritually for our children.

We often observe the disastrous results when parents work to provide material goods but neglect to provide the presence and guidance children take as signs of love. Harry Chapin's song "Cat's in the Cradle" speaks of a boy who wants to grow up to be just like his dad, but his dad never has time for him; as they both grow older, his wish comes true. The adult son has no time for his lonely father. These proverbs charge us to examine our desires, not only because they will direct our lives but also because they will be fulfilled. If our deepest desire is for a life lived wisely, we will have it, and if we wish to live in what the wise call folly, we will have that as well. Yet the proverbs of the sages will not leave us there, for they remind us of the rewards that come with wisdom and folly—rewards that come not only to us but to those who follow us.

To summarize, the proverbs of this chapter make clear that we are not called to leave an inheritance of wealth but a legacy that includes so much more, a way of life: "The righteous eat to their hearts' content, but the stomach of the wicked goes hungry" (13:25). But there is a caution: As we read, we may take the many contrasts of the chapter too lightly, putting ourselves on the path with the righteous too readily. These polarities are a teaching device, exaggeration to make a point, but we will miss the point if we fail to appreciate the various repetitions that we too are "prone to wander" and can be tempted to take little shortcuts in order to preserve our accounts or our reputations. To the sages, outright rebellion is not the enemy so much as compromise. The fact that the wisdom writers worked so hard to make these contrasts stark and clear shows that human nature often loses sight of their clarity and makes fuzzy choices.

DISCIPLINE OF DESIRE. As we have seen, the proverbs of this chapter gather around the central contrast drawn in the last pair of sayings. The last word in each compares the one who loves and administers "discipline" (*musar*, 13:24) with the wicked one who only craves and goes "hungry" (*tebsar*, 13:25). It is the discipline of loving instruction that makes the difference between a "longing fulfilled" (13:12, 19) and "craving" that is not (13:2, 4). We who read these proverbs today are called to receive this discipline, shaping our lives around it so that we offer it to those who come after us as a legacy.

In other words, the teaching of these ancient sages invite us to a *discipline of desire*, affirming that it is good to enjoy the world God has made and given us as a home. We do not need to feel guilt or shame about the delight of our senses of sight, hearing, touch, smell, and taste, we need only to set that delight in its home of wise living. If our desires are a combination of the delight of our senses and the cultural framework that shapes our experience of them, we can speak of desires that are educated, instructed in values of love and justice by these witty and memorable sayings.[15]

(1) The proverbs teach us to temper our pleasure in this good world with honesty and humility (13:10–11), diligence and faithfulness (13:4, 15, 17). Infants seek total and immediate gratification until they are taught otherwise, yet commercial media would rather we stay in a state of perpetual immaturity. Commercials and programming alike tell us that we must have more than we have, and we must have it right away. "The world is one great object for our appetite, a big apple, a big bottle, a big breast, we are the sucklers, the eternally expectant ones, the hopeful ones—and the eternally disappointed ones."[16]

Let's face it, we live in a culture that tries to turn all it can into a commodity, even "real life." I'm speaking here of the television show *Real World*, which puts a group of young adults together in a home and starts the cameras rolling, hoping for some conflict and drama to attract viewers. As I write, the latest version of the program is set up in a trendy neighborhood of Chicago. When some residents hit the streets to protest that this mediated vision of life was decidedly controlled and *un*real, they were whisked away by police, but not until they invited the "actors" to come and join them in the real world. The protesters knew that cameras rarely go to the poorer parts of the city, except to report a fire or crime. Does anyone want to listen to the concerns of people who are not young and hip?

The proverbs about eating can be set in the contemporary context of consumer culture and instruct us in the art of discerning what we take in, including the media diet that urges us to consume more of everything, including itself (I am embarrassed to think of the number of times I have gone without hours of needed sleep to flip around the channels, watching nothing in particular). Again, the question is not so much *what* we consume but *how* we go about fulfilling desires, the purpose behind our actions. We must also examine the outcome of our choices, asking whether they move us closer to a life of love and faithfulness or away from that life. As an example, consider the Lord's Supper,[17] itself a form of eating that celebrates God's good gifts as it holds up Christ's life of disciplined desire: "yet not my will, but yours be done" (Luke 22:42).

---

15. This discussion is inspired by T. J. Gorringe, *The Education of Desire: Toward a Theology of the Senses* (Harrisburg, Pa.: Trinity Press International, 2001), 91–94.

16. E. Fromm, *The Art of Loving* (London: George Allen & Unwin, 1962), 91; quoted in Gorringe, *The Education of Desire*, 93.

17. "In the Christian tradition it is above all the eucharist which exists to do this disciplinary and educative work. . . . It has to be both affirmative of the physical body, and of the earth, and *for that very reason* hostile to all forms of consumerism" (Gorringe, *The Education of Desire*, 104).

(2) We have seen that the discipline of desire comes as we choose to "walk with the wise" (13:20), learning the ways of wisdom from both teachers and companions. A friend of mine likes to say that we can tell what we will be like in five years by looking around at the people we choose to spend time with. Their concerns will become ours and will influence even the way we look at the world around us. Stephen Fowl has shown that ethical concerns push interpreters to pursue particular interests in their work of biblical interpretation, but also that those ethical concerns are to be understood in terms of real communities in particular historical situations. In part, the concerns of those communities determine which interests receive attention.[18] In other words, our work of interpretation is influenced, at least in part, by the way we assess the situations that confront us.

The sayings about the rich and poor challenge us to try to see life through the eyes of those who have less than we do. In Chicago, where I live and teach, a newspaper called *Streetwise* is sold by people who earn sixty-five cents of the dollar price. The mission statement of the paper reads: "To empower men and women who are homeless or at risk of being so as they work towards gainful empowerment and self-sufficiency." The self-sufficiency held up here is not that of boastful trust in riches but the hope of being able to work and receive reward for their labors—a longing fulfilled rather than a boast. The paper shows how life looks to those who do not enjoy the privileges of wealth and influence, let alone the comforts of home and pantry that we take for granted. It reports local and national news with a focus on how decisions and policies affect the lives of persons who earn low income.[19] Where you stand influences what you see.

Are the poor always righteous, the rich always wicked? Not in the book of Proverbs, and not in the world we inhabit either. Just as the homeless of Chicago work to make their voices heard, some time ago another group with considerable means gathered to reflect on the responsibilities of wealth. The conference speaker invited them to seek out a "wisdom partner" to help with discerning how best to use such wealth, but also to form a deep friendship with someone who does not reap benefits from the present economic system. Friendships help broaden one's perspective; a wisdom friend is able to discern motives behind actions, particularly impulsive actions that may be motivated by false guilt rather than grace. Seeing life through the eyes of

---

18. S. Fowl, "The Ethics of Interpretation or What's Left Over After the Elimination of Meaning," in *The Bible in Three Dimensions: Essays in Celebration of Forty Years of Biblical Studies in the University of Sheffield*, ed. D. J. A. Clines, S. E. Fowl, S. E. Porter (Sheffield: JSOT Press, 1990), 379–98.

19. *Streetwise*, 8/22 (May 30–June 5, 2000).

someone excluded by the system clarifies its purposes and failures.[20] In other words, one needs help to gain a healthy perspective on wealth. To acquire wisdom's outlook, we need friendships with persons from all walks of life.

Recently I attended a conference of teachers, many of whom had chosen to work in poorer school districts. Their insight into what it means to have a heart sick from hopes deferred challenged me to learn about wealth by listening to the poor. My conversations with the woman who sells me *Streetwise* week after week are not deep, but I have learned something about the cares of finding adequate medical treatment for children in the public aid system. Like those conversations, the cumulative effect of this cluster of proverbs challenges the adequacy of our own outlook as it encourages us to "walk a mile in another's shoes." They also prod readers with truths held in tension. While holding up the virtues of work and its rewards of wealth, these sayings also warn us away from a simple, one-sided view of life that equates wealth and virtue. They also warn us about pride and pretense, the first steps toward the greater dangers of violence and injustice.

(3) We have noted a twofold aspect to the discipline set out in Proverbs 13. Readers are told to learn discipline for themselves and offer instruction to others. In the same way, those who walk with the wise are rewarded with good things and leave good things to others. Material goods are not separated from matters of wisdom and virtue; rather, they are united. If it is a mistake to equate wealth and virtue, it is also misguided to separate them so that the wealthy are not included among the righteous. If things were that simple, there would not be the need for so many proverbs! As it is, the collection of proverbs urges readers to leave not a hoard but a legacy, for it is the combination of wealth and wisdom that endures (13:23).

An ancient version of "you can't take it with you" can be found in Psalm 49, in which the singer claims to "speak words of wisdom" and "give understanding" in proverb and riddle (Ps. 49:3–4). The psalm asks why it is that we become afraid when people boast of their wealth and riches, since no one can buy their way out of death (49:5–12), "the fate of those who trust in themselves" (49:13). The psalmist, however, trusts in God, who will redeem life from the grave and take the singer to himself (49:15). This, he says, is understanding; those without it are like the beasts that perish (49:20; cf. v. 12).

Put another way, Psalm 49 agrees with Proverbs that while circumstances around us may be complicated and hard to read, the choice before us is more simple than we think. The way we live reveals whether or not we have placed our futures in God's hands. A life spent focused on accumulation shows that

---

20. Haughey, *Virtue and Affluence*, 85–87.

we trust in our own powers to build a hedge against whatever may come—
folly indeed! Likewise, it is folly to think that we can leave that kind of security to our children if we name them in our wills but fail to pass on wisdom,
which allows them to "eat to their heart's content" (Prov. 13:25).

It is not easy to prescribe a course of action based on these principles,
because not everyone has great material possessions to leave and not everyone has descendants to leave it to, but everyone can think of those who can
benefit from our giving. "Longing fulfilled" can be sweet for others as well as
ourselves, and we can become the means by which they are fulfilled—
sweetness indeed. The efforts of some may be focused on matters of food,
shelter, and economic opportunity; others may focus on teaching and counsel, but each is a part of the church that as a corporate body seeks to leave
its legacy of disciplined desire.

Proverbs 14:1–35

¹ THE WISE WOMAN builds her house,
    but with her own hands the foolish one tears hers down.
² He whose walk is upright fears the LORD,
    but he whose ways are devious despises him.
³ A fool's talk brings a rod to his back,
    but the lips of the wise protect them.
⁴ Where there are no oxen, the manger is empty,
    but from the strength of an ox comes an abundant
        harvest.
⁵ A truthful witness does not deceive,
    but a false witness pours out lies.
⁶ The mocker seeks wisdom and finds none,
    but knowledge comes easily to the discerning.
⁷ Stay away from a foolish man,
    for you will not find knowledge on his lips.
⁸ The wisdom of the prudent is to give thought to
        their ways,
    but the folly of fools is deception.
⁹ Fools mock at making amends for sin,
    but goodwill is found among the upright.
¹⁰ Each heart knows its own bitterness,
    and no one else can share its joy.
¹¹ The house of the wicked will be destroyed,
    but the tent of the upright will flourish.
¹² There is a way that seems right to a man,
    but in the end it leads to death.
¹³ Even in laughter the heart may ache,
    and joy may end in grief.
¹⁴ The faithless will be fully repaid for their ways,
    and the good man rewarded for his.
¹⁵ A simple man believes anything,
    but a prudent man gives thought to his steps.
¹⁶ A wise man fears the LORD and shuns evil,
    but a fool is hotheaded and reckless.
¹⁷ A quick-tempered man does foolish things,
    and a crafty man is hated.

¹⁸The simple inherit folly,
>   but the prudent are crowned with knowledge.
¹⁹Evil men will bow down in the presence of the good,
>   and the wicked at the gates of the righteous.
²⁰The poor are shunned even by their neighbors,
>   but the rich have many friends.
²¹He who despises his neighbor sins,
>   but blessed is he who is kind to the needy.
²²Do not those who plot evil go astray?
>   But those who plan what is good find love and
>   faithfulness.
²³All hard work brings a profit,
>   but mere talk leads only to poverty.
²⁴The wealth of the wise is their crown,
>   but the folly of fools yields folly.
²⁵A truthful witness saves lives,
>   but a false witness is deceitful.
²⁶He who fears the LORD has a secure fortress,
>   and for his children it will be a refuge.
²⁷The fear of the LORD is a fountain of life,
>   turning a man from the snares of death.
²⁸A large population is a king's glory,
>   but without subjects a prince is ruined.
²⁹A patient man has great understanding,
>   but a quick-tempered man displays folly.
³⁰A heart at peace gives life to the body,
>   but envy rots the bones.
³¹He who oppresses the poor shows contempt for
>   their Maker,
>   but whoever is kind to the needy honors God.
³²When calamity comes, the wicked are brought down,
>   but even in death the righteous have a refuge.
³³Wisdom reposes in the heart of the discerning
>   and even among fools she lets herself be known.
³⁴Righteousness exalts a nation,
>   but sin is a disgrace to any people.
³⁵A king delights in a wise servant,
>   but a shameful servant incurs his wrath.

Original Meaning

THIS CHAPTER BEGINS with a contrast between the wise and foolish woman, a contrast similar to that made earlier between personified Wisdom and Folly. This allusion to the conclusion of the instructions in Proverbs 9 suggests that we are entering the conclusion of another lesson or section.[1] This allusion also alerts us to look for other references to the speeches of Wisdom and her antitype, Folly. The prominence of the phrase "the fear of the LORD" (14:2, 16, 27; cf. 9:10) leads the reader back to Wisdom's calls to her feast of knowledge (1:20–33; 9:1–12). The rejection of that invitation again is characterized as the mocker (14:6, 9; cf. 9:7–8; 13:1).

A number of words repeat themselves throughout the chapter, so it is not possible to propose an outline that highlights them all. The following outline is offered to help us see the flow of the chapter and its most significant repetitions:

The wise and foolish compared (14:1–7)
The prudent and foolish compared (14:8–15)
Fear of Yahweh, life, and refuge (14:16–27)
Kings, subjects, and servants[2] (14:28–35)

The Wise and Foolish Compared (14:1–7)

VERSES 1 AND 3 go together as signaled by the repetition of "wise" and "fool/foolish"; the difference between the two is explained in verse 2.[3]

14:1. The contrast here between building and tearing down sums up the sages' view of life's choices. Although we all make foolish choices and slap our foreheads from time to time, the sages speak here of our main direction in life, the point on the horizon that we set our sails to reach. As we imagine this wise woman building a house with her hands, attentive readers are drawn to the description of 9:1, that Wisdom has "built her house; she has hewn out its seven pillars." In fact, the first line is nearly identical to that of

---

1. Whybray, *The Composition of the Book of Proverbs*, 100–101, although it is not apparent that the verses that follow are written in the form of an instruction as he claims.

2. After Scoralick, *Einzelspruch und Sammlung*, 223–26; see also Scherer, *Das Weise Wort und Seine Wirkung*, 143–58, who, following different key words, divides this way: vv. 1–2 , 3–9 ("fool"), 10–14 (Heb. *leb*, "heart"), 15–18 ("simple" and "prudent"), 19–22 ("evil"), 23–25, 26–27, 28–35. Following the words "way" and "good" one can also divide: vv. 1–7, 8–13, 14–18, 19–22, 23–25, 26–27, 28–35. No single outline encompasses all of the catchwords; see comments at 14:14.

3. Garrett, *Proverbs*, 140.

9:1, but here it is "a wise *woman*" who builds the house. We may have a transition to the human appropriation of Wisdom's example (cf. 24:3–4; 31:21, 27).[4] The word for "tears down" is used in 11:11 for the city overthrown by the mouth of the wicked (see also "build up" and "tear down" in Jer. 1:10; 24:6; 42:10; 45:4).

14:2. The walk of the wise in 13:20 is here shown to be both upright and God-fearing. The contrast with the fool who "despises" (*bwz;* cf. 1:7) sounds like the prologue, but here the proverb makes explicit that this decision rejects Yahweh, who offers wisdom. We will see that the phrase "the fear of the LORD" occurs more often at the beginning and end of sections in Proverbs, and there are twice as many occurrences in the first half as in the second half of the book. The verbal form "fears the LORD" repeats in 14:16 (cf. 3:7), and two proverbs concerning "the fear of the LORD" show up at 14:26–27.

14:3. The contrast between a fool's "talk" (lit., "mouth") and a wise person's "lips" is linked to their rewards, punishment, or protection. The phrase translated "rod to his back" can also be rendered as "rod of pride." Whereas the rod is the parent's responsibility in 13:24, here it is the consequence of the fool's choice.

14:4. Another metaphoric proverb that stands out from its context reminds the reader of others (10:26; 11:22); the "abundant harvest" echoes that of the poor farmer of 13:23. Translation of the word "empty" or "clean" is difficult. Garrett proposes "grain," so that the line reads, "No oxen, a crib of grain." That is, if you have no ox, you will have more grain in the crib to feed the smaller livestock. But the point of the contrast is that it costs grain to keep an ox, but with the ox there is a greater return on the investment. What is the "crib"—a feeding trough or a storage place? Most agree it is the feeder, so that the empty crib means one has no oxen to feed.[5]

Either way, it is clearly better to have an ox in order to increase harvest, even if it requires some investment in feed. Today, we would speak of operating expenses and the fact that one must spend money to make money. The metaphor also speaks a word of humility, for as one needs the help of the ox to produce a harvest, so one needs the help of wisdom to succeed in life.

14:5. The theme of speaking continues from 14:3, but here the issue is lying and bearing false witness (cf. Ex. 20:16); this proverb contrasts false and faithful witnesses (cf. Prov. 12:17; 13:5). The false witness is (lit.) a "lie

---

4. Van Leeuwen, "Proverbs," 138, takes this as a shift from cosmic to human wisdom, the wise woman emulating the work of wisdom, perhaps "building a house" through childbearing.

5. Murphy, *Proverbs*, 103.

breather" or one who "breathes out lies" (cf. 14:25; also 6:19; 12:17; 19:5, 9). The false witness is like a club or sharp arrow (25:18); in a legal setting, that person will do great harm.

14:6. Verses 6–9 may be gathered around the inclusio of the "mocker," a key word in wisdom's speeches (*leṣ*, 9:7–8, 12). Verses 6–7 are paired around the lack of wisdom in the mocker and the fool, linked by the catchword "knowledge." Clearly the "seeking" of the mocker is a pretense, much like that of the one who feigns riches in 13:7. By comparison, knowledge comes quickly and easily to the one who has cultivated discernment (cf. *nabon* in 14:33), for it is this quality that the mocker lacks.

14:7. This proverb depicts another frustrated search for wisdom, linked with the previous verse; if mockers have not found wisdom, neither will knowledge be found with the fool. The company of fools has already been called harmful (13:20). "Lips" links the saying with 14:3 and continues the theme of foolish talk. "Walk" makes a contrast with the upright walk of 14:2. Woman Folly is also without knowledge (cf. 9:13); it is notable that she calls to those going on their "way" (*derek* in 14:2, 8, 12, 14). Once again, the proverbs recognize that the company one keeps will have its influence. Taken together, one can learn better alone than with the help of a fool.

The Prudent and Foolish Compared (14:8–15)

THE FIRST AND last verses of this section examine the wisdom of the "prudent" (*ʿarum*) and may form a chiastic pattern[6] held together by the catchwords "upright" (14:9, 11, 12), "heart" (14:10, 13, 14), and "way" (14:12, 14).[7] These proverbs develop the theme that appearances are not always as they seem, so that those who choose folly deceive no one but themselves.

14:8. The contrast in this saying between the "wisdom of the prudent" and the "folly of fools" (cf. 14:24) is completed with an unexpected contrast between thoughtful consideration of the way one walks and deception. Both are key themes in this chapter ("way," 14:2, 12, 14; "deceit," 14:2, 5, 25), and the combination here suggests that those who give thought to their way practice honesty in their words and deeds.

14:9. Verses 9 and 10 bring together two different thoughts about community. Even while the goodwill of people who seek peace is to be preferred to mocking, there is still an element of loneliness that comes to all. In verse 9, the contrast stands between a scornful attitude toward reconciliation and

---

6. Garrett, *Proverbs*, 142–43, sets in pairs vv. 8/15, 9/14, 10/13, 11/12 around the theme that life is deceptive and outward joy can end in grief. See comments on 14:14 for a different chiastic structure in 14:14–22.

7. Scoralick, *Einzelspruch und Sammlung*, 223.

a way of life that rarely needs it. The "goodwill" of the second line may refer to God's "favor" (*rason*, so NRSV), leading some to suggest that God mocks the fools with guilt.[8] The TNK takes the Hebrew *ʾašam* to mean that fools have to pay guilt offering money to maintain good relations: "Reparations mediate between fools; between the upright, good will." Ross nicely paraphrases, "Folly offends, but wisdom makes amends."[9]

14:10. This proverb is one of five sayings in this chapter about the "heart" (*leb*; cf. 14:13–14, 30, 33) and presents a rare picture of the inner life and emotions (cf. 14:13; the heart typically is recognized as the seat of intentions). All of life's experiences of bitterness and joy are depicted; the second line intensifies the idea of the first ("no one" is [lit.] "no stranger"). The saying appears to counterbalance the picture of communal harmony of 14:9. Even if it is good when brothers and sisters dwell in unity (Ps. 133:1), our inner lives are finally our own. Even while our lives are shared with others, our deepest thoughts and feelings remain hidden. Only God ultimately knows what is in the heart (Prov. 17:3; 21:2; 24:12).

This verse stands out as unusual, both in its lack of contrast and in its exploration of a psychological matter. It makes no prescription, but its observation does offer the reader wisdom to carry on through life. The saying illustrates how deceptive appearances can be, for there is always more than meets the eye.

14:11. The Hebrew word for "flourish" typically refers to plants that sprout or bud, but it also describes the increase of God's people, both Israel (Isa. 27:6) and the righteous (Ps. 72:7; 92:12–13; Prov. 11:28).[10] "House" and "tent" are paired as synonyms, not as contrasts; instead, "house" reminds the reader of 14:1 and the similar contrast between building and destroying.

14:12. Verses 12 and 13 are linked by the catchword "end" (*ʾaḥᵃrit*). Another contrast of appearance and reality, the key word "way" points to the choices that require foresight, while the "end" describes outcomes, rewards, and reality. The contrast between that which "seems right" (*yšr*; cf. 14:2, 9, 11 with overtones of "straight") and the actual end of "death" reminds the reader of wisdom's words (8:36; 9:18). This saying is repeated in 16:25. A somewhat different contrast is found in 12:15: "The way of a fool seems right to him, but a wise man listens to advice."

14:13. The "heart" sayings (cf. 14:10, 14, 30, 33) taken alone offer a picture of the inner emotional life, but in context of this chapter, they urge us

---

8. Van Leeuwen, "Proverbs," 140.
9. Ross, "Proverbs," 985.
10. *TWOT*, 734 (# 1813).

to take what we see of external appearances with a grain of salt. Facades fall, and time brings changes. This famous proverb is intended to be read in association with 14:12, as the repetition of its "end" in Hebrew (*ʾaḥᵃrit*) indicates. The two parts of the saying embrace the whole of human experience: Laughter may hide present heartache, while joy may in time be replaced by grief. When read alongside 14:10, the first and second lines correspond— the first on the theme of inner hurt, the second on the word "joy." Together they show how even joy has its costs; sometimes joy must remain private and hidden, and often it is temporary.

14:14. The "faithless" are (lit.) "those whose hearts have turned," linking this proverb with the heart saying in 14:13. In the book and in this chapter in particular, there are at least two uses of the word "heart," one for the seat of intentions (as here) and another as the seat of emotions and secret thoughts (vv. 10, 13). It is not clear if a cause-and-effect relationship between intentions and emotions is intended. The key word "way" suggests that this verse also be read with verse 12 as a reflection on final outcomes; the two serve as a frame that complements the long-term viewpoint of verse 13.[11] The word "good" links this verse with 14:19 and 22 and may mark a structure.[12]

14:15. This proverb bears striking similarity to 14:8, indicated by repetition of "consider" (*ᶜarum*), "gives thought" (*yabin*), and "steps" (*ʾašur; derek*, "way" in v. 8). If the folly of fools deceives, one can always find people who are easy to deceive, especially the "simple" who have not learned to distinguish wisdom from folly or right from wrong. These are the naive people that Wisdom tried so desperately to reach (9:4, 16), but Folly was not far away, mimicking Wisdom's call as she followed it with lies (9:13–18). By contrast, "prudent" people do their own thinking and can discern what is true. The "prudent" and the "simple" appear again in 14:18.

---

11. Clifford, *Proverbs*, 142, reads "his deeds" on the basis of Hos. 12:2; so also Murphy, *Proverbs*, 102. If one reads the MT as it is vocalized, "from on it" translates it in parallel with "ways" in the first line.

12. Three uses of the word "good" join together two mirror structures:

v. 14 The *good* have their fill of their deeds
  v. 15 *Prudent* give thought to their steps
    v. 16 *Fools*, arrogant and restless
    v. 17 *Foolish*, quick tempered and crafty
  v. 18 *Prudent* crowned with knowledge
v. 19 The *good* will have evil ones bow
  v. 20 Poor shunned by *neighbors*
  v. 21 Whoever despises *neighbor* sins
v. 22 The *good* find love and faithfulness

Fear of Yahweh, Life, and Refuge (14:16–27)

THIS UNIT IS framed by the phrase "fear of the LORD" and centers on the theme of reward for righteousness, especially that of honorable standing. The "fear of the LORD" proverbs that conclude this unit promise life and security (vv. 26–27).

14:16. Verses 16–17 are linked by images of hair-trigger temper and folly, and they are framed by the simple/prudent distinction in 14:15 and 18. If prudent persons consider their steps (v. 15), they turn from evil (v. 16). The two words that describe the fool do not give themselves easily to translation. (1) "Hotheaded" describes the fool who "meddles" in a quarrel (26:17); the NRSV has "throws off restraint" for this impulsive person. Setting the term in contrast with "fear" in the first line, this person knows no fear but should, for there is a difference between those who consider what they are doing and those who simply react. Egyptian wisdom literature held up the "silent man" as more mature than the "heated man," who could always be counted on to blurt out anger and folly. (2) "Reckless" translates the Hebrew word for "trusting" or confident, as in trusting in Yahweh (but see 11:28; 28:6, where it is used for trusting in riches and self). Some translators use "arrogant and over-confident" for the pair.

14:17. The comparison here is between one who does foolish things on impulse and one who does evil that has been carefully planned and premeditated, a product of scheming. Both ends of the temperament spectrum lead to bad ends. The intended message of the contrast may be that as bad as rash and foolish behavior is, it can be forgiven more easily than premeditated wrong. The word "hated" (*yiśśane'*) appears again in 14:20, translated as "shunned."

14:18. The "simple" and "prudent" of 14:15 reappear, this time receiving the consequences for the choices they made; the simple receive folly as an heirloom while the prudent "are crowned with knowledge." The crown here is more a decoration of valor than a sign of rule. Some propose to emend "inherit folly" to something like "adornment" or "ornament," but strong support is lacking.[13] In both lines of the saying, the rewards not only correspond to the qualities of "folly" and "prudence," they foster and nurture them. The terms remind the reader of the prologue and the speeches of personified Wisdom in chapter 1.

14:19. The only righteous/wicked saying in the chapter, this contrast is again between rewards, using the familiar image of the good serving the evil (cf. 14:14, 22). The word for "bow down" (*šaḥu*) reminds the reader of Joseph's

---

13. Murphy, *Proverbs*, 102.

brothers, who bowed before him when they met in Egypt. The proverb and its imagery offer hope to those who too often see the good bowing down before the power of an evil person.

14:20. Verses 20 and 21 are linked by the repetition of the word "neighbor" and the theme of the "poor" and "needy." When read together, the main contrast is between the self-interested love shown to the rich and the selfless kindness shown to the poor. The contrast in verse 20 points up the inequity; the poor who need friends have none, while those who need little have many. This sharp critique is heightened by the use of the word "neighbor." In ancient Israel, neighbor love included leaving the edges of one's field for gleaning, honest and just dealing, and correction (Lev. 19:9–19). Jesus called anyone who has need a deserving "neighbor" (Luke 10:25–37).

The word "shunned" (śnʾ) is the same word for the crafty who are "hated" (14:17). The two proverbs point out the irony that we "hate" schemers, yet at the same time we can love the rich and shun the poor, perhaps because we have not looked more closely at our inconsistencies. Other sayings about riches make the dispassionate observation that wealth brings with it the promise of security (10:15) and friends (19:4, 6), even while these benefits may be short-lived.

14:21. The implicit point of 14:20 is spelled out here, that it is "sin" to "despise" one's "neighbor" by failing to help in time of need (the word "despise" is used in 14:2 for rejecting Yahweh and his way). Verses 2 and 21 are similar in intent and should be read together, as if to say that to despise one's neighbor is to despise Yahweh. The saying turns the focus away from the experience of the poor in 14:20 to the responsibility of those who help or fail them. The rich may have many friends, but the one who is kind is "blessed" or happy (ʾašre). The theme of kindness to the needy is picked up in 14:31.

14:22. The last of the "good" sayings in this chapter (cf. 14:14, 19, 22) pairs good and evil in a contrast similar to 14:19. Those who plan evil are rewarded with going astray (cf. 7:25; 10:17; 12:26), so it is better to plan for good and enjoy its return in love and faithfulness. The Hebrew of the second line can also be read, "But love and faithfulness, those who plan good." The NIV footnote presents the option of "show love and faithfulness," consistent with other uses of the pair in Proverbs (ḥesed wᵉʾemet, 3:3; 20:28). The ambiguity may be intentional, that those who show these qualities receive their fruits in turn.

14:23. Verses 23–25 are linked by a theme; work brings wealth and even saves life, while mere talk or foolish talk only produces more of the same. The progression of ideas is similar to that found in 14:3–5. In 14:23 the contrast of mere talk and effort (with overtones of toil and sorrow; cf. ʾeṣeb in 10:22) is that of intention and follow through, emptiness and payoff.

14:24. As proof of 14:23, one only needs to look at the wealth of those wise enough to see the difference between talk and action; fools who cannot are left with the foolishness they began with. See 14:8 for another pairing of wisdom with the "folly of fools"; there, each quality is described, while here the focus is on reward, for like 14:23 the proverb ends with pockets empty. The image of a crown as a symbol of honor is associated with wisdom in 1:9 and 4:9.

14:25. In words similar to those of 14:5, this version of the saying contrasts the deception of the "false witness" with the *result* of the "truthful witness," the saving of life. The story of Naboth's vineyard reminds us of the death-dealing false witness. Are we to take a lesson here about the deadly power of lies? In a court of law we depend on the truthful witness to free innocent people, but there is more to the saying. Kidner takes it as a character sketch: "A man who will trim the facts for you will trim them as easily against you."[14] Therefore, "truthful" (*'emet*) can also be translated "faithful."

14:26. Linked together by the phrase "the fear of the LORD," verses 26–27 depict the results and benefits of this basic orientation to life. All four images correspond to the life-saving power of truth in 14:25; "the fear of the LORD" is a "secure fortress," "a refuge," "a fountain of life . . . that turns from death." The "fortress" is a confidence or reliance in which one trusts (the word is derived from *betaḥ*, "trust"). There is no contrast in this proverb, for the one who "fears the LORD" finds protection for self and for children. Given the dangers coming from those who plan evil and lie (14:22–25), a refuge that includes one's offspring, either as members of the household or as heirs who will benefit from an ancestor's trust and virtue, is even more welcome.[15]

14:27. This saying is virtually identical with 13:14, except that there the "teaching of the wise" is "a fountain of life"; here it is the "fear of the LORD," the attitude that makes one teachable. Fear of Yahweh is also one of the *outcomes* of such teaching. The contrast between life and death is familiar, but the surprise comes with the imagery. To animals, the difference between a spring of water and a net is life and death, but the human capacity to worship actually turns us from one to the other.

---

14. Kidner, *Proverbs*, 110.

15. It is not clear whether the reference to one's children should be read in the context of the book of Proverbs only; some reference to the "thousandth generation" may be intended. Clifford, *Proverbs*, 147, finds two meanings: one that God rewards a righteous person's family over generations (Ex. 20:6; Deut. 5:9), another that the parents pass on their own faith and devotion as a legacy.

Kings, Subjects, and Servants (14:28–35)

TWO SAYINGS ABOUT the king form the outer edges of what may be a chiasm:

A v. 28 *King's* glory
   B v. 29 *Exalt* [root *rwm*] folly
      C v. 30 *Heart* at peace gives life
         D vv. 31–32 Sayings on treatment and reward
      C' v. 33 *Heart* a home for wisdom
   B' v. 34 *Exalt* [root *rwm*] a nation
A' v. 35 *King's* delight

Of special interest is the appearance of royal proverbs, for each of the sayings in this section can apply to the responsibilities of monarch and the character qualities that are required. The last previous mention of kings in the book came in 8:15: "By me kings reign and rulers make laws that are just." From here on royal proverbs will continue to appear, often juxtaposed with sayings about "the LORD" (*yhwh*). The heaviest concentration comes at the start of the synonymous proverbs in chapter 16.

14:28. This saying is reminiscent of the ox in 14:4; one cannot claim to be much without acknowledging outside help. The larger the kingdom, the larger the wealth and status, but the second line turns the observation around to show that even a ruler's power is dependent on the quality of relationships in the kingdom. The contrast between many and none raises the question: How does a king lose subjects? The proverbs that follow answer the question. "Glory" translates a rare word typically used of Yahweh, leading readers to look for associations of God and king (Ps. 29:2; 96:9; cf. 1 Chron. 16:29; 2 Chron. 20:21, "splendor of his holiness").

14:29. A variation on 14:17, this proverb can be translated, "Long of nose/nostrils, great understanding; short of spirit/breath, one who exalts folly." The Hebrew word for anger describes a nose that grows hot (perhaps like that of an enraged bull); one short of nose or spirit is "quick-tempered" and associated with folly (cf. 14:17). If it is hard to believe that one displays wisdom by holding one's temper, the reverse picture of uncontrolled anger is certainly convincing.

14:30. Health or healing is mentioned once in every chapter from chapters 12–15 (12:18; 13:17; 14:30; 15:4). The contrast between a heart of "peace" (lit., "healing," *marpe'*) and "envy" (where passion and jealousy meet) is between that which promotes life and that which takes it. In this way, the thought is similar to that of 14:27, here focused on the virtue of contentment. Its lack can lead to intentions that ultimately bring death. Given the picture of the interior life offered in earlier proverbs about the heart (14:10, 13), it appears that the ancients knew that jealousy, passion, and envy eat one from the inside out, thus rotting the bones (cf. 6:34; 27:4).[16]

14:31. The final proverb of this chapter about "the poor" makes explicit what earlier sayings only implied (14:20–21), that mistreatment of the poor is equal to insulting the one who made them and cares for them. To honor the poor is to honor God, and this may be the "plan for good" of 14:22. To insult God is similar to "despising" him (cf. 14:2). Reading them together, we surmise that it is the absence of fear of Yahweh that gives a person the temerity to oppress the poor whom God loves. A similar idea appears in 17:5.

14:32. Verses 32 and 33 both present translation difficulties, in part because the literal reading of the Hebrew text produces meanings at odds with the general tenor of Proverbs. Death is always negative, and wisdom is never found with fools, yet in these sayings both assumptions seem to be contradicted.[17] Might it be that we have here a puzzle to solve, especially since it happens not once but twice, and that near the center of a chiastic structure? If so, we look to see that the surprise yields deeper insight. Verse 32 repeats the image of "refuge" from 14:26; here also the righteous are protected from the "calamity" that brings down the wicked. "The righteous have a refuge," presumably in God, that even death cannot shake.[18] Some interpreters follow the LXX and replace "death" with "integrity" (so NRSV), but the evidence is not compelling.[19]

14:33. The image of personified Wisdom "reposing" or being "at home" (so NRSV, *nuaḥ*; lit., "lodging") in the "heart" of a person may link the heart with the house that wisdom builds in 14:1. As the NIV footnote indicates, there is an alternate reading that follows the LXX, "but in the heart of fools she is not known." However, the Hebrew has no negative and reads "in the midst of fools," leaving it ambiguous whether wisdom is found *with* individual fools or *among* them when gathered. Either way, when we read with the Hebrew, Wisdom is with both the discerning and fools, yet she only stays with the former. Clearly Wisdom is seen calling out to all earlier in the book (chs. 1 and 9), but not all heed her call. She abides with those who

---

16. R. E. Clements translates "envy" (*qin'ah*) as "bad feelings": "A calm disposition gives life to the body, but bad feelings make the body ill" (*Wisdom in Theology* [Grand Rapids: Eerdmans, 1992], 79).

17. Garrett, *Proverbs*, 147.

18. Kidner, *Proverbs*, 111, allowing that the Israelites did not have "too advanced a doctrine of death," recognized that Job shows occasional glimpses of hope and that the righteous of the Psalms commit themselves to God in death (Ps. 31:15 after Delitzsch).

19. Clifford, *Proverbs*, 142, reads with the Heb. "death," citing the Dead Sea scroll 4QProv[b] in support. For arguments against reading with the LXX, see Heim, *Like Grapes of God Set in Silver*, 189–91.

respond to her, and it is her presence that makes for a peaceful and healthy heart (14:30).

We may find a solution to the puzzle of this strange pair of proverbs by reading them together, noting that the righteous have a safe place in death and that wisdom has a place to lodge in the heart of the discerning. In other words, give wisdom a place to dwell, and the righteous will have a place to hide. Might wisdom also be made known as the wicked are brought down? This certainly corresponds to the images of life and death found in chapters 1 and 9. In addition, we will see in the Bridging Contexts section that these two proverbs also juxtapose the matters of individual righteousness with collected folly and wickedness, perhaps anticipating the similar juxtaposition in 14:34 and 35.

14:34. Verses 34 and 35 are linked by the theme of shame. To be righteous lifts a nation's reputation high, but sin brings it disgrace (cf. Ezek. 36:16–21). This verse springs a trap, for the second line starts to read like Proverbs 14:22b, where *ḥesed* means "love" (thus yielding here, "love of a people, sin"), though it takes on the rarer meaning "disgrace" or "shame" (cf. 25:10; also Lev. 20:17; Ps. 52:1), even while it exposes a sinful people's true love.

14:35. The second of the royal sayings (cf. 14:28) and the second of a pair on shame (cf. 14:34), this proverb implies that a good kingdom requires good citizens, righteous people, and prudent servants. Both king and citizenry can profit from this counsel. A king will want to choose wise counselors, not merely those who flatter and say what the king hopes to hear. A people may wish for good character qualities in their leaders, but they ought to hold themselves to the same high standards. This may be a jab at the common assumption that honest and forthright character is always a good idea for someone else. The words for "wise" and "shameful" are the same as in 10:1, used there in reference to a son. We must be faithful members of our families and our communities, neither excluding the other.

CONNECTIONS. As we have already seen, the many repetitions of words and phrases that draw the individual proverbs into clusters allow no overarching structure to emerge. Rather, the series of connections are more like the homespun artwork many of us made at summer schools and camps. Some will remember driving nails into a board and wrapping strings of yarn around the nails in all sorts of combinations, the lines of the yarn forming a pattern. So here, the many lines of catchword and metaphoric connection tie together varied themes, outlining a pattern of wise and godly living. As the individual proverbs touch on the themes of truth telling, faithfulness, and kindness, the lines of connection also shape a pattern of right relationship with neighbors, rulers, and Yahweh.

(1) One way to examine these connections is to look for themes that tie clusters together. So 14:1–7 speaks of building with the hands, walking with the feet, and speaking with the mouth. These verses show how talk that carries truth and knowledge builds and protects, while false talk brings punishment (14:3). But why is a proverb about the work of the ox set among these sayings (14:4)? Readers are left to mull over this puzzle and decide on the connection. To my mind, the empty manger symbolizes the mocker's lack of wisdom and the fool's lack of knowledge (14:6–7), showing that the wisdom of truthful speaking (14:5) is as necessary for living as an ox is for a good harvest. Implicit also is a word about interdependence: People cannot make their way on their own, and those who try, deceiving and breaking down personal relationships in other ways, sever themselves from relationship with Yahweh (14:2). The capacity of honesty to build relationships is a principle that works just as effectively today as in Bible times.

(2) The next collection (14:8–15) shows that people who craft deceptions clearly have not thought through the consequences of their actions. Prudence is the ability to consider one's ways and their outcomes, and this capacity for forethought loosely ties the sayings together. Fools mock at practices of honesty and reconciliation, believing perhaps that self-made people do not need to stay in good standing with others as long as they get what they want. But as the heart has its reasons that are not always known or revealed (14:10, 13), so this appearance of independent trail blazing seems right until its hidden end of death is finally revealed (14:12). Today, as then, the lone ranger is more myth than reality. Appearances, the prudent person learns, can deceive.

(3) Prudence is associated with wisdom in the next cluster (14:16–27). The prudent are crowned with knowledge (14:18) as a form of honor, and they will even receive honor from evil persons (14:19); fools, by their quick-tempered and scheming ways, alienate others and God (14:16–17). This emphasis on standing in community extends to the way one treats the poor, for diligence in earning wealth must be matched with equal diligence in faithfulness to neighbors (14:20–24). Security and abundant life in the end come not from any quest for gain but in the fear of Yahweh (14:26–27). Prudence and faithfulness, then, are two complementary aspects of wisdom, for the first looks out for benefits to the self while the second considers the benefits of one's behavior for others. Wisdom balances self-care with loving self-sacrifice.

(4) Even kings must recognize the social aspects of wisdom, and so two proverbs about the king frame a recapitulation of the chapter's themes (14:28–

35). While it is common knowledge that a king's reputation stands or falls by the size of his people and armies, the proverb also implies that the king is dependent on those "little people," perhaps more than he realizes (14:28). Thus, the virtues of patience, understanding, contentment, and kindness make a leader strong, not weak (14:29–31). To abuse the poor is to despise Yahweh, who should be feared (14:31; cf. 14:2); conversely, righteousness brings with it a refuge that extends even to one's death (14:32; cf. 14:26–27).

Wisdom makes herself known, whether or not she is invited, as she builds great nations and teaches lowly servants (14:33–35; cf. 14:1). Kings, servants, and subjects all do well to be taught by wisdom, not only to learn the practice of honesty, prudence, and faithfulness with one another, but also to bring delight to the King of all creation (14:35). Therefore, the reader learns that the book of Proverbs is directed not only to the wise son (that young person, male or female, learning family responsibility from parents), but also to the wise citizen and the wise king.[20]

The personal and the political. The collection of proverbs in chapter 14 shows us that the personal always intersects with the political. Or we might say the personal and political intertwine—what is good for the individual is good for the people. Therefore, the house that wisdom builds and indwells is both the heart and the nation (14:33–34). These sayings encourage us to look at both and see their interrelation. To talk about kings and politics is to talk about the moral health of a nation, measured in biblical terms by its treatment of the poor.

The same concern for justice and mercy found here can be seen in the Prophets and in Psalms. In particular, Psalms 45–53 also intertwine the themes of wisdom and just rule. The king is praised not only for splendor and majesty but also for truth, humility, righteousness, justice, and loving righteousness and hating wickedness (Ps. 45:3–7). While this just rule provides prosperity for the nation, "God is our refuge and strength" sounds the counterpoint: "Though everything give way, we will not fear" (46:1–2). Yahweh is the King of the earth to whom all the kings belong (47:3, 7, 9)—kings of the earth who fear the city that God makes secure (48:4–8).

These psalms that praise Yahweh as ruler of heaven and earth are followed by psalms of wisdom and lament. Psalm 49 claims to speak words of wisdom in the form of proverb and riddle, exposing the folly of trust in riches or trust in self and explaining that wealth helps no one when death comes calling. The entire nation is called to repentance in Psalm 50, particularly the

---

20. Throughout the ancient Near East, kings sought wisdom from the gods to rule rightly and successfully. See L. Kalugila, *The Wise King: Studies in Royal Wisdom as Divine Revelation in the Old Testament and Its Environment* (CBOT 15; Lund: Liber Läromedel/Gleerup, 1980).

wicked, who "hate ... instruction" and use the mouth for evil and tongue for deceit, thus forgetting God (50:17–20). Psalm 51 quotes the repentance and confession of the king as he prays to learn wisdom in the inmost place (51:6). Next comes a denunciation of the wicked man who plots destruction with a deceitful tongue (52:1–4), quoting evildoers or fools who say, "There is no God" (53:1). In sum, Psalms 45–48 appear to be gathered as national songs that celebrate the king, the Lord, and the city where both dwell and rule in righteousness. Psalms 49–53 set that righteous rule in the context of wisdom and its enemies, deceit and foolish atheism.

The ordering of these psalms suggests that Israel believed God's rule could be embodied in a just and righteous rule of king and city, but they also knew that evil could lead anyone astray, even the king. The seductive powers of riches and double-dealing can turn the heart against God and neighbor alike, and these psalms, in harmony with the proverbs, describe that turning astray as folly, the rejection of wisdom's instruction. Like these psalms, the proverbs in Proverbs 14 and the entire book show that the personal and political dimensions of righteousness are inseparable. The personal virtues that build a society exalt a nation and delight a king (14:34–35), and their absence harms everyone, especially the evildoer.

Refuge and "the fear of the LORD." To summarize, the theme of just and righteous government in Proverbs 14 follows the same trajectory as that of the Psalms, holding up the just society while recognizing that it will always be under attack from without and within. If there is any refuge to be had from this attack, it is found in "the fear of the LORD"; all four references to Yahweh in this chapter use that phrase. While the first two define that fear as walking uprightly (14:2, 16), the pair at 14:26–27 name the benefits of confidence, refuge, and life that accompany it. In other words, the proverbs of this chapter speak of fear of Yahweh as right living that results in safety and trust.[21] There is a surprise reversal in the idea that in fearing one finds security, but the sayings reminds us that fear of Yahweh encompasses a wide range of human responses. This fear is more than emotion; it is also reverence and obedience that leads one to walk rightly before God. It is more than the upright life; it is also a safeguard against all that would cause us fear.[22]

The human person is meant to live in fear of God; if we forsake this fear that brings us safety, we will be afraid of everything else. If we direct our fears

---

21. There do not seem to be other occurrences in the book, but the refuge is a key image in Psalms, usually in the context of enemies (Ps. 46:2; 61:4; 62:8).

22. Clements has proposed that "fear of the LORD" was first associated with the worship of Israel but was later extended to have a wider and more universal appeal (*Wisdom in Theology*, 58–64).

to the one we can trust, all other fears will not be able to storm the strong tower. This basic insight of wisdom does not come naturally but must be learned: "Come, my children, listen to me; I will teach you the fear of the LORD" (Ps. 34:11). This psalm recommends turning from speaking lies and other evils, using words similar to that of the proverbs: "The eyes of the LORD are on the righteous. . . . The LORD redeems his servants; no one will be condemned who takes refuge in him" (34:15, 22). This psalm brings the two aspects of this fear together. We must turn from evil toward righteousness, but also trust that God will protect the righteous from those who would do evil to them. One might fear the schemes and attacks of the wicked, but the psalms and proverbs recommend "fear of the LORD" instead.

While the promise of these proverbs is confident and assured, the sages who brought them together were anything but naive; their view of final outcomes was shaped by the realization that God-fearers are never exempt from pain or persecution. The refuge of Yahweh is no guarantee against harm. Barbara Brown Taylor urges preachers to remember this when speaking of the Scriptures:

> If the Bible is not a book about admirable men and women, neither is it a book about a conventionally admirable God. It is a book in which wonderful and terrible things happen by the power of an almighty God, whose steadfast love for us does not seem to preclude scaring the living daylights out of us from time to time.
>
> People who claim to have no fear of the Lord have clearly not read the Bible. Someone needs to sit them down with a selected reading list that includes the ten plagues sent upon Egypt, the murder of Sisera, the slaughter of the Amalekites and the prophets of Baal, and perhaps the mauling of forty-two boys by two she-bears in the name of the Lord. If they protest that these are stories about what God does to bad people, then they should read the book of Job straight through, and if they insist that their God is the God of the New Testament, then they should study the passion narratives in each of the four gospels and see what happens to those who obey the will of God. We can run but we can't hide: if early death on a cross is how God rewards a well-beloved son who knows no sin, then what hope is there for the rest of us?[23]

The point is well taken that fear of Yahweh and its refuge exempt no one from danger, for the well-loved Son in his fear of God found a refuge in death (14:32). His resurrection becomes a refuge for us all.

---

23. B. Brown Taylor, *The Preaching Life* (Cambridge/Boston: Cowley Publications, 1993), 59.

Contemporary Significance

TEACHING STRATEGIES FOR Proverbs 14 could take one proverb and unpack the dynamics of comparison and contrast, or one could take a section (following one of the outlines above) and demonstrate the connections of theme and image. Still another approach, the one I follow here, brings together proverbs with a common phrase or theme (such as the four "fear of the LORD" proverbs) and expounds them, keeping the insights of the rest of the chapter close at hand. We have seen that fear of Yahweh is found in proverbs that speak of walking rightly (14:2, 16) and taking refuge (14:26–27) as two sides of the same coin. We will look at these in reverse order.

Taking refuge. Having spoken of the fear of Yahweh that redirects our fears of life's dangers, especially those that come from enemies, we also have seen how the language and outlook of the proverbs resonate with that of the psalms. With a view to final outcomes, the wise person looks to God when under attack. After suffering a series of persecutions of his own, the Hungarian composer Zoltán Kodály found a paraphrase of Psalm 55 written by a sixteenth-century poet and preacher from his hometown and set it to music. The lyrics highlight the similarities between the themes of the proverbs and the psalms:

> When as King David sore was afflicted,
> By those he trusted basely deserted,
> In his great anger bitterly grieving,
> Thus to Jehovah pray'd he within his heart.

> Better it were to dwell in the desert,
> Better to hide me deep in the forest,
> Than live with wicked liars and traitors
> Who will not suffer that I should speak the truth.

> Violence and strife rage fierce in the city,
> Mischief and malice, envy and sorrow,
> Boasting of riches, pride of possession;
> Ne'er in all the world saw I such deceivers!

> So in Jehovah I will put my trust,
> God is my stronghold and my comforter;
> I cast my burden alway, alway on the Lord.
> He will not suffer the righteous to be mov'd.

> As for the righteous, Thou doest preserve them,
> They that shew mercy, shelter find in Thee.

Those that are humble Thou doest raise on high.
Those that are mighty Thou scatter'st and destroyest.

These words King David wrote in his Psalter,
Fifty and fifth of prayers and of praises,
And for the faithful, bitterly grieving,
As consolation, I from it made this song.[24]

As Psalm 55 encouraged this preacher in time of trouble, so the proverbs hope to instill a similar outlook in us that "the faithless will be fully repaid for their ways, and the good man rewarded for his" (14:14). We can succumb to a cynical resignation that there is no point in doing good when rewards of bonus and promotion go to those who don't seem to care. We may not decide to compromise or cut corners ourselves, but we can lose our hope that the good way is the best way to life's rewards when we see they pass us by. We can end up dragging ourselves through our days, hopeless, angry, or sullen. We may need the encouragement of friends when our own trust runs low, and we may need to speak up for ourselves (a concept not foreign to these proverbs). They not only teach wisdom but also to use these observations drawn from everyday life to encourage those who have begun to walk wisdom's way to stay on that path.

Walking rightly. Moreover, even if we are not facing such discouragements ourselves, a growing awareness of the pervasive presence of evil described in the proverbs can also sensitize us to harsh treatment of others. The contrasts in Proverbs 14 pit fairness and truthful speaking against evil scheming and lying, reminding readers of the prophets. Isaiah's vision of a world restored not only gave sight to the blind and hearing to the deaf, but showed the humble and needy how to rejoice in Yahweh. For "the ruthless will vanish, the mockers will disappear, and all who have an eye for evil will be cut down—those who with a word make a man out to be guilty, who ensnare the defender in court and with the false testimony deprive the innocent of justice" (Isa. 29:20–21). Jeremiah castigated those who defrauded for gain: "Like cages full of birds, their houses are full of deceit; they have become rich and powerful and have grown fat and sleek" (Jer. 5:27–28a).

If, in ancient days, one could use the legal system to cheat the poor, we must ask ourselves if similar temptations present themselves today—and, of course, the poor tell us they do. Whether such cheating takes the form of negligent landlords or corporate restructuring that benefits stockholders at the cost of low-income jobs, kindness to the needy (14:21) requires justice first

---

24. Zoltán Kodály, *Psalmus Hungaricus*, in *Program Notes* (Grant Park Festival; June 18, 2000).

and charity second. Whoever "oppresses the poor shows contempt for their Maker, but whoever is kind to the needy honors God" (14:31).

In our day, questions of social justice turn off some believers because they are convinced that such talk is a form of theological liberalism, but a read through a book like *Cry Justice*[25] and its collection of the many biblical texts about rich and poor can put such fears to rest. For those who are concerned and want to get involved, the prospect is daunting, for how can one person do anything about the enormity of individual and corporate greed that is out there? While the answers are not simple, a commitment toward exploring them makes a good start, and the proverbs offer some suggestions.

(1) We can offer kindness as recommended in Proverbs 14 by simply being the friend the needy are so often without (14:20). This verse astutely observes that the rich make many friends, but it is costly to be a friend to someone who is poor. A quick look at our schedules may tell us that while we do not actively oppress anyone, neither do we go out of our way to help. One way to test our commitment to biblical values is to ask how much of our thoughts and energies are directed toward helping others in need, working for justice, and alleviating hunger. Another is to gauge how much time we actually spend in contact with people in need.

As I write, a heat wave has descended on Chicago that is almost as strong as the one that killed over a hundred people in 1995. Since that time a system of emergency services has been set up to check on elderly persons in stifling apartments and bring them to cooling centers in their neighborhoods. The mayor made a speech reminding the people of Chicago that the system is set up for those who do not have anyone to look after them. "Please," he pleaded, "don't call us to go over and visit your family and friends. Check on them yourselves!"

What is true in an emergency situation is just as true for the ongoing concern of poverty. Jesus had an answer for the one who asked, "Who is my neighbor?" (Luke 10:25–37). He also said that we are to think of those who are hungry, thirsty, sick, or in prison as more than our neighbor; they are the very presence of Jesus himself (Matt. 25:31–46). "For you know the grace of our Lord Jesus Christ, that though he was rich, yet for your sakes he became poor, so that you through his poverty might become rich" (2 Cor. 8:9) are words that Paul spoke in the context of caring for those in need. "Whoever is kind to the needy honors God" (Prov. 14:31).

(2) We can offer kindness by refusing to despise a neighbor in need. In the context of Proverbs 14, the word "despise" most likely refers to the atti-

25. R. Sider, ed., *Cry Justice: The Bible on Hunger and Poverty* (Downers Grove, Ill.: Inter-Varsity Press; New York: Paulist Press, 1980).

tude that leads one to defraud and cheat another, but we might also ask ourselves to what degree we look down on poorer neighbors as somehow lacking in the intelligence or drive that would bring them a better job or living situation. "God helps those who help themselves" is not found among the biblical proverbs, and it should never be used as a club to beat down those who do not have the access to education and opportunity that many of us have had. Our kindness to others begins with the attitude we bring to our relationship with them. When we find ourselves saying, "There but for the grace of God go I," we had better believe that we are talking about grace, not our own merits or advantages.

We can begin to show kindness to the poor by recognizing that they exist. I have often heard the story of Jairus and the woman with the hemorrhage preached with the accent on Jairus's fear that there would not be enough time for his daughter if Jesus took time to listen to the woman (Mark 5:21–43). But what did this penniless woman think just a few minutes earlier when she saw her last hope walking away with the well-to-do leader of the synagogue? Time was running out for her, and yet she would not call out to him. Could it be because she knew that the poor are shunned, even by their neighbors? Did Jesus look at Jairus when he said *"Daughter*, your faith has healed you"? Today, that acknowledgment of the poor can come as we make room for their needs in our budgets of time and money—both our personal budgets and that of our churches. Moreover, remembering the emphasis on life together in the sayings on neighbors and kings, we can ask ourselves how well our elected officials are doing in remembering the needy.

One final thought: I also notice that in this story, the woman is filled with fear and Jesus must tell Jairus not to be afraid. It is part of human nature to be afraid. We fear that which is bigger than we are. We fear when we face what we cannot control, what we cannot manage; it is an accurate assessment. Yet there is fear that rules us and leaves us feeling helpless, lost, alone, and there is a fear that leads to faith. Our fears can become signposts or better invitations to faith, redirecting our fears. In other words when we are afraid, we might ask ourselves, "If I'm afraid of this, what does God want me to believe about him?" If we fear him, we are *not* afraid; we are learning to have faith. Our fears can also become incentives toward neighbor love, for they can remind us to ask what someone with fewer advantages than ourselves might fear. For them, as well as for us, "in the fear of the LORD one has strong confidence, and one's children will have a refuge" (14:26 NRSV).

Proverbs 15:1–33

❧

¹ A GENTLE ANSWER turns away wrath,
   but a harsh word stirs up anger.
² The tongue of the wise commends knowledge,
   but the mouth of the fool gushes folly.
³ The eyes of the LORD are everywhere,
   keeping watch on the wicked and the good.
⁴ The tongue that brings healing is a tree of life,
   but a deceitful tongue crushes the spirit.
⁵ A fool spurns his father's discipline,
   but whoever heeds correction shows prudence.
⁶ The house of the righteous contains great treasure,
   but the income of the wicked brings them trouble.
⁷ The lips of the wise spread knowledge;
   not so the hearts of fools.
⁸ The LORD detests the sacrifice of the wicked,
   but the prayer of the upright pleases him.
⁹ The LORD detests the way of the wicked
   but he loves those who pursue righteousness.
¹⁰ Stern discipline awaits him who leaves the path;
   he who hates correction will die.
¹¹ Death and Destruction lie open before the LORD—
   how much more the hearts of men!
¹² A mocker resents correction;
   he will not consult the wise.
¹³ A happy heart makes the face cheerful,
   but heartache crushes the spirit.
¹⁴ The discerning heart seeks knowledge,
   but the mouth of a fool feeds on folly.
¹⁵ All the days of the oppressed are wretched,
   but the cheerful heart has a continual feast.
¹⁶ Better a little with the fear of the LORD
   than great wealth with turmoil.
¹⁷ Better a meal of vegetables where there is love
   than a fattened calf with hatred.
¹⁸ A hot-tempered man stirs up dissension,
   but a patient man calms a quarrel.

¹⁹The way of the sluggard is blocked with thorns,
  but the path of the upright is a highway.
²⁰A wise son brings joy to his father,
  but a foolish man despises his mother.
²¹Folly delights a man who lacks judgment,
  but a man of understanding keeps a straight course.
²²Plans fail for lack of counsel,
  but with many advisers they succeed.
²³A man finds joy in giving an apt reply—
  and how good is a timely word!
²⁴The path of life leads upward for the wise
  to keep him from going down to the grave.
²⁵The LORD tears down the proud man's house
  but he keeps the widow's boundaries intact.
²⁶The LORD detests the thoughts of the wicked,
  but those of the pure are pleasing to him.
²⁷A greedy man brings trouble to his family,
  but he who hates bribes will live.
²⁸The heart of the righteous weighs its answers,
  but the mouth of the wicked gushes evil.
²⁹The LORD is far from the wicked
  but he hears the prayer of the righteous.
³⁰A cheerful look brings joy to the heart,
  and good news gives health to the bones.
³¹He who listens to a life-giving rebuke
  will be at home among the wise.
³²He who ignores discipline despises himself,
  but whoever heeds correction gains understanding.
³³The fear of the LORD teaches a man wisdom,
  and humility comes before honor.

Original
Meaning

THIS FINAL SET of the contrasting proverbs in chapters 10–15 comes to a crescendo with the frequent appearance of Yahweh proverbs, particularly in the closing of 15:25–33. Yahweh knows the thoughts and actions of the wicked and righteous and responds accordingly. Looking back to the prologue (1:7), the last proverb of chapter 15 commends "the fear of the LORD" as an instructor in wisdom (15:33). No obvious structure or outline shows itself in this chapter, although there is some sense that the second half recapitulates the first.[1] The outline proposed here shows that some proverbs serve as links that tie sections together (15:8, 11) and that smaller clusters can be imbedded in larger ones.

Words and Speech (15:1–8)
Yahweh Sayings (15:8–11)
Death and Hatred/Life and Love (15:11–18)
    "heart" sayings (15:11–15)
    cheerfulness (15:13–17)
    eating and feasting (15:14–17)
    "good" sayings on contentment (15:15–17)
    "better than" sayings (15:16–17)

Sluggards and Fools (15:19–24)
    "joy" sayings (15:20–23)

Yahweh Sayings (15:25–33)
    "hear" sayings (15:28–32)

Words and Speech (15:1–8)

IN THIS CLUSTER of sayings gathered around the theme of speaking and listening, proverbs about the soothing reply, teaching, healing, and even prayer are included.

15:1. The first saying of this chapter picks up the topic of anger from 14:35 and turns the focus toward speech that turns away wrath (cf. 15:2). It may be that this proverb, like the one before, speaks to the king's wrath, but the advice is well taken in most situations; just as a gentle response calms anger, a hard word provokes it. The Bible has many examples; Nabal's inhospitality and Abigail's appeal is probably the most famous (1 Sam. 25:1–35). However, the gentle answer is not weak; a soft tongue is powerful enough to break bones (Prov. 25:15).

15:2. Another saying on the topic of speaking, this one distinguishes the wise and foolish by what their mouths produce. We rarely use the word "gushes" for something good, whether we are speaking of blood or emotion, and this is also true when we are talking about folly. The image com-

---

1. Whybray, *The Composition of the Book of Proverbs*, 106, sees two halves in 15:5–19 and 20–33, the second half resembling the instructions of chs. 1–9. Garrett, *Proverbs*, sees two corresponding sections in 15:1–17 and 15:18–16:8 based on the verbal links between 15:1 and 18 ("wrath," *ḥemah*, and "anger," *ʾap*) and the similarity of proverbs on true wealth (15:17 and 16:8). Heim, *Like Grapes of Gold Set in Silver*, 192–205, divides at 15:18–19 but sees a number of smaller clusters throughout the ch. (vv. 1–4, 5–12, 13–18, 19–23, 24–27, 28–33).

pares speech to water or some other rushing liquid—too much spouting out too quickly, neither controlled nor contained. Knowledge, by contrast, is (lit.) "made good" by the tongue of the wise, perhaps by taking the time and effort to make it attractive; when it comes out, its product is worth keeping. It comes out in moderation, not excess, so that nothing is lost.[2]

15:3. Human tongues speak and heavenly eyes watch. "Wicked" and "good" is a merism, spanning the range of human behavior to make the point that God not only sees all but judges all. The Hebrew root for "good" (*tob*) links the saying with the "tongue of the wise" in 15:2, taking speech as representative of a person's intentions and way of life. The emphasis is on God's knowledge, and recompense is only implied. By contrast, in speaking of the Egyptian god Thoth, *The Instruction of Amenemope* warns: "His eyes encircle the Two Lands; when he sees one who cheats with his finger, he carries his livelihood off in the flood."[3] But Proverbs rarely draws a direct line between outcomes and God's action; the exception in 22:12 proves the rule.

15:4. This proverb on speaking contrasts the "tongue that brings healing" or promotes health with the tongue that "crushes the spirit" (cf. 15:1–2). Speech that does damage is deceitful; by implication, then, speech that heals is truthful. One is a "tree of life," the other is literally twisted like a crooked branch. The tree of life is only found in Proverbs; Genesis 2:9; 3:22–24; and Revelation 2:7; 22:2 (cf. Ezek. 47:12). In Proverbs, it is associated with wisdom (Prov. 3:18), the fruit of the righteous (11:30), and a longing fulfilled (13:12). "Healing" (*marpe*) or perhaps calming (after the related Heb. root *rph*) is typically associated with wise speech (4:20–22; 12:18; 13:17; 14:30) and is mentioned once in every chapter from 12–15.

15:5. Even the most helpful speech must be accepted in order to do its work; as in the instructions, the one who rejects "discipline" (*musar*, cf. 1:7) is a fool. Here the discipline is paired with "correction," stressing that aspect of teaching central to the chapter (cf. 15:10, 12, 31–33). Wisdom to speak and teach others is learned in listening, a sign of "prudence" (cf. 12:16, 12:23; 13:16; 14:8). Note the similarity of 15:5–6 to 10:1–2, possibly marking the beginning and ending sections of the contrasting proverbs.

---

2. The emendation of the Heb. for "commends" (NIV) to "drips" (NRSV) in order to create a better parallel with "pours out" is unnecessary. The parallelism of Proverbs often uses *difference* and unusual pairings to communicate meaning. A similar contrast of key terms appears in 15:14.

3. *The Instruction of Amenemope*, in Lichtheim, *AEL* (XVII:10), 156. The phrase "cheats with his finger" refers to a dishonest scribe.

15:6. The first righteous/wicked saying in the chapter (cf. 15:9, 28–29) contrasts possessions with payback; one is "treasure," the other, "trouble."[4] Only the righteous receive rewards that one would like to keep and share. The saying in 10:2 is the reverse of this picture; the wicked may gain treasures, but they profit little in matters of life and death.

15:7. Like the speech saying of 15:2, this proverb contrasts the "knowledge" of the "wise" with the lack of that knowledge in the "hearts of fools." An intimate connection between lips and the heart is assumed, for the sages knew that what we say has its source in our hearts. Here the idea is extended; the desire to spread knowledge as an antidote to folly is the mark of a wise person and a caring teacher. Sayings about the "heart" gather in 15:11–15, 28–30. The reference to prayer that pleases Yahweh in 15:8 adds this proverb to the cluster; it is treated below as one of the Yahweh proverbs in 15:8–11.

Yahweh Sayings (15:8–11)

THREE SAYINGS ABOUT Yahweh's view of human affairs form an envelope around a proverb about final outcomes.

15:8. The second of the righteous/wicked sayings (cf. 15:6) is about proper worship. Sacrifice in itself is not spoken against here, nor does the saying hold up prayer as superior. Sacrifice by itself is nothing; it is the "sacrifice *of the wicked*" that Yahweh finds abominable. Like right sacrifices, prayers are pleasing when offered by those whose walk is upright or straight (cf. Ps. 51:16–17). Worship may never be divorced from our day-to-day actions (Isa. 1:10–17; 29:13; 59:1–2). What is detestable is "an abomination to the LORD," as echoed in the next proverb (Prov. 15:9; cf. 15:26; 16:5).

15:9. In this second saying that uses the words "detests" and "wicked," the truth of 15:8 is made more explicit. The scene shifts from acts of worship to the affairs of daily life, affirming that they are inseparable. "The LORD detests the way of the wicked," yet we should probably not assume a "hate sin, love the sinner" contrast is at work here. Instead, the proverb contrasts between two paths, indicated by use of the words "way" and "pursue" (the contrast extending to 15:10).

15:10. There are two connections with 15:9: the one who leaves the "path" of righteousness (cf. "way" in v. 9a) "hates" discipline (cf. "loves" in v. 9b). The warning is not just for the wicked; whoever wishes to stay on the path had better prepare for correction or reproof (cf. 15:5, 12, 31–33). How-

---

4. Clifford, *Proverbs*, 149–51, contrasts possessions safe in the house with the harvest in the field that was not gathered: "In the house of the righteous are great possessions, but the harvest of the wicked is in peril."

ever unpleasant it may be, correction is preferable to death. There are echoes of wisdom's speeches here (1:29–32; 8:32–36; 9:6–8).[5]

15:11. "How much more" (a fortiori) sayings are infrequent in Proverbs. Instead of arguing via contrasts, they take an accepted truth and apply it to a new situation. In this case, all agree that Yahweh knows, sees, and understands the mysteries of "Death and Destruction" (cf. "die" in 15:10). If these causes of uncertainty and terror are simple matters to Yahweh, easily examined and explained, then it is no great wonder that he searches and knows the secrets of the human heart.[6] Whereas in 15:3 Yahweh seems to be watching in every place, examining everyone's deeds, here the interior regions of the human person are exposed. God not only looks on behaviors, but the intentions that motivate them (cf. 1 Sam. 16:7).

Death and Hatred/Life and Love (15:11–18)

VERSE 11 IS DISCUSSED above, for it also fits in the previous cluster, functioning as a hinge. In this cluster, each proverb but one (15:12) uses the word "heart." Perhaps the cluster includes the first use of "heart" in 15:7; those sayings that do not use the word are similar in theme, especially on the reactions of love and hate toward either wisdom or wicked behaviors (15:8–10). The many overlapping themes of this chapter weave a rich tapestry of life lived in joy and contentment, yet death, poverty, and oppression are always close at hand (15:11, 15). The sayings do not intend to justify the plight of the poor but rather to restrain readers from taking advantage of them for gain.

15:12. The "mocker" appears in wisdom's speeches and a number of individual sayings (1:22; 9:7–8; 13:1; 14:6, 9). Like the one who leaves the path (15:10), the mocker "resents" (lit., "does not love") correction and proves it by failing to "consult the wise." One becomes wise through both association and instruction, and the mocker avoids both. If the two sayings on correction form a frame around 15:11, the intent may be to assure readers that perverse intentions of the heart are not always secret (cf. 14:10, 13). Mockers make their intentions known right away.

---

5. "Stern discipline" uses the word for evil or trouble (ra^c); it is not clear whether the discipline will lead the wanderer from death or bring it. The question is whether to translate v. 10a as a nonverbal clause, "discipline is hard" (Clifford, *Proverbs*, 149; "bad in the eyes of," cf. 1 Sam. 29:7) or as an adjective, "severe punishment" (Whybray, *Proverbs*, 228); the latter is more likely.

6. The NIV note records the Heb. terms used here. To the Israelites, *Sheol* and *Abaddon* were synonyms for the place of the dead (cf. Job 26:6). *Abaddon* comes from the Heb. word for destruction. Both *Sheol* and *Abaddon* are (lit.) "before the LORD," leading the translators to add "lie open" for clarity (cf. TNK, "lie exposed").

15:13. Both verses 13 and 14 begin with the word "heart"; verse 13 is (lit.) "a heart of joy makes good the face." This proverb repeats phrases taken from 15:2 ("makes good" of knowledge) and 15:4 (the "crushed spirit"; cf. 17:22; 18:14). The saying sounds like a health and medicine report from the evening news, but it means to show that the difference between a heart that rejoices and one full of sorrow can be seen on the face and sensed in the spirit. This proverb does not contrast external joy with internal sorrow but rather the wide range of our emotional states and their effects. Again (cf. 15:12), that which is deep within often does leak out.

15:14. Like the previous proverb, this one also begins with the word "heart." The pairing of "knowledge" with "mouth of fools" and "folly" is echoed in 15:2; a similar comparison of heart and mouth is made in 15:28. Whereas folly and evil gush from the mouth in those proverbs, here the mouth of the fool feeds on folly, perhaps its own. One can choose to act on the basis of an understanding heart or an unthinking appetite. The proverb implies that a heart that seeks knowledge will find it; folly, by contrast, is hardly gourmet fare. Verses 14–17 form another cluster around the theme of eating and feasting (cf. 13:2–4, 23–25).

15:15. Connected to the previous verse by the image of the feast, this saying completes the contrast begun there. The "cheerful heart" is (lit.) the "good heart"; while the translation "cheerful" may offer a contrast with the "wretched" days of the oppressed (*raᶜ*, "evil, trouble"; cf. 15:10), a "good heart" may also connote a contented and trusting heart (or even a "discerning heart" after 15:14). This last of the heart sayings sets the stage for another pair of sayings on contentment in 15:16–17.

15:16. Verses 16–17 are a pair of "better than" sayings[7]; both begin with *ṭob* ("better") and both end with *bo* ("with it").[8] In each line, the negative component is matched with a positive. Thus, having "a little" (a negative) can come with "fear of the LORD" (a positive), and the sum is "better than" the positive of "great wealth" since the negative of "turmoil" often comes "with it," especially if the wealth is gained fraudulently. The saying points out that things are never as simple as they may seem. Mitigating factors may make

---

7. With this pair, the "better than" sayings begin to appear more frequently (12:9; 15:16–17; 16:8, 19, 32; 17:1; 19:1; 21:9, 19; 25:7, 24; 27:5, 10; 28:6). I count only those proverbs that begin with *ṭob* ("better") in the first line and the comparative *min* ("than") in the second. Van Leeuwen, "Proverbs," 153, includes 8:11 and 19, where wisdom is better than wealth. See T. Perry, *Wisdom Literature and the Structure of Proverbs* (University Park: Pennsylvania State Univ. Press, 1993), for the fourfold structure of comparisons.

8. Note the similar pairing in *The Instruction of Amenemope*, AEL ch. 6 (IX, 5), 152: "Better is poverty in the hand of the god, Than wealth in the storehouse; Better is bread with a happy heart, Than wealth with vexation."

having little preferable to having much; by implication, "fear of the LORD," like wisdom, is worth more than gold or jewels (cf. 3:13–15; 8:10–11). "Fear of the LORD" connects this saying with the pair at 14:26–27.

15:17. This second "better than" saying extends the idea that humble circumstances are not to be despised. While the best situation would be to have both meat and love, if we must choose, a good relationship is always more important than material gain.[9] When read on its own, the saying depicts conflicted demonstrations of hospitality; there can be plenty on the table but scarce goodwill (cf. 17:1). When read together with 15:16, some of the compensations of poverty stand out.[10] Taken together, 15:15–17 redefine what is to be considered a good feast, namely, the cheerful heart reminding the reader of Wisdom's sumptuous table in chapter 9.

15:18. The comparison here shows that one's response to a situation influences it for good or bad. While some people typically create dissension, others can quiet it down. "Hot-tempered" and "patient" sound like qualities of temperament one is born with and cannot change, but this saying urges self-control, similar to 15:1. One chooses how to respond, just as one chooses to keep a good heart, fear Yahweh, and love (15:15–17).[11]

Sluggards and Fools (15:19–24)

VERSES 19–24 APPEAR to take a chiastic pattern formed by repetition key words:

A *Path* of the upright (v. 19)
  B *Joy* of a wise son, joy of folly (vv. 20–21)
    C Plans and counsel (v. 22)
  B' *Joy* of an apt reply (v. 23)
A' *Path* of life (v. 24)

15:19. The saying seems unconnected to its immediate context apart from the image of the path (cf. 15:24; see also 15:9–10). We have met the sluggard before (6:6–9; 13:4), and we will meet him again[12] as he appears

---

9. Or, as Clifford, *Proverbs*, 153, puts it, "a meal becomes a feast because of the joyous fellowship of the guests rather than because of the food."

10. McKane, *Proverbs*, 484; Whybray, *Proverbs*, 231.

11. See the similar advice from *The Instruction of Amenemope*, in Lichtheim, *AEL* (V, 10–15), 150: "Don't start a quarrel with a hot-mouthed man, Nor needle him with words. Pause before a foe, bend before an attacker, Sleep (on it) before speaking. A storm that bursts like fire in straw, Such is the heated man in his hour."

12. The sluggard appears in 6:6, 9; 10:26; 13:4; 15:19; 19:24; 20:4; 21:25; 22:13; 24:30; 26:13–14, 16.

throughout Proverbs as a fool who inspires laughter, at least at the start. It may be that coming after the praise of patience, this saying emphasizes that patience is not to be confused with passivity and its negative outcomes. The surprise comes in the contrast between a sluggard and the upright, for it implies that the lazy one is not upright, that is, not ethically responsible. What picture is conjured by a hedge of thorns? Thorns and briers in the path certainly slow the way and make traveling miserable; they may be a sign of folly, for who would choose such a route? They are also a sign of neglect (cf. 24:30–31). Thorns and briers are associated with evil in Micah 7:4: "The best of them is like a brier, the most upright worse than a thorn hedge."

15:20. Verses 20–21 are paired by use of the Hebrew root for "joy" (śmḥ). Note the similarity of verse 20 to the first proverb of the collection (10:1), nearly identical except that this son "despises" his mother whereas in 10:1, he brings her grief.[13] The second line of 15:20 implies the link between wisdom and love; if the fool despises his mother, then the wise son's gift of joy is a sign of love for his parents (cf. "father" in 15:5). One never leaves the family, even in entering relationships with God and community.

15:21. Folly is (lit.) "a joy" (cf. 15:20) to one who "lacks heart"; the "straight course" links this proverb with 15:19. This proverb itself implies that folly has its delights, but the person of understanding is not misled. Only a fool finds joy in the foolishness of putting self and pleasure first, not considering the consequences of actions or caring about the effects on self or others.

15:22. Just as destinations are reached by walking straight ahead (15:21), so goals are met when plans are submitted to the wisdom of others. Others can often spot flaws or shortcomings that we cannot, and to fail to consult them is to court trouble. Plans "fail" and are frustrated (lit., "broken"). The point is not to gather as many opinions as possible in a flurry of indecision but to consider more opinions than one's own. A wise person listens to advice (cf. 11:14; 12:15); fools like Rehoboam rejected counsel (1 Kings 12:8–13). Certainly the principle applies to the counsel wisdom offers (Prov. 1:25, 30) as well as to the counsel of Yahweh (cf. Ps. 32:8).

15:23. The first line might also be translated, "Some may find joy in the answer of their own mouths," describing those who like to hear themselves talk. This reading follows the idea of 15:22, that some people take no one's

---

13. This repetition of the words "wise," "foolish," "joy," "father," and "mother" may mark the beginning of the end of the contrasting proverbs. The theme of laziness in 15:19 also appears in 10:4–5.

counsel but their own. By contrast, a "timely word," that is, one that comes from outside one's own perspective, is desirable. However the proverb is translated, it celebrates the wisdom that knows how to speak the right word at the right time. This saying reminds the reader of the famous "seasons" poem in Ecclesiastes 3:1–8, that there is a "time to be silent and a time to speak" (Eccl. 3:7). "Joy" connects this saying with Proverbs 15:20–21, the "reply" (ma^ᶜneh, "answer") with 15:1 and 16:1.

15:24. Here is another "path" saying (cf. 15:9–10, 19). The downward path goes in the opposite direction of the path of life, it ends in "the grave" (še'ol; cf. 15:11). "Upward" is not so much a reference to heaven or life eternal as to the path that avoids untimely death or the death-dealing forces of hunger and sickness.[14] At root, everyone wants "life," but too many pursue it in ways that lead to death. Surely this saying brings us back to the most basic contrast of the proverbs, the ends toward which our lives are directed, the way we will travel.

Yahweh Sayings (15:25–33)

THE SECTION IS tied together by the significant number of Yahweh sayings, thus associating his judgments with the benefits of God-fearing wisdom.

15:25. The house of the righteous with its wealth and security (15:6) seems to be in view as the house of the proud and perhaps powerful is brought down (cf. 14:1). By contrast, the widow's boundary stone is the symbol of all that is humble and vulnerable about poverty. In Scripture, the moved boundary marker comes to stand for all injustice against weaker persons (cf. Deut. 19:14; 27:17; Hos. 5:10).[15] Yahweh makes sure it continues to stand right where it is (cf. Prov. 22:28; 23:10–11). So in the songs of Hannah and Mary, Yahweh brings down the high and mighty and lifts up the lowly (1 Sam. 2:1–10; Luke 1:46–55). It is the wise way of life that leads upward, not the proud way of lifted hearts and eyes (Prov. 15:24).

---

14. Clifford, *Proverbs*, 154, cites Deut. 28:43 as evidence that up and down can be symbolic of success and failure. Life and death in Proverbs take on what Clifford calls "metaphorical dimensions." Life implies blessing, enrichment, long life, good relations, reputation, security, and wealth. Death implies curse, deprivation, loss, short life, bad reputation, insecurity, and poverty. See also R. J. Clifford, "Proverbs as a Source for Wisdom of Solomon," in *Treasures of Wisdom: Studies in Ben Sira and the Book of Wisdom, Festschrift M. Gilbert*, ed. N. Calduch-Benages and J. Vermeylen (Leuven: Leuven Univ. Press, 1999), 255–63.

15. The example was common throughout the ancient Near East. See *The Instruction of Amenemope*, in Lichtheim, *AEL* (VII: 11), 151: "Do not move the markers on the borders of fields, Nor shift the position of the measuring-cord. Do not be greedy for a cubit of land, Nor encroach on the boundaries of a widow."

15:26. In this Yahweh saying, the theme is again his opposition to those who turn from him. He finds the "thoughts" (*maḥšᵉbot*, "plans" in 15:22) of the wicked to be a detestable abomination (cf. 15:8–9). The second line reads (lit.) "pure, pleasant words" (cf. 16:24; "compliments," 23:8), perhaps an association with acceptable sacrifice. There is some question whether "pure" should describe the speaker or the words/thoughts; if the latter, the line reads, "but pleasant words, acceptable (or pure)." Read alongside 15:25, the saying highlights Yahweh's look at intentions (cf. 15:3, 11) that motivate right and wrong behaviors. A negative example follows in 15:27; in 3:17, wisdom's ways are pleasing or "pleasant" (*noᶜam*).

15:27. The greedy person thinks only of gains, not consequences. Thus, the one "greedy for gain" (or "unjust gain," 1:19; 28:16; cf. Jer. 6:13; 8:10; Ezek. 22:7; Hab. 2:9) neither sees nor cares how those actions bring trouble to the family (cf. Prov. 11:29). The "bribe" (*mattanah*, "gift") plays on the desire for power (18:16; 19:6; 21:14); one can choose to hate the bribe or, as the proverb implies, to hate one's own "house" or family.

15:28. Verses 28–29 form a pair of righteous/wicked contrasts. The first, one of the "heart" sayings of the chapter (15:7, 11, 13, 14, 15, 30), compares the foresight of the righteous heart that "weighs its answers" by an internalized standard against the impulsive speech of the wicked that "gushes" forth evil like a broken dam. A similar comparison in 15:14 implies that if one pays attention to the intentions of the heart, then the speech of the mouth will bear the fruits of wisdom. When that inner work is ignored, the mouth pours out folly and its close cousin, evil. The verb and syntax of 15:28b is similar to 15:2b: "The mouth of the fool gushes folly."

15:29. This companion to verse 28 turns its attention from the workings of righteous and wicked hearts to Yahweh's response to both kinds. "Far" is not so much a measure of distance as of disposition; the wicked stay far away from God, and they are repaid in kind. The "prayer of the righteous" drives the point home, since readers assume the wicked do not pray. If we read 15:28 and 29 together, the evil speech of the wicked is the counterpart to the prayers of the righteous, which are Yahweh's delight (15:8).

15:30. Verses 30–32 are linked by catchword *šmᶜ* ("hear") in "news" (i.e., what is heard, 15:30), "listens" (15:31), and "heeds" (15:32).[16] In the first of the three, the direction of 15:13 is reversed; here a "cheerful look" from another (lit., "light of the eyes") makes a heart joyful. Similarly, good news gives health (lit., "puts fat") to the bones. The heart guides a person's words and actions, but it is also receptive of kindness from others. The condition

---

16. Van Leeuwen, "Proverbs," 152, observes that the heart, ears, eyes, mouth, and lips were all considered "organs of understanding" in Israel's oral culture.

of the heart influences a person's health (cf. 14:30). The "light of the eyes" is not explained; the parallel with the good news suggests that it refers to positive communication brought either by a messenger or a teacher (see 15:31 for a corrector or teacher). Set in the context of this chapter, the proverb is about messages that come from the good heart and bring health and life to those who receive them. If we look to the context that follows, we must include life-giving rebuke (15:31).

15:31. It is not stated whether the "rebuke" is given with a "cheerful look" (15:30), but we do recognize that it is an invitation. The one who "listens" (šmᶜ) to it finds a home among the wise. Thanks be to wise ones who make that invitation appealing and persuasive! Like 15:30, the two parts of this saying do not present a contrast; rather, the second line expands the thought of the first line. Rebuke brings life because it brings wisdom; in addition, it brings a place to live, a "home with the wise." If there is any contrast, it is in the reversal it brings to 15:12. Hating correction, the mocker will not go near the wise, as we also heard in wisdom's final speech (9:8). This key theme continues in the next proverb (cf. 15:5, 10).

15:32. This saying begins with words similar to 13:18, describing "the one who ignores discipline." It is also the companion piece to 15:31 (cf. 15:5, 10, in which "discipline" and "correction" are also paired). Those who ignore discipline not only disrespect others such as the wise, they hate themselves. Conversely, to "gain understanding" is to respect and love oneself. The thought echoes 9:12 (lit.): "If you are wise, you are wise for yourself." The proverb also connects with 15:30, in that the one who heeds (lit. "hears") correction "gains understanding" (lit., "heart"; cf. "lack judgment [heart]" in 9:4).

15:33. The second mention of "the fear of the LORD" in this chapter, like the first (15:16), compares what is "great" with what is "little." In this saying, however, what seems small leads to what is greater or better. Fear of Yahweh, a stepping down from self-rule (becoming small), is instruction in wisdom, and the proverbs often show how learning wisdom increases one's standing in the community. In the same way, before one is honored, one must learn humility. Whereas 15:16 spoke of material gain, this verse speaks of an increase in status. The first line incorporates terms from 1:7,[17] while the second line is identical with 18:12b (on "humility," see 3:34; 16:19; 22:4). Thus, the last proverb of the antithetical collection not only lacks a contrast; it also looks for like-minded companions—backward at the prologue and forward to the synonymous collection.

---

17. The first line reads, "The fear of the LORD, instruction of wisdom," leaving the translators somewhat puzzled as the NIV footnote indicates. Something like "instruction in wisdom" (NRSV) or "school of wisdom" (JB) renders it well. The LXX has "wisdom and instruction."

Bridging Contexts

AMONG THE MANY tones sounded by these proverbs, three themes draw them together and bring the collection of contrasts to a crescendo: (1) new insights into speaking and listening as functions of the heart, (2) repeated statements that Yahweh sees and understands all of those heart functions, and (3) multiple images of life lived in fear of Yahweh, a life of "cheerfulness" and "joy." We will look at each in turn, remembering that nearly half of the sayings in the chapter speak to matters of teaching and gaining knowledge.[18]

Speaking and listening. The importance of speaking and listening comes up again and again. The proverbs that mark the beginning and middle of the chapter exalt the patient person whose "gentle answer turns away wrath" and "calms a quarrel" (15:1, 18). In between are sayings about a wise tongue that "commends knowledge" and "brings healing" (15:2, 4), the "apt reply" and "timely word" that bring joy (15:23), and the "good news" that gives health to the bones (15:30).

Two aspects of communication are in view here: managing situations of conflict and the communication of knowledge through teaching. Social interaction and business dealings always have an element of conflict and difference of opinion, but conflict can be aggravated or it can be calmed, depending on how one answers. The wise person knows how to get at the matters of concern and work toward solutions so that all parties involved are reasonably satisfied. Fools, thinking only of their own interests, throw gasoline on the fires of conflict, leading others to respond in kind. Not "weighing answers" (15:28) to consider their effects, fools "gush" folly and its resulting evil (15:2, 28); rash speech is rarely profitable.

While there are times when we must overcome our tendencies to stay quiet just for the sake of getting along, impulsive words of anger never accomplish what we hope and usually bring regret. Wise persons not only make sure their words do not provoke a situation, they also learn to speak words that bring peace.[19] However, one does not come by such wisdom naturally, and it must be learned by listening to the wise words of others; teaching takes place by example as well as formal instruction. These proverbs not only urge us to listen and learn but also to become examples and teachers ourselves, always considering the good of all as the best way to achieve good for ourselves.

---

18. Whybray, *Proverbs*, 225.

19. It is no surprise, then, that self-help books with titles like *Coping with Difficult People* are popular (R. M. Branson, *Coping with Difficult People in Business and in Life* [New York: Ballantine, 1981]).

The work of learning wisdom takes place in the heart, for the wise heart informs the lips that spread knowledge (15:7), makes the face cheerful (15:13), seeks knowledge (15:14), and weighs answers (15:28). The heart can be cheered by good interaction with others (15:30), and this cheer provides a continual feast (15:15). Therefore, these sayings recognize that the intentions of the heart cannot be hidden for long, especially from Yahweh (15:11). A wise person recognizes the need to store good intentions there, particularly the humility and fear of Yahweh that leaves one open to teaching (15:31—33). While the need for a renewed or transformed heart sounds again and again throughout the Old and New Testaments, proverbs such as these seem to have been the inspiration for Jesus' teaching on good and bad fruit (Matt. 12:34—37, TNIV):

> For out of the overflow of the heart the mouth speaks. Good people bring good things out of the good stored up in them, and evil people bring evil things out of the evil stored up in them. But I tell you that people will have to give account on the day of judgment for every empty word they have spoken. For by your words you will be acquitted and by your words you will be condemned.

Believers should always reflect on the effects of their words, but they should also take the next step and examine the intentions and desires of the heart that inform them.

What Yahweh sees. The proverbs of this chapter affirm that Yahweh sees and understands the workings of the human heart. This chapter contains nine Yahweh sayings (15:3, 8—9, 11, 16, 25—26, 29, 33; nine more cluster in 16:1—11). Two "fear of the LORD" sayings come at the middle and end of the chapter. Most of the Yahweh proverbs deal with what pleases and displeases the One who sees all, even the intentions of the heart. Beginning with verse 11, these sayings move from behavior to matters of the inner life, adding that God sees them too. Therefore, just as the real work of learning wisdom takes place in the heart, so Yahweh examines the intentions that are stored there (15:11), sorting out the thoughts that are detestable and pure (15:26) and befriending the righteous while opposing the wicked (15:25, 29).

There is some implication that while we humans often value good looks and talent as the qualities that matter, Yahweh looks beyond appearances to reflect what is within. Even the prophet Samuel was fooled by appearance and stature when he saw the eldest of Jesse's sons. In reply, Yahweh said to Samuel, "The LORD does not look at the things man looks at. Man looks at the outward appearance, but the LORD looks at the heart" (1 Sam. 16:7).

Two of the nine Yahweh sayings in the chapter point to the appropriate heart response, "the fear of the LORD." Like the humility that comes before honor, humble reverence and obedience teach wisdom (Prov. 15:33)—a treasure so great that it multiplies the net worth even of those of modest means (15:16). These two sayings imply that desirable commodities such as wealth and honor are never separated from the attitude that we bring with them or use to acquire them. If we choose fear of Yahweh, we will practice humility and make peace; if we do not, we may have wealth, but pride and contentiousness will bring turmoil and endanger our houses (15:16, 24). If we must choose, it is better to have a little and keep what is truly valuable (15:16—17). Those open and willing to be instructed and learn have the richest fare, whether the table is as sumptuous as wisdom's feast (9:2—5) or as simple as a plate of greens. Wisdom and fear of Yahweh, as we have seen throughout Proverbs, are both the requirements and the goals of wisdom teaching, both beginning and end.

Life lived in the fear of Yahweh. Life lived in Yahweh's presence is a feast of cheerfulness and joy. For every image of the turmoil and trouble of the wicked, there are corresponding pictures of happiness, cheer, and rejoicing. Moreover, it is striking that these images of gladness are not associated with riches, honor, or status but rather with simple pleasures of life together. "The cheerful heart has a continual feast" even when there is little, if it is accompanied by the fear of Yahweh and love (15:13—17).

A wise son brings joy to his father (15:20), and an apt reply brings joy to both speaker and hearer (15:23). Folly may be a joy (root *śmḥ*) to the one who lacks heart (*leb*; NIV "judgment"), but a cheerful look brings the heart joy (15:21, 30). The proverbs here resonate with the observation of C. S. Lewis that nothing lasts forever except God and the people he has given to us. Sadly, the folly that tempts us all attempts to get us to love things and use people when it should be the other way around.

In commending the simple pleasures of wise living, the proverbs of this chapter sum up this life lived in fear of Yahweh with the word "good" (*tob*). The tongue of the wise makes knowledge "good" (15:2), just as the happy heart makes "good" the face (15:13); the "good" heart has the continual feast (15:15). Like a timely (lit., "good") word (15:23) and "good news" that brings health (15:30), the better life of moderation and love is also "good" (15:16—17). The eyes of Yahweh keep watch on the "wicked and the good" (15:3), for Yahweh finds any incursion of evil that would spoil that good to be detestable, an abomination (15:8—9, 26). Here is why God hears the prayer of the righteous but detests the sacrifices of the wicked (15:8, 29), why God opposes the proud and tears down their houses (15:25); their way of folly spoils and ruins this world, which God created for good. In answer to Marcion's declaration that a loving God would not judge or condemn the wicked, Tertullian wrote about this portrait of Yahweh:

What a prevaricator of truth is such a God! What a dissembler with his own decision! Afraid to condemn what he really condemns, afraid to hate what he does not love, permitting that to be done which he does not allow, choosing to dictate what he dislikes rather than deeply examine it! This will turn out an imaginary goodness.[20]

Thus, the contrasts we have seen again and again between the righteous and the wicked are meant to show us what true goodness looks like— goodness of life to be sure, but even more important, the goodness of God, who will not allow his intentions to be thwarted forever.

POWER OF SPEECH. The principles we have discerned in this chapter about wise speaking, the heart's desires, and the goodness of life lived in the fear of Yahweh translate easily into the concerns of our own day, and preachers and teachers may be surprised to find examples in every walk of life. These sayings on speech commend gentleness and truthfulness. Such speech turns away wrath (15:1), brings healing (15:4), and calms quarrels (15:18).

Yet such speech often involves stating uncomfortable truths in the form of rebuke and correction (15:31–32). Eva Jefferson Patterson is a civil rights attorney in the San Francisco Bay area. During the turbulent time of the late 1960s and early 1970s, she became the first African American president of the student government at Northwestern University. After the shooting of four students at Kent State University, she led thousands of students in a peaceful strike; Northwestern was the only campus in the Chicago area that did not shut down. A few days later, she confronted a small group of students heading toward the building that housed the ROTC building. They carried torches, intending to set the building on fire. Patterson convinced the group to turn around, saying, "These torches remind me of torches in another place and time." By using the imagery of racially motivated violence, she was able to calm their anger and move them to reconsider their action.[21]

On the other side, I once heard a rhetorical critic who is also a Viet Nam veteran speak about the ways societies talk themselves into war. He studied the famous speeches of Roosevelt and Churchill, Johnson and Nixon, editorials from those time periods, and art. When he published his findings, he

---

20. Tertullian, *Against Marcion* 1.27, in *Ante-Nicene Fathers*, ed. A. Roberts and J. Donaldson, quoted in E. Achtemeier, *Preaching Hard Texts of the Old Testament* (Peabody, Mass.: Hendrickson, 1998), 5.
21. N. Deenen, "Eva Jefferson Patterson," *Cross Currents* (Spring 2000), 10–15.

was surprised to receive requests to speak and consult from sports teams, corporate executives, and foreign military advisors! Our human capacity to influence and persuade can be used to quiet conflict or to stir it up.

Intentions of the heart. However, these proverbs do more than simply urge us to watch what we say and how; they also inspire us to examine the intentions of our hearts. We should take those occasions when we are inclined to speak harshly as opportunities to reflect on our motives for speaking and to ask whose interests we have at heart. We may find that our motives are more complicated than we imagined, that we want what is right but all too often seek what benefits us at the expense of others. A heart that weighs its answers will also remember that little with love is better than meat with hatred (15:17, 28).

Connections. These proverbs also urge us to make the connection between listening to instruction and speaking wisely. That is, they require of us a willingness to admit when we are wrong. Someone who is willing to "stand corrected" is less likely to get agitated and quarrel, more likely to hear another person's point of view, more able to build trust with another, and better able to speak. The interweaving of these images of speaking and listening, teaching and learning implies that learning is not finished once a person goes on to speak and teach others.

Preachers especially need to heed this call to a humble, teachable spirit. We may have correction to offer, but if it is offered in anger with harsh words or self-righteousness, we may be caught in an irony Jesus encountered. Throughout the Gospels he was opposed by religious leaders who wanted to do the right thing but did it in a way that alienated the population and the Son of God. A similar irony in our day is that we can be talking about the right things and alienating our listeners with judgment and crankiness. How can we balance the Lord's hatred of evil with love for our listeners? Let us never forget that in a sense everyone teaches—some in pulpits, some in schools, some at family tables, and some through friendship (I have been deeply influenced by friendship with wise elders).

We should note too that the chapter begins with the potency of a gentle answer and ends with the honor that comes to humility. One can speak softly yet authoritatively. If the message is not heard by those who love swagger and bluster, we can take hope that if we chose not to play with that form of fire, we may keep it from spreading.

The full life. Therefore, these proverbs of joy and feasting mingled in with proverbs of judgment can shed new light on what it means to love what God loves and hate what God hates. The self-denial taught here is not a denial of the good life God intends but rather a "renunciation of a self-directed life, for the very purpose of attaining a far greater fullness under the direction of God."[22] This fullness, says Paul Tournier, is the fullness of attaining maturity and bearing much fruit, as Jesus promised to those who would abide in him (John 15:5). Thus, it is that the tongue of the wise that brings healing is a tree of life (Prov. 15:4). Fear of Yahweh is better than a great treasure, and it comes before any great honor. In other words, while wisdom promises to fulfill one's desires for provision, long life, and honor, it does not come if those things are put first. Instruction and humility, contentment with adequate provision—these are the indications of a heart that fears God.

As the number of contrasting proverbs decreases and the synonymous proverbs begin to dominate the collection of 10:1–22:16, chapters 15 and 16 present a number of transitional clusters that blend the two kinds of proverbs. So the contrasts in 15:29 and 32 together tell us that Yahweh is far from the wicked, but that those who ignore instruction and correction even hate themselves. The synonymous proverbs of 15:30–31, 33 present the positive picture of one who listens to others and fears Yahweh, finding a home among the wise. Having made the contrast between the two ways of life as clear as possible, the sages of Proverbs now present the beauty of wisdom in harmonious colors. Drawing together this chapter's proverbs about the joys of wisdom and its contentment (15:17, 23, 30), the composer Michael Torke said about his work *Four Proverbs*:

> Proverbs, especially poetic and witty ones, make me laugh, and I write music to celebrate that state. Wisdom can be both fun and responsible, I see no contradiction. Ethical questions can weigh us down. Here they have lift, inspiriting intense shots of happiness.[23]

Even as these sayings depict a maturity of life that enjoys fullness and bears its fruit, so those who know the life of wisdom have a growing sense of knowing God's mind and heart, even as God knows theirs. They begin to value what God values; they begin to see the truth in this teaching and the benefits of walking in his way. They yield and are richly supplied; they surrender and are set free.

The contentment that comes when one surrenders a self-determined life of achievement and acquisition for one that offers good work and good rewards is better than any hoard of selfish riches. It is striking that the connections between instruction (*musar*) and Yahweh's oversight of human affairs sound very much like the instructions of chapters 1–9, but also here Yahweh's

---

22. P. Tournier, *The Seasons of Life*, trans. J. S. Gilmour (Atlanta: John Knox, 1976), 33.
23. Liner notes, M. Torke, *Book of Proverbs/Four Proverbs* (London: Decca Records, 1994, 1999).

presence is more strongly felt and receives greater emphasis. As the proverbs tell us more and more about Yahweh and his intentions and desires, we will find ourselves all the more wanting the same. "Better a little with the fear of the LORD than great wealth with turmoil" (15:16).

Proverbs 16:1–33

❧

¹ TO MAN BELONG the plans of the heart,
    but from the LORD comes the reply of the tongue.
² All a man's ways seem innocent to him,
    but motives are weighed by the LORD.
³ Commit to the LORD whatever you do,
    and your plans will succeed.
⁴ The LORD works out everything for his own ends—
    even the wicked for a day of disaster.
⁵ The LORD detests all the proud of heart.
    Be sure of this: They will not go unpunished.
⁶ Through love and faithfulness sin is atoned for;
    through the fear of the LORD a man avoids evil.
⁷ When a man's ways are pleasing to the LORD,
    he makes even his enemies live at peace with him.
⁸ Better a little with righteousness
    than much gain with injustice.
⁹ In his heart a man plans his course,
    but the LORD determines his steps.
¹⁰ The lips of a king speak as an oracle,
    and his mouth should not betray justice.
¹¹ Honest scales and balances are from the LORD;
    all the weights in the bag are of his making.
¹² Kings detest wrongdoing,
    for a throne is established through righteousness.
¹³ Kings take pleasure in honest lips;
    they value a man who speaks the truth.
¹⁴ A king's wrath is a messenger of death,
    but a wise man will appease it.
¹⁵ When a king's face brightens, it means life;
    his favor is like a rain cloud in spring.
¹⁶ How much better to get wisdom than gold,
    to choose understanding rather than silver!
¹⁷ The highway of the upright avoids evil;
    he who guards his way guards his life.
¹⁸ Pride goes before destruction,
    a haughty spirit before a fall.

¹⁹ Better to be lowly in spirit and among the oppressed
    than to share plunder with the proud.
²⁰ Whoever gives heed to instruction prospers,
    and blessed is he who trusts in the LORD.
²¹ The wise in heart are called discerning,
    and pleasant words promote instruction.
²² Understanding is a fountain of life to those who have it,
    but folly brings punishment to fools.
²³ A wise man's heart guides his mouth,
    and his lips promote instruction.
²⁴ Pleasant words are a honeycomb,
    sweet to the soul and healing to the bones.
²⁵ There is a way that seems right to a man,
    but in the end it leads to death.
²⁶ The laborer's appetite works for him;
    his hunger drives him on.
²⁷ A scoundrel plots evil,
    and his speech is like a scorching fire.
²⁸ A perverse man stirs up dissension,
    and a gossip separates close friends.
²⁹ A violent man entices his neighbor
    and leads him down a path that is not good.
³⁰ He who winks with his eye is plotting perversity;
    he who purses his lips is bent on evil.
³¹ Gray hair is a crown of splendor;
    it is attained by a righteous life.
³² Better a patient man than a warrior,
    a man who controls his temper than one who takes
        a city.
³³ The lot is cast into the lap,
    but its every decision is from the LORD.

Original
Meaning

CHAPTER 16 MARKS a shift from a collection of contrasting proverbs (10:1–15:33) to one comprised mostly of synonymous sayings (16:1–22:16). There is no subheading to distinguish a separate section, but the Masoretic scribes of the eleventh century did place a note marking 16:7 as the center of the book. Of the 375 sayings in Proverbs 10:1–22:16, there are fifty-five (just under 15 percent) that name "the LORD" (*yhwh*). The greatest concentration of these Yahweh proverbs falls in this transition from one collection to the next—nine such proverbs in chapter 15 and eleven in chapter 16. Moreover, nine of ten verses in 15:33–16:9 are Yahweh proverbs, a subunit that Whybray calls a "theological kernel." The statements about the king that follow are interpreted through this focus on Yahweh's righteous character and rule.[1]

Yahweh sayings (16:1–9)
King sayings (16:10–15)
Wisdom better than gold (16:16–19)
Wisdom sweet on the lips (16:20–24)
Evil fire on the lips (16:25–30)
Patience, reverence, and endurance (16:31–33)

This outline points up an example of dove-tailing: Verses 1–9 include one non-Yahweh proverb about riches and "injustice" (*loʾ mišpaṭ*, v. 8), while verses 10–15 have one nonroyal proverb about Yahweh's justice (*mišpaṭ*, v. 11 [NIV "honest"]).[2] The key image of the "way" appears in all but one of the clusters (*derek*, vv. 9, 17, 25, 31).

Yahweh Sayings (16:1–9)

EACH OF THE Yahweh sayings in this cluster probes a little more deeply into his sovereign involvement in human affairs; that which was only suggested in the previous chapters is here brought into better view. Therefore, careful readers will look for new insights into the mystery of God's ways as they come to terms with each new saying.

16:1. The chapter begins in the same way as the one before, with a saying about an "answer" (*maʿᵃneh*, 15:1). Whereas the earlier proverb stressed the responsibility of speakers for their answers, this proverb takes a wider view. Human hearts (the seat of intentions) plan, but the words that come forth are somehow from Yahweh.[3] If his wide-ranging sight and knowledge are repeated and emphasized in chapter 15, here a greater truth is presented, and

---

1. R. N. Whybray, "Yahweh Sayings and their Contexts in Proverbs 10:1–22:16," in *La sagesse de l'Ancien Testament*, ed. M. Gilbert, 2d ed. (Leuven: Leuven Univ. Press, 1990), 153–65. Whybray extends this observation to other examples of Yahweh sayings: 12:2–3; 14:1–2; 15:16–17; 18:10–11. He also believes that an older, secular wisdom is reinterpreted by the Yahweh sayings, but one need not accept the historical argument to appreciate this literary feature.

2. See Heim, *Like Grapes of Gold Set in Silver*, 208–9, who divides into clusters: vv. 1–8, 9–11, 12–15, 16–30.

3. We are taking heart and tongue here as source and conduit, but it is possible that they constitute a merism for all of human action (Clifford, *Proverbs*, 157).

it is confounding: Humans act according to their intentions, but God is somehow at work in those acts of word and deed.[4] The saying tantalizes, leaving the reader looking for more proverbs on the theme.

16:2. The second Yahweh saying again contrasts human and divine perspectives. Human assessments are limited and often distorted. The capacity for self-deception comes through in the image of one's ways being "innocent" (*zak*, "pure"; cf. 21:8; 20:11)[5] in one's own eyes. "Motives" (*ruḥot*, "spirits") are "weighed," presumably by Yahweh (21:2; 24:12; cf. 1 Sam. 2:3). The shift in metaphor reminds the reader of the famous phrase "weighed in the balances and found wanting" (Dan. 5:27). Egyptian tombs often sketched a life history in pictures, culminating in the weighing of the heart. If the heart was lighter than a feather, the individual was allowed into the next life. The interaction of the two lines in this proverb suggests that Yahweh is better able to discern our motivations than we are, hence the need for wisdom and instruction in standards outside of ourselves.

16:3. Again intention and deed are juxtaposed (as in v. 1). Here deeds are (lit.) "rolled over" toward Yahweh in trust (cf. Ps. 22:8; 37:5). As a result, plans and intentions are "made solid" (Prov. 4:26; 12:3); so also Yahweh makes steps "firm" (16:9). Recognizing his presence in everyday affairs, we might paraphrase: "Plan, pray, then act."

16:4. Like verse 2, the Hebrew begins with "all" (*kol*). Just as Yahweh weighs motives and plans, his purposes are established while those of the wicked fail in disaster. A counterpoint to the previous verse, this proverb reminds us that trust in God's plan is no guarantee for our desires but rather a reciprocal relationship between God's intentions and our own. Ultimately, Yahweh does what he purposes (or "answers"),[6] even while there are those who seek to work out their purposes, purposes that are contrary to Yahweh's.

16:5. Repeating and extending the thought of verse 4, the wicked meet disaster because they are proud of heart (cf. 15:25) and detestable (11:20–21). Once again, what has been hinted at earlier now comes to full light. The wicked do not undo God's intentions for the world by opposing his inten-

---

4. *The Instruction of Amenemope*, AEL (XVIII:16–17), 157: "The words men say are one thing, The deeds of the god are another." Murphy, *Proverbs*, 120, 124–25, claims the ancients saw the problem but refrained from trying to resolve it.

5. Pure olive oil was to be used for the lamps in the tabernacle (Ex. 27:20; 30:7–8; Lev. 24:2).

6. Hubbard, *Proverbs*, 235, makes it clear that the word either denotes "for his purpose" from the word to exert oneself (Eccl. 1:13; 3:10; 5:19) or "with its answer" from the more common verb (Prov. 1:28; 15:28). In the order of creation, each action receives its appropriate response or answer. Yet Yahweh responds also; if there is any overlap, it would be that just as God "answers" evil with judgment, so the creation has its own "answers" built in.

tions; rather, God opposes them because they are an abomination to him. Kidner reminds us that the sage lets the proud lead the seven abominations of 6:17, "in the very worst company ... whom he doubtless thanks God he does not resemble."[7]

16:6. "Love and faithfulness" are the classic pair that describe Yahweh's relation to us. Both terms refer to steadfast love that does not forget to do kindness. It weathers hard times. It is a quality of human character in 3:3 and a reward in 14:22. Yet this quality always shows itself in action, in *doing* love and faithfulness to another (cf. Gen. 47:29; Josh. 2:14).[8]

The contrast of punished pride is sin atoned (lit., "removed by exchange"). The word is not used in its typical ritual sense here (cf. Gen. 32:20; Isa. 28:18), although the ancients probably heard some reference to the sacrificial system (cf. 1 Sam. 15:22), following on the ideas of abomination and acquittal in Proverbs 16:5. "Fear of the LORD," the key theme of the book, takes on new significance here as both motivation and means for avoiding moral evil (cf. 16:17).

16:7. Friendship with Yahweh spills over into friendship with others. It is not stated whether this is an instance of cause and effect, as though peace with enemies is a reward, or whether the goodness of one's ways works like the words of the wise, which create calm instead of turmoil. "Peace with God, peace with others" might be a paraphrase of the proverb that stands in the very center of the book (cf. 16:2).

16:8. Tucked within the series of Yahweh proverbs is this "better than" saying similar to those found in the middle of the previous chapter (15:16–17; cf. 17:1). As part of a pair with verse 7, this saying makes clear that ways that please Yahweh may or may not bring great gain with them, but they will be accompanied by righteousness and justice (two of the cardinal virtues of 1:3). The point is not to glorify poverty but to deal with life's complexities. Because interests sometimes conflict, one should learn to choose righteousness and justice over profit—certainly because it is better but ultimately because it pleases Yahweh. Dare we go on to say that this implies that we care about justice, even for those who are not in our immediate circle?

16:9. A variation on the theme of 16:1–3 and using similar vocabulary, this saying compares the "heart" that plans a person's way to the work of

7. Kidner, *Proverbs*, 118.

8. The reader might ask whose love and faithfulness atone for sin. The NIV translation reflects the parallel in Heb.; "through love and faithfulness" and "through fear of the LORD," suggesting that human faithfulness is in view. Yet it is not clear that the same subject is meant for both lines of the proverb. It could be argued that, following Yahweh's hatred of pride in 16:5, his love and faithfulness are meant here (cf. Ps. 25:10).

Yahweh, who confirms or establishes the steps (the same Heb. words are used for "succeed" in 16:3 and "way" in 16:2). A person makes plans, and if the wisdom of the previous sayings has been heard, then there is a wonderful balance between human plans and God's oversight of the outcome. With a wisdom perspective, the two are in cooperation, not conflict.[9]

King Sayings (16:10–15)

A SERIES OF PROVERBS about the king upholds the virtues of honest speaking and just dealing. Four of these sayings alternate between the king's displeasure (16:12, 14) and pleasure (16:13, 15).

16:10. The first of the royal proverbs is followed by a Yahweh saying. Just as one overlaps pieces of cloth before sewing a seam, so this section inserts one of the royal proverbs before concluding the series of Yahweh sayings in verses 1–11. Likewise, a Yahweh saying stands in this section of royal sayings. The overlap reflects the biblical view that kings discharged their duties as appointed representatives of God's rule on earth. Lips and mouth are frequently paired; here they point to the king's responsibility to speak judgments that enact "justice" (a play on two meanings of *mišpaṭ*; cf. 16:8).[10] In this context, the witness to God's rule may be taken as an ideal picture of divine guidance (cf. 2 Sam. 14:17, 20; 1 Kings 3:9), and so the king's decisions can rightly be called "inspired" (lit., an "oracle").

16:11. As the king's just decisions are inspired, so also "honest" (or "just," *mišpaṭ*; cf. 16:8, 10) balances and scales are of Yahweh (11:1; 20:10, 23; cf. Deut. 25:13; Mic. 6:11). The figurative language of the second line relies on the common understanding that some merchants used two sets of weight stones, one for buying and one for selling. By stating that all honest weights are Yahweh's work, the proverb suggests that even when there is human intent to deceive, God's justice will eventually win out (cf. Prov. 16:1–2).

16:12. Connecting verses 11 and 12 are the similarities between the Hebrew spellings of "bag" (*kis*) and "throne" (*kisseʾ*). This righteous/wicked say-

---

9. Murphy, *Proverbs*, 121, looks to 19:21; 20:24; and Jer. 10:23 and concludes that the proverb affirms human helplessness before God. While I do not disagree, it seems to me that the picture of these proverbs is more optimistic about the real action of those who walk in God's "way."

10. The word for "oracle" (*qesem*) is unusual in this context; it typically refers to practices of divination that were outlawed (Num. 23:23; Deut. 18:10–14; 1 Sam. 15:23; Ezek. 21:21). Yet Balaam spoke only the oracle message given from God (Num. 22:18, 35, 38), and a similar sort of inspiration is in view here. Whether we translate "inspired judgments" or "oracle," the implied truth is clear: Yahweh, who works out everything for his own purpose (Prov. 16:4), can also ensure that justice is brought about through his representative, the king.

ing also juxtaposes the "detestable" with that which establishes or makes sure. Through a subtle use of vocabulary, the work of the king and Yahweh are intertwined. As the king shares Yahweh's abhorrence to the deeds of the wicked, the throne is established (25:5; see also 14:34; cf. Ps. 89:14; 97:2). Righteousness and justice are the only foundations for a stable government; a corrupt one will eventually fall.

16:13. This saying is connected to the previous one by the word "righteous" (*ṣedeq,* trans. "honest"). If the throne is established through righteousness, then kings will want to surround themselves with persons who speak that way. Just as kings detest the wrong, they love those who do right (12:2). Taken together, verses 12 and 13 hold up the virtues of speaking honestly.

16:14. Verses 14 and 15 work together to give poetic expression to the king's power over life and death. The wise take this knowledge to heart and extend the analogy to their relationship with the heavenly king. Just as kings find pleasure in honesty, they also hate its opposite. The stimulus of the king's anger is not mentioned, only its result—death. Wise persons know how to assuage anger (cf. 15:1, 18), and they know how to speak the truth so that it need not be aroused. Wise people like Joseph (Gen. 41), Daniel (Dan. 2), and Abigail (1 Sam. 25) knew how to speak in the presence of a king. The word for "appease" (*kpr*) appears in Proverbs 16:6 as "atone." Again, while the context is not that of the religious cult, readers would likely hear the overtones.

16:15. In contrast with wrath that brings death (16:14), here two weather metaphors describe the life-giving powers of the king. The juxtaposition of opposites—the sun that shines brightly and a dark rain cloud—surprise the reader with their similarity; both are welcome and necessary for a good crop.[11] "Favor" (cf. 17:7; also 8:35; 10:32; 11:27; 12:2; 14:9, 35; 18:2) and the image of a bright face (Ps. 4:6; 44:3; 89:15; cf. Num. 6:25) often are used of Yahweh.

Wisdom Better Than Gold (16:16–19)

TWO "BETTER THAN" sayings (16:16 and 19) hold up wisdom and humility as more valuable than riches. While some see common emphases on gaining and teaching wisdom throughout 16:16–23,[12] there does seem to be some

---

11. Two possible meanings for the word "brightens" (lit. "in the light of a king's face"), "smile" and "show favor" may overlap, even as we would say, one's "face lit up." So Job said "When I smiled at them they did not turn aside, nor did they cause my shining face to fall" (Job 29:24). M. I. Gruber, *Aspects of Nonverbal Communication in the Ancient Near East,* Studia Pohl, 12/II (Rome: Biblical Institute Press, 1980), 557–58.

12. Whybray, *Proverbs,* 246, believes that these verses form a mini-instruction, similar to those found in chs. 1–9.

distinction as the section moves from the motivations for acquiring wisdom (16:16–19) to the process of transmitting it (16:20–24).

16:16. Not much has been said in this chapter about wisdom apart from the calming influence of a wise one (16:14). Yet everything that has been said about Yahweh and the king is now taken as evidence for the supreme value of wisdom. Because it is a currency of life and death (16:4–5, 14–15), wisdom is to be desired above wealth. The form is not quite that of a "better than" saying (cf. 16:8, 19), but it does share its theme that gain without the integrity of wisdom loses its value, a theme also heard in the instructions (3:14; 8:10–11).

16:17. Another motif from the instructions is the highway by which one walks "straight" (*yašar*, "upright"), but this straight way also turns away from evil (cf. 16:6). A person guards the way and in so doing watches over life as well ("way," *derek;* cf. 16:9, 25, 31). While some interpreters take the "evil" to refer to evil deeds and others misfortune, in either case the promise of "life" brings the point home. Echoes of wisdom's promises to protect the traveler come to mind here (2:11–12; 3:21–24; 4:10–13).

16:18. Continuing the theme of road travel, this saying depicts one who does not watch the way out of arrogance (cf. 16:5, where "lifted" or "exalted" is used). "Spirits" or "motivations" (*ruah* for both) are weighed by Yahweh. The terse Hebrew of this saying could read, "Before destruction, pride, and before stumbling, a haughty spirit." The synonymous lines repeat the picture of arrogant people raising themselves up, only to trip and fall low.

16:19. This "better than" saying continues the theme of treasures worth more than gold (cf. 16:16). A companion to verse 18, the saying is linked by the repetition of the words "pride" and "spirit" and the contrast between the high and lowly. How can we imagine it is better to be humble and poor than proud and rich? The answer is in the quality of the communities that are contrasted here. We can imagine the two gatherings: one in which goods are divided, but with gloating and perhaps even a hint of resentment at having to share; the other where there is no wealth to divide, only joyful sharing of the meager provisions and company. Certainly one community is false while the other is real.

Wisdom Sweet on the Lips (16:20–24)

RELATED TO 16:16–19 on virtues that accompany wisdom, this cluster stresses matters of giving and accepting wisdom teaching. Two of the proverbs recommend "pleasant words" (16:21, 24).

16:20. One solitary Yahweh saying stands among these wisdom proverbs of speaking and listening. The happiness of trusting in Yahweh stands in clear contrast with pride and plundering (16:19; cf. Prov. 1; also Ps. 1).[13] The word translated "gives heed" (root *śkl*) appears also in Proverbs 16:22 ("understanding") and 23 ("guides"). "Trust" (cf. 3:5) is an active confidence; more than believing in God's protection and provision, trust believes that God's way is the best way and so gladly follows it. Murphy translates the conjunction as "but" and makes this a "how much more" saying: "Whoever ponders a word will find good, but whoever trusts in Yahweh, happiness!"[14]

16:21. This proverb begins a series on wisdom and speaking. The connection between heart and lips is made once again, here to demonstrate how reputation can also enhance teaching. If the first line stresses the fruits for the wise one, the second stresses the effect on others. Once again, the charge to gain wisdom carries with it a second charge to pass it on to others by means of persuasive teaching (lit., "sweetness of lips"; NIV "pleasant words").

Coming on the heels of Yahweh and king sayings, is this verse a suggestion that the king should also be a teacher? Perhaps the figure of Solomon is in view here, a model for all wise persons—if he had just stayed on course! The proverbs on teaching then speak both to rulers and those who serve them. The NIV text note shows that the Hebrew can be translated two ways (cf. 16:23; also 1:5; 4:21; 7:21; 9:9; Deut. 32:2; Isa. 29:24).

16:22. In the last of the "fountain of life" sayings (10:11; 13:14; 14:27; 16:22), the contrast is between "understanding" and "folly" along with each one's results, "life" and "punishment." The word for "punishment" (*musar*) is typically used for instruction or discipline; punishment is a rare meaning of this word (13:24; 22:15). Is the sense of the proverb that the fool is chastised, or that folly is the only instruction they know, so don't bother to teach them (cf. 26:4–5)? Both are possible, but the contrast with the fountain of life lends weight to the first interpretation.[15]

16:23. Repetition of the words from verse 21 ("wise," "heart, " and "pleasant words promote instruction") signals the connection with this saying about wise hearts and pleasant words, good for body and soul (cf. 16:24). The "understanding" (*śkl*) of verse 22 is here used by the heart that imparts understanding or "guides" (*śkl*) the mouth. The first line presents the conclusion, the second line the evidence. The second line could be translated "adds learning to the lips,"[16] perhaps a reference to the ongoing learning of the wise (cf. 1:5).

---

13. Whybray, "Yahweh Sayings," 164, believes this Yahweh saying interprets 16:16–19.
14. Murphy, *Proverbs*, 117.
15. Clifford, *Proverbs*, 161, applies Occam's razor, choosing the ordinary meaning of *musar* ("discipline") as the simplest solution: "As long as perverse folly is the discipline of fools, they will remain fools and eventually bring retribution on their heads."
16. Heim, *Like Grapes of Gold Set in Silver*, 216.

16:24. Honey is the subject of a number of sayings (24:13; 27:7). Expanding the idea of "sweet words" from verse 21, these pleasant words are also sweet to the soul or "palate" (so NJB; *nepeš* can mean throat, desire, or taste) and healing to the bones. "Appetite" in 16:26 (also *nepeš*) connects the goodness of honey with satisfaction of hunger, while honey itself is the symbol for the teaching that brings life (cf. 16:17), a sign that all is well.

Evil Fire on the Lips (16:25–30)

NEGATIVE IMAGES DOMINATE this cluster, particularly the villainous person. Note that many key words from 16:20–24 recur but as a mirror image of evil ("way," "mouth," "lips"), especially the reversal of "finds good" (*ṭob*, "prospers") in 16:20 to "not good" (*lo' ṭob*) in 16:29.

16:25. A verbatim repetition of 14:12, this verse also echoes the theme stated in 16:1–9. One can choose the way that seems right or straight to the eye, but such vision is often impaired (16:2). Only by choosing Yahweh's ways (16:7) can we be sure we are on the right path (cf. *derek*, "way," in 16:9, 17; "life" in 16:31). Following the proverbs on teaching, this saying also states our need for an external reference point by which we set our course.

16:26. Because this proverb makes an observation without judgment, it is difficult to understand. However, the repetition of the word *nepeš* ("appetite") from 16:24 (where it is translated "soul") suggests that we compare the overflowing sweetness of the honeycomb with the intense hunger that motivates a worker. A similar intensity of motivation should drive the quest for wisdom. If there is a way that leads to death (16:25), there is a course of action that leads to life. While some scholars look for help in the toil passages of Ecclesiastes 3:9; 4:7–8; 6:7, the reverse picture of the sluggard of Proverbs 6:6–11 may be in view, for it too is followed by the portrait of the scoundrel (6:12–19).

16:27. Verses 27–29 each begin with the Hebrew word for man (*'iš*) and add a new description; the "scoundrel," "perverse," and "violent" man are all the same person. Like the portrait of the scoundrel in 6:12–19, this evil person's thoughts, words, and actions are intent on hurting others. If a laborer toils to feed self and family (16:26), a scoundrel "plots" (lit., "digs a pit") to entrap the unsuspecting, working not to provide for himself but to take what others have. The second line likens evil speech to this action, adding that it also burns like fire. A "scorching fire" quickly spreads, destroying everything in its path as it burns out of control. On a trip taken ten years after the great fire in Yellowstone National Park, I was surprised that one could still see the sprawling graveyards of fallen trees.

16:28. The second description of the evil man names him as "perverse," turning to his speech that stirs up strife and alienates friends. The similarity between the two lines is the absence of goodwill and unity. The difference is that one can do it loudly as one stirs up dissension or quietly and secretly through gossip and tale-bearing. Both are equally devastating to community (cf. 26:20 and 22; also 18:8).

16:29. This saying and its images of seduction, enticing (with overtones of "making simple"), and leading victims down a bad path remind the reader of 1:10–19. Yet the seduction is that of violence! Perhaps this description of the scoundrel has saved the memory of the violent gang for last, pulling the trump card of this archenemy of community. A strong contrast stands here between the teacher who spreads health and peace and the "teacher" who spreads division and finally violence by word and example (cf. 4:14–17). The phrase "not good" may point to the antithesis of choosing wisdom; every other occurrence of the word "good" (*ṭob*) associates it with wisdom's way (16:8, 16, 19, 20, 32). Enticement is ultimately deception that pretends to be speaking good when in fact it is "not good."

16:30. The last description of the wicked man gets to the heart of the chapter's theme, summing up the intentions that motivate all these behaviors. It is not clear whether the nonverbal signals are meant for evil colleagues or as friendly but deceptive signs; perhaps they are a form of the enticement mentioned in verse 29. The image of pressing both the eyes and lips seems to be a common act of "perversity," linking this verse with the dissension and gossip of verse 28. In the instructions of chapters 1–9, such a person was dangerous to the health of the community. Here, this person may also be a menace to the working of justice in the court (cf. 16:13).

Patience, Reverence, and Endurance (16:31–33)

FOLLOWING THE REVOLTING portrait of the evil person, these verses return to the way of wisdom, highlighting the values of righteous living, patience, and, by implication, fear of Yahweh.

16:31. The young man of 4:9 was told to honor wisdom and expect the reward of a "crown of splendor"; here the crown is shown to be the gray head that comes with long life, itself a sign of honor (Lev. 19:32). The point is that long life is a reward for walking the righteous way (*derek*; cf. Prov. 16:9, 17, 25) even when one wants to quit. The only other choice is the way that seems right but really leads to death (16:25).

16:32. The last of the "better than" sayings in this chapter does not speak directly of material gains (cf. 15:16–17), although taking a city may involve some sharing of plunder (16:19). If humility in peace is better than pride in conquest, then patience is better than strength, for patience and self-control are their own forms of power (14:29; 15:18). Better to exhibit self-control than to control others. In an age when kings used stone reliefs to depict their prowess in war, this praise of the patience that maintains social order may have been shaped to surprise hearers with its common sense.

16:33. The last proverb in the chapter once again contrasts divine and human perspectives (cf. 16:1–5). People cast lots in order to discern Yahweh's will and so hope to find success. Most likely, "lot" refers to the use of Urim and Thummim (Ex. 28:30–31; Lev. 8:8; 16:8–10); among other uses, lots were used to make decisions about going to war (cf. Num. 27:21; 1 Sam. 23:9–12).[17] The "decision" (*mišpaṭ*) is a judgment, and Yahweh's judgments are for justice (*mišpaṭ*, Prov. 16:8) and honesty (16:11). A "lap" (*ḥeq*) is formed by the folds of one's garment. Thus, both lots cast into the folds and weight stones drawn out of the bag point to Yahweh's desire for decisions that reflect his will (cf. 16:11). Like the opening proverbs, however, the role of human planning in the final outworking of God's plans is left in mysterious tension.

Bridging Contexts

COMING AT THE MIDPOINT of the book, the proverbs of chapter 16 draw composite portraits of scoundrels and fools but also of wise teachers and rulers who recognize the strong presence of Yahweh in everyday affairs. Like the medieval diptych, these figures are juxtaposed like pictures in a hinged frame: Yahweh and the king in verses 1–15 and the wise teacher and scoundrel in verses 20–30. Thus, we must look to see how these portraits illuminate one another.

God and king. The first distinguishing feature of the chapter is the concentration of Yahweh sayings, the strongest in the entire book. These proverbs draw a portrait of a God whose intentions for good cannot and will not be thwarted. The proverbs of verse 1 and those that follow are often taken as a negation or minimization of human intentions, as in the motto "a person proposes, God disposes." Yet the reverse is the case; somehow human initiative and divine purposes work together in a way that does not diminish either. How else can human actions have real consequences such as success and punishment, as these sayings show?

The sages lived, as Klyne Snodgrass suggests, between two truths,[18] and this observation seems consistent with the strategy of the proverbs. Between

---

17. Hubbard, *Proverbs*, 238, takes Acts 1:21–26 as illustrating the proverb. The human cast chose Matthias, but the story goes on to show that God chose Paul. The sailors in Jonah 1:7 cast lots to find the source of the trouble and discern God's will. In Prov.18:18 the lot makes decisions that settle disputes and keeps opponents apart.

18. K. Snodgrass, *Between Two Truths: Living with Biblical Tensions* (Grand Rapids: Zondervan, 1990).

two sayings a truth comes forth that is greater than the sum of its parts. Interpreters differ on the significance of this binocular view of life, some suggesting that our plans must depend on God if they are to succeed,[19] others that God's purposes are accomplished in the end even when ours are not in line.[20] To an extent, both can be faithfully drawn from these sayings, but what comes through most clearly is Yahweh's passion for righteousness and justice and his commitment to realize those desires. Verse 8 makes the statement most clearly, even though it is the one proverb in the series that does not name "the LORD." We will see that its claim, "better a little with righteousness," sums up the mind of God.

We are to share this mind of God, thinking like him and sharing his desires. "Fear of the LORD" becomes both the motivation and the means to turn from evil, as does Yahweh's commitment to "love and faithfulness" (cf. Ex. 34:5–7).[21] Fear of Yahweh and trust in God's forgiveness go hand in hand, saying, "Has no one condemned you?... Then neither do I condemn you.... Go now and leave your life of sin" (John 8:10–11). Here again, God's intentions are fulfilled as we renounce sin and walk in ways that please him (Prov. 16:7).

The "better than" saying of 16:8 and its companions in 16:16 and 19 serve as qualifiers for the promises of health, wealth, and honor we find throughout the book. Wisdom has its rewards but also its requirements, and so we need these qualifiers when we listen to preachers of prosperity and victory. The "better than" proverbs teach us that if we have to choose (as is often the case in real life), we ought to choose "fear of the LORD" (15:16), love (15:17), righteousness, and justice (16:8). Paradoxically, we choose for God, betting with our lives that we will not lose in ways the wicked do, and in so doing we find that our choices are not as stark as we imagined.

The math of the proverbs shows that wise living adds a great deal to even modest amounts. While the choices between good and evil are sharply contrasted in the proverbs, they are not necessarily choices between our desires and God's. Instead, we find that our deepest desires are met, or transformed or redirected, as we grow in our understanding of God and want what God wants. The theme is carried through in the portrait of the just king, a harmonic counterpoint to this picture of God.

We have seen that Yahweh sayings and the royal sayings overlap in what seems to be an intentional design. The only saying that does not name Yahweh in 16:1–9 is about righteousness and justice (16:8), and the only

19. Whybray, *Proverbs*, 240.

20. Ross, "Proverbs," 1,002–3.

21. Van Leeuwen, "Proverbs," 159, finds here an allusion to the self-naming speech of Yahweh before Moses, set in the story of Israel's sin with the golden calf.

saying that does not name the king in 16:10–15 is a Yahweh saying about honest scales (16:11), a symbol of the king's righteousness (16:12) and justice (16:10). Setting the proverbs of Yahweh and the king side by side, we see a number of parallels signaled by catchwords:

- Yahweh *weighs* motives and intentions (16:2), and a just set of *weights* and scales are his doing (16:11).
- Yahweh *establishes* human plans (16: 3, 9) even as the king's throne is *established* through righteousness (16:12).
- Human pride is *detestable* to Yahweh and brings punishment (16:5), just as kings *detest* wrongdoing with a wrath that brings death (16:12).
- Human ways can be *pleasing* to Yahweh (16:7) just as kings take *pleasure* in honest lips (16:13).
- Loyalty and faithfulness *atone* for evil (16:6) while wisdom knows how to appease (= *atone*) the king's wrath (16:14).
- Most important, the repetition of work (*maʾᵃśeh*) is used for human plans submitted to Yahweh (16:3) as well as the human decision to carry a bag of honest weights (16:11).

The king is identified with Yahweh as an authority, one who holds life and death in hand; he must ensure that justice is done on this earth. In this way, the king is the right hand of God. The juxtaposition of the portraits of divine and human rule suggests that Yahweh's purposes are carried out whenever human authorities decide to value what God values. If those rulers and authorities fail, Yahweh will still see that justice is done, but his first choice is kings and subjects who share God's desire for goodness. Using a common form of the proverb, we might paraphrase, "Better a good king who establishes right dealings throughout the land than a bad king who makes the LORD establish justice and righteousness."

In Israel's history, the story of the kings and the eventual conquest of the land show how painful this work of Yahweh can be. Yet the delightful story of Joseph and his brothers (Gen. 37–50) shows another outcome as human intentions for evil are taken up into the greater work of God. Both pictures of God's work in human history affirm that his intentions will be established, even though the way it works out may not be known in advance or evident for quite some time. The two portraits of God and king work together like a diptych; together the proverbs of 16:1–15 affirm the principle that godly authority not only establishes God's purposes on earth, it establishes our purposes, bringing success and prosperity to a community.

Wisdom and humility. Following the twofold portrait of God's will done "on earth as it is in heaven," a smaller section is framed by sayings that hold wisdom and its accompanying humility to be "better than" any form of riches or wealth (16:16–19). The echo of "better a little with righteousness" in 16:8 indicates the importance of a theme we have also heard repeated throughout the book. Between these two comparisons, a pair of proverbs about traveling draw a contrast between the one whose way avoids evil and the one who stumbles over the sin of pride. The juxtaposition of pride and the temptations of wealth is not surprising, for we who use the sociologist's term "status symbols" know that every age has used wealth and its appointments to signify superior strength and intelligence.

Yet here is the rub, for people in every age can and will be tempted to choose the power of gold over wisdom and its responsibilities. So also the pride that comes with it can move us to plunder others, to take what they have as spoils of war, even if it is done via corporate means and its false rhetoric. Remember the "greed is good" speech from the movie *Wall Street?* The associations of wealth, arrogance, and evil in these proverbs let the reader draw the rest of the picture of destruction, making humble identification with the oppressed all the more attractive.

Just as the earlier chapters of Proverbs laid out luxuries associated with robbery and adultery (1:10–19; 7:14–20), so here those riches are associated with arrogant pride, urging us again to choose wisdom over gold or jewels (2:4; 3:13–15). However, in these proverbs we find temptations that are close to home, temptations to financial gain as a source of pride. That pride can be seen as arrogance that leaves God out of the picture, trust in our own capacities to make our way, and pride in the power we can exercise over others in order to get what we want. As we make progress through Proverbs, then, we find the problems associated with illegitimate use of wealth speaking more and more to our daily lives.

The wise teacher and the scoundrel. Another pair of portraits takes shape as the image of the scoundrel in 16:25–30 helps us look back and recognize the figure of a wise teacher in 16:20–24. The teacher is also a learner, one who "seeks to understand a matter," one who find what is "good." This person stands in strong contrast with the violent man, who leads others down a way that is "not good" (16:29). Wise in heart, this teacher speaks pleasant words that increase learning (16:21, 23) and bring healing, sweetness like a flowing honeycomb (16:24). Readers imagine a person whose openness to learning and correction make that one a good teacher, one who is convinced of the life-giving power of good words.

Is not a teacher one who passes on what has been learned so that we may learn it also? Not so for the one who takes the way that merely "seems right" (16:25; cf. v. 2). Guided only by principles generated by the self and its interests, this person speaks fire that stirs up conflict and alienates friends (16:28). Perverse and twisted (16:28, 30), this person walks a crooked path that is "not good" and ends in death (16:25). Scoundrels speak, not to spread knowledge but to conceal their own evil thoughts and plans.

Set in the context of the chapter, it seems that the king is confronted with the choice to be a teacher or a thief. Certainly the Old and New Testaments present many examples of both kinds of rulers. The principle at the heart of the contrast is the connection between openness to learning and speech that teaches, that is, speaking that imparts life to others. The exaggeration of the contrast shows us how our lives can major on giving or taking, on loving others or abusing them. The proverbs ask us to choose the overall course of direction for our lives so that we can bring the everyday decisions into line. Hunger motivates action (16:26); the question is what sort of action will we choose?

Final victory. The final three verses of this chapter hardly seem related to one another, yet there is a common thread of final victory. The virtues of a lifelong commitment to righteousness yield a long life (16:31), the one who commands control of self is the true conqueror (16:32), and lots of chance point to the final decision of Yahweh (16:33). Human will can be directed toward faithfulness, longsuffering, and a determined openness to God's will.

The sages of Israel did not choose to engage in disputes over free will and sovereignty but rather set the two truths side by side and left it for us to reflect on the nexus. Perhaps *freedom* is a better word for the two sides of this coin, for there is a human freedom that plans, decides, initiates, and responds, but there is a divine freedom that has its say in the outcome of events. An increasing awareness of God's freedom to fulfill his intentions can move us to bring our intentions into alignment with God's.

The final proverb brings together the element of chance in the casting of lots with the sure execution of Yahweh's purposes. Human choices are not made less important by considering the sovereignty of God; rather, their true importance is shown. Perhaps in reading the proverbs of this chapter, we are to recall that the evil men at the start of the book hoped to entice a young learner down the wrong path (16:29; cf. 1:10, 15), saying, "Throw in your *lot* with us" (1:14). If ever there were a statement of foolish pride (16:5, 18–19), it is this one, claiming to hold the future in its hands, yet completely unaware that the decisions of the lot are "from the LORD."

THE CONCENTRATION OF Yahweh sayings in this chapter brings us face to face with the mysteries of freedom; humans who are free to make plans and execute them may or may not recognize that God is also free to accomplish his will, yet both are nonnegotiable facts of life. To ignore either is to live an unbalanced life, for too great an emphasis on God's freedom may lead to passivity while too great an emphasis on human freedom may lead to pride. In ways that are left for the reader to discern, the overlap of the Yahweh and king sayings in this chapter becomes a model for wisdom in the lives of all readers.

Yahweh and authority. In this series of proverbs, the king is identified with Yahweh as an authority, one who holds life and death in hand. As we have seen, the king is also the right hand of God, responsible to his subjects, to make sure that justice is done on this earth. But, like every subject, the king is responsible to God, and to exercise God's authority, the king must also demonstrate godly character shaped after God's hatred of evil and his unrelenting opposition to those who practice it. As a subject himself, the king must practice honesty in speech and conduct. To betray that charge, then, is to fail in the duties as ruler and subject both.[22] Authority looks two ways, to the purposes of God and to the welfare of those ruled. When the look turns toward self and its gains and security, responsibility is betrayed and disaster follows.

The view of royal authority in Proverbs, therefore, suggests that every person must learn to be second in command if he or she is to exercise leadership well. The sin of pride rears its head when one rejects responsibility for others as a responsibility before God. It is arrogant to assume that one rules but is not ruled, or that one answers to no one but oneself. The biblical story of Joseph and his family offers one example of a boy who dreamed of others bowing before him but finally bowed before his father. As second in command to Pharaoh, he also learned that he was second in command to God and eventually said so to his brothers (Gen. 45:8–9; 50:18–19). So too the centurion in the Gospel story spoke of his own authority while deferring to the greater authority of Jesus (Luke 7:1–8). For this reason, the identification of wisdom with humility and lowliness comes out in many of the proverbs in this chapter.

Readers will recognize their own situations of responsibility and temptations to serve the interests of self. We recognize that nearly everyone is granted some authority in life, some responsibility for leadership. Parents, church committee chairs, elected officials, managers, and pastors all exercise authority that is to work for the good of those being served.[23] Here in this

---

22. See Deut. 18 and 1 Sam. 8 for the limits on kingly authority.

23. Hubbard, *Proverbs*, 232–53, treats this from the viewpoint of believers' response to dual authority, illustrated by Israel's exile in Babylon, Daniel's service in the king's court, and Jesus' words about giving only what Caesar owns to Caesar (Matt. 22:15–22; Mark 12:13–17; Luke 20:20–26).

set of Proverbs is the servant leadership that Jesus had in mind when, after washing his disciples' feet, he said in John 13:13–17:

> You call me "Teacher" and "Lord," and rightly so, for that is what I am. Now that I, your Lord and Teacher, have washed your feet, you also should wash one another's feet. I have set you an example that you should do as I have done for you. I tell you the truth, no servant is greater than his master, nor is a messenger greater than the one who sent him. Now that you know these things, you will be blessed if you do them.

Leadership of this sort thinks of its work as serving both the heavenly king and his subjects. Authority like this never thinks of power as something we hold over people and use to get things done, but rather as that which gets underneath and lifts up those who need support and encouragement.

To speak of the God-given responsibilities of leadership is not to say that the king's decisions are infallible (16:10); rather, like the cast of the lot, the king's words are to indicate the will of God. Therefore, in this ideal statement of the king's role, those lips and mouth will not betray justice. For this reason the army of Israel vetoed Saul's decision to put Jonathan to death. Saul had decreed that no soldier could eat before the battle was won, and Jonathan's reversal of that command came to light when Saul cast lots. But Saul's decree and the lot were overturned as the men recognized the hand of God in Jonathan's victory (1 Sam. 14:1–48).

Implications of leadership. If the first fifteen proverbs of the chapter present a picture of leadership exercised in full recognition of God's authority over human history, the second half of the chapter offers a series of implications. (1) This servant leadership rejects pride in favor of humble identification with the lowly and oppressed (16:18–19). More than a simple and superficial acknowledgment that God loves one and all, this work of leadership actually foregoes personal gains when the needs of others require it. In this way, one holds wisdom as more valuable than gold (16:16).

The journalist and television personality Malcolm Muggeridge spent half a lifetime ridiculing the pretenses of political power and pride before he came to see that the real danger of the age of modernity was materialism, calling its neon signs for "Gas, Drugs, Beauty, Food . . . the *logos* of our time, presented in sublime simplicity." A series of interviews with Mother Theresa and witnessing her humble identification with the poor of India finally convinced him to embrace the Christian faith he had kept at bay since boyhood. According to one of his biographers, "the more he thought about the moral decay of the West the more he agonized about his own recalcitrant sins. 'The only wish I have left in this life,' he confided in his diary, 'is that there should be burnt out of me all egotism, all pride, all lechery, all greed. . . . I want my being's dwindling flame to burn clearly and steadily, with no smoky spurts, until it flickers out."[24] Here Muggeridge saw in his own life the link between pride and greed that so worried the sages of Proverbs.

(2) Servant leadership listens, learns, and teaches, using "pleasant words" to bring both instruction and encouragement. Such leadership never rules by fiat but rather hopes to share insights and discoveries to persuade, not coerce. A commitment to do everything possible to help others see one's reasons brings a sweetness to a leader's words. Likewise, a commitment to listen and stay open to new information and insights makes the words that are finally spoken that much more persuasive.

Most of us are familiar with the survey that ranked personal integrity and the ministry of preaching as the two most important roles of a minister.[25] Would parishioners know that by watching us work? Proverbs' emphasis on speaking can apply to all, for at least in theory, all can speak out for justice in a participatory democracy. This vision of a fair and equitable society is as challenging as it is exciting, for one can sense that these sages knew about backroom deals and greased palms that appear in every form of government. Thus, ministers and members of congregations can consider how they may lend their voices when a just word is needed. Sadly the same survey of parishioners ranked "leader for social justice" eighteen out of twenty-one! Pastors and teachers of the church can also take the challenge of these proverbs to help the members of their congregations "preach good news to the poor . . . bind up the brokenhearted . . . proclaim freedom for captives and release from darkness for the prisoners" (Isa. 61:1; cf. Luke 4:18–19). It takes a lot of work to inform, teach, and persuade in leadership, but the results are worth it.

(3) The virtues of patience and endurance proves that leadership is really about servanthood, for if it were not, we would all quit whenever our needs go unmet or our plans are frustrated (16:31–32). We demonstrate patience when we keep at our work even when it seems unrewarding or unproductive, or when we hold on to the principles of servanthood even though we know some good old-fashioned authoritarianism would do the trick. We all face the human desire to hold power over our environment and other people so that they may serve our desires.

Some years ago, a pop group had a hit with the title "Everybody Wants to Rule the World." In one way or another we all wish to set up petty

24. G. Wolfe, *Malcolm Muggeridge: A Biography* (Grand Rapids: Eerdmans, 1995), 311–12.
25. N. Shawchuck and R. Hauser, *Leading the Congregation: Caring for Yourself While Serving the People* (Nashville: Abingdon, 1993), 116.

kingdoms (esp. in churches); the mark of leadership is recognizing that tendency and taking steps to manage it. If not, we can imagine that the kingdom really is ours and react terribly when it is threatened. Even with the best of intentions we can make the mistake of assuming that what we want is what is really best; we are really in trouble when we are willing to go to war over it.

The military imagery of the final proverbs may be more appropriate to our situations than we think, identifying the competitive spirit that crops up so easily. One way to counteract our tendencies toward building up kingdoms of self is to yield up our Palm Pilot calendars and five-year plans to God. We can examine them closely, recognizing that our plans may reflect more of our own desires than God's. At the same time, we can trust that God will take our prayers seriously when we ask, "Your kingdom come, your will be done, on earth as it is in heaven."

The proverbs of this chapter are realistic. They acknowledge the temptations to evil and recognize that some people will give in to them, but they are also realistic in their optimism. They confidently assert that Yahweh will have his way with this earth he has made, even when some would head off on their own. As symbols of this confidence, two proverbs about scales and lot-casting ask us to look closely at two hand-held bits of technology, one to ensure fair dealing between humans, the other to determine a future course of events. The scale can be perverted and the decision of the lot misinterpreted or ignored, but if Yahweh is behind the weighing of stones and the weighing of spirits, there can be no final deception or perversion.

Proverbs 17:1–28

1 BETTER A DRY CRUST with peace and quiet
 than a house full of feasting, with strife.
2 A wise servant will rule over a disgraceful son,
 and will share the inheritance as one of the brothers.
3 The crucible for silver and the furnace for gold,
 but the LORD tests the heart.
4 A wicked man listens to evil lips;
 a liar pays attention to a malicious tongue.
5 He who mocks the poor shows contempt for their Maker;
 whoever gloats over disaster will not go unpunished.
6 Children's children are a crown to the aged,
 and parents are the pride of their children.
7 Arrogant lips are unsuited to a fool—
 how much worse lying lips to a ruler!
8 A bribe is a charm to the one who gives it;
 wherever he turns, he succeeds.
9 He who covers over an offense promotes love,
 but whoever repeats the matter separates close friends.
10 A rebuke impresses a man of discernment
 more than a hundred lashes a fool.
11 An evil man is bent only on rebellion;
 a merciless official will be sent against him.
12 Better to meet a bear robbed of her cubs
 than a fool in his folly.
13 If a man pays back evil for good,
 evil will never leave his house.
14 Starting a quarrel is like breaching a dam;
 so drop the matter before a dispute breaks out.
15 Acquitting the guilty and condemning the innocent—
 the LORD detests them both.
16 Of what use is money in the hand of a fool,
 since he has no desire to get wisdom?
17 A friend loves at all times,
 and a brother is born for adversity.
18 A man lacking in judgment strikes hands in pledge
 and puts up security for his neighbor.

¹⁹ He who loves a quarrel loves sin;
   he who builds a high gate invites destruction.
²⁰ A man of perverse heart does not prosper;
   he whose tongue is deceitful falls into trouble.
²¹ To have a fool for a son brings grief;
   there is no joy for the father of a fool.
²² A cheerful heart is good medicine,
   but a crushed spirit dries up the bones.
²³ A wicked man accepts a bribe in secret
   to pervert the course of justice.
²⁴ A discerning man keeps wisdom in view,
   but a fool's eyes wander to the ends of the earth.
²⁵ A foolish son brings grief to his father
   and bitterness to the one who bore him.
²⁶ It is not good to punish an innocent man,
   or to flog officials for their integrity.
²⁷ A man of knowledge uses words with restraint,
   and a man of understanding is even-tempered.
²⁸ Even a fool is thought wise if he keeps silent,
   and discerning if he holds his tongue.

Original Meaning

ALTHOUGH THE INDIVIDUAL sayings of this chapter seem to have little in common as compared with the arrangement of the previous chapter, some central themes emerge upon a second look. The picture here works a bit like the "magic eye" illusions: If one looks straight at the details of the design, little else appears, but if one steps back a bit and lets the details merge, a larger image takes shape. Running through a melange of sayings about families (households) and larger communities are the twin themes of strife and unity. Proverbs about speech habits like gossip and quarreling are intertwined with proverbs about handling money (bribes and pledges) to show their connection with wisdom's goals of justice and harmony.

The chapter begins with situations of humble status and means (17:1–2) and ends with recommendations to keep words few (17:27–28). The implicit "less is more" philosophy of these sayings urges us to match moderation in speech and acquisition with extravagant generosity and faithfulness. While it is possible to hoard one's goods and sin against those who have little, there is no possibility of spending too much on righteousness, justice, and uprightness (cf. 1:3).

The Yahweh sayings at 17:3 and 15 divide the chapter in two, each half concluding with sayings about restraint (17:14, 27−28) and right judgment (17:15, 26). A number of sayings in the second half repeat themes begun in the first, often with the same vocabulary ("bribe" in 17:8, 23; "ruler/official" [*nadib*] in 17:7, 26; "love" in 17:9, 17). The satires on the fool, some in clusters,[1] crystallize what is said in the other sayings, providing clues for reading the proverbs that follow.

> Yahweh, Watching and Testing (17:1−15)
>> Households, sons, and brothers (17:1−6)
>> Eloquent fools and lying rulers (17:7−11)
>> Dangers of fools and folly (17:12−15)
>
> Wisdom, Always Close at Hand (17:16−28)
>> Fools and money, brothers and friends (17:16−20)
>> Suffering fools in secret (17:21−24)
>> Fools thought wise when silent (17:25−28)

The fool brings grief to parents and danger to the community; thus, the chapter also shows movement from household sayings (17:1−6), to community sayings (17:7−20), to a mixture of both (17:21−28).

Households, Sons, and Brothers (17:1−6)

WHILE THE CONNECTIONS between verses 1−6 are not immediately apparent, the family setting of verses 1−2 and verse 6 provide the context for the middle sayings about attitude.

17:1. The main contrast of a dry crust[2] with feasting is qualified by the accompanying quiet versus "strife." As in other "better than" sayings (e.g., 15:16−17; 16:8), the qualities of a loving home, peace, and quiet are set above material gains. Note that the saying does not pit poverty against wealth but rather sets each in a context, concluding that the emotional costs of strife may even be greater than the wealth one gains. "Feasting," as the NIV text note indicates, is (lit.) "sacrifices," presumably the *šalom* offering, which

---

1. The distribution of "fool" sayings does not indicate any overarching structure, although Heim sets off 17:10−16 and 17:21−25 on this basis (17:1−9, 10−16, 17−20, 21−25, 26−28); see his *Like Grapes of Gold Set in Silver*, 232−34. See also Scherer, *Das Weise Wort und Seine Wirkung*, 251−52, who divides 17:2−3, 4−9, 10−13, 14−15, 16−22, and 17:23−18:8.

2. Cf. 28:21, where the crust of bread is a sign of poverty (R. N. Whybray, *Wealth and Poverty in the Book of Proverbs* [Sheffield: JSOT Press, 1990], 14−15).

promoted good relationships through sharing.[3] The irony is plain: If the goal of harmony is not met, what good is a sumptuous table?

17:2. Like verse 1, this saying is also about life in a household, so it might be paraphrased, "Better a wise servant than a shameful son." Status, like material prosperity, means little if it is not matched by wise character. Servants and sons alike can be shameful (10:5; 14:35), and in this saying neither is privileged. "Rule" links this saying with 16:32 (*mšl,* "controls"). On dividing inheritance, see Deuteronomy 21:17; on slaves inheriting wealth, Genesis 15:2—3.

17:3. "Tests" here is set in parallel to the crucible and furnace that removes impurities and tempers the metal, naming "the LORD" as tester and the heart as tested. The Hebrew saves "the LORD" for last, creating a chiastic pattern that enhances the sense of suspense and climax.[4] In 27:21, a person is tested by praise; while not stressful, such a test does reveal one's true colors. If there are no precious metals, the crucible will show it; if there are no characteristics of wise character, the test will show that also.[5]

17:4. Two parallel descriptions of a wicked listener demonstrate a lack of testing (cf. 17:3). It is ironic that one who lies can be taken in by the same sort of deception in others. A good heart will discern, but evil persons will accept anything as long as it is in line with their own purposes. The pungent metaphors of evil lips and malicious tongue suggest that you can tell how someone will speak by noting what he or she chooses to listen to. In other words, if a person finds gossip delicious, it's a good bet that such an individual will spread it just as quickly. Kidner paraphrases, "Evil words die without a welcome."[6]

17:5. Evil lips are at work when the poor are ridiculed or someone's misfortune becomes an occasion to "gloat" (lit., "rejoice"). Is this one of the wicked messages that verse 4 has in mind? Attitude is an action waiting to happen, and so the way we view others determines the way we will treat them. Perhaps it is the attitude of pride in one's own merits that offends Yahweh and will not go unpunished (16:5; cf. 14:31; 22:2; 29:13).[7] Even as

---

3. Kidner, *Proverbs,* 122, sees ironic play on the *šalom* offering in the phrase "sacrifices of strife"(Deut. 12:11, 21; 1 Sam. 20:6; see also 1 Sam. 1:3—7).

4. T. P. McCreesh, *Biblical Sound and Sense: Poetic Sound Patterns in Proverbs 10—29* (Sheffield: JSOT Press, 1991), 109—12.

5. Clifford, *Proverbs,* finds the image of refining in Ps. 26:2; 66:10; Jer. 9:6; esp. Zech. 13:9.

6. Kidner, *Proverbs,* 123.

7. Whybray, *Poverty and Wealth,* 41—42. Whybray believes that these proverbs do not see poverty as something that should be abolished, but they do tell the rich to remember that the poor are not theirs to be exploited; the poor belong to God.

Yahweh identifies himself with the poor, Jesus said that what we do to the least, we do for him (Matt. 25:40).

17:6. This saying repeats the Hebrew words for "crown" and "splendor" from 16:31. The recycling of images is a common literary technique in Proverbs, and here the signs of age and righteousness are used to describe the potential joys of family life, a reversal of the images of family disappointment (cf. 17:1–2). Long life and the blessing of children are universally desired (Ps. 127:3–5), and so the surprise of the proverb comes in the pride children take in their parents. Perhaps an encouragement to set a wise example is implied in this statement of the ideal.

Eloquent Fools and Lying Rulers (17:7–11)

A SATIRE ON the fool heads up this section (17:7), the first of a number that are scattered throughout the chapter (17:10, 12, 16, 21, 24, 25, 28).

17:7. The ruler's obligation to be honorable is here made vivid by comparison with the fool's arrogant speech. The saying is difficult to translate, primarily because the word for "arrogant" or "eloquent" (see NIV text note) means "remaining" or "excessive."[8] Some follow the NIV note and translate "fine words" (e.g., NRSV), while others follow the LXX (*pista*, "faithful") and translate "honest."[9] Honest lips are a fitting counterpart to lying, but Proverbs do not always use strict parallels in making comparisons. Here the point of comparison is what is "unsuited" or not fitting, and so the picture of an empty head trying to speak to things he knows nothing about seems more consistent with the satires on the fool.

In either case, the climax in the saying comes with the "how much more"; it is even worse to find lying lips with a leader or noble (although it happens more often than we would wish!). The wordplay on "fool" (*nabal*, cf. 1 Sam. 25:5) and "ruler" (or "noble," *nadib*; cf. Prov. 19:6; 25:7) also appears in Isaiah 32:5: "No longer will the *fool* be called *noble* nor the scoundrel be highly respected."

17:8. Just as the noble should not lie, neither should a judge or any other authority be vulnerable to a "bribe." In making an observation about life, the bribe (lit., a "stone of favor") is likened to magic, so effective are its powers. The saying is descriptive and does not commend the practice of paying bribes, so here perhaps is another satire, something like the folly of the magician's apprentice. If this power should come to hand, it is bound

---

8. N. M. Waldman, "A Note on Excessive Speech and Falsehood," *JQR* 67 (1976): 142–45. The phrase *śᵊpat yeter* has some connotation of "arrogant overbearing speech," with the overtone of "false speech." By analogy, see Ps. 31:19; Prov. 26:28.

9. Murphy, *Proverbs*, 126–27; Scott, *Proverbs*, 108.

to be misused and bring disaster. The Hebrew word for "succeeds" (*śkl*) in other contexts means "understanding," "discerning," or even "wise" (17:2; cf. 16:22–23).

17:9. It may be that the theme of misuse or overdoing a matter continues from verse 8. Here the comparison between one who forgets a transgression (cf. 10:12) and one who keeps bringing it up or repeats it to others (cf. 10:18) makes a common observation about friendship and families. "Separates close friends" uses the same Hebrew as 16:28. Is this tale-bearing another form of perverse speech? The observation leads to the general truth that it is better to forgive and forget.

17:10. While it is usually wise to let an offense go rather than to dwell on it, this saying holds up the value of a loving rebuke. One can confront a wise person and expect a change in behavior, but not from the fool, for whom a hundred blows are not persuasive enough. While beatings were a common part of educational practice in the ancient world, this contrast between the effective force of words and a beating should be kept in mind when reading the sayings that seem to advocate corporal punishment.[10] The point here is that blows *won't* work if words won't.

17:11. While some will receive a rebuke, others will not and just keep going headlong into evil. The use of physical force in this case is not corrective but restraining. It keeps the evil person from doing more harm. "Rebellion" implies service to a lord or king, and this evil person "seeks" rebellion rather than love (root *bqš*; cf. 17:9). The "merciless official" (or "cruel messenger") reminds the reader of the king's wrath, a "messenger of death" (16:14). While a wise person will appease that wrath, here the evil person only provokes it. One can seek reconciliation or one can seek rebellion; the choice is clear.

Dangers of Fools and Folly 17:12–15

THE DANGERS OF fools and evil persons juxtaposed throughout this cluster suggests that the two are not as removed from each other as we might think.

17:12. Although Yahweh's wrath is often linked with bears (2 Kings 2:23–34; Hos. 13:8), it is the greater danger of human folly that is in view here (cf. Prov. 28:15). While not in the form of a "better than" saying, this proverb does compare two encounters to point out a surprising lesser evil; literally, this verse reads: "Let one meet a bear robbed of cubs and not [or

---

10. So also *Ahikar* 6.83, "A blow for a serving-boy, a rebuke for a slave-girl, and for all your servants, discipline!" J. Lindenberger, "Ahiqar: A New Translation and Introduction," *Old Testament Pseudepigrapha* (Garden City, N.Y.: Doubleday, 1985), 2:498; *ANET*, 428.

rather than] a fool with folly."[11] The salt of the proverb compares the danger of a bear *without* her cubs to fools whose folly goes *with* them wherever they go. Still there is more than meets the eye, for readers may ask, how did the bear lose her cubs? If any would be foolish enough to take them, they would be dangerous persons to be around, especially when the bear comes charging!

17:13. Another proverb about the returning effects of evil (cf. 17:11), this ancient version of "what goes around, comes around" might be paraphrased, "evil for good, evil forever." Here the focus on the house suggests that an individual's choices have consequences for family, although the principle can also apply to one's community. The juxtaposition with a vivid proverb about dangerous folly (17:12) implies that evil in its shortsightedness is just plain dumb.

17:14. Just as water cannot be brought back under control once it is released, so a quarrel has a life of its own that can escalate beyond anyone's expectation. The solution is to leave things as they are, to let a matter go (cf. 17:9). If the image is that of a sluice gate for irrigation (11:25; cf. Isa. 58:11),[12] the life-giving effects of getting one's responses under control is underscored.

17:15. The common theme of Yahweh's hatred of evil is here applied to legal resolutions of disputes (cf. 17:14). Judges are responsible to convict the guilty and clear the innocent; both false judgments are equally detestable (an abomination) in Yahweh's eyes. One can surmise in the background the gain that such corrupt judges receive. The Hebrew roots for "righteous" and "wicked" (cf. Deut. 25:1) link this saying with the righteous/wicked contrasts of chapters 10–15.

Fools and Money, Brothers and Friends (17:16–20)

MONEY CANNOT BUY wisdom, but it can be used wisely. In the hands of a fool, money is useless (17:16) and can be easily lost (17:18). It is better to be rich in love and faithfulness (17:20).

17:16. The point of this satiric proverb is two-sided: It is folly to think one can buy wisdom since it is a gift of God and must be acquired through study (2:1–6), and even if wisdom could be bought, the fool lacks the sense (lit., "heart") to know what to do with it. The sharp juxtaposition of having

---

11. T. R. Schneider, *The Sharpening of Wisdom: Old Testament Proverbs in Translation* (Pretoria: Old Testament Society of South Africa, 1992), 143; GKC, 113cc, 152g. The emendation of *bᵊʾiš* to *beyᵊʾušo* or *beyᵊʾušah* ("in her desperation") is not attested in the versions and is not convincing; S. E. Loewenstamm, "Remarks on Proverbs 17:2 and 20:27," *VT* 37 (1987): 221–24.

12. Scott, *Proverbs*, 111; Clifford, *Proverbs*, 106.

money and lacking sense makes it clear that heart, both as "desire" and "mind" (NRSV), is the prerequisite for learning wisdom. Some see a dunce showing up at the door of a teacher with fee in hand, but evidence for this in Israel is lacking. Rather, we see a fool who does not know what to do with good things like money, responsibility, or even a proverb (26:6–9)!

17:17. In Hebrew, "one who loves at all times" comes first and is followed by the descriptor, a "friend" (or "neighbor"). The comparison of "all times" in the first line and the times of "distress" in the second suggests that friends can, by choice, do what is expected of family. Here concerns of household and community are drawn together (cf. 17:13). The saying implicitly rebukes those who claim friendship but are nowhere to be found when they are needed.

17:18. This saying presents a counterpoint to the two that have gone before. Here another person who "lacks heart" (NIV "judgment") concerning financial matters uses his "hand" to prove it (cf. 17:16). The proverb in between praises the "friend" (*rea^c*, 17:17) who is there in tough times, even if it involves money, but such help to a "neighbor" (*rea^c* in this verse) is fool-hardy when it endangers one's estate. If verse 17 recommends generosity in neighbor love, verse 18 warns that the borrower may become lax and default, leaving the one who offers help needing help instead.[13] While no proverb approves of the practice of surety, when taken together, this proverb pair advises readers to avoid trouble, not a neighbor in need.[14]

17:19. At first reading, this proverb seems to say that quarreling is a sin, and so we should turn from quarreling. The word order in Hebrew, how-ever, reads: "The one who loves an offense [NIV "sin"] loves a quarrel" (cf. 17:9, which uses the same Heb. words for "offense" and "seeks").[15] If lov-ing or holding onto an offense leads one to build a "high gate" (presumably to keep away neighbors), one trusts in a false hope. Better to have good rela-tionships with neighbors than the best security system. If you don't have goodwill with your neighbors, nothing else you do will help (cf. 17:18; 13:10). The contrast between loving neighbors (17:17) and loving strife (17:19) is strong. If the "high gate" also refers to architecture that is elevated to impress, the symbolism of "high" sets the builder above neighbors, a dangerous attitude.

---

13. On pledges, see 6:1; 11:15; 17:18; 20:16; 22:26; 27:13. See also the similar warning in Sir. 19:15–16, 20: "Do not forget the kindness of guarantor, for he has given his life for you. A sinner wastes the property of his guarantor, and the ungrateful person abandons his res-cuer.... Assist your neighbor to the best of your ability, but be careful not to fall yourself."

14. A. Scherer, "Is the Selfish Man Wise? Considerations of Context in Proverbs 10:1–22:16 with Special Regard to Surety, Bribery and Friendship," *JSOT* 76 (1997): 63.

15. Garrett, *Proverbs*, 161, notes the reverse of v. 9, from one who "seeks love" to one who "seeks breakup," translating *šeber* as "breakup" instead of "destruction."

17:20. This proverb is one of the many sayings that link "heart" and "tongue" to represent the whole person's thoughts and actions. It stresses results; this person not only fails to "prosper" ("find good" [*ṭob*]; cf. 16:20) but falls into "trouble" (*raʿah*; 17:4, 11, 13). The deceitful tongue (lit.) "turns over" or, as one translator put it, is "double-tongued."[16]

Suffering Fools in Secret (17:21–24)

SATIRES ABOUT THE fool appear at 17:21, 24, and 28; the sayings in this section examine the effects of folly in the secret places of life, comparing grief and gladness.

17:21. If verse 20 depicts the effects of folly on the person who practices it, this proverb reminds us that the effects spread throughout the family (17:2; cf. 10:5) and to others as well. The proverbs that precede this one stress responsibility, but it is doubtful that the father of a fool is to be held responsible for the son's wayward folly. However, it is clear that the effects are devastating, even drying the bones (as the next proverb shows).

17:22. The "cheerful heart" is one that rejoices (root *śmḥ*), linking this saying with the one before; the grief of the fool's family is countered here with the positive effects of joy. Unlike the "perverse heart" of 17:20, this heart makes for "good" (*ṭob*). Can we say that the rejoicing heart knows contentment and gratitude while the perverse heart schemes to gain more no matter how? In Proverbs, the "crushed spirit" is brought on by heartache (15:13) and is hard to bear (18:14).

17:23. The theme of making right judgments appeared in 17:15, but the term "justice" (*mišpaṭ*) was last seen in chapter 16, where it refers to the king's judgment, the just balance, and Yahweh's decision (16:10–11, 33). "In secret" translates "from the bosom or pocket," most likely a reference to a "bribe" (cf. 17:8) that is brought out from a secret place (cf. 21:14). Like the hidden heart that reveals its conditions in word, deed, and even the condition of the body, so a bribe given in secret does its damaging work; a perverse heart (17:20) works to pervert justice.

17:24. This saying contrasts the person who keeps wisdom nearby and the fool who looks everywhere else for answers. The ambiguity of the phrase "eyes of the fool, to the ends of the earth" has puzzled commentators, who have suggested that the fool suffers from a short attention span, or is prone to ambition and greed. Most likely we are to remember that Wisdom called out to all in the public square, yet was only heard by a few (1:20–33; 9:1–12). The satire should be read in light of the other satires, particularly the fool

---

16. Clifford, *Proverbs*, 163.

who hopes to buy wisdom in 17:16. The "discerning" person (*mebin*) appears also in the satire of 17:10.

Fools Thought Wise When Silent (17:25–28)

FOOLS BRING THEIR families grief, and injustice pains a community; therefore, the virtue of restraint in word and deed is a first step toward wisdom. The concentration of wisdom terms in verses 27–28 leads to the surprise of a fool who is considered wise and discerning.

17:25. The second of the sayings about "bearing" (root *yld*, 17:21) a foolish son, this variation on the theme adds the "bitterness" of the mother to the father's "grief" (cf. 10:1; 19:13; 29:15). A Sumerian proverb expresses a similar regret: "A disorderly son, his mother should not have given birth to him. His god should not have created him."[17]

17:26. Even worse than condemning those who have done no wrong ("the righteous"; cf. 17:15; Deut. 25:1–3) is flogging "officials" (*nadib*) for doing what is right; the term for "integrity" is used for walking straight. Just as "lying lips" are not fitting for a "ruler" (*nadib*, Prov. 17:7), the punishment of a righteous ruler is inappropriate. The proverb recommends fair judgment for all members of society.

17:27. This saying presents two signs of a person who has gathered "knowledge"—that one moderates both words and temper. These conjure up the image of a person who knows when it is best to hold back words and control one's response to anger. "Restraint" is to consider or give thought to one's words. The even-tempered person is "cool of spirit" (NRSV).

17:28. The recommendations of verse 27 on holding back words continues; to "hold his tongue" is (lit.) "shut his lips." Of course, appearances can deceive, but the observation confirms the wisdom of practicing self-discipline. Reserve and restraint are so powerfully communicative that even fools can appear wise. That fools cannot remain silent for long comes out in 15:2 and 18:2. The repetition of "wise" and "discerning" seems to reverse the contrast of 17:24.

Bridging Contexts

AS WE HAVE noted before, the collection of synonymous proverbs in chapters 16–22 present a somewhat more complicated picture of the business of living together, asking readers to use what they have learned through their study of the instructions and contrasting

---

17. B. Alster, *Proverbs of Ancient Sumer: The World's Earliest Proverb Collections*, 2 vols. (Bethesda, Md.: CDL Press, 1997), 1:32 (1.157).

proverbs to decide what is best in a given situation. Thus, the first and last proverbs of this chapter present some of the ironies and contradictions of life as it unfolds before us. Just as a rich table may not be desirable when there is strife, so a fool can appear wise by practicing the first principle of wisdom, self-control. The varied proverbs present scenes of family strife, communities of love and justice, reflections on having much and having little, and the practice of restraint as a first step toward wisdom.

Conflict and strife. The theme of conflict and strife appears in 17:1 (and perhaps 17:2[18]). Surely the tension between parents and foolish offspring results in some yelling and screaming (17:21, 25). Some people, it seems, actually love a quarrel and, believing that fences make good neighbors, keep themselves as distant from others as possible (17:19). There is another picture, however, for in 17:6 family members realize they are each other's greatest inheritance, and 17:17 takes the ideal of family support and harmony and applies it to neighbors and friends of the larger community. Other proverbs show that many will seek love instead of destruction and cover over an offense instead of spreading it around like a talebearer (17:9, 14).

My own memories of living next to a retiree bring this positive picture home. A wooden fence separated our urban postage-stamp backyards, more for a sense of privacy than anything else. In summer, we could hear what went on in each other's backyards and houses, even what was on TV! Like it or not, we lived together, and so we both worked at offering help whenever we could and heading off potential conflicts before they grew into something bigger. Nothing happened on our block that this fellow did not see, and because we were on good terms, he was always looking out for our welfare, even keeping our front lawn watered and green. His old-fashioned approach to being a neighbor taught me a great deal.

Perhaps it is within families that conflict hits the hardest. At first readers may be surprised at the picture of a house filled with both feasting and strife, but news stories of domestic violence and family conflict over large inheritances remind us that having much often creates the desire to have more. The proverbs of wealth and poverty (17:1, 5, 17, 18) only imply what James stated directly in James 4:1–3:

> What causes fights and quarrels among you? Don't they come from your desires that battle within you? You want something but don't get it. You kill and covet, but you cannot have what you want. You quarrel and fight. You do not have, because you do not ask God. When you

---

18. Whybray, *The Composition of the Book of Proverbs*, 111.

ask, you do not receive, because you ask with wrong motives, that you may spend what you get on your pleasures.

James wrote to a Christian community in deep conflict, and the sages of the proverbs knew what can happen as well. Yet again, their collection includes the reverse picture of the friend who loves at all times, based on the ideal of family who stand by in time of trouble (17:17). Therefore the family and neighbor proverbs do present a model of what a larger community may become when the well-being of all is held higher than gains for self. In the fall of 2001, the American people were awed by the commitment and sacrifice of so many as the World Trade Towers fell before their eyes. But they were equally dismayed to learn that during that same time, the executives of a major corporation lied to its investors and employees, claiming that stocks were growing as those executives sold off their declining shares.

Love and justice. For this reason, implicit throughout this chapter is an emphasis on the twin virtues of love and justice. Just as the Creator is insulted when the poor he made are mocked (17:5), so he is disgusted when legal verdicts are perverted, sometimes with a bribe (17:8, 15, 23), always for some sort of personal gain. Ever vigilant, this is Yahweh who tests hearts to see if their intentions are pure (17:3), looking for love that rejoices in righteousness, not poverty (17:5, 22). This is the God of justice, who looks to see that righteousness is not rewarded with evil (17:13, 15, 26) and that evil is not rewarded with good (17:20). Thus, we can test and examine our own hearts. If it is love that looks out for a neighbor in time of need, it is justice that makes sure that no one falls into need because of greed. The malicious and double tongue deceives for its own gain, but truthful lips and upright rulers give the reader a sense of hope (17:7, 26).

There are only two Yahweh sayings in chapter 17 (three if we count v. 5, which calls God "Maker"), yet their common theme of testing sets a tone for the chapter. Just as Yahweh tests all hearts, so also some are charged with testing members of the larger community. If strife comes before the judge, that judge had better not pervert justice or take bribes. To call the wicked righteous or the righteous wicked is an abomination to the Lord, who judges the judges. Here again in this chapter, Yahweh watches human affairs to see whether hearts and words live up to the standards of love and justice.

In our own day, we may ask whether the economic scenarios of these proverbs can speak to the varieties of conflicts we experience. We know that family conflicts are not always about money and that conflicts in the church often appear to be about secondary matters (e.g., the color of curtains or the kind of music used in worship). Still, the challenge for contemporary readers is to discern how such conflicts can be traced to failures of love and justice. We bristle or blush when we realize a conflict is really about winning, having what we want without care for what the other wants or needs. While it is certainly not wrong to go after what we want, we learn here that we can rarely act on our desires free from consideration of others. Some sense of balance and fairness is necessary, making the discernment of wisdom teaching all the more crucial.

The wisdom of restraint. As we exercise love and justice, we are really practicing a form of self-restraint; that is, we hold back on some of our desires when we realize that taking for ourselves also means taking from another. Likewise, we hold back on all that we might say when we discern that such restraint is for the good of our relationships with others. We know that we cannot just let anger fly whenever things don't suit us if we want to have friends, just as we know it is not fair always to let others have their way at our expense (17:27–28). If it is wrong to engage in excesses of taking or speaking, the wisdom of restraint knows when to do both, again using the standards of love and justice to decide.

The proverbs of this chapter seem to relate the two, particularly around the matters of speech. Liars like to hear the kind of malice they spread, just as words can harm by mocking the poor and crowing over the troubles of others (17:4–5, 20). Some may tell lies and boast, but we can hold back from saying bad things about others, even if there is cause (17:7, 9). We must remember that words, like waters, cannot be gathered once they are spilled; such restraint and discretion keeps quarrels from breaking loose and causing destruction (17:14, 19). Yes, sometimes less is more (cf. 17:1)!

Perhaps this is the basic principle that fools fail to see, for the satirical proverbs shine their light on the fools' desire for possessions that are inappropriate. In other words, fools run after certain possessions but lack the important ones. The fool may have (or pretend to have) a gift of gab (17:7) but lack common sense, or scruples, or both. The fool may have money (17:6) but doesn't know that it cannot buy wisdom. The fool looks for wisdom everywhere but where it might be found (17:24; cf. James 1:5–8). The only thing the fool really owns is folly (Prov. 17:12) and the grief it brings to parents (17:21, 25). Three of the fool satires show a person hoping to buy wisdom (17:10), not knowing where to look for it (17:24), and finally practicing wisdom in some small measure (17:28). Is this a sign of small gain or redemption for the fool?

If so, then the fool illustrates the difference between living in ignorant isolation and the joys and responsibilities of living in healthy relationships with family and neighbors. The fool's silence can be an example to the wise who really would take their connections to others seriously. To sum up, the proverbs ask us to think of ourselves as if we were intimately related, not independent. This principle is stated baldly in the next chapter: "An unfriendly man pursues selfish ends; he defies all sound judgment" (18:1). But in addition, these proverbs also present repeated examples of virtuous lives of justice, love, and self-control that enable persons to live together, for how else can the virtues be enjoyed?

The story of Joseph and his family (Gen. 37–50) reminds us that these virtues are learned, not innate. Keeping these proverbs in mind, readers of that story might ask: What would have happened if Joseph had kept his dreams to himself? Was the conflict with his brothers over the inheritance or simply Joseph's desire to stand above them? Were they concerned over the money or their father's favoritism? We cannot say for sure, but we do know that Joseph's folly was matched by his brothers, bringing grief to their father.

But we also see that Joseph grew in wisdom, learning to speak wisely to jailers and kings. After testing the hearts of his brothers, he found that Judah had learned to care about his father's welfare, offering himself as a slave so as not to cause his father any more pain. In response, Joseph decided to cover up the offense against him and let it go. "And now, do not be distressed and do not be angry with yourselves for selling me here, because it was to save lives that God sent me ahead of you" (Gen. 45:5). This beautiful story of the forgiving grace of God also speaks to what works in our communities, a generosity of spirit that refuses to put the good of one before the good of all.

CONFLICT, CONFRONTATION, **and resolution.** Perhaps we should begin our discussion of contemporary life by facing facts. The evangelical church is just as prone to bitter conflict as the rest of the world, perhaps even more so. I recently heard one estimate that 30 percent of our churches need serious help. No wonder Jesus prayed for the unity of the church—he knew what was coming! We need not lament or paint overly bleak pictures of the situation, however, for I doubt that things are much different today from any other time in history. Conflict and its roots in inordinate desire have always been with us.

What is unique in today's situation is the tendency for people to leave churches when things get too hot, for we all know of people who hop from church to church carrying stories about how awful the previous one was. We can bemoan a lack of commitment, but more likely the issue at stake is the way conflict is managed. If, as we often quote, "everyone wants to rule the world," then issues of justice and fairness will always arise. Thus, the question is, will they be handled wisely or foolishly, with cries for a pound of flesh or with generosity?

A number of the proverbs gathered in this chapter recommend the curious blend of generosity and forgiveness (17:9, 14) with a reticence in words that at times seems downright stingy (17:27–28). While commitment to a community, warts and all, is a first step,[19] it is the practice of honest confrontation and forgiveness that helps imperfect groups of imperfect people hang together. Better the riches of kindness than those of feasting.

Better, that is, if we have to choose. The film version of *Babette's Feast* presents scene after scene of glorious fine food to make the point that love and generosity can sit at a wonderful table too. Fleeing the violence of nineteenth-century France, Babette has come to work for the elderly daughters of a local minister. These pious sisters make porridge out of stale bread crusts to feed the poor and are unstinting in their devotion to them. Unfortunately, the flock their father founded in their small village has been increasingly divided, dredging up sins of the past and throwing them in each other's faces.

Babette has made her home with these people, and her only connection with her homeland is the purchase of an annual lottery ticket. One day she wins a fortune in the lottery and asks to prepare a dinner in celebration of the late minister's one-hundredth birthday, but the sisters and the village are worried that their father will not approve of the lavish menu she plans, especially the wine! As the delicious meal progresses, however, hearts warm and loving words are exchanged. Only later do the sisters learn that Babette had once been a great chef in Paris and that she has spent all her winnings on the meal. Babette has caught the truth of the proverb that the sisters and their friends have missed, namely, that it is generosity of spirit that makes the table joyful, not the quality of the fare (17:1).

So our hearts are tested (17:3), for it is there, where our deepest intentions and desires lie, that who we really are becomes known. If our hearts are instructed in wisdom's ways, we know how to be generous when needed and also when to hold back. Both can be practiced in the context of faithfulness to parents and siblings, neighbors and friends. Such faithfulness can be shown in good times and bad, as various proverbs show. In good times, we can speak and act in ways that cover offenses and do not provoke them. If the goal is a "quiet house," then the place to begin is with ear and tongue, neither listening to malicious talk (17:4) nor producing it (17:5).

---

19. D. Gill, *Being Good: Building Moral Character* (Downers Grove, Ill.: InterVarsity, 2000), 43–61. Gill recommends commitment to a community and its mutual work of building character.

The context of the gathered proverbs makes one wonder whether both these proverbs are references to the way we talk about the poor ("Can you believe the way they live?") or anyone with problems ("Did you hear about poor so and so's ____ [affair, divorce, business failure, problems with kids, etc.]"?). Likewise, if we find ourselves secretly rejoicing in the news of someone's misfortune, we know we have some inner work to do. Somehow, that response suggests that we feel cheated in some way, perhaps because some expectations of life have gone unfulfilled. As we become aware of these inner reactions, we can also practice the inner generosity of wishing another well while refraining from any comment at all.

Speech that is loving and just practices restraint in various forms. The worst offense is lying (17:7) and bribing to buy the words of another (17:8), but lesser errors include repeating offenses (17:9). Instead, we can practice honest and loving confrontation (17:10), just as Jesus taught (see Matt. 18:15–20 on confrontation; Matt. 5:23–26 on making amends).

I said *loving and honest* confrontation because it is so easy to turn a confrontation into a quarrel. One editorial I read pointed out the temptations to "flame" that come with e-mail, for it has never been so easy to write harsh and angry words and then press "Send." Traditional wisdom has always advised that we write our letters and then read them another time before sending them off. The song "Letter That I Wrote" speaks of the letters written that were never intended to be sent, only written to get the burden out on the table, to blow off steam, or to achieve clarity. Singing as a wronged lover, the lyrics recall the singer's struggle to find the right words to express herself, "Though the words were not for you to hear." Then, after sitting down to write the letter, the singer "fell sleeping as the sun sank in the west."[20]

Thus, it may be that wisdom's blend of generosity and restraint will teach us how to be a friend at all times—one born for adversity, certainly helping those in need but also weathering disappointments in relationship. We may need more help with the latter because so many in our day feel wounded and let down in our churches, sometimes because expectations are too great, sometimes because love and justice have failed. Wisdom, living in these proverbs, teaches us what is best, most valuable, and deeply satisfying, helping us learn when it is right to make gifts and loans and when to cancel debts of all kinds. Most of all, we need help in learning to give generously of understanding, kindness, and forgiveness and when to hold back words that tear us apart.

---

20. R. and L. Williams, "Letter That I Wrote," from *Devil of a Dream* (Sugar Hill Records, 1998).

Proverbs 18:1–24

¹ AN UNFRIENDLY MAN pursues selfish ends;
   he defies all sound judgment.
² A fool finds no pleasure in understanding
   but delights in airing his own opinions.
³ When wickedness comes, so does contempt,
   and with shame comes disgrace.
⁴ The words of a man's mouth are deep waters,
   but the fountain of wisdom is a bubbling brook.
⁵ It is not good to be partial to the wicked
   or to deprive the innocent of justice.
⁶ A fool's lips bring him strife,
   and his mouth invites a beating.
⁷ A fool's mouth is his undoing,
   and his lips are a snare to his soul.
⁸ The words of a gossip are like choice morsels;
   they go down to a man's inmost parts.
⁹ One who is slack in his work
   is brother to one who destroys.
¹⁰ The name of the LORD is a strong tower;
   the righteous run to it and are safe.
¹¹ The wealth of the rich is their fortified city;
   they imagine it an unscalable wall.
¹² Before his downfall a man's heart is proud,
   but humility comes before honor.
¹³ He who answers before listening—
   that is his folly and his shame.
¹⁴ A man's spirit sustains him in sickness,
   but a crushed spirit who can bear?
¹⁵ The heart of the discerning acquires knowledge;
   the ears of the wise seek it out.
¹⁶ A gift opens the way for the giver
   and ushers him into the presence of the great.
¹⁷ The first to present his case seems right,
   till another comes forward and questions him.
¹⁸ Casting the lot settles disputes
   and keeps strong opponents apart.
¹⁹ An offended brother is more unyielding than a fortified city,
   and disputes are like the barred gates of a citadel.

20 From the fruit of his mouth a man's stomach is filled;
      with the harvest from his lips he is satisfied.
21 The tongue has the power of life and death,
      and those who love it will eat its fruit.
22 He who finds a wife finds what is good
      and receives favor from the LORD.
23 A poor man pleads for mercy,
      but a rich man answers harshly.
24 A man of many companions may come to ruin,
      but there is a friend who sticks closer
      than a brother.

WHILE A NUMBER of the proverbs of this chapter deal with the behavior and attitudes of the rich and poor, most of the sayings focus on use of words. A number of fool satires focus on speech habits that bring negative response. Although some proverbs treat matters of wealth and power, it is office of judge rather than king that is in view. Readers are asked to become more and more discerning as they interpret these proverbs and discover how their apparent disorganization points to a greater and richer unity. The themes that emerge with close study both echo the insights of previous chapters and provoke new thoughts and deeper insights.

The outline proposed here is based on similarities of topic and theme, recognizing that not every saying fits into the cluster.[1]

Sayings on speech and fools (18:1–8)
Sayings on strength, safety, and pride (18:9–12)
Sayings on speech and disputes (18:13–19)
Sayings on speech and its rewards (18:20–24)

Sayings on Speech and Fools (18:1–8)

THE MAJORITY OF these proverbs are about speech and its effects; all are concerned with the attitudes and actions that destroy relationships and community.

---

1. Meinhold, *Die Sprüche*, 1:296, divides using the key word "brother" in vv. 9, 19, 24; vv. 1–9 on perverse speech; vv. 10–19 on strengths that come to the wise; vv. 20–24 on speech and friends.

18:1. The "unfriendly" one is (lit.) a "separated" person who simply "seeks desire."[2] In other words, individualists like this one isolate themselves from other people with no thought for their concerns and needs. "Defies" translates the same word as "breaks out" in 17:14; the only other occurrence of this word in the Old Testament carries the basic sense of "quarrel" (20:3). After all that has been said in chapter 17 about family and community, the picture of isolation and quarreling here continues the theme of behaviors that bring strife.

18:2. Even as the unfriendly or "isolated" person of verse 1 "defies" (root *glʿ*) sound judgment, so this fool only "delights in airing his own opinions" or (lit.) "revealing [root *glh*] what is in his heart [*leb*]." The point of comparison is the self-centered and lonely universe each inhabits; the first quarrels with wisdom, the second refuses to hear it (cf. 18:15). Such people never engage in conversation, only monologue. Interested only in showing what he knows, the person in this verse accomplishes just the opposite. Ironically, he does "reveal his heart," for speech always reveals character (cf. 12:16, 23; 13:16).

18:3. As independent and isolated as the characters of verses 1 and 2 might hope to be, they are not free from the reaction of the community. "Contempt" goes with the wicked everywhere they go, as the repetition of "comes" in Hebrew suggests. Likewise, shameful actions come with the corresponding "disgrace" (cf. 3:35).

18:4. The first line states that any person's words are "deep waters," leaving the reader to wonder how to situate the saying. Are deep waters good or bad? The second line makes a contrast[3]; the fountain or spring of wisdom is a bubbling brook, waters that run neither still nor deep. While we say that "deep thoughts" are profound, in much of Scripture deep things are hidden[4] and surfaces deceive. Therefore, words, like deep waters, can mislead. The context of chapter 18 demonstrates the negative characteristics of a fool's speech (18:2, 6–7), and morsels of gossip go down to the inmost parts (18:8). The contrast with a flowing "fountain of wisdom" reminds readers of the fountain of life (10:11; 13:14; 14:27; 16:22).

---

2. The LXX reads *prophaseis* ("pretexts"), as in Judg. 14:4, yielding "the estranged person seeks pretexts" (Clifford, *Proverbs*, 169), or "a schismatic person seeks an opportunity for a quarrel" (Garrett, *Proverbs*, 164). The Heb. text makes good sense and can be left as it stands.

3. Some, however, take the second line as apposition to the deep waters; "words express a person's thoughts, bringing them to the surface" (cf. 20:5) (Clifford, *Proverbs*, 170). Goldingay, "Proverbs," 600, argues that nowhere in Proverbs do humans have their own inner resources of wisdom, so the proverb highlights a "contrast between human evasiveness and wisdom's sparkling clarity."

4. See 20:5, where "deep waters" are hidden from view; wisdom is also deep and hidden (Job 12:2; Eccl. 7:24); and the "deep lip" is a metaphor for unintelligible speech (Isa. 33:19; Ezek. 3:5–6). The deep pit of illicit sex (Prov. 22:14; 23:27) also hides its deadly effects.

18:5. Perhaps this saying is linked to the idea of deceptive words in verse 4. Here, a judge can show partiality to the wicked by (lit.) "lifting the face," an idiom for the verdict of "not guilty," pronounced as the accused gets up from bowing before the judge. Likewise, the judge can turn away or pervert justice for the righteous (17:23; cf. Isa. 10:2; Lam. 3:5). This proverb echoes the statement that one should not clear the guilty and condemn the innocent (Prov. 17:15), and "not good" echoes the statement on justice in 17:26 (also 16:29; 19:2; 20:23; 24:23; 25:27; 28:21).

18:6. The next two proverbs are paired on the *speech* of the fool (cf. 18:4). Unlike the false judgments depicted in verse 5, the fool receives a just and painful sentence. A companion piece to verse 2, here the results of the fool's babbling comes to light; it brings strife (cf. 17:1), and that discord can also come to blows. It is not certain whether the blows are the result of a fight or the punishment that is sometimes mentioned in wisdom literatures of the ancient Near East, perhaps from a court sentence (cf. 19:29).

18:7. It is one thing to get into a fight or wind up in court, another to face complete ruin. This saying intensifies the picture of 18:6 in the form of a chiastic structure. The lips not only bring strife (v. 6a), they are a snare on one's soul (or life, v. 7b). The mouth not only calls out for blows (v. 6b), it brings complete undoing (v. 7a; cf. 10:14; 13:3). If 18:6 notes the reaction of others (cf. 18:3), this verse makes it clear that the fool has no one to blame but himself.

18:8. This saying about listening goes with 17:4. There is also much in common with 18:4, particularly the "words" in the saying and the motion of "going down" deep (cf. 26:20 on "gossip"; 20:27, 30 on "inmost parts/being"). The word for "choice morsels," (*mitlahᵃmim*) appears in Proverbs only here and in the identical saying of 26:22; it is used in other Old Testament contexts for grumbling or murmuring (Deut. 1:27; Ps. 106:25; Isa. 29:24). McKane's paraphrase compares the words with "tidbits" that are "swallowed up and remembered." He argues that the "belly" is a reservoir of words and the seat of memory.[5] Are we to conclude that these tidbits of gossip go down deep to where human intentions lie? If so, they may be stored for evil purposes.

Sayings on Strength, Safety, and Pride (18:9–12)

THIS SMALL CLUSTER gathers around the themes strength and safety, symbolized by the high fortress and the assaults that come against it—negligence, trust in riches, and pride.

---

5. W. McKane, "Functions of Language and Objectives of Discourse According to Proverbs 10–30," in *La sagesse de l'Ancien Testament*, ed. M. Gilbert, 2d ed. (Leuven: Leuven Univ. Press, 1990), 185. See also idem, *Proverbs*, 374–75.

18:9. Previous sayings have spoken of the disastrous effects of laziness for both the sluggard (6:9−11) and those who employ one (10:26). "One who is slack" lets drop what is in the hands, but the destruction that results from such negligence is no accident. "Oops!" will not cut it. For a similar excuse and the phrase "partner to him who destroys," see 28:24. Both sayings point to the persistent capacity humans have for self-deception.

18:10. Verses 10−11 are linked by the images of fortress-like security—one real, one false. Someone in danger, even the slacker of 18:9, would want a place safe from destruction. Although the righteous are threatened with miscarriage of justice (18:5) and other ill effects of wickedness and folly, Yahweh is the strong tower, high and inaccessible to enemies (cf. 28:25b; 29:25b). The phrase "name of the LORD" occurs only here in Proverbs, but frequently in the Psalms it is a sign of refuge (Ps. 20:7; 61:7−8; 124:8; 142:7). Here, the righteous are (lit.) "set on high" (*niśgab*).

18:11. Linked with the saying before by the word "high" (*niśgab;* here, "unscalable"), the contrast between trust in wealth and faith in the name of Yahweh stands out clearly. The difference, of course, is that wealth is only a strong city and high wall as "they imagine it," adding a new twist to the imagery of 10:15a. Readers are reminded of the "high gate" of 17:19.

18:12. This proverb comes as a capstone to the previous sayings about high and safe places (18:10−11), for here we learn that hearts can be "proud" (lit., "lifted high"). Yet this rise is only a precursor to a "downfall," a breaking or destruction (cf. 18:9). The second line provides the happy reversal, in that "humility" or lowliness comes before "honor."[6] It seems that either attitude leads inexorably to its opposite (cf. 11:2). We know that life does not always work out that way to our eyes, but it happens often enough for it to become a story that needs a proverb to name it. The first line echoes 16:18a and the second echoes 15:33b.

Sayings on Speech and Disputes (18:13−19)

THE SAYINGS OF this cluster gather around the two themes of speaking and resolving conflicts in a legal setting. Also scattered throughout are images of strength and weakness, continuing the sequence that began in 18:10.

18:13. There is a distinct difference between lowliness (18:12) and shame. One is self-imposed, the other is determined by others. If pride goes before downfall, then speaking without listening goes before an exposure of folly and shame. As in 18:2, fools choose not to hear, only to be heard. Put another

---

6. Clifford, *Proverbs,* 171, says it well: "Honor is given, not taken." He cites Ps. 132:1, noting the emphasis falls not only on attitude but on action.

way, they only like to hear themselves talk. One way to exhibit humility is to listen carefully.[7]

18:14. "Spirit" (*ruaḥ*) is the first word in each line. The contrast between a spirit that holds up and one that weighs down suggests that the typical role of the spirit, working as a supportive friend in sickness (and other difficulties?), is reversed when that spirit itself is crushed down. It cannot hold one up; instead, it becomes a crushing weight itself. When the body is weak, the spirit offers strength; but what if the spirit itself is weak (cf. Matt. 26:41)?[8] The connection between spirit and body links the proverbs that mention the crushed spirit (15:13; 17:22).

18:15. Each line ends with the word "knowledge" (*daʿat*), setting in parallel the ear of the wise that seeks knowledge and the heart of the discerning that acquires it. We have seen the connection between heart and tongue, the heart being the wellspring of what a person says, but here the heart is a recipient of what the ear seeks out. There may be some implication that the ear of the wise not only searches for knowledge but it does so by sorting out knowledge from folly. We are aware of selective listening that can tune out noise or other conversations at a party. Here the ear seeks knowledge so that it can be received and internalized to good effect. What a contrast to the intake of gossip in 18:8!

18:16. A descriptive proverb that leaves its opinion unstated, this verse simply states that a gift opens, or "makes wide," the way for someone, specifying the goal—to come into the presence of "the great," someone of higher status who perhaps can bestow a favor. If the ear of 18:15 seeks to acquire knowledge, the gift only seeks to buy access to power (cf. 19:6). We may distinguish the influence of a gift from the contract of a bribe (15:27; 17:8, 23), although the two seem synonymous in 21:14.

18:17. Another descriptive proverb, this one comes with a sharp observation and implicit recommendation. As there are always two sides to every story, it is better to wait until both are heard before passing judgment (Deut. 1:6—18). Unlike the previous saying, this observation on social life depicts a situation of conflict, not goodwill. The social setting is some legal dispute, signified by the word *rib* for "his case" and the technical use of "right" (lit., "righteous," *ṣaddiq*).

---

7. Is there a judicial context here? Murphy, *Proverbs*, 136, says no, but one could argue that the general principle certainly applies to the judgments mentioned in 18:17—19.

8. R. E. Clements, *Wisdom in Theology* (Grand Rapids: Eerdmans, 1992), 80, suggests that unlike physical illness, which is often temporary, "deep emotional hurt may be much more lasting and injurious in its effects." The implication is clear that inner hurt is worse than physical sickness and "far more difficult to heal."

18:18. The lot in this context is used for guidance in settling a dispute, which links this saying with verse 17. Read in this context, this proverb suggests sometimes it is impossible to determine who is in the right. It is also possible, however, that this saying simply says that there are times when the lot is the most objective means of settling a conflict. Read in the larger context of Proverbs, one is also reminded that Yahweh's decisions are compared with the lot, and perhaps there is some sense that the lot gives the decision over to God (16:33). The words "dispute" is repeated in the next verse, as is the idea of "strong."

18:19. Disputes occur between neighbors (18:17), but also between brothers. This saying observes that such conflicts are especially strong and intractable. It may be because the sense of betrayal is so great; one expects the brother to stand with, not against, so sibling conflict is the worst example of good relations perverted. This saying repeats the phrase "fortified city" from 18:11; is there an implication that good relationships are to be chosen over the appearance of security in wealth? The second line adds that disputes in general are also impregnable. These disputes are sometimes caused by one who plots evil (6:14; 26:21) or by a contentious spouse (19:13; 21:9, 19; 25:24; 27:15).

Sayings on Speech and Its Rewards (18:20–24)

THE SAYINGS OF this group touch the ways we talk with one another and their effects. The theme is also implied in the proverbs about loving relationships with wives and friends like brothers (18:22, 24).

18:20. Back to the topic of speech, this saying might be paraphrased, "we'd better be able to stomach what we say." Fruit and harvest present the imagery of eating, and the use of the word *beṭen* for stomach links this saying to 18:8, another proverb about "eating words." This proverb does not specify whether one will be filled with bad or good, but other sayings in the book confirm our hunch. The quality of the fruit that goes in the mouth depends on what comes out (1:31; 12:14; 13:2)—or, as we say, people will "eat their own words."

18:21. This saying ends with the word "fruit" (*pᵉri*), just as verse 20 begins with it. From what has been said in this chapter, the tongue clearly has power over life and death, depending on how it is used. It is harder, however, to understand what it means to love the tongue. Most likely, the one who loves the tongue understands its power and uses it for good, and so the fruit mentioned in both verses is probably good fruit. What was left ambiguous in verse 20 is specified here.[9]

---

9. Clifford, *Proverbs*, 173, looks to grammar to conclude that the feminine suffix "it" refers to life and death as a distributive. The result, then, is you eat what you choose, either

18:22. At first, this proverb seems to be a truism that is out of place in the chapter, but the strangeness invites a closer look. Chapter 18 has a number of sayings and single lines that are repeated throughout the book, but this is the only verse that repeats nearly verbatim a verse from chapters 1—9. Wisdom says of herself in 8:35 (common words are italicized): "For *whoever finds* me *finds* life *and receives favor from the* LORD." These are the only two verses in the Hebrew Bible that use the word "find" (*mṣ*ʾ) two times in one verse.[10] Why should the finding of a wife, good as it is for a man, be linked with receiving God's favor? The connection with Wisdom's words about herself in 8:35 reminds us that wisdom is a gracious gift of God, a sign of blessing and favor, yet available to all who ask for it (Prov. 2). As Wisdom calls out and offers herself, so does Yahweh; yet humans must seek her and Yahweh diligently.[11]

18:23. Readers can take each line of this proverb separately and find a description of life. More often than not, the poor must plead with someone who holds power over them, while the rich can answer harshly to those of lower status. Read together, the hierarchy in any such conversation between rich and poor shows itself (cf. 22:7). Is this another false use of the power of wealth as in 18:11, an example of pride as in 18:12? It is difficult to discern the economic status of the speaker of the proverb, but one can detect a note of censure against the rich. One might expect the rich man to answer kindly or gently or in some other gracious manner.[12]

18:24. In contrast to the previous verse, where there is no friendship, this saying compares many "friends" (cf. 14:20)[13] to "one who loves" (ʾ*oheb*) and sticks close like a brother. Even as an offended brother can become an unyielding fortress (18:19), so a faithful brother hangs on dearly (17:17). Here is the reverse image of the "unfriendly" person who separates himself

---

life or death (cf. Deut. 30:15—20). J. G. Williams, *Those Who Ponder Proverbs: Aphoristic Thinking and Biblical Literature* (Sheffield: Almond Press, 1981), 45—46, sees the principle of retributive justice at work.

10. D. C. Snell, "Notes on Love and Death in Proverbs," in *Love and Death in the Ancient Near East: Essays in Honor of Marvin H. Pope*, ed. J. H. Marks and R. M. Good (Guilford, Conn.: Four Quarters, 1987), 165—68. Only two verses in Proverbs mention love and death, 8:36 (one after 8:35) and 18:21 (one before 18:22). Therefore, the two pairs bear an even greater similarity.

11. R. E. Murphy, "The Faces of Wisdom in the Book of Proverbs," in *Mélanges bibliques et orientaux en l'honneur de M. Henri Cazelles*, ed. A. Caquot and M. Delcor (Neukirchen-Vluyn: Neukirchener Verlag, 1981), 337—45.

12. Whybray, *Wealth and Poverty in the Book of Proverbs*, 116—17.

13. The first line of the proverb is ambiguous and difficult to translate. "May come to ruin" can be translated "may keep one company," yielding: "Some friends play at friendship" (NRSV).

in his selfishness (18:1; cf. 17:19). The word "loves" is repeated from 18:21; one who loves the power of the tongue will also love friends and neighbors.

Bridging Contexts

THE CHAPTER BEGINS with a proverb about selfish isolation and ends with one about friendship so close it looks like family. In between these reflections on social life are a myriad of images, some puzzling and some disturbing. Readers today are challenged to spot the thematic threads that tie these images together as well as the primary contrasts. The negative pictures of foolish speech with its strife are answered with the possibility of finding a friend like a brother and a good wife, a symbol of wisdom. Each theme explores the many ways we humans act to draw near to one another in love or separate ourselves into lonely worlds of our own making.

The words of the mouth. The proverbs of chapter 18 make it clear that the isolation, self-centeredness, and poor judgment of verse 1 make themselves known through acts of speaking, as shown in verse 2. Fools have no desire to listen, only to spout their own views. The words of the mouth, like deep waters, can hide and deceive, and words like these are far removed from the life giving words of wisdom (18:4). Words can be partial to the wicked (18:5), bring strife and calamity to the fool (18:6—7), and damage both the reputation of others as well as the lives of those who have an ear for it (18:8).

Readers then find that negative images of speaking and listening give way to more positive pictures. Fools speak first and listen never (18:13, 23), yet the heart and ears of the wise seek out knowledge (18:15), patiently listening to both sides of the story (18:17). Another pair of proverbs wryly observes that one's mouth eats the "fruit" that the same mouth produces; that is, one bears the consequences for good or bad of what one does with words (18:20—21).

We who pay much attention to what we eat (or at least are told we should) may need to be reminded that the ancients were less concerned with the nutritional value of foods and more concerned with the immediate effects of eating. While they did not have the science and health reports that appear in our daily newspapers and TV broadcasts, they did know when eating left them with a feeling of well-being and when eating made them sick. They knew that some things were better to eat than others and that spring waters were best for drinking. So the symbolism of these proverbs reminds us that we may find gossip tasty, but what we really need are the life-giving waters of wisdom (18:4, 8). They tell us that what we hear and say will go deep into "the inmost parts" (*beṭen*, 18:8; also "stomach" in 18:20), so we need to take care. If today we are rightly focused on eating well for good health, the sages ask us to keep in mind that the talk we choose to consume also works for our good or ill.

But we also know that our words can either draw us together or pull us apart, so two proverbs remind us that self-absorbed prattling is likely to lead to words of disagreement and then to blows (18:2, 6). Language by its very nature is dialogical, said the Russian writer Bakhtin.[14] We are always "answering" (18:13, 23) the speech of others, even if only in our minds, and the dialogue is meant to draw us out of ourselves to include others and their way of looking at things. The root of the word "communication" is to "have in common." Heart speaks to heart, and if all goes well, there will be a sharing of minds. If we do not acknowledge the social nature of language, a gift of God meant to establish his *šalom* of harmonious relations,[15] then we will separate ourselves in selfishness (18:1) and risk bringing disgrace on ourselves (18:13; cf. v. 3).

Speaking to would-be teachers, James advises that the tongue is like a bit on a horse or a rudder on a ship; if we can control it, we are able to keep the whole body in check, yet no one has achieved complete mastery. It is a power, capable of setting a forest on fire or corrupting a whole person, especially through boasting and cursing others (James 3:1–6, 9–12). Likewise, the sages of Proverbs observe that life and death are in the power of the tongue (Prov. 18:21) and warn of the dangers of pride (18:12). James may have had these proverbs in mind as he wrote: "But the wisdom that comes from heaven is first of all pure; then peace-loving, considerate, submissive, full of mercy and good fruit, impartial and sincere. Peacemakers who sow in peace raise a harvest of righteousness" (James 3:17–18).

The wisdom of these proverbs encourage us to set aside speech that is isolating, proud, and ultimately destructive in favor of speech that joins people together in humility and concern (18:12, 24). The principle of listening before answering in matters of dispute (18:13, 15, 17) can be extended to include all forms of listening that hopes to draw others near and to lift them up in love. If boasting alienates, careful listening creates strong bonds.

Pride and humility. The problem of pride is stated directly in 18:12, but other examples of pride (lit., the "heart lifted high") and contrasts between high and low, up and down, run throughout chapter 18 (esp. vv. 9–12). We have seen that one who is slack is one who lets things drop or fall, thus destroying and bringing things down (18:9). The name of Yahweh is a strong

---

14. M. M. Bakhtin, *The Dialogic Imagination: Four Essays*, trans. C. Emerson and M. Holquist (Austin: Univ. of Texas Press, 1981).

15. Q. J. Schultze, *Communicating for Life: Christian Stewardship in Community and Media* (Grand Rapids: Baker, 2000).

tower in which the righteous are "set on high" for safety (18:10; cf. 2 Sam. 22:3; Ps. 46:7, 11; Isa. 33:16), but the rich only imagine that their wealth is a "high" wall (Prov. 18:11; cf. 17:19). The antidote to such pride is the humility or lowliness that comes before being lifted up in honor (18:12).

Contrasts such as these are implicit in other proverbs of this chapter, for the use of language itself often reflects hierarchies in which some end up higher or better than others.[16] We see that a gift allows the giver into the presence of someone greater, while the lowly poor have only pleas for mercy to offer the rich (18:16, 23). Centered in it all is the false exaltation of pride, a heart lifted up; therefore, fools are proud when they should be ashamed. Paraphrasing what we have learned from the Gospels, we see the irony that in raising up self, one displays folly, but in taking a low road, one demonstrates wisdom. So Jesus "did not consider equality with God something to be grasped ... and being found in appearance as a man, he humbled himself and became obedient to death—even death on a cross!" (Phil. 2:6–8).

Lowliness, the willingness to walk the downward way of the cross,[17] can also remedy the conflicts and disputes depicted in Proverbs 18:12–19. One need not, like the offended brother (18:19), be unyielding, fortified like the proud of 18:11. Instead, one's openness to resolve conflict also shows one's willingness to go one down instead of one up. So also, the lot settles disputes when both sides agree to its outcome (18:18)—that is, if all efforts to listen and discern the right in a matter have failed (18:13, 15, 17).

But what of the crushed spirit?[18] Is there perhaps a difference between a chosen spirit of lowliness (18:12) and the spirit that has been beaten down and is therefore unable to fulfill its function of helping a person bear up? In other words, Christlike humility chooses downward mobility for self, not for others, and therefore forces it on no one. If anything, one

---

16. K. Burke, *A Rhetoric of Motives* (Berkeley: Univ. of California Press, 1969); and "Definition of Man," in *Language As Symbolic Action: Essays on Life, Literature, and Method* (Berkeley: Univ. of California Press, 1966), 15: "To the extent that a social structure becomes differentiated, with privileges to some that are denied to others, there are the conditions for a kind of 'built in' pride. King and peasant are 'mysteries' to each other. Those 'Up' are guilty of not being 'Down,' those 'Down' are certainly guilty of not being 'Up.'"

17. H. J. M. Nouwen, *Letters to Marc About Jesus* (San Francisco: Harper and Row, 1988), 39–50.

18. The connection between spirit and body links the proverbs that mention the crushed spirit (15:13; 17:22; 18:14). A cheerful heart does good, but heartache crushes the spirit (15:13), and a crushed spirit dries the bones (17:22). That connection with the heart may lie in the background of 18:14 as well, for the heart shows up in 18:15 (see also 12:25). Perhaps we can say the spirit is that which enlivens a person; when it leaves or when it is bitter or crushed, its life-charging capacities are negated.

would side with the one who would not crush the bruised reed or snuff out the dim wick (Isa. 42:3). The chosen spirit of lowliness is rewarded in Proverbs 29:23: "A man's pride brings him low, but a man of lowly spirit gains honor." Again, one only receives honor when it is not considered something to be grasped.

The benefits of commitment. The cultivation of wise speaking and lowly attitude lead the reader to the benefits of right relation as typified in the good wife and the friend like a brother. In the last few verses of the chapter, words like "favor," "mercy," and "love" (the friend of 18:24 is "one who loves") begin to sketch a picture of life lived in full awareness of the presence of God and God's gifts. While some acknowledge that we are on the receiving end of God's many graces, others pretend not to see.

Two consecutive lines (18:23b—24a) speak of the rich person who speaks harshly and the person with many friends who comes to ruin (perhaps the same person; cf. 19:4). The juxtaposition suggests that some think they need little from others, but it is the one who looks for a life companion and works at being a lifelong friend who finds favor from Yahweh (18:22, 24b). Typically, the gifts wisdom bestows are related to long life, wealth, and honor, but here, Yahweh's gifts include spouse and the friend who sticks close. While many friends can fill our address books, as we in America know all too well, only a few, maybe even just one, loves in a way that causes us to stop in wonder and gratitude.

Moreover, the one who finds a wife finds what is good (18:22; cf. 12:4; 19:14; 31:10—12; see also 16:20; 17:20; 19:8, where "prospers" means "finds good") and "receives favor from the LORD" (cf. 2:5; 3:4; 12:2). The verbal links we observed earlier between 18:22 and 8:35 suggest that finding such a wife is also a symbol of finding wisdom (cf. 1:28; 3:13; 8:17; 10:13; 24:14), as in Proverbs 31:10: "A wife of noble character who can find? She is worth far more than rubies."

In addition, if the good wife is a sign of finding wisdom, then perhaps the friend, the one who loves and stays closer than a brother, also reminds us of the one whose name is a strong tower (18:10). Certainly the one who loves at all times, even through adversity (17:17), shows how wisdom is lived out in the life of a willing and open person. But perhaps the image points beyond, for Christians through the centuries have seen here a picture of Jesus, our brother in the faith. Status and its hierarchies may drive us apart, as 18:23 shows, but the love and commitment of 18:22 and 24 point to wisdom that unites, itself a symbol of divine love. In sum, the gifts of married love and friendship ultimately point back to the source, to the One who cares for us more than we can ever know.

As we ask ourselves how these teachings of Proverbs on dialogue, lowliness, and commitment carry over into our own day, we remember that the enemies of bad speaking, pride, and isolation, have always been with us. It may even appear that, like mutating bacteria, they continue to take on new forms in order to proliferate and wreak havoc in every age. Thus, we must ask ourselves how these negative and positive images of community life present the principles by which we can intentionally work toward life that is less impersonal and more deeply satisfying, not to mention faithful to God's intentions. The forms of folly in every age yield to the practices of wisdom.

What to do with talk. For starters, let us burn into our minds the picture that all of our practices of speaking and listening end up in the "inmost parts" or "stomach" (18:8, 20–21), and let us make a conscious effort to reject gossip and other forms of put down. We can further imagine that saying or listening to such talk is like eating junk food[19]—tasty perhaps, but ultimately empty and even harmful. Do we really want mean-spirited and critical words to churn around inside us? Daily vigilance over what we say and hear are akin to habits of healthy eating. Such habits need not be cultivated with an attitude of superiority (after all, we know how hard diets are to keep), but rather by asking those around us to help with the hard work of taming the tongue and becoming faithful listeners. The other side of this practice is speaking a word of honest confrontation when there is a legitimate concern, choosing loving correction over back-biting.

Recalling that fools only desire to hear themselves talk, we must also cultivate the habits of real dialogue, drawing others out in order to hear their points of view and, when appropriate, engaging in spirited debate. Too often our churches encourage a culture of superficiality that assumes that we must all agree if we are to get along, or at the least extend tolerance to one another (whether or not such efforts are sincere). Here is what M. Scott Peck calls "pseudo-community," the attempt to join with others without practicing emptiness that is releasing our expectations of each other.[20]

The value of real honesty can be surprising. Studs Terkel reported the story of C. P. Ellis, a textile worker who grew up learning to blame others for most of his problems, especially his financial struggles. A second-generation

---

19. Van Leeuwen, "Proverbs," 173.

20. M. S. Peck, *The Different Drum: Community Making and Peace* (New York: Simon & Schuster, 1987). Peck claims that groups typically move through the four stages of pseudo-community, chaos, emptiness, community.

member of the Klu Klux Klan, he attended interracial civic meetings and was extremely vocal about his feelings toward other races. As a result, he was asked to work on policy projects with a black woman. The more the two worked together, disagreeing at every turn, the more they began to see clearly into each other's lives. Each was criticized by their respective communities, and the children of both were harassed at school. Ellis's mind began to change, and he eventually ran for president of his union to promote equal treatment of workers, reporting that he had listened to tapes of Martin Luther King's speeches with tears in his eyes.[21] We can do more than hold back critical words and reject gossip; we can listen to others and learn what life is like for them. Listening like that can keep us from answering harshly before we have heard (18:13, 23).

Moving down, not up. We can be on the lookout for ways to practice the principle of moving downward instead of climbing upward. The upward mobility of pride is different from recognitions of excellence that come with promotions and awards. One serves the community, the other the concerns of the self, especially when moving up requires stepping on or over others. In other words, the problem of pride is its isolation and lack of concern for others, not the lift that comes with well-deserved success and accomplishment.

Sports coaches know the difference between the player who wants to be a star and those who want to play their best to help the team succeed. The New England Patriots surprised the 2002 Super Bowl audience when they insisted on being introduced as a team instead of as a series of individual players, and they surprised the audience again when they went on to beat the favored St. Louis Rams! No, team spirit does not always guarantee victory, yet the gesture of the group introduction made them winners of another sort before they even took the field. By contrast, those who seek to build a fortress of wealth rebuff the poor with a harsh answer, driving them away (18:10–12, 23). The downward way of wisdom, then, is a way toward others, and we can test our motives and decisions by asking if they lead us closer to others or away. If away, we should be watching out for pride.

After explaining the descending way of the cross from Philippians 2 to his nephew, Henri Nouwen spoke of his home country, the Netherlands:

> I have noticed one thing in particular: increasing prosperity has not made people more friendly toward one another. They're better off,

21. S. Terkel, *American Dreams: Lost and Found* (New York: Ballantine, 1981), 221–33, quoted in R. Anderson and V. Ross, *Questions of Communication*, 3d ed. (Boston/New York: Bedford/St. Martin's, 2002), 246–47.

but the new-found wealth has not resulted in a new sense of community. I get the impression that people are more preoccupied with themselves and have less time for one another than when they didn't possess so much. There's more competitiveness, more envy, more unrest, and more anxiety. There's less opportunity to relax, to get together informally, and enjoy the little things in life. Success has isolated a lot of people and made them lonely. It seems sometimes as though meetings between people generally happen on the way to something or someone else. There's always something else more important, more pressing, of more consequence. . . . And the higher up you get on the ladder of prosperity, the harder it becomes to be together, to sing together, to pray together, and to celebrate life together in a spirit of thanksgiving.[22]

For that reason, Nouwen decided to give up his career of teaching at schools like Yale and Harvard and went to live at L'Arche, a community in which volunteers live with mentally disabled adults. Nouwen never argued that everyone should do the same, only that they consider the love that moved the Son of God to follow the descending path to poverty and the cross and make decisions about life and career in prayerful communion with him.

Notice that in the view of life that Nouwen describes, the pursuit of individual affluence means that we are all on our own, with no one to trust but ourselves.[23] Such is the vicious circle of materialistic pride, self-centeredness, and isolation that leaves each of us clamoring to get all we can to hedge our bets against the future. The downward way of wisdom holds the support of a spouse or friend as more valuable. Is it coincidental that wealth is depicted as a fortress, perhaps inspiring the conflicts between brothers that are stronger than a city (18:18–19)? Just as an attacking lion isolates an animal from the herd for attack, so the circle of pride and self-reliance isolates us so that we might be destroyed (18:12).

---

22. Nouwen, *Letters to Marc About Jesus*, 42–43.

23. B. Schwartz, "A New Wake-up Call," in *In Trust* (January, 2000), 29–30. Schwartz reviewed a book by D. G. Myers entitled, *The American Paradox: Spiritual Hunger in an Age of Plenty*, and found the argument convincing, even though the book left him wondering *why* people are so materialistic. "Could it be because Americans have learned that they can't count on anyone but themselves to provide things like health care and education for their families? . . . It seems to me that there is a causal relationship between the policies that have made us affluent and our growing unhappiness. In our pursuit of wealth, we have removed constraints on business and allowed the social safety net to erode. The ideology of the free market is one of individualism, materialism, and freedom from constraint, and the ideology infects everything it touches."

These proverbs hold out the strength of relationships as more secure than that of isolating wealth, which is likened to a fall. What do we really want—a pile of wealth or one who loves? A happy side-benefit of this move away from isolated pride and toward others is the increase in trust, without which no one can live.

On friendships. As a result, we can prayerfully take on a firm conviction that friendships truly are more valuable to us than silver and gold, and we can ask for grace to practice the twin virtues of gratitude and commitment. Gratitude is the antidote for the insecure striving after the false props of wealth and status. Thanksgiving orients us to things as they are, dispelling the fantasies of imagined security. Whenever we pray and give thanks at the table, we are not only rejecting that false sense of trust in our own achievements and stockpiles, we express our trust in the one we have asked to "give us this day our daily bread." In the same way, we can give thanks often for our friends, grateful that God has provided for these needs as well.

Do we live as though we believe the adage that no person is poor who has friends? Can we name those with whom we have been friends for more than a few years and name the tests that such a friendship has survived? Giving thanks for our friends may be especially important when they have hurt us or let us down (or perhaps even when we find them irritating—of course, they would never think the same of us!). This is not to say that we do not confront when it is needed or even end a relationship that is too self-serving to qualify as a friendship, but we first express our commitment to our friends by giving thanks for them and what they have meant to us so far.

We can also give thanks to those friends who give us opportunities to serve and move outside of ourselves. If the false security of wealth isolates and sets its bearer above others, there is also an isolation that comes not from material plenty but from having nothing materially to give. Although media images of retirement hold out travel, sunny climes, and beautiful surroundings as the standard of success, the aging often are lonely in our culture, in part because they are learning to live on less, achieve less, and apparently have nothing to offer unless one would count the life experiences that could teach the young. Their experience of living and even of learning how to die is generally not seen as valuable by younger persons, who do not see the need to think that far ahead.[24]

---

24. S. Hauerwas with L. Yordy, "Captured in Time: Friendship and Aging," in *A Better Hope: Resources for a Church Confronting Capitalism, Democracy, and Postmodernity* (Grand Rapids: Brazos, 2000), 173–87. Much of the discussion here is drawn from this article.

As we said earlier, there seems to be a difference between the giving of gifts to earn access to the great (18:16) and the gifts that are given from the life-long companions of spouse and friends (18:22, 24). The distinction between a friendship based on advantage or pleasure and one based on the mutual desire for growth in character is as old as Aristotle. Yet the two need not be so finely divided; the advantages and pleasures of a friend who is also concerned for our best good, even our growth in godly wisdom, are considerable. Christians of an earlier age viewed friendship as an important discipline for growth in the Christian life: They encourage practice of Christian virtues, build up the church as the body of Christ, and enhance friendship with God.[25]

Therefore, friendships between the aging and the young can be extremely enriching, as the popularity of the book *Tuesdays with Morrie* shows. Even as older Christians can be called on to give freely of their experience, wisdom, and perspective, their understanding of what is truly valuable in life, the young can call them to responsibility and ongoing commitment that is more than the appeal for help with church committees and suppers. At a number of times in my life, I have been a member of smaller churches, and there I was struck by the interchange between generations that so often gets squeezed out in age-specific church programming. Hauerwas and Yordy urge, "we must continue to be present to those who have made us what we are, so that we can make future generations what they are called to be."[26]

In other words, the generations need each other for conversations in wisdom, and the conversation most likely should not flow only from old to young. The very movement of the book of Proverbs itself shows that after a period of listening and taking in, young learners are encouraged to enter into spirited dialogue with the proverbs, perhaps a model for the dialogue we are to have with one another in the church.

The richest of conversations will often take place in the context of friendships that have developed over years. If the sages placed the proverbs on good marriage and loving friendship in proximity with one another, could it be that some sense of each as lifelong and life-giving is intended? So the monk Aelred spoke of the "iron that sharpens iron" that comes in godly friendship: "Friendship cannot even exist without grace. Therefore, since eternity thrives in friendship, and truth shines forth in it, and grace likewise becomes pleasant

---

25. "Friendship excels everything . . . for friendship is a path that leads very close to the perfection which consists of the enjoyment and knowledge of God, such that [one] who is a friend of man is made into a friend of God, according to what the Savior said in the Gospel: 'Now I will not call you servants but my friends' [John 15:15]." Aelred of Rievaulx, *Spiritual Friendship*, trans. Mark F. Williams (Scranton, Penn.: Univ. of Scranton Press, 1994), quoted in Hauerwas with Yordy, "Captured in Time," 180.

26. Hauerwas with Yordy, "Captured in Time," 185.

through friendship, you be the judge whether you should separate the name of wisdom from these three."[27]

In a culture that appears to thrive on pride, isolation, and the insecurity that shows itself in bad speech habits, Christians, safe and secure in the name of Yahweh, the strong tower (18:10), have the confidence and freedom to form committed friendships. In those friendships we learn to step down from our self-imposed pedestals to befriend those who appear to have nothing to give, and in turn are surprised to find that in so doing we become truly rich.

---

27. Aelred of Rievaulx, *Spiritual Friendship*, quoted in Hauerwas with Yordy, "Captured in Time," 186.

Proverbs 19:1–29

¹ BETTER A POOR MAN whose walk is blameless
  than a fool whose lips are perverse.
² It is not good to have zeal without knowledge,
  nor to be hasty and miss the way.
³ A man's own folly ruins his life,
  yet his heart rages against the LORD.
⁴ Wealth brings many friends,
  but a poor man's friend deserts him.
⁵ A false witness will not go unpunished,
  and he who pours out lies will not go free.
⁶ Many curry favor with a ruler,
  and everyone is the friend of a man who gives gifts.
⁷ A poor man is shunned by all his relatives—
  how much more do his friends avoid him!
 Though he pursues them with pleading,
  they are nowhere to be found.
⁸ He who gets wisdom loves his own soul;
  he who cherishes understanding prospers.
⁹ A false witness will not go unpunished,
  and he who pours out lies will perish.
¹⁰ It is not fitting for a fool to live in luxury—
  how much worse for a slave to rule over princes!
¹¹ A man's wisdom gives him patience;
  it is to his glory to overlook an offense.
¹² A king's rage is like the roar of a lion,
  but his favor is like dew on the grass.
¹³ A foolish son is his father's ruin,
  and a quarrelsome wife is like a constant dripping.
¹⁴ Houses and wealth are inherited from parents,
  but a prudent wife is from the LORD.
¹⁵ Laziness brings on deep sleep,
  and the shiftless man goes hungry.
¹⁶ He who obeys instructions guards his life,
  but he who is contemptuous of his ways will die.
¹⁷ He who is kind to the poor lends to the LORD,
  and he will reward him for what he has done.
¹⁸ Discipline your son, for in that there is hope;
  do not be a willing party to his death.

¹⁹ A hot-tempered man must pay the penalty;
   if you rescue him, you will have to do it again.
²⁰ Listen to advice and accept instruction,
   and in the end you will be wise.
²¹ Many are the plans in a man's heart,
   but it is the LORD's purpose that prevails.
²² What a man desires is unfailing love;
   better to be poor than a liar.
²³ The fear of the LORD leads to life:
   Then one rests content, untouched by trouble.
²⁴ The sluggard buries his hand in the dish;
   he will not even bring it back to his mouth!
²⁵ Flog a mocker, and the simple will learn prudence;
   rebuke a discerning man, and he will gain knowledge.
²⁶ He who robs his father and drives out his mother
   is a son who brings shame and disgrace.
²⁷ Stop listening to instruction, my son,
   and you will stray from the words of knowledge.
²⁸ A corrupt witness mocks at justice,
   and the mouth of the wicked gulps down evil.
²⁹ Penalties are prepared for mockers,
   and beatings for the backs of fools.

Original Meaning

THIS CHAPTER OPENS with the alternating themes that closed chapter 18: integrity of speech and the relation of wealth and friends.[1] We see then that it is possible to work with a section of proverbs that begins in one chapter and ends in another, just as the figures of mockers and sluggards that appear in this chapter continue into 20:1–4. Sayings on the poor cluster at the beginning (19:1, 4, 7) and middle (19:17, 22); the first and last of these are "better than" sayings about the poor and integrity (19:1, 22). The contrasting picture of the false witness and punishment also comes at the beginning (19:1, 5, 9) and end (19:28–29). Sayings about knowledge begin and end the chapter (19:2, 25, 27), while sayings about the fool appear only in the first half (19:1, 3, 10, 13). The figures of the fool, the sluggard, and the mocker help the reader identify proverbial clusters.

---

1. Garrett, *Proverbs*, 169–71, marks 18:22–19:14 as a section based on the inclusio of proverbs about the good wife.

Fools, friends, and false witnesses (19:1–9)
Fools, rulers, and families (19:10–14)
Sluggards and discipline (19:15–24)[2]
Mockers and knowledge (19:25–29)

These figures and the key terms instruction/discipline (*musar*), knowledge, and the parental voice remind the reader of the instructions of chapters 1–9 and their urgent plea that the son "listen to advice and accept instruction" (19:20; cf. 19:27).

Fools, Friends, and False Witnesses (19:1–9)

THESE PROVERBS JUXTAPOSE pictures of folly and the evil of false witness with the friendships of the wealthy and poor. A proverb about gaining wisdom stands out from its context.

19:1. The "better than" sayings typically speak to matters of poverty and wealth (cf. 15:16–17; 16:8; 17:1) or satirize the fool (17:12); this is the first to combine the themes. The contrast is surprising, for one expects "rich" to parallel "poor" (cf. 28:6).[3] However, a blameless walk and a crooked tongue mix metaphors in typical proverbial style, the path of the feet and words of the mouth serving as expressions of either wisdom or folly. Most striking is the juxtaposition of folly and perversity, an association that has only been implied before. Verses 1–3 are linked together by the vocabulary of feet walking on the path and the theme of the destructive results of folly.

19:2. This saying is linked with verse 1 by the repetition of "good" (*tob*) and the metaphor of walking. The two lines work independently and as a pair; "zeal" or "desire" (NRSV)[4] needs the guidance of "knowledge" or it will walk in a way that is "not good." One manifestation is the "hasty" feet that "miss the way" ("miss" uses a typical Heb. word for "sin," *ḥaṭṭaʾ*). By implication, the proverb holds out patience and caution as knowledgeable companions of desire.

19:3. The "way" that was implied by "walk" in verse 1 and the Hebrew for "feet" in verse 2 is named here; it is the "overturned way," a metaphor translated by NIV as a "ruined life" (the verb may have overtones of the "perverted way"). The second line may intentionally move in two directions. The heart that rages against Yahweh is certainly the source of all folly, but

---

2. A chiastic structure takes shape in vv. 15–24 based on key words and themes: laziness (vv. 15, 24), life (vv. 16, 23), poor (vv. 17, 22), discipline (vv. 18, 20–21).

3. Clifford, *Proverbs*, 174–75, emends the second line to read "than one walking on a crooked way though he is rich" (on the basis of 28:6), but Proverbs has a number of verses that are nearly identical but for one variation (cf. 19:5, 9). Murphy, *Proverbs*, 141, reads with Heb. text and notes that the LXX does not have the verse.

4. Meinhold, *Die Sprüche*, 2:310–11, takes *nepeš* as "life," not desire.

it may also be a result. The fool, having ruined his life all by himself, now wants to blame God for his misfortune![5]

19:4. Verses 4–7 cluster around the themes of wealth/poverty and friendship. A contrast between "many friends" and the only "friend" that deserts (lit., "is separated"; cf. 18:1) highlights the poor person's plight. So far, the description of the one with wealth and friends is neutral, yet reader's sympathies are directed to the isolated poor; the plenty of the rich seems merely unfair, not culpable. Yet the proverb points out the painful truth that most would rather be a friend to the rich. More than anything else, the proverb is an indictment of unreliable friends (cf. related sayings in 18:23–24).[6]

19:5. The saying seems unrelated to its context, but the theme of true and false speech returns from 19:1 and 18:20–21. If one gains wealth or courts friendship through falsehood, that perverse use of speech will eventually be repaid. False words and lies are often paired to denote the betrayal of the neighbor/friend relationship. The proverb is nearly identical with 19:9; parts of it appear in 6:19; 12:17; 14:5, 25; 19:9; 21:28. The theme is stated with variation in 19:6–7.

19:6. In what appears to be a neutral description like that in verse 4, the two lines compare a "ruler" who can dispense favors with one who seeks favors by giving "gifts." Yet the friendship is hollow for both parties, being based only on self-interest and personal gain. The plurals "many" and "everyone" highlight the contrast with the deserted friend of 19:4 and 7. The poor have nothing to give or to buy friends with (cf. 18:16, 23), a bitter observation on relationships.

19:7. The Hebrew of the first line resembles that of verse 6b ("Everyone is the friend") so that it can be translated, "Everyone of the poor man's brothers shuns him," setting up a contrast similar to verse 4. In this unusual proverb of three lines, the last is most troublesome to translate, as the NIV text note indicates.[7] Whatever we choose to do with the third line, the point of the

---

5. Cf. Sir. 15:11, "Do not say, 'It was the Lord's doing that I fell away'; for he does not do what he hates."

6. Proverbs tends to speak of results of poverty, not its causes. While laziness is one sure cause of poverty, the proverbs on the topic often focus on response and generally recommend kindness to the poor. Murphy, "Excursus on Wealth and Poverty," in *Proverbs*, 260–64.

7. The Heb. reads something like "pursuing-words-not-these." The NIV follows Scott, *Proverbs*, 115, in relating the extra line to the saying, but Scott also emends to read, "When he follows them they speak angrily to him." Most commentators take the line to be corrupt, perhaps a leftover half of another saying. The LXX includes another couplet, which creates a very different proverb: "Everyone who hates his poor brother shall also be far from friendship. Good understanding will draw near to them that know it, and a sensible man will find it. He that does much harm perfects mischief; and he that used provoking words shall not escape."

first two lines is clear and expands the picture of verse 4. The poor person is deserted even by relatives, so it is not unexpected that friends also keep their distance. Juxtaposed with the friendship of wealth in verse 6, this proverb resembles the saying of our song, "Nobody knows you when you're down and out." It is a portrait of superficial friendship, practiced even by one's family. Another "how much more" proverb appears in 19:10 (see also 11:31; 15:11; 17:7; 21:27).

19:8. An upbeat saying intrudes on this unhappy series of proverbs, assuring the reader that those who acquire "heart" or sense (here translated "wisdom") care for themselves; it is a way of loving one's own life (*nepeš* can be translated "soul, life, self" as well as "desire, zeal"; cf. 19:2). The one who "keeps" understanding prospers (lit., "finds good," reminding the reader of the man who finds a wife, 18:22; cf. 16:20; 17:20). Contrasted with the shallow and self-serving attention given to the wealthy and powerful, there is an element of surprise in this advice, for it does not urge readers to become better friends but to care for self. However, if anyone gets understanding and wisdom, this self-care will certainly lead to the good of family and neighbors.

19:9. This proverb is virtually identical with verse 5 except for a substitution of "perish" for "not go free." Readers are challenged to discern why the repetition is made when most of the other verses in the cluster speak of favors and help. This crime of perjury is more than a preference for the rich over the poor, it is outright attack. It is not stated whether the recompense comes from the legal system or in the form of final judgment from Yahweh.

Fools, Rulers, and Families (19:10–14)

IN THIS SECTION proverbs about fools and families hold up the quality of wisdom (*śekel*, 19:11, 14) in wise persons and wives. Such wisdom knows how to control one's own temper and how to keep it from flaring up in others.

19:10. Another "how much more" saying (cf. 19:7) compares the fool living in luxury to the apparently unthinkable situation of a slave ruling over a prince (cf. 30:21–23). Yet wisdom thinking allows for just this reversal, at least in a household where the servant is wise and the son shameful (17:2).[8] Experience confirms the truth of the picture; fools usually do not live in luxury, but sometimes exceptions prove the rule. As the second line shows, however, it certainly is not fitting! The proverb may point to the more fitting chain of events in verse 9.

---

8. Whybray, *Proverbs*, 278, notes that Zimri, who assassinated the king and came to power, was called a servant (*ʿebed*, 1 Kings 16:1–13; cf. 2 Kings 9:31).

19:11. Verses 11–12 are linked by the theme of anger and forbearance. The virtue of "patience" is here associated with wisdom (cf. the root *śkl* for the "prudent wife" in 19:14). The patient person is (lit.) "long of nose," meaning that it takes a long time for the nose to get hot in anger (cf. 16:32). It is one's glory to overlook an offense (cf. 17:9) instead of seeking strife (cf. 17:19; 29:22). Ironically, it is when we seek to protect our honor or status by quarreling that we stand to lose it the most.

19:12. This second saying on anger (19:11) returns to the subject of rulers (19:10). Readers may conclude that this king stands in contrast with the wise person of the previous saying. Other proverbs about the king's anger mention death (cf. 16:14–15; 20:2), and here the image of grass wet with life-giving dew contrasts sharply with the lion heard growling, perhaps hidden in the same grass. If it is wise to practice patience and restrain one's anger, it is also wise to do everything possible to keep from provoking anger in one more powerful.

19:13. Verses 13–14 contrast the "quarrelsome wife" with the "prudent wife," each verse also including a mention of parents and estate. The first line of this proverb is easier to grasp than the second. A fool for a son spells calamity for a father who hopes he will grow up to care for the family and its businesses (17:2). If that father has counted on that help for the family's survival, the son who sleeps during harvest (10:1–5) will leave the family destitute. The continual dripping of the quarrelsome wife is not like the annoyance of a leaky faucet; the dripping roof is destructive and dangerous,[9] a fitting parallel for the ruin of the foolish son. "Quarrelsome" most likely refers to relationships in the community, the strife that drives neighbors apart.

19:14. Note that typically, Bible readers quote the second line without the first, but here (as in 19:13) the words "father" and "wife" appear in the first and second lines respectively. The contrast suggests that one inherits wealth and house from family, but the wife who does one good is a gift of God (cf. 18:22). Again the mysterious correspondence between decision and blessing is held up but not explained (cf. 16:1, 33). The contrast between the quarrelsome wife (19:13) and the one who is prudent (root *śkl* = "wisdom" in 19:11) extends the picture of the happy and prosperous home.

Sluggards and Discipline (19:15–24)

VERSES 15–17 REPEAT the key words of verses 2 (*nepeš*, "zeal, desire"), 3 (*derek*, "way"), and 4 (*dal*, "poor") in the same order, suggesting that the chapter divides into two halves. The emphases on a father's "discipline" as an antidote to laziness and lying reminds the reader of the instructions of chapters 1–9.

---

9. Garrett, *Proverbs*, 170.

19:15. Even as the happy and prosperous home comes as a gift (19:14), it requires diligence and hard work or the estate can be lost. Perhaps readers are to see the shameful son in this picture of laziness (Prov. 19:13; cf. 10:5). The Hebrew for the "shiftless man" can be translated "the desire [*nepeš*; cf. v. 2] of the indolent," so that as laziness *only* brings on sleep, the appetite of the indolent goes hungry. "Deep sleep" usually comes from God (*tardemah*, Gen. 2:21; 15:12; 1 Sam. 26:12; Job 4:13; 33:15).[10] In the creation story, Adam's deep sleep ends as he awakes to meet his wife, a gift from God (Prov. 19:14). Here it is the result of slack hands that end up empty (10:3–4; 12:27).

19:16. "Instructions" is (lit.) "command" (*miṣwah*; cf. 6:23; 13:13), a word often used of parental teaching (2:1; 4:4; 7:2). In the context of Proverbs it points to the directions for living that one ignores at one's peril. To refuse their guidance is to despise one's way, to be careless about where one walks. A double use of the Hebrew word "keep" (*šmr*) in the first line can be translated "one who keeps instructions keeps one's life" (*nepeš*, "life, person, desire"; cf. 19:15).

19:17. Instead of a describing of the poor person's destitute lot (19:4, 7), here the proverb show a poor person helped by a neighbor who shows kindness. Because Yahweh repays such good work, the saying calls this interaction a loan to God (14:31; 17:5). While the poor often cannot repay, Yahweh always can—not as the return for some kind of seed-faith investment but as a general reward for righteousness and its alignment with wisdom. The picture of plenty for all is central to the teaching of *torah* (Deut. 15:1–11).

19:18. The words "discipline" and "son" in the first line remind the reader of the instructions of chapters 1–9, where discipline (*musar*; cf. 19:20) carries the double meaning of instruction and correction (sometimes even punishment), the emphasis depending on context. However, while those instructions were directed to the son, here the proverb urges parents to exercise such discipline "for in that there is hope," the possibility for a good outcome.[11] The proverb recognizes the possibility of a bad outcome, which is set out in the second line. This can be woodenly translated, "and to kill him, do not lift your soul/desire" (*nepeš*; cf. 19:2, 15, 16). While some understand the discipline as corporal punishment (cf. 13:24; 23:13–14), others see it as an alternative to execution (cf. Deut. 21:18–21).[12]

---

10. Clifford, *Proverbs*, 177.

11. The NRSV translates, "*while* there is hope." The difference is not great, the one stressing urgency, the other stressing motivation.

12. The NIV rightly captures the sense rendered by Scott, *Proverbs*, 116, "And do not indulge him to his own destruction." To fail to discipline is to hate one's son; to instruct is to love (13:24). Murphy and TNK put it more strongly, urging fathers to keep their anger in check, as does Clifford, *Proverbs*, 175, "Do not be intent on killing him."

19:19. The second person ("you") of the previous verse continues, as does the theme of rescue. Just as "you" might rescue a son with vigilant discipline, so "you" might be called on to rescue (or even pay the fine of) a person of wrath. However, there is a big difference between teaching someone while there is "hope" and bailing out someone who will not learn, for you will have to do it again and again. The saying not only recommends the value of a cool temper, but it also offers advice on handling the one who has not cultivated it. If a person has not learned self-discipline (19:18), then no kind of rescue will ever be effective.

19:20. This third proverb to use the second-person imperative offers more general advice, not to the parents but to the young. "Discipline" (*musar*) and "in the end" remind the reader of 19:18, while the practice of listening to advice stands in sharp contrast with the hot temper of 19:19. In fact, the goal of becoming "wise" might be defined as living with the end in view; the Hebrew speaks of "your end." If the phrase points to the end of life, then wisdom is a lifelong project, not a job order that one fulfills and moves on. There is also some hint that one becomes wise in order to teach others.

19:21. Like the Yahweh sayings of 16:1–4, 33, this proverb contrasts human and divine purposes, moving from the "many plans" to the one that will "prevail" or stand (*taqum*). Yahweh's "purpose" is his counsel (*ʿesah*, "advice"; cf. 19:20), perhaps suggesting that to listen to wise human counsel is to also be receptive to the counsel of the Lord. Once again, the proverb urges its readers to consider final outcomes and ends.

19:22. The last of the five sayings about the poor in this chapter (19:1, 4, 7, 17, 22) resembles the first, a "better than" saying about the poor person who does not lie (cf. 19:1). The Hebrew of the first line can actually be read two ways, depending on the translation of the word *ḥesed*. While this term is usually used for kindness and faithfulness (esp. of Yahweh), in some contexts it is used for shame (Lev. 20:17; Prov. 14:34). If "shame" is used, then "desire" takes on the negative charge of "greed" (cf. NIV text note).[13] The reading of the NIV, however, draws a contrast between human fidelity and the faithlessness of the liar. The "liar" is elsewhere a corrupt witness (6:19; 14:5, 25; 19:9; 21:28). Therefore, it is better to be poor and honest than to have great gain through lies (cf. 19:1; cf. 19:5, 9).

19:23. The last of the Yahweh sayings in this chapter returns to a familiar topic, human response to one whose counsel stands (cf. 19:21). The first line can be translated, "Fear of the LORD—to life!" "Life" (*ḥayyim*) denotes the

---

13. Two other proverbs begin with the same Heb. word (*ta'awah*): 11:23 ("desire") and 21:25 ("craving").

sense of life lived to the full, including a long life of health, prosperity, and honor, the primary motivators of the instructions. In the second line, this life is pictured as a traveler who has found lodging that satisfies (food and a place to rest the head) and is safe (not bothered by evil or trouble, *ra*^c). For a traveler, to lie down in safety and rise up again was no small thing (cf. 6:22). Thus, to fear Yahweh is to fear nothing else.

19:24. In contrast with the verse before, this proverb lampoons one who goes unsatisfied (cf. the identical proverb in 26:15). Like the picture of laziness and hunger in 19:15, this satiric saying imagines one who even finds the effort of eating to be too much. The contradiction may hold the key: Most sluggards do want something for nothing; here, the irony of sloth comes out in a humorous sight that hides the stinger. Although no one is really that lazy, the exaggeration shows that sloth will leave one hungry.

Mockers and Knowledge (19:25–29)

THESE PROVERBS FEATURE the negative example of the "mocker" (19:25, 28, 29) to aid the parent's instruction about learning or missing "knowledge" (19:25, 27).

19:25. The contrast is plain; beat a mocker as an example to the simple, because the mocker is beyond learning. The bite of the saying is that of the two, only the simple have the hope of learning "prudence" this way. But if you correct an *understanding* person with words, that same person will *understand* (root *byn*) knowledge (cf. 19:27, which repeats the word "knowledge," and the similar proverb of 17:10). The mocker reappears in 19:28–29.

19:26. The symbolism of this proverb makes sense when read in reverse: The shameful son (cf. 19:13) brings ruin on the house, which is tantamount to robbing father and evicting mother. The proverb may be hyperbolic, like the saying on the sluggard (19:24) and the parable of the son who threw away half his father's estate (Luke 15:11–24). Yet Jesus also had harsh words for the Pharisee's practice of Corban (Mark 7:9–13), so the danger of failing to honor and care for parents is real (Deut. 5:16), especially when the son's foolishness has left the parents destitute.

19:27. This saying is unusual in that it not only speaks in second person, but it addresses the son. If we read it in context, the proverb then speaks in the voice of the parents who were just wronged in the previous verse. The two lines are linked by a repetition of similar sounding imperative verbs, italicized in my translation as, "To cease *to listen* [*lišmoa*^c] to instruction my son, is *to stray* [*lišgot*] from words of knowledge." The warning is a counterpoint to 19:20, where the words "listen" (*šma*) and "instruction" (*musar*) appear. The image of stepping away from "knowledge" appears in 19:2 (cf. 19:25). In Proverbs, a young learner can be led astray by another woman, a sign of one's own folly (5:20, 23), wine and beer (20:1), and evil men (28:10).

19:28. This enigmatic proverb incorporates images scattered throughout the chapter; the corrupt witness breathes lies (19:1, 5, 9, 22) and in so doing mocks the very idea of justice (19:25, 29). "Gulps down evil" is ambiguous, pointing to the greedy appetite of the wicked but also hinting at final rewards (cf. 18:20–21). Desire without knowledge is not good (19:2), for you may swallow poison!

19:29. Linked with the previous saying by the repetition of "justice" or judgment (root šp̄ṭ, "penalties") and "mock," this saying delivers the payback that the reader has been waiting for. Mockers receive the very justice they once spurned, penalties that are "prepared" or stored. The beatings of 19:25 will take place, and while they may not instruct the mockers or fools (17:10; 26:3), they will teach one willing to watch and learn that God's justice is not mocked (19:5, 9).

OF THE MANY and varied scenes presented in this collection of proverbs, a number of repeated words and themes stand out. As we tried to understand each proverb as it might be heard in its original setting, we observed that (1) the repeated emphasis on discipline and instruction sounds very much like the parental teaching of Proverbs 1–9, (2) the sayings about the rich and poor speak about integrity and friendship, and (3) the five Yahweh sayings keep the Lord at center stage.[14] In sum, as we turn to consider the significance of these proverbs for today, we see that their teaching on integrity and truthfulness speak to our dealings with wealth and neighbors, all in the sight of Yahweh, who loves justice and establishes his counsel.

Discipline and instruction. The matter of parents teaching sons and the repetition of the term "knowledge" (19:2, 25, 27) remind us of the instructions of chapters 1–9 and the teaching that will resume at 22:17. The emphasis on knowledge stands out in the proverb ("It is not good to have zeal without knowledge, nor to be hasty and miss the way," 19:2), and we have seen that "zeal" translates a word that is often used for life and life's desires (*nepeš*). We might therefore conclude that desire and its passions must be accompanied by wisdom's kind of knowledge or it will be "not good."

---

14. Scherer, *Das Weise Wort und Seine Wirkung*, 277, sees three kinds of sayings or themes (*Schwerpunkte*): didactic sayings, Yahweh sayings, and economic sayings.

But those who get wisdom love their souls (*nepeš*, 19:8); just as those who obey instructions love their lives (*nepeš*, 19:16), the desire (*nepeš*, 19:15) of the shiftless goes hungry without it. In previous chapters we have spoken about the "discipline of desire," which sets our God-given passions and desires within the boundaries of wisdom's framework of love and justice. So here, the echoes of the parent's lessons to the son (chs. 1−9) remind us again that this discipline of desire is a lifelong project, for adult sons and daughters can bring joy or ruin to their parents (19:13, 18).

The linked proverbs in 19:25 and 27 remind us that we never outgrow the need to "accept instruction" and that what counts is being wise "in the end." We cannot be sure how adults of old received this instruction; perhaps it came from the extended family, perhaps from trusted friends. For adults today, this may speak to the need to talk about our working lives, our family and community responsibilities, and the development of our inner lives, yet many Christians find it difficult to locate other believers with whom they can discuss such things freely without fear of judgment. We should be more intentional in seeking out such groups and in providing them.

It is also striking that two grotesque examples of negative behavior also make a return appearance from the instructions. Two figures from chapter 6, the sluggard and the scoundrel, typify passive dependence and active betrayal, both forms of resisting wisdom's instruction (cf. 12:17−27). So here the sluggard's "mouth" goes empty for lack of effort while the "mouth" of the wicked gulps down evil (vv. 24, 28). Yahweh especially hates the lying tongue and the false witness who pours out lies, a figure repeated twice here (19:5, 9; cf. 19:28; also 6:16−19). In fact, it is better to be poor than to gain material wealth in this way, for what everyone desires is "unfailing love," the consideration of others practiced by those who receive instruction (19.1, 22; cf. 20:6). Today, just as it was then, laziness and treachery are variations on a stubborn refusal to learn from others or to love them. Fools listen to and care for no one but themselves.

Integrity and friendship. A number of proverbs in the chapter explore the relationship between friendship with the rich and friendship with the poor. While the instructions of chapters 1−9 did not deal specifically with the matters of wealth and poverty, they did warn against those behaviors of violence and lying that are often motivated by greed. Earlier collections of the individual proverbs compared the lives of the poor and rich, as in 13:8, "A man's riches may ransom his life, but a poor man hears no threat." But here we see that bribes and gifts buy one's way into success and win many friends (19:6; cf. 17:8; 18:16), while the poor person is shunned by friend and family alike (19:4, 7). Therefore, the one who is kind to the poor lends to the Lord, who will pay back what the poor cannot.

Wealth makes friends, as Jesus reminded us (Luke 19:6). The question is, whom do we desire for our friends? If the poor have no friends and the one who gives gifts has many, we naturally conclude that friendship of this sort is superficial and fair-weathered. Yet to make friends with the poor by kindness is to make friends with God; so Jesus told us the King takes every kindness done to the least as done for him (Matt. 25:31–46). Friendship like this continues through good times and bad (Prov. 17:17).

We may take it as a sign of our own importance to have friendships with the well-connected, but wisdom reminds us that the most important friendships are those we make with those who have nothing to give in return. Jesus said in Luke 14:12–14 (cf. 6:32–36):

> When you give a luncheon or dinner, do not invite your friends, your brothers or relatives, or your rich neighbors; if you do, they may invite you back and so you will be repaid. But when you give a banquet, invite the poor, the crippled, the lame, the blind, and you will be blessed. Although they cannot repay you, you will be repaid at the resurrection of the righteous.

The gifts that win many friends can be given to the powerful or they can be put on deposit with the Lord. The corrupt witness, the gifts, and the bribes all speak to rewards of another kind, and the general theme of payback runs throughout the chapter, through the punishment of the lying witness (19:5, 9) and the just judgments prepared for the mockers (19:29). We might conclude that every use of our money has its paybacks, it rewards, and the proverbs gathered here instruct us that wisdom pays better returns. We may find ourselves in positions where we have to deal with those in authority over us (19:10, 12), yet to believe that our own well-being is only wrapped up in theirs is to engage in the most foolish of thinking. We can put the question this way: Whose friendship do we really want? We can court the rich and powerful and forget the poor, but if we do, we will also pass by the Lord, who chooses to identify with them.

The Lord at center stage. The five proverbs that name Yahweh ("the LORD") in this chapter affirm again and again that just as we want to have the king for our friend, so we should want to remain friends with Yahweh above anyone else. Yet the fool's heart rages against him (19:3), even though it is his purpose that prevails (19:21). For those who fear him, Yahweh grants the gift of a good wife (19:14), repays kindness done for the poor (19:17), and brings life, satisfaction, and safety (19:23).

The chapter also implies that Yahweh is a judge whose justice will not be mocked. Fools can rage against him and pervert their way (19:3), but false witnesses will not go unpunished (19:5, 9), and mockers will suffer the penalties prepared, just as beatings are prepared for the backs of fools (19:29). Given the association between the king and Yahweh observed in chapter 16, can we infer that the description of Yahweh in this chapter is much like that of the king, his anger like the roar of a lion and his favor like dew on the grass? If so, then here is another reminder that to court any king but Yahweh is to fall into the deepest folly.

"But a prudent wife is from the LORD" (19:14b). Remembering that a previous proverb on finding a wife (18:22) points back to personified wisdom, the gift of God (8:35), readers will see here a similar link between parental teaching that prepares the young man to choose the right kind of wife and the personified figure of wisdom as that life partner (cf. 31:10–31). The symbolism suggests that embracing wisdom becomes the passage to adulthood, so that one moves into maturity by choosing wisdom as a lifelong companion. This is not to jettison the plain sense that a prudent wife is from Yahweh (so are prudent husbands!) but to recognize that these echoes of the parents' lectures of chapters 1–9 use the same literary strategy that links coming of age with embracing the way of wisdom. So parents can pass on houses and wealth (19:14) and even their teaching (19:20, 27), but Yahweh is the source of the wisdom that brings life.

OUR RELATIONSHIP to the poor. Like parents teaching their son, the proverbs of this chapter would have us receive instruction and correction with the express goal of educating our desire (*nepeš*) with knowledge (*daʿat*, 19:2, 25, 27). While it is nowhere stated this way, we may infer that the parents' lectures of chapters 1–9 have given way to the teaching of the larger community, and it is this correction the parents recommend to their son.

From where will such correction come? Certainly it will come from the negative examples of this chapter—the fool in luxury, the sluggard in poverty, the lying witness, acts against family (evicting mothers and deserting brothers), a preference for the rich with gifts that will buy favor. But such correction can also come from those very persons who are so often shunned and overlooked; perhaps it will be the poor who will tell us the truth about the way our society and our churches work. It is better to be poor with integrity, better to be poor than a liar (19:1, 22). Of course it is better to have integrity *and* enough to live on, but if we have to choose, character comes first. This is not to say that those who go without do so out of choice, for we know that most do not. Still, could it be that poor people also know and see in ways that would be instructive for us? If we will let them, those who know deprivation will become our teachers.

The work of Robert Coles[15] has shown us that when a person lends an interested ear, children and adults who know poverty will speak about their lives in a way that teaches and moves. Coles went to live among migrant farm workers and heard children struggling with profound questions of faith and innocent suffering while he heard adults give eloquent testimony to a strong faith. One woman said:

> If someone offered me a million dollars, and said I could have all I want to eat for myself and my children, but I'd have to stop thinking about Him and start thinking of myself only, then I'd know I was in real trouble. I'd start worrying about myself. I "hope" I would. I hope I'd remember Jesus. He warned us about thinking about ourselves and not Him. He asked a lot of us.[16]

When Coles turned his attention from the children of poverty to those from affluent backgrounds, to his surprise he found that the fruits of such privilege were a mixture of pride and anxiety, the same that he realized were in his own heart. His five books on those interviews, *Children in Crisis*, won a Pulitzer Prize, but more important, they helped Coles gain a sense of his own mission. Trained as a psychiatrist, he went on to teach courses in literature to Harvard business students, medical students, law students—any and all who were expected to enter the workforce and become a success. Those students testified that the novels they read together confronted them with questions of what was most important in life. One spoke of his encounter with the truth "that we're always in danger of talking one line and living another—and the more successful we are, the more the danger."[17]

Thus, by listening to children, parents, and students, Coles and others like him give voice to both rich and poor and their experience of life, the truth has a better chance of being told, and as a result, we receive instruction. We also reject false witness when we allow everyone's story to be heard instead of only a few: "What [a person] desires is loyalty" (19:22). One way to show that faithfulness to others is to turn our attention toward their stories and allow them to examine our own. Here is one step we can take toward knowledge that will discipline our desires.

---

15. An excellent introduction to Coles's life and work can be found in P. Yancey, *Soul Survivor: How My Faith Survived the Church* (New York: Doubleday, 2001), 87–118.

16. Ibid., 103.

17. R. Coles, *The Call of Stories: Teaching and the Moral Imagination* (Boston: Houghton Mifflin, 1989), 125–26.

Yet we know that it will not do to simply listen to the lives and stories of the poor, for what they need are friends (19:4–7). I take that in the most general sense to mean that friends are those who care about their welfare: "What a person desires is loyalty." Some will show their friendship with the poor through works of compassion, others as they work and call for justice. But whatever form it takes, a commitment to be there for those who often feel as if they have no one who cares for them can be the greatest contribution the church and its Christians can make. To be present is to acknowledge that those people exist. To stay away is to believe and propagate the tacit lie that they do not exist, perhaps itself another form of false witness.

Henri Nouwen came to realize that friendship like this is the purpose for which we were created. One of the twentieth century's most significant writers on Christian spirituality, with teaching posts at Yale and Harvard, Nouwen told gatherings of ministers that at the end of life, God would not ask him how many books he had written but rather how well he had loved his neighbor. As he taught pastoral theology to those who would become ministers in the American church, he became concerned about the connection with the "other" America, the continent to the south. "I knew that God's voice could not be heard unless it would include the voices of the men, women and children of Latin America." For six months, therefore, he lived in Bolivia and Peru to discern whether God might be calling him to live and work there.

Nouwen's thoughts and impressions of that time are recorded in his journal, published under the title *¡Gracias!*, a title that gave testimony to the grace of God and Nouwen's thanks for all he had learned during that time. As he reflected on the richness of life among those who had so little, he began to experience a poverty of his own, a shortage of thanksgiving. He concluded his time by reflecting that the "poor are a eucharistic people, people who know how to say thanks to God, to life, to each other." Recognizing that all of life is a gift, he concluded that it is all given so that we can say thanks:

> A treasure lies hidden in the soul of Latin America, a spiritual treasure to be recognized as a gift for us who live in the illusion of power and self-control. It is the treasure of gratitude that can help us to break through the walls of our individual and collective self-righteousness and can prevent us from destroying ourselves and our planet in the futile attempt to hold onto what we consider our own.[18]

Nouwen's emphasis on gratitude reminds us that the Yahweh sayings in Proverbs 19 tell us that God will not be outgiven. Lend to the poor and you

---

18. H. J. M. Nouwen, *¡Gracias! A Latin American Journal* (San Francisco: Harper and Row, 1983), 147, 188.

will be repaid in full; fear Yahweh and you will rest safely, untroubled by worry (19:17, 23). Does this mean that we will never make a bad loan or suffer any setbacks? Of course not. But it does mean that this life of God-fearing wisdom will lead us to see that what we do have is a gift, not a privilege, and we will find that we need much less than we think.

There are many angles on this matter of receiving instruction throughout the chapter, but it really does boil down to the education, or better the discipline, of our desires. I suspect that we carry no small measure of guilt over our desires, for we know that often we are silly putty in the hands of marketers, that we feel a sense of deprivation when it appears that our friends are doing better than we are. We hear of saints who have chosen to forgo the comforts of wealth and privilege, and we feel guilty for not wanting to let go, or we talk ourselves out of guilt and say that God calls us to different paths.

These proverbs remind us that our desires are not bad but they can be uninformed, or better undisciplined. They tell us that desires not informed by knowledge are "not good" and that in our haste to fulfill our wants we can easily misstep. Proverbs would have us learn another way. Instead of worrying about how well we are doing, we can worry about how well those with less are doing. Seeing that what we have is a gift, we are free to give it again.

Proverbs 20:1–30

¹ WINE IS A MOCKER and beer a brawler;
  whoever is led astray by them is not wise.
² A king's wrath is like the roar of a lion;
  he who angers him forfeits his life.
³ It is to a man's honor to avoid strife,
  but every fool is quick to quarrel.
⁴ A sluggard does not plow in season;
  so at harvest time he looks but finds nothing.
⁵ The purposes of a man's heart are deep waters,
  but a man of understanding draws them out.
⁶ Many a man claims to have unfailing love,
  but a faithful man who can find?
⁷ The righteous man leads a blameless life;
  blessed are his children after him.
⁸ When a king sits on his throne to judge,
  he winnows out all evil with his eyes.
⁹ Who can say, "I have kept my heart pure;
  I am clean and without sin"?
¹⁰ Differing weights and differing measures—
  the LORD detests them both.
¹¹ Even a child is known by his actions,
  by whether his conduct is pure and right.
¹² Ears that hear and eyes that see—
  the LORD has made them both.
¹³ Do not love sleep or you will grow poor;
  stay awake and you will have food to spare.
¹⁴ "It's no good, it's no good!" says the buyer;
  then off he goes and boasts about his purchase.
¹⁵ Gold there is, and rubies in abundance,
  but lips that speak knowledge are a rare jewel.
¹⁶ Take the garment of one who puts up security for a
    stranger;
  hold it in pledge if he does it for a wayward woman.
¹⁷ Food gained by fraud tastes sweet to a man,
  but he ends up with a mouth full of gravel.
¹⁸ Make plans by seeking advice;
  if you wage war, obtain guidance.

¹⁹ A gossip betrays a confidence;
    so avoid a man who talks too much.
²⁰ If a man curses his father or mother,
    his lamp will be snuffed out in pitch darkness.
²¹ An inheritance quickly gained at the beginning
    will not be blessed at the end.
²² Do not say, "I'll pay you back for this wrong!"
    Wait for the LORD, and he will deliver you.
²³ The LORD detests differing weights,
    and dishonest scales do not please him.
²⁴ A man's steps are directed by the LORD.
    How then can anyone understand his own way?
²⁵ It is a trap for a man to dedicate something rashly
    and only later to consider his vows.
²⁶ A wise king winnows out the wicked;
    he drives the threshing wheel over them.
²⁷ The lamp of the LORD searches the spirit of a man;
    it searches out his inmost being.
²⁸ Love and faithfulness keep a king safe;
    through love his throne is made secure.
²⁹ The glory of young men is their strength,
    gray hair the splendor of the old.
³⁰ Blows and wounds cleanse away evil,
    and beatings purge the inmost being.

Original Meaning

THEMES OF DISCERNING intentions and reading the behaviors of others weave throughout this collection of proverbs that includes six Yahweh sayings (20:10, 12, 22–24, 27), four royal sayings (20:2, 8, 26, 28), and two versions of the proverb about differing weights and measures (20:10, 23).[1] These reflections go beyond the practical skills of living life to pondering its mysteries. Readers will observe that more and more proverbs read like a riddle—teasing, provoking, and stimulating thought.

Foolish behaviors of brawling and loafing (20:1–4)
Discerning hidden intentions through behavior (20:5–9)

---

1. Whybray, *The Composition of the Book of Proverbs*, 114–17, takes 20:20–21:4 as a thematic group containing seven Yahweh sayings, all but one arranged in triads, mixed together with royal proverbs.

Seeing as Yahweh sees (20:10–12)
Business practices, foolish and wise (20:13–17)
Counsel, not cursing (20:18–21)
Judgment, divine and human (20:22–30)[2]

Foolish Behaviors of Brawling and Loafing (20:1–4)

THE WORD "MOCKER" links 20:1 with 19:25–29. It also functions as a hook-and-eye link between that section on acquiring wisdom and this section on demonstrating wisdom.

20:1. Just as the last five proverbs of chapter 19 describe the trouble caused by a human mocker, so here wine is personified as a mocker, perhaps to compare it to the one who will not learn (19:25–27), who laughs at justice only to receive just penalties (19:28–29). More important, those who are "not wise" are "led *astray*" (*šgb*) by this mocker, just as the one who stops listening to instruction *"will stray* [*šgb*] from the words of knowledge" (19:27; cf. 5:19, 20, 23; 28:10). The use of *šgb* suggests that to stagger from drink is to err both in one's steps and one's judgment (Isa. 28:7). The "brawler" (*homeh*) is loud and noisy, like the foolish women of Proverbs 7:11 and 9:13. This proverb recognizes that alcohol can impair one's judgment (cf. 21:17; 23:29–35; 31:4–5) and therefore compares it to two figures known to be a negative influence.

20:2. Continuing the association of noise and danger from the previous verse, the king's wrath is here likened to a lion's roar. The wise take warning, but fools provoke it and pay with their lives (lit., "sins against his soul," *hoteh napšo*; cf. 19:2). The first line is nearly identical to 19:12, except for the word "wrath" in place of "rage." The earlier verse added a word about the king's favor as life-giving dew, whereas here the threat of death is made explicit.

20:3. Juxtaposed with the warning about provoking kings is a more general warning against quarreling in any form, a reverse of the sequence in 19:11–12. The contrast between the person who is careful to avoid an argument and the one quick to find it reminds the reader that character has its tendencies or typical behaviors. "Honor" (*kabod*, "glory, reputation"; cf. 3:35; 11:16; 15:33; 18:12; 25:27; 26:1, 8; 29:23) comes to the one who keeps clear of quarrels but not to the fool. Implied is the wisdom of the one and the shame of the other (17:14, 19; 18:1). The bite of the saying may be that

---

2. Scherer, *Das Weise Wort und Seine Wirkung*, 286–93, takes 19:2–20:21 and 20:22–22:3 as major sections, dividing 19:28–20:1; 20:2–12, 13–19, 20–21, 22–24, 25–30 as subsections. Heim, *Like Grapes of Gold Set in Silver*, 267–87, parcels 19:25–20:4; 20:5–13; 20:14–19; 20:20–21:4.

those who quarrel will not gain the respect they fight for but will actually lose standing in the community.

20:4. As in 19:11–13, the two antitheses of wisdom are quarreling and laziness. "In season" is the time after the fall rains when one plows and sows seed for next year's harvest. The comic example of the sluggard who makes no preparation but still looks for a result recommends both foresight and industry (cf. 6:8). Coming after 20:3, it may also recommend shifting one's energies away from conflict and toward something more productive.

Discerning Hidden Intentions Through Behavior (20:5–9)

THESE PROVERBS OBSERVE that behavior reveals character and intentions, yet discernment in such matters is not easy; it requires skill and understanding.

20:5. This proverb itself, like deep water, is difficult to fathom. Like water from the bottom of the well, human "purposes" (ʿesah, "counsel"; cf. 8:14; 19:20; 21:30) can be drawn out if one has the proper equipment—in this case, "understanding." Similar to the proverb in 18:4, this comparison is between the hidden recesses of the human heart (ʿesah, cf. Isa. 29:15) and wisdom's access to them. The saying is probably a paradigmatic teaser, introducing those that follow on the intention of the heart (esp. Prov. 20:9).

20:6. This proverb on faithfulness recalls the friendship themes of the previous chapter (19:4, 6–7, 22). "Unfailing love" (ḥesed) in the first line and "faithful" (ʾemunim) in the second use terms for human loyalty that are often associated with Yahweh, but the point here is that few among us live up to that standard. "Who can find" testifies that such friends are rare (cf. 31:10; cf. Job 6:14). Read along with Proverbs 20:5, this proverb suggests that careless or deceptive speech cannot hide its purposes for long.

20:7. The counterpart to the previous verse, the saying assures readers that whoever walks in integrity (19:1; 28:6) is called a ṣaddiq ("righteous one"); blessed are the descendants who share in the honor. Here is a legacy or inheritance one cannot sell, buy, or lose (cf. 10:7; 13:22; 17:2). "Children" can also be the beneficiaries of a parent's faith (14:26).

20:8. Another royal saying (cf. 20:2, 26, 28), this one depicts the king as a judge. In the ancient world it was assumed that royal decisions required wisdom sent from the king's god (cf. Ps. 72).[3] Three images serve as symbols of this judgment: the throne (Prov. 16:12; 20:28; 25:5; 29:14), the threshing

---

3. L. Kalugila, *The Wise King: Studies in Royal Wisdom As Divine Revelation in the Old Testament and Its Environment* (Uppsala: CWK Gleerup, 1980), 127. Wisdom as a royal prerogative is a prevalent motif in ancient Near Eastern texts, but the Old Testament affirms that the only source of such wisdom is Yahweh.

floor, and the eyes that see and perceive rightly. "To judge" (*din*; cf. Gen. 30:6; Deut. 17:8) corresponds with "winnows," a picture of sorting out wheat and chaff (Prov. 20:26; cf. Ps. 1:4–6), but this verb can also mean to scatter, as if the king were throwing evil away. Unlike the righteousness that shows itself to the public (cf. Prov. 20:7), evil is often more furtive, sometimes even posing as righteousness, and therefore it must be found out. The king's work of discernment is akin to that of Yahweh, who judges in righteousness to vindicate the righteous and the poor (29:7; 31:5, 8; cf. Ps. 7:8; 9:4; 140:12; Isa. 3:13).

20:9. More than a statement that all humans sin, the rhetorical question asks who can find someone who has been cleaned and purified from sin (*mehatta'ti*, "from my sin"), with the implied answer that such people are rare (cf. 20:6). The point is not so much that there are people who claim to be without sin (1 John 1:6; cf. "pure" in Prov. 16:2; "right" in 21:2), but that there are more people who claim to have dealt with it than really have. The proverb is a statement of personal accountability, suggesting that the righteous do not need to have the king find them out (20:7–8) but will root out unrighteous behavior for themselves.

Seeing As Yahweh Sees (20:10–12)

THIS TRIO SETS a puzzling proverb about children between two others about seeing the way Yahweh sees.

20:10. In the midst of sayings on the shadiness of the human mind and heart comes this saying that puts things in the clear duality of the proverbs. The point is set in two pairs, (lit.) "a stone and a stone, an ephah and an ephah." In other words, there are measures, and then there are measures, only one of which is true (cf. Lev. 19:35–36; Deut. 25:13). If the wicked are winnowed out like chaff (Prov. 20:8), then false measures are also rejected as an abomination (*to'ahah*, cf. 20:23) to Yahweh, who sees and knows the difference.[4]

20:11. Interpretation of this verse is troubled by translation problems. The first line could read, "Even by his actions a young man deceives," but the NIV should be followed as more true to common experience.[5] The theme of pure and right character in 20:9 continues into this saying, the question being how a person's character is recognized. The "child" (*na'ar*, 7:7; 22:15) is most

---

4. T. R. Schneider, *The Sharpening of Wisdom: Old Testament Proverbs in Translation* (Pretoria: Old Testament Society of South Africa, 1992), 200, believes the proverb is a riddle like 10:26 and 11:22, but the brain teaser comes in reading the proverb in its cluster, not in the proverb itself.

5. See TNK, Van Leeuwen, "Proverbs," 186, and Clifford, *Proverbs*, 180, 183, for translations that stress deception. Clifford translates (cf. Gen. 42:7; 1 Kings 14:5, 6): "In his actions even a boy can playact, though his deed be blameless and right."

likely the young man who does not fare well in this book. While some take the proverb to mean that a person's character is revealed in early childhood or adolescence and that this makes a case for careful teaching (true as each thought may be), the point is that whether old or young, actions reveal character to those who have learned the wise art of discernment.

20:12. The figure of "ears that hear, eyes that see" is used throughout the Old and New Testaments to signify careful attention and discernment, just as Jesus said, "If any have ears to hear, let them hear." The form of this proverb is similar to 20:10. The duality of ears and eyes is similar to stone and ephah; the second line repeats the name of Yahweh together with the phrase "both of them" (*gam-šᵉnehem*). Whereas differing weights are abomination to God, he made eyes and ears to perceive and understand, and he is pleased when they do. The opposite may be seen not so much in blindness as in the eyes closed in sleep (20:13), a figure for the refusal to acquire wisdom.

Business Practices, Foolish and Wise (20:13–17)

FOUR PROVERBS ON business practices restate the values of hard work, honesty, wise speaking, and careful dealing that have appeared throughout the book, especially in proverbs about laziness and pledges.

20:13. The contrast as translated by the NIV communicates the point but loses some of the flavor; the one who sleeps could become dispossessed or lose the inheritance (*yaraš;* cf. 23:21; 30:9), and readers know that the sleeping son is shameful (10:5; 19:15). The second line can be translated, "open your eyes and be satisfied with bread," the word "eyes" linking the proverb with 20:12. Perhaps another wise use of the eyes is in mind here rather than simply staying awake, for the cultivation of discernment is both a form of diligence and a key to success.[6]

20:14. The saying raises the question: Can there be disinterested communication? Can one speak for reasons other than gain? The proverb answers the question with words similar to the differing sets of weights in 20:10; here there are two kinds of speaking, one for negotiating and one for boasting. The goods are weighed by differing standards depending on whether one is a buyer or an owner. Perhaps the saying implies that both the depreciation and the boasting are exaggerated. Thus, the saying relates to others on the theme of not taking words at face value (20:6, 9).[7]

---

6. For this reason Heim, *Like Grapes of Gold Set in Silver*, 272–73, puts the proverb with 20:5–13.

7. Murphy, *Proverbs*, 152, thinks that a boast after a deal "is not a very convincing sign of victory!"

20:15. Coming on the heels of verse 14, the "rare jewel" (*keli yeqar;* cf. Isa. 61:10) of "lips that speak knowledge" suggests that there is a more profitable way of speaking than haggling and boasting. Is there disinterested speech? Yes, but it is rare (cf. Prov. 24:4; Jer. 15:19). "Abundance of rubies" shows that compared with knowledgeable lips, even precious rubies are plentiful (Prov. 3:15; 8:11; 20:15; 31:10), perhaps a connection with "food to spare" in verse 13. The proverb asks, What do we value the most?

20:16. The proverbs consistently disapprove of making pledges (6:1; 11:15; 17:18; 22:26–27; 27:13), perhaps because of the possibility of sharp dealing and other forms of evil (Ex. 22:25–26; Amos 2:8). The saying may be a parody on the teaching of Deuteronomy 24:10–13, 17, that one should not take another's garment in security or at the least should give it back on a cold night. Ironically, one who makes an unwise pledge may well have given his shirt, for he will surely lose it (cf. Prov. 22:27).[8] The "wayward woman" of the second line is translated in harmony with the nearly identical 27:13. This line can also be read, "Seize the pledge given as surety for foreigners."

20:17. "Sweet to a man, the bread of falsehood" translates the proverb woodenly, but it also reminds the reader of Woman Folly's promise of stolen water and bread eaten in secret (9:17), particularly coming after terms similar to the names of the "stranger" and "wayward woman" in verse 16 (cf. *zarah* and *nokriyyah* in 5:20). One expects the stomach to be filled with gravel, not the mouth, but it is fitting that false speech fills the mouth that produces it with dirt and stone. "Sweet" (*careb*) links this proverb with the "security" (*carab*) of verse 16 (cf. "avoid," *lo' titcarab* in 20:19).

Counsel, Not Cursing (20:18–21)

THE PROVERBS OF this cluster contrast the wisdom of seeking advice for careful planning with sins of speech that betray trust and dishonor families.

20:18. The story of Hushai and Ahithophel proves that wars are won (and lost) by strategy, not strength (2 Sam. 15:32–37; 16:15–17:23). The terms for external wisdom and counsel have been recommended before: *cesah* (Prov. 1:25, 30; 8:14; 12:15; 19:20–21; cf. 21:30) and *tahbulot* (1:5; 11:14). Both terms appear in 24:6: "For waging war you need guidance (*tahbulot*), and for victory many advisers" (*cesah*). While not every ancient reader would be in the position to wage war, the principle of seeking counsel goes well with the

---

8. A. Scherer, "Is the Selfish Man Wise?: Considerations of Context in Proverbs 10:1–22:16 with Special Regard to Surety, Bribery, and Friendship," *JSOT* 76 (1997): 64, finds an "ironical connotation" that the guarantor is so foolish that the loss of the garment doesn't trouble him. Read in its literary context on property (20:12–21), this saying describes a man who uses wisdom in judging which business practices are "insecure or even dubious."

general theme of not knowing another's motives or even one's own (cf. 20:5). Here the emphasis is on not knowing all the details or possible outcomes of a situation; for that reason one should seek out advice, practical and ethical, from one who speaks words of knowledge (20:15).

20:19. Read next to verse 18, this proverb suggests that one should seek guidance, not gossip. Therefore, it says to treasure the friend who gives sage advice instead of the latest dirt, who helps you think through your plans and does not reveal them to others. The practical wisdom of this observation teaches that if you hear a confidence, someone else will probably hear yours.[9]

20:20. Here is another description of damaging speech (20:3, 6, 9, 14, 16, 17, 19), but unlike the previous proverb on gossip, this saying concludes with a metaphor instead of an imperative. The extinguished "lamp" can refer to the light that goes out when it is most needed, but it may be a metaphor for losing one's life. The shameful son has appeared throughout the book (see esp. 19:26), but according to the Mosaic law, the man who curses parents deserves the death penalty (Ex. 21:17; Lev. 20:9). The metaphor leaves it for the reader to decide whether a real execution is intended (cf. Prov. 13:9). The Hebrew for "pitch darkness" appears as "dark of night" in 7:9, where danger comes to the one who did not take his parents' advice (cf. 20:18).

20:21. This proverb is linked to the one before by the theme of family and estate, for a disgraceful son is tempted to take a shortcut to the inheritance (cf. 17:2). There is some difficulty with "quickly gained" since the marginal note in the Hebrew text (the *qere*), "gotten by greed," makes more sense than the text itself (*ketib*) for this rare word.[10] Whether the inheritance is gained quickly or greedily, the point of the proverb is that inappropriate behavior at the start cannot lead to blessing, divine or human, at the end (cf. 20:17). Choices have predictable outcomes.

Judgment, Divine and Human (20:22–30)

FOUR OF THE six Yahweh proverbs of this chapter are set in this cluster around the theme of judgment and discernment, again with a focus on the king who winnows out the wicked (20:26; cf. 20:8).

---

9. The word for "avoid" echoes the sound and spelling of "security" and "sweet" (20:16–17, root *ʿrb*). Although it may be best to avoid unwise pledges and the sweetness of false gain, the wordplay may be more a display of wit than guidance for reading.

10. Clifford, *Proverbs*, 185, translates "greedily guarded" after an Arabic cognate to keep the *ketib* (text as written), while the LXX follows the *qere* (marginal emendation). Certainly the idea of greed makes more sense, but both options leave much to the imagination. How does one gain an inheritance greedily, or hurriedly for that matter?

20:22. The first of a trio of Yahweh sayings[11] comes after the list of wrongs in 20:10–21, particularly the mention of "the end" in verse 21. One expects Yahweh to repay evil, but instead he "delivers" (*yošaᶜ*, "saves") the one who hopes in him. Common to crime and the desire to avenge it is the illusion that humans are masters of their way, exercising complete control and free of moral constraints. When injured, we are tempted to act every bit as unlawfully in response—"See how you like it!" Just as wisdom teaches us to hold back our words in general, here words of vengeance are warned against specifically.[12] In their place, the proverb recommends patience for those who have been wronged.

20:23. A variation on 20:10 (cf. 11:1), the Hebrew of this proverb sets the word "detests" (*toᶜabah*, "abomination") first. The repetition of the differing weight stones may signal that all the evil acts listed after verse 10 have not gone unnoticed, for Yahweh's displeasure is repeated as well. Typically, the word for "dishonest" is used for intentions and speech (*mirmah*; e.g., 12:5, 17, 20).

20:24. This second in a pair of Yahweh sayings also presents a variation on a theme treated in earlier chapters, that humans plan their way but Yahweh directs the steps (16:9). As in 20:23, it begins with a truth about Yahweh as the background against which another statement will take shape. If human steps are directed by Yahweh, then how can we understand our own way? The simple and implied answer is to get wisdom from Yahweh. If verse 23 suggests that humans are under moral obligations and constraints, verse 24 sets limits on both human power and human understanding. The juxtaposition of human plans and intentions with God's sovereign action in human affairs is not meant to discourage planning or activity but rather to guide it. The wise do well to seek counsel about this plan (20:18), listening instead of making rash or hurtful statements (20:19–20).

20:25. The metaphor of the trap should register with anyone who has made a promise, only later to wish he or she had been more careful. The proverb literally reads, "A snare to one who declares holiness, and only after making vows, considers it." The rash declaration that something is holy to Yahweh reminds readers of Jephthah's costly "vow" (*neder*, Judg. 11:30–40), which demonstrates that words can become a "trap" (*moqeš*, cf. 12:13; 18:7).

20:26. Like 20:8, this royal saying ascribes the power to "winnow out the wicked" to the king. The "threshing wheel" was used to crush husks of grain

---

11. Whybray, *Proverbs,* 298, and *The Composition of the Book of Proverbs,* 115, marks off 20:20–21:4, counting seven Yahweh proverbs in fifteen verses, all but 20:27 set in groups of three.

12. Van Leeuwen, "Proverbs," 187, notes that this verse does not recommend pacifism, since divine justice is typically carried out by human authorities (Ps. 72; Rom. 13:1–7).

---

so that the pitchfork could toss up the chaff to be blown away. The metaphor carries elements of judgment and repayment, just as kings in the ancient Near East were often depicted as driving their chariots over their enemies. Yet this king is not called mighty but "wise," hinting at his powers of discernment. To "winnow" is also to scatter the chaff to the winds; just as Yahweh scattered the people of Israel in exile (Jer. 31:10), so this wisdom is also power.

20:27. The association of the king's discernment and judgment seen in the previous verse continues here; just as the king winnows out wicked, so Yahweh searches out the inner regions, seeking wickedness to drive it out. The image of God's light searching human interior spaces fits in well with neighboring proverbs on the interior life (20:5–6, 8–9, 26) and the sages' fascination with the effect of that inner life on human behavior (20:24–25).

The NIV text note indicates that the first line phrase is not easy to decipher (lit., "lamp of the LORD, breath/spirit of the human"). The question is whether the lamp searches the spirit (NIV) or is to be identified with it (NIV text note). Most commentators take the latter approach: "The human spirit is the lamp of the LORD."[13] That our inmost secret places are not hidden from Yahweh is never disputed (15:11; 16:2; 17:3; 18:8; 21:2), and some liken the breath that fills our bodies to the lamp that lights dark chambers.[14]

A second question follows: Is the lamp a symbol for God's knowledge of us or for our own self-knowledge and conscience, or for both?[15] The key in my view is the link between that which is hidden in deep waters (20:5) and dark rooms (20:27; cf. Jer. 17:10). Wisdom allows a person to do what the lamp does—to reveal what is hidden.[16] The reappearance of "inmost being" in Proverbs 20:30 suggests that while blows will purge evil, the discernment of wisdom can accomplish the same through teaching and self-correction.

---

13. Scott, Murphy, and TNK take the human breath as the lamp; the NRSV also, calling it spirit. Clifford, *Proverbs*, 186, suggests that human "lifebreath," the "gift of God," courses throughout the body as a claim; all of its regions belong to him and are under his scrutiny.

14. "Spirit" (*nišmat*, cf. Job 26:4) is the "breath of life" in Gen. 2:7 and 7:22; the "breath of the LORD" in Isa. 30:33 and Job 32:8. "Inmost being" (*hadre–beten*, the inner chambers of belly) appears in 18:8; 20:27; 20:30; 26:22 (cf. "chambers of death," 7:27; "chambers of riches," 24:4).

15. Van Leeuwen, "Proverbs," 188, notes that lamps and breath both give life in the Bible, and so the metaphor can point to both God's knowledge of the human and human self-knowledge as a gift of God, not simply one or the other.

16. S. E. Loewenstamm, "Remarks on Proverbs 17:12 and 20:27," *VT* 37 (April, 1984): 221–24. Lowenstamm proposes to read "lamp" as a participle of *nir* ("to break up, to plow"). The word "search" can also mean to dig (cf. Job 3:20), so he translates, "God ploughs and examines the soul of man, searches all the inmost chambers."

20:28. The famous pair of "love and faithfulness" (*ḥesed* and *ʾemet*), split up in 20:6, is reunited here. If the former saying took a pessimistic look at the human capacity for love and faithfulness, here the sages observe that kings depend on them for security. It is not clear whose love and faithfulness bring this security, but more likely the primary reference is to the king's character, with perhaps a secondary reference to the faithfulness of the court and citizenry. The pair of love and faithfulness is often used to describe God, and its use here may imply another source of support. The overlap of king and Yahweh is prominent in both this chapter and larger subsection of 20:16–22. The same throne that winnows out evil (20:8) is protected by love.

20:29. Time offers every young person an exchange; if strength is spent wisely, the return is a long life, symbolized by the gray (lit., "hoary"; cf. 16:31) head. Does the saying encourage old and young alike to take a look at the glory of the other? Just as a great king is kept safe by love and faithfulness, so wisdom grants every person a measure of glory.

20:30. Even as Yahweh's lamp searches out the "inmost being" (*ḥadre–beṭen*, "the inner chambers of belly"; cf. 20:27), so blows and beatings purge the "inmost being" of evil. The juxtaposition of discernment and judgment that runs throughout the chapter (see 20:8, 26) suggests that one can either acquire the capacity for discernment to discipline self or fail to learn discernment and suffer the discipline of another who has. Translators are not certain about the one verb in this saying, which may mean simply "to rub."[17]

THE MANY DOUBLED proverbs and images of this chapter suggest that a clue for reading can be found by attending to the repetition. So we observe that two pairs of royal proverbs (20:2 and 8; 20:26 and 28) frame two clusters of Yahweh proverbs (20:10 and 12; 20:22–24 and 27), with a list of speech sins running throughout and gathering at the center: quarrels (20:3), self-deception (20:9), sharp bargaining (20:14), unwise pledges (20:16), falsehood (20:17), tale-bearing (20:19), cursing (20:20), threat (20:22), and rash vows (20:25). We also notice that there are two proverbs about the king's winnowing (20:8, 26), two on Yahweh's hatred for false weights and measures (20:10, 23), and two on the

---

17. Clifford, *Proverbs*, 181: "Blows and wounds *come upon* the wicked." Von Soden proposes "insult" for "cleanse" and "scar" for "beatings," interpreting the proverb to mean that malice leaves a scar on the inner character, but the proposal requires some emendation based on Aramaic (see W. von Soden, "Kränung, nicht Schläge in Sprüche 20:30," *ZAW* 102 [1990]: 120–21).

sluggard who goes without food (20:4, 13).[18] Therefore we will look at Yahweh's work of watching and searching, the king's work of winnowing, and the failure to work by sluggards of all kinds, especially those who do not discipline their speech.

Yahweh's work of watching and searching. The Yahweh proverbs of this chapter (and the next, 21:1–3) reassure the reader that God watches, searches, and knows when weights are different and knows when hearts are not in line with his purposes. Moreover, he will deliver those who reject revenge in favor of waiting and trust (20:22); yet, in ways that are mysterious and difficult to understand, a person's steps are "from the LORD" (*mey°hwah*, 20:24; cf. 16:1–4; 19:21). Extending the teaching of earlier chapters that God's purposes will stand and not be thwarted, the sayings of this chapter add new insight into Yahweh's examination of human purposes. Recognizing that many boast of faithfulness and purity (20:6, 9), these proverbs suggest that God knows our own hearts better than we do. For that reason the guidance of his gift of wisdom is indispensable (20:24).

The king's work of winnowing. Like Yahweh, the wise king also judges, winnowing out evil with his eyes and winnowing out the wicked with a threshing wheel (20:8, 26). That king's wrath is like a lion's deadly roar, yet love and faithfulness make the throne secure—perhaps a sign that the righteous king's purposes will also be established. This portrait of the king suggests that he is a man of understanding who can draw out the purposes and intentions of persons from the deep well of human hearts (20:5). Behavior is a good indicator of character, but the discerning person is also able to see through boastful and deceptive speech, even as Yahweh knows when someone is carrying two sets of weights.

Moreover, lips that speak knowledge, though rarer than gold and rubies, are worth more than both (20:15), suggesting that this discernment is not only good for protection against evil but also for speaking and teaching the wisdom of the right way, perhaps in the form of counsel and advice (20:18). Once again, the royal proverbs show that the king is the human model of Yahweh's intention to establish righteousness, justice, and equity on the earth (cf. ch. 16). While the responsibilities of the king to enact these characteristics of the good society apply to political leaders today, we have noted before that they also are important for anyone who carries responsibility for leadership.

On sluggards. The pair of proverbs on the sluggard hints at his failure to use the eyes that God gave him (20:12), for he would have food to spare if

---

18. Other doublets appear on "honor" and "glory" (20:3, 29) and on "love and faithfulness" (20:6, 28).

he kept his eyes open instead of sleeping (20:13). Instead, he fails to plow and looks for a harvest that never materializes (20:4). Contrasted with the wise king who winnows evil with his eyes, the symbolism suggests that the foolish sluggard has neglected to learn the art of discernment and therefore cannot even take care of himself, let alone others. If the wise king ensures that justice prevails, the sluggard's inattention does nothing to prevent the social disorder depicted at the chapter's center. Unwise pledges, fraudulent gain, gossip, cursing, threats, and rash vows are all signs of two kinds of failure: the lack of self-understanding and discipline (20:6, 9, 27) and the failure to restrain others from doing harm with their words and actions (20:8, 26, 30).

The proverbs of chapter 20 together suggest that if we will not allow the lamp of Yahweh to search our inner being and drive out the darkness of sin, more extreme forms of external discipline are required. Put another way, the symbolism of this chapter's collection of proverbs sets out both internal self-discipline and the external discipline of law and judgment. The first is always preferred, but experience told the sages that both are necessary.

However, the speaker in Psalm 1 was not sad that the law had been given; rather, he celebrated it as a resource for meditation. The one who meditates on the law of Yahweh will not be led astray by mockers of any sort, human or alcoholic (Ps. 1:1; cf. Prov. 20:1). That person will stand in the judgment, the assembly of the righteous, while the wicked will be blown away like winnowed chaff (Ps. 1:4; cf. Prov. 20:8, 26). The psalmist is a person who knows that Yahweh watches and that wickedness will perish (Ps. 1:6; cf. Prov. 20:27). Therefore, rather than being led astray by strong drink, the wise will choose to be led in the way of the righteous.

POWER AND WISDOM. The sayings in the chapter touch on drunkenness, brawling, laziness, and cheating, which to our ears may sound more like country music or a cowboy movie than holy Scripture! It may be intentional that two of these proverbs speak of honor and glory (the honor of avoiding strife in 20:3 and the glory of youthful strength juxtaposed with the splendor of gray hair in 20:29). Both recommend the life of wisdom that rejects the foolish, greedy, and shortsighted behaviors that make up so much of this chapter's collection of pictures. Strength may be the glory of youth, but it is the wisdom symbolized by the gray head that leads both young and old away from the deception that we can do whatever we want, "because we can."

There may be something about the unwarranted boast of power in the many negative speech acts listed in this chapter: "Do not say, 'I'll pay you back'" (20:22) reminds the reader of Lamech's boast (Gen. 4:23–24) and the warning of James against boasting of tomorrow's deeds (James 4:13–17). Jesus warned against oaths, telling his listeners that "you cannot make even one hair white or black" (Matt. 5:36; cf. James 5:12). The Yahweh proverbs in particular carry a message about the folly of assuming that our limited power allows us to act in ways that have no limits. In other words, because our powers over the future are set within limits, our behavior must also find its way within a set of limits, moral guidelines that teach us to not act as though we believe we have power over one another. The idolatry of sin is imagining we have ultimate authority to make our own way and therefore to exercise ultimate authority over our behavior, becoming a law unto ourselves. It begins in boasting when our talk is bigger than the strength we actually have.

Marva Dawn and Eugene Peterson express their concern for such an unrealistic sense of effectiveness in *The Unnecessary Pastor*, using the word "unnecessary" to challenge what the culture, we ourselves, and our congregations often presume is most important for pastoral ministry: leading, managing, and getting things accomplished. Part of the problem, they observe, is a confusion between two kinds of language: *scientia*, words that describe an abstract reality, usually to exercise power over it, and *sapientia*, words that enter into reality, experiencing and expressing it in relationship with it, interacting with reality rather than pushing it into submission. It is the language of relationship, the difference between science and wisdom. The former depersonalizes knowledge, the latter makes it personal. The view we choose about knowledge determines our attitude toward it; we can look at knowledge as information or knowledge as wisdom.[19]

The view we take of knowledge will ultimately write our job descriptions. If, in our ministries, we believe that it is most important to achieve a growing membership roster, an increase in program development with its accompanying budget, we may be doing the right things for the kingdom but for the wrong reasons, and we may be missing opportunities to address the misunderstandings of power and effectiveness that the sages worked so hard to correct. But if in our many activities we are also teaching people the difference between success and faithfulness, the difference between self-deception and self-awareness, and most important the difference between lips that speak knowledge (20:15) and lips that boast, curse, and defraud (20:6, 9, 14, 17, 19, 20), seeking to make the difference known in our lives, then by God's grace, we may find our steps directed by the Lord and, as a result,

---

19. M. J. Dawn and E. Peterson, *The Unnecessary Pastor: Rediscovering the Call*, ed. P. Santucci (Grand Rapids: Eerdmans, 2000), 132–37.

understand our way (20:24). Here is one way we can allow the lamp of Yahweh to search our inmost being.

Self-examination. The proverbs about the king's winnowing eye can also alert us to the need to examine motives and root out boasting and other forms of self-deception (20:8, 26). The capacities of the human heart in this regard are astounding. The church needs ministers and leaders who are good at smelling the proverbial rat but who also make themselves available to offer positive advice and counsel (20:18) to those who will seek it. Put simply, we need one another, not only to offer insight and fresh perspective on our plans but also to tell us when we are kidding ourselves, especially if we seek justifications for our sins.

As an extreme example of the human tendency to hide from the truth, we might consider the films of Errol Morris. In *The Thin Blue Line*, a murderer talks about his wild behavior as a young man: "I wasn't doing nothing but hurting myself." Morris calls the moment "one of the most ironic lines I've ever put on film, and people never comment on it. . . . Whenever I hear the line, I think, 'Not quite. . . . [You've hurt] others as well.' This moment of self-knowledge seems to be a moment of self-deception." A later film, *Mr. Death: The Rise and Fall of Fred A. Leuchter Jr.*, recounts Leuchter's efforts to prove that the gas chambers at Auschwitz were not used for executions; his report is often cited by those who deny that a Jewish holocaust took place.[20]

Again, the church and its leaders do their job when they teach the importance of self-examination and confession and when they risk stating the obvious by declaring some behaviors right and others wrong. So, for example, someone might hear the proverb that food gained by fraud only tastes sweet for a while (20:17) and wonder who wouldn't know that already, yet pastors and other counselors of the church can testify that embezzlements and extramarital affairs are only some of the forms that self-deception takes. Remembering that the king winnows out the wicked, we can appropriate its example, not to eliminate all sinners from the church but to use the discipline of the church to redeem and restore those who might otherwise be lost. Teaching can be preventative, but it can also be corrective.

Diligence and discipline. Finally, the example of the sluggard can be a motivation toward diligence and discipline in general, but especially toward the development of discernment of our own spirits. If the proverbs of this chapter recommend openness to the searching lamp of Yahweh and the wise and discerning counsel of others, they also urge believers to "understand [their] own way" (20:24), as difficult as it may be. Perhaps the best way to

---

20. P. T. Chattaway, "The Self-Deception of Mr. Death," *Books and Culture* (January/February 2000), 5.

495

practice wise speaking is to learn to speak truth to ourselves, praying for eyes that see and asking that we become aware of the dark areas in our inner being.

This may be what Jesus had in mind when he called the eye the "lamp of the body," reminding us to be sure that our eye is good, so the body will be full of light (Matt. 6:22–23). Daily prayer for self-understanding need not be a sign of self-hatred or despair but a mark of growing perception of grace, as the famous hymn testifies, "Once I was blind, but now I can see."

The proverbs of this chapter are, like the purposes of the heart, deep waters, difficult to fathom (Prov. 20:5). Their reflections go beyond teaching the practical skills of life to pondering its mysteries, optimistic that what is dark can become a little more light and the unknown can indeed become known, if only in part. As they urge their readers to meditate on the wonders of God's work within human society as well as the human heart, they also help us become less of a mystery to ourselves.

Proverbs 21:1–31

‌❧

¹ THE KING'S HEART is in the hand of the LORD;
　he directs it like a watercourse wherever he pleases.
² All a man's ways seem right to him,
　but the LORD weighs the heart.
³ To do what is right and just
　is more acceptable to the LORD than sacrifice.
⁴ Haughty eyes and a proud heart,
　the lamp of the wicked, are sin!
⁵ The plans of the diligent lead to profit
　as surely as haste leads to poverty.
⁶ A fortune made by a lying tongue
　is a fleeting vapor and a deadly snare.
⁷ The violence of the wicked will drag them away,
　for they refuse to do what is right.
⁸ The way of the guilty is devious,
　but the conduct of the innocent is upright.
⁹ Better to live on a corner of the roof
　than share a house with a quarrelsome wife.
¹⁰ The wicked man craves evil;
　his neighbor gets no mercy from him.
¹¹ When a mocker is punished, the simple gain wisdom;
　when a wise man is instructed, he gets knowledge.
¹² The Righteous One takes note of the house of the wicked
　and brings the wicked to ruin.
¹³ If a man shuts his ears to the cry of the poor,
　he too will cry out and not be answered.
¹⁴ A gift given in secret soothes anger,
　and a bribe concealed in the cloak pacifies great wrath.
¹⁵ When justice is done, it brings joy to the righteous
　but terror to evildoers.
¹⁶ A man who strays from the path of understanding
　comes to rest in the company of the dead.
¹⁷ He who loves pleasure will become poor;
　whoever loves wine and oil will never be rich.
¹⁸ The wicked become a ransom for the righteous,
　and the unfaithful for the upright.
¹⁹ Better to live in a desert
　than with a quarrelsome and ill-tempered wife.

²⁰ In the house of the wise are stores of choice food and oil,
  but a foolish man devours all he has.
²¹ He who pursues righteousness and love
  finds life, prosperity and honor.
²² A wise man attacks the city of the mighty
  and pulls down the stronghold in which they trust.
²³ He who guards his mouth and his tongue
  keeps himself from calamity.
²⁴ The proud and arrogant man—"Mocker" is his name;
  he behaves with overweening pride.
²⁵ The sluggard's craving will be the death of him,
  because his hands refuse to work.
²⁶ All day long he craves for more,
  but the righteous give without sparing.
²⁷ The sacrifice of the wicked is detestable—
  how much more so when brought with evil intent!
²⁸ A false witness will perish,
  and whoever listens to him will be destroyed forever.
²⁹ A wicked man puts up a bold front,
  but an upright man gives thought to his ways.
³⁰ There is no wisdom, no insight, no plan
  that can succeed against the LORD.
³¹ The horse is made ready for the day of battle,
  but victory rests with the LORD.

THIS CHAPTER BEGINS and ends with sayings about Yahweh's purposes and victory. In between are proverbs gathered into clusters about final outcomes and rewards. Some, like the proverbs on laziness (21:5, 25), love of pleasure (21:17), and a quarrelsome wife (21:9, 19), do not fit into this general framework.[1] A single observation on the power of gifts and bribes stands out from its context (21:14).

Yahweh looks at the heart (21:1–3)
Sins of a proud heart, lies, and violence (21:4–8)
Final outcomes and judgments (21:9–19)

---

1. Whybray, *Composition*, 117–18. Whybray calls 21:1 and 21:31 a frame, but Goldingay, "Proverbs," 601, puts 21:30–31 in a frame with 22:16. It may be the case that 21:30–31 works as a hinge that links the chs. and their clusters.

Examples of wise moderation and strength (21:20–23)
Sins of pride and power (21:24–29)
Yahweh's victory (21:30–31)[2]

Yahweh Looks At the Heart (21:1–3)

THREE PROVERBS TIE together Yahweh's relationship to the king with Yahweh's desire for integrity.

21:1. The royal sayings in chapter 20 spoke of the king's powers of discernment and judgment; here the emphasis is on the greater purposes of
God. Even the king is a subject of Yahweh, for the seat of human intentions,
the heart, is in Yahweh's hand. Just as water is directed to a good purpose by
digging irrigation ditches and building dams, so the king's heart will follow
the directives of Yahweh to establish his purpose of justice.[3] The history of
Israel and its erring rulers shows that the king was never a puppet. Thus, this
proverb describes the ideal situation of the good king who wisely responds
to guidance. Theme and vocabulary remind the reader of 16:1. The threefold rhythm of the Hebrew, "channels of water, heart of the king, in hand of
the LORD," echoes the grouping of three Yahweh proverbs in the previous
chapter (cf. 20:22–24).

21:2. Like the similar proverb of 16:2, this saying, like 21:1, links a person's ways to the heart that directs them. As skilled as we humans are in jus-
tifying our own ways, believing we are right ("straight," *yašar*), it is Yahweh
who weighs the heart to get an accurate measure of its intentions. Intentions of the heart are also deep waters (20:5), and although the wise can
draw them out, there are limits. Yahweh alone can determine what is known
and what is hidden from a person's own self-perceptions.

21:3. The final proverb of this Yahweh cluster moves from the intentions
of the heart to the action it directs. Deeds are not to be placed in a special category but describe the way everyday dealings with others ought to take place.
Everyday deeds that are "just" and "right" are (lit.) "chosen by the LORD" over
special religious actions such as sacrifice. The comparison does not demean
devotional practices but does observe that it is easier to have sacrifice without
right living than it is to have right living without religious practice. Thankfully,

---

2. These proverbs do not fit neatly into any pattern. Scherer, *Das Weise Wort und Seine Wirkung*, 302–33, divides larger sections 20:22–21:3; 21:4–29; 21:30–22:16. The smaller clusters as identified by Scherer are: vv. 1–3, 4–12, 13–16, 17–21, 22–24, 25–29, 30–31. Heim, *Like Grapes of Gold Set in Silver*, 282–304, places vv. 1–4 in a larger section 20:20–21:4; the rest of the ch. is divided vv. 5–8, 9–19, 20–29, 30–31.

3. Garrett, *Proverbs*, 179, adds that this divine guidance does not rule out the need for counselors (cf. 20:18).

believers do not have to choose. If we did, however, the proverb reminds us that Yahweh has had plenty of experience with people who believed that sacrifice was enough (21:27; Jer. 7:1–11). Perhaps this proverb parallels Proverbs 16:3, urging us to commit our work to Yahweh in righteousness.

Sins of a Proud Heart, Lies, and Violence (21:4–8)

CONTRASTED WITH DOING "what is right and just" (21:3), this catalog of deviations resembles the list of abominations of 6:17–19.[4] The first, a "proud heart" (21:4), can be said to inspire all the others that follow as the "lamp" or light that guides the wicked.

21:4. The translation of "lamp" is a conjecture, since the Hebrew vowel points yield "tillage" or "plowed ground," but here the emendation to "lamp" after 24:20 is warranted.[5] What is clear from the saying is the negative association of pride with sin, for the wicked take as their guiding light the conceit that they can judge what is right. Believing that what is right for them is all that matters, they do not care what is acceptable to Yahweh (cf. 21:3). Throughout Scripture, haughty eyes and arrogant kings will be brought low (Isa. 2:11, 17; 10:12), but kings who reject arrogance are promised a long dynasty (Deut. 17:20).

21:5. One would expect to find laziness as the opposite of "diligence," as in 12:27, but here "haste" is another form of laziness. "The plans of the diligent" points up the significant contrast that haste usually comes from lack of foresight or preparation (cf. the sluggard of 20:4). Haste in general is disapproved throughout Proverbs (20:21; 29:20), but here the contrast of "poverty" with "profit" may point to a scheme designed to make a fast buck.

21:6. Connected with the previous saying by the theme of profit (perhaps the quick and easy kind), this saying equates treasures obtained by deceit with things transitory and deadly. The two enemies "fleeting vapor" (cf. Eccl. 1:2) and "deadly snare" (cf. Prov. 18:7) negate human desires for permanence and security, often expressed in Proverbs as a long life. As in 21:5, the end result of the lying tongue is poverty. The NIV text note reports the change from the Masoretic text's "those who seek death." Following the LXX and the Vulgate, the phrase "snares of death" (cf. 13:14; 14:27) can be read with slight emendation.

21:7. The "violence of the wicked" is not specified. Throughout the Old Testament injustice and lies are forms of violence that bring their own reward,

---

4. Whybray, *Proverbs*, 307, links 21:4 with 6:17.

5. Murphy, *Proverbs*, 157–59, translates "the tillage of the wicked is sinful." But 24:20 does name a "lamp of the wicked" that is snuffed out. Clifford, *Proverbs*, 189, translates "the lamp of the wicked will fail," drawing a contrast with the lamp that does not go out in 31:18.

but actual physical violence is probably in view here. The irony that the wicked's own violent behavior "will drag them away" creates the picture of a person caught and dragged like a fish in a net (Hab. 1:15) and extends the metaphor of the snare from Proverbs 21:6. "To do what is right" is (lit.) "to do what is just" (*la⁽ᵃ⁾śot mišpaṭ*), using vocabulary that links this saying with 21:3. Those that refuse to do justice for others will have it done to them.

21:8. The contrast between a "guilty" person (*zar*) and an "innocent" one (*zak*, "pure") is not so clear in the Hebrew text, where the word for guilty is often translated "strange."[6] The contrast between ways that are crooked ("devious," *hᵃpakpak*) and straight ("upright," *yašar*) is clear and should guide the reading (cf. 21:2). Character and deeds match more often than they do not.

Final Outcomes and Judgments (21:9–19)

PROVERBS ABOUT CONSEQUENCES and judgments are collected between the frame of similar proverbs on the "quarrelsome wife." The larger section could be divided in two by the strange appearance of a proverb about bribes and anger in 21:14.

21:9. The humor in this proverb and its companion in verse 19 breaks up the seriousness of the sayings on pride and injustice that come before and after. Obviously someone took pleasure in creating new variations on the formula to intensify the comparisons. It is better to live in a leaky house (19:13; 27:15), no, better to live on the roof of the house (21:9=25:24),[7] no, better to live in the desert and not even have a house (21:19), than to live with a quarrelsome wife. This woman is known for her ability to stir up conflict—a sign of folly also for a quarrelsome man (20:3).

21:10. The Hebrew uses body images; the *throat* or desire (*nepeš*) of the wicked craves evil, and the neighbor will find no mercy in those *eyes* (*bᵉ⁽ᵉ⁾naw*). How then can anyone expect such a person, centered only on self and desires, to show mercy to a neighbor? This person only craves, never gives. We readers expect desire (*nepeš*) to crave acquisitions and pleasures, but we do not expect to learn that evil becomes a desirable end in itself. Whatever the motivation, some people simply enjoy doing wrong. The bite of the saying is that no one can live anywhere near such a person, perhaps a link with 21:9.

21:11. This proverb assumes that the mocker will not learn, even when punished with blows (cf. 19:25; 20:30). Nevertheless, even a "simple" (lit., "naive") person can learn from the example. The same dynamic is at work

---

6. So TNK: "The way of a man is tortuous and strange."

7. Scott, *Proverbs*, 125, believes the corner of the roof is a small room or shelter used for guests (2 Kings 4:10).

when the young man's parents quote personified Wisdom's threats against the mockers in 1:20—33. Better still, the wise person will learn from instruction, not physical punishment (cf. 1:5; 9:9, 12). Therefore, both forms of discipline are worthwhile, though in different ways. The word "instructed" (*śkl*) appears in 21:12 as "takes note."

21:12. Continuing the theme of punishment from verse 11, the "evil" (*raᶜ*) craved by the wicked in 21:10 is rewarded with their "ruin" (*raᶜ*, "trouble, evil"; cf. 21:7). The NIV text note shows that "the Righteous One" translates *ṣaddiq* here; that is, the One who brings ruin is Yahweh. Throughout the wisdom writings it is God who overthrows the wicked and frustrates the words of the unfaithful (cf. Job 12:19; Prov. 22:12).[8] The catchword *śkl* ("observe") links Proverbs 21:11 and 12; whereas the wise observe to be instructed, Yahweh observes to judge.

21:13. Those who give no mercy (21:10) receive none. Just as the cries of the poor go unanswered, this saying leaves it to the reader to conclude that Yahweh will shut his ears to those who did not listen to the poor. This proverb completes the picture of 21:11—12; Yahweh will bring to ruin those who cause the ruin of others, and he will not help those who do not help the poor. The threat is similar to wisdom's bitter promise: "Then they will call to me but I will not answer; they will look for me but will not find me" (1:28; for the positive statement of the principle, see 19:17). The "cry of the poor" may be their ever-present need or their response to a specific injustice (cf. 21:14—15).

21:14. Read together with verse 13, this proverb hints that some people may be willing to give a gift or bribe to soothe human wrath but will not make a gift to the poor to avert divine anger! Both lines of this saying emphasize the hiddenness of the bribe-gift, the secrecy most likely a sign that it is given to pervert justice (17:23; cf. 1 Sam. 12:3; Job 36:18; Amos 5:12). It is not clear whether the anger mentioned is the king's (Prov. 20:2), a judge's (17:15; 18:5), or that of some other person. The point is that it is one thing to accept a settlement for personal damages and quite another to take payment to ignore someone else's just cause.

21:15. The picture of justice victorious in broad daylight is in view here as both the righteous and evil see the outcome, a reverse of the secrecy of gifts and bribes in verse 14. It is not clear whether everyday fair dealing or

---

8. Most translations and commentators agree. Clifford, *Proverbs*, 191, observes that the righteous never punish the wicked in Proverbs, only God does (13:6; 19:3). However, Garrett, *Proverbs*, 181, argues that *ṣaddiq* is always used of humans in Proverbs and notes the parallel use of *śkl* in vv. 11 and 12. Therefore he translates, "A righteous man observes the house of the wicked, how wickedness brings it to ruin," but he has to emend "ruin of the wicked" to do so.

just court decisions are in view here, but the "terror" of the "evildoers" is a clue that some sort of judgment is at work (cf. 10:28–29). It is not their downfall that brings joy to the righteous but the fact that justice is done.

21:16. In line with verses 11–15, the image of the "path" or "way" (*derek*) here illustrates final outcomes; a traveler who strays from the good path will not end up in a good place. The "company of the dead" is (lit.) the "assembly of the *rᵉpaʾim*" (2:18; 9:18), the shades that populate the netherworld, a sure sign that the traveler is not just lodging for the night—this journey is over!

21:17. The saying is chiastically structured around a repetition of "one who loves." In the first line this person loves "pleasure" (lit., "rejoicing," *śimḥaḥ*; cf. 21:15); in the second, "wine and oil." The connection with the rejoicing in 21:15 leaves the reader asking what might be wrong with wine and oil, gifts of God that gladden the heart (Ps. 104:15). First, it seems that this "love" empties the purse; to love wine and oil and not the work that produces them is shortsighted and eventually leaves one wanting (cf. Prov. 20:4). Moreover, this love is a reversal of other priorities. One who seeks justice and virtue will also find life's enjoyments, but one who puts those ahead of virtue will end up missing them both.

21:18. Interpretations of this enigmatic proverb vary widely, perhaps because the matter of "ransom" touches on the heart of the Christian doctrine of atonement. However, in the ancient world a ransom was a payment of compensation for damages (6:35; 13:8) or some other crime (Ex. 21:30; cf. Num. 35:31), a way for individuals to pay their debt to society with a ransom. Throughout Proverbs the righteous are rescued from the trouble that rightly comes on the wicked instead of them (Prov. 13:8; 11:8). Therefore, the point is not so much that the righteous need a ransom for crimes or guilt but that the wicked will receive *their* just reward, a theme that connects 21:15–18. Money also links a number of the proverbs, for like a ransom, a gift or bribe can soothe anger (21:14), but one can pay for pleasures and become poor (21:17).[9]

21:19. Unique among the quarrelsome wife sayings, this proverb brings the household imagery to a climax (see comments on 21:9); better to be alone, living without a house in the desert, than in a miserable domestic situation. "Ill-tempered" may not describe the wife's personality but the general state of vexation in such a house. Like its near neighbor in verse 9 ("better to live"), this satiric proverb stands out from its context, presenting the reader with a riddle about its significance. Perhaps it extends the metaphor of the foolish and loud woman from Proverbs 9 to say, "Choose your life partner carefully, choose wisdom!"

---

9. Persons becoming ransom for others appears in Isa. 43:3–4; Jesus' saying on ransom in Mark 10:45 reverses the expectation that the righteous will not suffer.

Examples of Wise Moderation and Strength (21:20–23)

FOUR PROVERBS OFFER positive examples of wisdom as a mirror reflection of the sins of 21:10–18.

21:20. Linked with the previous proverb by the image of the household, this wise one (cf. 21:11) stores up the knowledge and the goods he acquires. The "stores of choice food" are (lit.) "desirable stores" or "precious treasures."[10] This saying contrasts the wise one who practices moderation and foresight and the fool who swallows everything in gluttony and shortsightedness. Like 21:17, this proverb urges control of appetite and thrift as two cures for gluttony. However, read along with Ecclesiastes 2:18–19, the proverb could be a "somber comment on the ephemeral nature of wealth," for one may gather goods only to leave them to a fool to squander.[11]

21:21. Another saying about possessions and virtues, this proverb pictures a person who seeks the qualities of "righteousness" (*ṣᵉdaqah*; cf. 21:15; 20:7) and "love" (*ḥesed*; cf. 19:22; 20:6). In seeking these virtues, one also finds the three primary desires of the proverbs: life, prosperity, and honor (cf. 3:16; 22:4). One cannot do better than to find long life, wealth enough to share, and a good name in the community.[12] By implication, this is the same "wise" person of 21:20 and 22.

21:22. Another saying about the "wise" (cf. 21:20), here the victorious wise one brings down a city along with its signs of great power, warriors, and stronghold. The last Hebrew word, "they trusted it," is key, pointing out the confidence placed in strength and numbers and contrasting it with the wise person's trust in God.[13] The wise one knows how to use the power of counsel and words, but he also recognizes its limits.

21:23. This proverb plays on the word *šmr*, translated in the NIV as "guard" in the first line and "keeps" in the second: "one who guards mouth and tongue, one who guards self from troubles." The image of keeping watch ties this saying to 21:22 and its guarded stronghold, implying that

---

10. Clifford, *Proverbs*, 192, takes it as fine wine after 1 Chron. 27:27. The same ambiguity of terms shows up as "vineyard of wine" (NASB) or a "pleasant vineyard" (NRSV) in Isa. 27:2. The decision to emphasize edible goods may have been influenced by the "wine and oil" of Prov. 21:17.

11. Whybray, *Proverbs*, 313.

12. "Prosperity" is a variation from the Heb. text that repeats "righteousness" (see the NIV footnote). The LXX does not read "righteousness," and a number of commentators (McKane, Scott, Murphy, Clifford) omit it altogether. Garrett, *Proverbs*, 183, maintains it, taking it as an abbreviated repetition of "righteousness and love" from the first line, meaning that those who seek those virtues will find them.

13. See the similar stories of Eccl. 9:13–16 and Ahiqar, whose wisdom in answering an enemy's riddle saved the city from destruction.

it is harder to guard one's speech than a city (yet the wise are up to the challenge; cf. 16:32).

Sins of Pride and Power (21:24–29)

A SERIES OF proverbs on sins that follow out of pride (21:24; cf. 21:4) concludes with a pair of Yahweh proverbs on human limits of power.

21:24. The character of the mocker is further exposed. Such a person will not learn (21:11; cf. 19:25) because of pride and arrogance (cf. 21:4; also 11:2; Obad. 1:3; Hab. 2:5). "Overweening pride" may be translated "fury of pride," describing the rages that come on one who exercises no control over mouth and tongue (cf. Prov. 21:23).

21:25. The first of a pair of proverbs on the sluggard's craving explains why that appetite will be "the death of him." The focus is on the hands that "refuse to work." There is a reversal here; appetite that does not motivate a person to work (16:26) will ultimately lead to other means of satisfying it. The wicked person "craves evil" (cf. 21:10; Ps. 112:10), though a number of proverbs use the same word for the "desire" of the righteous (*ta²ªwat*, Prov. 10:24; 11:23; 13:12, 19; 19:22; Ps. 10:17; 21:2). The difference is in the object of the desire as well as the means used to obtain it. How often laziness and gluttony go together!

21:26. The picture of one who craves all day long (21:25) is contrasted with one who practices continual giving. This contrast between an appetite that cries for more and a person able to give without saying "that's enough" may describe the wise one of 21:20. A righteous person like this does not shut his ear to the poor (21:13). We may go further and say that if the righteous give without sparing, the giving goes beyond what one has to spare.[14]

21:27. Evil deeds have been named "detestable" throughout Proverbs, so certainly the hypocritical sacrifices of a wicked person will draw the same response from Yahweh (cf. 21:3). It is even worse if the sacrifice is brought to serve another purpose, even though the proverb does not specify what such "evil intent" might be. Jesus' example of those who give to the poor with trumpets blaring is one example of seeking favor from those who are watching (Matt. 6:2). Read alongside the picture of generous giving in the previous verse, this offering also begins to look like a bribe (cf. Prov. 21:14).

---

14. Some commentators (e.g., Murphy, *Proverbs*, 157) hold that the subject of the first line need not be the sluggard of 21:25 but anyone whose appetite takes control. Clifford, *Proverbs*, 193, keeps the two proverbs independent to preserve the integrity of each, yet adds a word about appetite: "What keeps normal people alive kills sluggards, for they cannot lift their hands to their mouths to feed themselves (cf. 19:24)."

21:28. The first line is familiar and most likely represents a theme in variation (cf. 19:5, 9). The second line is meant to carry the punch of the proverb, but unfortunately it is not clear. The Hebrew text as it stands reads, "the one who listens will speak forever," which the NIV footnote paraphrases, "but the words of an obedient man will live on."[15] In this reading, the one who hears might be an honest witness who reports correctly what was heard, or an honest judge, or perhaps any discerning listener. "Destroyed forever" translates the phrase differently to preserve the parallel with the line before,[16] but the first reading makes good sense that the discerning person will endure (cf. 21:23).

21:29. As translated, this proverb draws a contrast between those who make their way by putting up a hard and impenetrable front with those who reflect on their ways, the latter depicting an attitude of openness. The second line again presents translation problems, for the Hebrew text (*ketib*) reads "establishes his ways" (cf. 16:9), while the Hebrew marginal note (*qere*) reads "considers his way" (cf. 14:8; 20:24). Whether the translation reflects a teachable attitude or its outcome is not as important as the contrast with the "bold front" or "brazen face" of the wicked (cf. 7:13).[17] The last Hebrew word in each line carries the bite of the proverb. One attends to *his face*, the other to *his way*; one attends only to the self and its preservation, the other to the larger picture of life lived uprightly, in harmony with Yahweh's creation and community.

Yahweh's Victory (21:30–31)

21:30. THERE IS a sort of "wisdom . . . insight . . . plan" that betrays the first principle of true wisdom (1:7), namely, choosing to set oneself "against the LORD" rather than to fear him (Ps. 5:5; 36:2).[18] Perhaps we can better say that any wisdom of this sort "is no wisdom" at all. Set in the literary context of this cluster, the proverb's threefold repetition of "is no" (*ʾen*) emphasizes the limits of human endeavor, recognizing the foolish pride that inspires the behaviors listed in Proverbs 21:24–29. The terms "wisdom,"

---

15. Variations on the reading include: "but an accurate one will testify again" (Clifford); "but one who listens will have the last word" (Murphy); "but the one who really heard will testify with success" (TNK); "but a good listener will testify successfully" (NRSV).

16. D. A. Garrett, following Dahood, replaces "speak" with "drive out," translating "and whoever listens to him will be driven out forever" ("Votive Prostitution Again: A Comparison of Proverbs 7:13–14 and 21:28–29," *JBL* [1990]: 681–82).

17. Garrett, ibid., takes this to be the equivalent of a "bold-faced lie."

18. "Can succeed" is (lit.) "before" (*neged*) Yahweh, which the TNK translates: "No wisdom, no understanding, no advice is *worth anything* before Yahweh" (italics added).

"insight," and "plan" may have military connotations that are made more explicit in the next verse.

21:31. The war horse is both strong and constrained, a symbol of human power. Riders can harness a horse and even prepare it for battle, but victory belongs to Yahweh, not the one who pulls the reins (Ex. 15:1, 21; Deut. 20:1; Ps. 20:7; 33:17; 37:9; Jer. 51:2). Common to this proverb and the one before is the theme of human effectiveness—intellectual effort in preparing and planning and physical prowess. The two proverbs name different but related errors: The first and most obvious is to go against God; the second and more subtle, to forget to thank God for victory and trust in your own foresight and strength. The parallelism in both verses reminds the reader of the mysterious relationship between human initiative and divine purposes that have come to the forefront in this second half of the collected proverbs (Prov. 16:1–22:16).

ONE OF THE most notable features in the chapter is the paired recurrence of themes and keywords. While we cannot be certain that their presence indicates an intentional structure, it is notable that two sets of Yahweh proverbs (21:1–3 and 30–31) frame a collection of paired themes that fall into a mirror pattern, namely, the upright way (*yašar* and *derek* in 21:2, 29), sacrifice (21:3, 27), pride (21:4, 24), and the quarrelsome woman (21:9, 19).

Puzzling sayings about "the Righteous One" and the gift given in secret fall in the middle (21:12, 14), while "righteous" and "righteousness" appear throughout, often in contrast with the wicked (21:3, 12, 15, 18, 21, 26). Throughout the first half of the chapter, the phrase "do justice" appears three times (*ʿᵃsoh mišpaṭ*, 21:3, 7, 15); in the last of these, the righteous rejoice when that justice brings terror to the evildoers. The theme of judgment and reversal echoes throughout the cluster of proverbs at 21:12–15, a theological center, assuring that the righteous will be vindicated and the wicked judged. But how does this relate to the mysteries of Yahweh's purposes in 21:1–3 and 30–31? And why does a strange proverb about gifts and bribes stand near the middle of this chapter?

Yahweh and human beings. It may be that the pairing of word and theme suggests a strategy of looking for the proverb's mate to find the key to its meaning. If we consider that small clusters of proverbs are paired this way, we can compare the two sets that name "the LORD." The first trio of Yahweh proverbs tells us that he knows the human heart, weighing its motives and knowing when right actions do not accompany acts of worship like sacrifice.

The two Yahweh proverbs that conclude the chapter stress that no powers, intellectual or physical, can stand against him, so that even kings who mount horses must grant that victory belongs to Yahweh, not their own strength or cunning. Knowledge and rule are the boundaries within which wise living must remain. To believe one can stand against Yahweh is foolish pride; to think one can deceive and go undetected is foolish self-deception. Either choice is out of touch with reality.

Yet it is this self-deceiving pride that led the unnamed pharaoh of the Exodus to play games with God, tricking the Hebrews time and time again and finally chasing the released slaves with horses and chariots. The narrative puzzles and tantalizes us as we read that God hardened that king's heart (Ex. 10:1), but this is not the picture we have here in Proverbs 21:1. Rather, God turns the king's heart like the watercourse. The metaphor suggests that he guides but does not dictate the king's actions, directing them to a good purpose.

It is not clear whether 21:1 speaks of Israel's king or kings in general, but we may try to find a general principle. If a king will acknowledge God's knowledge and guidance, the fruits of righteous wise living will be watered and grow.[19] But if a king should ask with Pharaoh, "Who is the LORD, that I should obey him" (Ex. 5:2), then the struggles and destruction of the wicked are played out instead. So in the Exodus narrative, neither Pharaoh's wise men nor his horses and armies were able to stand against Yahweh (Ex. 7:10–13; 14:23–30; Prov. 21:30–31).

Yet Pharaoh was as forthright as he was hard; few of Israel's king's were so honest in their refusal to listen and learn. Some, like Saul, thought that one could replace teachability and obedience with sacrifices and still claim loyalty, but as Samuel reminded Saul, "Does the LORD delight in burnt offerings and sacrifices as much as in obeying the voice of the LORD? To obey is better than sacrifice, and to heed is better than the fat of rams. For rebellion is like the sin of divination, and arrogance like the evil of idolatry" (1 Sam. 15:22–23; cf. Prov. 21:3–4, 24, 27).

The Yahweh proverbs of this chapter not only call its readers to humility and teachability, they offer the hope that those who choose Yahweh's guidance of wisdom will live a life directed to good purposes—in the case of the king, ensuring justice for others; in the case of the ordinary reader, a passion for justice and fair dealing that shapes our desires. In interpreting the

---

19. Another clue may come from the use of channeled waters in 21:1 and the reverse in 5:16, waters flowing loose and undirected in the street, a sign of folly and refusal to learn. If the symbols are used consistently, channeled water is purposeful water, while water spilled in the streets is water put to no purpose at all but wasted.

principle of these proverbs for our own times, we must reject all forms of pride and deception, weighing the motives of our hearts by Yahweh's standards of righteousness and justice.

Desire. A number of the proverbs of this chapter treat the familiar topic of desire, most conspicuously the pair on craving that depicts the wicked who crave evil and the sluggard who simply craves for more (21:10, 25–26). Of the two pictures, we may find ourselves having more in common with the sluggard, for as we have seen throughout Proverbs, the sluggard is lazy about all kinds of work, including the labor of learning wisdom. Moreover, we recognize some of the sluggard's inclination to put appetite above everything else. We also remember that the book of Proverbs often juxtaposes the one who loves evil with the sluggard (6:6–19), perhaps to remind us that we face a variety of temptations.

Common to both is the exaltation of desire above everything else. The wicked will make a fortune with a lying tongue, employ violence and devious ways (21:6–8), present false sacrifice and false witness, and do all this with a bold front (21:27–29). The sluggard, by contrast, is easily spotted, not only by laziness but also unbounded craving. The sluggard rejects labor; the scoundrel is full of energy but rejects a moral code. Both reject love for neighbor, for the ideal righteous person of Proverbs is not only moral and industrious but a charitable person (21:26). Again, we see that evil and lazy persons express their craving differently, but both disregard the neighbor and fail to give. Thus, while some "love wine and oil" and foolishly devour all they get (21:17, 20), the wise store it, perhaps with the intention to share.

In sum, the two pictures work together to show us that while some are vulnerable to temptations that do our neighbors active harm, many more are prone to lazy indifference to their need and failure to give and care. Both, in a sense, shut their ears to the cry of the poor (21:13). In seeking to appropriate the principles of these proverbs for our own day, we must ask whether we are primarily tuned to the cry of our desires or the cry of the poor.

Other proverb pairs. Two other proverb pairs stand out in this chapter: the pair on the quarrelsome wife (21:9, 19) and a less obvious pair on payment and ransom (21:14, 18). While we may take the first pair of "better than" proverbs as ancient examples of satire (remembering that there is a quarrelsome man who kindles strife in 26:21), we recognize the truth common to both, that it is better to live alone than to live in unrelenting conflict.

The second of the two proverbs adds the description "ill tempered" (*ka°as*), using a word that typically refers to the fool who shows his "annoyance" (12:6), who brings "grief" to his father (17:25), and whose "provocation" is heavier than stone and sand (27:3).[20] As provocation is the sign of the fool, the proverbs suggest that to live with such a woman is to live with a fool; for that reason it is better to live alone. Moreover, in the symbolism of proverbs, if the young man is not to *become* a fool, he must seek out a good and wise woman, making wisdom his life partner. In Proverbs 31 that woman does a man good, but here one does not wish to share a home with a woman who shows such signs of folly. The principle of reversal may be at work in this picture of a man who chooses folly only to spend his life trying to get away from its effects.

Interestingly, the apparently unrelated proverb about gifts and bribes in 21:14 falls in the middle of this section framed by the two proverbs on the contentious woman, five proverbs before it and five after. In between are proverbs that depict a series of sins (21:10, 13, 14, 16, 17) and proverbs about justice (21:11, 12, 13, 15, 18). The "ransom" of 21:18 is the last of a series of reversals; the wicked who want to ruin others are themselves brought to ruin by the "Righteous One" (21:12), the one who hears no cry will not be heard (21:13), and justice, when accomplished, brings terror to those who terrorized the righteous (21:15).

Yet the proverb on the secret gift and bribe shows no such reversal and makes no moral statement (21:14). Instead, it simply observes that secret gifts and bribes do calm the anger of others, leaving readers to imagine such a situation, perhaps a bribe given to tell someone to stay quiet and let others take a fall. Yet while it is true that there are payments that divert wrath and soothe anger, only a fool believes that secret gifts and bribes can work over the long haul.

Moreover, there is a similar observation on the joys of eating "secret" bread and stolen water in Proverbs, and it is made by the foolish woman (9:17). Verse 18 looks at another sort of payment, a "ransom" of the very life of the wicked for the righteous. Read in the context of chapter 21, then, the bribes that undo the righteous (21:14) are themselves undone by an unspecified ransom (21:18), presumably from Yahweh, who weighs hearts and whose purposes stand (21:1–3, 30–31).

In sum, it seems that the pairs of proverbs on vexing women and compensating payments are pieces of a puzzle that fall into place when the folly common to both is observed. Foolish people cause strife, and foolish people believe that illicit payoffs can resolve it. The final ransom in 21:18 hints at Yahweh's work of reversal; what the wicked wish on others comes on them

---

20. In the song of Moses, the word is used four times as Yahweh's son Israel angers him with idols (Deut. 32:16, 19, 21, 27). In the song, Moses also chastises Israel for rejecting wisdom and trusting in their own battle strength (Deut. 32:28–30; cf. Prov. 21:30–31).

instead, a principle we saw in Proverbs 1. The appearance of foolish women and wicked men may signal readers to look back at previous warnings against the wicked men who leave straight paths to walk dark ways (2:13–15) and the woman of seductive words whose paths lead down to death (2:16–19; 9:18).[21]

The pair of proverbs at 21:30–31 warn us that there is always potential for a battle between our wills and God's will, a potential characterized by those whose ways are right in their own eyes and those who give thought to their ways (21:1–3, 29). To incorporate this principle into our own situation, we must observe the dangerous follies of our own day and keep an eye out for the ways that point to our own struggle to submit ourselves to God's will.

THE PRINCIPLE OF REVERSAL. As we seek to translate the message of these collected proverbs for our own day, we recognize that some of the misdeeds depicted here are closer to our own situations than others. While it is true that only some people will resort to bribes and ill treatment of neighbors to get what they want, most of us are more vulnerable to the sins of omission. So, for example, even if we do not actively take advantage of the poor, we do often fail to hear their cries and act on their behalf (21:13). However, common to both is the principle of reversal, that what we do to or for our neighbors will eventually come back to us.

The various reversals in the chapter can provide a model for our application of the principle, anticipating the Golden Rule as Jesus taught it. Certainly Jesus' application of the principle behind these proverbs, "Do to others what you would have them do to you, for this sums up the Law and the Prophets" (Matt. 7:12), gives us reason to consider the effect our actions have on others and ourselves. We might ask ourselves, "What would I want done to me," because given the nature of things, it just might come back on our heads!

We can also make helpful applications if we reverse the negative pictures and put the corresponding virtues into our lives. Thrift and moderation are the reverse of gluttony (21:20). Generous giving is another reverse of gluttony (21:26), but perhaps it also is a reverse of self-serving gifts and bribes (21:14). A guarded tongue (21:23)—that is, speech that considers its effect on others— is the reverse of the lying tongue and perhaps also of insincere worship (21:6,

---

21. Interestingly, the word for "spirits of the dead" (*r*p*a*ᶜ*im*) is used to describe the ways of the woman in 2:18 and 9:18, and then only once again in 21:16: "A man who strays from the path of understanding comes to rest in the *company of the dead*."

27). In all there is a principle more well known than practiced, that in seeking the good of others, we find that good comes to ourselves (21:21).

Succeeding in life. When we have finished this work of translation, we may find ourselves wondering why it is that so many find self-centered living attractive when it is proven time and time again that this way of life is ultimately self-defeating. Put another way, we may ask why our culture has turned selfish pursuits into virtues. We may find that temptations to pride are more subtle than we imagined and that they require a certain level of self-deception. So, for example, if we were to count the number of hours we devote to advancing our careers or our status, we may be surprised. This is not to say that all achievements and successes are wrong or that the only humble way to live is one of passive self-resignation. Rather, when we set the goals and achievements of life above God's desire for a kingdom of *šalom*, we get off course. It is one thing to succeed in life, it is another to live for success.

In his best-selling book, *Bobos in Paradise*,[22] David Brooks traces the history and development of two competing views of success and their synthesis at the end of the twentieth century. In days past, bourgeois society with its conventional wealthy lifestyle was satirically and sometimes bitterly countered by the bohemian lifestyle, which rejected both wealth and manners, preferring instead to emphasize freedom of mind and spirit. If the one stressed material success, the other emphasized self-actualization. The conflict appeared to reach a climax in the social turmoil of the 1960s; many remember the hippie disdain for conventional values and quest for freedom. In the 1980s we saw the rise of young urban professionals, and the yuppie lifestyle stressed hard work and conspicuous consumption.

As the twenty-first century dawned, argues Brooks, the two were melded into one well-educated, overachieving, and conspicuously consumptive character, someone who is every bit as concerned to make a self as to make money. The BOBO, or Bourgeois Bohemian, is an amalgam of the upper-crust establishment of the first half of the century and the counterculture that sprouted and took root in the second (although the two movements are much older than that). What Brooks found especially interesting is the conflicted attitude this new upper class carries about its success. Although increased access to higher education has led to a greater number of high-salaried professionals, this new upper class takes pains to distance itself from crass consumerism.

> This class is responsible for more yards of built-in bookshelf space than any group in history. And yet sometimes you look at their shelves

---

22. D. Brooks, *Bobos in Paradise: The New Upper Class and How They Got There* (New York: Simon & Schuster, 2000).

and notice deluxe leather-bound editions of all those books arguing that success and affluence is a sham: *Babbit, The Great Gatsby, The Power Elite, The Theory of the Leisure Class.* This is an elite that has been raised to oppose elites.[23]

It seems, then, that the bourgeois goals of material success and conspicuous consumption have not been nullified by bohemian aspirations to freedom and self-discovery. Rather, the latter has been assimilated, so that many of the ideals of community or charity that were left in either view have been muted, if not forgotten. Just as conspicuous consumption was not rejected as much as transformed, the ideals of social justice have been absorbed and thereby neglected. Brooks ends his book with a call for new political and social engagement: "Healthy self-interest becomes self-absorption if it is detached from larger national and universal ideals."[24]

Once again, as we seek to appropriate the lessons of the proverbs, we remind ourselves that the strong contrasts in these sayings symbolize the choices that stand before us, even as we recognize that the contrasts are not always so clear in real life. It has been said that the reason we need so many proverbs is because life itself comes to us in so many diverse and complicated ways. Proverbs allow us to look at the situations of our lives and ask: Is what is true in this proverb true in this situation as well? Thus, the reappearance of righteous/wicked contrasts reminds the reader of the proverbs collected in chapters 10–15 and their insistence that the two ways lead to different ends.

Giving and justice. If we are to appropriate these lessons of proverbs, we must also remember that none of us is perfectly righteous or purely wicked, yet the temptations depicted in these sayings call us to examine ourselves and ask which virtues we would like to have characterize our lives. Of the many mentioned in this chapter, two are prominent: the habit of giving and the love of justice.

As an antidote to laziness and craving, the proverb recommends giving "without sparing" (21:26). Peter Gomes found an example of such giving in a woman named Oseola McCarthy, a laundry worker who somehow managed to save $300,000 and then gave it to a historically black college for scholarships. In 1996, McCarthy was given an honorary degree by Harvard University, along with Walter Annenberg, who had made the largest individual contribution to higher education.

When it came time to present the honorary degree to Miss McCarthy in the wake of Ambassador Annenberg's, the university

---

23. Ibid., 41.
24. Ibid., 272.

marshal began, "Mr. President, we have with us today another phil-
anthropist. . . ." The choice of words was deliberate, and more than
her gift, Oseola McCarthy has given new life to the notion that phil-
anthropy proceeds not from great resources, or in response to great
need, but out of great love.[25]

Gomes observes that the habit of giving distinguishes the righteous in unexpected ways.

As an antidote to acts of evil that fail to love neighbor (or worse, to harm
neighbors without concern), the proverbs hold out love for justice. The triumph of justice stands out in 21:11–15, but that cluster is framed with the
consequences that come to those who harm others (21:5–7, 16–18). If we
reverse that picture of evil, we can look for ways to love justice and pursue
it in our daily existence. Let's be honest and admit that we feel the most
anger and resentment when we ourselves have suffered a wrong, yet too
often we silently stand by when it has been dealt to another.

There are two senses of justice. One is for daily interactions that reminds
us, as did John the Baptist, don't lie, don't cheat, don't gouge (Luke 3:10–14).
In our everyday exchange of money, goods, and words, we can ask ourselves:
Have I been fair? Is this deal straight or crooked? The other more complicated meaning of justice has to do with acting to ensure justice *for others.* Some
choose to work through political action, others choose to protest, and still others believe that teaching values of fairness and equality will make a difference.

As part of a city-wide program, Marilyn Scott, an African-American library
worker, not only read a story about racial prejudice to a first grade class, she
told them about her own experiences of rejection. The children were asked
why people would do such things, and in thinking of answers, they also
imagined what their own responses would be. At the end of the session, they
were asked, "So what would you do to stop somebody from hurting somebody's feelings like that?" Nearly every hand in the class went up and each
child was called on, some more than once, until every suggestion was heard.
Scott then told them, "You've got the right to speak up. . . . That's what these
lips and tongue are for."[26] In sum, cultivating a habit of giving and a love for
justice does more than reject the path of evil, it seeks to "overcome evil with
good" (Rom. 12:21).

---

25. P. Gomes, *The Good Book* (New York: William Morrow, 1996), 307–8, quoted in
Homiletics, 13/1 (January–February 2001): 46–47.

26. J. Hughes, "Boulder Reading Effort Aims to Turn Page on Racism," *Denver Post* (Feb.
26, 2002).

Proverbs 22:1-16

¹A GOOD NAME is more desirable than great riches;
    to be esteemed is better than silver or gold.
²Rich and poor have this in common:
    The LORD is the Maker of them all.
³A prudent man sees danger and takes refuge,
    but the simple keep going and suffer for it.
⁴Humility and the fear of the LORD
    bring wealth and honor and life.
⁵In the paths of the wicked lie thorns and snares,
    but he who guards his soul stays far from them.
⁶Train a child in the way he should go,
    and when he is old he will not turn from it.
⁷The rich rule over the poor,
    and the borrower is servant to the lender.
⁸He who sows wickedness reaps trouble,
    and the rod of his fury will be destroyed.
⁹A generous man will himself be blessed,
    for he shares his food with the poor.
¹⁰Drive out the mocker, and out goes strife;
    quarrels and insults are ended.
¹¹He who loves a pure heart and whose speech is gracious
    will have the king for his friend.
¹²The eyes of the LORD keep watch over knowledge,
    but he frustrates the words of the unfaithful.
¹³The sluggard says, "There is a lion outside!"
    or, "I will be murdered in the streets!"
¹⁴The mouth of an adulteress is a deep pit;
    he who is under the LORD's wrath will fall into it.
¹⁵Folly is bound up in the heart of a child,
    but the rod of discipline will drive it far from him.
¹⁶He who oppresses the poor to increase his wealth
    and he who gives gifts to the rich—both come to
    poverty.

Original Meaning

FEAR OF YAHWEH (22:4) makes a significant appearance in this collection, which includes two pair of Yahweh sayings, each with a saying in between (22:2–4, 12–14). The appearance of *ʿšr* ("riches, the rich") in 22:1, 2, 4, 7, and 16 may be the clearest indicator for reading this section as a unit, though there are some indicators of smaller clusters.[1] Proverbs about the training of a young man (*naʿar*; NIV "child") and the relations of rich and poor are juxtaposed at verses 6–7 and 15–16. The terms and themes of verses 9–16 fall into a mirror pattern that links proverbs about rich and poor (vv. 9, 16), driving out trouble (vv. 10, 15), and speaking (vv. 11–14). No one outline can capture the complex web of interaction between the collected proverbs; connections and relationships overlap like threads woven together to form a rope. Because the proverbs about riches are concentrated in verses 1–7, we make the following divisions, using titles that describe the concentrations, not every proverb in the section:

Proverbs about riches and consequences (22:1–7)
Proverbs about speaking and judgments (22:8–16)

Proverbs About Riches and Consequences (22:1–7)

MOST OF THE proverbs about riches are clustered here, interspersed with proverbs about rewards and consequences.

22:1. Each line of this "better than" saying makes a comparison. The first line places the Hebrew word for "choosing" (*nibḥar*; NIV "more desirable") at the beginning. It can be translated: "A good name is to be chosen rather than riches" (NRSV). If one chooses riches above all else, the actions that follow will break relationships of trust and tarnish one's name. Wealth in itself is not condemned in Proverbs, but it is always secondary to honorable relationships and reputation. The "good name" (*šem*) implies that good character will make itself known around town. "Esteemed" (*ḥen*) uses a word translated elsewhere as "favor" (3:4; 13:15; 28:23) or "grace" (1:9; 3:34; 4:9); it is translated as "gracious" in 22:11.

22:2. Reputation is to be preferred above riches (22:1), but there are to be no preferences between rich and poor. To make such distinctions is to dishonor Yahweh, the "Maker of them all" (cf. 14:31; 17:5; 29:13). The proverb

---

1. Interpreters have not come to agreement on the divisions. Scherer, *Das Weise Wort und Seine Wirkung*, 320–33, divides 22:1–10, 11–16; Heim, *Like Grapes of Gold Set in Silver*, 304–11, divides 22:1–5, 6–16; Whybray, *The Composition of the Book of Proverbs*, 119, argues that vv. 1–6 come together as an instruction to the young.

does not say that Yahweh makes anyone rich or poor, for poverty and wealth often are a result of sinful human preferences (22:16).

22:3. The key to this verse can be found in the contrast between the "prudent" one (singular) and the "simple" ones (plural), hinting that the majority is not always right. The prudent one practices foresight, looking ahead to see the consequences that issue from choices (12:16, 23; 14:8, 15, 18; and here 22:3 [cf. 27:12]). The word for "danger" (*ra'ah*) is translated as "evil, wicked" (11:19, 27; 16:27, 30; 17:13; 24:1, 16) or "trouble, harm" (1:33; 3:29–30; 13:21; 16:4; 27:12), depending on context; both meanings may be intended here. The prudent, knowing the effects of evil, see it coming and hide, while the simple, not even knowing the danger (chs. 1; 7; 9), walk straight toward it (cf. 22:5).

22:4. The familiar trio of desirables, "wealth and honor and life," comes to those who seek higher ideals and lower status. Many translators set "humility" as primary and "fear of the LORD" as appositional, rendering something like "the consequence of humility, fear of the LORD," but the two related attitudes can be taken as complementary. "Riches" links this verse with verses 1–2. Can we also read a link with verse 3, that fear of evil and fear of Yahweh go together?

22:5. Just as the fear of Yahweh leads to desirable attainments, so the path of the "wicked" (lit., "a crooked person," a play on the path image) leads to dangers of "thorns" that hinder and wound, as well as "snares," the symbol of death. To avoid the path is to avoid the dangers, an observation of cause and effect similar to verses 3–4. One who is vigilant guards the "soul" (*nepeš*), although this word can be translated "life" or "desire."[2] The ambiguity lets readers conclude that those who guard their desires and appetites also guard their lives.

22:6. Linked with "path" in verse 5 by the catchword "way" (*derek* in both cases; cf. also 22:3),[3] the first imperative in this chapter urges parents to start a youth on the right way. The second line predicts the likely outcome, "when he is old, he will not turn from it." Remember that a proverb is not a promise; therefore, this one is no guarantee for any method of parenting. It should never be interpreted so caring parents whose offspring give up the faith or get into trouble are at fault. The verb "train" (*ḥnk*) often denotes dedications

---

2. Clifford, *Proverbs*, 196, takes the basic sense of *nepeš* as "throat," a reference to human speech: "Proverbs regards speaking as the most characteristic human activity. In this saying it stands for human activity as such. The message, to keep safe, speak rightly." However speech does not appear in this section until v. 11.

3. The topics of training and the poor (vv. 6–7) follow in same sequence in vv. 15–16, forming an inclusio (Garrett, *Proverbs*, 187).

of various kinds[4] and may refer to the initiation of the young man into adulthood.[5] The word for the youth, *na'ar* (NIV "child"), is used seven times in Proverbs (1:4; 7:7; 20:11; 22:6, 15; 23:13; 29:15) and elsewhere for young adults (Gen. 14:24; 37:2).

"Way he should go" is (lit.) "at the beginning of his way" (*darko*); thus, four views on the proverb have been proposed. The moral view stresses the *good* way; the vocational view stresses the *position* a young man would take in society or court; the personal aptitude view stresses the learner's *capacities*; and in the personal demands view, the proverb ironically observes that a *spoiled* child will never change.[6] In my judgment, the proverb speaks not so much of early childhood training as of the initiation to adulthood and the teaching of its expectations and responsibilities.

22:7. In strong contrast to the picture of equality in verse 2, this saying depicts life as it is usually observed. The rich rule over poor, with implication that only one party has access to the power that money brings. The second line adds that those who borrow, whether by necessity or choice, put themselves under that power. Many commentators take this saying as a warning to the poor against borrowing,[7] but perhaps a more general observation about the responsibilities of power is intended (cf. 22:9, 16; 18:23).

Proverbs About Speaking and Judgments (22:8–16)

IN THIS CLUSTER, proverbs about right speaking commingle with sayings about the judgments that come on the foolish and wicked.

---

4. The term describes the initial use of buildings in Num. 7:10; Deut. 20:5; 1 Kings 8:63; 2 Chron 7:5. Abraham sent out his initiated men to rescue Lot (Gen. 14:14). The word uses the same root as that used for Hanukkah, the celebration of the rededication of the temple in the intertestamental era. So the NIV footnote presents the alternative reading, "Start."

5. T. Hildebrandt, "Proverbs 22:6a: Train Up a Child?" *Grace Theological Journal* 9/1 (1988): 3–19; reprinted in *Learning from the Sages: Studies on the Book of Proverbs*, ed. R. Zuck (Grand Rapids: Baker Book House, 1995), 277–92. Hildebrant's understanding of the root *bnk* is influenced by S. C. Reif, "Dedicated to HNK," *VT* 22 (1972): 501.

6. See Hildebrandt, "Proverbs 22:6a," 14–16, who proposes a fifth view, in which the young man is initiated into the *status* of a highborn squire of the court. "The intent then of this verse addresses a late adolescent's entrance into his place in adult society. This should be done with celebration and encouragement—giving him respect, status and responsibilities commensurate with his position as a young adult" (p. 3).

7. Murphy, *Proverbs*, 165, claims the proverb "has more bite if it is directed to the poor . . . since it warns them that they must strive to be independent, or they will lose their freedom to their creditors." However, in context, the proverb is also a goad to those who have a solid place in society, those in a position to lend. Both parties are responsible—the potential borrower to avoid borrowing, the lender to be kind with that rule, remembering that a good name is more desirable than riches (22:1) and that Yahweh is Maker of rich and poor (22:2).

22:8. This version of "you reap what you sow" (cf. Job 4:8; Gal. 6:7) extends the idea of responsibility from Proverbs 22:7. One can share with the poor or oppress them (22:9, 16), but each action will receive the same treatment in turn. The most difficult part of the translation is the last word; the "rod of his fury" will either finish, fail, or by extension, "be destroyed."[8]

22:9. Continuing the theme of just rewards from verse 8, the giving of bread and the blessing of generosity will receive good in return. The "generous man" is (lit.) "generous of eye," the opposite of one who has a bad eye and hoards things (23:6; 28:22).[9] The attitude behind this sharing with the poor obviously has more in common with 22:2 than with 22:7 and 16 (cf. Deut. 15:9–10; 2 Cor. 9:8 on cheerful giving).

22:10. The logic of the first line works also for the second: Get rid of the troublesome person, and the trouble goes with him ("strife" and "quarrels" come from the same Heb. root, *dyn*). The mocker has made a number of appearances toward the end of this collection (19:25; 20:1; 21:11, 24), but he, like folly (22:15), should not be accepted or tolerated. The proverb does not advocate the suppression of conflict, only unnecessary arguing. Whereas many conflicts can be worked out with attention to proper process, not all are due to misunderstanding. "Sometimes," said a humorist, "people just act like jerks."

22:11. The person who practices wise and good speech is not driven out like the mocker (22:10) but is welcomed by the king. The connection of heart and lips has been made throughout proverbs. Here "gracious" uses the same word as "esteemed" in 22:1 (*ḥen*). The king would want a friend or counselor with qualities such as these (cf. 16:13).[10]

22:12. Linked with verse 11 by the theme of speaking, this saying makes a strange contrast between the "words of the unfaithful" and "knowledge" guarded by Yahweh. In Proverbs, the Lord watches or guards (*nṣr*) to protect (2:8) or to judge (24:12); here judging makes a better parallel with the frustration of the unfaithful (cf. 11:3). Yahweh not only judges how "knowledge" leads one to live, he "frustrates"(*slp*) wicked persons (21:12) as well as

---

8. The same phrase is used of Yahweh's judgment in Lam. 3:1. Van Leeuwen, "Proverbs," 198, finds a close parallel in Isa. 14:5–6, in which Yahweh breaks the ruling rod of wicked oppressors like Babylon. Clifford, *Proverbs*, 197, thinks the rod is a threshing flail, one stick attached to another to beat out grain (cf. Isa. 28:27), an image consistent with the agricultural metaphor of the first line. In any case, it is not the rod of discipline in 22:15 and 23:14, for it is viewed positively in those proverbs.

9. Jesus' parable of the workers in the vineyard quotes the generous landowner who asks, "Are you envious (of evil eye) because I am generous (good)?" (Matt. 20:15).

10. Clifford, *Proverbs*, 195, suggests that the king should be the subject of both lines: "The king is a friend to the pure-hearted; one gracious of lips is his companion."

wickedness and folly itself (11:3; 13:6; 19:3). Some see a legal reference in the word "knowledge" similar to that in 29:7, translating "the eyes of the LORD watch over a lawsuit."[11]

22:13. This satire depicts a sluggard industrious enough to concoct a far-fetched story in hopes of avoiding work. Although few real excuses are as wild or transparent as this one, the scene reminds readers that Yahweh can tell whether one's words come from knowledge or deception (22:12). Although this proverb appears unconnected to its context,[12] there may be a subtle link with the next proverb about the predatory adulterous woman, who was last seen in the "streets" (7:12; cf. 5:16).

22:14. The strange (*zarot*) or "adulterous" woman has not appeared throughout the collected proverbs. But just as the adulterous woman and Woman Folly appeared at the conclusion of the instructions (7:1−27; 9:13−18), so the smooth-talking woman (cf. 23:27) appears at the conclusion of this collection of proverbs.[13] Added here is the news that this fate is somehow associated with Yahweh's wrath. We would expect the one who falls into the pit of her words will incur that wrath (cf. 22:12), but we get the reverse! Foolish choices in one area influence others (22:15), and only those who stray from Yahweh's way will be susceptible to her seductive danger.

22:15. It was a youth (*na͑ar*), not a child, who fell into the trap of the adulterous woman in chapter 7, and the *na͑ar* now appears in this proverb that follows hers. Better the rod used for discipline than a trap of sin and death (13:24; 23:13−14; 29:15)—though this rod can also be symbolic of parents' teaching (*musar*, "discipline"). Words from 22:5 ("far"), 22:6 (teaching the *na͑ar*), and 22:8 ("rod") link this proverb with others on training and judgment.

22:16. This proverb describes an anti-Robin Hood, who takes from the poor and gives to the rich. In the parallelism of the Hebrew, the two lines of the proverb each follow an action with a result: The one who oppresses the poor increases his wealth, and the one who gives to the rich comes to want. The question is whether the second result, "come to poverty," does apply to "both," since in Hebrew, there is no word "and" joining the two lines. The ambiguity may be intentional, even a reflection of life's own ambiguities, but

---

11. D. W. Thomas, "A Note on *da͑at* in Proverbs 22:12," *JTS* 14 (1963): 93−94. So also Clifford, *Proverbs*, 198, who notes that a bribe undermines the words of the innocent in a trial or subverts a just cause (Ex. 23:8 and Deut. 16:19). So God "watches over the plans of the human hearts and subverts lying words."

12. Whybray, *Composition*, 120.

13. Van Leeuwen, "Proverbs," 199, notes the positive image of woman as a well in 5:15−20. Without water, a well becomes a dangerous pit (cf, 23:27)!

in the context of Proverbs, even a simple observation can have its sting. So it may be that the proverb uses irony to describe the same person—an operator who first takes advantage of the poor to make oneself rich and then uses that wealth to buy more illegitimate influence. That cycle will be broken, for as Knox aptly puts it, "Oppress the poor for thy enrichment, and ere long a richer man's claim shall impoverish thee."[14] In the final proverb of this first collection, oppressors wake up to find they have become one of the group they oppressed![15]

AS WE READ the last of the individual proverbs collected in chapters 10–22, we expect the conclusion of a major section to draw our attention to its most important themes. Here proverbs about responsible adulthood stand side by side with proverbs about teaching and discipline, many of which use words and pictures from the instructions of chapters 1–9.[16] Verses 10 and 15 in particular suggest that one can forgive a young person's folly, but if it is not driven out (like a mocker), it can turn to evil. When that happens, it is not only the young who suffer but also the family and the whole community, especially its poor. Together, these proverbs present their closing argument that one can either become a student of wisdom and a gracious member of adult society or an example of folly and a curse to society.

Wisdom training for youth. Verses 1–7 present a list of attitudes and qualities that characterize the wise one, recognizing the value of honor and equality above that of riches (22:1–2) and practicing prudence and watchfulness (22:3, 5) as a result. Common to all are the humility and fear of Yahweh that bring riches, honor, and life (22:4). These qualities do not come without intentional guidance, and so 22:6 recommends giving the young a good start. The reappearance of terms from the book of instructions reaffirms the importance of teaching upcoming generations, a theme that runs throughout Proverbs. Although it is nowhere stated directly, this collection of proverbs holds out the expectation that those who learn will eventually take their turn as teachers (22:6, 15; cf. 4:1–9; 9:7–9).

---

14. Quoted in Kidner, *Proverbs*, 149.

15. The four sayings that have the phrase "come to poverty" are of a kind. Behaviors that lead to poverty are mistreating the poor by withholding instead of giving (11:24), laziness (14:23), lack of planning and haste (21:5), and favoring rich over poor (22:16). The first and last deal with treatment of rich and poor, the other two treat laziness and haste.

16. Whybray, *Composition*, 119–20. Many of the symbolic figures of the instructions appear: the "unfaithful" or wicked man, the sluggard, and the strange woman (22:12–14).

The *na'ar* ("youth, young man"; NIV sometimes uses "child") appears seven times in Proverbs, twice in this chapter (1:4; 7:7; 20:11; 22:6, 15; 23:13; 29:15). In the prologue (1:1–7), the book indicates that it is designed to teach the young the right way (1:4) so that they do not stray onto deadly paths (cf. 7:7). The end of this present collection places the spotlight on the youth's learning once again, stressing the need for teaching (22:6) and the correction of "discipline" (*musar*, 22:15). Later references to that correction also speak of the rod that drives folly away, for a beating is better than death (23:13; 29:15). If the rod of discipline drives folly far away from the youth's "heart" (22:15), it does so to nurture the love of a "pure heart" that will win over the king (22:11). The king's love for purity is like that of Yahweh, who watches over knowledge (22:12). In sum, the discipline of correction will save the youth from the path of the wicked (22:5) and make a way for responsible service to king and community (22:11).

Verse 6 is no promise that every parent's efforts to teach and guide children will be successful (see comments), but it is a warning that those who neglect this teaching court trouble. Parents, therefore, should not take the proverb as judgment, for as we saw in the instructions of chapters 1–9, the parental teachers place responsibility for learning on the shoulders of the son (2:1–6; 9:6–12). While there are many differences between the educational methods of the instructions and our own, we also observe that the ancients did not define growth into adulthood in terms of individuation and distance from families but rather the assumption of responsibilities for the family and the neighboring community.

This orientation toward community is a welcome correction to the individualism that so often confuses independent judgment with self-centeredness. I recently saw a teen sitcom in which a young woman struggled to please her friends and family, each expecting her to attend a different college. The plot was resolved when she announced that she wanted to make her own choice and had her wishes acknowledged. So far, so good; but when viewers hear the actress ask "What do I want to do?" they may also need a reminder that self-determination is not the same thing as self-indulgence. Growing up and making decisions about college and career does not mean that one can also choose whether or not to consider the needs of neighbors or take responsibility to care for the poor (22:9). In the view of the sages, maturity includes both independent decision-making and the making of new commitments that match independence with interdependence. Education, public and Christian, must strike a tender balance between encouraging independence and fostering connectedness. According to Proverbs, the test of a solid education of our young is the concern they show for the poor.

Wealth and poverty. The book of Proverbs does not present a systematic treatment of the topic of wealth and poverty; instead, it integrates it into its vision of wisdom. For example, in many cases, the poverty of the sluggard is used to illustrate the truth that choices have consequences. The purpose is not to describe the origins of all poverty but rather to warn against a life of folly.[17] Neither the poor nor the rich are idealized, for both stand as equals before their maker (22:2). Both can hear the call to wisdom and fear of Yahweh, and both can choose to shut their ears to it. Poverty and wealth are extreme situations of life that can lead people away from God (30:7–9), while generosity to the poor is an expression of true wisdom (cf. 31:20).[18]

Certainly we should never use 22:2 to support a fatalistic acceptance that "the poor you will always have with you" (cf. Matt. 26:11), an attitude that Jesus never taught or encouraged. The whole of Scripture denounces the ongoing presence of poverty as a witness to the sin of a people. The purpose of the text is not to excuse us from responsibility but rather to read it in its context of justice and care. Wealth is a blessing of Yahweh, but it is to be acquired and used as a fruit of wisdom.[19] In other words, wisdom must set the guidelines for how money is gained and used. The poor are not to be exploited in commerce or forgotten in their need.

The section begins with a proverb about honor and ends with one of shame, both calling for a proper attitude toward wealth and riches (22:1, 16). Two other pairs juxtapose proverbs about teaching and proverbs about relations of rich and poor (22:6–7, 15–16). In addition, the frequent mention of rich and poor throughout implies that a primary objective of this teaching is an understanding of wealth and its power, an understanding that leads to fair and generous treatment of the poor. If humility and the fear of Yahweh bring wealth (22:4), the arrogant reverse of those attitudes will eventually result in poverty (22:16).

If 22:6–7, 15–16 were placed to form an inclusio that frames all that comes between,[20] then we who read these proverbs centuries later can see that what they say about speaking is connected to the theme of justice

---

17. T. Longman III, *How to Read Proverbs*, 120, finds seven themes in the proverbs on wealth and poverty: (1) God blesses the righteous with wealth; (2) foolish behavior leads to poverty; (3) the wealth of fools will not last; (4) poverty is the result of injustice and oppression; (5) those with money must be generous; (6) wisdom is better than wealth; (7) wealth has limited value.

18. L. J. Hoppe, *Being Poor: A Biblical Study* (Wilmington, Del.: Michael Glazier, 1987), 92–97.

19. R. E. Murphy, "Proverbs: 22:1–9," *Int* 41 (1987): 398–402.

20. Garrett, *Proverbs*, 187.

and compassion. Speech that mocks in pride is not the gracious speech that wins the king (22:10–11); likewise, faithless words and lazy excuses will not please Yahweh (22:12–13). Those who turn from God's way will be vulnerable to what is most dangerous of all, words of seduction—here symbolized by the mouth of the adulteress, a pit, a trap that destroys. The way we speak also says a great deal about the way we think about riches and the poor.

Therefore, as we seek to apply these proverbs to our own day, we must remember that the sages did not separate good speaking from issues of fairness and justice. As Lemuel's mother reminded him, kings are to speak out for justice for the poor (31:1–9), but the responsibility is ours as well. If we are to watch our words, we must do more than look to see how our words affect the people we like to be with, people of similar social and economic status. We must also recognize the power of words to educate others about decisions that affect the poor and to speak out for justice. In practical terms this means not only speaking out for the needs of the least privileged members of society but also teaching the coming generation to care about their concerns. If we can encourage a new generation to love generosity and justice, we have done our job well.

Yahweh proverbs. Finally, as we conclude our study of this first collection of individual proverbs, we note the strategic placement of two sets of Yahweh proverbs, each with a seemingly unrelated proverb in between (22:2–4, 12–14). The first pair speaks of attitude. To recognize that rich and poor are both creations of Yahweh is to exhibit humble fear of Yahweh. The second pair speaks of Yahweh's watching over the words spoken by the unfaithful, watching also as the unfaithful suffer his wrath in the form of seductive words. In the middle of the first pair is a proverb about seeing trouble and hiding from it; in the middle of the second pair is a proverb about hiding from work and responsibility.

If there is good news to be heard, it is that God has made the wise way known and has made wisdom's rewards clear in the form of strong contrasting choices. We can choose to value a good name above riches (22:1) or to value riches above good relations (22:16), but we cannot claim we do not know that one is better than the other. Just as Yahweh wants us to become students of wisdom so we can teach it, he also sets the example of a teacher by laying out clear choices and consequences. Those consequences are not rewards for our merits or failings but rather natural responses to our choices for wisdom or against it. Yahweh our teacher also ensures that correctional discipline takes place.

CHOICES. WILLIAM WILLIMON, Dean of the Chapel at Duke University, preached a sermon on "a good name is more desirable than great riches." To the students, he issued a challenge:

Form two lines at Commencement, and ask people who graduate from here to choose one of these paths into the future. One line leads to riches, the other to a good name. Which line will be longer? Don't call it "riches," for things are usually only a means to some other end, but call one path "power," and the other "a good reputation." Which line would be longer? I know of someone who, upon graduation, had decided to give himself to the task of teaching in an inner-city school. "I've wasted two years in that school," he said. "Now I've got to face facts, move on. I've lost some of my idealism, my early naivete. I'm going to apply to law school." Yes, face facts. Get in step with the way the world works. And the way the world works is, "Choose power, riches, things, and if there is any free time left over when you get home from the office, work on your reputation."[21]

The proverbs gathered at the end of this collection state again and again that our choices about riches say the most about our choices for or against wisdom. Moreover, these proverbs not only assert that integrity of wisdom must be taught and learned, they also make clear that both teacher and learner share responsibility for that process. Elders are responsible for teaching the young (22:6, 15), but the young are responsible for internalizing the knowledge and values of their teachers. Love of integrity (a "pure heart," 22:15) and love of neighbor shown in the sharing of bread (22:9) are matters of individual choice. But, as one of my teachers was fond of saying, those choices are "personal, but not private." These proverbs are designed to persuade individuals to learn wisdom and love its characteristics, though the goal of such persuasion is interrelatedness—relationship, not isolation. The wise person is a connected one.

Individual versus corporate. Yet sometimes these emphases on individual responsibility can create the opposite effect. A worst-case scenario produces the self-made person who believes, "God helps those who help themselves," confusing the proverbs of Ben Franklin with those of the Bible! While it is true that the biblical proverbs continually ponder the mysterious interaction of divine action and human response, a misreading of this

---

21. W. H. Willimon, "Where Are You Headed? A Bit of Proverbial Wisdom (Proverbs 22:1)," *Pulpit Digest* (March/April 1998), 71–76 (quote from p. 73).

principle suggests that people bring all their troubles on themselves, but this is never taught in Proverbs. Folly will bring its consequences, but not all negative consequences are the result of folly. As we seek to apply these proverbs, we must be careful to remember that individual responsibility is not the cause of every problem, nor is it the solution. How many times have we heard ourselves say, "If they would just...."

The many proverbs about the poor that cluster in this final section remind us that the rich often have power over the poor and sometimes abuse that power (22:7, 16). This practice of gaining and distributing wealth contrary to the ways of wisdom cannot exist without a system, that is, a network of relationships in which oppression is allowed to go unchecked. While the presence of systemic sin is not directly stated in these proverbs about education and uses of wealth and power, it is everywhere implied.

Individualistic explanations or solutions to the gap between rich and poor can overlook the problems of corporate sin, an ironic perversion of the proverb's sense of community relationships. Richard Mouw argues that as heirs to the fundamentalist legacy, we share many of that movement's strengths, particularly its emphasis on biblical authority and evangelistic urgency. However, we have also inherited some weaknesses or negative expressions of its traits: an anti-intellectualism that prefers action over reflection, an otherworldliness that overlooks the possibilities for positive social change in the here and now, and a separatistic spirit that often criticizes other Christian bodies before seeking to understand them.[22]

About that second matter of otherworldliness, Mouw is concerned that we evangelicals often speak of a "personal evangelism" in contrast to a "structural" or "social" understanding of gospel witness. Why, he asks, is it personal evangelism to ask an alcoholic to break free of enslavement to drink, yet it is something different if we ask believers to give up some deeply ingrained gender biases and racial prejudices? Further, why is it often not considered a gospel witness to call for changed practices of local and national economies as well as government institutions such as education? He follows his questions with an example:

> Back in the days of South African apartheid, I often illustrated the importance of addressing the structural dimension of human life by imagining a miraculous result from a single effort at mass evangelism. Suppose Billy Graham were to hold a crusade in South Africa, and every single person in the country, whether by being physically present at the meeting or by watching on television, were to make a per-

---

22. R. Mouw, *The Smell of Sawdust: What Evangelicals Can Learn from Their Fundamentalist Heritage* (Grand Rapids: Zondervan, 2000), 24.

sonal commitment to Jesus Christ as Savior and Lord. Would this cure South Africa of its racism? No. The next morning all the apartheid apparatus would still exist. Laws would have to be rewritten. Prejudices would have to be unlearned. The educational system would have to be reformed. The evangelical slogan "changed hearts will change society" is clearly inadequate in such a situation. To be sure, the motivation to bring about change can result from millions of individual wills being redirected toward the love and service of a divine Savior. But individual conversions do not automatically bring about structural change.[23]

While the proverbs of this chapter do not directly address the problem of corporate or institutionalized sin, the contrast between a king who loves integrity and a person who oppresses the poor (22:11, 16) implies that personal sin, like spilled wine, often seeps its way into social structures, staining everything it touches. Yet those who hope to hold a high view of Scripture and submit themselves to its teachings do not always see it that way, particularly when it comes to linking economic injustice with racial prejudice.

A recent study of attitudes toward race among white evangelical Christians in America concluded that the evangelical movement's understanding of individual free will and responsibility, along with the importance it places on personal relationships, leads many Christians to conclude that racism is a problem of sinful persons, not social structures, and that the problem can be solved if those at fault were to repent and take steps to treat others better. The authors conclude that these ideas and values actually work to perpetuate a racially divided society rather than improve it.

> Most white evangelicals, directed by their cultural tools, fail to recognize the institutionalization of racialization—in economic, political, educational, social, and religious systems. They therefore often think and act as if these problems do not exist. As undetected cancer that remains untreated thrives and destroys, so unrecognized depths of racial division and inequality go largely unaddressed and likewise thrive, divide, and destroy. The solutions evangelicals propose and practice—though in many ways unique in modern America, and much needed as far as they go—simply cannot make much headway in the face of these powerful countercurrents that undercut and fight against their well-intentioned, individualistic solutions.[24]

---

23. Ibid., 123.

24. M. O. Emerson and Christian Smith, *Divided by Faith: Evangelical Religion and the Problem of Race in America* (Oxford/New York: Oxford Univ. Press, 2000), 170.

The authors quote from their interviews to support their claims. When asked if America has a race problem, one woman answered, "I think we make it a problem. . . . Well, people have problems. . . . It's just people. People are gonna have arguments with people. I feel like once in a while, when an argument happens, say between a black guy and a white guy, instead of saying, 'Hey, there's two guys having an argument,' we say it's a race issue." One respondent was especially direct: "We don't have a race problem, we have a sin problem."[25] The authors recommend that evangelicals temporarily set aside their preference for action and urgency and take time to consider the problem from many perspectives, especially that of African Americans, before promoting any strategies.

As a first step, we can examine our own attitudes toward individualism and collective responsibility. The authors of *Habits of the Heart* took their title from a phrase in Tocqueville's famous work *Democracy in America*. His description of American individualism, written in 1835, sounds remarkably familiar:

> Individualism is a calm and considered feeling which disposes each citizen to isolate himself from the mass of his fellows and withdraw into the circle of family and friends; with this little society formed to his taste, he gladly leaves the greater society to look after itself. . . . There are more and more people who, though neither rich nor powerful enough to have much hold over others, have gained or kept enough wealth and enough understanding to look after their own needs. Such folk owe no man anything and hardly expect anything from anybody. They form the habit of thinking of themselves in isolation and imagine that their whole destiny is in their hands. . . . Each man is forever thrown back on himself alone, and there is danger that he may be shut up in the solitude of his own heart.[26]

A decade after *Habits of the Heart* was released, the authors observed that our culture's concern for adolescent independence may have adverse effects. "American individualism resists more adult virtues, such as care and generativity, let alone wisdom, because the struggle for independence is all-consuming."[27] Calling for a "civic membership . . . [that] points to that critical intersection of personal identity with social identity," they also cite Lester Thurow's distinction between an establishment and an oligarchy:

---

25. Ibid., 69–70, 78.

26. A. de Tocqueville, *Democracy in America*, trans. George Lawrence, ed. J. P. Mayer (New York: Doubleday, Anchor, 1969), 506, 508; quoted in R. N. Bellah et al., *Habits of the Heart: Individualism and Commitment in American Life*, updated ed. (Berkeley: Univ. of California Press, 1985, 1996), 37.

27. Ibid., xi.

An establishment seeks its own good by working for the good of the whole society (noblesse oblige), whereas an oligarchy looks out for its own interest by exploiting the rest of society. Another way of putting it would be to say that an establishment has a strong sense of civic membership while an oligarchy lacks one.... An oligarchy taxes itself least; an establishment taxes itself most.... We need at least a portion of the overclass acting as a true establishment if we are to deal with our enormous problems. If the members of the overclass can overcome their own anxieties they may realize that they will gain far more self-respect in belonging to an establishment than to an oligarchy.[28]

"A good name is more desirable than great riches." While the church must act to overcome racial divisions and ensure equal opportunity and access, we must first examine our own ideas and opinions about these matters and consider our attachment to individualistic understandings of wealth and success. We must ask if there are ways that the very economy that provides us with jobs and income sets a good name above riches or whether it takes from the poor and gives to the rich. In other words, we may come to see that our economy works like the greedy individual of Proverbs 22:16. Because attitude is incipient action, we must work at both levels, and so the importance of the teacher.

Conclusion. I have argued that the collected proverbs of chapters 10–22 reaffirm the call of wisdom presented in chapters 1–9, but do so by calling young learners to responsible adulthood. Such maturity discerns the dynamics of power and wealth and acts wisely through the example of sharing bread (22:9), speaking graciously (22:11), and teaching these ways of wisdom to the young (22:6, 15). In so doing, wise believers will remember that Yahweh teaches the way of wisdom but also looks to see how it is practiced. Some will become full-time teachers, and some will model and teach as part of their work as police officers, health-care providers, attorneys, mechanics, and politicians. Yet all are called to pass on what has been learned.

The other day I got a call asking if I would serve on the Christian Education Board of my church, planning the programs and courses for children, youth, and adults. Realizing that it is one more way to become a teacher and a chance to introduce Christians to the issues of personal and social responsibility cited above, I decided to say yes. But my work of responding to these proverbs has just begun.

---

28. Ibid., xiii, xxxi; citing L. Thurow, *Head to Head: The Coming Economic Battle Among Japan, Europe, and America* (New York: Warner, 1992).

Proverbs 22:17–29

¹⁷ PAY ATTENTION AND listen to the sayings of the wise;
  apply your heart to what I teach,
¹⁸ for it is pleasing when you keep them in your heart
  and have all of them ready on your lips.
¹⁹ So that your trust may be in the LORD,
  I teach you today, even you.
²⁰ Have I not written thirty sayings for you,
  sayings of counsel and knowledge,
²¹ teaching you true and reliable words,
  so that you can give sound answers
  to him who sent you?
²² Do not exploit the poor because they are poor
  and do not crush the needy in court,
²³ for the LORD will take up their case
  and will plunder those who plunder them.
²⁴ Do not make friends with a hot-tempered man,
  do not associate with one easily angered,
²⁵ Or you may learn his ways
  and get yourself ensnared.
²⁶ Do not be a man who strikes hands in pledge
  or puts up security for debts;
²⁷ if you lack the means to pay,
  your very bed will be snatched from under you.
²⁸ Do not move an ancient boundary stone
  set up by your forefathers.
²⁹ Do you see a man skilled in his work?
  He will serve before kings;
  he will not serve before obscure men.

Original Meaning

THE SHIFT FROM individual sayings to the address of a teacher in 22:17 tells us that we have entered a new section of the book, one that spans 22:17–24:22. We set this section apart here because (1) there is a new title, "the sayings of the wise" (22:17); (2) the style returns to the instruction-like writing we encountered in chapters 1–9; and (3) a generation of biblical scholarship has drawn comparisons between 22:17–23:11 and the Egyptian *Instruction of Amenemope*, noting similarities and differences in form and content.

(1) The new title, "the sayings [words] of the wise," not only marks the transition to a new section but also to the final third of the book.[1] Of the seven superscriptions in Proverbs (1:1; 10:1; 22:17; 24:23; 25:1; 30:1; 31:1), all but the first two make mention of sages other than Solomon. Perhaps we have here a sign that the final third of the book preserves an ongoing tradition of wisdom that was cultivated and passed on by "the wise," "the men of Hezekiah" (25:1), Agur (30:1), and Lemuel (31:1). This final third of the book is similar to what has gone before, yet distinct in form and content (e.g., in its insertion of riddles and numerical sayings).

(2) In some ways, the style of these "words of the wise" leaves readers with the impression that we are starting over again, for these instruction-like sayings are followed by a collection of individual proverbs (25:1–29:28), just as we saw in the first two-thirds of the book (1:1–9:18, followed by 10:1–22:16). For this reason readers approach the final third of the book as a recapitulation of what has gone before, but also as a review that adds new developments to the familiar content.

Mention of the "sayings . . . of the wise" in the prologue (1:6) may give us a clue that we are at a new level of teaching that takes what has been learned in the first two rounds and puts it to use. For example, readers find new attention to the matter of table manners and excess eating and drinking (23:1–35), perhaps meant to prepare a young sage for service as a teacher, ambassador, and advisor to rulers. If earlier chapters stressed the importance of gaining wisdom and learning to master its literary forms, these chapters review all that while adding new and more challenging material.

(3) Comparison with the Egyptian *Instruction of Amenemope* also draws our attention to similarities and differences with what has already been taught in Proverbs. The manuscript of this Egyptian instruction was discovered in the late nineteenth century, but when it was published in 1923, similarities with this section of Proverbs led some scholars to suggest direct influence. For example, comparison of Proverbs 22:17–18 with *Amenemope* 3:9–16[2] shows

---

1. See the outline of Proverbs in the introduction. A similar title, "These also are sayings of the wise," appears in 24:23, where it marks the transition to a smaller section.

2. "Give your ears, hear the sayings, Give your heart to understand them; It profits to put them in your heart, Woe to him who neglects them! Let them rest in the casket of your belly, May they be bolted in your heart; When there rises a whirlwind of words, They'll be a mooring post for your tongue" (Lichtheim, *AEL*, 2:149).

the use of "your ears," "hear," "heart," "beneficial/pleasant," "in your belly," and "on your tongue/lips."[3]

Moreover, because *Amenemope* was written in thirty chapters, biblical scholars began to read the difficult *šilšom* ("three days ago") as "thirty," even though the Hebrew text does not include the word for "sayings" (22:20) and no attempt to delineate those thirty sayings has won wide acceptance.[4] Even as we remember that Solomon's wisdom was compared with the wisdom of the east and of Egypt (1 Kings 4:30), we also observe significant differences between the Hebrew and Egyptian texts; similarities in content end at 23:11. Moreover, only thirty-two of the eighty-six verses show close relationship; there is more in the "sayings of the wise" than is to be found in *Amenemope*. Finally, points of contact with *Amenemope* run throughout Proverbs and are not limited to these words of the wise. For example, both texts speak of poverty and piety as better than wealth with conflict (e.g., 15:16−17 and *Amen.* 9:5ff.).[5]

In assessing any possible influence from *Amenemope*, we remember that two dynamics are at work. (1) The points of connection between Proverbs and *Amenemope* are also common to the larger body of ancient Near Eastern wisdom literature, so one can make too much of the parallels. (2) We must acknowledge that there is a greater concentration of these points of contact in *Amenemope* than in other examples of ancient Near Eastern wisdom literature, even though the themes are often treated differently in each work.[6] Thus, there appears to be some influence, indicating that the composer, if not also the audience, knew of the Egyptian work, but direct influence and borrowing is not as certain as many scholars claim. (3) The most important point of comparison is the purpose each was written to serve; if *Amenemope* was

---

3. G. E. Bryce, *A Legacy of Wisdom: The Egyptian Contribution to the Wisdom of Israel* (Lewisburg,, Pa.: Bucknell Univ. Press, 1979), 101−2. Bryce concludes there are varying degrees of Egyptian influence on phrases and concepts, some more direct than others, and he recognizes that some parts of the "sayings of the wise" show no influence.

4. The LXX reads *trissos* ("three times"), and the TNK has a "threefold lore." Could this be taken as an introduction to the last third of the book?

5. Murphy provides a balanced assessment of the question in *Proverbs*, 290−94, and *The Tree of Life*, 23−25. See also J. H. Walton, "Cases of Alleged Borrowing" in *Ancient Israelite Literature In Its Cultural Context* (Grand Rapids: Zondervan, 1989), 192−97; Whybray's review of research in *Proverbs: A Survey of Modern Study*, 6−14, 78−84.

6. J. Ruffle, "The Teaching of Amenemope and Its Connection with the Book of Proverbs," *TynBul* 28 (1977): 29−68; reprinted in R. B. Zuck, *Learning from the Sages: Selected Studies on the Book of Proverbs* (Grand Rapids: Baker, 1995), 293−331. Ruffle concedes that half of the first part of the sayings of the wise treat the same subjects as *Amenemope*, and after granting that this seems more than coincidental, he suggests that an Egyptian scribe working in Solomon's court may have used a text that was part of his early training. Differences could be attributed to a combination of rhetorical purpose and foggy memory.

written as an instructional guide for those preparing for public service, we can then look for a similar purpose in the "sayings of the wise."[7]

A good number of these instructions are phrased as admonitions ("Do not"; cf. 3:7–12, 27–31), pointing out behaviors and associations that should be avoided. Many also come in paired verses, one for the admonition, one for the motivation. While we make no attempt to discern thirty sayings, the use of the admonition does offer some clues about structure and the mirrored repetition of themes in the second half of chapter 22.

> Pay Attention, Give Sound Answers to One Who Sends (22:17–21)
> Sayings of Counsel and Knowledge (22:22–29)
>> Do not *exploit the poor* (22:22–23)
>> Do not *make friends* with the hothead (22:24–25)
>> Do not strike hands in *pledge* (22:26–27)
>> Do not *move the boundary stone* (22:28)
>> The skilled one will serve *kings* (22:29)

While the opening and closing sayings speak to matters of service (22:17–21, 29), the admonitions in between warn against exploitation of innocent neighbors (22:22–23, 28) and bad associations (22:24–25, 26–27).

Pay Attention, Give Sound Answers to One Who Sends (22:17–21)

22:17. THE INSTRUCTION style resumes in 22:17, although the address, "My son," will not appear until 23:15. A prologue of sorts includes a call to attention and motivations for learning, much like the prologue of 1:1–7, yet this introduction is not as comprehensive as the preview to the entire book. Three imperatives make up the charge: "pay attention," "listen" (lit., "turn your ear and hear"), and "apply your heart" (cf. 2:1–2), linking hearing with the seat of human intention and purpose. "Sayings of the wise" (cf. 1:6) is parallel with "what I teach" (lit., "my knowledge"), identifying this teacher as one of the wise or someone who teaches using words.

22:18. The motivation in verse 18 envisions a "pleasing" (*naᶜim*; cf. 23:8; 24:4) outcome; sound teachings stored in the heart[8] will find expression in wise speech that blesses and teaches others. "All of them ready on your lips"

---

7. Goldingay, "Proverbs," 602. Clifford, *Proverbs*, 200, notes that Amenemope exemplifies a later form of Egyptian instruction that "displays a new inwardness and a quest for serenity.... The ideal is not achievement but contemplation, modesty, compassion, and serenity." See also Lichtheim's comments in *AEL*, 2:146.

8. "Heart" here is the "inner parts" of previous sayings (*beṭen*; cf. 18:8, 20; 20:27, 30; 26:22).

assumes that one brings out of the storehouse of teaching a synthesis, wisdom that is perhaps greater than the sum of the parts (cf. Matt. 13:52).

22:19. Verse 19 warns that knowledge and wisdom are necessary for successful living, but they are not the source of one's confidence; teaching is to inspire trust in Yahweh, integrating intellectual study and faith.[9] The second line of verse 19 repeats the second person "you," and the emphatic concluding words, "even you," surprise the reader; they seem to say, "Yes, I'm talking to you, not somebody else. Trust in the LORD."

22:20. The famous translation issue of verse 20 (see comments above) should not obscure the purpose of the verse, namely, to introduce these "written" sayings of counsel and knowledge. For the first time in Proverbs, oral teaching has given way to teaching by means of text. "Counsel" here is a plural noun, the means by which "knowledge" is transferred from teacher to learner.

22:21. Verse 21 sets out a secondary goal for teaching these "true and reliable words,"[10] that is, to show how one might return reliable words in answer to one who sends (cf. 18:13; 24:26). This reference to "him who sent you" brings to mind earlier sayings about messengers, both bad (10:26) and "trustworthy" (13:17, root *'mt*; cf. 25:13; 26:6, where the topic appears again). *Amenemope* also speaks of the messenger (*Amen.* 1:5–6). Thus, we conclude that one function of these teachings is to prepare a young man for some sort of diplomatic service. One schooled in wisdom must be prepared to give an answer when representing a king or official, knowing what to say not only in terms of content but also in terms of style and speaking with eloquence that "is pleasing" (22:18). The two purposes (trust in Yahweh and skill in answering for [or to] a king or official) are complementary, not mutually exclusive. Sages who served as courtiers answered to two authorities, as did Joseph, who advised Pharaoh but ultimately served Yahweh.

Sayings of Counsel and Knowledge (22:22–29)

22:22–23. THE "SAYINGS of counsel and knowledge" (cf. 22:20) in 22:22–29 are a series of admonitions, each paired with a reason or motivation; each begins with the Hebrew negative *'al* ("do not"). Verse 22 continues the emphasis on fair treatment of the poor that was so prominent in 22:1–16 and

9. Clifford, *Proverbs*, 206, notes that *yhwh* is the center word in 22:17–21.

10. The word "truth" is unusual and rare, perhaps Aramaic (cf. Dan. 2:47; 4:37). It may refer to the "truthful integrity with probity" that inspires confidence. A. Cody, "Notes on Proverbs 22:21 and 22:23b," *Bib* 61 (1980): 418–26. The Heb. text repeats the roots of "reliable words" in the second line. "Words of truth" is allowable in both instances (Garrett, *Proverbs*, 196).

throughout the sayings (10:15; 14:31; 17:5; 19:4, 17; 21:13). The word "exploit" is translated "rob" (*gzl*, 4:16; 28:24) in its other contexts, suggesting that exploitation is one way to take what belongs to another.

The syntax of "because they are poor" has puzzled translators. While the poverty of these people is reason enough to treat them kindly, most likely the phrase chides the exploiters who see their powerless prey as easy pickings; they crush the poor in court (lit., "at the gate," where legal matters were decided). Ironically, those who try to use the system to do wrong will find out that they are called to an even higher court. The double use of *rib* in "take up their case" (22:23; lit., "strive a striving"; cf. 23:11) echoes the voice of the prophets, who portray Yahweh as judge, prosecutor, and executor (Isa. 1:17; 3:13; 19:20; 41:21; Jer. 2:9; 25:31; Hos. 4:1; Mic. 6:2; 7:9).

22:24-27. The matched sections of verses 24–25 and 26–27 present familiar warnings about avoiding certain persons and practices, juxtaposing new motivations. A number of the proverbs warned against a "hot-tempered man" (cf. 15:18; 19:19), but describing this person's influence as a snare is new, reminding the reader of the invitation to violence in 1:10–19. The "pledge" (22:26) was compared with a trap in 6:1–5 (cf. 11:15; 17:18; 20:16 = 27:13), but here the teacher warns against repossession. Here too, taking a pledge is a form of bad association.[11] Just as one stands to lose in associating with a hothead, so one can lose all in a bad pledge; having your "bed [snatched] from under you" is like our losing the "shirt off your back." Here is the clearest reason for the warning, as if the teacher saying, "Your creditors will show the same 'mercy' that so many show to the poor, for you will become one of the poor yourself."

22:28. The prohibition here against moving the boundary stone stands alone, with no accompanying motivation or reason (a reason is given in the similar 23:10). The personal pronoun emphasizing "*your* forefathers" implies that the person on the other side of the property line is kin. The only other reference to the boundary marker in Proverbs names the widow (15:25; cf. Deut. 19:14). To move that marker for financial gain is therefore to defraud those most vulnerable. If Proverbs 22:24–25 and 26–27 are about self-protection, the surrounding verses (22:23 and 28) are directed toward protecting and caring for the powerless of society.

22:29. A three-line saying in verse 29 interrupts the series of prohibitions with a rhetorical question and answer that holds up excellence and pride in work. Mind your own business, it seems to say, neither cheating the poor or

---

11. The word "debts" is a new addition to the teaching on pledges. Its root only occurs here and in Deut. 24:10, where it is translated as "loan." If the loan is to someone who is poor, no security is to be taken.

getting mixed up in bad company. Do your work well and live well, and you will have the king as your employer, a coveted association (cf. 23:1). If earlier proverbs about the king stressed his responsibilities for executing justice and his capacities for discerning evil intention (22:8), these instructions give advice about working for such a person. One advances through competence and integrity, not cunning or careerism.

WE BEGIN WITH two observations about structure. (1) Similar sayings about boundary markers in 22:28 and 23:10 possibly define the boundaries of a larger section (see comments on ch. 23). (2) Another possible structure is a mirror repetition of themes in verses 17–29: service (22:17–21, 29), exploitation by means of the legal system (22:22–23, 28), and bad associations (22:24–25, 26–27). We may take each of the three themes in turn.

Service. The sayings at the beginning and end of this small section urge the learner to "pay attention," either by listening (22:17) or by looking (22:29). In each case, the goal is to learn those attitudes and practices that will prepare one for effective service to one who sends (22:21), perhaps the king himself (22:29). The first of the sayings highlights the "sayings of the wise," the teachings that the learner stores in the inner parts so they are ready to be spoken on the lips (22:18). As we have seen, these teachings foster trust in Yahweh as well as the capacity to return reliable words to the one who sends (22:19–21). Perhaps this facility with wise words is the skilled work of verse 29.[12]

In any case, the teacher makes it clear that learning and storing these teachings prepares one for service that involves the proper use of words, making sure they are "reliable" words (twice in the Heb. of 22:21). Words such as these not only speak the truth, they do so in the spirit of faithfulness—faithful to what serves the interests of the employer and the common good (assuming that they are not different!).

In bringing these principles into our own day, we must keep in mind that learning wisdom prepares us to speak wisely, to speak in ways that are faithful to those we serve—both those we work for and those for whom we have responsibility. It may be that like the sages of old, we are called upon to teach, to give advice and counsel, or simply to represent the concerns of another. In short, the sages of old were responsible both for maintaining and

---

12. The word for "skilled" (*mahir*) describes one who is speedy, or by extension, diligent and attentive. Ezra, was a scribe skilled (NIV "well versed") in the law of Moses (Ezra 7:6); the king's singer of Ps. 45:1 was a "ready scribe" (NRSV) or "skillful writer" (NIV).

teaching the words of the wise and for putting them to work in daily practice of advising and representing.

Today, it is hard to find the occupation that does not require this aspect
of wise speaking. Lawyers, physicians, and educators have this written into
their job descriptions, but who of us does not need these skills for knowing
how to find the best ways to get the job done and preserve good relationships at the same time? A secretary I know works for an office of student services at a nearby college. She is charged with instructing, advising, and
serving the concerns of the constituency that includes students and potential employers who may hire them.

Exploitation. Two admonitions against exploiting the poor and moving
the boundary stone both warn against using systems that were set up to protect property in order to steal it. The means used to take advantage of the
poor and needy are not stated in 22:22, only that it is done "at the gate,"
where disputes should be settled fairly and not on the basis of special favors
or bribes. Likewise, to move a boundary stone is to acquire property illegit-
imately (22:28); just as the community met at the gate to ensure fair dealing,
so the community of ancestors set up the boundaries to ensure that land
stayed with its owners. Yahweh takes up the case of the poor (22:23), so
one may assume he too looks after boundary disputes.

Servants of the royal court had access to power and influence that could
easily be abused for private gain, just as in public service today. These two
admonitions assume that one who has learned from these teachings will do
more than stay clear of such abuses, for they will also be watchful to stand
against them. This principle links with the conclusion of the individual sayings in 22:16, that those who oppress the poor to increase wealth or give of
that wealth to the rich for power and influence will come to ruin.

James reminds his readers how easy it is to fall into the trap of favoring
the rich over the poor, adding that the rich exploit the poor and use their
influence to drag them into court (James 2:1–9). Whatever our venue of service and employment, we are called to serve the neediest and weakest persons, not only refusing to abuse them but also doing all we can to protect
them from those who would. This principle also applies to the way we treat
others at our jobs. A well-known story tells of the exam that medical interns
were given in which they had to write the name of one of the hospital's jan-
itors. Likewise, the principle applies to corporations and governments. In
our world of larger and larger circles of business and professional relationships, it is not easy to spot neglect and abuse, but even the commitment to
become aware of such issues is a step forward.

Bad associations. The two admonitions that form the center of this
mirror structure warn against bad associations with hotheads and borrowers

(22:24–27). The danger of the first is taking on that person's quick-tempered ways and later paying the price for them. The danger of the second is taking on responsibility for another's debts and possibly paying that price. In both, the caution is well taken that choosing associates means choosing their behaviors and attitudes, but also the consequences that result from them.

Previous proverbs warned against the dangers of hot-tempered people, especially getting caught in their wreckage: "A hot-tempered man must pay the penalty; if you rescue him, you will have to do it again" (19:19). If we were to articulate the positive teaching that is implied, it is like another proverb: "He who walks with the wise grows wise, but a companion of fools suffers harm" (13:20). Parents who keep watch on their kids' choice of companions are not only looking out for their immediate welfare, they are teaching them how to make such choices in the future, especially if they provide good models.

The point of these warnings against pledges cannot be that we are not to loan or give to needy neighbors. Rather, the sages suggest that we not become needy by pledging foolishly. Said another way, if you don't have the means to loan, you don't have the means to pledge. Pledge as though you were giving over what you have, and don't make promises you don't intend to keep. Become a judge of character, because you are pledging on the assumption that the person will pay back and not leave you in the lurch. Moses taught that a loan to the needy should be made without interest. If a coat is taken in pledge, it should be given back at night when it gets cold; perhaps this is an argument against taking a pledge from the poor at all (Ex. 22:25–26; cf. Deut. 24:10–13).

Jesus even advised his followers, in the context of not resisting evil, turning the other cheek, and walking the second mile: "Give to the one who asks you, and do not turn away from the one who wants to borrow from you" (Matt. 5:42; cf. Luke 6:30). Reading these words with the sages' teaching in mind, we see that Jesus encouraged making loans, even if a person had the potential to go bust. "If you lend to those from whom you expect repayment, what credit is that to you? Even 'sinners' lend to 'sinners' expecting to be repaid in full. But love your enemies, do good to them, and lend to them without expecting to get anything back" (Luke 6:34–35).

If this is the good we should do our enemies, how should we treat our poor neighbor? "Do not be hardhearted or tightfisted toward your poor brother. Rather, be openhanded and freely lend him whatever he needs" (Deut. 15:7–8; cf. Ps. 37:26; Prov. 19:17). The warning against foolish pledges should be set in the biblical context that loans are to be made on the basis of care, not on the potential for repayment. The point of the warning is akin to the warning against close friendship with the hothead; in seeking to apply these principles in our day, let us remember that choosing companions is equal to choosing their ways and their potential problems.

IN SUM, THIS first section of the "sayings of the wise" extends the themes of previous chapters by calling learners to faithful and diligent service, a service that rejects greedy and impetuous ways. The call comes with the reminder that this service not only pleases employers and neighbors but also Yahweh, who will take up the case of the poor and all who are abused. We have tried to understand what it means to "give sound answers" (lit., "return reliable words"), concluding that it means keeping one's speech in line with the content and tone of wisdom teachings. Such speaking can take the forms of teaching, advising, and even advocating for fair treatment of others. Today, the need is as great as ever for "giving sound answers" to the problems that vex our culture and our churches. In short, the words "of the wise" are needed more than ever before, and they ought to come not only from pulpits and Christian education forums but also from Christians who speak eloquently and persuasively in the public square.

Addressing the age. Two dimensions of the issue stand side by side. (1) The emphasis on a tradition that is passed on from one generation to the next speaks of mastery that comes from apprenticeship, learning the venerable texts while internalizing and then reproducing their ideals of character. (2) The "sound answer," or return of reliable words, suggests that the teaching applies the principles that have stood the test of time to contemporary questions and concerns. While the accent in Proverbs falls on the first emphasis, we dare not ignore the need to connect the wisdom of the ages with contemporary issues. Christian education classes can invite those who explore the fields of science, ethics, and law to work with nonprofessionals toward the integration of faith and learning. Clergy and church leaders can use their training in theology to pose questions and work together toward answers.[13]

Stated more plainly, it is necessary and important to offer classes in Bible and spiritual life, but it is just as important to tackle the hard questions of our

---

13. D. F. Morgan, *The Making of Sages: Biblical Wisdom and Contemporary Culture* (Harrisburg, Pa.: Trinity Press International, 2002), 73, believes that too many clergy delegate the task of education or shirk it altogether. "In the contemporary period, the fact that lay leaders take over the responsibility for teaching means, as one explanation, that it is seen as unimportant by clergy who do not want to do it."

time. Such discussions can bring together clergy who are the custodians of the Christian tradition with those scholars and scientists who have, over the course of time, inherited the sage's role of the curious observer. In other words, the twofold role of the sage as tradition-bearer and practitioner seems to have been divided in our own day between the clergy/theological custodians and the professionals, who observe, explore, and seek to generate new knowledge.[14]

Perhaps the church should sponsor conversations in the spirit of a public forum that offers insight and help for the issues of the day. If so, then the church as a body might fulfil the role of the fledgling sage, passing both the "reliable words" of tradition and answering with "reliable words" that respond to ever-changing circumstances. For example, few churches were interested in the beliefs of Islam until the attacks of September 11, 2001, which left people asking why so many Muslims were so angry. Since then, experts in Islamic studies have been busy speaking to churches and community groups. In the same way developments in medical technology call for deliberation about ethics of research and availability of health care.

Why should such discussions be left to the academy when they affect the lives of everyone? Ought not the church to initiate them and make them accessible to the general public? In applying the call to learning that opens the words of the wise, we can teach teaching individuals how to learn and return "reliable words" in their daily work and community life, but we can also call the church to provide a similar service to its members and the larger community.

The rich and poor. Certainly one of the most vexing problems awaiting address by the evangelical church is a moral climate that is at best only mildly disturbed by the growing gap between rich and poor. Yet this concern was first and foremost in the minds of those who produced the words of the wise and Proverbs.[15] We have seen that there are those who will use legal systems for purposes opposite of those they were designed for, and some will even use positions of authority to take advantage of the poor and weak. The wise one rejects all such temptations to petty and dishonest gain, but he also remembers that Yahweh takes up the case of those who have been crushed

---

14. Ibid., 76–83. Drawing from various studies in the history of education in the West, Morgan distinguishes the traditional model of apprenticeship and character formation (*paideia*) from the newer model and its goal of specialization in an area of knowledge and research (*Wissenschaft*). Can we encourage interaction between the two in church and public forums?

15. H. C. Washington, *Wealth and Poverty in the Instruction of Amenemope and the Hebrew Proverbs* (SBLDS 142; Atlanta: Scholars Press, 1994). Washington argues that Proverbs, like Amenemope, reflects a heightened awareness of the poor in society.

and plundered. Therefore, to respond as God does is to become an advocate for the poor, using whatever resources and authority are available to offer mercy and work for justice.

Christian individuals and churches both can test their "wisdom quotient" by asking how much of their resources of time, wealth, and energy go toward improving the situation of those caught in poverty. Churches especially demonstrate their wisdom learning by sharing this basic disposition so important to the Law, the Prophets, and the Writings. Giving to missions and hunger relief agencies is a wonderful start, especially when it is followed by local involvement. If the church does not know what to do, it can always call local agencies and ask what kind of help is needed. This much is clear: If the sages of old spoke to the concerns of wealth, poverty, and justice, we do well to emulate their example.

Friendships and partnerships. Finally, the warnings against bad associations warn us that friendships and partnerships are never neutral. If we are to become a people who learn, preserve, and teach these wisdom traditions, we are more likely to succeed if we link arms with even-tempered people who take responsibility for their actions rather than hotheads and nonneedy borrowers. Does this mean we are always to steer clear of angry types and never consider making a loan? Not necessarily, for the principle at the heart of these warnings is unwise commitment to those who do not share wisdom's purposes.

Christians debate over what it means to "be separate" from the world and its lusts, but clearly these warnings do not negate Jesus' command to be salt and light in the world (Matt. 5:13–16). In the same way the apostle Paul explained that believers cannot avoid all associations with immoral people without leaving this world; they are, however, to avoid association with people who claim to be believers but lack self-control in their sexuality, speech, and appetite (1 Cor. 5:9–11). He advised his hearers, "Do not be yoked together with unbelievers" (2 Cor. 6:14). In other words, Paul reformulated the sage's principle, stating that the close association of Christian fellowship is incompatible with behaviors devoid of Christian commitment. Certainly those who are concerned only for their own well-being make poor companions and models.

We may not be in the position of a ruler, a servant to a ruler, or any of its contemporary equivalents, but the sages' counsel to speak wisely, act justly, and avoid partnerships with those who do not is sound advice for all of us. "He has showed you, O man, what is good. And what does the LORD require of you? To act justly and to love mercy and to walk humbly with your God" (Mic. 6:8).

Proverbs 23:1–35

¹ WHEN YOU SIT to dine with a ruler,
  note well what is before you,
² and put a knife to your throat
  if you are given to gluttony.
³ Do not crave his delicacies,
  for that food is deceptive.
⁴ Do not wear yourself out to get rich;
  have the wisdom to show restraint.
⁵ Cast but a glance at riches, and they are gone,
  for they will surely sprout wings
  and fly off to the sky like an eagle.
⁶ Do not eat the food of a stingy man,
  do not crave his delicacies;
⁷ for he is the kind of man
  who is always thinking about the cost.
"Eat and drink," he says to you,
  but his heart is not with you.
⁸ You will vomit up the little you have eaten
  and will have wasted your compliments.
⁹ Do not speak to a fool,
  for he will scorn the wisdom of your words.
¹⁰ Do not move an ancient boundary stone
  or encroach on the fields of the fatherless,
¹¹ for their Defender is strong;
  he will take up their case against you.
¹² Apply your heart to instruction
  and your ears to words of knowledge.
¹³ Do not withhold discipline from a child;
  if you punish him with the rod, he will not die.
¹⁴ Punish him with the rod
  and save his soul from death.
¹⁵ My son, if your heart is wise,
  then my heart will be glad;
¹⁶ my inmost being will rejoice
  when your lips speak what is right.
¹⁷ Do not let your heart envy sinners,
  but always be zealous for the fear of the LORD.

¹⁸ There is surely a future hope for you,
and your hope will not be cut off.
¹⁹ Listen, my son, and be wise,
and keep your heart on the right path.
²⁰ Do not join those who drink too much wine
or gorge themselves on meat,
²¹ for drunkards and gluttons become poor,
and drowsiness clothes them in rags.
²² Listen to your father, who gave you life,
and do not despise your mother when she is old.
²³ Buy the truth and do not sell it;
get wisdom, discipline and understanding.
²⁴ The father of a righteous man has great joy;
he who has a wise son delights in him.
²⁵ May your father and mother be glad;
may she who gave you birth rejoice!
²⁶ My son, give me your heart
and let your eyes keep to my ways,
²⁷ for a prostitute is a deep pit
and a wayward wife is a narrow well.
²⁸ Like a bandit she lies in wait,
and multiplies the unfaithful among men.
²⁹ Who has woe? Who has sorrow?
Who has strife? Who has complaints?
Who has needless bruises? Who has bloodshot eyes?
³⁰ Those who linger over wine,
who go to sample bowls of mixed wine.
³¹ Do not gaze at wine when it is red,
when it sparkles in the cup,
when it goes down smoothly!
³² In the end it bites like a snake
and poisons like a viper.
³³ Your eyes will see strange sights
and your mind imagine confusing things.
³⁴ You will be like one sleeping on the high seas,
lying on top of the rigging.
³⁵ "They hit me," you will say, "but I'm not hurt!
They beat me, but I don't feel it!
When will I wake up
so I can find another drink?"

A SERIES OF snapshot pictures of meals, home schooling, and seduction present the would-be servant of the king with a guide to resisting temptation through identification with the parents' teaching. Repetition of the key words "heart" (*leb*, 23:7, 12, 15, 17, 19, 26, 33, 34 [lit., "heart of the sea"]) and "eye" (*ʿayin*, 23:5, 6, 26, 29, 31, 33) urge the young leader to take care what each takes in. Warnings, prohibitions, and depictions of drinking and eating together urge this young person to exercise discipline over desire. The organization of the chapter draws together common themes and images.

Deceptive Delicacies and Fleeting Riches (23:1–8)
    Do not crave the ruler's delicacies (23:1–3)
    Do not weary yourself with riches (23:4–5)
    Do not crave the stingy person's delicacies (23:6–8)

Teaching and Traditions (23:9–14)
    Do not speak to fools or move the boundary stone (23:9–11)
    Do not withhold discipline (23:12–14)

Signs of Wisdom That Bring Parents Joy (23:15–21)
    Be wise, fear Yahweh (23:15–18)
    Be wise, avoid drunkards and gluttons (23:19–21)

The Seductions of Sex and Wine (23:22–35)
    My son, give your heart to me, not the harlot (23:22–28)
    Do not gaze at wine (23:29–35)

Deceptive Delicacies and Fleeting Riches (23:1–8)

TWO VIGNETTES ABOUT a table of delicacies frame a warning about the pursuit of riches.

23:1–3. The mention of a ruler in verse 1 links this series of sayings with previous teachings on service (cf. 22:21, 29), and the double mention of "delicacies" in verses 3 and 6 suggests that verses 1–8 are interrelated as well. The juxtaposition points out the contrast between skilled work that serves and selfish gluttony.

In verses 1–3 it is the ruler who "serves" a meal, yet that ruler is still in charge—an aspect of the situation that the guest is to "note well."[1] The NIV note indicates that the line may be translated "who [*not* 'what'] is before you"

---

1. The root *byn* can mean "discern." Other uses of the root in the ch. translate as the nouns "wisdom" (23:4) and "understanding" (23:23).

since the relative pronoun *ʾ͏ašer* is ambiguous. The double meaning can encompass the whole situation, including both food and host. Putting a knife to the throat is not a threat of death but rather holding a knife to one's desire, for the word *nepeš* can mean "throat" or "appetite."[2] The "delicacies" uses the same word for the savory food Jacob cooked to deceive his father (Gen. 27:17, 31); certainly this "food is deceptive," for it is (lit.) the "bread of lies."

Some think that the host is testing the guest, looking for signs of discipline and self-control and thus making the offer of hospitality insincere (cf. 23:6–8).[3] Certainly a ruler would look for someone who is not ruled by appetite (cf. 23:20–21), for such a person will show integrity and diligence in work. But is the host's intention all that is false about these delicacies? It is also true that we can allow "delicacies" and the status they bring to cloud our judgment, tempting us to make them the goal of life instead of faithfulness and love. Therefore, if the delicacies are a symbol for desire, ambition, and even pride, is this ruler deceptive or has he acquired a wise perspective on riches? Such a wise person would affirm the teaching of the sayings that follow.

23:4–5. These two verses on riches develop the theme of desire and deception, so the connection with the ruler's table in 23:1–3 is clear. A wordplay on the Hebrew root for "fly" (*ʿwp*) in the first and last lines of verse 5 urges readers not to let their eyes fly to riches, because as soon as the eyes land on them, they also will sprout wings and fly. The image seems to say, "Let your eyes stay put on that which lasts instead of flying around to fleeting riches."[4] Like the "bread of lies," riches are also deceptive (23:3); therefore one should not become weary in their pursuit but have the "wisdom" (root *byn*, as in "note well" in 23:1) to know when to stop or "show restraint" (cf. 23:2).

23:6–8. Framing the instruction on riches is another vignette about sitting down to eat, but this time the host's character is clearly stated. He is (lit.)" bad of eye" (NIV "stingy"), in contrast to the generous person with a good eye (cf. 22:9; 28:22). Like the ruler of 23:1, he also has a table of deceptive delicacies (cf. 23:3), for he says, "Eat and drink," but does not mean it. Perhaps this is a grudging host who sees an unexpected guest as an imposition instead of a chance to show hospitality, halfheartedly offering

---

2. The phrase might be translated, "Put a blade to your throat if you are not master of your appetite."

3. In Proverbs "lies" typically pour out of a false witness (6:19; 14:5, 25; 19:5, 9).

4. Whybray, *Wealth and Poverty in the Book of Proverbs*, 94–96, notes the shift in emphasis from the individual proverbs where justly acquired wealth does last, and only hasty or quick riches are condemned.

the welcome that was so important to ancient oriental culture.[5] Therefore, the teacher advises not moderation but total avoidance: "Do not eat" (23:6). People usually vomit from eating too much, but in this case even a little of this food will not stay down, so everything is lost—the meal and the compliments.[6]

Like chasing riches that fly away (23:4−5), craving these delicacies only leads to loss and emptiness. The "compliments" are (lit.) the "pleasing [words]" of 22:18, which the wise student stores on the advice of the teacher. Here, however, they are put to a wrong purpose, namely, flattery for greedy gain instead of wise servanthood. Together, the three teachings of 23:1−8 make it clear that meals are about a lot more than food. Usually a meal is a sign of hospitality and friendship to all who come by; yet there are other meals where either guest or host is tested, where motives other than friendship are present. Just as Woman Wisdom offered a banquet of life and Woman Folly a meal of death (9:1−18), so here food and appetite are used as metaphors for the attitude one brings to riches and the kind of "teaching" one desires.

Teaching and Traditions (23:9−14)

THREE SEEMINGLY UNRELATED prohibitions treat the topic of folly, the first and last offering different perspectives on teaching. Sometimes words are wasted on fools and cheats, but stern discipline can be effective.

23:9−11. Two prohibitions warn against unwise word and deed. A number of sayings in Proverbs caution against speaking wisdom to fools, who will reject it (9:7−8; 26:4−5), and the theme of wasted words connects the saying in 23:9 with the one before. Just as one should take care in speaking at the table, so one should take care when speaking to a fool who will not listen to instruction (contrast 22:17).

The teaching on the ancient boundary stone (23:10; cf. 22:28) does not mention the forefathers who set it up, only the fatherless who have no one to speak for their rights. To encroach on their land by moving a boundary marker is to disturb a family inheritance. Yet they have a strong "Defender,"

---

5. Clifford, *Proverbs*, 210−11, thinks the opposite, that uninvited guests are the "thieves who will suffer the same consequences as those who rob the poor in *Amenemope*, ch. 11. They cannot keep their unjust gain." *Amenemope* reads, "A poor man's goods are a block in the throat, it makes the gullet vomit."

6. The extensive footnote in the NIV shows the difficulty of translation. It is not certain whether we are to read the word as "calculate" (*ša'ar*; TNK " like one keeping accounts") or "puts on a feast" (NIV note), or as another word that means "hair" (*śe'ar*, NRSV, following the LXX, "for like a hair in the throat"; *Amenemope* 11, "a block in the throat"). Although the translation is uncertain, the point about restraint is clear.

a kinsman redeemer (*go'el*),[7] who will take up their case (*rib*); the *rib* is a controversy or wrong that must be set right. The fatherless do have kin after all, just as the poor have a defender in Yahweh (cf. 22:22–23; 15:25). Systems of law were created to protect the poor and defenseless; the legal terminology suggests that anyone who misuses the system to abuse them will have it used against himself instead.

23:12–14. A renewed call to attention repeats the words "heart" and "ears" from 22:17, this time with a call to "apply" oneself to instruction and knowledge. The word for "instruction" (*musar*) is translated as "discipline" in 23:13, for both verbal teaching and the correction of the rod are considered instruction. The first use directs the young student (*na'ar* [NIV "child"] denotes a young man) in the right way, the second steers the student from the wrong way.[8]

As we have said about previous references to the rod, the teaching of verses 13–14 are not an endorsement of corporal punishment as much as a call to the responsibility of teaching and correcting. To "punish" or strike in this way is (lit.) to "deliver his soul from *še'ol*," as the NIV text note indicates (cf. 1:12; 7:27; 9:18; 15:24); such is the fate of those who fall in with violent men or consort with foolish women. Whereas earlier in Proverbs, the young person was warned to avoid such people, now the student must become a teacher who also warns others (cf. 23:26–28). Those who are urged to receive instruction (3:11) must also pass it on. As the famous proverb says, "Those who teach learn twice."

Signs of Wisdom That Bring Parents Joy (23:15–21)

PARENTS EXPERIENCE JOY when their offspring choose their wisdom over the influence of drunkards and gluttons.

23:15–18. Like the group of sayings in 23:12–14, admonition follows an address, here once again the typical "my son." Two conditional sayings work individually and as a pair in verses 15 and 16. The repetition of "heart" unites the first two lines around the theme of gladness (cf. 10:1): "If *your* heart is wise, then *my* heart will be glad." Gladness continues into verse 16, where the teacher's whole "inmost being" rejoices at this meeting of wise heart and upright speech.

---

7. The *go'el* is one who steps in on behalf of the family to execute some sort of responsibility of redemption by paying a debt (Lev. 25:48ff.), buying back land (Lev. 25:25ff.), exacting a debt, avenging blood (Num. 35:12ff.) or, in the case of Yahweh, redeeming those who are in trouble (cf. Job 19:25; Jer. 50:34); see *TWOT*, 300.

8. In the ancient world, the rod became a symbol of correction, that which beats folly out of the fool (cf. 22:15). Those punishments are preferable to death, as the wordplay on "not die" and *še'ol* shows. "If I beat you, my son, you will not die; but if I leave you alone, [you will not live]"; *Ahiqar*, line 82 in J. Lindenberger, "Ahiqar: A New Translation and Introduction," *Old Testament Pseudepigrapha* (Garden City, N.Y.: Doubleday, 1985), 2:480–507.

The second line of verse 17 and the first line of 18 begin with the same phrase (*ki ʾim*), linking zeal for "fear of the LORD" with "future hope" (cf. 24:19–20; Ps. 37; 73).[9] Wisdom first looks to Yahweh, then toward the prosperity of others with improved vision. "Envy" and "zeal" are both derived from the same word (*qanah*) for an intense feeling of love and desire. Because this emotion is often expressed as jealousy, we can speak of being jealous of other persons (Prov. 24:1, 19) or jealous for God (23:17). This explicit mention of Yahweh comes near the middle of the "sayings of the wise," which place a pair of Yahweh proverbs near the beginning and the end.

23:19–21. The theme of keeping the heart continues from verses 15–18. To listen and receive teaching is to be wise, say these parents (cf. 23:15), to keep the heart on the "right" (*yašar*, "straight") path.[10] The negative examples may have been inspired by Deuteronomy 21:20: "They shall say to the elders, 'This son of ours is stubborn and rebellious. He will not obey us. He is a profligate and a drunkard.'" The warning combines fears of gluttony and laziness; the "drowsiness" may come from the wine or simply from love of sleep. Like the table scenes of Proverbs 23:1–11, this teaching calls for restraint when encountering food and drink that fail to nourish or satisfy, as well as independent thinking in the face of peer pressure.

The Seductions of Sex and Wine (23:22–35)

THE SEDUCTIONS OF illicit sex and overindulgence in wine are juxtaposed to point up the traps and destruction brought on by each.

23:22–25. Having warned the young learner about negative influences in 23:17–21, the parental teachers again speak of gladness at their son's wise choices (23:25; cf. 23:15–16). The first and last lines of this section end with the Hebrew phrase "gave you life/birth," once for father (23:22) and once for mother (23:25). A charge to receive a parent's counsel in adulthood is implied in "do not despise your mother when she is old" (23:22); certainly the grown-up Lemuel received (or at least remembered) his mother's teaching (31:1–9).

In the same way, this young man is told to buy truth and not sell it, treasuring it for a long, long time. He is to do the same with "wisdom" (cf. 23:15,

---

9. The second line of v. 17 does not translate easily. Some interpreters carry the personal emphasis of "sinners" into the next line, supplying a subject for fear of Yahweh: "but rather those who revere Yahweh at all times" (Clifford, *Proverbs*, 202).

10. The Heb. allows for subtle differences in translation—"keep your heart on the right path" (NIV, taking "heart" as the subject of the verb) or "walk the way of your heart" (Murphy, *Proverbs*, 172, following Heb. word order, with "heart" as construct/object), also paraphrased as "walk on the path your own heart chooses" (Clifford, *Proverbs*, 213). Whatever the translation, the main point of choosing wisdom over peer pressure remains clear.

19, 24), "discipline" (*musar*, cf. 23:13—14), and "understanding" (root *byn*; cf. 23:1, "note well"; 23:4, "have the wisdom"), honoring his parents by honoring their teaching. The charge is backed up with a motivation in 23:24—25. Parents' rejoicing is in each of the four lines, the verbs for "great joy" (*gil*) and "delights" (*yiśmaḥ*) repeating in a chiastic pattern.

23:26—28. The parent's teaching on the heart (cf. 23:12, 15—18) resumes with the evocative phrase in 23:26, "My son, give me your heart." To give the heart is to entrust it to the one who will direct it through *teaching*, although some affection is certainly involved. The father is also an *example* as he asks the son to observe "my ways" with "your eyes." What is seen with the eye is stored in the heart, so the father urges the son to let his eyes "keep" (*tiroṣnah*, "be pleased with") his ways.

The motivation for this charge is the danger of the prostitute or harlot (*zonah*, 6:26; 7:10; cf. Deut. 23:18), whose promiscuous ways are a deep pit (cf. Prov. 9:18; 22:14). The warning stands in parallel with one about the "strange woman" (*nokriyyah*, 2:16; 20:16), who is off limits. She lies in wait like a bandit, a common image in Proverbs (1:11, 18; 2:12—22; 7:12; 12:6; 24:15), multiplying her victims (cf. 2:22).[11] Just as those who are not careful to watch their ways can fall into a pit, so they can be easy picking for predators who wait along the back roads.

23:29—35. Another warning about drunkenness (cf. 23:20—21) takes the form of a satire, using key words from the chapter ("eye"; "beat" or "punish," 23:13—14, 35; "end," *aharit*, 23:18, 32) to make a summary point. A series of rhetorical questions begins with general descriptions of woe and sorrow and ends with the hangover problem of eyes that are bloodshot (or bleary, cf. 23:29). If we have a riddle in 23:29, the answer is provided: The person who has these problems is the one who lingers over wine.

Therefore, the teacher warns, "Do not gaze at wine" as it shines red, sparkling in the cup, going smoothly down the throat, seductive as any wayward woman.[12] Yet what goes down smoothly bites like a snake "in the end"

---

11. The phrase "multiplies the unfaithful" is difficult to translate. Clifford, *Proverbs*, 205, following TNK, suggests, "She destroys the faithless," after Zeph. 1:2—3. Whybray, *Proverbs*, 340, notes two meanings: (1) passive participle, "deceived" or "betrayed"; (2) collective noun meaning "treachery"; trans., "She repeatedly acts treacherously toward men."

12. The poem personifies the wine, depicting it as "giving its eye" (*yiten ʿeyno*) that sparkles or winks at the one who stares at it, thus suggesting a form of seduction. See 6:24—26 for a similar enticement based on visual appearance (esp. the eyes in 6:25), and the role played by the senses in the seduction of 7:6—23. Is it a coincidence that teachings on the wayward woman and seductive wine are juxtaposed here as drunkenness and seduction in ch. 5 (cf. the key word *šgh*, "intoxicated" or "staggering" in 5:19—20, 23)? See also the comparison of love with wine in Song 7:9.

(cf. 23:18, where "future" is *aḥarit*). The "bite" refers to the list of wine's stupefying effects: visions (23:33), reeling (23:34), and the dangerous combination of dulled senses mixed with bravado (23:35). "I can take it!" says the drunk; feeling invincible, he is actually going down like a boxer who has taken too many blows. The "high sea" is (lit.) "the heart of the sea" (*leb-yam*, 23:34), which is actually the low point of the wave as one sinks down, a contrast with the "head" (*roʾš*) or top of the mast, perhaps intended to compare seasickness to drunkenness, or possibly the hangover.[13] The braggart claims he is not hurt, but in reality he is addicted to this form of self-abuse (23:35).

WE HAVE SEEN that the key words "heart" (*leb*, 23:7, 12, 15, 17, 19, 26, 33, 34) and "eye" (*ʿayin*, 23:5, 6, 26, 29, 31, 33) appear throughout this part of the "sayings of the wise," restating and developing the truth of previous chapters. What the eye takes in is stored in the heart: "My son, give me your heart and let your eyes keep to my ways" (23:26). The father's touching plea calls for an identification with parental teaching, values, and view of the world. But this learning can be perverted if the eyes are led astray by that which seduces, especially wine, for the "eyes will see strange sights" and the "mind [heart] imagine confusing things" (23:33).

Dangers of undisciplined desire. These typical themes of ancient instructional literature are developed in the sayings about uncontrolled eating and drinking and the need for discipline (*musar*, 23:12–13). Food and drink can deceive, so the young learner is warned not to "crave delicacies" (23:3, 6) or to "linger over wine," which can make one stupid and miserable (23:29–35). In between these warnings, the parents plead with their son to make them glad by becoming wise (23:15–25), adding yet another warning that foolish gluttony and drunkenness only make one poor (23:20–21). It takes wisdom and discernment to recognize drunkenness and gluttony for what they are, to see the trap that hides under the bait. Therefore, to bring the wisdom teaching of these instructions into our day, we can reflect on the new information these sayings present about deception and the hidden dangers of undisciplined desire.

(1) The three vignettes about deceptive delicacies and riches in 23:1–8 speak to gluttony, because the lack of control over appetite marks one as

---

13. Murphy, *Proverbs*, 177, directs the reader to Ps. 107:27 for a similar description of the highs and lows of a stormy sea.

self-centered and unfit to serve. People sometimes say that it does not matter if their leaders practice personal morality as long as they work for the public good, but the sages of Proverbs will have none of it. They do not distinguish the shrewd but indiscreet leader from the righteous but naive one. For them savvy and righteousness go together. Jesus had no patience for those who would use leadership to serve themselves, chastising the Pharisees for their topsy-turvy values: "Woe to you, blind guides! You say, 'If anyone swears by the temple, it means nothing; but if anyone swears by the gold of the temple, he is bound by his oath.' You blind fools! Which is greater: the gold, or the temple that makes the gold sacred?" (Matt. 23:16–17).

The sages in Proverbs insist that the pursuit of good but transitory things like food and money makes a poor goal for life. After reading that riches grow wings to fly away, it is hard to know who is more to be pitied, the stingy one whose "heart is not with" guests or the craving one who eats his delicacies only to get sick and lose them (Prov. 23:6–8). "Have the wisdom" to cease such pursuits, we read (23:4), or we will spend all our energies chasing the wind. Instead, we must constantly remind ourselves that the wisdom of Proverbs is primarily about managing our desires.

Can we really let wisdom guide what we want in life and how we go about getting it? Unfortunately, trained by media culture, we want everything, and thus we make everything into a commodity. According to Greg Miller and Michael Real, the baseball players' strike of 1994 marked the turn toward a new understanding of sports in America, one in which individual free agency and its promise of sky-high salaries finally took precedence over the more traditional values of teamwork and excellence. One might argue that professional sports have always been about money, but Miller and Real insist that the rejection of baseball's "grand narrative" of dedication and sacrifice (as typified by Lou Gehrig), along with the increased role of broadcast media in hyping the drama of the ball games and negotiation games, and the commitment to unconstrained capitalism are signs of an emerging postmodern consciousness.[14]

To speak in this way, however, is merely to describe the current signs of an age-old problem. Jesus told the parable of the workers in the vineyard after the rich man walked away sad, unable to let go of what he had to give to the poor. When Peter reminded Jesus that he and the others had left everything to follow him, Jesus laid out their reward; they would sit on thrones and judge the twelve tribes of Israel and give out rewards to everyone else. But, he added, they would have to know how those rewards will

---

14. G. R. Miller and M. Real, "Postmodernity and Popular Culture: Understanding our National Pastime," in *The Postmodern Presence: Readings on Postmodernism in American Culture and Society*, ed. A. A. Berger (Walnut Creek, Calif.: AltaMira, 1998), 17–34.

be distributed: "Many who are first will be last, and many who are last will be first" (Matt. 19:30).

This parable about a landowner who hires laborers to work one hour and pays them the same as those hired in the morning brings the point home. The early morning workers grumble that the treatment is unfair. They should be worth more, they say, and the landowner answers: "Don't I have the right to do what I want with my own money? Or are you envious because I am generous?" (Matt. 20:15). "Envious" translates a Greek phrase that literally translates "evil of eye," the description of the stingy man in Proverbs 23:6 (cf. 23:17). The point is clear: God wants us to give generously; we want to be sure we get what we are worth. We are the greedy host and the greedy guest. We crave delicacies. We are "always thinking about the cost" (23:7).

(2) Worse than simply craving and striving after riches is throwing away wise words and grasping for the property of others. Instead, those who apply themselves to learn can also offer discipline (23:9–14). Two views of instruction stand in tension: "Do not speak to a fool" who will spurn the teaching, but "do not withhold discipline" from those who might receive it. Wisdom learning includes knowing how to discern when correction will be effective or wasted (cf. 26:4–5). Certainly it is better to receive correction, even when painful, than to fall into the kind of folly that moves a boundary stone and will summon the strong Defender (23:10–11). This warning seems out of place among these sayings on teaching and learning, but we have seen that Yahweh is often named when the poor are being cheated or oppressed (cf. 22:22–23).

The placement of this saying suggests that discipline that saves the soul from death also averts Yahweh's judgment.[15] How are we to teach in this way—holding up Yahweh as the defender of the poor while we work at teaching and correcting, encouraging discipline of thought and deed, and hoping our children and students will learn to discipline their desires? It seems to me that the image of a God who comes to the aid of the poor connects with the inner sense of justice that drives so many of the good/evil movies about cops and superheroes. We should instruct our children to identify themselves with this Defender. This possibility of identifying with Yahweh in his view of things and in his purposes may just restore the motivation to learn that is so absent from much of education.

In my limited experience, students of junior and high school age do not see why it is wrong to center their lives around material goods, for it does

---

15. The boundary saying is one of a pair in the "sayings of the wise," and their appearance may mark off a chiastic section. This mirror pattern would pair the boundary sayings (22:28; 23:10–11), the skilled worker and the fool (22:29; 23:9), and the two tables (23:1–3, 6–8), placing the fleeting riches at the center (23:4–5).

not seem to hurt anybody. However, the potential for craving to turn to grasping and its potential for injustice and abuse of the poor may provide motivation to learn. Strong teaching of this sort may be the analogy of the rod of punishment we are to practice today.

(3) Verses 15–25 are framed with the joy of parents over a young adult who learns wisdom. Twice the son hears it is better to be wise, better than to envy sinners or join with drunkards and gluttons. Interestingly, these words about associations show that their children's identifications are at stake here. If they identify with the parents by embracing their teaching, the parents are glad. But if they join with the dissolute or even envy the lives of sinners from a distance, there is the danger of a short life of poverty.

Thus, the very first instruction of Proverbs insisted that one chooses one's life by choosing one's associations, for there the father warned his son not to go with "sinners" or to accept their invitation (1:10). As we said in the comments on 22:24–27, the principle here is not avoiding all those we might call sinners (after all, we are sinners too) but rather refusing to join with them in their goals or the paths they walk on to reach them. The point is not to reject people but the ways they represent. We today need godly wisdom to figure out the subtle stray paths we must reject. Hard as it is to stay away from obvious sins, it is even harder to avoid those subtle temptations of desire, the ways we indulge ourselves to our detriment, much like one who eats or drinks too much.

The goal, as we have seen throughout Proverbs, is to point the heart in the right direction (23:19)—away from undisciplined desire and toward wisdom and fear of Yahweh. The parallelism of 23:17 suggests that the affections of our hearts can be expressed as envy or zeal. By examining our reactions, we can look to see whether our hearts envy and crave or whether they experience zeal and joy. When we are feeling a lust for more, we can know we are on the wrong path. What, then, does this say for a culture that is never satisfied?

(4) The call for identification with one's parents and their dedication to wisdom continues into the sayings on women and wine (23:26–35), for the father prefaces them by saying, "Give me your heart." If the son is responsible to keep his own heart on the right path (23:19), he learns it by giving his heart to another, attending to the parents' teaching and example. The popularity of wisdom figures like Yoda in *Star Wars* and Gandalf in *Lord of the Rings* should encourage us that we are not on the wrong track if we speak about external and internal discipline with our kids. Certainly the teaching that compares envy and lust with zeal and joy is tested by temptations of sexual pleasure apart from lifelong emotional and spiritual commitment, or temptations of drunken feelings of freedom and being invincible.

In popular discourse, sexual addiction has taken its place alongside substance addiction as another powerful force that overpowers and pulls people away from paths that would lead to their deepest desires. While Proverbs never uses the language of sexual addiction, this teaching does emphasize the deadly power of sex out of bounds, and perhaps the juxtaposition of sexual lust and drunkenness is meant to point out the similarities. "Do not gaze at wine" sounds like a warning about gazing at a lustful woman. The father wants the son's heart; he has it if the son watches his ways to emulate them, letting his eyes keep to those ways. But if the young man looks at the woman or the glass of wine, he will not be watching his own way and will be caught unaware. Perhaps this is why the teacher says that this woman is a deep pit or a bandit lying in wait and that wine is like a snake or an attacker (23:35; cf. 24:1).

In addition, these seductive pleasures also threaten to hold power over us and make us captive. In our desire to be free of constraints, we become slaves of our desires. Wisdom in this sense is like Paul's freedom in Christ; in it we find ourselves able and even empowered to choose the right way (Gal. 5:1, 13).

The discipline of the heart. In sum, this section of the words of the wise frames the earnest teaching of the parents with examples of desire out of bounds, most notably gluttony and drunkenness. "My son," the teacher says, "give me your heart, keep your eyes on me, for you may look aside to delicacies, you may envy sinners, you may join with drunks and gluttons, you may give your heart to prostitutes, you may be seduced by the eye of wine. To go with any of these is to reject your parents who gave you life, but to seek wisdom is to love them even as you grow into independence."

The parents' teaching is about discipline of desire, but it is also about the use of the heart in two important senses: a heart can be filled with wise teaching to direct one's paths (23:26), but a heart can also experience the affections of envy and greed, or zeal and joy (23:15–17). For this reason, the teachers repeat what has been said to link it with something new (in good biblical fashion). Here they repeat the warnings against the adulterous women and violent men (cf. 2:12–22) and juxtapose them with warnings against less obvious distractions like excesses of eating and drinking. The teaching moves from subtle failures at the ancient business lunch to rock bottom failures like the drunkard.

The prevention and remedy is discipline, learned from proper identification with models and internalized. In this way, the sages used the word "heart" to speak to both our intentions and affections. If the student's heart is pointed in the right direction (ways and zeal), then the parents' hearts will rejoice. As in the earlier instructions, the young steward is still asked to choose.

THE SAGE WHO spoke to his son, "Give me your heart," would say the same to us, urging us to keep our eyes on wise ways of living, to understand the connection between eyes and heart as well as the heart's capacity to express our intentions and affections. In contemporary terms, we can apply these insights as we reflect on our pursuits, name those areas that require discipline, and set out specific plans for walking in the ways of wisdom.

Reflection on our pursuits. We can practice regular reflection about our activities and pursuits as well as the effect they have on our inner lives. As we think about the examples in this chapter, we may be struck with some of the differences between ancient dinner etiquette and our own, but even more surprised at the similarities. Craving after the deceits of luxurious food and riches is still with us, though in different forms. For us, the riches do not always fly away, but the satisfaction that they are supposed to bring does. David Meyer calls this "soaring wealth and shrinking spirit 'the American paradox.' More than ever we have big houses and broken homes, high incomes and low morale. In an age of plenty, we feel spiritual hunger."[16]

Certainly a first step in the right direction is taking an inner inventory of our pursuits and the satisfaction they bring. This is not to say that only what satisfies is good; rather, it is an attempt to turn things around, to seek what is good because it satisfies. In our age of plenty, when many middle and upper class people do not struggle for basic needs and economic survival, if a pursuit is not satisfying, this can be a sign that we are into something bad.

Students in a seminary course were asked to pretend it was their seventieth birthday and write a letter about their lives, particularly how they lived and used their money. The professor was struck that the students wrote letters that expressed a deep faith and a growing sense of compassion for a needy world. The letter exercise, say Christine and Tom Sine, is also one way to set our hearts in the right direction and keep our eyes on good practices. The letter could be followed with an assessment of time remaining until age seventy and the steps needed to bring one's life into line with that goal.[17]

Areas that require discipline. We can name those areas of life in which our desires may need the discipline of wisdom. Throughout Proverbs we have seen that our desires are never negated or labeled as bad, but the dangers

---

16. D. C. Meyers, "Wealth, Well-Being, and the New American Dream," *Enough: A Quarterly Report on Consumption, the Quality Life and the Environment* 12 (Summer 2000): 5, quoted in C. Sine and T. Sine, *Living on Purpose: Finding God's Best for Your Life* (Grand Rapids: Baker, 2002), 36.

17. Sine and Sine, *Living on Purpose,* 70–71.

of pursuing them irresponsibly are always before us. The warnings against gluttony and drunkenness, juxtaposed with the seductions of illicit sexuality, make an old connection. Movies like *Big Night*, *Like Water for Chocolate*, and *Chocolat* have established a genre in film that is at least as old as the Song of Songs and its description of kisses like wine. Arguing from research and his own counseling practice that sexual appetites are more difficult to control for men while women have more problems with appetites for food, Karl Scheibe wonders if at root men tend to seek power while women more often seek acceptance, both to feed ego needs.[18] Certainly it is not the physical needs that move us to action, as an earlier generation of psychologists claimed, but rather our symbolic needs for success and significance.

> We are far more easily sated in our bodily appetites than we are by images and tales of romance and banquet. The major psychological truth about human beings is not that they are driven by needs for food and for sex, but rather that human imagination has transfigured eating into gastronomy and sex into eroticism.[19]

If it is a quest for some nonphysical satisfaction that moves us, the proverbs instruct us about the subtle or not-so-subtle dangers of gluttony, moving from poor table manners to the outright dissipation of the drunkard. While not stated as such, they also warn us against the dangers of addictions to food, sex, work, and a host of other substances and experiences that feed us in ways that have nothing to do with our bodily needs. By pointing out the painful and even deadly consequences of appetites that know no bounds, they show that we are either masters of our desires or they are masters of us. This is not to argue that sheer force of will is called for; every twelve-step group acknowledges a higher power and the need for accountable relationships with peers.[20] But given the potency of desire and its strength and persistence, we must recognize the potential for addiction in all of us, and it is appropriate to view it as sin.

New priorities. Can addiction also describe a society that refuses to practice self-control over desires? Certainly the many testimonies collected by Christine and Tom Sine say so. They especially quote those who say that liv-

---

18. K. Scheibe, *The Drama of Everyday Life* (Cambridge, Mass.: Harvard Univ. Press, 2000), 113, 122–23. "Whatever the origins of these differences in genes or in culture, women do not accumulate as much money as men, and men do not accumulate as many clothes. No male counterpart can be found for Imelda Marcos's collection of 3,000 pairs of shoes." However, Scheibe said little about alcoholism that seems to make no gender distinction.

19. Ibid., 116.

20. K. Miller, *Sin: Overcoming the Ultimate Deadly Addiction* (San Francisco: Harper and Row, 1986).

ing to give rather than accumulate produces a deeper sense of satisfaction than they thought imaginable, as if they found what they were created to do and experience. As an antidote to our addictive culture, they call believers to take the off-ramp from the fast track and create a mission statement that sets new priorities for their lives. To keep the heart on the right path, they recommend writing the personal or family mission statement, a practice made popular by Stephen Covey.[21] They recommend peeling back the busy schedules that leave us frantic and overtired for a time of reflection and writing a statement that reflects the good life, that is, the life given away.

For the Sines it means working as consultants to churches, sharing their own experiences of mission work and helping those Christian bodies dream up new ways to meet needs. For others like Max Depree of DePree Leadership Center, it means running a business in a way that puts caps on executive salaries and seeks to raise the wage of the lowest paid workers. For others, it involves weekly investment in community service or annual mission trips.

Reflecting on our pursuits, recognizing and dealing with addictions, and setting a mission statement to guide us are just three ways to put the new teaching of the sages to work in contemporary life. This much is clear: Given that the quality of life is so poor for so many in our world and that our efforts to achieve satisfaction by having plenty have failed miserably, putting a knife to our throats (desires) doesn't sound like such a bad idea at all.

---

21. S. R. Covey, *The Seven Habits of Highly Effective People: Restoring the Character Ethic* (New York: Fireside, 1989), 106–9, 137–43.

Proverbs 24:1–34

¹ DO NOT ENVY wicked men,
    do not desire their company;
² for their hearts plot violence,
    and their lips talk about making trouble.
³ By wisdom a house is built,
    and through understanding it is established;
⁴ through knowledge its rooms are filled
    with rare and beautiful treasures.
⁵ A wise man has great power,
    and a man of knowledge increases strength;
⁶ for waging war you need guidance,
    and for victory many advisers.
⁷ Wisdom is too high for a fool;
    in the assembly at the gate he has nothing to say.
⁸ He who plots evil
    will be known as a schemer.
⁹ The schemes of folly are sin,
    and men detest a mocker.
¹⁰ If you falter in times of trouble,
    how small is your strength!
¹¹ Rescue those being led away to death;
    hold back those staggering toward slaughter.
¹² If you say, "But we knew nothing about this,"
    does not he who weighs the heart perceive it?
Does not he who guards your life know it?
    Will he not repay each person according to what he
        has done?
¹³ Eat honey, my son, for it is good;
    honey from the comb is sweet to your taste.
¹⁴ Know also that wisdom is sweet to your soul;
    if you find it, there is a future hope for you,
    and your hope will not be cut off.
¹⁵ Do not lie in wait like an outlaw against a righteous
        man's house,
    do not raid his dwelling place;
¹⁶ for though a righteous man falls seven times, he rises again,
    but the wicked are brought down by calamity.

¹⁷ Do not gloat when your enemy falls;
    when he stumbles, do not let your heart rejoice,
¹⁸ or the LORD will see and disapprove
    and turn his wrath away from him.
¹⁹ Do not fret because of evil men
    or be envious of the wicked,
²⁰ for the evil man has no future hope,
    and the lamp of the wicked will be snuffed out.
²¹ Fear the LORD and the king, my son,
    and do not join with the rebellious,
²² or those two will send sudden destruction upon them,
    and who knows what calamities they can bring?

²³ These also are sayings of the wise:

To show partiality in judging is not good:
²⁴ Whoever says to the guilty, "You are innocent"—
    peoples will curse him and nations denounce him.
²⁵ But it will go well with those who convict the guilty,
    and rich blessing will come upon them.
²⁶ An honest answer
    is like a kiss on the lips.
²⁷ Finish your outdoor work
    and get your fields ready;
    after that, build your house.
²⁸ Do not testify against your neighbor without cause,
    or use your lips to deceive.
²⁹ Do not say, "I'll do to him as he has done to me;
    I'll pay that man back for what he did."
³⁰ I went past the field of the sluggard,
    past the vineyard of the man who lacks judgment;
³¹ thorns had come up everywhere,
    the ground was covered with weeds,
    and the stone wall was in ruins.
³² I applied my heart to what I observed
    and learned a lesson from what I saw:
³³ A little sleep, a little slumber,
    a little folding of the hands to rest—
³⁴ and poverty will come on you like a bandit
    and scarcity like an armed man.

Original Meaning

THE CHAPTER DIVIDES into two parts: the conclusion of "the sayings of the wise" in 24:1–22[1] (cf. 22:17) and an appendix that begins, "These also are the sayings of the wise" (24:23–34). Themes that repeat in 24:1–22 include the house and using strength to help others instead of bringing them down; in 24:23–34, images of house and field are juxtaposed with more instructions about dealing with neighbors. While Yahweh sayings appear at the beginning, middle, and end of the "sayings of the wise,"[2] no direct or indirect mention is made in 24:23–34, although blessings and poverty are named (24:25, 34). If this section was written to teach those heading into public service, the symbols of the legal system ("the gate," 22:22; 24:7) and emphases on speaking (22:21; 24:7) that frame the "sayings of the wise" call not only for personal integrity but also for using power to speak for those who have none (24:5–12, 23–26). The structure continues along the lines of paired sayings on a theme.[3]

> Advocacy, Not Envy (24:1–12)
>> Do not envy the wicked (24:1–2)
>> By wisdom a house is built and filled (24:3–4)
>> By wisdom one grows in power (24:5–6)
>> Fools, schemers, and weaklings (24:7–10)
>> Rescue those heading for death (24:11–12)
>
> Trust and Hope, Not Violence or Gloating (24:13–22)
>> Wisdom nourishes like honey (24:13–14)
>> Do not lie in wait for the righteous (24:15–16)
>> Do not gloat when enemies fall (24:17–18)

---

1. Clifford, *Proverbs*, 199, proposes a three-part structure to "the sayings of the wise": 22:17–23:11, addressed to those starting a career; 23:12–35, speaking to the concerns of youth; 24:1–22, depicting the destinies of the righteous and the wicked.

2. Something of a mirror structure appears, matching the pairs of *yhwh* sayings at beginning and end (22:19, 23; 24:18, 21), a pair that indirectly names Yahweh (23:11; 24:12), and a charge to fear Yahweh near the middle (23:17).

3. V. A. Hurowitz, "An Often Overlooked Alphabetic Acrostic in Proverbs 24:1–22," *RB* (2000): 526–40, argues that 24:1–22 are set apart by the acrostic form. The proposal involves a number of emendations and changes, including placing v. 9 after v. 10. Hurowitz believes that the verses then fall into a mirror structure: A and A' (vv. 1–2, 19–22), B and B' (vv. 3–4, 15–18), C and C' (vv. 5–6, 13–14), D and D' (vv. 7–8, relocated v. 9), with X (vv. 10–12) at the center. In my opinion, one can observe literary features such as mirror repetitions without insisting on a tightly organized structure that requires making changes in the Heb. verse order.

Do not fret or envy evildoers (24:19–20)
Fear Yahweh and the king (24:21–22)

Diligence and Honesty, Not Partiality (24:23–34)
Judge rightly, kiss the lips (24:23–26)
First the field, then the house (24:27–34)

Advocacy, Not Envy (24:1–12)

BENEFITS AND RESPONSIBILITIES of wisdom are described by the metaphors of
house (24:3–4), military strength (24:5–6), and city gate (24:7). The wise are
to rescue their neighbors, not scheme against them (24:1–2, 8–10).

24:1–2. This pair of sayings recapitulates the teaching of 23:15–21.
Themes of envy (23:17) and bad company (23:20) reappear as the learner is
warned against those who use heart and lips to do violence instead of what
they were created for, namely, to speak rightly in the fear of Yahweh (23:15–
18). The choice of companions often begins in the desire to emulate. But what
kind of company can one have with people who think and speak about trouble? What is there to envy except easy gain?

24:3–4. The association of wisdom with building a house has appeared
in previous parts of the book (9:1; 14:1), but here includes the contributions of "understanding" and "knowledge." By these a house is not only
built and established, it is filled with treasures "rare and beautiful" (cf. 3:15;
8:18). Wealth may be obtained by violence and deceit (24:1–2; cf. 1:13),
but only by wisdom does one have a place to live. This theme is picked up
in 24:27–34; without wise work in the field, the house will be empty. While
warnings against greed and threats of danger have been associated with
wealth in other parts of the book, here the motivations are like those of
Woman Wisdom, who holds life in one hand and wealth and honor in the
other (3.16).

24:5–6. Again, components from the previous sayings are brought
together; here the wise one, stronger than the fortress (21:22), and many
counselors (11:14) together give advice for war (20:18). The interaction
between 24:5 and 6 sets some limits on the power of the wise; to wage war,
get guidance (*taḥbulot*) and advisors.[4] The might of the wise is not solitary, nor
is wisdom gained in isolation, but only through the teaching of others. The
theme of strength in 24:5 does not become victory until the last line.

24:7–10. Following the glowing portrait of wisdom in 24:3–6, a series
of anti-wisdom portraits of the fool, the schemer, and the weakling make

---

4. This is the last occurrence of *taḥbulot* in the book (cf. 1:5; 11:14; 12:5; 20:18). "Increases
strength" reminds the reader of increasing learning in 1:5.

---

related arguments. If guidance and counsel help one win a battle, the fool has none to give at the gate, where public decisions and judgments are made (24:7). Just as one can speak to cause violence and trouble, it is also possible to be silent when justice calls for a wise word. A Sumerian proverb says, "The one who knows but does not speak is a fool."

Verses 8–9 are linked by the catchword "scheme," bringing together the "master of schemes" (ba⁻al mᵉzimmot) and the "schemes of folly" (zimmat ʾiwwelet; cf. the fool of 24:7; 22:15).[5] Strong language links this figure with the detested (lit., "abomination") mocker, one who makes plans as though there were no one to call those plans to account. The one who falters in 24:10 is one who has little strength (cf. 24:5); the repetition of the root for "trouble" (srr) allows for a literal translation, "You let down in the day of trouble; troubled, your strength!" This saying may be the climax to 24:1–10, but it also continues into the pair at 24:11–12. If so, then your strength has faltered when you have been called on to help others.

24:11–12. A pair of sayings call the wise to use strength in times of trouble (cf. 24:10) for those who are being led to death and are staggering (or yoked) for slaughter, rescuing them and holding them back (ḥśk; cf. 10:19; 11:24; 13:24; 17:27; 21:26; 24:11). The reason for the death march is not stated, and interpreters have suggested that these people are led astray by folly or have been unjustly accused at the gate, thus needing a voice to speak for them.[6] An unusual verse of four lines again names the one who watches and repays (24:12; cf. 23:10–11). The rhetorical questions (cf. 23:29) make it clear that the first line is a falsehood; one cannot claim "we did not know" to the one who knows. There are no valid excuses for standing idle when it is possible to help. The fourth line restates a common theme, that Yahweh will pay back according to deeds. What is new here is that the threat is directed at the reader, not some wicked third party.

Trust and Hope, Not Violence or Gloating (24:13–22)

WISDOM IS COMPARED to honey, sweet and nutritious; those who eat it have a future, unlike the wicked. Four prohibitions build on this truth and warn against unwise actions and reactions.

24:13–14. A pair of sayings compare the sweet taste of honey and its nourishment to the goodness of wisdom that builds, fills, and fortifies a house

---

5. The uses of mᵉzimmah in chs. 1–9 are positive ("discretion, discernment" in 1:4; 2:11; 3:21; 5:2; 8:12), but in the individual proverbs and here (24:8–9), it takes on the negative cast of "crafty" or "scheming" (12:2; 14:17).

6. Hubbard, *Proverbs*, 373, lists three righteous acts that deliver from death: to thwart oppression of the poor, foil false arrests, and break up gang violence.

(24:3, 5, 7; cf. 16:24; Ps. 19:11; 119:103; see also Prov. 5:13; 25:16, 27). Most important, the learner will "know" (cf. 24:12) that this honey of wisdom makes a future in which hope is not cut off (23:18; 24:20). Jonathan demonstrated his wisdom when he tasted honey (1 Sam. 14:24—45), Samson the opposite (Judg. 14:8—20).

24:15—16. The first of a series of four prohibitions (24:15—21) again warns against violence (cf. 24:2), particularly violence at the house or dwelling place (perhaps the house of the wise one; cf. 24:3—4). "Lying in wait" reminds readers of the violent men of 1:11 and the forbidden woman (7:12; 23:28). Both "wicked" (*rašaʿ*, "outlaw") and "righteous" (*ṣaddiq*) are named in the first line of 24:15; verse 16 repeats the terms, contrasting their destinies the same way the individual proverbs of chapters 10—15 did. The righteous may fall, but they rise again—not like the wicked, who are brought down for good (cf. 4:19; Jer. 6:15; 8:15; 20:11).

24:17—18. However, we must not gloat over that downfall; "stumbles" uses the same Hebrew root as "brought down" in 24:16 (*kšl*). Yahweh, who sees and knows hearts, will find it "evil" (cf. 24:12). Since there are many proverbs on the fate of the wicked, it is strange to see this prohibition against a natural reaction. Yet the problem is the same as that of 24:15—16, for in each case, one seeks or is made glad by the misfortune of another. Yahweh would rather have us rejoice over rescues (cf. 24:11—12) and leave matters of judgment to him (see 24:19—20).

24:19—20. At first sight, this pair of sayings appears simply to repeat motifs from other parts of Proverbs, particularly 23:17—18 (cf. 24:14). But like the previous pair, it speaks to internal responses to the wicked; our reactions to their successes and failures reveal much about ourselves and our own desires. If 24:17—18 tell us not to rejoice at the misfortunes of the wicked, these tell us not to worry when they succeed. If the wicked have no future, if their lamp is put out (13:9; 20:20; cf. Isa. 43:17), why exert ourselves? Being righteous is one thing, but the next step is trusting in that ultimate judgment when life does not move in predictable ways.

24:21—22. The climax of the first "sayings of the wise" collection recommends what we have come to expect as central, "the fear of the LORD" (cf. 23:17); here it is joined with "fear ... the king." The reverse of this fear is not courage but foolhardy rebellion. Like the descriptions of the wicked in 24:16—17, 20, the rebels' downfall is certain, but it comes suddenly, beyond expectation and prediction ("Who can know"; cf. "know" in 24:14). The dangers of bad association have been highlighted throughout the words of the wise (22:24—27; 23:20—21; 24:1); this final word assures us that there is no alliance that can withstand the wrath of God and king.

Diligence and Honesty, Not Partiality (24:23–34)

A NEW SECTION begins with the title, "These also are sayings of the wise." It is distinct from the "sayings of the wise" (22:17–24:22) in what it lacks: There is no father's address to son or any mention of Yahweh or wisdom. It does present further instruction on right judgment and a first-person moral tale in which a sage reports on a learning experience (cf. 4:3–9; 7:6–23; also Ps. 37:35–36).[7] The two overlap in something like a dovetail joint.[8]

24:23–26. The second line of 24:23 sets the tone for the section: To pervert judgment (lit., "to recognize faces") is "not good" (cf. Deut. 1:17; 16:19; Prov. 28:21). The image of blindfolded justice continues this ancient tradition that a case is not judged on the basis of who is involved (or what they can do for the judge). Verse 24 expands this idea: To say to "the guilty" (*rašaʿ*, "wicked"), "You are innocent" (*ṣaddiq*, "righteous") uses the familiar pair (cf. 24:15–16) to show how judgments are returned. Those who turn in a favorable verdict will receive a bad one from peoples and nations, a euphemism for unanimous public opinion.

Following this pair of sayings on false judgment, verses 25–26 present a picture of those who judge rightly (*mokiḥim* is related to *tokaḥat*, "rebuke, correction"). For such people, it will "go well" (*naʿam*, "pleasing," 22:18). On them "will come . . . rich blessings" or blessings of good (*tob*), echoing the "not good" of 24:23. Verse 26 is short and vivid: Lips that speak truth are like lips that kiss. The kiss in the ancient world communicated loyalty as well as affection. The honest answer comes from one who (lit.) "returns words that are right" (cf. cf. 22:21).[9] Interpreters debate whether the legal context of 24:23–25 determines the meaning.[10] The main comparison is that of doing good for another with one's lips, a strong contrast to the deceitful lips of 24:28.

---

7. Whybray, *The Composition of the Book of Proverbs*, 145–47; *Proverbs*, 356. The LXX places this section after 30:14.

8. Meinhold, *Die Sprüche*, 2:410, proposes a three-part parallel structure: A (vv. 23–25, 28), B (vv. 26, 29), C (v. 27, 30–34). Garrett, *Proverbs*, 201, has a simpler proposal that is supported by the repetition of "lips" in verses 26 and 28: A (vv. 23–26, 28–29), B (vv. 27, 30–34).

9. "Honest" (*nekoaḥ*) is a rare word, used only eight times in the Old Testament, most often by the prophets as a synonym for that which is right (Prov. 8:9; Isa. 30:10; 57:2; 59:14; Jer. 17:16).

10. J. M. Cohen, "An Unrecognized Connotation of *nšq peh* with Special Reference to Three Biblical Occurrences," *VT* 32 (1982): 416–24. Cohen translates, "He that gives forthright judgment will silence all hostile lips," based on the image of pressing lips together to kiss or to keep silence. The latter meaning is attested in the rabbinic literature. However, to do so, Cohen has to bring in "hostile" by imposing the context of the law court. In other contexts, the honest words simply refer to telling the truth (Clifford, *Proverbs*, 217).

24:27–34. An extended teaching on fields and their upkeep frames a pair
of prohibitions against false witness and vengeance. The proverb about work
in 24:27 recommends putting first things first; before building the house of
security, comfort, and rest, prepare the fields and secure an income (cf. 27:23–
27). The house is a frequent metaphor for wisdom in Proverbs, especially in
this chapter, for by wisdom the house is built and filled (24:3–4). It is folly,
therefore, to have a house to live in but no provisions to live on.

This direct imperative to work is framed with two sayings about lips, honest and deceitful (24:26, 28). In addition, the prohibitions in 24:28–29 warn
against two forms of bad speech: witnessing against one's neighbor without
cause (cf. Ex. 20:16; Deut. 5:20) and threatening to return harm when there
is cause to do so.[11] Perhaps the first speaks to the aggressor who hopes to take
advantage of the legal system, the second to the victim. It is possible that the
two are related; someone might present false testimony as a way of getting
revenge. Yet the assurances of Proverbs 24:15–20 remind readers that Yahweh
oversees the matters of justice and reward, forbidding any attempt to take
vengeance into one's hands (cf. 20:22; 24:12).[12] Repayment only escalates, so
here is perhaps the basis for Jesus' teaching on turning the cheek and loving
the enemy (Matt. 5:38–48; cf. Prov. 24:17–18; also 15:1).

The appendix to the "sayings of the wise" ends with a look at the sluggard's
neglected field (24:30–34; cf. 10:4; 20:4, 13).[13] This second teaching on the
work of the field (cf. 24:27) offers a first-person description of the thorns,
weeds, and broken stone wall. Note the repetition in "see" (*hinneh*, 24:31; not
trans. in NIV) and "I looked ... I saw" (*hzh,*, 24:32). Although the sluggard "lacks
judgment" (lit., "heart" [*leb*], 24:30), the speaker takes this sight to heart and
learns its "lesson" (24:32, *musar*, the final use of this word in Proverbs).

The wise man then repeats the proverbial saying of 6:10–11: "A little
sleep, a little slumber, a little folding of the hands to rest—and poverty will
come on you like a bandit, and scarcity like an armed man."[14] This time,
however, the warning comes from one who has learned to look and learn,
who does not need to be told, "Go to the ant, sluggard, consider its ways
and be wise" (6:6; cf. 22:29). Juxtaposing this inductive lesson on vineyard
keeping with teaching on righteous speaking suggests that diligence in

---

11. The terms "without cause" and "deceive" appear in 1:10–11, where the bandits
"entice" (cf. 16:29) the young man to attack a "harmless soul" ("for no reason," *hinnam*; cf.
3:30; 26:2).

12. McKane, *Proverbs*, 575, argues that vengeance becomes a cruel taskmaster that in the
end will destroy us.

13. On the sluggard, see also 6:6, 9; 10:26; 13:4; 15:19; 19:24; 20:4; 21:25; 22:13;
26:13–16.

14. The NIV text note shows that the translation "vagrant ... beggar" is also permissible.

both demonstrates wisdom and is essential for successful living. Negligence in either area exacts a high price. So Jesus calls wise those stewards who look after the house and its servants, and he calls wicked those who forget the master, beat the servants, and indulge in overeating and drinking (Matt. 24:45–50).

Bridging Contexts

THE FINAL THIRD of the "sayings of the wise" and the appendix that follows combine the concerns of the instructions (chs. 1–9) and the individual proverbs (chs. 10–22), bringing together direct teaching on the actions of the wicked with indirect teaching on the life of wisdom, symbolized in metaphors of the house and the sluggard. The sayings of this chapter teach us about envy and its antidotes, advocacy, trust, and diligence.

Envy and its antidotes. Envy afflicts us all, but it can be countered with advocacy for those in need. Verses 1–12 set out positive and negative instructions: Do not envy the wicked who prey on others, but protect and deliver the weak instead. Stand against the deeds of the wicked as you stand up for your neighbors. The symbols of home, military might, and the city gate communicate security and safety, directing the reader to wisdom where true security is found. Envy is more an attitude than an action, desiring what others seem to have and wanting to be with them or like them (24:1; cf. 24:19).

Yet attitudes lead to actions, and the attitudes of the wicked result in violent schemes (24:8–9); to envy their lives is to take on their ways and displease Yahweh (cf. 3:31–35). Could it be that we also envy the security that seems to come to the wicked? Certainly the psalmist said so, for after confessing that his feet almost slipped, he described his envy that the wicked seem to have no struggles. They are free from sicknesses, burdens, and human ills, and they increase in wealth (Ps. 73:1–5; cf. Prov. 24:12). But after entering the sanctuary, the psalmist realized that the wicked themselves are short-lived and that envy had grieved his heart (Ps. 73:17–22).[15]

In translating the teaching of the sages into counsel for our lives today, we must note that attitudes not only inform our actions, they circle back to work their influence on the life of the heart. In our day, we may not be troubled by the success of those who act unjustly; we usually despise politicians, executives, or accountants who betray public trust in order to swell their

---

15. See also J. C. McCann, "Wisdom's Dilemma: The Book of Job, the Final Form of the Book of Psalms, and the Entire Bible," in *Wisdom, You Are My Sister*, ed. M. L. Barre (CBQMS 29; Washington, D.C.: Catholic Biblical Association of America, 1997), 18–30.

own pockets. But we do envy those who through talent and fame seem to live lives that do not extend beyond their own comforts and desires. Who wouldn't want to be a highly paid model, actor, or athlete after seeing all the good things that come their way?

Perhaps we also feel cheated that these rewards go to some but not to us. Looking at what we do not have, we forget that so many have so much less. As an antidote, these sages recommended acquiring the treasures of wisdom and using them to look out for others, holding back those who are heading toward death. In our envy of those who have so much, have we neglected those who are worse off than ourselves? "Deliver them," says the sage, for no one can claim ignorance; lack of attention is no excuse.

Envy is a power, but so is wisdom; battles are won—not on strength and weapons alone but on counsel and strategy (24:5–6). Action directed toward a wrong goal can sometimes be worse than no action at all. Therefore, we must also recognize that we need wisdom to point us in the right direction and to give us confidence that we are empowered in our movement toward good goals. The reference to power suggests that we stand against evil, speaking rightly when others speak falsely and resisting those who take what little others have in order to enrich themselves. The positive example of wisdom's strength encourages us to speak against the wicked one, who opens his lips to speak mischief (24:2), and against the fool, who does not open his mouth when a righteous word is needed (24:7). It may even mean to speak out that our culture is going the wrong way when it promotes envy's lies that "one can never be too rich or too thin."

Again, this teaching sets out two paths with no foot traffic in between. We can either envy the wicked or we can take our stand against their violence. As these teachers portray it, neutrality is not an option. "If you falter in times of trouble, how small is your strength" (24:10). In sum, we must take the counsel against envy of the wicked and use it to teach us about envy in general. Envy will either drive us toward the wicked and their indifference or toward those who need someone to speak and act on their behalf. The sages tell us to take our eyes off the prosperous and put them on those who need us.

Trusting God and king. True wisdom is a power unlike any other, for it never abuses, even as it cannot be abused. Other forms of power can be perverted, and the teachers present their warnings in 24:13–22. The lecture begins with the metaphor of nourishing honey. Just as honey is sweet to the taste, wisdom is sweet to "the soul" (or "life," *nepeš*, 24:14); one who enjoys it has a future, unlike the wicked (24:16, 20). Step one, therefore, is obvious enough: Do not lie in wait against the house of the righteous, especially if that house is established by wisdom (24:3, 15), for you will fail. The righteous fall and rise, even seven times; the wicked only fall once. But when the wicked fall, step two is more challenging: Do not gloat or rejoice, and (we may infer) certainly do not work to bring it about. Why become like them? Better to trust in the work of Yahweh.

Surprisingly, the sages instruct us to practice emotional indifference to the wicked, or at least to refuse to indulge our reactions to their fortunes. If we are not to envy their rise, neither are we to be glad at their fall. Perhaps this response is important because there is an ever-present danger of becoming like them in attitude and action. If we are not to plot violence, neither are we to seek vengeance for it (24:15–18). Leave those who do violence to God and the king, and they will take care of them (24:21–22).

It is folly to attack the righteous, for they will rise; it is folly to rebel against Yahweh and the king, for they will not be overcome (cf. Ps. 2). To do so is foolish, for it is a rejection of Yahweh's righteous rule. So the young David refused to stretch out his hand against Yahweh's anointed, even though King Saul meant to do him harm; at most, he would only damage a corner of his garment and steal his spear (1 Sam. 24:1–13; 26:1–25). Absalom, by contrast, not only sought to kill the king; he stole the favor of the people by proclaiming their every grievance as righteous (2 Sam. 15:1–12).

Perhaps here too is the basis for Jesus' teaching on turning the other cheek, refusing to resist an enemy (Matt. 5:39), as well as the basis for the teaching that we are to overcome evil with good (Rom. 12:21). In Bible survey classes, we always have interesting discussions about the bloody Bible that glories in the conquests in Exodus and Joshua. Answers to the problem of war in the Old Testament do not come easily, but some things are clear: Murder was always distinguished from warfare, yet underneath it all is the awareness that the two are both rooted in violence. Peter Craigie put it well when he said, "Violence begets violence and nothing else."[16]

If it is true that the righteous have a future and the wicked do not (a reverse of our common perceptions), then we see that both life and death are not in our keeping. Therefore we will not take vigilante action but will rather trust the larger wisdom of the community, including that of the king. The teaching of the sages assumes that the king will act rightly; if he does not, a new scenario comes into play, as is written in the history of Israel. "Do not rebel," in this context, means do not seek to overthrow a just system for your own gain.

Every saying in 24:15–22 makes some reference to the fate of the wicked, and so we look to see what is new and expanded here, especially the

---

16. P. C. Craigie, *The Problem of War in the Old Testament* (Grand Rapids: Eerdmans, 1978); see also T. R. Hobbs, *A Time for War: A Study of Warfare in the Old Testament* (Wilmington, Del.: Michael Glazier, 1989).

surprising teaching of 24:17–18. What Yahweh will do, who can know? He will bring calamity, but he may turn from wrath. Thus, we are to learn to weep at the death of the wicked, not rejoice. God told Jonah, who "fretted" over the plant (Jon. 4:1, 4, 9; cf. Prov. 24:19), not to fret over his plan to save Nineveh. He told Ezekiel that he takes no pleasure in the death of the wicked (Ezek. 18:23). Here is a warning against vengeance and the toll it takes on our souls. If it takes wisdom to trust that the righteous will rise, it also takes wisdom to believe that the wicked will not. It is wrong to seek the harm of the righteous, but it is equally wrong to seek the harm of the wicked. Vengeance is a real desire, and, like all desires, it must submit to discipline.

Translating the principle of these teachings for our own situation, we recognize that vengeance and *Schadenfreude* (joy at the troubles of one's enemy) can be the ugly mirror image of envy; both display a lack of confidence in Yahweh's rule and overestimate our own strength. The final words of 24:22 in Hebrew, "Who can know," set limits on even the knowledge of the wise (24:4–5). There is One who knows and weighs hearts, and that One will repay (24:12). Our role is to deliver those in need, not to punish the wicked. While some may take advantage of another, we also may make too much of our power to avenge wrongs. This teaching is an argument in support of the systems of jurisprudence, as flawed as they are, and perhaps the first steps toward an ethic of nonviolent resistance to evil. We are never to respond to evil by plotting or even hoping for evil in return (cf. 24:28–29). Our response takes root in trust.

Diligence. Finally, the sages once again use the example of the sluggard to teach diligence. The appendix to the "sayings of the wise" (24:23–34) combines direct teaching on jurisprudence with indirect teaching on laziness through the metaphor of the overgrown field. The direct teaching speaks to judges and plaintiffs alike; it is not good to show partiality in judging or to call the wicked righteous, nor is it good to bear false witness against the neighbor or to plot revenge (24:28–29). In both cases, the honest answer, the straightforward word, is like a kiss on the lips (24:26), as self-interest is set aside in favor of truth and as a wise one speaks truth instead of plotting to do wrong or repay a wrong (cf. 24:1–2, 8–9, 15–22).

It may seem strange to interweave this teaching with advice about fields and houses, but the phrase "build your house" (24:27) directs the reader to wisdom that is indispensable for the task (24:3). If the house is a symbol for acquiring wisdom in heart, mind, and practice, then right speaking in the community, a proper response to neighbors both righteous and wicked (holding back the unjust word), is like preparing the fields first or putting the most important tasks first. Perhaps this is another way of saying that the work of wisdom comes before any other work; to neglect it is to allow one's life to become overgrown with all sorts of thorns and weeds. If it is wisdom that fills the rooms of the house (24:4), laziness invites poverty to come like a bandit (24:34), and to be poor in wisdom and heart is to be poor indeed.

The indirect teaching of the field metaphor brings home the point of 24:13–22 as well as the entire teaching of the "sayings of the wise" (22:17–24:34). Wisdom comes first, and all else follows: "Wisdom is supreme; therefore get wisdom" (4:7). In the individual proverbs, we saw that the sluggard is like stinging vinegar and smoke to the one who hires him as a messenger (10:26). Here a sluggard is one who has not learned to take care of himself, to serve an employer, or to be a responsible member of a community. To be lazy about the matters of wisdom is to make a mess of everything else. Just as a fool heads for bed without having prepared the field and goes against the basic principles of life and survival, so fools ignore the values of wisdom and truth in word and deed and find themselves in an overgrown tangle of weeds.

ATTITUDES. Three striking metaphors of house, honey, and field commend the life of wisdom in the face of temptations to seek other paths to the good life. The sages who passed on these teachings recognize that those who spurn wisdom or choose evil often enjoy great success and provoke our envy, and that envy may be the reason why we hope they will fall. The wise ones of old also recognize that these responses are natural, even as they counsel us to do what is unnatural—to look for those who need rescue, to forego the pleasure of revenge, and to accomplish all that through the power of right speaking. We have observed that in general, power is subject to perversion and abuse, but the power of wisdom is by definition directed to building community life, not destroying it, protecting others instead of seeking their downfall.

Whence comes violence and greed, envy and revenge, except from a feeling of emptiness and a sense of shortfall? These teachings remind us that in choosing wisdom, we acquire a home and stores aplenty, that we have food that is delicious and nourishing, and that these come with responsibility to watch over our fields and work them. If we teach against envy then, we must also teach about the house and its treasures; if we speak against vengeance, we must also speak about the rich taste of honey and its future hope; and if we speak against laziness and irresponsibility, we must speak about the blessings that come on those who are diligent to speak and judge rightly. In other words, we who preach and teach are charged to point toward the fullness and richness that so many pass by in their pursuit of vanities. Hard work indeed!

So, for example, we have said that we may or may not envy the wicked, but we certainly envy the rich and famous. In a recent television interview, the actor Michael J. Fox spoke about coming to terms with his diagnosis of Parkinson's disease. He went through all the stages of grief: denying, raging, bargaining, drinking to beat depression, and finally coming to accept the limitations of his life. He said the illness shook him out of the fantasy that he lived in a world that only answered "Yes" and pushed him to confront the conflicts with friends and family that the fantasy produced. Recognizing that his powers were not unlimited, he turned his attention away from the world of accomplishment and acquisition and toward starting a foundation to keep the disease from exacting its toll on others.

Fox also identified the irony that the losses that came with the illness also brought gains of insight and maturity. Purposefully moving in his seat to minimize the involuntary motions that come with Parkinson's, he said, "When I could not be physically still, I finally learned to become inwardly still." If the fantasies of a powerful and acquisitive life can seduce an actor to a sense of exaggerated self-importance, we can see that it would easily tempt others to actually wish others evil or even plot violence and harm. It is better, say the sages, to steer clear of any envy of power that destroys and embrace the power that builds and establishes (24:3–4).

Power and service. A problem remains: Is not that power of wisdom a power for winning wars (24:5–6), and are not victories in war simple triumphs of the will? We have also seen that the metaphor of battle is about struggling against the naked exercise of power, a battle for the soul, and no one has understood that better than Charles Colson. Given a "second life" after being released from prison, Colson founded the Prison Fellowship ministry to work for restoration instead of recrimination in our penitentiary systems.

A few years after writing *Born Again*, Colson wrote a series of columns for the Prison Fellowship newsletter, calling them "my struggles to confess Christ 'where the battle rages.'" He quoted Athanasius' call to stand "*contra mundum*— against the world" and the words of John Wesley: "Making an open stand against all the ungodliness and unrighteousness which overspreads our land as a flood is one of the noblest ways of confessing Christ in the face of his enemies."[17] One of those columns was entitled "The Problem of Power," warning Christians that "worldly power is not inherently evil, but it is inherently corrupting," and adding that political idealists and religious leaders alike can become captive to maintaining political access instead of service.[18]

---

17. C. Colson, *Who Speaks for God? Confronting the World with Real Christianity* (Westchester, Ill.: Crossway, 1985), 12–13.
18. Ibid., 38–41.

Speaking of his days in the White House, he remembered that he was especially struck by religious leaders who thundered like prophets as they rehearsed what they would tell the President, only to become quiet lambs when led into the power and prestige of the Oval Office.

The paradox, Colson later wrote, is that loving service is a form of power that stands in direct opposition to the power of the world that seeks to control. Therefore, the first step toward service and advocacy is to release the need for control. Colson cited Solzhenitsyn's discovery that in surrendering all illusions of control of his safety and comfort in the gulag, he became free of his captive's power. Also citing Paul, "My power is made perfect in weakness ... when I am weak, then I am strong" (2 Cor. 12:9–10), Colson recalled his own experience of visiting the largest prison in Peru, encouraging the Christians there, and then having access to speak to the government's highest leaders about the prisoners. "They wanted to meet me, not because of any power or influence I had, but because of our work in the prisons.... Whatever authority I had in speaking to these powerful men came not from my power but from serving the powerless."[19] Colson spoke of his desire to "rescue those being led away to death," whether they live in prisons or presidential mansions.

Thus, we come back to the goal of this little manual of public and political service, to serve those in power and those in need, and more particularly to serve both by speaking honestly. We serve when we tell the truth about ourselves, when we insist that truth be told with regard for others, and when we refuse dishonest testimony and insist that right judgments be spoken. Service to those in power must not be at the expense of the powerless. The purpose of this set of writings was stated at the start, to teach true and reliable words so that sound answers might be returned (22:21). The same truth is stated at the end: "An honest answer is like a kiss on the lips" (24:26).

In the view of the sages, the basic commitment to speaking truthfully is the best way to demonstrate fear of God and king; to fail in that commitment to speak honestly is to have no foundation for anything else. If the "words of the wise" and its appendix have anything to teach us, it is that serving honestly and faithfully is hard work, that the snares and temptations are always before us, and that they are often hidden under the camouflage of seeking what appears to be good. It is natural to act out of greed, envy, or a desire for vengeance, for it appears that we only want what is good. However, we will be surprised to learn that faithful service is the path toward what is good, even as we learn that it is in giving that we receive.

---

19. C. Colson, "The Power Illusion," in *Power Religion: The Selling Out of the Evangelical Church*, ed. M. S. Horton (Chicago: Moody Press, 1992), 29–30; reprinted from *Kingdoms in Conflict* (New York and Grand Rapids: W. Morrow and Zondervan, 1987).

Proverbs 25:1–28

These are more proverbs of Solomon, copied by the men of Hezekiah king of Judah:

²It is the glory of God to conceal a matter;
  to search out a matter is the glory of kings.
³As the heavens are high and the earth is deep,
  so the hearts of kings are unsearchable.
⁴Remove the dross from the silver,
  and out comes material for the silversmith;
⁵remove the wicked from the king's presence,
    and his throne will be established through
      righteousness.
⁶Do not exalt yourself in the king's presence,
  and do not claim a place among great men;
⁷it is better for him to say to you, "Come up here,"
  than for him to humiliate you before a nobleman.
What you have seen with your eyes
⁸   do not bring hastily to court,
  for what will you do in the end
    if your neighbor puts you to shame?
⁹If you argue your case with a neighbor,
  do not betray another man's confidence,
¹⁰or he who hears it may shame you
  and you will never lose your bad reputation.
¹¹A word aptly spoken
  is like apples of gold in settings of silver.
¹²Like an earring of gold or an ornament of fine gold
  is a wise man's rebuke to a listening ear.
¹³Like the coolness of snow at harvest time
  is a trustworthy messenger to those who send him;
  he refreshes the spirit of his masters.
¹⁴Like clouds and wind without rain
  is a man who boasts of gifts he does not give.
¹⁵Through patience a ruler can be persuaded,
  and a gentle tongue can break a bone.
¹⁶If you find honey, eat just enough—
  too much of it, and you will vomit.

¹⁷ Seldom set foot in your neighbor's house—
   too much of you, and he will hate you.
¹⁸ Like a club or a sword or a sharp arrow
   is the man who gives false testimony against his
      neighbor.
¹⁹ Like a bad tooth or a lame foot
   is reliance on the unfaithful in times of trouble.
²⁰ Like one who takes away a garment on a cold day,
   or like vinegar poured on soda,
   is one who sings songs to a heavy heart.
²¹ If your enemy is hungry, give him food to eat;
   if he is thirsty, give him water to drink.
²² In doing this, you will heap burning coals on his head,
   and the LORD will reward you.
²³ As a north wind brings rain,
   so a sly tongue brings angry looks.
²⁴ Better to live on a corner of the roof
   than share a house with a quarrelsome wife.
²⁵ Like cold water to a weary soul
   is good news from a distant land.
²⁶ Like a muddied spring or a polluted well
   is a righteous man who gives way to the wicked.
²⁷ It is not good to eat too much honey,
   nor is it honorable to seek one's own honor.
²⁸ Like a city whose walls are broken down
   is a man who lacks self-control.

Original Meaning

"ALSO THESE ARE proverbs of Solomon" reads the Hebrew literally, but this superscription also names a second king, "Hezekiah king of Judah," and it credits his men with preserving these proverbs. Just as two kings are named in this superscription, so also many of the sayings in 25:1–29:27 are meant to be read and interpreted as pairs, one shedding more light on the other. Most interpreters find a two-part structure in the section as well: a concentration of nature similes in chapters 25–27 and contrasts between the righteous and the wicked in chapters 28–29.

Moreover, the message of chapters 25–27 is directed toward servants and messengers, while many of the sayings of chapters 28–29 are addressed to rulers.[1] In the middle of this section is a pastoral poem (27:23–27) that also speaks to the responsibilities of kings and servants. Similes and comparisons take on the quality of riddles. The difficulty of translating these proverbs also leads to much head scratching, as the NIV text notes indicate.

Chapter 25 forms a subsection with repetition of words at the beginning and end ("glory/honor" and "search out/seek" in vv. 2, 27; "honey" in vv. 16, 27).[2] Van Leeuwen presents a structure that alternates between sayings and admonitions (S and A) as well as the dimension of good and evil (+ and -):[3]

Introduction: S + (vv. 2–5)
I   A–(vv. 6–10)
    S + (vv. 11–15)
II A. A–(vv. 16–17)
    S–(vv. 18–20)
II B. A + (vv. 21–22)
    S–(vv. 23–27)

However, two characters, the king and the neighbor, figure prominently throughout. Sayings about right speaking and neighbor love bring court and common together:

Kings and honors (25:1–7)
Neighbors and testimony (25:8–10)
Rulers and words (25:11–15)
Neighbors good and bad (25:16–20)
Waters and words (25:21–26)
Honey and honor (25:27–28)

Kings and Honors (25:1–7)

PROVERBS ABOUT THE king and honors explore the mysteries of authority and status.

25:1. The phrase "proverbs of Solomon" is identical with 1:1 and 10:1, but here it specifies that "these also" (lit.) were "copied by the men of

---

1. See the outline of the book of Proverbs in the introduction.

2. G. Bryce, "Another Wisdom 'Book' in Proverbs," *JBL* 91 (1972): 145–57; and *A Legacy of Wisdom: The Egyptian Contribution to the Wisdom of Israel* (Lewisburg, Pa.: Bucknell Univ. Press, 1979), 135–62. Bryce proposes a structure that alternates between praise of the king and condemnation of the wicked: king, vv. 2–3; wicked, vv. 4–5; king, vv. 6–15; wicked, vv. 16–26.

3. R. C. Van Leeuwen, *Context and Meaning in Proverbs 25–27* (SBLDS 96; Atlanta: Scholar's Press, 1988), 64–65. Meinhold, *Die Sprüche*, 2:416, includes v. 28.

Hezekiah king of Judah." The Hebrew root of the verb "copy" (ʿtq) carries the idea of moving (cf. Gen. 12:8; 26:22), perhaps in moving the sayings from another collection to this one, perhaps in passing the sayings on to others. The mention of Hezekiah's men points to a tradition of collecting and arranging the sayings to be passed on to another generation.[4]

Many of these proverbs speak of kings, but Hezekiah and Solomon had more than that in common. Both are remembered for their wonderful exploits of leadership but also for leaving kingdoms that did not survive them. Solomon's was split, Hezekiah's lost, each downfall taking place after their reigns. The allusion calls readers to pay attention to those character qualities and practices that build up community life instead of tearing it down.

25:2. Previous introductions to "proverbs of Solomon" were followed by instructions to sons (1:8; 10:1), but here the focus is on the king, and this theme continues through verse 7. Kings find glory in searching out matters that God has concealed, not in conquests or in great accumulations of wealth.[5] Kings were recipients of divine wisdom in the ancient Near East,[6] and so Solomon asked for such wisdom (1 Kings 3:16–28); thus, nothing was hidden from him (1 Kings 10:3).

Each of the two lines of this proverb begins and ends with the same Hebrew words; it can be translated: "Glory of God to conceal a matter, but glory of kings to search out a matter." The word for "matter" in most other contexts means "word" (*dabar*), but can we not say that God conceals secrets of creation in both? It may be that the wise make clever sayings to mimic the recalcitrant secrets of the created order; they hide truth in order to reveal it, or in this case, to invite seekers to investigate. It is also a king's duty to search out matters of truth in human affairs, "winnowing out evil with his eyes" (20:8).

25:3. Kings may search out a matter (25:2), but their own hearts are unsearchable, as high as the heavens and deep as the earth. Just as no one can fathom all there is to know of creation or the greatness of Yahweh, who brought it into being (Job 5:9; Ps. 145:3; Isa. 40:28), so the heart of the king is never fully known, perhaps even to himself (Jer. 7:10). But why is this important? (1) It

4. M. Carasik, "Who Were the 'Men of Hezekiah' (Proverbs 25:1)?" *VT* 44 (1994): 289. Carasik believes that the superscription is a canonical allusion to Hezekiah's story in 2 Kings 18–19.

5. The word for God (ʾlohim) is only used in two other proverbs, both with the verb "to find" (mṣʾ): knowledge of God (2:5) and favor of God and humanity (3:4). God is the one who knows where hidden wisdom is found, leaving humans to search it out (Job 11:7–10; 28:3, 11, 20–21).

6. L. Kalugila, *The Wise King: Studies in Royal Wisdom as Divine Revelation in the Old Testament and its Environment* (CBOT 15; Lund: LiberLäromedel/Gleerup, 1980).

shows that the king's breadth and depth of understanding are great. (2) God and king are associated in Proverbs 24:21−22 with a warning about not knowing the calamities they can bring—we dare not imagine that we can figure them out. However, the God who conceals also reveals what we should know and obey (Deut. 29:28−29). To paraphrase Mark Twain, it is better to follow what we do understand rather than worry about what we do not.

25:4−5. These two proverbs are linked by the catchword "remove" or drive out, as well as by parallel form and repetition of Hebrew sounds. Although each saying can stand alone, the first states the general principle while the second names the specific situation of rebellion and judgment treated in the previous chapter (24:21−26; cf. 16:12; 20:28; 29:14). The puzzle of "material" that comes out of (or "from," NIV text note) the smith's fire may best be understood as a technical term that encompasses both the refining and the casting of the metal, used for the calf that came out of the fire (Ex. 32:24) and the weapon "forged" (Isa. 54:16−17).[7] No one prefers a corrupt government any more than anyone wants impure silver; it is in this sense that the throne is "established through righteousness." The king searches out matters (Prov. 25:2) so that he can remove wickedness from his presence.

25:6−7. A prohibition and a "better than" saying are paired by not only theme but also by the terms for up and down, small and great. The saying in verse 6 is also linked with verse 5 by the phrase "king's presence" (cf. 25:1−3; 22:29). If the king will not tolerate the wicked, neither will he tolerate sycophants and hangers-on who hope to gain something by hobnobbing with people of status and means. The prohibition is clear: Do not put yourself in the company of the great; let the king bestow that honor. If you claim it for yourself, you will be put in your place, (lit.) "a lower place before a noble" (cf. 16:19; 29:23); it is better to choose humility than to be humiliated.[8] There are three "do not" prohibitions in 25:6, 8, and 9, with three corresponding instances of shame in the eyes of others for being too proud, litigious, or talkative. It is better to show restraint in all three cases, to hold back and take your time.

Neighbors and Testimony (25:8−10)

THESE THREE SAYINGS move matters out of the royal court and into community, warning against hasty lawsuits and reckless testimony against a neighbor.

---

7. R. C. Van Leeuwen, "A Technical Metallurgical Usage of *yṣ'*," *ZAW* 98 (1986): 112−13, takes v. 5 as a paradigm for the whole chapter.

8. Clifford, *Proverbs*, 221, points out that it is also possible to translate "to humble yourself" or "lower yourself," preserving the up and down imagery.

25:8. As the verse division and text note show, verse 8 is not an easy one to translate. Does the line "what [or who] your eyes see" refer to the nobleman of verse 7 or a matter brought too quickly to court (see NIV text note)? There is a connection with verses 6–7; just as one should not move too quickly to a high position, so one should not be too quick to contend that one is right before a judge. Your neighbor may prove you wrong (cf. 18:17; 11:12).

25:9–10. "Your neighbor" (*re'eka*) and "argue your case" (*rib*) and "shame" link verses 8 with verses 9 and 10, as does the prohibition followed by "lest" (*pen*). If it is foolish to go before legal authorities too quickly, it is also possible to speak rashly when the time comes to argue a case. Unrelated assaults on character come easy when one has damaging secrets to divulge, but such attempts at disgrace usually backfire. The result is shame plus a bad reputation that never goes away.

Rulers and Words (25:11–15)

METAPHORS OF JEWELRY and weather describe words, both loving and careless.

25:11–12. Rather than misuse speech in mistaken testimony or slander (cf. 25:8–10), words are meant to be spoken at the right time for good purposes. Just as a jewelry maker sets a finely wrought apple of gold into its silver setting, wise people know how to bring the right word to a situation. Each displays a beauty that is the mark of a skilled artist. What is the "word aptly spoken"?[9] It can be a word of reproof or correction, yet it must find a receptive listener (15:23).[10] The sender must be careful not only to craft persuasive words but also to exercise discernment in determining when it is best to speak and when to keep silent.

25:13–15. A proverb about the power of persuasive speaking is preceded by a pair of sayings about personal reliability, all three together showing the difference between speaking faithfully and falsely. It is not clear whether the cool snow comes from the skies during a late harvest or from the high mountains during the summer harvest. Either way, the point of comparison is the refreshment it brings, similar to the refreshment one feels when one has confidence in a messenger (cf. 25:25; also 13:17; 22:21).

---

9. Some translate "aptly" as "finely wrought." Garrett, *Proverbs*, 207, makes an interesting case that the dual form of the word might be read as "on its wheels," the two wheels being like the two lines of the proverb.

10. Here is an appreciation for the role of the hearer in communication: the "receptor reigns" (C. H. Kraft, *Communication Theory for Christian Witness*, rev. ed. [Maryknoll, N.Y.: Orbis, 1991]).

Gifts promised but not given are (lit.) "false" (NIV "he does not have," 25:14; cf. 25:18; 26:28). This verse reminds readers of previous sayings about gifts and influence (18:16; 19:6; 21:14). Yet attempts at influence can fail or backfire; it is better to be a person of patience (lit., "long of nose," i.e., slow to anger, cf. 14:29; 15:18; 16:32) and gentleness. The soft tongue that breaks a bone (25:15) speaks of quiet determination that persuades. To be quiet and slow to anger is not a sign of weakness but of power (cf. 16:32).

Neighbors Good and Bad (25:16–20)

AFTER DESCRIBING THE words that persuade a ruler, the attention returns to issues of speaking and living with one's neighbors.

25:16–17. Like the pair at 25:4–5, here a metaphor is applied to a specific situation. Another saying on temperance recognizes that honey is a treat few will refuse (24:13), but the taste can, as the abbot said to Romeo, become "loathsome in its own deliciousness." The intense flavor that makes honey so desirable is also what demands moderation (23:1–3, 6–8). Just as too much of a good thing becomes the opposite, so friends and neighbors are good, even sweet, as long as visits are not too frequent or too long. The phrase "too much of xx" is repeated to underline the point, as is the admonition to (lit.) "make rare" one's steps, using the root often translated as "precious" for stones or jewels (3:15; 20:15; 24:14).

25:18–20. This trio of sayings uses experiences of pain to describe people who cannot be trusted or counted on. Linked with the verse before by the repetition of "neighbor," verse 18 compares weapons designed for war with false testimony, which is also designed to injure (Ex. 20:16). Unlike the soft tongue that is strong enough to break bones (Prov. 25:15), weapons like these are meant to coerce, not persuade. Bad teeth and lame feet cannot be relied on to do their jobs; moreover, they are often painful. Therefore, trusting in unfaithful people is a lot like bearing down on a sore foot or trying to eat with an aching tooth; the word for "unfaithful" may even denote treachery (*bgd*, 25:19; cf. 11:3; 21:18).

One who sings songs to a heavy heart (25:20) probably does not mean to cause pain, but the poor timing has the effect of pulling off a needed coat or dissolving soda with vinegar (cf. 25:11–12 on right timing).[11] In each case, what is needed is lost or missing, particularly the word of comfort or understanding. Each action is inappropriate and therefore hurtful.

---

11. The LXX has "vinegar on a wound" (followed by NRSV), similar to the vinegar on the teeth (10:26).

Waters and Words (25:21–26)

IMAGES OF WATERS good and bad illustrate the importance of speaking well and doing good.

25:21–22. Rather than taking away a needed coat or singing songs to the sad, one should practice kindness, even to one's enemies, giving food to the hungry and water to the thirsty (cf. 25:25). Jesus spoke of kindness to one's enemy, quoting this proverb and the ancient tradition it represents,[12] as did the apostle Paul (Matt. 5:43–48; Rom. 12:17–20).

But what does it mean to heap burning coals on the enemies' head? Three of the four lines of Proverbs 25:21–22 are clear, so we should keep Yahweh's reward for kindness to enemies at the forefront as we try to make sense of a puzzling image. Interpretations have for the most part followed one of two options set forth in antiquity: the burning coals either symbolize "burning pangs of shame" that lead to repentance (Augustine and Jerome) or the final punishment of an enemy who refuses to be reconciled, even after being fed (Origen and Chrysostom).[13] The search for a similar practice in ancient Near Eastern culture has discovered a variety of practices: Coals placed in a tray were carried on the head as a gift to the poor or as a sign of repentance; burning coals were also placed directly on the head to punish, to heal wounds, or to relieve suffering for a person dying of rabies!

Whatever the ancient referent, the solution seems to be in the reversal of the expected; just as songs to a troubled heart are out of place (25:20), so is kindness to an enemy. If a gentle tongue can break bone (25:15), so kindness is a power that overcomes any enemy, like dumping hot coals on an invading army trying to scale a wall (Ps. 140:9–10). Even if one's enemy hates this show of love, takes it as judgment, or finds his head burning with shame, at least Yahweh approves and will reward it.

25:23–24. Two sayings about anger and quarreling imply that paying attention to how one speaks can make a difference. The saying in verse 23 not only requires interpretation of the comparison but also asks the reader to make a connection with the other saying about wind and rain (25:14). The sly tongue is (lit.) a "hidden" (*sater;* cf. "conceal," *str,* in 25:2) tongue, which some take to be whispering or backbiting. Others believe the north wind, which usually does not bring rain in Israel, is also "hid-

---

12. *Amenemope,* 5:1–9, in Lichtheim, *AEL,* 2:150: "Don't raise an outcry against one who attacks you, Nor answer him yourself.... Lift him up, give him your hand. Leave him (in) the hands of the god; Fill his belly with bread of your own, that he be sated and weep."

13. See S. Segert, "Live Coals Heaped on the Head," in *Love and Death in the Ancient Near East: Essays in Honor of Marvin H. Pope,* ed. J. H. Marks and R. M. Good (Guilford, Conn.: Four Quarters, 1987): 159–64.

den."[14] Secret words about others will be heard and produce their results, and so anger and quarreling may drive an embattled spouse out of the house (25:24). The quarrelsome wife proverbs symbolize folly, a contrast to the wife who earns her husband's praise (31:10—31; see the discussion of the identical 21:9).

25:25—26. A pair of similes compare good and bad sources of drinking water to the positive and negative experiences of life. To people who relied on messengers instead of e-mail, good news from a faraway land was like cold water on a parched throat. The news might be of family, or it might be about the success of a king's army. The word for "cold" is rare; its root is used only six times in the Old Testament, and the only other occurrence in Proverbs associates cool temper with restrained speech (17:27). Both verse 25 and the saying in verse 13 bring together images of cool refreshment with a messenger.

As refreshing as a cold drink can be, it is not always available, however; sometimes the source is contaminated. Verse 26 plays on expectations; one expects a spring to provide drinkable water and one expects the righteous to remain true to character. Ezekiel rebuked both the Egyptian pharaoh and the leaders of Israel for stirring up the water with their feet, making it muddy and unusable (Ezek. 32:2; 34:18). Whether the "righteous man who gives way to the wicked" is a victim or someone who fails to stand for righteousness and protect others (cf. Prov. 24:11), the outcome for those who need the clear water of fair treatment is the same.

Honey and Honor (25:27–28)

TWO PROVERBS ABOUT self-discipline and restraint use metaphors drawn from the field and the city. Honey again is used to recommend moderation (cf. 25:16), but this time in comparison with seeking one's own honors (lit., "the search of their glory is glory," or "to seek glory upon glory," repeating the roots *ḥkr* and *kbd* from 25:2).[15] If kings find their glory in searching out the

---

14. Garrett, *Proverbs*, 209, paraphrases the difficult grammar: "As a cold wind gives birth to rains, so cold looks give birth to a storm of slander."

15. Bryce ("Another Wisdom 'Book,'" 145–57) observed an inclusio, in which nearly every root of 25:2–3 repeats in 25:27. Efforts to read the difficult Hebrew and account for the differences in the ancient versions have led some to emend the text. One that follows Latin Vulgate translates, "It is not good to eat too much honey, and he who searches for glory will be distressed" (or "oppressed") (A. A. Macintosh, "A Note on Proverbs 25:27," *VT* 20 [1970]: 112–14). Garrett, *Proverbs*, 210, emends to read, "But seeking out difficult things is glorious," comparing the bad of excess sweets with the good of unraveling the sages' riddles. The translation itself is a riddle that humbles the interpreter!

matters of wisdom and right rule, so should those who read these sayings, forsaking the quest for honor (25:6–7).[16] A person who does not know when to stop eating honey or to refrain from seeking accolades is a person who lacks self-control—not only troublesome to others but also dangerous to self, vulnerable like a city breached by attackers. Self-discipline is self-defense. This teaching on glory and folly continues into the next chapter.

CHAMPIONING RESTRAINT. If anything characterizes this new section of proverbs, it is a riddling quality, each pair or cluster of sayings asking: How is x like y? Metaphors of general experience are applied to particular situations, as "too much of a good thing" is first compared to eating honey and then to visiting and self-promotion.

Sayings about the king and neighbor are also set side by side, the proverbs about neighbors proving that kings can provide good government but they cannot legislate a culture of fairness and concern. The sages never made a false split between personal character and a good society; kings and citizens alike are responsible to "remove the wicked from the king's presence" (25:5). There are no different sets of ethics for kings, courtiers, and subjects, and the ethical principles laid out here still find a place in our status-seeking and self-serving culture of consumption.[17] The sages who brought together these proverbs saw the dangers and recommended the practice of restraint, reflection, and "searching out" matters of wisdom and fairness. In particular, the sayings of this chapter recommend restraint of our tendencies toward self-advancement and of our tendencies to do violence to our neighbor.

(1) A first form of restraint is holding back on self-promotion, neither putting oneself forward in the king's presence nor gorging on one's own honors (25:6–7, 27). It is better to wait for the call to move up than to be told to move down, as Jesus made clear in his teaching on banquet seating (Luke

---

16. R. C. Van Leeuwen, "Proverbs 25:27 Once Again," *VT* 36 (1986): 105–14, translates, "To eat much honey is not good and to seek difficult things is (no) glory." This translation reads the "not" in the first clause as a double-duty negative (GKC 152, p. 478 n.1) and brings the theme in line with Job 11:7–10; Sir. 3:21–23; 7:4–7; and *Ahiqar* 47, "Do not despise that which is your lot, nor covet some great thing which is withheld from you."

17. W. Brueggemann, *Theology of the Old Testament*, 718–20, speaks of a "metanarrative of military consumerism," by which leaders and citizens alike are persuaded that well-being and happiness are secured by acquiring goods and using whatever force is needed to protect them. In his view, the Old Testament provides resources for another narrative, or "counter-testimony." See also R. Clapp, ed., *The Consuming Passion: Christianity and the Consumer Culture* (Downers Grove, Ill.: InterVarsity, 1998).

11:45; 14:7–14). The many references to up and down throughout the chapter do more than illustrate the ancients' understanding of social hierarchies; they remind us that we too are not as democratic and egalitarian as we wish to believe. We are caught up in hierarchy when we wish to be higher or better than another in accomplishments or acquisitions.

Excellence is praiseworthy, but the dangers of competition are always near. Seeking the higher place usually means that someone else has to be put lower (James 2:1–4), whereas taking the lower place lifts up both the neighbor and ourselves (James 4:6–10; cf. Eph. 4:2; 1 Peter 5:6). The sages recommend not only knowing one's place in the scheme of things but voluntarily taking the lower place by being slow to anger and quick to serve (Prov. 25:21–24). Moreover, they set proverbs about righteousness and humility side by side at the beginning and end of the chapter (25:4–7, 26–27) to remind readers that they are fruits of the same tree (cf. 3:34; 11:2; 15:33). It may be that the association with Hezekiah is intended to remind us of the king who showed off his treasures and struggled with pride (2 Kings 20:12–21; 2 Chron. 32:24–33).

(2) A second form of restraint holds back from doing harm to a neighbor. A number of the sayings call for patience in dealing with rulers and neighbors, waiting and practicing caution. Warnings about anger come in the cautions against hasty lawsuits and disclosures (25:8–10, 18) as well as the sly or "hidden" tongue and quarrels (25:23–24). The proverbs on lawsuits point out the irony that attempts to defame one's neighbor often bring shame on the witness instead. If the ancients knew how easy it was to speak and act in the heat of anger with neighbors one had to see everyday, how much more are we inclined to act rashly in encounters with those we do not know in supermarkets and on the streets.

Still, these proverbs are about the wrongs done to neighbors, those who count on us to treat them well; failure there is especially hurtful. The sages call for neighbor love and then go one step farther—teaching love for one's enemy, doing good to one who may have done harm (25:21–22). Jesus continued to teach this tradition of kindness to the enemy, adding that one should settle matters quickly before going to court and that one confront an individual before bringing the matter to the elders and congregation (Matt. 5:43–48, 25–26; 18:15–17; Luke 12:57–59). Therefore, holding back from anger also has an active component of seeking to resolve differences. The practice also heeds earlier sayings about not rejoicing in an enemy's fall (Prov. 20:22; 24:17–18); if God will judge the wicked, we are relieved of that responsibility.

Persuasive words. In place of lawsuits, the sages recommended persuasion and patience (25:15). The gentle tongue that breaks bones is a sign that words can be effective, even with someone who has more authority and power. Gentle words do more than win someone to a position, they win the other person as well. Force someone to do your will and you will have an enemy; persuade that person and you will have a friend. So false testimony works like a club, a sword, and an arrow, winning the battle and destroying any possibility for relationship (25:18).

The sages compared persuasive words to finely wrought jewelry to speak of their beauty and value. So, for example, Nabal's wife, Abigail, skillfully spoke and persuaded David against killing her husband when the man returned evil for David's good. She spoke of Nabal's folly, the strength of David, and the possibilities for regret. David said to Abigail, "Praise be to the LORD, the God of Israel, who has sent you today to meet me. May you be blessed for your good judgment and for keeping me from bloodshed this day and from avenging myself with my own hands" (1 Sam. 25:32−33). Wise speaking includes holding back troublesome words and speaking those that counsel and persuade. Persuasion sometimes takes the form of a rebuke, wise words that point out what one needs to see but cannot for any number of reasons (Prov. 25:15−16). The one who rebukes is wise, realizing the need for mutual correction. If the listener sees the same need, then that one is wise as well.

To persuade, one must be found credible by the hearer; therefore, a trustworthy messenger is refreshing to a master (25:13), but this aspect of character is woven throughout the sayings. The classical rhetoricians spoke of rhetorical *ethos* (good sense, good character, and good will) as a necessary third component of persuasion. One needs the finely wrought words of a truthful message and one needs an open listener, but without a speaker who is seen as trustworthy, nothing happens. We are persuaded by speakers we approve of and perceive as honest and competent; we take criticism and correction from those we believe are on our side.

A reputation for trustworthiness comes from reliability and sensitivity, but the absence of these is devastating. If there are some who are nowhere to be found when needed, there are others who come and do exactly the wrong thing (25:19−20). Trust is built by having the good sense to know what is required and the good will to do it. My father would rely on his record when seeking to persuade his friends or me, asking, "Have I ever steered you wrong?" He did not mean that he never made a mistake, only that he could be counted on to give counsel that would help.

In sum, the sayings of the chapter gather around the theme of holding ourselves back from excess consumption, self-advancement, and rash conflict. Holding ourselves back, we can be free to develop qualities of faithfulness, trustworthiness, and charity that do good to neighbor and enemy alike. The practice of restraint—holding back words and actions and moderating our intake of good things—allows us time for reflection so that we, like the kings of old, may search out matters, separating dross from silver and removing self-interest from our lives.

 RESTRAINT AND REFLECTION are the sages' remedies for self-centered and unwise living. On a personal level I know I need to cultivate the habit of pausing to ask whose interests are being served in a particular decision or action. Too often I have found that actions I thought were loving were not seen the same way through another person's eyes. So also our communities, governments, and churches can also act in self-deceiving ways—all the more reason to consult with those outside our circles for "a word aptly spoken" (25:11).

Knowing when to speak. Opportunities to restrain ourselves from self-promotion are probably the most obvious (25:6–7), but this does not mean that one sits on the sidelines of life, never moving out to share one's gifts and talents. Instead, we can keep watch for attempts to use our talents (not to mention friends and connections) in competitive and unseemly ways. A friend worked in an office that promised a cash prize to the employee who had the best idea for improving operations. The office staff said they did not want to compete, pooled their ideas into a videotaped skit, and used the money for a victory party. Who walked away the winner?

So also we can be quick to use damaging testimony against another (25:8–10), in and out of court, perhaps to settle a score, perhaps to lift ourselves up by putting another down. Does this mean we should never come forward with what we have seen and heard? Of course not, especially when the common good requires it. But the first step is often bringing a private word of correction to the person who needs it. In other cases, when rebukes are not heard or the danger of repeat offense is too great to risk, charges must become public.

The warning against hasty litigations and slanders is not easily applied to matters of sexual abuse of minors. Careers and lives have been ruined by charges that turned out to be the product of imagination or an attempt at revenge or mischief. However, recent exposures of sexual abuse among clergy and other guardians of public trust have shown that it is possible to err by remaining silent, especially if it is done with the intention of protecting personal or institutional interests. The proverbs' recommendation to avoid hasty action reminds us to take care to verify charges and examine motives.

Better to have a word like a beautiful ornament than to bring false testimony, make false promises of gifts, or sing false hopes to a heavy heart

(25:11–20). If inappropriate words are best withheld, the good words of teaching and correction can be held in temporary reserve, waiting for the right time and right audience. Better to be trustworthy and faithful, bringing refreshment and not pain (25:13, 19). The right word, given at the right time, can be used to teach, uplift, encourage, and even challenge. Having a track record of words and deeds that benefit others opens the way to bring a correcting word, and we know we have established such trust when people ask for our perspective. A friend pays good money to attend a weeklong workshop to improve her musicianship on the string bass. She asks her teachers to be brutally honest, and they are honest, but not without encouragement that she will become a better player.

When our comments are not requested, we can ask permission to share them. I remember a graduate seminar that was particularly rough on a student presenter, and I remember being impressed when another member of the class asked, "Would you like to hear more about this aspect of your paper, or do you have enough to work with?" Granted that it is hard to answer a question like that with "No," asking it gave attention to the relationship as well as the message. Speakers that have earned the public's trust can also bring words that inspire and challenge. If Franklin Delano Roosevelt told a nation in desperate economic times that they had nothing to fear but fear itself, Martin Luther King reminded their sons and daughters that his people had suffered hard times throughout American history. The ancient rhetoricians spoke of *kairos*, the right time to speak a word of encouragement or rebuke.

Self-control. If it is better to hold back harmful words and keep good ones in reserve, it is also better to have the defense of self-control than to lack its discipline and protection. It is better to hold back from seeking honors than to eat too much honey and get sick (25:27–28, 16). In the tradition of the church, gluttony was named one of the seven deadly sins, but gluttony is not the same as overeating. Rather, it is a spiritual problem of isolation, a turn inward that acknowledges no need for God and community. Its excesses reveal that one is eating and drinking alone, with neither thanksgiving nor responsibility. If the blessing of food and drink is most clearly seen in the communion meal that binds us to the Lord and his family the church, then the abuse of that good gift is the kind of eating that takes place without sharing and without receiving the gift of food from the hands of another. According to William S. Stafford:

> In gluttony the power of sin comes to focus on food and drink. There is a succession of stories of wrong eating in the Bible, from the fruit in the Garden of Eden, eaten so that the human pair might be "like

God," to the morsel taken by Judas before he went out into the night to betray Jesus. Those stories go to the heart of what the Christian tradition means by sin. Those meals were eaten by human beings who wished to define their identities and purposes by displacing God.[18]

However, 25:28 reminds us that to lack self-control is to be like a city without walls to protect it from attack. So also, the ancient understanding of gluttony warns us that it is like going into battle alone, a parade example of folly. It helps us understand the problem of excess, and it warns us of the dangers of self-aggrandizement and the isolation it brings. If it is possible to head too often to the neighbor's house (perhaps for help or a meal?), it is also possible in our days of individually microwaved dinners to foster a false sense of independence and security. The self-reliant person can also turn out to be lonely.

Love for enemies. It may be better to live alone on the corner of the roof than in the house with a quarrelsome wife (or husband, 25:24), but that is not how Yahweh meant it to be. It is better to be able to offer a wise word and to put a curb on one's own interests. Best of all, say the sages, is the show of kindness that needs no moderation, namely, giving food and drink even to our enemies rather than hoarding it for ourselves. So the one saying in the chapter that speaks of Yahweh's reward calls us to return good for evil (25:21). What better way to learn to discipline our self-seeking ways than to err on the side of kindness? Certainly Jesus had this in mind when he told his followers to go two miles and turn both sides of the face, although the ways this will work itself out in life are always surprising.

To illustrate the exercise of inexplicable grace in communication, Quentin Schultze tells two true stories. The first is of a couple who lost their son to a drunk driver. Consumed with the desire for revenge, they saw that the young man was prosecuted to the fullest extent of the law. However, as they learned more about his life, they began to see that the man had never received the support and care that they had given to their son. Over time, they invited their son's killer to share meals in their home as an expression of their growing love. The other story concerns a man who lost his son in a gang shooting. When he learned that one of the men convicted for the crime had been sitting in the car, he went before the judge to ask for mercy.[19]

---

18. W. S. Stafford, *Disordered Loves: Healing the Seven Deadly Sins* (Cambridge/Boston: Cowley Publications, 1994), 21. The seven deadly sins are: gluttony, lust, avarice, anger, envy, sloth, and pride. Stafford shows how we are susceptible to each and offers disciplines that lead us to grace and healing.

19. Q. J. Schultze, *Communicating for Life: Christian Stewardship in Community and Media* (Grand Rapids: Baker, 2000) 31—33.

We may show love for enemies with food and drink or with words of grace and kindness, but in every case, we learn to give and in so doing find what we really need. Restraint, reflection, and proper action—the sayings of this chapter hold out reserve and discernment as crucial for social life and personal character. Like the kings of Proverbs, we too are called to "search out a matter," that is, to investigate the situations of life to discern truth from falsehood and make responses that are faithful and wise.

Proverbs 26:1–28

¹ LIKE SNOW IN summer or rain in harvest,
  honor is not fitting for a fool.
² Like a fluttering sparrow or a darting swallow,
  an undeserved curse does not come to rest.
³ A whip for the horse, a halter for the donkey,
  and a rod for the backs of fools!
⁴ Do not answer a fool according to his folly,
  or you will be like him yourself.
⁵ Answer a fool according to his folly,
  or he will be wise in his own eyes.
⁶ Like cutting off one's feet or drinking violence
  is the sending of a message by the hand of a fool.
⁷ Like a lame man's legs that hang limp
  is a proverb in the mouth of a fool.
⁸ Like tying a stone in a sling
  is the giving of honor to a fool.
⁹ Like a thornbush in a drunkard's hand
  is a proverb in the mouth of a fool.
¹⁰ Like an archer who wounds at random
  is he who hires a fool or any passer-by.
¹¹ As a dog returns to its vomit,
  so a fool repeats his folly.
¹² Do you see a man wise in his own eyes?
  There is more hope for a fool than for him.
¹³ The sluggard says, "There is a lion in the road,
  a fierce lion roaming the streets!"
¹⁴ As a door turns on its hinges,
  so a sluggard turns on his bed.
¹⁵ The sluggard buries his hand in the dish;
  he is too lazy to bring it back to his mouth.
¹⁶ The sluggard is wiser in his own eyes
  than seven men who answer discreetly.
¹⁷ Like one who seizes a dog by the ears
  is a passer-by who meddles in a quarrel not his own.
¹⁸ Like a madman shooting
  firebrands or deadly arrows
¹⁹ is a man who deceives his neighbor
  and says, "I was only joking!"

20 Without wood a fire goes out;
  without gossip a quarrel dies down.
21 As charcoal to embers and as wood to fire,
  so is a quarrelsome man for kindling strife.
22 The words of a gossip are like choice morsels;
  they go down to a man's inmost parts.
23 Like a coating of glaze over earthenware
  are fervent lips with an evil heart.
24 A malicious man disguises himself with his lips,
  but in his heart he harbors deceit.
25 Though his speech is charming, do not believe him,
  for seven abominations fill his heart.
26 His malice may be concealed by deception,
  but his wickedness will be exposed in the assembly.
27 If a man digs a pit, he will fall into it;
  if a man rolls a stone, it will roll back on him.
28 A lying tongue hates those it hurts,
  and a flattering mouth works ruin.

Original
Meaning

THE SECOND CHAPTER of the proverbs of Solomon "copied by the men of Hezekiah" helps readers "search out matters" by comparing fools (26:1–16) and troublemakers (26:17–28; cf. 25:1–2 and the introduction to ch. 25). The chapter begins with proverbs about what is and is not "fitting"[1] and closes with proverbs about just rewards, naming consequences that are fitting. Those who learn wisdom, therefore, observe wisdom's laws of nature and social life and learn to make decisions appropriate to that which is "fitting" for the situation.

The sayings of the chapter assemble into four negative character sketches of the fool, the sluggard, the quarreler, and the deceiver, although it could be argued that verses 17–28 describe the speech habits of the same evil person.[2] Readers are to learn to recognize these types, not only to protect themselves from such people but also to protect themselves

---

1. B. Waltke, "Old Testament Interpretation Issues for Big Idea Preaching," in *The Big Idea of Biblical Preaching: Connecting the Bible to People*, ed. K. Willhite and S. Gibson (Grand Rapids: Baker, 1998), 41–52. Waltke finds the "big idea" of what is fitting (and not fitting) for the fool is the key to preaching this chapter.

2. Whybray, *The Composition of the Book of Proverbs*, 123–24, separates the quarreler and the deceiver.

from their own folly and bad intentions. The wise one must know how to deal with them all.

Fools and Sluggards Wise in Their Own Eyes (26:1–16)
No glory for fools (26:1–12)
No work for sluggards (26:13–16)

Quarrelers and Deceivers (26:17–28)
Careless and quarrelsome speech (26:17–22)
Hateful and deceptive speech (26:23–28)

Fools and Sluggards Wise in Their Own Eyes (26:1–16)

TWELVE PROVERBS OFFER instruction on avoiding or dealing with people like the fool, for the way one handles a fool can be foolish or wise in itself. The phrase "wise in his own eyes" (26:5, 12, 16) links the portraits of the fool and the sluggard.

26:1. The first three sayings about the fool are linked in their use of simile and form. There are three components to each saying, the last describing the actual folly. The first proverb imagines weather out of order: Snow does not come in summer, rain is not welcome during harvest, and so glory should not come to a fool ("glory," *kabod*, links with 26:8; cf. 17:7; 19:10; 25:27). Kings find glory in searching out matters, exploring the natural and social orders (25:1), but such work is too high for a fool, one of many reasons the fool should not expect any honors.

26:2. The second three-part saying (cf. 26:1) examines the reverse of honor, the curse. If verse 1 depicts natural order out of whack, verse 2 depicts the order as it should be—undeserved curses do not stick because, like glory to a fool, they are not fitting. The metaphors of fluttering sparrows and swallows depict birds one never sees at rest (23:5); so also an "undeserved [*ḥinnam*, lit., "for nothing"; cf. 1:11; 24:28] curse" never lands. The saying seems out of place, the only one of the first twelve verses that does not use the word "fool." Yet birds that dart are in danger (7:23; cf. 1:17; 6:5) as are birds that stray from the nest (27:8), suggesting that cursing has dangers of its own.

26:3. After showing that honor is not fitting for a fool (cf. 26:1), this three-part proverb states what is fitting: Whips make horses move, halters lead donkeys, and rods punish fools (cf. 10:13). If a rod is recommended, it is assumed that the fool is no smarter than these beasts of burden, beyond convincing by argument. More advice on dealing with the fool comes in verses 4–5.

26:4–5. This famous pair of contrasting sayings show that it is not always easy to know how to make a fitting response to a fool. It is not possible to determine whether one or both of these proverbs existed independently, although it is possible that one called out the response of the other. People often bring together dueling proverbs to show that one size does not fit all: "The early bird gets the worm, but the second mouse gets the cheese." Being wise in one's own eyes is dangerous (26:12), so perhaps the appropriate "answer" of 26:5 is the rod of 26:3, while the "answer" of debate or correction would be foolish (26:4). Both would ensure that the fool who does not listen receives no glory (26:1; cf. 9:7–9; 23:9; 29:9).

The shift from second person to third person in 26:5b may show some concern for the fool, hoping that his arrogance will be exposed and lead to a change.[3] Some argue that the point is not so much on what is fitting but on the teacher's dilemma: Although one should not have to enter into dialogue with the fool, it is the sage's job.[4]

26:6. A chiastic structure unites verses 6–10, matching proverbs on hiring or sending the fool (26:6, 10) and the "proverb in the mouth of the fool" (26:7, 9); a second proverb about glory for the fool stands at the center (26:8; cf. v. 1).[5] With the possible exception of verse 7, each depicts some sort of violence or danger. Verse 6 presents another set of threes, perhaps to indicate inappropriate action as in verses 1–3. Sending messages by unreliable types has come up before (10:26; 13:17; cf. 22:21; 25:13). It is not clear whether the harm described is done to the sender or to others, but the former is more likely.

26:7. The comparison repeats the idea of nonfunctional feet and legs from verse 6 (cf. 25:19) as well as the idea of words carried by a fool. Just as the lame cannot use their legs, so a fool cannot use a wise saying and therefore cannot be a good servant and carry a message. Anyone can memorize a collection of sayings (or principles or rules) and apply them inappropriately, just as C. S. Lewis knew that a "scholar's parrot may talk Greek." It takes wisdom to craft and deliver an apt word (25:11).

26:8. The point seems obvious; in contemporary terms, giving glory to a fool is like loading a gun. Giving honor is not only inappropriate for the fool (26:1), it is also dangerous. And there may be more here; tying the stone in the sling makes it ineffective, and the one who swings it could get hurt. Similarly, the fool who thinks he is wise is a danger to himself and others, but mostly to himself.

3. T. Hildebrandt, "Proverbial Pairs: Compositional Units in Proverbs 10–29," *JBL* 107 (1988): 210–11.

4. K. Hoglund, "The Fool and the Wise in Dialogue," in *The Listening Heart: Essays in Wisdom and the Psalms in Honor of Roland E. Murphy, O. Carm.*, ed. K. G. Hoglund et al. (Sheffield: JSOT Press, 1987): 161–80.

5. Garrett, *Proverbs*, 212.

26:9. The thornbush in the drunkard's hand (lit.) "goes up" in his hand. This ambiguous verb can either mean that the thorn goes up to pierce the drunkard's hand or that it goes up in his hand as a weapon (NEB, NRSV). Yet a thornbush does not make for a very dangerous weapon, and this may satirize the fool and his pretense to wisdom. The second line is the same as that of verse 7, perhaps to show that when spoken by a fool, a proverb has little effect.

26:10. Images of piercing weapons and wild drunkards link this proverb with the one before, but it also summarizes verses 6–10: Sending a fool creates danger for all (26:18). The Hebrew text is difficult to translate, as the many variations in the ancient versions attest.[6] The second line repeats the Hebrew consonants for "hire" (*śoker*, lit., "and hires a fool and hires a passerby"), but the same letters can be read, "and hires a fool or a drunkard passing by" (cf. *šikor* in 26:9).

26:11–12. The last two of the fool sayings describe people who are apparently incapable of learning. Fools repeat their folly, and those who think themselves wise are even worse off. Is there more to the metaphor of verse 11? Vomit is typically a sign of folly in Proverbs (23:8; 25:16), so the dog's actions make holding on to folly seem particularly distasteful. The last of the fool sayings in verse 12 presents a surprising climax. As dangerous as the fool might be, there is more chance that the fool will learn than someone "wise in his own" eyes, completing the thought of verse 5 and warning that the dangers of folly are never far from the would-be sage. The second line is repeated in 29:20.

26:13–16. These verses present a series of vignettes on the sluggard, three that demonstrate his laziness, the fourth to show that like the fool, he is "wise in his own eyes." We have met the sluggard before (6:6–9; 10:26; 13:4; 15:19; 19:24; 20:4; 21:25; 22:13; 24:30). His fearful claim about lions in the streets, identical to 22:13, is a transparent attempt to avoid going out to work.

Verse 13 reports what the sluggard *says*; verse 14 indicates that he *does* even less. The only motion one will see is his turning in bed, satirically likened here to a door on its hinge. He will not go through the door to find work; he will only mimic its motion so he can stay put.

Yet even a sluggard needs nourishment. In fact, the proverbs often portray him as someone who works too little and eats too much. The picture of a hand that is buried or hid in the dish suggests a deep scoop, but even this

---

6. D. C. Snell, "The Most Obscure Verse in Proverbs: Proverbs 26:10," *VT* 41 (1991): 350–56. Snell's proposal, "A great one makes a fool of everyone, and a drunkard is a fool (even) of passers-by," has not been widely adopted.

effort is left off since now he is too tired to bring it back to his mouth (26:15). This saying paraphrases 19:24; the first lines are identical, but the punch in the second line is different, adding the attribution "too lazy" or "weary."

Although the proverbs have associated the sluggard's behavior with folly, he does not see it that way, and perhaps this is his greatest folly of all. He is "wise in his own eyes," the hopeless status described in verses 5 and 12. The "seven" may be a sign of collective strength or an allusion to the Mesopotamian myth of seven sages who brought culture and learning to the human race before the great flood.[7]

Quarrelers and Deceivers (26:17–28)

THE SECOND HALF of chapter 26 is organized into four subunits of three proverbs,[8] each cluster defined by catchword and theme. It may be that readers are to supply the phrase "wise in his own eyes" at the conclusion of each triad, just as it was repeated throughout the first half of the chapter (26:5, 12, 16). The first two groups are linked by the theme of quarrels (26:17–19, 20–22), the second two by the theme of deception (26:23–25, 26–28). If the quarreler stirs up strife and conflict, the deceiver tries to smooth it over with lies. Troublemakers have been set next to the sluggard in Proverbs before (6:6–19; 15:18–19; 19:24–25; 20:3–4; 24:28–33).

26:17–19. Terms from these three sayings ("quarrel," "fire," "deceive") appear throughout the rest of the chapter. The chapter's second proverb about dogs (26:17; cf. v. 11) will remind some readers of President Lyndon Johnson grabbing his hound dog by the ears, but most of us would avoid provoking a dog that way. It is needless and causes pain for all involved (esp. if the dog bites), just like hasty quarreling (25:8–10; 15:18; 20:3; 22:24–25).[9] Continuing the theme of verse 17, the extended saying of verses 18–19 depicts one who does not take seriously the ruinous effects of his actions. The first part of the comparison requires the whole verse to describe the mad (or reckless) person who shoots fiery darts, arrows, and death (cf. 25:18).

26:20–22. Three proverbs about gossip, quarrels, and damage extend the theme of verses 17–19. Gossip is the wood for quarrel's fires, so remove the fuel and the fire goes out (26:20). But the potential for monetary gain in legal disputes ("strife" uses the term *rib*; cf. 26:17) traces the problem to the

---

7. Clifford, *Proverbs*, 233.

8. Van Leeuwen, *Context and Meaning in Proverbs 25–27*, 116–19.

9. A number of commentators (Clifford, Murphy, and Van Leeuwen) divide the verse after "passer-by," making the dog that one passing by. The repositioning is important since the same Heb. root is repeated in the word "meddle" (*ʾbr*). The double sense of "passing by" and "meddling" is important to the punch of the proverb.

real source, the "man of quarrel" who feeds the fire. Taken together, one can see the need to excise both the behavior and the person who stirs up quarrels, just as one takes away wood to put out a fire. If quarrels can be profitable, morsels of "gossip" can be tasty, going down to the inmost parts; the metaphor may indicate that they have a negative influence on one's mind and heart (cf. 26:24; see the comments on the identical proverb in 18:8).

26:23–25. Three proverbs develop the theme of deception from verses 18–19, describing it as an attractive surface that hides the ugliness lying beneath. The image of glaze on clay is straightforward enough (26:23), but translators differ on whether the Hebrew "silver dross" (see NIV text note) should be emended after a related Ugaritic term to "glaze." Dross removed by a smelter would look like silver when overlaid on clay, but no one would be fooled. In the same way, glaze is only a cover. "Fervent lips" are literally "burning" like flaming arrows (cf. 26:18; also 16:27; Ps. 7:13), scattering the thoughts of an evil heart. In Proverbs 26:24, the lips of a malicious man hope to disguise the deceit of the "heart" (lit., "inner being"; cf. 26:22).

The "malicious man" (26:24) is (lit.) "one who hates" (śnʾ; cf. 26:26, 28). His speech can be charming, even beautiful, like glittering silver dross, but it conceals seven abominations (26:25; cf. "seven" in 26:16 and the seven abominations in 6:16–19). In the same way, an enemy may multiply kisses (27:6).

26:26–28. Three examples of evil deeds that backfire begin with the ultimate end of deception (cf. 26:19, 23–25). Malice or "hatred" (26:26; cf. v. 28) cannot be hidden for long; when it is exposed, everyone in the assembly will know (cf. 5:14). Getting caught in a trap set for others is a common motif of Psalms as well as Proverbs (Ps. 7:15–16; 57:6); the stone will "return" just as the dog returns (šwb; cf. Prov. 26:11) to vomit. So also, the false tongue not only hurts others, it hurts itself because it leads to its own ruin. "Hates" repeats the same root as "malice" in verse 26 and "malicious" in verse 24 (śnʾ); flattery for gain is just one of hate's lying strategies.

Bridging Contexts

LEARNING TO LIVE WISELY. The sayings of chapter 26 are tied together by the theme of discerning what is fitting, and so each of the four characters show us how to avoid their habits and the trouble they cause. Van Leeuwen calls verses 1–12 a "treatise on the hermeneutics of wisdom, how one uses proverbs in ways that are fitting. Thus one learns to read proverbs and in turn, to read life."[10] The strategy extends to the

---

10. Van Leeuwen, *Context and Meaning*, 99.

rest of the chapter, for each character has not learned to read either and so is unable to match learning and life. The fool, the sluggard, the quarreler, and the deceiver each illustrate a lack of perception that fails to discern what is required for the life of wisdom. In some cases, the intentions are downright evil: "The lips of the righteous know what is fitting, but the mouth of the wicked, only what is perverse" (10:32).

The "undeserved curse does not come to rest" like the flitting birds because it is "for nothing" (*ḥinnam*, 26:2). This takes the reader back to 1:17, in which the wicked are like birds unaware of a baited trap. Just as they did not know that their violent deeds would come back upon them, so the characters of this chapter become the victims of their own folly and evil (26:27). All that has been said between that first chapter and this one has helped us understand the biblical irony that "what goes around comes around." Through the many instructions and proverbs, we have come to understand how that circle of folly works, but in reading them we also learn how we might make a wise response, doing good so that it may circle back to us.

Moreover, in these later chapters of the book, we also move from taking the clear directions of the parents' instructions to learning how to discern wise action for ourselves. We have observed that the proverbs of chapters 26–27 put more emphasis on the responsibilities of servants and messengers, while chapters 28–29 stress the responsibilities of kings (see comments in ch. 25). Therefore, we may set the proverbs of this chapter in the context of responsibilities for discernment that fall to servants, messengers, and employers but also to neighbors and community leaders.

The dangers of lack of wisdom. What stands out to readers in this chapter's collection of proverbs is that fools and evildoers cause damage and trouble, not only for themselves but also for many others. Curses (26:2), cut-off feet, violence drunk like wine (26:6), slings (26:8), thorn bushes (26:9), archers (26:10), firebrands, arrows and death (26:18), fire and strife (26:19–21, 23), and pit and stone (26:27) are all intertwined with acts of speaking, illustrating the devastating power that words grant to those who use them for harm.

However, these proverbs go on to show that while they may do damage, all words used without the guidance of wisdom ultimately fail. Each of the four characters misuses the power of speaking, trying to "do things with words" that he cannot. The fool wants to use the proverbs of the wise, but he can only speak folly (26:7, 9). The sluggard wants to answer discretely, but he can only make up fantasies that people see through (26:16, 13). The quarreler wants to use strife and gossip to his advantage, but he only succeeds in spreading fire (26:18–21); the deceiver wants to be smooth as glaze, but he cannot hide the evil in his heart (26:23–26). Each attempts to harness the power of words, only to be overpowered in the process. Fools only fool themselves. Evildoers bring evil on themselves. These character sketches help us recognize our own pretenses and bad intentions, revealing how transparent, futile, and dangerous they can be.

The sayings on the fool appear to be directed to a person who is also foolish enough to hire one as a messenger; both should know that such an honor is not fitting, even if the fool desires it. The dangers are clear, and the one who sends is responsible for the damages, at least in part (26:6–10). The proverb pair on answering the fool presents two goals: (1) We are to keep ourselves from "becoming like him," and (2) we are to keep the fool from thinking he has become like the wise (26:4–5). We must weigh the dangers to self against the benefits that might come to another. We can avoid the path of the fool by "searching out matters" (25:2) and not taking on those too great for us, and we can hold back from giving assignments to those not suited for them. One way that a reader of proverbs can become a reader of life is to become a judge of character, an ancient principle that applies today. If we value wisdom, we will look for it in others and encourage it when we find it.

Before they are sent anywhere, fools (who are wise in their own eyes) need both the rod and the appropriate answer, symbols for bringing teaching and correction together (26:3–5). We have seen that proverbs, the sayings that provoke insight and persuade, are limp and ineffective in the mouth of a fool (26:7, 9), who can recite them but does not understand them. If sages and messengers of old used proverbs in their conversations with rulers, they needed to learn how to use the right one at the right time and to follow their instruction, or the results could have been disastrous. The adulterous king David sent a proverb to his general Joab to keep secret their conspiracy to kill Uriah: "The sword devours one as well as another." David paid the price for his folly and sin as he heard his judgment pronounced in a parable (2 Sam. 11:25–12:14).

In a sense, those who send and those who are sent have much in common. Although few of us will hold something like that ancient job of messenger, the role of using our own knowledge and insight to represent another person or tradition extends into most of our lives. Diplomats and executives may be charged with representing governments and corporations, but the task of faithful representation also falls to teachers, who must understand their field of study to pass it on—and that includes teachers of the gospel. The call to learn and teach involves critical reflection, the ability to bring principles and life situation together, and so one cannot simply recite accumulated knowledge; it would sound like a proverb in the mouth of a fool.

A colleague in graduate school told me that she always started a new course asking what she needed to learn from it and how she would go about connecting it to her work. Teachers sometimes ask their students to set such goals, often in the form of a learning covenant. The point is to ask teachers and students alike to bring together accumulated knowledge and its application to ever-changing life settings. Such is the work of teaching wisdom, and in a sense, all who teach in schools, churches, and homes are called to it.

There seems to be precious little wisdom with the sluggard who works so hard to avoid work. Thus, sending a sluggard on a mission is like putting vinegar to the teeth and smoke to the eyes (10:26). Part of the problem is foolish pride, for this one too is wise in his own eyes, wiser than those who know how to answer and perhaps beyond any hope of learning (26:12, 16).

Throughout Proverbs, the sluggard has warned readers of the dangers closest to them, especially the danger of avoiding the important matter of learning wisdom. The danger is real, though hidden; no violent images are used in this set of sayings apart from the imagined lion in the streets, and even this is more humorous than frightful. The only lion the sluggard will meet in the "road" and "streets" is Woman Wisdom (cf. 1:20; 8:1–3; 9:3–4), and, of course, he avoids her at all costs. Yet perhaps here is why the sluggard represents the greatest danger for us—pride's close cousin, complacency, is hard to recognize. Each appearance of the sluggard reminds us that learning wisdom is hard work, requires constant attention, and yields greater rewards than those of late mornings in bed and half-eaten food. The sluggard is a kind of fool, and so these two figures, wise in their own eyes, warn us of similar tendencies toward pride and complacency in our lives.

If the fool and sluggard do not get it, so also the evil pair of characters in 26:17–28 do not understand how to read "what is fitting" out of life. They do not understand that "what goes around comes around," and so they try to use the power of words for evil ends, only to have their evil turn back on them. If it is dangerous to hire a fool, it is also dangerous to ignore the follies of the quarreler and deceiver. If fools and sluggards are wise in their own eyes, proud and complacent, these two are also, believing they are slick and smooth. Yet just as the fool and sluggard are exposed for what they are, so these characters are eventually found out, but it is better to recognize them before they do their damage.

Those who deceive, quarrel, and gossip think they are smarter than their neighbors, to whom they lie and say, "I was only joking!" (26:18–19). They are like archers shooting firebrands, just as those who gossip are like those who "kindle strife" as if it was a campfire. A fire in a fireplace can provide a welcome haven for a neighbor, but when used against the neighbor to set fire to house and property, fire is a dangerous thing indeed. So is the pretense of neighbor love. The images of this particular brand of folly all speak of covering evil over with pleasing appearances—attractive glaze, charming speech, and flattering or smooth words (26:23, 25, 28), pretending friendship when in fact the intent is hatred (26:24, 26, 28).

Each proverb's exposure of this pleasing deception of goodwill and the ugly reality of hatred accomplishes the work of 26:26; it exposes wickedness in the assembly. The seven abominations that accompany the hate of this person's heart are perhaps an answer to seven who can answer discretely (26:16). Like the sluggard, these people too are wise in their own eyes, yet not wise enough to see that they will be exposed and will be caught in their own traps. Appearances can be deceiving; thus, readers must sharpen their skills of character assessment, rooting out such pretense in their own lives and steering clear of it when it appears in others.

Perhaps the strategy of the sages who put these proverbs together set the buffoons next to the liars to show that they are not that far apart. Both pretend to wisdom, one by speaking proverbs, the other by speaking falsehood. Neither knows what is fitting, and so just as dogs return to eat what their stomachs rejected, so the stone turns back to crush the one who set it in motion (26:11, 27). Both believe that they are wise, but more tragic are those who believe they are slick enough to put one over on those they call friends. To speak lies, however beautiful they may sound, is to speak foolishly.

Thus, the ancient rhetoricians criticized those who used the art of persuasion to make themselves appear great or make the wrong appear right; they saw that it was possible to use words for effect but not for love. In the same way, Paul addressed the quarrels and divisions of the church at Corinth with teaching on wisdom and humility (1 Cor. 1:10–11). While interpreters debate whether Paul had ancient practitioners of rhetoric in mind when he set preaching of the cross against words of human wisdom (1:17), it is clear that he rejected what he called fine words and words of wisdom, reminding the Corinthians that not many of them were of high status or wise (1:26). In the end, Paul dismissed fine-sounding words of secular wisdom because they led to pride and quarrels. Instead, he presented Christ:

> For I resolved to know nothing while I was with you except Jesus Christ and him crucified. I came to you in weakness with great fear and trembling. My message and my preaching were not with wise and persuasive words, but with a demonstration of the Spirit's power, so that your faith might not rest on human wisdom but on God's power. (1 Cor. 2:2–5, TNIV).

Paul's words remind us how quickly any quest for wisdom can turn inward, elevating our own accomplishments rather than looking to the work of God in Jesus. They also remind us that we can set aside our quest for honors or advantages and open ourselves to the one who loves us in spite of our pretenses. It is a sign of wisdom to know the three principles of this chapter: to know what is fitting, to realize that one gets what one gives out, and to apply these truths to the practice of communication. The characters of this chapter show us that it is folly to try and become facile with words if we forget the importance of wisdom, humility, and honesty.

DANGEROUS VERSUS CAREFUL TALK. If we are to apply the principles of these proverbs to our own day, we may as well admit that at times we have all played the fool or the troublemaker to some degree. Who has not sought honors by dropping a name or an accomplishment in hopes of fishing some word of praise out of the conversation? Who has not said an unkind word, either to another in a quarrel or about another in gossip, hoping to prove that we are right or better than the one singed by the fire? So it is that we often speak to lift ourselves up or, failing that, to at least stand on top of somebody else; if honor will not come to us, let dishonor come to another.

The problem is that we are messing with the basic chemistry of communication and are in danger of blowing up the lab, hurting others as well as ourselves. In high school I had a lab partner who wanted to prove he was smart by messing with the procedure, concocting something that he thought would get a bigger reaction than our lab book prescribed. He got a reaction, but not the one he expected. The teacher saw what was going on, told both of us to sit down, gave us a lecture on safety, and then gave us both zeros for the day. Looking back, that penalty was much easier to take than catching a piece of lab beaker in my face. "A whip for the horse, a halter for the donkey, and a rod for the backs of fools" (26:3). The basic chemistry of communication says that bad talk brings bad results, so we should be grateful when it does not blow up in our faces.

There are two ways that we can put aside dangerous talk and avoid its dangers. (1) The first is to practice and teach the reverse of the fool's pride and strive for humility in speaking. Rather than trying to show off concerning what (or who) we know, we can try to find out about the things we do not know, learning from others all we can about this world of ours and its workings. Curiosity about life is almost always rewarded in ways that boasting and preening are not. Of course, there are times in life when it seems that pretenders and sluggards are rewarded, but the general principle of humility holds—nothing earns honor more than working for goals higher than praise.

If we are in an endeavor only for the honor it brings, we will surely be disappointed.

If a fool believes he is wise enough to use a proverb, the sluggard believes he is wiser than seven; worse than giving honor to a fool is giving honor to oneself the way the sluggard does (26:1, 5, 8, 12, 16). Thus, the fool tries too hard to earn honors by parroting proverbs, and the sluggard thinks he can craft clever tales to serve his purposes. The sluggard is a kind of fool, and so these two figures, wise in their own eyes, warn us of similar tendencies toward pride and pretense in our lives.

Here is the danger of letting our words reveal that we are wise in our own eyes. It keeps us from paying attention, leading us to forget that our knowledge of the facts is always limited. Therefore, we should not be saying, "I know what to do," but rather always asking, "What is the best thing to do in this case? How can I exercise discernment in this world of limited perceptions and partial knowledge?" I once heard a speaker tell the story of a man on a subway who seemed oblivious to the raucous behavior of his children. When someone asked him why he did not make them sit down and stay quiet, he apologized and answered that they were coming from the hospital where his wife had just died. He needed a word of comfort, not correction.

While the requirements of wisdom do not change, the way they are applied to situations is fluid, and a humble appreciation for care with words will mark us as wise. Just as fools are unaware of their folly, so they that deem themselves wise are in danger of the same (cf. Eccl. 7:23–25). Although Yahweh is not named in this chapter's collection of proverbs, the recurring phrase "wise in his own eyes" sends readers back to Proverbs 3:1–10, where parent pleads with their son to keep the teaching and commands, especially that of love and faithfulness, hoping that he will "win favor and a good name in the sight of God and man" (3:4), will trust in Yahweh instead of his own understanding (3:5), will fear Yahweh instead of being wise in own eyes (3:7), and will honor Yahweh with wealth instead of using it to aggrandize self (3:9).

(2) The second way to practice good communication is to reject the troublemaker's deception and cultivate loving honesty within ourselves and with those around us. We need honesty with ourselves to uncover when our anger at another is really jealousy or a quarrel about some superficial matter is really about some deeper hurt from the past. We can catch ourselves trying to sugarcoat our words when we really want to say something hurtful. The break can give us a chance to collect ourselves so we can go back lovingly to confront the real issue.

While the deceits described in these proverbs seem designed to steal a neighbor's reputation or property, the principle of setting aside dishonesty, gossip, and quarrels carries over into our interactions with family and neighbors, and even with God. How much conflict in our churches could be avoided with honest and loving confrontation? We can be ruthless with ourselves but also firm with others, calling them to account when we believe they are less than honest.

Envy and jealousy. When we quarrel and gossip, what is it we think we lack? Sometimes we believe we need more material goods and get jealous, probably more often what we believe we lack is status and the esteem of others. Hatred and honesty seem to be in opposition here, for the motivation for these deceptions is hate (*śnʾ* in 26:24, 26, 28). If we hate someone simply for having what they have, we have experienced the mortal sin of envy, as described by William S. Stafford: "Envy is resentment of the good another person enjoys, with hatred of the other person for having it. It moves beyond the shallower deadly sins toward something worse: ill will pure and simple, the hatred of good because it is good."[11]

Envy fails to recognize two truths: (1) that we are created beings, depending on God for all that we are and have, our gifts and our talents, and (2) that God's distribution of those gifts and talents makes us depend on one another as well. What one has, another needs, but if we assume that we must have it all, we reject that dependence on God and each other and set ourselves up for envy, hatred, and potential acts of malice. It is better to thank God for what we have and then go on to thank God for what our neighbors have, accepting that our gifts, like our wisdom, have limits. If the fool refuses to accept the limits placed on wisdom, the one who hates refuses to accept the limits of our gifts and acquisitions—no one can have it all. Thanksgiving can help with that acceptance. What we may sense as lack can drive us to depend on God and be open to receive help from a neighbor.

Therefore, we can be honest with ourselves if we find that we resent what others have in the way of talents, possessions, lifestyles, and family. When we lie, quarrel, or gossip, we can recognize the underlying hatred and envy, looking also to see if it is accompanied by any hurt. Joseph's brothers hated him and envied the place he had in his father's heart, but that bitter root grew out of the hurt caused by favoritism. Recognizing that we are prone to envy and its hatred can help us uncover some of our own deceptions (even self-deceptions) before they do damage and are exposed. The worker who lies to a colleague and claims it was all a joke can identify his own sense of

---

11. Stafford, *Disordered Loves*, 93–94. The discussion that follows is adapted from this work. The word "envy" is derived from the Latin *invidia*, the "evil eye" or curse that people of ancient Rome gave to those who had success or beauty they did not, believing the look would bring misfortune or even death.

deprivation. The student eager to spread the news of a rival's mistake can recognize her desire to take that rival's place. The habitual quarreler can identify the inner needs that motivate the disputes. Moreover, when we see these forms of hate in others, we can take steps to expose it in confrontation, to take another aside before things get worse, before the lab blows up.

Perhaps it is envy that moves the sluggard to think himself wiser than seven who can answer well, and perhaps it is laziness that keeps the troublemaker from dealing with his own envy and hatred. Yet just as the fool and sluggard are exposed for what they are, so these characters are eventually found out, though it is better to recognize them before they do their damage. These character sketches help us recognize our own pretenses, revealing how transparent, futile, and dangerous they can be.

Appearances can be deceiving, and so readers are encouraged to sharpen their skills of character assessment, rooting out such pretense in their own lives and steering clear of it when it appears in others. Instead, we can take Paul's recommendation and seek to know Christ, "in whom are hidden all the treasures of wisdom and knowledge" (Col. 2:3). Recognizing that in him we have the "riches of God's grace that he lavished on us with all wisdom and understanding" (Eph. 1:7–8), we can look for what is fitting instead of what serves us, recognize that while evil attracts evil, good is returned with good, and that both can be practiced in the way we talk to one another. If we value wisdom, we will nurture it within ourselves, look for it in others, and encourage it when we find it. We will try to lift up others instead of ourselves, a theme that is explored in the next chapter.

Proverbs 27:1–27

¹ DO NOT BOAST about tomorrow,
for you do not know what a day may bring forth.
² Let another praise you, and not your own mouth;
someone else, and not your own lips.
³ Stone is heavy and sand a burden,
but provocation by a fool is heavier than both.
⁴ Anger is cruel and fury overwhelming,
but who can stand before jealousy?
⁵ Better is open rebuke
than hidden love.
⁶ Wounds from a friend can be trusted,
but an enemy multiplies kisses.
⁷ He who is full loathes honey,
but to the hungry even what is bitter tastes sweet.
⁸ Like a bird that strays from its nest
is a man who strays from his home.
⁹ Perfume and incense bring joy to the heart,
and the pleasantness of one's friend springs from his
earnest counsel.
¹⁰ Do not forsake your friend and the friend of your father,
and do not go to your brother's house when disaster
strikes you—
better a neighbor nearby than a brother far away.
¹¹ Be wise, my son, and bring joy to my heart;
then I can answer anyone who treats me with contempt.
¹² The prudent see danger and take refuge,
but the simple keep going and suffer for it.
¹³ Take the garment of one who puts up security for a
stranger;
hold it in pledge if he does it for a wayward woman.
¹⁴ If a man loudly blesses his neighbor early in the morning,
it will be taken as a curse.
¹⁵ A quarrelsome wife is like
a constant dripping on a rainy day;
¹⁶ restraining her is like restraining the wind
or grasping oil with the hand.
¹⁷ As iron sharpens iron,
so one man sharpens another.

¹⁸ He who tends a fig tree will eat its fruit,
     and he who looks after his master will be honored.
¹⁹ As water reflects a face,
     so a man's heart reflects the man.
²⁰ Death and Destruction are never satisfied,
     and neither are the eyes of man.
²¹ The crucible for silver and the furnace for gold,
     but man is tested by the praise he receives.
²² Though you grind a fool in a mortar,
     grinding him like grain with a pestle,
     you will not remove his folly from him.
²³ Be sure you know the condition of your flocks,
     give careful attention to your herds;
²⁴ for riches do not endure forever,
     and a crown is not secure for all generations.
²⁵ When the hay is removed and new growth appears
     and the grass from the hills is gathered in,
²⁶ the lambs will provide you with clothing,
     and the goats with the price of a field.
²⁷ You will have plenty of goats' milk
     to feed you and your family
     and to nourish your servant girls.

THE "PROVERBS OF Solomon copied by the men of Hezekiah" (cf. 25:1 and the introduction to that chapter) go on to explore themes of friendship and trusting relationships. The first twenty-two verses (the number of letters in the Hebrew alphabet) gather into groups of two, although the relationship between some pairs is more clear than others (27:5–6, 15–16). The last five verses form a longer poem that uses pastoral imagery to describe the rewards of care and diligence.

Praise and rebuke (27:1–6)
Family and safety (27:7–12)
Bad neighbors and quarrelsome wives (27:13–16)
Iron to iron, face to face (27:17–22)
Care for one's animals[1] (27:23–27)

---

1. Meinhold, *Die Sprüche*, 2:449, uses the three-line sayings as section markers (27:10, 22, and 27).

The pastoral poem of verses 23–27 provides the positive answer to the first proverb, "Boast not about tomorrow, for you do not know what a day may bring forth." It challenges our superficial assumptions about human self-sufficiency, skills, accomplishments, or anything else that might displace our need to love and depend on family, neighbors, and even the plants and animals of God's good earth. Boasting isolates and has the potential to destroy; healthy interdependence nurtures. These challenges to our misguided individualism also come with a number of surprise reversals: Friends may wound, and enemies may kiss (27:6).

Praise and Rebuke (27:1–6)

IN BETWEEN SAYINGS about boasting and praise (27:1–2) and wounds and kisses (27:6–7) are reminders that folly and jealousy always bring others down.

27:1–2. The first proverb pair is connected by the Hebrew root for "praise" (*hll*), urging readers to reject the negative "boast" in favor of "praise" from the mouth and lips of someone else. Related to the proverbs about "honor" and the fool, this pair uses a format similar to that of 26:4–5; the initial prohibition of "do not" is followed by an admonition "do." "You do not know" (27:1) is surely an indictment in a book about wisdom (see 27:23 for what one should "know"). Any boast about what we will do finds its limit with the unknown.[2] A friend of mine often says, "You never know—you or I may not be here tomorrow." Both lines of verse 2 state the reverse of boasting, praise from an "other" (*zar*; cf. 5:10, 17; 14:10)[3] or "someone else" (*nokri*), followed by the negative—not one's own mouth and lips. In Proverbs, lips were made for building up one another with teaching and correction, not for building up ourselves.

27:3–4. Like the fool satires of 26:1–3, this pair takes a threefold form of comparison. The weights of stone and sand in verse 3 are not the little markers the ancients used on their scales but reminders of the sweaty work of lifting heavy loads and carrying them on one's back (27:3; cf. 26:27). The fool's provocation is even heavier, harder to bear, more burdensome than sand and rocks put together. A play on the word *kabed* (lit., "weighty") sets the "honor" that is not fitting for the fool (cf. 26:1, 8) against his true character; the vexation a fool brings is weighty but not an honor (cf. 27:18). Just

---

2. The Egyptian instructions use the theme. *Ptahhotep*: "One plans the morrow but knows not what will be" (Lichtheim, *AEL*, 1:69). *Amenemope*: "Do not lie down in fear of tomorrow: 'Comes day, how will tomorrow be?' Man ignores how tomorrow will be" (Lichtheim, *AEL*, 2:157).

3. However one should not put up security for a "stranger" (*zar*; cf. 6:1; 11:15; 20:16).

as boasting is a burdensome form of folly (27:1, 3), so the raging fires of anger and fury are small matters compared with the quiet burn of jealousy (6:34; 14:30; cf. the discussion of envy in ch. 26). We may think ourselves burdened by the folly of others, but who among us has not been knocked down by our own jealousy?

27:5–6. Two proverbs about correction reverse common expectations, telling us what we already know but pointing out the irony we often miss. The contrasts of verse 5 are plain, but the wit of the proverb leads one to ask why "open rebuke" is better than "hidden love." We might say that hidden love is no love at all, for it does the loved one no good; reproof, even if it comes with anger (27:4), is painful but profitable. Hiddenness can be a sign of wisdom when one does not blurt out every thought, but it can also be a sign of hatred, as verse 6 shows. The enemy who kisses is (lit.) "one who hates" (root *śnʾ*; cf. 26:28; "malicious" in 26:24, 26); "multiplies" or "excessive" denotes some form of deception.[4] Friendship sometimes brings praise (27:2) and sometimes wounds (27:6; cf. 20:30), but those wounds are also faithful ("trusted," *ʾmn*).

Family and Safety (27:7–12)

FRIENDS CAN BE like family; to ignore them is to be like a bird that strays from the nest and heads for danger.

27:7–8. The theme of reversed expectations continues into this pair of proverbs about rejection. One whose hunger is satisfied literally walks past or tramples honey (5:3; 16:34; 24:13; 25:16, 27), while someone who strays from home is like the bird that leaves the safety of the nest. However, if you are hungry, even the bitter tastes sweet, and so we should be glad for the homes we have. It is not clear why leaving home is a problem, because the word "strays" is difficult to translate; in some biblical contexts it means "fly away" (16:2; Nah. 3:17), in others, "flee" (Ps. 31:11; Isa. 21:5), and in still others, "wander" (Job 15:23; Hos. 9:17). It may be that the hunting practice of beating bushes to drive out birds is in view (Isa. 16:2). Just as every other bird in Proverbs is in some sort of danger (Prov. 1:17; 6:5; 7:21–23), so here a young man leaves the nest of security and heads toward potential harm (cf. 27:12). Together, the proverbs warn against taking anything for granted.

27:9–10. Like the previous pair, a proverb about sweetness (*matoq*; cf. 27:7) is followed by one about home and family, each depicting a welcome reception.[5] The sweet smells of perfumed oil and incense cause the heart to

---

4. N. M. Waldman, "A Note on Excessive Speech and Falsehood," *JQR* 67 (1976): 142–45.

5. Garrett, *Proverbs*, 217, sees an ABAB pattern in vv. 7–10, although I would argue it may continue into vv. 11–12, where gladness is followed by the error of "going" (cf. vv. 8, 10).

rejoice (*śmḥ;* cf. 27:11), just as the sweetness of a friend and neighbor is better than one's own counsel (cf. 24:13–14). The extended proverb of verse 10 combines an admonition with a "better than" saying, twice repeating the word "neighbor" from the verse before (*reʿa;* cf. "friend," 27:9). Neighbors like this make sure that they follow up their earnest counsel with support in a time of need. "A friend loves at all times, and a brother is born for adversity" (17:17). Neighbors, like family, are precious and should not be rejected or abandoned (cf. 27:8). The Hebrew word "day" (*yom,* 27:10; lit., "day of your disaster") may link this proverb to verse 1, reminding readers that a day may bring calamity.

27:11–12. These proverbs are linked by contrasting wisdom and prudence, and like the pairs at verses 7–8 and 9–10, satisfaction is followed by the error of "going." The address "my son" has not appeared since we left the "words of the wise" (23:15, 19, 26; 24:13, 21), and this is the last one we will see until Lemuel's mother instructs him (31:2). If this son learns wisdom, his father will rejoice ("wise" in 27:11 falls in the middle of the twenty-two verse acrostic; cf. 10:1; 13:1; 15:20; 23:15); "joy to the heart" repeats the phrase from 27:9, and "father" appears in 27:10.

"Contempt" in Proverbs is typically directed toward the Maker (14:31; 17:5) and his poor children; by a similar identification, contempt for the father can be silenced by the son's wisdom and virtue (Ps. 119:41–42). The saying about "danger" in Proverbs 27:12 is nearly identical to 22:3. In this context it implies that a father is also glad to see his son exercise prudence and "hide" (*str;* cf. 27:5) than to be simple and walk right into trouble (cf. 1:8–27; 7:1–9; 9:1–6, 13–18).

Bad Neighbors and Quarrelsome Wives (27:13–16)

Unpleasant experiences with neighbors and household make a strong contrast with the positive sayings on friends and family that have gone before.

27:13–14. A proverb pair about treating strangers like neighbors and neighbors like enemies shows that friendly actions are inappropriate when they do too much. Certainly rash pledges of security have been named a danger throughout Proverbs (cf. 1:15; 6:1; 17:18; 22:26–27), but taking a chance by doing this neighborly deed for a "wayward woman" or a "stranger"[6] is clearly out of place. In any case, the one making the loan should take the garment as security (something not done for a poor neighbor, Deut. 24:10–13) because it may be all the payment he will ever see.

---

6. The nearly identical proverb in 20:16 has an alternate reading "foreigners" (*nokerim;* cf. "someone else" in 27:2) instead of "wayward woman" (*nokriyyah*); the NRSV follows this reading and translates 27:13, "seize the pledge given as surety for foreigners." The Hebrew text makes sense as it stands.

Blessing a neighbor too early and too loudly (27:14) may be more a sign of insincerity than disregard for peace and quiet (cf. 27:9–10; 1 Sam. 13:10). Regardless of the social context understood by original readers, what is meant as blessing is taken as curse (*qll*, Prov. 26:2; cf. Ps. 109:17–18), a sign of hostility.

27:15–16. If the loud neighbor is annoying, worse is the quarrelsome wife, here again compared to a leaky and potentially dangerous roof (cf. 19:13); like the constant dripping, the arguments seem to have no end. Two other metaphors expand the picture of trouble in verse 16, but translation is difficult. (1) "Restraining" can also be translated "hiding" or even "storing like treasure."[7] (2) It is not clear what the Hebrew of the second line means (lit., "oil—his right hand—meets/calls"). Most solutions propose unusual idioms[8] or emendations; perhaps it is best to say that just as wind cannot be shut away, so the hand makes a poor container for oil. The point is clear that little can be done with a contentious person, female or male (cf. 26:21).

Iron to Iron, Face to Face (27:17–22)

THE KEY WORD "face" (27:17, 19) stresses the importance of knowing other people in order to discern their motivations.

27:17–18. Two proverbs speak about good relations with neighbors and employers. In verse 17, the point is clear enough; we all want friends who will keep us sharp through challenging conversation and personal feedback. The comparison with striking iron points out the need for two to hone the edge (cf. Ezek. 21:14–16); one (lit.) "sharpens the face [cf. Prov. 27:19] of his neighbor" (*rea^c*; cf. 27:9, 10, 14).

The imagery of verse 18 is straightforward also, for it is common knowledge that those who tend a garden enjoy its produce. Bringing the two proverbs together and setting them in context, readers learn that it is by serving well *and* keeping the employer sharp that servants receive the "honor" (*kabed*, 27:18; cf. 26:1, 8, "heavy" in 27:3) that so many seek (27:1–2).

27:19–20. Like the pair at verses 17–18, a saying about "face" is followed by one about eating. The Hebrew "face to face" of verse 19 mirrors the "iron to iron" of verse 17, and it is possible to read "one human heart reflects another" (NRSV); the translation of the NIV implies that the heart is the

---

7. The Heb. letters *ṣpn* can also be read "north," so the LXX translates, "The north wind is sharp, but it is called lucky." A similar wordplay may be at work in 25:23–24.

8. Because oil was a medium for fragrance in the ancient world, Garrett, *Proverbs*, 220, translates, "He who keeps her keeps wind, and he will call [her] the perfume of his right hand," so as to say a quarrelsome wife is like an expense that does him little good, a contrast to the good wife of Prov. 31. Clifford, *Proverbs*, 236, translates, "the oil on her hand announces her presence," suggesting that like strong perfume, her contentious character cannot be hidden.

---

reflection of that same person's character.[9] Both readings are possible, but the first fits the chapter's theme of friendship more closely. Sheol and Abaddon (see NIV text note on v. 19; cf. 15:11; 30:16), those abodes of death, were always hungry, ready to swallow anything that lives. So the avaricious appetite of humans is compared to that which destroys. The parallel use of body parts draws the contrast ("man," *ʾadam*, in both 27:19–20); if kind hearts can reflect one another in friendship, it is also true that greedy eyes can devour another's life.

27:21–22. The words "praise" and "fool" of 27:1–3 appear in this proverb pair, creating a frame at the beginning and end of the twenty-two-verse acrostic. The word "tested" does not appear in Hebrew but it is implied by the image in the first line; crucibles and furnaces test metal ores, revealing what they contain and separating what is valuable from dross (cf. 25:4). The NIV translation suggests that the way we react to the praise of others reveals our motives, honorable and dishonorable (cf. 17:3). Other translations take the "mouth of his praise" as the community's assessment of character: "A person is worth what his reputation is worth" (NJB; cf. 12:8).

Verse 22 presents another metaphor of processing natural material. Unlike the crucible and furnace that separate, a mortar and pestle grind grain that has already been removed from its husk by the thresher. The point is that folly cannot be separated from the fool, for it is too deeply ingrained. If verse 11 speaks of "wisdom" at the midpoint of these twenty-two verses, the last names the "fool" and "his folly."

Care for One's Animals (27:23–27)

27:23–27. UNLIKE THE COLLECTION of proverb pairs that precedes, these last five verses make up an extended poem, notable for the pastoral imagery that appears in all but one of its sayings (27:24). That saying about riches and crown is the only real proverb in this section, and it may provide the clue to the poem's meaning. The contrast of fleeting wealth and power with nature's ever-renewing provision teaches further lessons about faithfulness in relationships. This mini-instruction urges the listener to "know" the condition of the animals, foreshadowing the emphasis on knowing that appears in 28:2 and 22. In addition, verbal links suggest that this poem is a metaphor of wise rule, just as wisdom and the woman of worth exercise wise rule in the "house" with "servant girls" (27:27; cf.

---

9. Clifford, *Proverbs*, 236, following the LXX, reads, "face to face" instead of "reflects the face" (cf. Deut. 34:10; Ezek. 20:35); "words are the route to the core of the person." Garrett, *Proverbs*, 221, argues that just as the water is an exact reflection of a person's face, so the heart reflects what the person is. "In other words people have a basic consistency to them. . . . One should learn how to read people and thus learn whom to trust."

9:1–3; 31:15).[10] Ancient Near Eastern writings also tell us that kings of ancient Mesopotamia and Egypt were sometimes called "shepherds."[11]

Two charges to attend to one's animals in verse 23 repeat terms from verse 19. The person is to know the "condition" (lit., "face") of the flocks and set his "heart" on the herds, just as the wise study and know the human heart. The imperative "know" answers the warning of verse 1, "you do not know"—certainly an approach to the future that pleases Yahweh (cf. 29:7).[12] The emphasis seems to be on the interdependence between humans and their animals, not on compassion for them (cf. 12:10–11).

The charge to know is followed by a motivating reason in verse 24, stated in the negative: "Riches do not endure forever." Unlike a herd that will replenish itself if cared for, riches can be squandered and lost for good. So also a crown[13] is not guaranteed from generation to generation if a healthy relationship with the subjects is ignored (cf. 14:28). One never arrives at the place where work is not necessary. Images of harvest and plenty illustrate the rewards of proper attention to the farm, where gathering hay to feed the animals in turn provides homespun goods and fields in trade (27:25–26).[14]

Verses 26–27 describe the payoff for diligence, the second line of each describing the abundance that buys fields and feeds family and servants. "Plenty" in verse 27 translates the same word used for eating just "enough" honey in 25:16; having "enough" is for sharing, not gorging, so the servants who look after their employers should be cared for in turn (27:18). While some interpreters think the message of the poem was directed to landed young men called into service at the court,[15] the metaphor for attentiveness and diligence applies to many areas of life (cf. 2 Tim. 2:6).

---

10. R. C. Van Leeuwen, *Context and Meaning in Proverbs 25–27*, 133–43, takes the interplay between "house" and "kingdom/dynasty" as evidence that someone in Hezekiah's time believed that the monarchy was not inviolable (cf. 2 Sam. 7:1–17; Jer. 26:16–17; Mic. 3:12). B. Malchow, "A Manual for Future Monarchs: Proverbs 27:23–29:27," *CBQ* 47 (April 1985): 238–45, reprinted in R. B. Zuck, *Learning From the Sages: Selected Studies on the Book of Proverbs* (Grand Rapids: Baker, 1995), 353–60, argues that a royal instruction manual begins with 27:23–27 and extends to 29:27.

11. *ANET*, 159, 164, 265–66, 440, 443.

12. The emphatic idiom "be sure you know" is variously translated, "know [this] for certain," or "you shall surely know" (cf. Gen. 15:13; 1 Sam. 28:1; 1 Kings 2:37, 42).

13. Clifford, *Proverbs*, 237, along with a number of other interpreters, finds "crown" (*nezer*) out of place and emends to "treasure" (*ʾoṣar*), following Isa. 33:6 and Jer. 20:5.

14. This word for "grass" (*ʿśb*) only appears here and in 19:12, "A king's rage is like the roar of a lion, but his favor is like dew on the grass."

15. Hubbard, *Proverbs*, 418, takes this as a warning against get-rich-quick schemes and cites Ezek. 34. Perdue, *Proverbs*, 226–27, believes the sages who served at court may have been gentlemen farmers.

INTERDEPENDENCE. Despite translation difficulties and some uncertainty about the use of metaphors, we have seen that the themes of friendship and interdependence tie together the acrostic of verses 1–22 and the pastoral poem of verses 23–27. Repetition of the key term "know" draws the reader's attention to the link. If a person should not boast because one does not "know" the future, one should "know" the conditions of the flocks and herds that provide for the coming days (27:1, 23).

Likewise, key terms from verses 2–3 are repeated at the end of the acrostic. If one should let another offer "praise" in place of boasting, one should remember that with all "praise" comes testing (27:2, 21). If a "fool" is hard to bear, it is also true that a "fool" cannot be separated from his or her folly (27:3, 22). So also the sages who assembled this collection of proverbs drew words from the instructions ("Be wise, my son," 27:11) and put them together with proverbs and parts of proverbs that appeared earlier in the collections (27:12, 13, 15). Again and again, the proverbs themselves leave clues that they are to be read side by side, the interaction between like proverbs and themes offering richer insight for living. One who learns to bring like sayings together knows how to use them and is deemed wise (cf. 26:4–5, 7, 9).

In a sense, this strategy of juxtaposition carries over into our experience of life together. Just as proverbs take on richer meaning when they work together, so human beings are at their best when they come together around some greater purpose, be it worship, good works, or mutual edification. In the social outlook of Proverbs, we are not wise or whole unless we are related; the autonomous person is hardly a person at all. So it is for the church, the visible body of Christ. As William Willimon put it:

> It is difficult for Christians to imagine a truly isolated individual who is unattached to some communal, social framework. Even the person who says, "My behavior is my own business and no one else's" is thereby demonstrating his attachment to a community, namely, the community that fosters isolated, unexamined, lonely people whose only purpose is self-aggrandizement.[16]

So these proverbs elevate praise over boasting and the near neighbor over the distant relative, valuing those face-to-face relationships that refine

---

16. W. H. Willimon, *Pastor: The Theology and Practice of Ordained Ministry* (Nashville: Abingdon, 2002), 311.

us like precious metal and hone us sharp like iron blades. The matters of character are inevitably communal, for our hearts are both proved and improved through interaction. Read in their literary "communities," these sayings teach us to assess and encourage good character in ourselves, but also in others. The pastoral poem reminds us that we demonstrate good character as we live in committed relationships with one another.

Assessing and encouraging character. (1) To start, we can assess and encourage good character in ourselves. The proverbs on friendship use metaphor in ways that are difficult to apprehend, but we see that friendship meant more to the people that used the proverbs than simply helping each other materially. One person keeps another sharp through counsel and correction, but a worker also makes sure that the employer gets a hundred percent effort (27:17–18). Praise and rebuke both assume that there is excellence worth pursuing, that some behaviors are worthy of a good word and some need a "No." We assess and encourage good character in ourselves by setting aside boasting in favor of praise. This does not mean that we act only for complements, for that too is a form of boasting. It does mean that we strive for those characteristics that are praiseworthy, especially being a good neighbor, one as good as family.

Reversals of common expectations appear throughout the chapter. Acts of love may sting, and acts of betrayal may kiss one on the cheek (27:6–7). Perhaps, then, it is this deep understanding of relationships that moves a parent to call a child "wise" (27:12). We make our first steps toward wisdom when we learn that the sacrifices of neighbor love are not repaid in a this-for-that fashion but in the abiding commitment people develop for one another. Why else would some people say that their friends are like family to them (27:9–10)?

(2) Just as these proverbs call us to encourage good character in ourselves, they also invite us to assess and encourage good character in others. As we do so, we may find that praise and encouragement make boasting unnecessary. Although I may want to say nothing complementary to a braggart for fear of encouraging the offensive behavior, I am trying to learn to point out that person's good qualities, hoping to fill the need that motivates the boasting in the first place. If we must take care to avoid getting caught up in the fool's provocation, the quarrelsome person's strife, or our culture's encouragement of greed (27:3, 15, 20), we need not write off such persons entirely; they too need our commitment to their emotional, moral, and spiritual growth.

The reasons why people act as they do, contrary to much of what we see on television, are not easily interpreted, explained, or challenged, but this does not mean that we do not need to understand them. In our days of unrelenting loneliness and angry interaction, the cultivation of friendship is one way to encourage good character and make God's kingdom visible.

The pastoral poem. Whether the pastoral poem of verses 23–27 was directed toward rulers and their courtiers is a matter of debate, but for our purposes, it is important to remember that it was included in the biblical canon because its lessons on interdependence are for us as well. Just as the Israelites learned important lessons about pride and responsibility from the trials and triumphs of King David, his son Solomon, and their descendants, so people in Shakespeare's day were moved and instructed by his dramatic portrayal of kings from their history. The lives of the rulers became lessons for everyone. Therefore, although efforts to identify the original intended audience for this poem are important, we must also remember that wisdom's proverbs and instructions have a way of taking on a more universal appeal, and we will look for a similar strategy here.

The symbolism of the poem can yield a number of insights, but the primary and foundational message is the importance of nurture and care. So, for example, if rulers were encouraged to think of a kingdom as a farm that requires attention but yields a harvest, they would also think of the relationship between themselves and the people they ruled as mutually beneficial. They might read the poem's contrast between humble farm work and the acquisition of riches and power as the difference between cultivation and ownership.

So too in our day, we seem to be more caught up in acquiring the things of this world than with tending and maintaining a living system placed in our care. I think it is significant that in the Midwest, where I live, the business report appears on prime-time news, but to see the farm report, I would have to get up before daylight. I know that this is the time when farmers rise to start work, but to me it is also a sign of how our economy has changed over the last century, a sign of where we have placed more value.

Perhaps, then, the reversals of the chapter are at work, reversing our sense of what is most important and valuable. One would expect that riches are to be preferred over a barn of hay, or that being a ruler with servants is better than working the farm, but verse 24 reminds us that wealth and power do not endure or renew themselves. Moreover, we know from experience that they can cut off the one who possesses them from meaningful relationships, leaving one isolated and lonely—a phenomenon that receives much attention today. We may go so far as to say that one cannot really live without relationships that require nurture and care, for it is in that mutual giving and receiving that we find our true selves.

We noted that the term "plenty" may also be translated "enough" (27:27), enough for oneself but also enough to share. It is striking that the mention of "servant girls" leads the reader to the wise woman's care for the "servant girls" of her "household" (along with mention of "clothing" and "field" in 31:15–31), and the maids who are sent out to invite travelers to Wisdom's feast (9:1–4). Since both Woman Wisdom and the noble wife represent the life of wisdom, it is not an exaggeration to say that wisdom is "known" and recognized where people "know" and understand mutual interdependence, where there is always enough to share. Therefore—and this is important—it is our network of relationships that helps us decide how much is "enough." In our own day of disproportionate distribution of wealth among individuals and nations, we must rightly be concerned about our networks of responsibility and care. We must ask ourselves how we have become so desensitized to the world's need.

BILL MONROE, the originator of bluegrass music, spent his whole life taking his band and songs to every rural southern town his wood-paneled station wagon (later a bus) could take him. There is a story that in his last years, Monroe would hitch up a horse to plow the field in front of his home. He would plant seed, watch it grow, but never harvest, leaving the grain out for the birds and animals. Obviously a symbolic act, he plowed and sowed not because he needed the food; it was enough for him to feel a connection with the earth and its rhythms of life.

Monroe also had a strong sense that connection to the land implied connection to one's neighbors. While visiting a flea market, he picked up an old worn farm tool and said, "These were good people."[17] While it is possible to romanticize the rural life, it is striking that agrarian imagery has been used throughout the centuries to communicate important truths about interdependence and its implications for personal character and vocation.

"Enough." We have already examined the significance of these proverbs and the pastoral poem for personal character, particularly informing our notions of what is "enough." These writings challenge our way of looking at things, for we live in a time that portrays character in caricatures, and as a result, our choices seem forced. Stories in broadcast and print media make it seem as though one either lives for self, like a robber baron, or for others, like Mother Theresa. Yet most of us live and work in the daily grind of earning a living, loving and caring for our families, and trying to be good to our neighbors. We do not want excess, we want to have "enough." Still, in the

---

17. These stories come from interviews I've read and heard with former Bluegrass Boy Peter Rowan.

backs of our minds, we wish there could be a little more, just a little more to take the edge off our financial worries and make things a little easier.

It is therefore hard to see when that legitimate concern for well-being turns the corner into avarice, the immoderate desire for possessions that takes the means of material goods and makes them into ends, into gods. "And when a creature is made into a god, it becomes a devil."[18] The proverbs and poem of this chapter help us to see that there is an approach to life and possessions that sets them in proper perspective so that we realize that we need one another, not things we can own. It is possible, then, to have "enough" for ourselves and also to have plenty to share.

Our view of created things will determine how we act toward them. Adam and Eve were placed in the garden to till and keep it, but they could not bear the limitations of possession that were placed on them; they worked the garden but could not own it. William Stafford paraphrases Augustine's teaching that humans can treat created material possessions as substitutes for God:

> Things carry something of their maker with them, whether the maker is God or a human being. That "something" can be grasped for its own sake, apart from the maker; when it displaces God, it is idolatry. A woman who catches a reflected glimpse of God's beauty through a certain view of redwoods down a certain river may ignore God, take those trees as the beauty she seeks, and spend her life buying the property. This applies to human products as well; once we put our wisdom and spirit into them, it is possible to put them in God's place.[19]

Yet "riches do not endure forever, and a crown is not secure for all generations" (27:24), for only God and God's children are eternal. It is better to worship God instead of created things, and it is better to view God's children as neighbors and not competitors when it comes down to who gets what. Throughout its history, the church has seen its members express their faith in one of two ways: Some have chosen voluntary poverty, either for a limited time or a lifetime, while others have taken the path of stewardship, holding possessions as a trust. The first proclaim that all belongs to God by having little or no possessions, the second by holding them lightly.[20] The

---

18. P. Kreeft, *For Heaven's Sake* (Nashville: Thomas Nelson, 1986), 107. Kreeft adds, "An economic system based on money rather than natural wealth (land, food, houses) has no natural, built-in limit to the flames of avarice. Since the desire for artificial wealth (money) is infinite, the miser always wants more" (110).

19. Stafford, *Disordered Loves: Healing the Seven Deadly Sins*, 64–65.

20. Ibid., 71–72.

theme of care and nurture in these proverbs reminds us that our possessions will not love us, no matter how much we love them, but given the proper care, our neighbors will.

Work as service. A second and related principle of the chapter is that work is a form of service. We have seen the dangers of gluttony, literal and symbolic, and certainly work that does nothing but provide us with more than we can possibly enjoy is out of harmony with God's self-giving work in Christ. Paul reminded the Christians at Philippi to "look not only to your own interests, but also to the interests of others," pointing to Jesus who took the nature of a servant (Phil. 2:4). We do our work mindful that, at root, all our work is (or should be) loving service to others, and by analogy, service to the God who loves and cares for all his children, sending rain on the just and unjust (Matt. 5:45).

Some forms of work exploit the well-being of others, either by its product, as in the case of pornography and tobacco, or by unfair treatment of workers. Yet so many occupations do make some contribution to the well-being of others and therefore reflect the work of God in the world.[21] Therefore, we work to provide for our needs, but this is only part of our motivation. Provision and service need not be mutually exclusive.

As I write, a number of American companies are under scrutiny for over-reporting income, underreporting expenses, and engaging in good old-fashioned insider trading. Friends in the business community remind me that this is not the norm for the majority of companies, but the news does leave the public asking hard questions about the objectives of these corporations.

In a book titled *When Good Companies Do Bad Things*, the matter of mutual responsibility is translated in terms of the global business community, stressing the need for trust and accountability between three parties: businesses, the governments of the countries in which multinational corporations do business, and nongovernment organizations like Greenpeace that watch and comment on business practice. So, for example, European business leaders often ask why so many of their American colleagues do not seem to understand environmental responsibility: "What is it about American executives? They don't seem to care about the environment personally. You'd think they didn't have to breathe the same air or drink the same water everyone else does."[22]

One American executive answered that if thirty years ago businesses resisted, and twenty years ago they saw the need, only now is action starting

---

21. D. Atkinson, "A Christian Theology of Work," in his *Pastoral Ethics* (Oxford: Lynx Communications, 1994), 104—11.

22. P. Schwartz and B. Gibb, *When Good Companies Do Bad Things: Responsibility and Risk in an Age of Globalization* (New York: John Wiley & Sons, 1999), 118.

to take place; that, say these authors, is too long. If public campaigns against business practices can make accusations that border on caricature, the authors believe that there is some truth to be heard and that businesses often insulate themselves from hearing how these concerns affect real people. By interacting with public opinion and anticipating what might go wrong, companies can avoid being blindsided. One company learned this the hard way; it made plans to deal with environmental protection but was blindsided by accusations of racism in the organization.

By reviewing the public failures of a number of visible companies, the authors of *When Good Companies Do Bad Things* concluded that good companies *fail to prevent* bad things from happening by fostering a corporate culture that does not tolerate dissent, focusing exclusively on financial performance, discouraging employees in their efforts to integrate business and moral intelligence, not listening to organizations who disagree with them, and letting a commitment to a project overshadow all other considerations. In short, business leaders who do not consider ethical and social issues to be their responsibility do not set out to do wrong, but neither do they take the steps that are needed to do right. In the imagery of the pastoral poem, they do not pay attention to their flocks and herds or heed the other proverbs' teaching about mutual connection and correction. Holding out the positive value of honor and a good reputation, the authors sound like so many of these proverbs:

> A company attracts the best, brightest, and most committed employees not as a result of slick recruiting campaigns, but by creating a corporate reputation that makes the best people want to work there. Once the best people are working for the company, they will want to maintain their own self-respect, the company's image, and its reputation by continued improvement and innovation in social as well as business practices—a virtuous circle.[23]

The writers speak of integrity and integration. Not only must businesses and those who work for them act in honest and honorable ways, they must integrate what they do with the countries that host them. Their lessons reflect the proverbs: To ignore that we are related to one another and to God's creation is to court trouble; to recognize it is to live to the full.

In Charles Frazier's novel *Cold Mountain*, a young woman named Ada has fallen on hard times. Her intended is off fighting for the Confederacy and her father has died. The war economy has made the father's stockholdings

---

23. Ibid., 175.

worthless, leaving her with nothing but a small farm tucked away in the North Carolina mountains. Raised and educated in the city, Ada finds she can barely milk a cow, let alone churn butter or make cheese. The neighbors take pity and send over Ruby, a resourceful young woman whose father had left her alone in their shack when he joined up.

The two strike a deal, Ruby sharing her know-how, Ada working as an assistant as they put her farm in working order. "To Ada, Ruby's monologues seemed composed mainly of verbs, all of them tiring. Plow, plant, hoe, cut, can, feed, kill."[24] They would survive the winter, but only because Ruby paid careful attention to the weather as well as the signs of the moon and stars for planting and harvesting. Once in the fall, to check on how well Ada was learning, Ruby put her hands over her student's eyes and asked what she heard. Ada replied that she heard the wind in the trees.

> Trees, Ruby said contemptuously, as if she had expected just such a foolish answer. Just general trees is all? You've got a long way to go. She removed her hands and took her seat again and said nothing more on the topic, leaving Ada to conclude that what she meant was that this is a particular world. Until Ada could listen and at the bare minimum tell the sound of poplar from oak at this time of year when it is easiest to do, she had not even started to know the place.[25]

Wisdom shows itself in attention to details, but also in the understanding that the details of life work together, just as we were meant to do in the mind of our Lord and Creator.

---

24. C. Frazier, *Cold Mountain* (New York: Atlantic Monthly, 1997), 80.
25. Ibid., 228.

Proverbs 28:1–28

¹ THE WICKED MAN flees though no one pursues,
    but the righteous are as bold as a lion.
² When a country is rebellious, it has many rulers,
    but a man of understanding and knowledge maintains
        order.
³ A ruler who oppresses the poor
    is like a driving rain that leaves no crops.
⁴ Those who forsake the law praise the wicked,
    but those who keep the law resist them.
⁵ Evil men do not understand justice,
    but those who seek the LORD understand it fully.
⁶ Better a poor man whose walk is blameless
    than a rich man whose ways are perverse.
⁷ He who keeps the law is a discerning son,
    but a companion of gluttons disgraces his father.
⁸ He who increases his wealth by exorbitant interest
    amasses it for another, who will be kind to the poor.
⁹ If anyone turns a deaf ear to the law,
    even his prayers are detestable.
¹⁰ He who leads the upright along an evil path
    will fall into his own trap,
    but the blameless will receive a good inheritance.
¹¹ A rich man may be wise in his own eyes,
    but a poor man who has discernment sees through him.
¹² When the righteous triumph, there is great elation;
    but when the wicked rise to power, men go into hiding.
¹³ He who conceals his sins does not prosper,
    but whoever confesses and renounces them finds mercy.
¹⁴ Blessed is the man who always fears the LORD,
    but he who hardens his heart falls into trouble.
¹⁵ Like a roaring lion or a charging bear
    is a wicked man ruling over a helpless people.
¹⁶ A tyrannical ruler lacks judgment,
    but he who hates ill-gotten gain will enjoy a long life.
¹⁷ A man tormented by the guilt of murder
    will be a fugitive till death;
    let no one support him.

¹⁸ He whose walk is blameless is kept safe,
>   but he whose ways are perverse will suddenly fall.
¹⁹ He who works his land will have abundant food,
>   but the one who chases fantasies will have his fill
>   of poverty.
²⁰ A faithful man will be richly blessed,
>   but one eager to get rich will not go unpunished.
²¹ To show partiality is not good—
>   yet a man will do wrong for a piece of bread.
²² A stingy man is eager to get rich
>   and is unaware that poverty awaits him.
²³ He who rebukes a man will in the end gain more favor
>   than he who has a flattering tongue.
²⁴ He who robs his father or mother
>   and says, "It's not wrong"—
>   he is partner to him who destroys.
²⁵ A greedy man stirs up dissension,
>   but he who trusts in the LORD will prosper.
²⁶ He who trusts in himself is a fool,
>   but he who walks in wisdom is kept safe.
²⁷ He who gives to the poor will lack nothing,
>   but he who closes his eyes to them receives
>   many curses.
²⁸ When the wicked rise to power, people go into hiding;
>   but when the wicked perish, the righteous thrive.

Original Meaning

CHAPTERS 28 AND 29, the last two chapters of the proverbs preserved by "the men of Hezekiah" (25:1–29:27; cf. comments in ch. 25), have a character of their own, combining sayings on rule and government with proverbs about good relations with family and neighbors. Repeated words such as "understanding" (28:2, 5), "trusts" (28:25–26), and "way/walk" (28:6, 18, 26) draw the portrait of one who is fit to be a good neighbor and a good ruler. Central to chapter 28 is the appearance of the Hebrew word *torah* ("teaching, instruction, law"); each occurrence is preceded by some reference to the poor (28:3–4, 6–7, 8–9), ensuring that the idea of "neighbor" includes everyone.

Like the proverbs of 10:1–15:33, antithetic parallelism dominates, particularly the contrast between the righteous and the wicked.[1] Malchow has sought to demonstrate the redactional unity of chapters 28–29 by noting the exclusive use of two-line proverbs and the appearance of the words "wicked" and "righteous" at 28:1 and 29:27, the first and last verses of the unit.[2] Four other uses of the pair (28:12, 28; 29:2, 26) define the subunits of the section and interact with one another to present a statement about rule and use of authority. Each frame of verse pairs defines the theme of the section within (see also the comments in Bridging Contexts).

Responsibilities of kings and people to the poor (28:1–12)
Fates of the wicked and the righteous (28:13–28)

All three terms for ethical living first listed in the prologue (1:3) appear. The virtues of righteousness, justice, and uprightness/equity are praised, as are the people who exhibit these characteristics: "the righteous" (root *ṣdq*, 28:1), people of "justice" (root *špṭ*, 28:5), and "the upright" (root *yšr*, 28:10). The juxtaposition of this triad theme with rule and oppression and then prosperity suggests the three are interrelated; perhaps one's attitude toward possessions and power reflects where one stands on the triad.

Responsibilities of Kings and People to the Poor (28:1–12)

THE FIRST TWELVE proverbs of this chapter turn the spotlight on one's relationship with the poor and the teaching of God. Rulers and commoners alike can turn away from both, but only with disastrous consequences for the nation and themselves.

28:1. While some boast in their pride (27:1), the "righteous are bold as a lion"; the word for "bold" (*baṭaḥ*) is typically used for trust or confidence (28:25–26; 2 Kings 18:30; Job 40:2). Here righteous confidence is contrasted with the fear that plagues the wicked, always looking over their shoulders as they flee.[3] Readers recall the shepherd David, who faced lions and bears and praised Yahweh for his deliverance (1 Sam. 17:34–37).

---

1. The section is divided in two by the pastoral poem at 27:23–27 and is framed with a repeated juxtaposition of rulers and their God (25:1–2; 29:26–27). Goldingay, "Proverbs," 605, saw that chs. 25–27 contained "vivid pen-pictures," with few references to God or the righteous-wicked pair. Here in chs. 28–29 the "balance is reversed, and questions of morality and theology return."

2. B. Malchow, "A Manual for Future Monarchs," *CBQ* 47 (1985): 238–45. So also Meinhold, *Die Sprüche*, 2:464. Murphy, *Proverbs*, 213, 218, accepts Malchow's observations but not the conclusion; in his view, it is not a manual for rulers but the teaching of the sages.

3. Kidner, *Proverbs*, 168. Clifford, *Proverbs*, 243, looks to Lev. 26:17, 36, a curse for disobedience to the covenant, running even when the enemy has stopped giving chase.

28:2. Verses 2 and 3 both treat the topic of government through the metaphor of land. A "country" (*ʾereṣ;* lit., "land") is personified as "rebellious," one who acts like the wicked person of verse 1. A land of deficient character is cursed with a succession of rulers, making the nation vulnerable to attack. Surprisingly, the second line does not contrast rebellion with a people's repentance (cf. the famous 2 Chron. 7:14) but with a single person of "understanding and knowledge" (lit., "one who knows"; cf. *yadaᶜ* in Prov. 27:23). Rulers like this maintain order (cf. 29:4); the proverb assumes that a people will rebel unless led by a person of wisdom.

28:3. The natural image of torrential rain that flattens grain is clear enough, but the comparison to human affairs is less so. The Hebrew texts reads, "A poor man, and one who oppresses the impoverished," which has led some to emend "poor man" (*raš*) to "wicked ruler" (*rašaᶜ*) after the LXX (cf. NIV and NRSV). Rain that destroys the crop instead of watering it could describe a bad ruler (the reverse of one who "knows" the condition of the flock and cares for it, cf. 27:23–27). However, one poor person taking the opportunity to profit at the expense of another adds the bitterness of betrayal. The translation "ruler" is more likely, though not certain; if we do read "poor," this would be the only instance of the poor oppressing the poor in Proverbs.

28:4. Verses 4–5 should be read together, since the first line of each describes the absence of wise guidance and the rise of evil. The second lines (like the contrasts of 28:1–2) state that those who understand will also act to resist injustice. By implication, the righteous not only keep their ways straight but make sure others do the same, standing presumably with the strength of a lion (28:1). The word "resist" can be translated "fight"; in other contexts it is used for dissension (28:25; 29:22). A ruler certainly has responsibility and the power to take this action, but the charge is for all who "keep the law." Attitude toward "the law" (*torah*, "teaching, instruction"; cf. 28:7, 9; also 1:8; 29:18) makes the difference, for humans need a reference point outside themselves. In Proverbs, *torah* primarily refers to wisdom teaching, not the covenant instructions given through Moses. Yet the two are not far removed; to ignore this teaching is also to ignore that of Moses, especially when it involves mistreatment of the poor (28:3; cf. vv. 6–9).

28:5. Similar in form to verse 4, this saying contrasts those who "do not understand justice" with those who "understand it fully" (lit., "understand all things") because they seek Yahweh (cf. the "man of understanding" [root *byn*], 28:2). Once again we are reminded that the purpose of *torah* and understanding is to bring about justice (or "right judgment," cf. 1:3).

28:6. Verses 6–8 can be read together around the theme of possessions, for they describe persons who are either blameless and discerning or corrupted by wealth, perverted, gluttons, and cheats. The better-than saying of verse 6 replicates half of 19:1 by introducing a different second line; perversity there is heard from the fool's lips, whereas here it is seen in the rich one's perverse ways. In both cases the only essential possession is integrity.

28:7. "Keeps the law" echoes the second line of verse 4, where companionship is also a theme. One person is a friend to the wicked, another a friend of gluttons; both are unresponsive to parental instruction (cf. 23:20–21; 27:11; Deut. 21:18–21). A person can be discerning or disgraceful; the first understands a great deal (root *byn*; cf. Prov. 28:2, 5) and does much to preserve justice and order.

28:8. Gouging on loans may be one of the forms of the oppression mentioned in verse 3. Israelites were to charge no interest at all to those in great need, for to the poor, any interest would be "exorbitant" (Ex. 22:25; Lev. 25:36; Deut. 23:19). If one gets rich doing just that, the interest must be great indeed; it is poetic justice that the ill-gotten wealth goes to one who will give it back to the poor (cf. Prov. 28:27).

28:9. Poetic justice appears again in another *torah* saying that follows a saying about the poor (cf. 28:7, 9; 29:18). The return in kind for not listening to the law is a familiar motif in the prophets, but it also appears in wisdom's first speech (1:23–28); if you won't listen to God, God will not listen to you. This proverb suggests that everything about this person is an "abomination" (*to'ebah*; NIV "detestable") to God, even the act of prayer, for it is disingenuous.

28:10. This proverb presents a vivid picture of an evil person leading another along a path strewn with his own traps, reminding readers of 1:17–18, where evil men tried to lead the young man away from right living and toward a life of violence. Just as their plan backfired (26:27), so also here, but the blameless (28:6, 18) receive a good inheritance. The use of the term "upright" echoes the prologue of the book (1:3).

28:11. As it reads in Hebrew, this saying pits a rich person who thinks himself wise against a poor person. The NIV rightly translates the example as what "may" come from a rich man, for the saying does not indict every wealthy person; it does recognize that the temptation is there. One who is wise in one's own eyes has no fear of God or love of righteousness (cf. 3:7; 26:5, 12), for such people answer to no one. We would expect the contrasting poor person to be humble, with downcast eyes. Instead, this person is "discerning" (*mebin*; cf. 28:2, 5, 7), one who has eyes to see through the bravado (cf. 25:2).

28:12. Linked with verse 13 by the image of "hiding/concealing," this saying draws a contrast between loud rejoicing in the open and silent hiding to show how political power can be used to help or oppress (cf. 11:10; 28:28; 29:2, 16). People know that the character of a leader will have consequences for them, but the "triumph" of the righteous is not the victory of a political group or party. Rather, it is the people's exultation when righteous rule is established (cf. 28:2-5).

Fates of the Wicked and the Righteous (28:13-28)

CRIMES OF THEFT and the practice of greed that shuts its eyes to the poor will bring destruction, but the one who repents finds mercy. Yahweh is named or implied as actor throughout this cluster.

28:13. Verses 13 and 14 are linked by Yahweh's response to human choices. The image of hiding in verse 12 is repeated here in the "concealing" of sin (cf. 17:9); the remedy for this cover-up is to "confess" and "renounce" (*ʿozeb*; lit., "leave, abandon"). People may forgive a person who truly changes, but the phrase "find mercy" also looks for grace from another direction (cf. Num. 14:41; Ps. 32:1-5).[4]

28:14. If the previous saying hinted at divine grace, here human fear of Yahweh leads to blessing or happiness (*ʾašre*; cf. 8:34; 20:7; Ps. 1:1). Note the contrast between one who "fears continually"[5] and one who "hardens the heart." A hard heart knows no correction and therefore no change; it will hide, not confess (Prov. 28:13), a sure path to "trouble."

28:15. Verses 15 and 16 both deal with matters of unjust rule. Hard hearts do not know proper fear and make trouble for others as well (cf. 28:14). Two metaphors for a wicked ruler use the well-known behaviors of two fearsome animals. The lion roars and the bear charges (or, possibly, "ranges" or "roves" over a territory); whether the behaviors are linked to hunting or defending territory is not clear, but the first is most like a wicked ruler, who preys on the poor. In Proverbs, the king's wrath (presumably a *just* wrath) is like the lion's roar (19:12, 20:2); only here is the roar like a wicked person ruling over the helpless poor (*dal*; 28:8, 11; cf. v. 12).

28:16. Linked with the previous proverb by the theme of government, this saying presents a contrast between the tyrant who rules with (lit.) "great oppression" and the good ruler who (lit.) "makes long the days," that is, has a long life. One must choose how one defines greatness; the ruler who is

---

4. Whybray, *Proverbs*, 393, along with other interpreters, observes that this is the only verse in Proverbs that speaks of God's forgiveness of the penitent. Murphy, *Proverbs*, 216, looks to Ps. 32 and Job 31:33-34 for parallels and stresses the public nature of the confession. It is made before the community and God. "One can cover the faults of another (Prov. 10:12) but not one's own sins."

5. The word is not *yiraʾ*, as used in the phrase "fear of the LORD," but *paḥad*, "trembles" (Ps. 119:120; cf. Prov. 1:33; 3:25). "The LORD" is not written in the Heb. but is implied (cf. 14:16).

lacking in understanding and abundant in oppression has bet on the wrong horse.[6] The word for "ill-gotten gain" appears only at the start and middle of the book and finally here near its end (*beṣaᶜ*; cf. 1:19; 15:27).

28:17. Verses 17 and 18 both treat the subject of guilt and consequences. Although difficulties with translation and therefore with identifying the background to this proverb make interpretation provisionary, we know that the person "tormented" is (lit.) "oppressed by lifeblood" (28:3; cf. 14:31; 22:16).[7] The translation of "fugitive till death" is one way to make sense of "flees to a pit." While most agree on "let no one support him" as the concluding phrase, Proverbs often uses *tmk* for placing hands on a person, yielding, "Let no one touch him," in the sense of capture.[8] In either case, the warning against interference is clear, and thus the cities of refuge may be in the background (Ex. 21:12–14; Deut. 19:1–10). While the original context remains uncertain, clearly sins of blood start a justice in motion that cannot be derailed.

28:18. The one "whose walk is blameless" has appeared before, as has the matching contrast with the one "whose ways are perverse" or crooked (28:6, 10). Verse 10 also pictures one who "will fall"[9] into his own pit, although the word is not the same as that used here. The blameless are "kept safe" (or "saved," *yšᶜ*; cf. 20:22), although the protector is not named.

28:19. Read together with verse 20, this proverb makes a comparison of rewards. Not only is the wordplay on (lit.) "plenty of bread . . . plenty of poverty" a wry contrast in outcomes (repeating *yiśbaᶜ*, "filled"), the contrast of behaviors also sets staying home against riding off in pursuit of vanities. If the goals are empty at the start,[10] the final outcome will be also. This saying is nearly identical to 12:11 (except for the last two words in that proverb, "lacks sense").

28:20. Like verse 19, this saying asks its hearer to choose outcomes. Do you want to be blessed richly, or are you only in a hurry (*ʾaṣ*; cf. 19:2; 20:21; 21:6; 29:20) to get rich? The first requires faithfulness, the second abandons virtue to chase after material gains, cutting corners in work and ethics. Once

---

6. The word for prince (*nagid*) occurs only here in Proverbs; many commentators suggest that it overloads the line and may have been inserted by later scribes. On the basis of the Greek Septuagint, others recommend that "lacks judgment" be changed to "lacks revenue," thus motivating the oppression.

7. G. R. Driver, "Problems in the Hebrew Text of Proverbs," *Bib* 32 (1951): 192. Driver repoints the Heb. to read "a man *addicted* to bloodshed shall flee into the pit."

8. Clifford, *Proverbs*, 242.

9. There is some debate whether "suddenly" (lit., "at once") should be dropped on the basis of the LXX, which has "pit" (see NRSV). We withhold judgment and follow the Hebrew text with emphasis on the verb "fall."

10. Murphy, *Proverbs*, 217.

again, it comes down to aims in life; if one seeks the higher goal of virtue, other goods will come. But if one seeks the lower goal of possessions alone, even more will be lost, perhaps even one's integrity. The one who does "not go unpunished" in Hebrew will (lit.) "not be acquitted." The theme of riches is picked up again in verse 22.

28:21. The contrast in the saying is ironic. Although it is "not good" (cf. 18:5) to show favoritism in judging (lit., "recognize faces"; cf. 24:23; Deut. 1:17; 16:19), people will risk great penalties for small amounts of gain, even a piece of bread (cf. *lehem*, "food," in Prov. 28:19; cf. 20:17). We often see this with news reports of judges and elected officials who sell all for the pottage of bribery. Perhaps this is one of the ways one can hurry to get rich (cf. 28:20, 22).

28:22. In this second portrait of one who is "eager to get rich" (cf. 28:20; *bahal* can also mean "hurries"), the motivation appears. The "stingy man" is one (lit.) "of evil eye," that is, "miserly" (NRSV; cf. 23:6; "good eye" in 22:9), and will do anything to acquire assets. Given the context of the previous verses, readers are not surprised that what waits is not wealth but poverty. In God's economy, hoarding and acquisitiveness put riches in bags that are full of holes (Hag. 1:6), but that irony does not occur to this person who "is unaware" (lit., "does not know"; cf. Prov. 7:23; 9:18). Once again, a proverb makes clear that acquiring wealth just to hold onto it makes a poor goal for a life. What is condemned is not work or wealth but making them the center of one's life and everything else peripheral.

28:23. The reversal of this saying is like the one just before; what one hopes to get eludes the grasp, whether it be riches or favor. Rebuke in teaching and personal feedback may be costly to those who give it and painful to those who receive it (cf. 9:7–9; 27:5–6), but it pays back in time ("at the end"). However, flattery (cf. 6:24; 26:28) earns little real favor, although it is not clear whether the flattery is given with that end in mind or to gain some other unscrupulous advantage. In any case, the reversal shows that it is the honest tongue that earns favor, not a "smooth" one.

28:24. The point is in the comparison; while destruction is heinous in the view of the community, so is the act of cheating parents (cf. 18:9). The robbery is not specified, but one can imagine scenarios of mooching or usurping property. To do such a thing and say (lit.) "no transgression" (*'en pašaʿ*; cf. 29:16, 22) not only adds insult to injury, it betrays a seared conscience (cf. 30:20). Parents who have given of their means and very selves to their children deserve care when it is their turn in their later years. There is a lesson here about returning thanks and service to those who have given much.[11]

---

11. Murphy, ibid., 217, looks to the Decalogue and the concrete sayings 19:26; 20:20; 28:24; 30:11, 17.

28:25. This proverb and the one that follows are linked by the repetition of "he who trusts" (*boṭeaḥ;* cf. "confidence" in 28:1). The wordplay puts together greed (*raḥab nepeš,* "great appetite") and prosperity (*yeḏuššan,* "growing fat"; cf. 1:25; 13:4; 15:30; 28:5). Outcomes are also compared: Greed brings "dissension" (root *grh;* cf. 28:4; also 15:18; 29:22), trust brings prosperity. As in 28:14, Yahweh's presence is understood but not named in Hebrew.

28:26. The punch of this saying comes from what is left out of the syllogism. Those who trust in themselves (lit., "in his own heart"; cf. 3:5) are by definition "fools," headed for a destruction with no escape (cf. 28:18). To trust in one's own heart is to believe that one's own thoughts and intentions are sufficient guides to life, that they will lead us to what is good for ourselves. The sages knew better. Although it seems logical that we know our needs and can look out for our own best interests, nothing is further from the truth.[12] It is not specified whether the destruction is self-inflicted, imposed by Yahweh, or both.

28:27. If the greedy one defrauds, hoards, and comes to poverty (see 28:22, 25), one who gives to and cares for the needy suffers no want. The key is to be able to see need, but many prove unwilling to try, shutting their eyes. Here is no blessing (28:20) but curse (cf. 3:33; Deut. 28:20–27), perhaps a way of stating that one will be poor of health, status, and provisions. The "many [*rab*] curses" find their echo in the righteous in the next verse, who become many or "thrive" (*yirⁱbu*).

28:28. The picture of verse 12 is repeated, beginning with people in hiding (cf. 27:12), but then giving, as Paul Harvey would say, "the rest of the story." The wicked will perish, and not from natural causes; after that, the righteous will thrive (see comments on 28:27; cf. 29:2, 16).

Bridging Contexts

RULERS AND RIGHTEOUSNESS. Readers who are attentive to proverb placement and the arrangement of proverb clusters will note the righteous/wicked contrasts that form the framework of chapters 28 and 29 (28:1, 12, 28; 29:2, 16, 27). They may also notice that each of the middle four of these sayings cites the one that comes before, picking up where the other ends (all are also linked by use of the key word *rab*, root *rbb*, highlighted with italics):

- 28:12—When the righteous triumph, there is *great* elation; but when the wicked rise to power, men go into hiding.

---

12. Goldingay, "Proverbs," 605, suggests that trust in one's self turns one away from God and others and is thus doubly stupid.

- 28:28—When the wicked rise to power, people go into hiding; but when the wicked perish, the righteous *thrive*.
- 29:2—When the righteous *thrive*, the people rejoice; when the wicked rule, the people groan.
- 29:16—When the wicked *thrive*, so does sin, but the righteous will see their downfall.

These four verses relate the righteous/wicked contrast to the matters of government and its effect on the people, a topic treated directly in 28:2, 3, 15, 16 and 29:4, 14, 26, but also implied in the proverbs about righteousness, justice, and fair dealing (28:1, 5, 10; cf. 1:3). While righteous rule has appeared before as a fruit of wisdom (cf. 8:15–16; 16:10–16; 20:8, 26, 28; 25:1–6), the matter comes to center stage for the climax of chapters 28–29 and will be treated again in chapters 30–31.

The last two verses of chapter 28 link care for the poor and righteous rule. The choice between "many" curses and a "thriving" population of righteous people (28:27–28, root *rbh* in both cases) makes an age-old association of political thinking. If there are too many people who are poor and unjustly defrauded, government has not done its job. Verse 16 places responsibility on the monarch: "A tyrannical ruler lacks judgment, but he who hates ill-gotten gain will enjoy a long life." However, the rare term for "ill-gotten gain" is also used in proverbs that do not mention the king, appearing at the beginning and middle of the book (1:19; 15:27) and here near the end. The proverbs leading up to 28:16 juxtapose piety (28:13–14) and the devastating effects of wicked government (28:12, 15) in a way that adds this dimension of rule to the general concern for worship and ethics introduced at the very start of the book.

The two proverbs in this chapter that name Yahweh do the same, contrasting evil people who do not understand justice with those who seek Yahweh and understand all things (28:5)—a contrast between the one of great appetite who only stirs up a pot of strife with the one who trusts in Yahweh and (lit.) "grows fat" (28:25). It was every person's responsibility to live in righteousness, justice, and equity, but rulers had the additional responsibility to enact laws and judgments to accomplish the same.

Certainly the themes of rule and righteousness have their outworking in matters of economics and power, the dynamics of which are never separated. While the differences between the democratic governments of North America and the monarchies of Israel and the ancient Near East are many, certain principles do carry over into our day. One is the standard of measure by which governments are judged, ensuring justice for all its constituents and taking care that a deficient understanding of justice does not leave out the poor. Drawing from all that has been said in previous chapters, the proverbs of this collection make a strong connection between personal character and good government, not to claim that the issue is simple but to show that the concerns of wisdom permeate every level of society.

Therefore, while the proverbs will not advise us about means—for example, trickle-down economics versus strong government involvement, private versus federal action, government support of religious charities—they do hold out the standards of fair dealing and inclusion that help leaders and voters navigate their way through the details of living and working together. When United States president Jimmy Carter quoted Micah 6:8, "He has showed you, O man, what is good. And what does the LORD require of you? To act justly and to love mercy and to walk humbly with your God," his inaugural speech addressed the character of a people, not only his own leadership.

Therefore, Christians who seek to understand these proverbs will ask their leaders to exhibit good character—and not just in matters of personal holiness, such as marital fidelity, honesty, and rejection of ill-gotten gain. They will also ask their leaders to use their power and influence to establish the expectation of justice, mercy, and even humility throughout the land. For a start, the evangelical church can learn from its wins and losses in political involvement and broaden its agenda to include personal holiness and social justice, rejecting the false division between the two that biblical teaching frequently speaks against. Jesus criticized the Pharisees not for ignoring personal religious practices but for ignoring the weightier matters of justice, mercy, and faithfulness (Matt. 23:23; Luke 11:42 adds "love of God"). Could the Pharisees' problem of compartmentalization speak to a common human tendency? A faith that has no concern for fair and just treatment of the poor is found wanting (James 2:14–18; 3:13–18; 5:1–6).

Politics and faith. Yet the proverbs do not stop with the matters of righteousness, justice, and fair dealing in human relationships; they typically go on to talk about fear of Yahweh (cf. 1:3, 7), urging their readers to seek and trust in him (28:5, 25). In between the two Yahweh proverbs are others that imply his presence by mention of prayer, confession, and fear (28:9, 13, 14). In the sage's understanding, righteous rule and fear of God were inseparable.

Today, however, American Christians live in a pluralist society that separates matters of justice from matters of faith, even as it has traditionally made a distinction between church and state. That distinction has received greater attention in recent years as greater numbers of people representing other religions have joined the first immigrants to the land. Previous assumptions that Christmas nativity scenes can be displayed on civic property have been challenged because of increased recognition that Christians are not the only voice.

The relationship between American society and the Christian faith is complex and beyond the scope of our discussion, but a growing secularism is beyond dispute. Can Christians require their leaders to be people of faith as well, and is it in their best interests to vote for professing Christians? The proverbs do not answer such questions directly, for they assume that kings and queens will consider themselves answerable to the Lord as part of the royal charter. Two extremes certainly are to be avoided: to assume that faith necessarily makes one a better ruler and that a strict secularist cannot appreciate matters of justice as necessary for the common good. The relationship of Christians to the political scene will be taken up in the next section, but here we note that while one may love justice without a corresponding love for God, the proverbs show us that the reverse can never be true; one cannot claim to love God and have no interest in justice.

Avarice and rulers. More at the center of these proverbs, however, is the problem of persons in power using their positions for their own gain, richly illustrated in Israel's history and almost as frequently in today's local and national politics. The sages stress that the righteous will not only reject such practices but resist them (28:1, 4), knowing that wickedness will eventually fall (28:28; cf. 29:16) and that the righteous will do all that is necessary to oppose evil while they wait, sometimes hiding, sometimes standing strong as a lion (28:1, 28). Such concern to stand for what is right can be both personal and political. One can speak for fair treatment of a friend or of a whole people group, even speaking against governmental leaders when necessary.

Torah. While the mysteries of power and leadership are complex and never completely understood, what is clear here is the call to faithful character. The tradition was clearly communicated to Israel in the *torah* delivered through Moses, the basis of a covenant relationship between God and the people, a covenant that the people broke and Yahweh promised to restore (the New Testament points to the new covenant in Jesus). In Proverbs, the *torah* (teaching) is that of wisdom, not the covenant with Israel, yet that teaching is never in conflict with the *torah* of Moses. So, for example, if the commandment says to love your neighbor because "I am your God," the proverbs says to love your neighbor because it works better that way. The references to *torah* in chapter 28 show that there are good reasons for recommending the neighbor love of the covenantal *torah* through the teaching/*torah* of the proverbs.

THE CHURCH, RIGHTEOUSNESS, and politics. These proverbs of righteous character and righteous rule lie side by side, suggesting that whatever the differences between personal and political choices, the concern for fairness and compassion are sure guides for both. As Christians deliberate about their involvement in the political process, it is important to remember that these lessons about personal and corporate character must first be put into practice by the church.

Robert Webber reminds us that the early Christian movement was a countercultural movement, nonaligned with political powers. The early church was seen as subversive because the Christians would not say that "Caesar is Lord," reserving that phrase for Jesus and his kingdom. Webber recovers that stance of nonalignment, chiding Christians who align themselves with conservative Republicanism and liberal Democratic politics alike. He believes that Christians are citizens of another kingdom with another form of politics—

> the politics of forming and nurturing a society in the world that images the new creation through forming a people with Christian virtues and a Christian view of life. The social and political work of evangelicals is counter cultural. However, the calling of the church is not to "clean up America for God," but to be the church, a radical counter cultural communal presence in society. The ultimate question is not "How is America?" but "How is the church?"[13]

However true it is that Christians are first called to live as an alternate community to the ways of the world, balancing radical identification and distinction, Christians are also called upon to vote and serve as community leaders. They will be (or should be) asked to lend voice and muscle to the business of living in neighborhoods, towns or cities, and nations. While the church exists as a model of what might be, challenging and inspiring the rest of the community, its members are also faced with the daunting prospect of stating their views on matters social and political and of lending support to local civic bodies and service organizations.

We should cooperate and lend support when we can, but we should also speak when we disagree—and at root, Christians disagree with the rest of the world over the question of political authority, that is, who really is in charge. If we serve and speak as though we had no higher allegiance than the

---

13. R. E. Webber, *Ancient-Future Faith: Rethinking Evangelicalism for a Postmodern World* (Grand Rapids: Baker, 1999), 167–68. Webber adds that the early church lived in a tension between being separate from the world, identified with the world, and seeking to transform the world.

One who calls us to learn and live wisdom, we may be cheered, but we may also be jeered or something worse. William Willimon claims that

> the church is, for better or worse, God's answer to what is wrong in the world. Just let the church begin telling the truth, speaking the truth to power, witnessing to the fact that God, not nations, rules the world, that Jesus Christ really is Lord, and the church will quickly find how easily threatened and inherently unstable are the rulers of this world.[14]

Christians, wealth, and society. While comprehensive, this general distinction between Christian and secular views of authority guides but does not make decisions about positions on issues of the day. If these proverbial reflections on government and life together critique our separation of what is personal and political, they also challenge us to respond on both levels. Christians seeking to live under the tutelage of these sages' wisdom will make important choices about life vocation and lifestyles, but they will also have opinions that are exercised about matters corporate and societal.

(1) Just as the church should present itself as a community set apart from any others, yet in service of all, believers should make life choices that say no to the greed and climbing that characterizes so much of contemporary culture as well as refuse to shut their eyes to the poor (28:27), keeping them open to notice the overwhelming needs around us. One begins to reject the world's values and appetites by making room in one's life for those who have need. It is a matter of call—*vocare* or vocation.

John Westerhoff critiques the assumptions of modernity, including its attempt to eliminate dualisms. He claims that when the dualism of the material world and the spiritual world was abandoned in favor of material monism, vocation came to be understood only as a career. "When you ask people about their vocation, they talk about what they do to make a living."[15] There is a better way, says Westerhoff, for the Christian life of faith comes by living it, not by thinking about it:

> We are more apt to act our way to a new way of thinking than we are to think our way to a new way of acting. . . . Robert Bridges, a friend of the poet and Jesuit priest Gerard Manley Hopkins, so admired

---

14. Willimon, *Pastor: The Theology and Practice of Ordained Ministry*, (Nashville: Abingdon, 2002) 256–57. For this reason, Willimon adds that "because the consequences of Spirit-filled speech tend to be political, economic, and social, therefore *we must discipline ourselves to read Scripture congregationally, ecclessially, and therefore politically*, rather than therapeutically, subjectively, inductively, or relevantly, as the world defines relevance."

15. J. Westerhoff, "Westerhoff on Stewardship," *Giving* 3 (2001): 18–22.

Hopkins' faith and spirituality that he wrote him a letter asking how he might also have that experience of God. The return letter from this man of words contained just two words: Give alms.[16]

The funny thing about money is that we can give it away and draw close to God, or we can hoard it and find ourselves far away from him. Certainly the proverbs that name the poor in this collection intend to teach us something about the life of faith and the influence that money has in our lives, for good or for bad. Where did we ever get the idea that life was about getting all we can and maybe giving some away? Reversing those priorities may be better for our souls than we know.[17] It can be as simple as learning to give generously to those who are in need.

(2) Christians are challenged to support good government and work with it to resist evil in all its forms. If the principle is clear, the ways to work it out are not always easily articulated. It is clear that giving alms alone will not keep some from taking unfair advantage of the poor, and one way that Christians can open their eyes to the poor is to become aware of policies that impact people of low income, support those that help, and vote against those that work against them. Yet a recent survey of students at evangelical Christian colleges found that 77 percent agreed that "social problems are best addressed by changing individual hearts," and 55 percent agreed that "individuals are poor because of structural causes"; only 9 percent agreed that "social problems are best addressed by changing social institutions." They believed that the church should focus on personal morality (54 percent) more than social justice (12 percent).[18]

Certainly other issues come under the umbrella of righteousness and wickedness, but for these proverbs, the central issue is that greed and grasping exemplify wickedness, and when it is characteristic of political leadership, the results are devastating. Wickedness or righteousness alike can thrive and

---

16. Ibid., 19.

17. C. Sine and T. Sine, *Living on Purpose: Finding God's Best for Your Life* (Grand Rapids: Baker, 2002). The Sines cite Donald Kraybill in *The Upside Down Kingdom* (Scottsdale, Ariz.: Herald, 1990), 137: "Faithful stewards are fugal when calculating their own needs and generous in responding to the needs of others."

18. Yet only 35 percent agreed that "if enough people are brought to Christ, social problems will take care of themselves" (J. M. Penning and C. E. Smidt, *Evangelicalism: The Next Generation* [Grand Rapids: Baker, 2002]). The authors add: "Evangelical college students hold a social theology that reflects views historically associated with American evangelicalism. Evangelical college students still adhere to an individualistic world view, for they believe that social problems are best addressed by changing individual hearts than by reforming social institutions.... Social problems do not disappear because sin does not disappear even among those who are brought to Christ," 117-18.

wane, but the final outcome is that the wicked will "perish" (28:28). While the responsibility for these outcomes clearly belongs to Yahweh, people and their leaders are both responsible for establishing the environment in which righteousness gets the upper hand. This chapter is a challenge to develop wisdom's character, both as individuals and as a people.

Proverbs 29:1–27

¹ A MAN WHO remains stiff-necked after many rebukes
   will suddenly be destroyed—without remedy.
² When the righteous thrive, the people rejoice;
   when the wicked rule, the people groan.
³ A man who loves wisdom brings joy to his father,
   but a companion of prostitutes squanders his wealth.
⁴ By justice a king gives a country stability,
   but one who is greedy for bribes tears it down.
⁵ Whoever flatters his neighbor
   is spreading a net for his feet.
⁶ An evil man is snared by his own sin,
   but a righteous one can sing and be glad.
⁷ The righteous care about justice for the poor,
   but the wicked have no such concern.
⁸ Mockers stir up a city,
   but wise men turn away anger.
⁹ If a wise man goes to court with a fool,
   the fool rages and scoffs, and there is no peace.
¹⁰ Bloodthirsty men hate a man of integrity
   and seek to kill the upright.
¹¹ A fool gives full vent to his anger,
   but a wise man keeps himself under control.
¹² If a ruler listens to lies,
   all his officials become wicked.
¹³ The poor man and the oppressor have this in common:
   The LORD gives sight to the eyes of both.
¹⁴ If a king judges the poor with fairness,
   his throne will always be secure.
¹⁵ The rod of correction imparts wisdom,
   but a child left to himself disgraces his mother.
¹⁶ When the wicked thrive, so does sin,
   but the righteous will see their downfall.
¹⁷ Discipline your son, and he will give you peace;
   he will bring delight to your soul.
¹⁸ Where there is no revelation, the people cast off restraint;
   but blessed is he who keeps the law.
¹⁹ A servant cannot be corrected by mere words;
   though he understands, he will not respond.

²⁰ Do you see a man who speaks in haste?
>   There is more hope for a fool than for him.
²¹ If a man pampers his servant from youth,
>   he will bring grief in the end.
²² An angry man stirs up dissension,
>   and a hot-tempered one commits many sins.
²³ A man's pride brings him low,
>   but a man of lowly spirit gains honor.
²⁴ The accomplice of a thief is his own enemy;
>   he is put under oath and dare not testify.
²⁵ Fear of man will prove to be a snare,
>   but whoever trusts in the LORD is kept safe.
²⁶ Many seek an audience with a ruler,
>   but it is from the LORD that man gets justice.
²⁷ The righteous detest the dishonest;
>   the wicked detest the upright.

THE FINAL CHAPTER of proverbs collected by "the men of Hezekiah," like the others in the collection (25:1–29:27; see comments in ch. 25), intertwines reflections on rule and public character with general sayings about the moral life. While the latter clearly apply to all, the juxtaposition implies that they especially apply to rulers. Also, the insights on rule remind readers that we all wield power in some form to some degree and therefore need to handle it responsibly.

While chapter 29 does not fall into an obvious outline, the repetition of "thrive" (root *rbb*, "increase") in 29:2 and 16 and the recurrence of "wise/wisdom" in between (29:3, 8, 9, 11, 15) ties the first half together. The wise person sees righteousness and wickedness for what they are and makes the right choice. Verses 13–14 juxtapose sayings about Yahweh and the king near the middle of the chapter, as do verses 25–26 near the end, so we set our markers there.

Cycles of thriving righteousness and wickedness (29:1–16)
Discipline of sons and servants, justice for nations (29:17–27)

Other features point to an intentional arrangement. Verses 12–14 link long-lasting rule with discernment and justice.[1] Verses 15–21 present topics

---

1. Whybray, *The Composition of the Book of Proverbs*, 127–28, adds that vv. 10–17 may form a subsection on the need for kings to learn wisdom like everyone else.

in a leapfrog fashion, its key terms and themes showing up in every other verse: "child/son" (29:15, 17), "sin/no restraint" (29:16, 18), "discipline/ correct" (root *ysr*, 29:17, 19), "revelation/see" (root *ḥzh*, 29:18, 20), and "servant" (29:19, 21).[2] Verses 22–27 may take the form of an alphabetic acrostic (see discussion at v. 22). Key words and themes show up in proverbs about the people (29:2, 18) and the rise and fall of rulers, good and bad (29:2, 16; cf. 28:12, 28), showing the effects of one on the other in a more critical assessment of the work of kings. The Hebrew for "man" (*ʾîš*, 29:1, 3, 4, 6, 9, 10, 13, 20, 22, 26, 27) appears frequently throughout, suggesting that matters of living wisely are always both personal and public, never one or the other.

Cycles of Thriving Righteousness and Wickedness (29:1–16)

SOMETIMES THE WICKED rule, sometimes the righteous, but the wise know that the wicked will eventually fall. The wise ways of restraint and peace come to the forefront, for they are always in season.

29:1. The ox that would not bend its neck for a yoke became a symbol for recalcitrant Israel (Ex. 32:9; Deut. 9:6; 2 Kings 17:14; Isa. 48:4). We would expect "stiff-necked" (lit., "make the neck hard") to be in contrast with "broken," but like a clay jar that shatters (*šaber*), such a person is "destroyed," broken beyond repair. A rebuke is a wound (Prov. 27:5–8), but it is given to prevent something much worse. Those who refuse this means of prevention will be denied any means of restoration (cf. 6:15b, which repeats the second line of this verse).[3]

29:2. The contrast between the plural righteous people who "thrive" (*rbh*, lit., to "increase, become many"; cf. 28:28; 29:16) and the singular wicked person who "rules" suggests that these righteous people are the ones who really hold the power. People thrive when there is a single good ruler; they do not go into hiding (cf. 28:28) but rejoice. Clearly, one bad ruler can do great harm and cause many to groan. Wisdom and folly are never experienced in isolation, but their effects are especially pronounced when practiced by someone in authority.

29:3. This saying pits love of wisdom against visiting prostitutes, similar to the personifications of wisdom and folly that run throughout the book (4:6–9; 9:1–18; 31:10–31). A father finds joy in a son who lives well, raises

---

2. Strictly speaking, the leapfrog of key words only shows up in vv. 17–21, although "child/youth" (*naʿar*), repeats at vv. 15 and 21.

3. Malchow, "A Manual for Future Monarchs: Proverbs 27:23–29:27," 241, says that this verse is a centerpiece to chs. 28–29, similar to the function of 25:16 in 25:2–27; cf. Bryce, *A Legacy of Wisdom*, 142.

a family of his own, and passes on his parents' wise ways along with the estate (cf. 28:7). Conversely, a father's wealth can be squandered (lit., "destroyed"; cf. 19:9; 21:28), losing all the father has worked so hard to keep, both the wealth and the more precious possession of the son (cf. 5:7–10). Jesus told a story about such a lost son (Luke 15:11–32). In Proverbs, however, those who find wisdom find "wealth" (*hon*, Prov. 8:18), and happily in Jesus' parable, the son "came to his senses."

29:4. A second proverb contrasting good and bad rule joins with verse 2 to create a frame around the wise son saying of verse 3, perhaps a subtle reminder that kings also rejoice and grieve over their sons. The contrast between justice that brings stability (lit., "causes a land to stand") and evil that "tears it down" is clear. But the phrase that the NIV renders "greedy for bribes" is difficult, prompting a number of translations. The phrase reads a "man of that which is lifted up" (*terumot*, NIV "bribes"), an allusion to sacrifices of worship (Ex. 25:2–3). It is used here as a metaphor for rulers who help themselves to the "offering"—perhaps through taxes or by fraud (TNK). "Justice" (root *špṭ*; cf. Prov. 29:14, 26) is the highest responsibility of the king.

29:5. Following a saying about greedy kings comes this proverb about one who mistreats a neighbor. The flattery is certainly intended to cheat the neighbor in some way, but it is not clear whether "his feet" goes with the neighbor or the flatterer.[4] If the first, the contrast is between the smooth words of flattery (5:3; 7:21; 26:28; 28:23) and the harsh capture of the net. If the latter, the proverb is like our "what goes around comes around," consistent with the next proverb and the many references to traps in Proverbs (cf. 1:17–19; 26:27; 28:19).

29:6. The net spread out for others (29:5) is also the sin that traps the trapper. The contrast between one who is snared (*moqeš*; cf. 29:25) and one who rejoices (*sameah*; cf. 29:2) is that between the cry of a captured bird and the song of one who is free. Gladness or rejoicing is a common response to righteousness in Proverbs (cf. 13:9; 23:24–25).

29:7. A literal translation reads, "A righteous one knows the rights of the poor [cf. 31:5, 8], a wicked one does not understand such knowledge." The key to the saying is the word "know" (*ydᶜ*), which appears in both lines, reminding readers of the herdsman who is to "know" the condition of the flocks (27:23) and the ruler of understanding and "knowledge" (28:2). Both should be caretakers, authorities who make sure they know about human need and take steps to meet it (29:4, 13–14, 26). By extension, all who are

---

4. The NRSV removes the ambiguity of the translation: "Whoever flatters a neighbor is spreading a net for the neighbor's feet." The parallel structure of the proverb sets flattery directed *toward* (*ᶜal*) a neighbor against the net *for* (*ᶜal*) the feet.

righteous "know" the rights of the poor, but those who do not understand this knowledge are called "wicked." Strong words!

29:8. A series of character sketches in verses 8–10 is marked by the Hebrew word for "man" at the start of each verse (*ʾiš*; plural, *ʾanše*), pitting the "mockers" and "bloodthirsty men" against a single "wise man." This motif of incendiary fools and calming sages occurs throughout Proverbs, but here the picture is intensified by the presence of "men who scorn" ("mockers"; cf. 1:22) and the disastrous effects that spread throughout the city. Such people "stir up" (*yapiḥu*) the city like one who blows on a fire to inflame it. The saying is first of a series on the theme of speaking and listening (29:8–12).

29:9. The scope narrows in this second of three proverbs about types of "men" (see previous comment). The scene is a courtroom in which a wise man (lit.) "seeks justice" (root *špṭ*) from a "fool." The result is the same as in verse 8—not conciliation or settlement but more uproar, here fueled by more scoffing with the addition of raging. The wise may calm anger, but not the rage of a recalcitrant fool (26:3–5). When read together, the two proverbs imply that mocking (i.e., rejecting all external standards of behavior) inevitably leads to social upheaval.

29:10. The third character sketch (see comments on v. 8) looks at "bloodthirsty men" (lit., "men of blood"; cf. 2 Sam. 16:8). This saying is complicated by a difficult second line, which can be translated, "the upright, they seek his life." Typically, to seek one's life denotes an intent to kill (cf. 1 Kings 19:10; Ps. 63:10), but "the upright" may be the subject of the second line, creating a contrast; in this reading, the upright seek the life of the person of integrity, perhaps to save it.[5] Either way, the evil intent of the "bloodthirsty men" who hate integrity and the contrast with those who love it are clear (cf. Prov. 29:27).

29:11. This saying about self-control contains a number of idioms that give the interpreter pause. Translated literally, it reads: "A fool gives out all his breath/mind [*ruaḥ*; cf. 1:23], but the wise quietly holds it back." The saying is akin to the pair at verses 8–9: The fool lets everything out, including his folly, mockery, and raging, but the wise give their words beauty and persuasiveness by making them few (cf. 12:15; 13:3; 14:3; 15:7; 17:28).

29:12. As written in Hebrew, this proverb does not say that the officials *become* wicked, only that they *are* (lit., "all his officials, wicked"). Yet the sense of the NIV holds true, for the character of the ruler determines the character

---

5. Murphy, *Proverbs*, 219–20, translates, "Those who shed blood hate the blameless, but the upright seeks him out." G. R. Driver took "seek" (root *bqš*) as "make great or magnify," as in "but the upright magnify, make much of his life" ("Problems in the Hebrew Text of Proverbs," *Bib* 32 [1951]: 194).

of the court and even the nation. The implied admonition urges persons in authority to weed out the word of falsehood before it takes root (20:8).

29:13. The first Yahweh proverb of this chapter (cf. 29:25–26) levels the playing field between the poor and those who would take advantage of them (28:8; Ps. 72:14). The snap of the saying comes at the end of the first line when the "poor man" and the "oppressor" (lit.) "meet" (*pgš*; cf. Ps. 85:10). The poor person does not defer, the oppressor does not speak harshly (cf. Prov. 18:23), but both are silent before the one who made them (20:12; 22:2) and gave "light to the eyes." The imbalance of power is restored with one look at the One who gives them the ability to see each other.

29:14. This saying links with the one before on the theme of the poor; set in contrast to the person who oppresses them is the king who judges with fairness (or "faithfulness," *ʾemet*). Kidner catches the sense well: "The test of a man in power, and his hidden strength, is the extent to which he keeps faith with those who can put least pressure on him."[6] Association with Yahweh who judges the poor faithfully is strong, as is the theme of stability (29:4; cf. 20:28; Ps. 72:4–7, 12–14).

29:15. This saying contrasts teaching and correction, symbolized by the rod, with the child (or "youth," *naʿar*) "left to himself."[7] This proverb does not relegate administration of discipline to the mother (cf. the father in 13:24) but uses her to highlight the common motif of gladness and shame (23:21–25). There may be word/sound play on "rod" (*šebeṭ*) and "shame" (*mebîš*). The parent who does not give needed correction risks receiving unwanted shame.

29:16. The salt of the proverb is in the wordplay on *rbh*, to "multiply, become great" (28:28; 29:2). The NIV translates it as "thrive" to include the sense of ascending to power and the resultant increase in sin. One might paraphrase to say that the wicked rise, and so the proverb assures readers that the righteous will see their eventual downfall, brought on by their own folly and the intervention of God. In its literary context, this proverb on corporate character is equally applicable to courts and households (cf. 29:14–15).

Discipline of Sons and Servants, Justice for Nations (29:17–27)

SAYINGS ABOUT HOUSEHOLD discipline and community justice are juxtaposed, revealing how much each has in common with the other.

---

6. Kidner, *Proverbs*, 175.

7. It is not clear what "left to himself" (lit., "let go, sent out," *mᵉšullāḥ*) means; some take it as "unrestrained" (Murphy), "let loose" (Clifford), "neglected" (NRSV), or even "out of control" (TNK). The nuance of the word, here set in contrast with "discipline," is more like an animal left to graze (Isa. 27:10) than a bird driven from its nest by a hunter (Isa. 16:2).

29:17. The proverbs of verses 17–21 are linked by catchwords in a leapfrog fashion (see introduction). Akin to the saying at verse 15, this hopeful proverb stresses the positive aspect of "discipline"; if a son left to himself brings shame, the son who receives "discipline" ("instruction," root *ysr*; cf. 29:19; 19:18; 22:6; 31:1) gives peace and delight.[8] Again, what is given is returned in kind.

29:18. Although this proverb is well known, it is often misunderstood because of the varied translations. The KJV is familiar to many: "Where there is no vision, the people perish: but he that keepeth the law, happy is he." The NIV, making use of more recent scholarship, translates the troublesome first line by replacing "revelation" for "vision" and "cast off restraint" for "perish." The "revelation" (*ḥazon*)[9] is usually a prophetic vision (Isa. 1:1; Dan. 1:17; Hab. 1:1), yet this vision may be withheld in times of apostasy and crisis (1 Sam. 3:1; Lam. 2:9; Ezek. 7:26). Thus, the first line observes that when there is no such communication from God and his prophet, the people run wild like undisciplined sons (cf. Prov. 29:15–17; also Ex. 32:25).[10]

The second line narrows the focus to an individual who keeps the *torah* (certainly the teaching of the wise and possibly the *torah* of Moses) and is blessed or happy (*ʾašre*; cf. Ps. 1:1; Prov. 31:28). This saying does not elevate individual piety over social righteousness; rather, it observes that teaching, wisdom, and covenant are a constant resource for both. This proverb is too limited in its teaching if it is only taken as support for church programs and goal-setting.

29:19. A puzzling saying that seems to contradict all that has been said about teaching, this proverb appears not only to negate the influence of words but also to claim that understanding does not necessarily lead to an appropriate response. However, as one of two proverbs about servants in this chapter (cf. 29:21), the emphasis here falls on correction and even restraint (cf. 29:18). Servants were expected to follow orders, and at times more than a verbal prodding was necessary. While a servant may be wiser than a son (17:2; 29:15), the exception proves the rule. A wise person, perhaps a messenger to a ruler, was expected to "respond" or give an answer (22:21), but such learning is not in view here; a servant was to hear and do.

---

8. The Heb. roots for "peace" (or "rest," *nuaḥ*) and "delight" (*maʿadannim*, same root as "Eden") both appear in the description of the garden (Gen. 2:15).

9. The LXX reads "interpreter"; some emend the Heb. to a related word for "supervisor," but the principle of leadership is clear enough without disturbing the parallel of "vision" and "law."

10. Malchow, "A Manual for Future Monarchs," 242–43, takes it as a warning to aspiring rulers that the lack of such vision (cf. Job 4:12; 32:8–10; Prov. 2:6) is a cause of anarchy.

29:20. This proverb works on two levels—as a truth drawn from experience and as a piece of the mosaic of verses 17–21. The observation on the dangers of rash speech is simple enough, but to say that there is more hope for the fool who rages, mocks, and says everything that comes to mind (29:9, 11) is to use the hyperbole to show how serious this matter is (cf. the nearly identical 26:12). Certainly speaking without thinking is in view (10:19; 19:2), but in this context, the repetition of *hzh* (see, "revelation," 29:18) suggests that hasty speech ignores the constraints of the "law" (*torah*) as well as the practices of discernment that see and learn (22:29; 24:32).

29:21. The main contrast of this proverb is between beginning (lit., "from youth"; cf. 29:15) and end; one who does not discipline a servant at the start will have trouble later on. Interpreters wrestle with the word translated "grief," for it occurs nowhere else in the Hebrew Bible. The meaning is taken from the LXX, which differs from the Hebrew of this verse by making the youth wanton or reckless, not pampered. The NRSV opts for the more general meaning of "bad end." The proverb implies that discipline provided early on will lead to a happier ending.

29:22. The last five verses of chapter 29 take the form of a partial alphabetic acrostic; acrostics also appear at the conclusion of the words of the wise (24:1–22) and the words of Lemuel (31:10–31).[11] While a common theme is not immediately apparent, the linking of sayings about Yahweh and the king puts the primary focus on community justice (29:25–26). The first line of this verse is virtually the same as that of 15:18, a proverb that concludes with a picture of patience that calms quarrels. Here the second line adds a parallel picture of the hot-tempered person (lit., "master of wrath") who multiplies or increases transgressions (cf. 29:2, 16; 28:28). As wrath goes uncontrolled, so does its damage. Perhaps some wordplay was intended by following "grief" (*manon*, 29:21) with "dissension" (*madon*).

29:23. The contrast between high and low is enhanced by the repetition of the root *špl* ("low") at the center of the proverb. The word "pride" is used elsewhere for swelling waves (Ps. 46:4) that will eventually fall.[12] "Honor" (*kabod*; cf. Prov. 3:35; 15:33; 18:12; 26:1, 8) must come from another or someone else (25:27; 27:1–2); yet a "lowly spirit" does hold it fast (cf. 4:4; 5:22). Better to be called up higher than put lower (cf. 25:6–7).

---

11. V. A. Hurowitz, "Proverbs 29:22–27: Another Unnoticed Alphabetic Acrostic," *JSOT* 92 (2001): 121–25. The proposed acrostic is complicated but coherent. Simply stated, v. 22 begins with *aleph* and v. 27 with *tav*, with repeated words appearing in chiastic order: "man" (*ʾiš*, vv. 22, 27), "many" (*rab*, vv. 22, 26), "man" (*ʾadam*, vv. 23, 25), and "low/lowly" (root *špl*, v. 23).

12. Clifford, *Proverbs*, 255.

29:24. While the exact sense of this proverb is hard to determine, it is clear that the one who is friend with a thief (lit., "one who divides the take"; cf. 16:19) is no friend to himself (lit., "hates his own life/desire [*nepeš*]"; cf. 29:10). The second line can read "he hears an imprecation and does not tell," most likely an allusion to Leviticus 5:1: "If a person sins because he does not speak up when he hears a public charge to testify regarding something he has seen or learned about, he will be held responsible." To hold back testimony when it is called for is a crime of complicity, one that injures the community and, because it angers Yahweh, oneself.

29:25. The last verses of this chapter and the conclusion of the proverbs collected by Hezekiah's men (cf. 25:1) name Yahweh and king (cf. 29:13–14) and repeat the contrast between the wicked and righteous (cf. 29:2, 7, 16). The first of two Yahweh sayings contrasts fear of human power with "trust in the LORD" (cf. 28:25). The first line depicts that fear as a hunter's trap, but the second line speaks of protection, being set high above all dangers like a tower on a mountain (cf. 18:10–11; Job 5:11).[13] One can show kindness to enemies without fear, since Yahweh rewards (Prov. 25:21–22). Perhaps the legal context of the previous verse is still in view, warning judges to fear no person, great or small, "for judgment belongs to God" (Deut. 1:17, 29).

29:26. Another proverb about judgment (cf. 29:24–25) sets the typical pattern of appeal to a ruler against the ultimate source of justice, Yahweh. A person's first course of action is to reach the highest person in authority. This proverb does not look past that earthly authority but rather recognizes that role as a duty given by Yahweh and answerable to him. Perhaps some sense of limits on human judgment is implied as well; certainly the proverb lends assurance for those times when no justice from a ruler can be obtained.

29:27. Although this proverb sounds like a simple truism along the line of "dogs hate cats," there is more here than first meets the eye. Similar in theme to verse 10, the double use of the word "detest" ("abomination," *tocebah*) communicates more than a feeling of mutual distaste; instead, the two ways of life are totally incompatible.[14] Each line begins with that word; its initial *taw* comes last in the Hebrew alphabet, serving here to mark the end of the acrostic as well as the "proverbs of Solomon copied by the men of Hezekiah king of Judah" (25:1).

---

13. Whybray, *Proverbs*, 405, believes that such fear may lead to those behaviors that in Proverbs are compared to snares (pledges, adultery, violence).

14. The word is most often used with the LORD in Proverbs (e.g., 3:32; 6:16; 11:1, 20; 12:22; 15:8, 9, 26; 16:5; 20:10, 23; and perhaps 28:9), but also of kings (16:12), wisdom (8:7), fools (13:19), general reaction to mockers (24:9), corrupt judging (17:15), and "seven abominations" (26:25).

THE CONCLUDING SECTIONS of "the men of Hezekiah" draw together those sayings on neighbors, family, kings, people, and their God to demonstrate wisdom at work at every level of social interaction.[15] Nations need discipline, just like sons and servants (29:1); each needs teaching, correction, and even the threat of punishment or restraint when the first two are not heeded. The effects of wisdom and folly vibrate throughout the social network the way the entire spider web shakes when one strand is disturbed. Unrestrained sons disgrace and grieve their parents, but wise children bring them joy (29:3, 15, 17). Servants who are pampered instead of corrected bring problems, as do the officials of a ruler who listens to lies (29:12, 19, 21).

Rulers. The proverbs about rulers are like those that speak of the thriving of the righteous and the wicked (28:2, 28; 29:2, 16), showing that governments develop a character that is deeply felt by all the people. We can go so far as to say that they are in symbiotic relationship; people get the rulers they want and deserve, but a king can give stability to a nation by insisting that justice characterizes his rule (29:4, 7, 14, 18, 26). While this call to righteousness goes out to all the people (29:2, 27), a sort of trickle-down theory of righteousness is also at work in the sayings about the disciplinary role of the king. A wise ruler is like a wise parent, householder, or employer, who does everything necessary to teach, correct, and (when necessary) restrain.

In our day, we may have grown a bit too cynical about our expectations of leaders, believing that a certain amount of savvy requires some level of moral compromise as well. If national security is threatened, it is better to violate the civil rights of a few in order to ensure safety for the many. If a leader helps the economy get off the ground, why should we make a judgment on that leader's personal life? We make a distinction between the ethics of the kingdom and the *Realpolitik* that leaders face every day.

To make this claim is not to say that the choices facing national leaders are not painfully complicated or that it is always possible to act in a way that violates no standards whatsoever. It is to say that the human tendency toward self-serving behavior insinuates itself into actions, both individual and collective. These proverbs place a large share of the burden on leaders to bring the guiding rule of wisdom to the people. Similarly, it is a

---

15. Perdue, *Proverbs*, 239, suggests that the chapter sums up themes from chs. 25–29: the contrasts between righteousness and wickedness, and wisdom and folly, and the choice between the two poles that faces every ruler.

responsibility of a nation's people to reflect on its actions and to ask how well they conform to the standards of righteousness, justice, and fair dealing (1:3).[16]

There is mutual accountability implied in these proverbs, but the more direct teaching places responsibility squarely on the shoulder of rulers and others in authority, the people charged with the care and discipline of others. Thus, we may judge the character of our leaders by what they ask of us. Do they appeal to standards of fairness and compassion or only of our own interests? Again, the choices are not always as clear in life as the polarities of the proverbs, but the primary motivations of justice and self-interest often are; we can watch for these.

In each of the two parts of this chapter, proverbs about the king and Yahweh sit side by side, reminding readers that the shaping of personal and national character is never removed from the one who gives light to the eyes of rich and poor (29:13), sets those who trust on high (29:25), and brings justice to those who seek it (29:26). Rulers who serve as vice-regents to the King of heaven will judge the poor with faithfulness, not listening to lies (29:11, 13) or fearing any human influence or power (29:25); that one will have a throne that is secure. The contrast of snares and towers highlights the truth that fairness and justice bring the stability and security that armies and political strategies alone can never achieve.

Contrasts and comparisons. The first part of this chapter (vv. 1–16) is set apart by the repeated contrast between the righteous and wicked (vv. 2, 7, 16) and, more important, by five references to wisdom (vv. 3, 8, 9, 11, 15). Righteous rule benefits the people, especially the poor, but transgressions (perhaps against them) are many when the wicked rise to power and the people groan. So also mockers and fools inflame cities and upset assemblies, but the wise assuage anger, seek justice, and know when to exercise restraint (vv. 8, 9, 11). Children need correction if they are to love this wisdom, but the outcome is joy for parents instead of shame (vv. 3, 15).[17]

Images of violence are woven through this first part, vividly illustrating the outcomes that are much worse than the temporary pain of correction. The neck that will not bend to accept the yoke of correction will be broken forever (29:1). People and rulers alike are called to receive and give this correction; it may even be modeled in the sayings that are more critical of those in power. Earlier proverbs about rulers praised their godlike wisdom and

---

16. As noted in the introductory comments to ch. 29, all three Heb. roots from that verse appear in this chaper.

17. Murphy, *Proverbs*, 224, hypothesizes mistreatment of parents and says that such correction must have been needed!

powers of discernment, but these sayings are more akin to the reality of wicked rulers, a reality Israel knew firsthand.

If the first part of chapter 29 compares sons to people and their rulers, the second part (vv. 17–27) continues this format, juxtaposing a group on household discipline with the acrostic series of proverbs loosely gathered around justice in the community. Discipline of sons and servants at the start is necessary if householders are to have rest and avoid grief (vv. 17, 19, 21). So also a people that casts off restraint jettison *torah* as well as any learning that comes from "seeing" (vv. 18, 20); words in haste are only one form of unconstrained behavior (cf. 29:8, 10, 11–12). Anger and pride take their toll, but a lowly spirit is like the neck that bows to correction (29:22–23). Those who refuse to testify and protect the thief may do so out of fear of human reprisal, but in showing this respect for evil, such people hate themselves (29:13–14).

The series repeats the theme that has sounded again and again through the book: A people that practices justice is a people considered wise. As the people of Israel were getting ready to enter the land, Moses reminded them that they were a heavy burden indeed, "too heavy for me to carry alone" (Deut. 1:9). At the very start of his instructions to them, he reviewed the process of selecting leaders (Deut. 1:16–17), using words much like the concern of these proverbs:

> And I charged your judges at that time: Hear the disputes between your brothers and judge fairly, whether the case is between brother Israelites or between one of them and an alien. Do not show partiality in judging: hear both small and great alike. Do not be afraid of any man, for judgment belongs to God.

Moses' charge envisions small and great on the same playing field—no fear of any person, justice from God. This is the guiding vision that drove the sages (29:18) and their insistence that a people either moved toward this ideal of fairness and equality or away from it; either way, the corrective word was crucial. The word that gives this guidance, the *torah* of these proverbs, may have come from Moses and certainly comes from parents and sages. In any case, these proverbs agree with Moses that teaching (*torah*) directs, corrects, and, if need be, restrains and punishes to keep its people from destruction. In other words, the great contrast between the righteous and the wicked, the wise and fools, does not suggest that one is good and the other needs correction. No, all need to be taught, corrected, and held back from wandering toward destruction (cf. 24:11–12). Nothing is further from the contemporary mind.

NEED FOR WISE **discipline**. Everyone has a story about parents who love their children by drawing clear boundaries and enforcing them. My favorite story about such "tough love" comes from a friend who got a call from the police. His underage granddaughter and friends had been caught using fake identification to get into a night club and buy liquor, so he went down to the station. When he arrived, the officer in charge offered to take him to the room where the girls were waiting. "That's OK," he said, "let them stew in there a while." Then he asked the officer to tell him the whole story. After warnings were given and the girls were on their way home, they pleaded with him not to tell their parents, and the reason they had called him became clear. "Oh, no," came the answer, "everyone's parents are going to know about this."

Our stories about parents and children may be like those that gave rise to these proverbs about correcting sons and servants, and by extension, the correction of whole peoples. The leapfrog connection of sons (29:15, 17), people (29:18, 20), and servants (29:19, 21) remind us that we have to face the unpleasant duty of setting limits and enforcing discipline. In doing so, we risk being seen as less than tolerant, indulgent, and encouraging, but we will also be known as people who know the value of boundaries and guidance. As another election day draws near, my television is flooded with ads for candidates who portray themselves either as supporters of education and social welfare or tough-minded guardians who will reduce crime through better law enforcement and prosecution. Why must we be forced to choose between teaching and setting limits?

We have seen that the contribution of the collection of proverbs "copied by the men of Hezekiah" use juxtaposition to set examples of wise living in the domestic realm beside public and governmental examples of wisdom and folly. These proverbs, like those that came before, continue to stress the importance of wise and righteous character, but it is a mistake to assume that the polarities of wise and fool and the righteous and wicked mean that some people are simply good and some bad. The distinction, as we have seen again and again, is between those who respond to wisdom's guidance, correction, and restraint and those who do not. The sages were much too realistic to believe that only bad people need correction or that we would not need laws if we all were better people, better Christians. For this reason they knew that kings were responsible for ensuring fair dealing and that even they needed the guidance of wisdom and the accountability that comes with awareness of Yahweh's pervasive presence.

Misconceptions. Their wisdom corrects a number of misconceptions in contemporary culture. (1) Many believe that most decisions about behavior are a matter of personal choice; if it does not hurt anyone, why should something be called wrong? For starters, our vision may be limited (29:18, 20). The faulty logic of this way of thinking was exposed by a series of antidrug ads. Young men and women looked into the camera and said, "I killed a drug runner in Columbia"; "I bribed police"; "I helped so and so die of an overdose." By participating in the drug trade, all sorts of unspeakable crimes take place.

(2) A second, related misconception believes that the church should only speak out about sins of private morality, as if drug use, sexual immorality, abortion, and gambling only affect those who practice them. We believe we can ignore the matters of justice and fair dealing in our communities, yet this is precisely why Jesus criticized the Pharisees (Matt. 23:23, 25).[18]

I have watched the eyes of more than one congregation glaze over when I begin to preach and teach about matters of justice. I've tried to understand why this is so, and I have wondered that there is some suspicion that a concern for such matters betrays a drift toward a more liberal understanding of the faith and the Scriptures, when the case is exactly the reverse. While it is true that voices in secular society have called for human rights and fairness, this does not mean they are out of harmony with the Bible; rather, I think that we can document that the source of their inspiration was the church and the Bible.

(3) We believe that freedom is a higher value than responsibility. We are a society that wants to live without limits on our economy, our lifestyles, and other freedoms, and so we have often unconsciously identified those freedoms with freedom in Christ. This is not a call for a return to big government involvement in managing and delivering social services, only a reminder that sometimes our desires for freedom end up becoming freedom from social responsibility.

Church and government. If these are the misconceptions, what does this collection tell us about the life of the church, its mission in the world, and its involvement with the powers of government? (1) It calls Christian individuals to wise living that exerts its influence in ever-widening circles. Parents discipline children in their homes in the hope that their character will become evident wherever they go. Those who serve in political arenas will

---

18. R. C. Van Leeuwen, "Building God's House: An Exploration in Wisdom," in J. I. Packer and S. K. Soderlund, eds., *The Way of Wisdom: Essays in Honor of Bruce K. Waltke* (Grand Rapids: Zondervan, 2000), 210. "Since this neopagan society overwhelmingly shapes the media and forms of our communal life, the church's most difficult spiritual battles may not concern what we do in worship or in private. Rather, it is in our public, civic existence that we Christians are prone to sin and fall short of God's glory (Rom. 3:23)."

hold the twin emphases of righteousness and discipline in their work, the first to define the vision, the second the means.

(2) The church, the collected body of Christ, makes its influence felt through the same twin emphases, disciplining itself to display a righteousness that includes the traditional signs of morality, but also exerting a correcting influence on society by means of careful analysis and critique of public policy and cultural trends. Some of my friends write movie reviews, others participate in political think tanks. Still others enter the political arena by running for office or serving on community organizations. All are concerned with promoting righteousness that is both personal and public.

Opinions vary as to how Christian influence on society should work. While some in our communities harbor fears that Christians plan to take over everything from school boards to political offices and dictate norms for behavior and censorship, such fears have proven to be unfounded. Moreover, the coming generation of evangelicals, at least as reflected in surveys of students at Christian colleges, forms no monolithic picture. There is some identification with the Republican party, but there is also a wide range of opinions on specific issues, some more conservative and some more liberal, accompanied by a marked degree of tolerance. In many ways, these students criticize a church that has abandoned its role in public life.[19]

Others, such as Robert Webber, believe the church does well to recover the ancient tradition of standing separate from the world and condemning its evil practices by refusing to join in, identifying with the world by participating fully in all that does not require compromise, and seeking transformation by living as countercultural witness. For Webber, the role of the church is not to change the world but to be the church.[20]

While Christians will debate the most appropriate role for church involvement in matters of state, the vision of wisdom that permeates every level reminds Christian readers of the kingdom of God, which, like salt that preserves the world, clings insistently to a vision of peace and prosperity for all. In that way, the proverbs about the king's rule look beyond the successes and failures of human kings like Solomon and Hezekiah to the rule of Christ: "Endow the king with your justice, O God, the royal son with your righteousness" (Ps. 72:1). As the representatives of this king, the church will find ways to teach, correct, and support families and governments in their teaching for good and in their restraint of evil.

---

19. See Penning and Smidt, *Evangelicalism: The Next Generation*. This survey seeks to update the information gathered by J. Hunter in *Evangelicalism: The Coming Generation* (Chicago: Univ. of Chicago Press, 1987). See also the comments on Penning and Smidt in ch. 28.

20. Webber, *Ancient-Future Faith*, 164–73 (see also the comments on Webber's book in ch. 28).

Proverbs 30:1–33

T HE SAYINGS OF Agur son of Jakeh—an oracle:

This man declared to Ithiel,
to Ithiel and to Ucal:

2 "I am the most ignorant of men;
  I do not have a man's understanding.
3 I have not learned wisdom,
  nor have I knowledge of the Holy One.
4 Who has gone up to heaven and come down?
    Who has gathered up the wind in the hollow of his
      hands?
  Who has wrapped up the waters in his cloak?
    Who has established all the ends of the earth?
  What is his name, and the name of his son?
    Tell me if you know!

5 "Every word of God is flawless;
  he is a shield to those who take refuge in him.
6 Do not add to his words,
  or he will rebuke you and prove you a liar.

7 "Two things I ask of you, O LORD;
  do not refuse me before I die:
8 Keep falsehood and lies far from me;
  give me neither poverty nor riches,
  but give me only my daily bread.
9 Otherwise, I may have too much and disown you
    and say, 'Who is the LORD?'
  Or I may become poor and steal,
    and so dishonor the name of my God.

10 "Do not slander a servant to his master,
  or he will curse you, and you will pay for it.

11 "There are those who curse their fathers
  and do not bless their mothers;
12 those who are pure in their own eyes
  and yet are not cleansed of their filth;

651

¹³ those whose eyes are ever so haughty,
  whose glances are so disdainful;
¹⁴ those whose teeth are swords
  and whose jaws are set with knives
to devour the poor from the earth,
  the needy from among mankind.

¹⁵ "The leech has two daughters.
  'Give! Give!' they cry.

"There are three things that are never satisfied,
  four that never say, 'Enough!':
¹⁶ the grave, the barren womb,
  land, which is never satisfied with water,
  and fire, which never says, 'Enough!'

¹⁷ "The eye that mocks a father,
  that scorns obedience to a mother,
will be pecked out by the ravens of the valley,
  will be eaten by the vultures.

¹⁸ "There are three things that are too amazing for me,
  four that I do not understand:
¹⁹ the way of an eagle in the sky,
  the way of a snake on a rock,
the way of a ship on the high seas,
  and the way of a man with a maiden.

²⁰ "This is the way of an adulteress:
  She eats and wipes her mouth
  and says, 'I've done nothing wrong.'

²¹ "Under three things the earth trembles,
  under four it cannot bear up:
²² a servant who becomes king,
  a fool who is full of food,
²³ an unloved woman who is married,
  and a maidservant who displaces her mistress.

²⁴ "Four things on earth are small,
  yet they are extremely wise:
²⁵ Ants are creatures of little strength,
  yet they store up their food in the summer;

²⁶ coneys are creatures of little power,
  yet they make their home in the crags;
²⁷ locusts have no king,
  yet they advance together in ranks;
²⁸ a lizard can be caught with the hand,
  yet it is found in kings' palaces.

²⁹ "There are three things that are stately in their stride,
  four that move with stately bearing:
³⁰ a lion, mighty among beasts,
  who retreats before nothing;
³¹ a strutting rooster, a he-goat,
  and a king with his army around him.

³² "If you have played the fool and exalted yourself,
  or if you have planned evil,
  clap your hand over your mouth!
³³ For as churning the milk produces butter,
  and as twisting the nose produces blood,
  so stirring up anger produces strife."

THE FINAL TWO chapters of the book of Proverbs present "the sayings of Agur" (30:1) and "the sayings of King Lemuel" (31:1), two figures whose non-Israelite names appear nowhere else in Scripture. These superscriptions mark the sixth and seventh sections of the book (see the outline in the introduction), yet certain similarities of theme and vocabulary suggest that the two chapters are meant to be read alongside each other.

(1) Each chapter begins with discourse marked as an "oracle" (30:1−14; 31:1−9) and ends with an artful reflection on human experience, taking the form of numerical sayings (30:15−33) and an acrostic poem (31:10−31). The "oracles" are also introduced as "sayings" (lit., "words") of a foreign figure, either spoken by or to a "son" (30:1; 31:1). The content of each first section urges temperance (30:6−10; 31:3−4), presenting prohibitions (marked by ʾal, "do not") followed by a negative outcome (marked by pen, "lest"). The links at the beginning and end of this two-chapter unit put the emphasis on human response to God (30:1−9; 31:30).

(2) The end of chapter 30 and beginning of chapter 31 are connected. The word "king" is used four times at the end of chapter 30 (30:22, 27, 28, 31) and

four times at the beginning of chapter 31 (31:1, 3, 4). A charge to keep silent ("clap your hand over your mouth," 30:32) is followed by a charge to "speak up" (lit., "open your mouth," 31:8–9). The outcome of ignoring the first charge is evil and strife (30:32–33) and the outcome of heeding the second is fair judgment (31:8–9).

(3) We also notice similarities of image and theme, such as the adulteress who eats (with its overtones of ruin and devouring, 30:20) and women who consume strength and ruin kings (31:2–3). The contrast develops as the negative images of women in chapter 30 are answered by the positive images of chapter 31. While Agur laments that he has not learned wisdom (30:3), the woman of 31:26 opens her mouth to teach wisdom.

Therefore, it appears that chapters 30 and 31 are to be read together as a four-part conclusion to the book of Proverbs, just as chapters 1–9 served as its introduction. In fact, many of the figures of those chapters appear again in chapter 30: the bloodthirsty men (30:11–14; cf. 1:10–19; 2:12–15), the adulteress (30:20; cf. 2:16–19; 7:1–27), and the numerical sayings of chapter 6.[1] The number four also recurs throughout the chapter; while most interpreters divide it into two parts (30:1–14, 15–33),[2] the repetition of "four" suggests a different outline.

The Oracle of Agur (30:1–14)
>Knowledge of wisdom and the Holy One (four questions and answers; 30:1–5)
>Prohibitions and prayers (four "do not–lest" in series; 30:6–10)
>A generation of evildoers (four "a generation" in series; 30:11–14)

Numerical Sayings (30:15–31)
>Four that never say "Enough" (30:15–17)
>Four amazing ways (30:18–20)
>Four earth-shattering outcomes (30:21–23)
>Four small but wise creatures (30:24–28)
>Four stately in stride (30:29–31)

Epilogue on Pride and Strife (30:32–33)

The Oracle of Agur (30:1–14)

THE INTRODUCTION TO the "sayings of Agur" asks a series of four rhetorical questions, followed by one person's despair at finding wisdom and God. In

---

1. Meinhold, *Die Sprüche*, 2:496, finds an echo with ch. 3 and its emphasis on relationship with God (30:1–9; cf. 3:1–12) and neighbor (30:10–16; cf. 3:21–35).
2. The LXX places 30:1–14 before 24:23–34 and 30:15–33 after.

a sense, the "oracle" is actually a prayer in two parts, first for knowledge of God and second for a life lived before him in wisdom. The importance of proper speaking runs throughout this section.

30:1−5. A number of surprises await us in chapter 30. There is a new superscription that names a person previously unknown, "Agur son of Jakeh." The Hebrew words of this verse can either be translated or left to designate proper names.[3] The NIV text notes show that "oracle" can be read as "Massa," one of the sons of Ishmael (Gen. 25:14; 1 Chron. 1:30),[4] and "to Ithiel, to Ithiel and to Ucal," can be read as "I am weary, O God; I am weary, O God, and faint."[5]

Scholars have written much and agreed little concerning this translation, but since 1:6 promised that we would learn of (lit.) "the words of the wise *and their riddles*," we look for those riddles every time we see a section introduced by "words of" (cf. 22:17; 24:23; 31:1). So, for example, "to Ithiel" is a palindrome in Hebrew, a word that reads the same forward and backward (*l'yty'l*); the brainteaser gives a preview of what is to come and may hint that we are to look for the double meaning.

We should also note that reading the Hebrew as both words and names yields meanings that fit the context. "Oracle" makes sense if we think of wisdom as something revealed, a gift of God (31:1; cf. 2:1−6; Isa. 13:1; 14:28; Ezek. 12:10; Nah. 1:1; Hab. 1:1; Mal. 1:1), yet "weary" can describe one worn out from searching (cf. Prov. 2:1−6).[6] Perhaps this weariness comes from searching for wisdom apart from that given by God, or perhaps this is the cry of someone ready to receive God's gift of wisdom.

Agur's message begins with confession of ignorance: (lit.) "For more beast than man am I" (30:2). The beast was a sign of subhuman intelligence, a symbol used with the assumption that it is a capacity of human nature to

---

3. A distant possibility suggested by some is "Sojourner, son of Piety," but that does not clearly follow from the Heb. Agur translates as "I fear" in Deut. 32:27, "I dreaded the taunt of the enemy, lest the adversary misunderstand and say, 'Our hand has triumphed; the LORD has not done all this.'" The very next verse (32:28) reports that Israel was foolish, not wise.

4. "Massa" appears as an Arabian tribe in the Assyrian literature. See 1 Kings 4:30−31 for a reference to sages of the east.

5. The verbs for "weary" and "exhausted" are also paired in Jer. 20:9. "I am faint" most likely is derived from a passive sense of *'kl*, "to consume" (P. Franklyn, "The Sayings of Agur in Proverbs 30: Piety or Scepticism?" *ZAW* 95 [1983]: 238−52). E. Strömberg Krantz, "A Man Not Supported by God": On Some Crucial Words in Proverbs 30:1," *VT* 46 (1996): 548−53, reads, "God is not with him" for Ithiel.

6. Clifford, *Proverbs*, 260−61, notes the similarity of this vocabulary to oracles of Balaam (Num. 24:15−17) and David (2 Sam. 23:1)—"traditional language of seers recounting their vision."

perceive spiritual matters and to be in relationship with its Creator. To lack such perception is to be like an animal that is only concerned for its food and safety (cf. Ps. 73:21–22). It is not clear whether the speaker confesses that he has tried and failed or not tried at all, but this question motivates the reader to continue.

The couplet in verse 3 heads where we expect, the confessor declaring that he has not learned wisdom or gained knowledge of "the Holy One." Parallelism in this verse implies that to learn wisdom is to gain knowledge of God (cf. Prov. 9:10; Job 28:28). Some interpreters take Agur's words as skepticism that is then answered by the more positive view of verses 5–14,[7] but the entire oracle can be read as that of a sincere seeker. The terms "wisdom" and "knowledge" join with "understanding" in verse 2 to set out the sages' hope and goal for humankind (cf. Prov. 1:1–7).

Four questions in verse 4 initiate a series of "fours" that runs throughout the chapter; here four questions beginning with "Who" are followed by two that begin with "What." Certainly the "who?" questions are meant to be answered, "the Holy One" (30:3), but to what purpose?[8] "Knowledge of the Holy One" appears only here and in 9:10, a verse that names "the fear of the LORD" as its beginning. The repetition may direct the reader to learn of wisdom there, where it is preceded by a cosmic vision of wisdom at creation (8:22–31) and a picture of a wise woman, her house, and her maids (9:1–3; cf. 31:10–31). The deeds of the "Who" questions are those Yahweh accomplished by the agency of wisdom (3:19; 8:27). Most likely, "Who has gone up to heaven and come down" should also be answered with "the LORD," although the question implies that mortals have tried and failed (cf. Deut. 30:12; Bar. 3:29).

Many commentators find here a motif of ancient Near Eastern literature; common to many human attempts to ascend to heaven is the great gulf that separates the human and divine realms. Only the gods may possess power, wisdom, and immortality, and therefore no human has ascended to heaven and descended without bringing about disaster.[9] Others agree that these

---

7. J. L. Crenshaw, "Clanging Symbols," in *Justice and the Holy: Essays in Honor of Walter Harrelson*, ed. D. A Knight and P. J. Paris (Atlanta: Scholar's Press, 1989), 56–57.

8. The questions remind the reader of God's questions to Job in Job 38–41. Murphy, *Proverbs*, 228, finds sarcasm in "if you know," modeled after Job 38:18. Crenshaw, "Clanging Symbols," 57, thinks the questions and the phrase "if/surely you know" remind the reader of Job 38:5.

9. R. C. Van Leeuwen, "The Background to Proverbs 30:4aá," in *Wisdom, You Are My Sister: Essays in Honor of R. E. Murphy, O. Carm., on the Occasion of His Eightieth Birthday*, ed. M. L. Barré (CBQMS 29; Washington, D. C.: Catholic Biblical Association of America, 1997): 102–21. Van Leeuwen cites a number of biblical texts that assume this widespread motif:

questions are Agur's humble confession of his limitations, but they place the emphasis on divine power, not on human efforts to attain it.[10] Still others take the "gone up and come down" as a cross-reference to Genesis 28:12–13 and the angels ascending and descending on the stairway from heaven in Jacob's dream.[11] The second and third questions express wonder at the extent of a mighty grip (cf. Isa. 40:12).[12] The fourth shows that all of creation, heavens and earth, sky and sea, are under Yahweh's rule (cf. Ps. 2:8; 22:27; 67:7; 72:8; Isa. 52:10). Similar questions are posed by Amos, who answers, "The LORD is his name" (Amos 4:13; 5:8; 9:6).

It is the last question that gives us trouble, and even the Hebrew marks it as different, using not *mi* ("Who") but *mah* ("What"): "What is his name, and the name of his son?" Again, the answer to "his name" is clearly God, "the LORD," for it is repeated in the verses that follow (30:5–9; cf. 18:10). The identification of "his son" is trickier; interpreters have suggested that it may be Israel[13] or the king,[14] but the strongest implication from context is that it is any person who learns wisdom. In the book of Proverbs many lectures are addressed to "my son" while 3:11 reminds us that Yahweh teaches discipline like a father (cf. 31:2, 28).[15] The riddle-like form of the question leaves the matter open, but the emphasis on learning wisdom sounds clearly.

The questions imply that God acts to create and maintain a world, but God also speaks (30:5). "Every word of God is flawless." "Flawless" or fire-tested (*ṣĕrûpah*; cf. 27:1) here does not mean hardened like steel but rather that the quality of the metal has been "proved," so that all dross is removed. That pure word shows that God is a "shield" to those who take refuge (30:5), the

---

Gen. 11 (and perhaps 28); Amos 9; Isa. 40:12–14; Job 38:4–6; and esp. Deut. 30:11–12. Scott, *Proverbs*, 179, notes similarities with the Epic of Gilgamesh and the *Dialogue of Pessimism*.

10. Crenshaw, "Clanging Symbols," 56, revocalizes to read "assumed dominion" instead of "come down," adding emphasis to the central idea of sovereignty (cf. Ps. 139:8; also Prov. 25:3).

11. Skehan, *Studies in Israelite Poetry and Wisdom*, 41–43; Murphy, *Proverbs*, 228–29.

12. K. J. Cathcart suggests "fold in the garment" or "pocket" instead of "hollow of his hands" ("Proverbs 30:4 and Ugaritic *HPN*, 'Garment,'" *CBQ* 32 [1970]: 418–20).

13. Skehan, *Studies*, 41–43, translates Agur as "I am a sojourner" (Ps. 39:13), a mortal passing through this time on earth. Because Jacob described himself as a sojourner (Gen. 47:9), saw the ladder with angels going up and down (Gen. 28:12–13), and is called firstborn son (Exod. 4:22), Agur, like Jacob, is the every man of Israel, the son of Yahweh. The allusion is instructive, but the form *ʾagur* does not appear in the Old Testament as "I sojourn." It does appear with the meaning "I fear," as spoken by Yahweh in Deut. 32:27.

14. Van Leeuwen, "Proverbs," 256, cites 2 Sam. 7:14; Ps. 2:7; 89:26–27. See also Solomon's praise in 1 Kings 8:14–61; 2 Chron. 6:1–42.

15. Goldingay, "Proverbs," 606: "He is simply the only one who openly acknowledges ignorance because of the inherent mystery of the things of God."

phrase a near verbatim citation of David's song of praise (2 Sam. 22:31; Ps. 18:30).[16]

The next verse in David's song answers the question, "For who is God besides the LORD? And who is the Rock except our God?" (2 Sam. 22:32; Ps. 18:31). The theme of that song is deliverance from his enemies. So also in Proverbs 2:1–7, Yahweh, who gives wisdom, knowledge, and understanding from his mouth, is also a shield; thus, perhaps here is an encouragement to keep these promises in mind as an answer to Agur's despair.

30:6–10. The series of "fours" continues with four appearances of the phrase "do not" (*'al*), two as prohibitions to the reader ("do not add ... do not slander") and two as prayers to God ("do not refuse me ... do not give"); each of four descriptions of potential failure begins with Hebrew *pen* ("lest") and ends with a name of God.[17]

Verses 5–6 are linked around the theme of God's words. Any additions to those true and faultless words will prove false, and for that reason Agur asks God to protect him from the ever-present danger of falsehood and lies (30:8). If those words are "flawless" or pure, to add to them would add impurities or dross, and here that dross is named as falsehood. It is not clear whether the "liar" needs correction for false teaching about God or for believing lies about poverty and riches. Moses warned the people about adding to or subtracting from the commands of Yahweh, adding that if they would hear and obey, they would be considered wise and understanding (Deut. 4:1–8; 5:22; 12:32). To talk when we should be listening is never wise.

God's words are true, but human words can prove false. So the speaker offers the first prayer recorded in the book, making two requests of God: to keep falsehood and lies at bay and to provide daily bread (Prov. 30:8; cf. Ex. 16:1–36). If there is too much, one can forget God in pride (cf. Deut. 8:10–18); if there is too little, one may forget God's commands and steal (cf. Prov. 6:30–31). The falsehood expressed in "disown you" can also be read as "deny" or "renounce." "Name" is repeated from verse 4; to dishonor the name is (lit.) to "seize or take" it, perhaps in vain (cf. Ex. 20:7; Lev. 19:12; Deut. 5:11). We can say, then, that these two requests constitute a prayer for wisdom.

The theme of falsehood continues into verse 10, for slander of a servant is probably to bring a false report, just as Joseph brought a bad report about

---

16. R. D. Moore, "A Home for the Alien: Worldly Wisdom and Covenantal Confession in Proverbs 30:1–9," *ZAW* 106 (1994): 96–107. Moore argues that the citation of David's last words makes allusion to the Law and Prophets in order to lend legitimacy to wisdom's place in the canon.

17. Franklyn, "Sayings of Agur," 251, notes that although God is named throughout, Agur does not use the covenantal name *yhwh* until the end of the prayer.

his brothers (Gen. 37:2; cf. Ps. 101:5). Such bad talk brings a curse in return (*qll*; cf. Prov. 30:11), and one (lit.) "incurs guilt" that may require payment of restitution.[18] In sum, then, four prohibitions against false speaking follow the proclamation that God's word is fire-tested, true, and flawless. Warnings against evil speaking also occupy the sayings of 30:11–14, beginning with another saying about a "curse," the catchword that links 30:10–11.

30:11–14. Each of the next four verses begins with the Hebrew word *dor* ("generation"). Each describes "one of a generation" who rejects the way of wisdom, the opposite of God's intention for humankind (Ex. 3:15; Deut. 1:35; 32:5, 20; Ps. 95:10; Jer. 7:29). The word "curse" connects verse 11 with the one before; to curse parents is sinful in the Pentateuch (Ex. 20:12; 21:17; Lev. 20:9; Deut. 27:16) as well as the book of Proverbs (Prov. 30:17; 20:20). God's intention is shown by the sons of the wise woman of worth, who praise her (31:28).

Parallel lines in verse 12 present an ironic description of those "pure in their own eyes," who do not see that they are covered in filth (cf. 20:9; Isa. 4:4; 28:8). The Hebrew "his eyes" (*ʿenaw*) closes the first lines of verses 12 and 13 to describe pride; in verse 13 the eyes are (lit.) "lifted up" to look down on others (cf. Prov. 6:17; Ps. 18:27). Verse 14 is twice as long as the others, four lines illustrating arrogance that oppresses. These mouths not only speak evil, they eat unjustly. They devour the poor, a motif used often by the prophets but also by the psalmist, speaking of fools who devour the people like bread (Ps. 14:1–4).

Numerical Sayings (30:15–31)

THERE ARE FIVE numerical sayings in this section, all list "four" items. Four use a "three plus one" pattern. The numerical sayings are early examples of reflections on nature and society, distinct from the numerical lists in chapter 6 and elsewhere.[19] The sayings draw together observations on life and nature to illustrate various aspects of wisdom. The point of the comparison is not always easy to discern, and so each numerical saying works like a riddle. There is an alternating pattern between numerical sayings and seemingly unrelated single sayings (30:15, 17, 20).

---

18. The structure and grammar of vv. 6 and 10 are nearly identical, creating a frame around Agur's prayer. See a similar structure in Deut. 23:15–16: "You are not to turn over a slave to his master."

19. W. Roth, *Numerical Sayings in the Old Testament: A Form Critical Study* (VTSupp 13; Leiden: Brill, 1965); and "The Numerical Sequence x/x+1 in the Old Testament," *VT* 12 (1962): 300–311. Of the thirty-eight examples in the Old Testament and Sirach, twenty-one are poetic in form.

30:15–17. Coming on the heels of the "generation" sayings in 30:11–14, the leech's twin daughters, "Give! Give!" (perhaps inspired by the two mouths, one at each end of the leech), are repulsive and sobering metaphors for a greedy generation. Their "prayer" is the reverse of that in 30:7–9; this insatiable appetite makes a striking contrast with the request for "just enough."

The first of the following "three–four" sayings brings together four more leech-like consumers that will take all they can. "Enough" (repeated in 30:15 and 16) translates the Hebrew word for "wealth" or sufficiency (*hon*), but these figures do not know what the word means. "The grave" (*šeʾol*, Sheol) in verse 16 signifies the ever-present power of death,[20] always working to take another living being into its realm; like the closed womb, dry land, and fire, it does not produce, it only consumes (cf. 26:20–21).

Verse 17, while not a numerical saying, comments on the four insatiable consumers as well as the four descriptions of "a generation" that precede (30:11–14). Just as greedy generations devour the poor from the earth, so the one who (presumably from greed) mocks parents instead of caring for them will be eaten in turn (cf. 2 Sam. 21:10; 1 Kings 14:11). The terms "eye" and "father and mother" and the theme of disrespect goes back to Proverbs 30:11–13.[21] The eye can be insatiable also (27:20), but here it seems to be an arrogant and mocking eye that brings on the scavenging birds. The vultures are (lit.) "sons of eagles," using the same word for eagle found in 30:19.

30:18–20. The second of the "three–four" sayings brings together four phenomena about which the speaker says, "I do not understand," echoing the words of Agur's lament (lit., "I do not know them"; cf. 30:3–4). The first person "I" echoes the personal voice of the seeker (cf. 30:2–3). The riddle repeats the word "way" (*derek*; cf. 23:19, 26; 2:8–20), linking this riddle with the additional saying in 30:20.

But how are the four "ways" of verses 18–19 to be related, and what is the key to the puzzle?[22] Each of the first three relates its motion to its environment (an eagle in the sky, a snake on the rock, a ship on the sea), but the last one, a man (*geber*; cf. 30:1) with a woman, has more to do with relationship, a common topic of Proverbs (3:13–18; 8:17–21). The first three name the elements of creation: sea, earth, and "heavens" (*šamayim*; cf. 3:19–20; 8:22–29; 30:4).

---

20. Murphy, *Proverbs*, 235, observes that Sheol is not merely a place but a *"power that pursues every living thing."*

21. The theme of dishonoring parents in Proverbs finds its strongest statement here. The word for obedience could be translated "homage" after Gen. 49:10 (Clifford, *Proverbs*, 265).

22. Murphy, *Proverbs*, 235, thinks that the way of these travelers is "unrecoverable, mysterious, the way man and woman meet one another and become one." Clifford, *Proverbs*, 266, shows that the pairing of humans comes after description of a tripartite universe in Ps. 33:6–8 and 69:34 [35].

If all four creatures move in ways both wonderful and mysterious through God's created order (30:18), we also see that wisdom is needed to make one's way rightly, as the picture of the unrepentant adulteress in 30:20 makes clear.[23] Each of these wise travelers knows how to make its way in its part of the created order: Eagles don't try to swim, snakes don't try to fly, and ships that go on rocks are destroyed. Therefore men or women who despise the mystery of love and sex and move outside of its boundaries are like those who step out of their place in created order and cause the earth to tremble (30:21—23; cf. *derek*, "strength," in 31:3).[24] Here with the adulteress, just as in 30:14—17, eating is associated with behavior that is out of bounds, this time depicting a sexual appetite that knows no restraint (cf. 7:14—18; 9:16). Finishing one's improper eating by wiping the mouth characterizes someone who is both casual and proud in her ignorance.[25] The contrast between the wonder of 30:18—19 and the contempt of 30:20 is striking.

30:21—23. The numerical form of this third of the "three—four" sayings is reinforced as the word "under" (*taḥat*) is repeated four times. Just as the "way of an adulteress" (30:20) is out of step with the created order of wisdom, so the four items listed threaten to overturn that order. In ancient Near Eastern thinking, the earth shakes when the natural order is disturbed.[26] The "trembling" (30:21) of the earth is like the raging of the fool that disturbs peace in every sense of the word (cf. 29:9). Two male examples (the servant who comes to rule and the sated fool) have occurred before (19:10; cf. Eccl. 10:5—7), but not the unloved woman or supplanting maidservant. The four have an ABBA pattern that links rise in power and satisfied hunger, perhaps to show that each turn of good fortune is not accompanied by the character to match.

The unloved (lit., "hated") woman is variously understood as a divorced woman (Deut. 24:1—4), an older woman who finally finds a husband and gloats, or the wife who is second in line for her husband's affections, perhaps an allusion to the situation of Leah (Gen. 29:31, 33) or Hannah and Peninnah

---

23. T. Longman III, *How to Read Proverbs*, 45, takes "way" as a metaphor for sexual intercourse. So the adulteress contemptuously engages in sex without commitment, ignoring the covenantal commitments of this "way."

24. M. Haran, "The Graded Numerical Sequence and the Phenomenon of 'Automatism' in Biblical Poetry," (VTSupp 22; Leiden: Brill, 1972): 239—67. Haran argues that there is no connection with v. 20 apart from the catchword "way" and theme of sexual relations.

25. "Way" as illicit sexual relations appears in Jer. 2:23, 33; 3:13. Clifford, *Proverbs*, 266.

26. R. C. Van Leeuwen, "Proverbs 30:21—23 and the World Upside Down," *JBL* 105 (1986): 599—610, cites the Egyptian text "Nefertiti": "I show you the land in turmoil . . . I show you the master in need, the outsider sated, The lazy stuffs himself, the active is needy. . . . I show you the land in turmoil . . ." (Lichtheim, *AEL*, 2:139—45), and Isa. 14; Jer. 4; Joel 2; Amos 8. The world upside-down made right appears in 1 Sam. 2:1—10.

(1 Sam. 1:1—7; cf. Deut 21:15). In the view of the sages, there is an order to life, and as long as it is just and fair, it should not be disturbed.

30:24—28. As in other "three—four" sayings, the statement of the number also offers the key to the puzzle that follows. Readers are to ask: How are these things small and yet "wiser than the wisest?" It is not strength for ants, but rather foresight and preparation of provisions (cf. 6:6—8). It is not power for coneys (or badgers; cf. Ps. 104:18), but rather their ability to make a home where no one can touch them. It is not leadership for locusts, but rather their capacity to organize in great numbers and devour crops (Ex. 10:13—15; Joel 1:4—7). The lizard is also small and powerless; it can be caught in the hand yet it lives in the house of the powerful king.

The repetition of "creatures" (ʿam; lit., "people," 30:25—26) and "king" (30:27—28) signals that these small creatures teach great lessons about being a people, asking ancient readers: "What kind of people do you want to be— strong, led by a king? (cf. 30:29—31). You don't need that as much as you need wisdom." The power of the weak and the weaknesses of those in power are noted in comparison.

30:29—31. The final "three—four" saying names things "stately [lit., good, *ṭob*; cf. Ex. 22:4; 1 Sam. 15:9, 15] in their stride"; in slang, they are "walking good." Unlike the creatures of verses 24—28, the lion is mighty among the beasts, for he stands down to nothing. So also the rooster in the chicken yard and the he-goat in his pen, but perhaps readers are meant to see the irony that these are like big fish in a small pond. Each would run from a lion! Kings often took the lion as their emblem, so we are interested to see that the last of the four is a king; but looking more closely, we see it is a king with an army (lit., "standing before his people"). Even kings and their armies run when they are outnumbered and overpowered ,so readers may ask whether this king is more like a lion or a barnyard animal.

An alternate translation in the NIV text note pictures a "king secure against revolt," one who does not stand *before* his people but *against* his people when they rise against him (cf. 24:21—22). In either case, the pairing of "king" (*melek*) and "people" (ʿam) brings together words that were used twice in 30:24—28, suggesting that we understand these brave and stately four in light of the small and wise four. Again, power comes not from strength or numbers alone but from wisdom, especially the wisdom that fears God and acts uprightly (cf. 30:1—14). Any other view betrays its arrogance and pride, silly as a strutting rooster or billy goat.

Epilogue on Pride and Strife (30:32—33)

THE LAST OF the sayings is not introduced with numbers, although it lists three "churnings" in verse 33. The fool is one who lifts up oneself (*naśaʾ*; cf. the "lifted eyes" of 30:13). The word for fool is *nabal*, from which the name of Abigail's husband was taken (1 Sam. 25:25). Fools like this either exalt themselves or plan evil, and the two are not that far apart. The remedy in Hebrew is short and direct: "Hand to mouth!" (cf. Prov. 30:6, 10; Job 40:4–5). Speech is for defending others (Prov. 31:8–9), not for plotting and speaking evil (6:16–19).

The three lines of verse 33 are linked by the repeated phrase "churning ... produces" (*miṣ*) and a wordplay on "nose" and "anger," both from the same root (*ʾap*). The final word is "strife" (*rib*; cf. 3:30; 15:18; 17:1, 14; 18:6; 20:3; 26:21), the produce of folly and evil. There are three churnings, but we have come to expect a fourth. Perhaps the lack of a fourth signals that the advice can be heeded and that folly can be averted in favor of wisdom.

 IN THIS MOST challenging chapter of Proverbs, Agur's own words are the best guide to interpretation: "I have not learned wisdom" (30:3). Whereas chapter 31 will offer a mother's counsel on wise rule and a poem on the wise woman of worth, this collection of sayings presents vivid examples of folly and its fruits. Two exceptions are the certainty of God's fire-tested words (30:5) and the four small and wise creatures (30:24–28), examples of revealed and experiential wisdom. The sayings come to a climax in the words on leadership, suggesting that kings can either be wise and learn from God's word and creation or lift themselves up in pride and greed.

In seeking to discern the principles applicable for our day, we must look more closely at the place of these sayings in Proverbs and the larger canon of the Bible. We have seen that the four parts of chapters 30 and 31 work together to form a conclusion to the book. The words of these non-Israelite figures request and recommend the life of wisdom (30:1–14; 31:1–9), while the poetic forms of numerical sayings and acrostic illustrate it (30:15–31; 31:10–31).

Messages through biblical allusions. We have seen that Agur's questions in verse 4 praise Yahweh, but at the same time they also set limits on human aspirations and achievements. The answer to the question on his name (30:4) directs readers to the words of David, who affirms that Yahweh is God, a shield and refuge (30:5). The allusion points to David as the model of kingship, to whom all other kings were compared, the anointed one whom Yahweh promised to show unfailing kindness (2 Sam. 7:1–11). In this light, Agur laments his ignorance but does so as a seeker, one who asks questions that can be answered, particularly by Israel's tradition of royal covenant. The allusion to David's song turns our attention to the covenant God made with

David and his descendants, and we note that the king was called God's son (2 Sam. 7:11–17). The word in which David trusted was a word of covenant, of promise, and therefore of shield and refuge.

We do well to trust in that word also, setting limits on our own sense of wisdom, accomplishment, and significance.[27] Here also is a call to know Yahweh, a call that comes when human efforts have reached their end. The biblical wisdom traditions set divine knowledge and strength against all human ingenuity to encourage humility and worship. So also we can make sure that our preaching, teaching, and witness all proclaim the One whose knowledge and power show ours to be small and limited. Agur's lament and its allusion to the royal tradition move us to humility.

The section marked by four "do not" sayings (30:6–10) also present questions, this time in the form of requests for integrity and daily bread, keeping falsehood and lies, as well as the extremes of poverty and riches, far away (30:8). "Do not add to his words," recalls Moses' charge (Deut. 4:2), and the possibility of having too much and denying Yahweh stands at the center of Moses' last words (32:13–18). In this case, the "son" is Israel, the son who ate and grew fat, became prideful and greedy, and forgot God. Israel, the son whom God meant to be wise (4:5–6), became like the son who is a fool (*nabal*, 32:5–6; Prov. 30:32).[28]

All through Proverbs, the sages warn us of the dangers of excess, particularly those of greed and apostasy. Now we see the dangers of falsehood that denies the existence of God; it comes in word with the question, "Who is the LORD?" (cf. Ex. 5:2), or in such deeds as stealing and dishonoring God (cf. Hos. 4:1–2). If God's words are flawless, promises that are always kept, we too can look to see that our words have integrity, that promises to follow his way are kept.

Following the apostasy and stealing of Proverbs 30:7–10 are the marks of a generation that curses parents, denies any sin, looks on others in pride, and devours the poor (30:11–14). These examples of willful arrogance also direct readers to the "perverse generation" of unfaithful children, "foolish and unwise" (Deut. 32:5–6, 20, 28). Although Moses worried about the wor-

---

27. In fact, failure in covenant may explain why foreigners are given the last word in Proverbs (cf. Deut. 32:27–28), not Solomon or Hezekiah. Perhaps the great riddle of Proverbs is this covenantal rebuke of Solomon and Hezekiah and, by extension, its warning to all persons in leadership and authority.

28. T. Frymer-Kensky, "The Sage in the Pentateuch: Soundings," in *The Sage in Israel and the Ancient Near East*, ed. J. G. Gammie and L. G. Perdue (Winona Lake, Ind.: Eisenbrauns, 1990), 275–87, observes that in Deuteronomy wisdom is *studied*, noted by frequent use of the word *lmd* ("to study, learn").

ship of other gods, here the problem is practical atheism, the sure signs of a turn from knowledge and wisdom.[29] The curses Moses pronounced from Mount Ebal began with condemnation of idolatry, followed by curses for dishonoring father and mother, moving a boundary stone, and withholding justice (27:15–26). The extreme behavior of these "generations" in Proverbs warn us about these errors in their more subtle forms. Better to acknowledge "I am more beast than man" (Prov. 30:2, "most ignorant of men") than to be a beast who does not recognize it and thus brings great harm.

To bring the principle of this teaching into our day, we acknowledge the goodness of honoring parents, caring for the poor, and confessing pride, and we acknowledge that we exist as members of "generations" that can easily be led astray. As our popular culture becomes more "sassy" (its word for selfish), I see the need to join hands with people who consciously swim against the stream, those who practice care instead of indulgence.

In sum, the biblical allusions of 30:1–14 use the words of Moses and David to draw a contrast between an Agur's humility and a generation's harmful pride. By means of citation and allusion, the seeker Agur uncovers both the best and worst of Israel's history, and in this way becomes one of Israel's teachers. Sometimes an outsider can see matters more clearly than the children of God can.

Having enough. The second part of the chapter's teaching comes in the numerical sayings, starting with two, three, and four things that either cry "give" or never know when to say "enough." More striking are the related sayings that do not take the numerical form, sayings about the eye that mocks parents and the mouth of the adulteress (30:17, 20). These examples of folly stand out from their context as stark reminders that sin is both deadly and deceitful. The mocking eye and the disdainful mouth are examples of pride that cares little for the effects of its actions.

We have seen throughout Proverbs that to neglect care of one's parents is to hurt and dishonor them and that it is deadly for a young man to fall into the trap of the adulteress. In the same way, the hungers of the leech, Sheol, dry earth, and blazing fire also show the dangers of unrestrained appetite. If they have never learned to say enough, we who claim to serve a God who provides certainly can. As I write, nightly news reports question the high salaries paid to CEOs as they expose those executives who have been caught using inside information to line their own pockets.

---

29. Crenshaw, "Symbols," 63–64. "In God's sight persons who claim to possess knowledge of the Holy One but lack respect for parents, behave hypocritically, think too highly of themselves, and oppress the defenseless are in fact the real atheists of society; for they dissociate justice and the Holy."

As a contrast to that prideful mocking and casual consumption, a riddle asks how an eagle flies, a snake moves, a ship sails, and a man and woman court and commit (30:18—19). In place of pride comes humility, the sense that the world and the One who made it are greater than we can ever fathom, thus making all self-satisfied mocking and boasting ludicrous. We too can take care to watch for the connection of pride and insatiability, remembering that haughtiness and unrestrained hunger often travel together (30:20). Some will think me cranky, but when I see a mountainous SUV with a vanity plate that says, "I Want Gaz," and then hear a news report that we are using up earth's resources of ozone and forests faster than it can replenish them, I see another manifestation of our particular brand of American pride and appetite.

The last two numerical sayings seem to be of a kind, the first depicting the topsy-turvy world out of order, a world in which the servants are set above their masters, the second depicting the small and lowly who exhibit wisdom and power. If the first appears to uphold social order by bemoaning its disruption, the second seems to satirize it. A lizard is small and easily caught, but it shares the palace with the king! There is the folly of the small pretending to be great, but there is also the wisdom of the small who use their ingenuity to do great things. So the ants make up for their size with foresight that stores up food, the coneys make use of the strength of the rocks to find a safe haven, the locusts organize themselves into a devastating power, and the lizard finds a home wherever it wants.

So also the picture of four beings that strut carries a note of satire. A king with an army may be great, but there may be one even greater. If there were a "better-than" saying at the end of all this, it might be, "Better to be humble and wise than a fool who pretends to greatness." Humility is a virtue of which the church and the watching world never says, "Enough!"

Finally, the last of the sayings warns against two related expressions of prideful folly: exalting self and plotting evil (30:32—33). The cure for such evil speaking is to put hand to mouth and stop it. The series of three churnings shows such speech for what it is, a punch in the nose and a source of strife. The last of Agur's sayings commends humble quiet over words that puff up pride and stir up trouble, reminding the reader of the "six things the LORD hates" (6:16—19).

In sum, the numerical sayings link appetite with self-exaltation and contrast them with the wisdom that shows foresight, humility, and respect. The riddles and puzzles may confuse readers, but there is a certain pleasure in mulling over these sayings and unlocking their metaphors and allusions. Preachers and teachers may wish to take the chapter as a whole, pointing out the interrelated themes of pride and appetite, or they may wish to treat Agur's prayer and the numerical sayings separately, speaking first to revealed wisdom and second of godly wisdom born of experience and observation.

PRIDE AND HUMILITY. "If you have played the fool and exalted yourself ..." (30:32). All of the sayings of this chapter, Agur's musings and the numerical riddles, together illustrate the pervasive show of folly that can be summed up in the word "pride." The tradition of Christian spirituality named seven deadly sins, most of which appear in this chapter: gluttony, lust, avarice, anger, envy, acedia (often called sloth, the despair of life lived without God), and pride, the aggrandizing of self as though God did not exist.[30] Of the seven, pride was viewed as the most basic and the most dangerous, for it rejects God even as it refuses to submit or to receive grace. Pride will not obey, nor will it ever seek help. We miss the mark when we think of pride as only some sort of conceit or inflated self-image. Peter Kreeft reminds us:

> Pride is not first of all thinking too highly of yourself, because it isn't *thinking* first of all but *willing*, just as humility isn't thinking about yourself in a low way but not thinking of yourself at all. It's thinking less *about* yourself, not thinking less *of* yourself. Pride is willful arrogance, arrogating to yourself what is really God's.[31]

Agur saw this, lamenting his ignorance of wisdom and admitting that he did not know the Holy One (30:1–4). The sayings that follow warn against adding to God's holy words and living a life of falsehood (30:5–10). The numerical sayings illustrate the various forms of pride in its images of grasping and strutting. Insatiable hunger is symbolized by men who devour the poor and women who gulp down illicit sexual experience, but this same pride also inspires evil speaking, falsehood, cursing, and boasts. As we read the sayings, we may find our own lives reflected in these images; certainly they reflect much of what we see practiced in our culture.

Both kings and commoners of Israel fell victim to these sins of pride, and so the words of Moses and David echoed in the chapter point to God's covenant with a people, founded at Mount Sinai and reaffirmed with its leaders at Mount Zion. Both "sons," the people of Israel and their kings, were

---

30. See, again, Stafford, *Disordered Loves: Healing the Seven Deadly Sins* (Cambridge/Boston: Cowley Publications, 1994).

31. P. Kreeft, *For Heaven's Sake* (Nashville: Thomas Nelson, 1986), 98.

meant to be wise and live in faithfulness to that covenant, yet they broke covenant in a show of pride that led them to abandon God. Their lives were much like the negative examples of this chapter.

But in time another Son lived wisely in submission and faithfulness, doing what king and people did not, and that Son offered his life so that God might credit his wisdom and righteousness to us, so that in him we may find the grace to live wisely also. "What is his name and the name of his son? Tell me if you know!" (30:4). Christians who know Christ as the wise Son recognize that in him our follies of pride find forgiveness and healing. He teaches and empowers us to say "Enough!" to our illicit hungers and to put our hands to our mouths to stop violent speaking. Instead, recognizing that we are small and weak, we can seek the wisdom that the lowliest of God's creatures seem to understand. Humility, the antidote to pride, is not merely a confession of weakness. It is a source of great strength.

A wonderful illustration of wisdom that empowers the small comes from Jim Wallis, recalling a church service he witnessed during the time of apartheid in Cape Town, South Africa. A political rally had been scheduled at the cathedral, but when the government canceled it, Bishop Desmond Tutu said, "Okay, then, we're having church." The police came too, and they lined the walls of the church to intimidate the people in the pews. Tutu preached that day that apartheid would one day fall because it was evil. Then he spoke to the police: "You are powerful, but you are not gods. I serve a God who cannot be mocked." Then with a smile he said, "So since you've already lost, I invite you today to come and join the winning side."[32]

Courage like this comes from having a healthy assessment of who we are—limitations, sins, and all—but also in being able to see who God is as well. Pride subverts both, driving us to gobble all we can in insatiable hunger and to speak in ways that churn up anger and violence. Agur's oracle looks in another direction, at first in despair of having looked for wisdom without finding it, but then turning to the One who inspires wisdom by revealing a vision of himself. The One who gathers the wind in his hands and the waters in his cloak, the One who sets out the ends of the earth he has made, also calls us to see him, recognize him, and bow before him.

Such is humility, seeing clearly enough to recognize our smallness and God's greatness. As such, it is the hallmark of wisdom, the answer to pride and despair. "Humility is the opponent of both. It keeps us from despair as

---

32. J. Wallis, "Guest Essay: On the Winning Side," *World Vision Today* 4/1 (Autumn 2000): 31. Wallis adds: "Someday, by God's grace, we'll look into the eyes of wealth, power, greed, and indifference and say, 'You have already lost, so why don't you come and join the winning side?'"

well as from pride. The greatest virtue keeps us from the greatest vice. It is the greatest virtue in the sense that it is the first and foundational virtue."[33] So Agur's oracle and these numerical sayings come at the end of the book of Proverbs to remind us how pride keeps us from "the fear of the LORD . . . the beginning of knowledge [and wisdom]" (1:7 with 9:10).

---

33. Kreeft, *For Heaven's Sake*, 101.

Proverbs 31:1–31

THE SAYINGS OF King Lemuel—an oracle his mother taught him:

2 "O my son, O son of my womb,
    O son of my vows,
3 do not spend your strength on women,
    your vigor on those who ruin kings.

4 "It is not for kings, O Lemuel—
    not for kings to drink wine,
    not for rulers to crave beer,
5 lest they drink and forget what the law decrees,
    and deprive all the oppressed of their rights.
6 Give beer to those who are perishing,
    wine to those who are in anguish;
7 let them drink and forget their poverty
    and remember their misery no more.

8 "Speak up for those who cannot speak for themselves,
    for the rights of all who are destitute.
9 Speak up and judge fairly;
    defend the rights of the poor and needy."

10 A wife of noble character who can find?
    She is worth far more than rubies.
11 Her husband has full confidence in her
    and lacks nothing of value.
12 She brings him good, not harm,
    all the days of her life.
13 She selects wool and flax
    and works with eager hands.
14 She is like the merchant ships,
    bringing her food from afar.
15 She gets up while it is still dark;
    she provides food for her family
    and portions for her servant girls.
16 She considers a field and buys it;
    out of her earnings she plants a vineyard.

¹⁷ She sets about her work vigorously;
    her arms are strong for her tasks.
¹⁸ She sees that her trading is profitable,
    and her lamp does not go out at night.
¹⁹ In her hand she holds the distaff
    and grasps the spindle with her fingers.
²⁰ She opens her arms to the poor
    and extends her hands to the needy.
²¹ When it snows, she has no fear for her household;
    for all of them are clothed in scarlet.
²² She makes coverings for her bed;
    she is clothed in fine linen and purple.
²³ Her husband is respected at the city gate,
    where he takes his seat among the elders of the land.
²⁴ She makes linen garments and sells them,
    and supplies the merchants with sashes.
²⁵ She is clothed with strength and dignity;
    she can laugh at the days to come.
²⁶ She speaks with wisdom,
    and faithful instruction is on her tongue.
²⁷ She watches over the affairs of her household
    and does not eat the bread of idleness.
²⁸ Her children arise and call her blessed;
    her husband also, and he praises her:
²⁹ "Many women do noble things,
    but you surpass them all."
³⁰ Charm is deceptive, and beauty is fleeting;
    but a woman who fears the LORD is to be praised.
³¹ Give her the reward she has earned,
    and let her works bring her praise at the city gate.

Original
Meaning

THE FINAL CHAPTER of Proverbs is book-matched with chapter 30 (see comments there).¹ Like that one, this chapter begins with the "sayings" of a foreigner, an "oracle," which is then followed by artfully arranged poetry. The four-part unit of chapters 30 and 31 recaps the images and themes of the book, drawing them together into a comprehensive

---

1. The parts have a number of linking features. For example, the four prohibitions of the mother's teaching (marked by the Heb. negative ʾal) may echo the prayer of Agur in 30:7–10.

conclusion. Even as the book began with the "proverbs of Solomon son of David, king of Israel," so here a king receives instruction from his mother about choosing a life partner and the dangers of undisciplined sex and drinking.[2] A positive picture follows, presented as a woman of noble character who manages a household and earns praise.

The two parts of this chapter are linked as well: Both women are teachers (cf. 31:26), and the conversation in the royal palace is matched with the wisdom of the citizen's home.

> Kings Speak Out for the Poor (31:1–9)
>   A mother speaks to her son (31:1–2)
>   Rulers are not to drink and forget (31:3–5)
>   Give drink to the poor so they can forget (31:6–9)

> The Woman of Worth Brings Her Husband Good (31:10–31)
>   Nine-verse unit beginning with "noble character" and "husband" (31:10–18)
>   Two-verse unit repeating "stretches hand"–"palm" (31:19–20)
>   Nine-verse unit ending with "husband" and "noble character" (31:21–29)
>   Two-verse coda repeating "praise"–"work of her hands"[3] (31:30–31)

Moreover, if the acrostic is divided in two, the midpoint and conclusion put emphasis on the woman's community service (31:20 and 31).[4]

Kings Speak Out for the Poor (31:1–9)

A MOTHER'S LESSON to her son reminds the ruler to serve all the people, especially the poor.

31:1–2. A superscription introduces the "sayings of King Lemuel—an oracle," reminding the reader of the sayings of Agur, which are also called "an

---

2. Clifford, *Proverbs*, 271, puts it well: "The author transforms traditional warnings to rulers against the abuse of sex and liquor into an exhortation to practice justice . . . applicable to all who are tempted to turn authority into privilege."

3. After M. H. Lichtenstein, "Chiasm and Symmetry in Proverbs 31," CBQ 44 (1982): 202–11. Garrett, *Proverbs*, 248, proposes a different chiastic structure that puts v. 23 at the center, emphasizing the rewards that come to the man at the gate. The structure matches: Wife's high value (vv. 10, 30–31); Husband's good (vv. 11–12, 28–29); Wife's hard work (vv. 13–19, 27); Giving (vv. 20, 26); No fear (vv. 21a, 25b); Clothing (vv. 21b, 25a); Coverings and garments (vv. 22, 24); Public respect for husband (v. 23).

4. M. L. Barré, "'Terminative' Terms in Hebrew Acrostics," in *Wisdom, You Are My Sister: Studies in Honor of Roland E. Murphy, O. Carm., on the Occasion of His Eightieth Birthday* (CBQMS 29; Washington D.C.: Catholic Biblical Association of America, 1997), 207.

oracle" (*massaʾ*, see 30:1 for comments). While we are no more able to identify Lemuel than Agur, we do note that these sayings are not really Lemuel's
but his mother's, a reminder that women serve as teachers throughout the
book (1:8; 4:3; 6:20; 31:26). She repeats "my son" three times, the last translated either "son of my vows" or "the answer to my prayers" (see NIV text
note; cf. 30:16; 1 Sam. 1:11, 28).[5]

31:3–5. The four prohibitions that follow in verses 3 and 4 begin with
the negative *ʾal* and are followed by *pen*, "lest," in verse 5, describing the negative consequences. Kings are not to spend their strength on women; the
word "strength" (*ḥayil*) reappears as "noble character" in verse 10 (cf. 5:9–10;
12:4). Nor are they to spend their vigor on those who destroy kings; the
Hebrew for "vigor" is (lit.) "your ways," recalling the "way" of an adulteress
in 30:20. The concern over the distractions of harems and drinking and the
resulting impaired judgment were common throughout the literature of the
ancient Near East, including that of Israel.[6]

The ideal king protects the poor and defenseless, caring for them instead
of amassing wealth and building great palaces (Isa. 9:5; 11:2). Such rulers not
only refuse bribes and reject shady dealing, they rule to make sure that such
things are not done by anyone else so that the rights of the poor are not
deprived (NRSV "perverted").

31:6–9. Verse 6 reverses the picture of the previous warnings; instead of
"giving" (*ntn*, 31:3) strength to women, rulers are to give beer and wine as a
comfort to those who are perishing (31:6; cf. Gen. 5:29; Ps. 104:15). Note
also that the verbs "drink" and "forget" (Prov. 31:5) are repeated in 31:7; the
poor can drink and forget their poverty, for they are the ones who suffer.

Such a recommendation may surprise those who object to drinking in any
form, while others may be troubled by encouraging the poor to drink,

---

5. The first word before each "my son" is *mah* ("what"), so that the phrase might be
translated, "What is this, my son?" Some (TNK, NRSV) translate, "No, my son" and others,
"Listen," after Arabic use; see J. L. Crenshaw, "A Mother's Instruction to Her Son (Proverbs
31:1–9)," in *Perspectives on the Hebrew Bible: Essays in Honor of Walter J. Harrelson*, ed. J. L. Crenshaw (Macon, Ga.: Mercer Univ. Press, 1988), 15. The translation of this idiomatic use of
mah is difficult, leading to many different renderings: "What is important?" (Meinhold), or
"What are you doing?" (Clifford), or "What should I tell you?" (Garrett).

6. Meinhold, *Die Sprüche*, 2:518, lists the kings who fell to drink: Elah (1 Kings 16:8–14),
Ben-Hadad of Aram (1 Kings 20:16), and kings in general (Eccl. 10:17). The nations of
Ephraim (Isa. 28:1; Hos. 7:5) and Israel (Hos. 4:11, 18) are rebuked for succumbing to
drink that takes away understanding. On the problem of harems, see Deut. 17:17; 2 Sam.
16:20–22; 1 Kings 11:1–8.

7. M. H. Lichtenstein, "Chiasm and Symmetry in Proverbs 31," 204–5, explains that just
as the order of the words "wine" and "beer" are reversed, so their misuse is followed by the
opposite, i.e., its proper use.

especially those pastors and social workers who see the devastating effects of alcoholism in families. (1) We must recognize that total abstinence from alcohol was rare in the ancient world (as, e.g., in Nazirite vows), even while the problems of addiction to drink were recognized. (2) Behind this recommendation to give drink is a concern for responsible execution of judgment and care for the least powerful members of the kingdom. As Murphy puts it, instead of storing wine in his cellars, the king should offer it as comfort to those who hurt.[8] In my view, the "wine" is both a real comfort and a symbol of the fair judgment and rule that a king gives to his people (cf. 28:16; 29:14).

While we may be shocked to hear a suggestion of drinking to escape trouble, we should also note that in 31:5, "drink and forget" describe an irresponsible king who has no misery to forget, yet drinks anyway. Moreover, the offer of drink is not the only solution; we would be more concerned about this counsel were it not followed by the call to speak out for the poor.

In the Hebrew text, verses 8 and 9 both begin with the strong imperative, "Speak up" (lit., "open your mouth"). Certainly the theme of speech in Proverbs comes to fruition here. Above all, wise speech is speech that advocates for the rights of the poor. Kings are to make this part of their job description (e.g., 29:4, 14; cf. 16:13; 20:28; 25:5); note that in previous chapters this responsibility belongs to everyone. The Hebrew of verse 8 reads, "for the mute," that is, those "who cannot speak for themselves" and be heard. Then, as now, the rich and powerful had the voices that counted. Today, when E. F. Hutton speaks, everyone listens, but the cry of impoverished millions goes unheard.

In verse 9, "speak up" is repeated and defined: Good speech enables one to "judge [*špt*, the same root as the Heb. word for justice] fairly." Rather than deprive the poor of their rights (31:5), those who speak rightly will defend them. More than giving drink to cover over the misery of the poor (31:7), those who speak rightly work to remove the source of that misery.

The Woman of Worth Brings Her Husband Good (31:10−31)

THE BOOK OF Proverbs concludes with an acrostic poem that arranges key terms in a chiastic structure, the literary artistry reflecting the carefully ordered environment of home and world that Wisdom brings about (cf. 3:13−20; 8:1−36). Although the two parts of chapter 31 do not follow one another in the LXX, they do seem to speak to one another in the present arrangement. So, for example, while Lemuel's mother warns of the harm in spending one's "strength" (*ḥayil*, 31:3) in giving the wrong kind of attention

---

8. Murphy, *Proverbs*, 240−41.

to women, the poem begins with the good that a woman of "noble character" (*ḥayil*) can bring (31:10–12). Yet over the centuries, the poem has taken
on a life of its own. In Jewish tradition, it is recited by the husband to his wife
on Sabbath evenings,[9] and Christians are familiar with the reading on
Mother's Day. Certainly it was designed to persuade young men to seek a
good wife, but we also see this woman as another embodiment of wisdom,
similar to the personifications of Wisdom throughout the book.

31:10–18. The "wife of noble character" (*ʾēšet ḥayil*, "worth, strength") has
been mentioned before: "A wife of noble character is her husband's crown"
(12:4). We can also translate "a *woman* of noble character" after 31:29–30
and Ruth 3:11, observing that she enacts more roles than wife. "Who can
find?" communicates that faithful character is valuable because it is rare (cf.
Prov. 20:6), and the question may refer to the elusive nature of wisdom itself
(1:28; 8:35; Job 28:12–13).

From the start we are given a clue that somehow this poem is a summary
of all that has been said about wisdom in Proverbs. The first of the praises
describes this woman's character as a treasure (31:10), her worth measured
in precious stones ("rubies"), thus reminding readers of previous descriptions
of Wisdom (cf. 3:15; 8:11). Her husband recognizes her worth, for he "lacks
nothing of value [*šalal*, the same word that the violent gang used for "plunder" in 1:13; cf. 16:19]." What some would take by force comes to those
who seek what is most important.

"Brings him good" (31:12) in other contexts is translated as "repays" (3:30;
11:17; cf. Ps. 103:10; 119:17); in this woman, Wisdom's promises are fulfilled (Prov. 4:6, 8–9).[10] The first description of her work in verses 13–18
repeats significant terms in order: She works with her "hands" (lit., "palms")
and trades (root *sḥr*, 31:14, 17–18a), even into the night (31:15, 18b).[11] She
"sees" (*ṭaʿamah*, 31:18) or perceives that her trading is profitable, unlike the
beautiful woman who shows no "discretion" or the sluggard, more wise in his
own eyes than those who answer "discretely" (*ṭaʿam* in 11:22; 26:16). She is
like Wisdom, who is more profitable than silver (3:14).

In sum, this woman works and trades night and day to provide for herself and her household; she is as wise as the evil characters of chapter 30 are
foolish and self-centered. Moreover, she models the life of wisdom that Agur
has requested, repeating terms from the previous chapter. She ranges far and
wide to bring home food or "bread," just like merchant ships on the seas

9. B. L. Visotzky, "Midrash Eishet Hayil," *Conservative Judaism* 38 (1986): 21–25.

10. T. P. McCreesh, "Wisdom as Wife: Proverbs 31:10–31," *RB* 92 (1985): 25–46.

11. B. Waltke, "The Structure of the Valiant Wife (Prov. 31:10–31)," unpublished paper
presented at the Society of Biblical Literature Annual Meeting, 1999.

(cf. 30:19).[12] The word for "food" usually means "prey" (Ps. 11:5; Mal. 3:10). She provides for her house and maids (Prov. 31:15; cf. 27:7), in the same way Agur asked Yahweh to provide (30:8). She "considers" (31:16) a field to buy it, "planning" not for evil (30:32) but to use its produce and earnings (lit., "fruit of her hands"; 31:31) to plant a vineyard. She "sets about her work vigorously," for she (lit.) "girds her loins with strength" (31:17), the same word used to describe ants who have little "strength," yet store up and provide food (30:25).

31:19–20. The midpoint of the poem is set apart by a chiastic structure that repeats Hebrew words for "hands." The woman's hand "holds [*šlḥ*] the distaff,"[13] but she also "extends" (*šlḥ*) her hands to the poor (31:19a, 20b).[14] Her palms take hold of the spindle and open themselves to the needy (31:19b, 20a). The wordplay creates a contrast between the hands that close on her tools of production but open to share of her rewards with the poor (cf. 19:17; 22:9). She is the mirror reverse of the generation that wants to swallow up the "poor" and "needy" (30:14; cf. 14:31). The focus on hands carries over to 31:31 (lit., "work of her hands"), and the description of clothing extends through 31:21–22 to 31:25: "She is clothed with strength and dignity."

31:21–29. The husband and household appear twice, first as beneficiaries (vv. 21–25), then as those who praise her accomplishments of word and deed (vv. 26–29). The benefits are also presented in chiastic fashion, drawing attention to the honor that comes to the husband.

A v. 21 No fear of snows—household *clothed* in scarlet
  B v. 22 She is clothed in *linen* and purple
    C v. 23 Husband respected at the gate
  B' v. 24 She makes and sells *linen* and sashes
A' v. 25 Laughs at future—she is *clothed* in strength and dignity

This structure helps readers see that her work in making finished clothing of the yarn spun earlier gives her confidence for the future. The wordplay in 31:25 clothes her, not in the scarlet of her household (31:21)[15] but in "strength and dignity" (cf. 31:17). She is also clothed in linen and purple, materials both expensive and a sign of honor (Est. 8:15), but she also has linen to sell (Prov. 31:22, 24). At the center of this arrangement sits the husband,

---

12. McCreesh, "Wisdom As Wife," 43, finds a reflection of Solomon's ships in the "ships from afar" (1 Kings 9:26–28 = 2 Chron. 8:17–18; 1 Kings 10:22 = 2 Chron. 9:21).

13. The distaff holds the material being spun into thread by the spindle.

14. The "hand" (*yad*) extended as far as the elbow; thus the NIV, "opens her arms to the poor."

15. A number of commentators (Clifford, Murphy) prefer "double" (after the LXX) to "scarlet." Meinhold, *Die Sprüche*, 2:526, finds the color in Ex. 25:4; 2 Sam. 1:24; Isa. 1:18; Jer. 4:30.

honored at the gates where he sits with the elders, presumably to make deliberations and judgments (31:23; cf. v. 31). No connection is stated; it is implied
that this industrious wife does him good and brings him wealth, and so this
man is honored, perhaps for his own wisdom, perhaps for the good she
brings him. Some interpreters see a satire of the important but ultimately
useless "husband" (cf. 31:11; 25:6–7), but this ignores the important role
elders play in judging for the rights of others.[16]

Her words and deeds together bring her praise. The husband is not the
only one who speaks wisely, for she (lit.) "opens her mouth in wisdom"
(31:26; cf. v. 20), just as Lemuel was instructed in 31:8–9. The "faithful instruction" (*torat ḥesed*) is faithful in both senses of the word, true to the tradition
and to the marginalized people it serves. If the husband speaks for justice at
the gates, she does the same in the home (cf. 1:8; 6:20; 13:14). Therefore, if
we haven't already, we should make association with another person who
"speaks with wisdom" (1:21; 8:3).[17]

The sayings that follow in 31:28–31 refer to another kind of speaking, the
epideictic speech of praise ("praise" appears three times). The first two verses
(31:28–29) report the family's praise, the last two verses (31:30–31) the
praise of the unnamed teacher and crowd at the city gates. The last four
verses of the acrostic poem sound echoes of the first four. The terms "husband" and "noble" appear in the first two verses of each (31:10–11 and 28–
29) and the words "work" and "her hands" come at the end (31:13, 31). The
third verse in each sequence contrasts good done "all the days of her life" with
beauty that is fleeting (31:12, 20).

If the start of the poem lauds the good she brings to her husband, the
end rewards it with praise, from her children and her man. Presumably,
the men at the gate speak well also of this man's wife, and this adds to the
honor he receives (31:23). Her husband's praise outdoes Boaz in recognizing her worth (*ḥayil*, "noble things," 31:29; cf. 31:10; Ruth 3:11), holding her up as surpassing all. Small wonder, then, that Ruth follows Proverbs
in the Hebrew canon, for both women are examples of strength, resourcefulness, and loyalty.

---

16. This "lazy man" interpretation is at least as old as Delitzsch, *Proverbs*, 327–28. The
man "goes after his calling, perhaps a calling which, though weighty and honorable, brings
in little or nothing." However, Meinhold, *Die Sprüche*, 2:526, saw the echo of "gates" where
Wisdom speaks (1:21; 8:3), where the poor are to receive justice (22:22), and where a fool
has nothing to say (24:7).

17. The word for "watches over" (*sopiyyah*, 31:27) may be a pun on the Greek word for
wisdom (*sophia*), as suggested by A. Wolters, "Ṣôpiyyâ (Prov. 31:27) as Hymnic Participle
and Play on Sophia," *JBL* 104 (1985): 577–87. In my judgment, a contrast with the woman
who is never at home (7:11) seems more likely to have been the writer's intention.

31:30—31. Readers have heard throughout the book that charm and beauty can deceive and disappear, just like riches (31:28; cf. 6:25; 11:16, 22; 13:11; 21:6). More important than any beauty, charm, or even work is the fear of Yahweh, which shapes all that this woman is (31:30); having this fear, she has no fear of the future (31:21). While some interpreters read the Hebrew to argue that this woman *is* the fear of Yahweh, in my view, it is enough that each appearance of personified Wisdom in the book also mentions "fear of the LORD" (31:30; cf. 1:29; 9:10). We cannot miss the significance that the goal of wisdom teaching named at the beginning of the book (1:7) comes to fruition in this woman's character.[18] What else can we readers do but join in giving her "the reward she has earned" (lit., "the fruit of her hands")?[19]

ONCE AGAIN, we must seek to understand this chapter in light of the four-part structure of chapters 30 and 31 (see comments in ch. 30). So, for example, when we observe the frequency of cautionary sayings about the king in 30:21—31, we notice that 31:1—9 warns the king against self-indulgence and irresponsible rule. Moreover, Agur's prayer for knowledge of God and help in living well (30:1—9) is answered by a "woman of noble character," who models fear of Yahweh in her successful and charitable life (31:10—31).

Women as teachers and role models. The two parts of chapter 31 are linked together by women teachers and examples who help and influence men in positions of responsibility. While one takes his seat at the city gate among the elders, another sits on the throne to rule and judge (31:9, 23). The wisdom that instructs kings (8:14—16) and citizens (9:1—8) alike also brings them good (3:13—18). In this way, the two parts of the chapter do what the book does, bringing palace and gate together; wisdom is not for kings alone but for all of us in our varied positions of leadership and responsibility.

(1) The queen mother tells Lemuel to set aside wine, women, and song for the responsibilities of leadership, giving the needy what they need for comfort and aid and speaking out for their rights. To speak out is to speak

18. Recall that "fear of LORD" appears not only at the beginning and end of the instructions (1:7, 9:10), but also at the middle of the sayings and the book (15:33). McCreesh, "Wisdom as Wife," 25—46, adds other references to Wisdom's house and riches: 3:15; 8:18, 21; 24:3—4; see also 4:6—9 and 16:16.

19. Six of the seven words of 31:31 are also used in the poem: "give" (*natenah*, v. 24), "from fruit of" (*mippri*, v. 16), "her hand" (*yadeyah*, vv. 19 and 20), "praise" (*haltlah*, vv. 28, 30), "at the gates" (*bassearim*, v. 23), "her works," (*castah*, vv. 22, 24).

the word of decision that restrains and punishes cheating, fast dealing, and other subtle forms of stealing that often hurt the poor the most. Today, the injustice of Naboth's vineyard, stolen for the king's wine (1 Kings 21:1–28), reminds us of large-scale indifference to fair trade between nations, unequal opportunity in hiring and housing, and a few renegade CEOs. The conclusion to the book of Proverbs recognizes that the poor will be forgotten unless someone speaks for their rights and needs; then, as now, leaders were charged with making sure the poor were not cheated or overlooked.

Whybray may be right that there is no vision of equal distribution among these sages, no question about the social causes of poverty.[20] The ancients did not ask the larger questions about wealth and its distribution that sociologists and economists raise today; they simply wanted to assure that the rich and powerful did not take what did not belong to them. A look at a daily newspaper will confirm that it is a good place to begin today!

Throughout the book we have said that instructions for leaders speak to the roles of leadership that all of us exercise in our jobs, families, and voluntary associations. The standards of righteousness, justice, and equity (1:3) apply to every human interaction; thus, this concluding admonition reminds us that speech is the primary means by which such standards are realized. In the imagery of Proverbs, we can use our mouths for greedy consumption, or we can use them for just and compassionate speaking, in the halls of government or the business office.

(2) Moreover, the "wife of noble character" speaks with wisdom and faithful instruction (31:26), and she follows up those words with actions. If Lemuel's mother warned about giving strength (*ḥayil*, 31:3) away to women, this woman proves that there are those whose strength (*ḥayil*, 31:10) brings good, not harm, to their men. We should remember that we find here an image of a household manager that is both concrete and ideal. It is concrete in that these actions of an upper class wife reflect the actual "cultural experience of a social group of women."[21] It is also ideal, for these qualities are demonstrated to perfection. Can anyone live up to this standard?

We are faced with the problem of role models that can inspire but can also discourage; I know of one couple who threw out their Christian self-help

---

20. See Whybray, *Wealth and Poverty in the Book of Proverbs*.

21. E. L. Lyons, "A Note on Proverbs 31:10–31," in *The Listening Heart: Essays in Wisdom and the Psalms in Honor of Roland E. Murphy, O. Carm.*, ed. K. G. Hoglund et al. (JSOTSup 58; Sheffield: JSOT Press, 1987), 237–45. Lyons concludes from archaeological evidence that such a picture of life for Israelite women fits the premonarchic and possibly the postexilic periods. C. R. Yoder, *Wisdom As a Woman of Substance: A Socioeconomic Reading of Proverbs 1–9 and 31:10–31* (BZAW 304; Berlin/New York: Walter de Gruyter, 2001), finds correspondence with the later Persian period.

books because no matter how diligent and sincere their efforts, they were always found wanting. The poem seeks to inspire a desire for wise living, not perfectionism—but how are we to understand it?

Roles, activities, and character. The concrete aspects of the woman's good work are part of the reading of this poem, and they direct us to ideals worthy of emulation. So Madipoane Masenya observes that this portrait of an ideal woman reclaims endangered aspects of *bosadi* (womanhood) in South African culture: effective household management, care for the needy, and industry. It is an ideal that those women can emulate in the face of industrialization and cultural change, for many poor African women are left alone to farm unproductive land, hindering their traditional roles of caretaker and contributor. Moreover, the woman of Proverbs 31 reminds African readers what it means to be a person who cares for the community outside the nuclear family. Masenya cites the concept of *ubuntu* (*botho*/humanness), a fundamental respect for human nature as a whole, communicated by the Zulu saying, "A human being is a human being because of other human beings." She also describes the practice of sending young girls to visit those who are elderly and without family, bringing firewood, water, and food.[22] These concrete actions do speak to the larger ideals of character.

Such an approach to interpretation can put the emphasis where it belongs, on the biblical values of service and community. It can also remove some of our contemporary concern that this poem sets limits on the roles and activities available to women. As a portrait of a woman and her household, we recognize this poem has been used to praise and pressure women, but its root message of choosing love and following it through in actions makes a fitting conclusion to a book about wisdom. Speak well and let your actions speak as loudly, say the sages. Choose carefully when it comes to issues of personal character and companions. While it is true that the poetry was directed toward males and the good or bad that comes to them, women have always known it works both ways.

The practical counsel of Proverbs has helped generations of believers get their heads out of the clouds and down to the business of living as though the world really is inhabited by other people, a welcome antidote to the self-indulgent values of contemporary life. Women may find this woman of worth too perfect or too domestic, but her example of competent and caring activity carries through the ages into our own, inspiring men and women alike. "Who can find?" (31:10) receives its answer from Wisdom herself: "Whoever finds me finds life and receives favor from the LORD" (8:35). In sum,

22. M. Masenya, "Proverbs 31:10—31 in a South African Context: A Reading for the Liberation of African (Northern Sotho) Women," *Semeia* 78 (2002): 55—68.

the poem of praise sums up the teaching of the entire book concerning Wisdom, the good she inspires and brings to those who find her.

However, remembering that this is a book attributed to Solomon, we may wonder if the sages meant to draw our attention to the negative influence of Solomon's many wives and concubines (1 Kings 11:1–13); Solomon's wives turned his heart toward other gods, and Lemuel's mother warns against dissipation and forgetting. In my view, the chapter brings together positive roles of counsel and example: Lemuel's mother teaches the responsibilities of leadership, while the woman of noble character runs a household that increases in wealth, provides for its own, and reaches out in charity, a model of administration that any king might envy. Put another way, the symbolism of the acrostic poem not only points to the pursuit of Wisdom as lifelong partner, it also models a government that benefits all at the expense of none; it is like a prosperous and just kingdom. We may risk overstatement to say that the woman not only models the skill of administrating a household, she shows a king how to run a kingdom, doing that which Yahweh requires—providing for all.

The Lord of wisdom. Finally, this woman also represents the Lord of wisdom. We have observed that throughout Proverbs, female figures represent both Wisdom and Folly. Just as chapters 7–9 juxtapose Woman Wisdom with personifications of adultery and folly, so here Lemuel's mother warns against using one's sexual powers foolishly, giving that strength away to women (cf. 30:20) instead of finding a woman who contributes to one's good (31:12). Here, Wisdom's calls to receive her teaching and hospitality come together as the house Wisdom built with her hands is realized in this home of security and nurture (cf. 1:20–23; 8:1–11; 9:1–6).[23]

The descriptions of this woman's valor and strength have military overtones, reminding careful readers of the praise due a conquering king, perhaps even the king of heaven. Therefore, we are not surprised that the deeds of the noble woman show some reflection of the mighty deeds of Yahweh, who cares for the poor and righteous.[24] Thus, readers meet the wisdom of Yahweh in a mother's teaching and a wife's example, embodiment of the wise life that is both identified with Yahweh and yet distinct. While she is not

---

23. McCreesh, "Wisdom As Wife," 25–46. McCreesh highlights the call of Woman Wisdom in Prov. 1, 8, and 9. By ch. 9, the call has become an invitation to marriage (9:5; see also Song 5:1 on bread and wine).

24. A. Wolters, "Proverbs 31:10–31 As Heroic Hymn: A Form-Critical Analysis," *VT* 38 (1988): 446–57. So also Yahweh fights on behalf of the poor (cf. Ps. 112:10). Wolters notes that both Ps. 111 and 112 begin with *Hallelu Yah* and both mention fear of Yahweh—Ps. 111 giving the reason for the fear, the acrostic poem of Ps. 112 giving the picture of what it looks like in a faithful person's life.

Woman Wisdom, this final example of wisdom in feminine persona reminds readers of all of Wisdom's earlier appearances, a means by which Yahweh speaks to his people (1:20–33; 3:13–18; 8:1–36; 9:1–12).

So also, Yahweh is not Woman Wisdom and should not be called Wisdom or Sophia, although he is wise (see comments in ch. 1). Rather, we hear the voice of God through her words as well as through the wisdom of the instructions, proverbs, words of the wise, and their riddles (1:6). In this way, wisdom, like the historical narratives, the prophets, and the psalms, becomes another biblical means for God to communicate his person and intentions for his people.

 CONCERN FOR THE **poor as an element of wisdom.** Perhaps the most important aspect of the conclusion to the book of Proverbs is that both Lemuel's mother and the woman of noble character teach and model the orderly life of wisdom. Throughout the book, women have taught alongside men, fulfilling the vision of Genesis 1–2, man and woman together representing the image of God.[25] Therefore, just as we asked women to identify with the young man in his journey toward the wise life throughout the book, so we ask men to identify with the core values of these wise women. Let us be taught not only to live sober and responsible lives but also to "speak up for those who cannot speak for themselves" (31:8). Let us manage our affairs so as to provide well for family and stranger. In this way the public concerns of the queen mother and the private concerns of the wife of character come together.

Thus, we must listen with Lemuel as his mother urges responsible use of authority and power, serving not ourselves or those who can help us but those who have nothing to give in return. I'm concerned that collectively, we as Americans and members of an American church body can become the forgetful king that troubled Lemuel's mother. Thanks to the availability of media, entertainment can be cheaply enjoyed. The millions of Americans who watch the Superbowl and spend a few dollars each on beer and snacks add up to the millions that go to athletes and catchy TV commercials. My purpose is not to decry the few hours of entertainment the national holiday of Superbowl Sunday brings, but to wish that all of the effort and ingenuity that went

---

25. Goldingay, "Proverbs," 607, approves of TNK's translation, a "truly capable woman." He ascribes the words to Lemuel's mother, stressing that her teaching role resembles that of the mother as well as personified Wisdom. In his view, the poem encourages women to push the envelope of what is expected, since men need less encouragement to achieve.

into winning games, creating catchy commercials, and producing block-buster half-time shows went into speaking and acting on behalf of the poor who live right next door to us.

I know a couple who work with the Center for Student Missions, an agency that has a facility on the university where I teach. I was impressed that their idea of mission took high school kids to inner cities, not to faraway lands. In this way, the values of neighbor love are put into action that can be practiced at home; students learn to hear and speak for those who cannot speak for themselves. Their example proves that the private life of responsible and charitable citizenship and the physical care of visiting, feeding, and helping is always in season. So the center of the acrostic poem links the wise woman's industry with her charity (31:19–20). In the same way, Paul urged that persons work with their hands to have something to share with those in need, a practice he kept himself (Eph. 4:28; 1 Thess. 2:6–12; 2 Thess. 3:6–15).

Private and public life. Private and public life come together in the two women of this chapter, as do teaching and example. Lemuel is taught to keep a personal discipline to ensure that he executes his public charge. So also the man at the gate (hopefully speaking up for the poor) is helped by a woman who stretches her hands out to make cloth and embrace the poor. Why have we so often assumed that taking care of our own excludes taking care of the stranger? Or, to turn the question around, why do so many pour themselves out in ministry to the neglect of their families? Testimonies of parents who have taken their children along on mission trips show that such separation is needless and potentially harmful, for these children learn more about love and service by watching their folks than they would ever learn from their parents' teaching alone.

Moreover, for too long, this passage has been used to argue that women can only exercise their gifts and competence in the home or in some similar service; yet both women in this chapter follow the lead of Woman Wisdom in their concern for righteousness, justice, and equity that is both public and private (1:3; 8:14–16). In other words, while it is not inappropriate to read the text on Mother's Day, it is an inadequate way to interpret it. Reading and teaching the chapter on other Sundays of the church year, including both Lemuel's mother and the woman of substance, can help the church transcend the limitations imposed by American church culture.

I once visited a church where Mother's Day and Father's Day were occasions to celebrate the nurture that all adult members provided to the younger members of the church community. Every woman received a flower and every man received a citation to recognize the teaching, guidance, and affection given to the children, youth, and young adults of the church. So also, the whole chapter can also be read to encourage the church in its work of calling for justice and providing for those in need.

The call of God through Wisdom. As a conclusion to my comments on this book of Proverbs, I would like to reflect on the way that God speaks to his church through the counsels and examples of these wise women and the writings they bring to a close. Throughout the book we have seen that the direct teaching of lecture and counsel stands side by side with the indirect teaching of imagery, and here a mother's lecture and a wife's busy agenda together point the way to wisdom, just as Jesus our teacher and example directed his disciples and followers toward the kingdom of God. I hope, therefore, that Proverbs and other wisdom books may take their place alongside the stories, the commandments, and the psalms as another way that God speaks and guides his church toward faithful discipleship.

Too often we take our cues on guidance from the call stories. God appears to Abraham, Moses, and Jeremiah and gives directions—Moses and Jeremiah to go and speak, Abraham simply to go. We try to generalize from these stories to our own lives. They are especially applicable when someone senses a call to go and speak for God; how many ordination sermons have been preached from Exodus 1–3, Jeremiah 1, Isaiah 6, or Acts 9? However, the dynamics of the call to speak can also apply to the varied ministries of the church and daily life, not just to those of pulpit. Reading these stories, we might assume that we too will hear some sort of voice, audible or inner, that gives us a specific directive. But we should also keep in mind that God came to these people in ways they did not expect, and they did not always like what they heard. The call narratives are not the only biblical resource for teaching about guidance.

Throughout the book of Proverbs, it is not God but a woman who claims to represent God who reaches out to all who pass by, calling them to learn from her and rebuking those who do not (1:20–33; 9:1–12). Just as this woman offered to teach, so here at the book's end the woman of noble character teaches her household. Just as this woman invited travelers to a banquet, so here is a woman who provides food, shelter, and clothing. We have noted the similarities and suggested that this wise wife resembles Wisdom herself, the voice that God uses to summon and instruct listeners.

We may wish to hear the dramatic voice that calls us to some heroic action, but let's remember that Moses and Jeremiah would have been just as happy to be mistaken for someone else. Less dramatic, perhaps, is this picture of women teaching their sons and providing for their families, but as this picture sums up all that has been said about diligence, responsible choices, and just and compassionate relationships with neighbor, we hear God speaking. As God speaks, he calls us to listen to Woman Wisdom and to emulate her, symbolically making her our life companion. If we find this way of thinking strange, we can remember that we do the same with Jesus' life and teachings, calling him teacher and Lord (John 13:13).

Wisdom will teach Christ's church by word and example, and she will mediate the guidance of God—not by telling us what we are to do in a particular situation but by instilling in us the capacities to make such decisions for ourselves, based on the qualities of teachability, discernment, foresight, industry, honesty, charity, and fairness that will guide our attitudes and actions. A friend tells me that he cannot read through Proverbs quickly because it speaks too specifically and powerfully to his life; he has to slow down so the insights can take root. Therefore, I want to conclude this book with a plea and reminder that Wisdom's teaching in the instructions, proverbs, and riddles of this book deserve all the attention we can give them. "Let her works bring her praise at the city gate" (31:31)—and in the church as well.

Scripture and Apocrypha Index

Scripture Index

Scripture Index

Matthew		Luke		John	
5:45	617	**Luke**		**John**	
6:2	505	1:46–55	363, 401	1	36
6:19–25	132	2:40	303	1:1–14	42
6:19–24	237	2:52	119, 303	1:1–2	256
6:22–23	496	3:7–14	333	1:1	225
6:24	329	3:10–14	514	4:36	327
6:25–34	81, 331	4:18–19	429	8:10–11	423
7:12	511	4:19	303	9:1–5	133
7:15–21	298	4:23	22	11:44b	210
7:24	41	6:30	538	12:25	251
10:29–31	81	6:32–36	476	13:13–17	428
10:39	251	6:34–35	538	13:13	685
11:19	41, 90	6:35	194	15:5	409
12:34–37	405	6:38	329	15:15	463
12:42	41	6:39	22	19:40	210
13:44–46	147	6:43–45	298	20:7	210
13:44–45	237	7:1–8	427	**Acts**	
13:52–53	22	7:6–9	45	1:21–26	422
13:52	41, 534	8:10	22	9	684
18:15–18	332	10:25–37	379, 390	14:8–18	90
18:15–17	583	11:42	630	**Romans**	
19:30	552	11:45	582–583	1:5	90
20:15	519, 552	12:13–21	201	1:13	327
22:15–22	427	12:15	363	1:18–32	90
22:34–40	106	12:20	201	1:18	178
23:16–17	551	12:22–34	81	1:24, 26, 28	90, 178
23:23	630, 649	12:57–59	583	3:23	649
23:25	649	14:7–14	583	6:21	294
24:45–50	566	14:7–11	22	12:17–20	580
25:40	435	14:12–14	476	12:21	514, 568
25:31–46	390, 476	14:16–24	280	13:1–7	489
26:11	523	15	300	**1 Corinthians**	
26:41	452	15:11–32	639	1:10–11	599
27:59	210	15:11–24	473	1:24	42, 255, 258
Mark		15:13–14	160	1:30	255
3:23	22	15:19, 21	324	2:2–5	599
4:24–25	329	16:1–15	318	4:16	46
4:35–41	274	16:8	41	5:9–11	541
5:1–15	274	16:13	329	8:1	346
5:21–43	391	17:33	251	13	39
7:9–13	473	17:37	21	13:4–7	46
7:14–23	87	19:1–10	350	**2 Corinthians**	
8:31–37	87	19:6	476	6:14	541
8:35–38	251	19:9	311	8:9	390
10:45	503	20:20–26	427	9:8	519
12:13–17	427	22:42	367	12:9–10	572
12:28	130	23:53	210		
15:46	210				

703

Scripture Index

Subject Index

Subject Index

Bring ancient truth to modern life with the
NIV Application Commentary *series*

Covering both the Old and New Testaments, the **NIV Application Commentary** series is a staple reference for pastors seeking to bring the Bible's timeless message into a modern context. It explains not only what the Bible means but also how that meaning impacts the lives of believers today.

Genesis
This commentary demonstrates how the text charts a course of theological affirmation that results in a simple but majestic account of an ordered, purposeful cosmos with God at the helm, masterfully guiding it, and what this means to us today.

John H. Walton   ISBN: 0-310-206170

Exodus
The truth of Christ's resurrection and its resulting impact on our lives mean that to Christians, the application of Exodus is less about how to act than it is about what God has done and what it means to be his children.

Peter Enns   ISBN: 0-310-20607-3

Leviticus, Numbers
Roy Gane's commentary on Leviticus and Numbers helps readers understand how the message of these two books, which are replete with what seem to be archaic laws, can have a powerful impact on Christians today.

Roy Gane   ISBN: 0-310-21088-7

Judges, Ruth
This commentary helps readers learn how the messages of Judges and Ruth can have the same powerful impact today that they did when they were first written. Judges reveals a God who employs very human deliverers but refuses to gloss over their sins and the consequences of those sins. Ruth demonstrates the far-reaching impact of a righteous character.

K. Lawson Younger Jr.   ISBN: 0-310-20636-7

1&2 Samuel

In Samuel, we meet Saul, David, Goliath, Jonathan, Bathsheba, the witch of Endor, and other unforgettable characters. And we encounter ourselves. For while the culture and conditions of Israel under its first kings are vastly different from our own, the basic issues of humans in relation to God, the Great King, have not changed. Sin, repentance, forgiveness, adversity, prayer, faith, and the promises of God — these continue to play out in our lives today.

Bill T. Arnold   ISBN: 0-310-21086-0

1&2 Chronicles

First and Second Chronicles are a narrative steeped in the best and worst of the human heart — but they are also a revelation of Yahweh at work, forwarding his purposes in the midst of fallible people, but a people who trust in the Lord and his word through the prophets. God has a plan to which he is committed.

Andrew E. Hill   ISBN: 0-310-20610-3

Esther

Karen H. Jobes shows what a biblical narrative that never mentions God tells Christians about him today.

Karen H. Jobes   ISBN: 0-310-20672-3

Psalms Volume 1

Gerald Wilson examines Books 1 and 2 of the Psalter. His seminal work on the shaping of the Hebrew Psalter has opened a new avenue of psalms research by shifting focus from exclusive attention to individual psalms to the arrangement of the psalms into groups.

Gerald H. Wilson   ISBN: 0-310-20635-9

Proverbs

Few people can remember when they last heard a sermon from Proverbs or looked together at its chapters. In this NIV Application Commentary on Proverbs, Paul Koptak gives numerous aids to pastors and church leaders on how to study, reflect on, and apply this book on biblical wisdom as part of the educational ministry of their churches.

Paul Koptak   ISBN: 0-310-21852-7

Ecclesiastes, Song of Songs

Ecclesiastes and Songs of Songs have always presented particular challenges to their readers, especially if those readers are seeking to understand them as part of Christian Scripture. Revealing the links between the Scriptures and our own times, Iain Provan shows how these wisdom books speak to us today with relevance and conviction.

Iain Provan   ISBN: 0-310-21372-X

Isaiah

Isaiah wrestles with the realities of people who are not convicted by the truth but actually hardened by it, and with a God whose actions sometimes seem unintelligible, or even worse, appears to be absent. Yet Isaiah penetrates beyond these experiences to an even greater reality. Isaiah sees God's rule over history and his capacity to take the worst of human actions and use it for good. He declares the truth that even in the darkest hours, the Holy One of Israel is infinitely trustworthy.

John N. Oswalt   ISBN: 0-310-20613-8

Jeremiah/Lamentations

These two books cannot be separated from the political conditions of ancient Judah. Beginning with the time of King Josiah, who introduced religious reform, Jeremiah reflects the close link between spiritual and political prosperity or disaster for the nation as a whole.

J. Andrew Dearman   ISBN: 0-310-20616-2

Ezekiel

Discover how, properly understood, this mysterious book with its obscure images offers profound comfort to us today.

Iain M. Duguid   ISBN: 0-310-21047-X

Daniel

Tremper Longman III reveals how the practical stories and spellbinding apocalyptic imagery of Daniel contain principles that are as relevant now as they were in the days of the Babylonian Captivity.

Tremper Longman III   ISBN: 0-310-20608-1

Hosea, Amos, Micah

Scratch beneath the surface of today's culture and you'll find we're not so different from ancient Israel. Revealing the links between Israel eight centuries B.C. and our own times, Gary V. Smith shows how the prophetic writings of Hosea, Amos, and Micah speak to us today with relevance and conviction.

Gary V. Smith

ISBN: 0-310-20614-6

Jonah, Nahum, Habakkuk, Zephaniah

James Bruckner shows how the messages of these four Old Testament prophets, who lived during some of Israel and Judah's most turbulent times, are as powerful in today's turbulent times as when first written.

James Bruckner

ISBN: 0-310-20637-5

Haggai, Zechariah

This commentary on Haggai and Zechariah helps readers learn how the message of these two prophets who challenged and encouraged the people of God after the return from Babylon can have the same powerful impact on the community of faith today.

Mark J. Boda

ISBN: 0-310-20615-4

Matthew

Matthew helps readers learn how the message of Matthew's gospel can have the same powerful impact today that it did when the author first wrote it.

Michael J. Wilkins

ISBN: 0-310-49310-2

Mark

Learn how the challenging gospel of Mark can leave recipients with the same powerful questions and answers it did when it was written.

David E. Garland

ISBN: 0-310-49350-1

Luke
Focus on the most important application of all: "the person of Jesus and the nature of God's work through him to deliver humanity."

Darrell L. Bock   ISBN: 0-310-49330-7

John
Learn both halves of the interpretive task. Gary M. Burge shows readers how to bring the ancient message of John into a modern context. He also explains not only what the book of John meant to its original readers but also how it can speak powerfully today.

Gary M. Burge   ISBN: 0-310-49750-7

Acts
Study the first portraits of the church in action around the world with someone whose ministry mirrors many of the events in Acts. Biblical scholar and worldwide evangelist Ajith Fernando applies the story of the church's early development to the global mission of believers today.

Ajith Fernando   ISBN: 0-310-49410-9

Romans
Paul's letter to the Romans remains one of the most important expressions of Christian truth ever written. Douglas Moo comments on the text and then explores issues in Paul's culture and in ours that help us understand the ultimate meaning of each paragraph.

Douglas J. Moo   ISBN: 0-310-49400-1

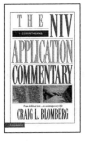

1 Corinthians
Is your church struggling with the problem of divisiveness and fragmentation? See the solution Paul gave the Corinthian Christians over 2,000 years ago. It still works today!

Craig Blomberg   ISBN: 0-310-48490-1

2 Corinthians
Often recognized as the most difficult of Paul's letters to understand, 2 Corinthians can have the same powerful impact today that it did when it was first written.

Scott J. Hafemann   ISBN: 0-310-49420-6

Galatians
A pastor's message is true not because of his preaching or people-management skills, but because of Christ. Learn how to apply Paul's example of visionary church leadership to your own congregation.

Scot McKnight   ISBN: 0-310-48470-7

Ephesians
Explore what the author calls "a surprisingly comprehensive statement about God and his work, about Christ and the gospel, about life with God's Spirit, and about the right way to live."

Klyne Snodgrass   ISBN: 0-310-49340-4

Philippians
The best lesson Philippians provides is how to encourage people who actually are doing quite well. Learn why not all the New Testament letters are reactions to theological crises.

Frank Thielman   ISBN: 0-310-49300-5

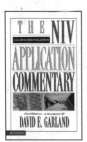

Colossians/Philemon
The temptation to trust in the wrong things has always been strong. Use this commentary to learn the importance of trusting only in Jesus, God's Son, in whom all the fullness of God lives. No message is more important for our postmodern culture.

David E. Garland   ISBN: 0-310-48480-4

1&2 Thessalonians

Paul's letters to the Thessalonians say as much to us today about Christ's return and our resurrection as they did in the early church. This volume skillfully reveals Paul's answers to these questions and how they address the needs of contemporary Christians.

Michael W. Holmes   ISBN: 0-310-49380-3

1&2 Timothy, Titus

Reveals the context and meanings of Paul's letters to two leaders in the early Christian Church and explores their present-day implications to help you to accurately apply the principles they contain to contemporary issues.

Walter L. Liefeld   ISBN: 0-310-50110-5

Hebrews

The message of Hebrews can be summed up in a single phrase: "God speaks effectively to us through Jesus." Unpack the theological meaning of those seven words and learn why the gospel still demands a hearing today.

George H. Guthrie   ISBN: 0-310-49390-0

James

Give your church the best antidote for a culture of people who say they believe one thing but act in ways that either ignore or contradict their belief. More than just saying, "Practice what you preach," James gives solid reasons why faith and action must coexist.

David P. Nystrom   ISBN: 0-310-49360-9

1 Peter

The issue of the church's relationship to the state hits the news media in some form nearly every day. Learn how Peter answered the question for Christians surviving under Roman rule and how it applies similarly to believers living amid the secular institutions of the modern world.

Scot McKnight   ISBN: 0-310-49290-4

2 Peter, Jude
Introduce your modern audience to letters they may not be familiar with and show why they'll want to get to know them.

Douglas J. Moo

ISBN: 0-310-20104-7

Letters of John
Like the community in John's time, which faced disputes over erroneous "secret knowledge," today's church needs discernment in affirming new ideas supported by Scripture and weeding out harmful notions. This volume will help you show today's Christians how to use John's example.

Gary M. Burge

ISBN: 0-310-48620-3

Revelation
Craig Keener offers a "new" approach to the book of Revelation by focusing on the "old." He stresses the need for believers to prepare for the possibility of suffering for the sake of Jesus.

Craig S. Keener

ISBN: 0-310-23192-2